MAZDA

MAZDA6
2003-11 REPAIR MANUAL

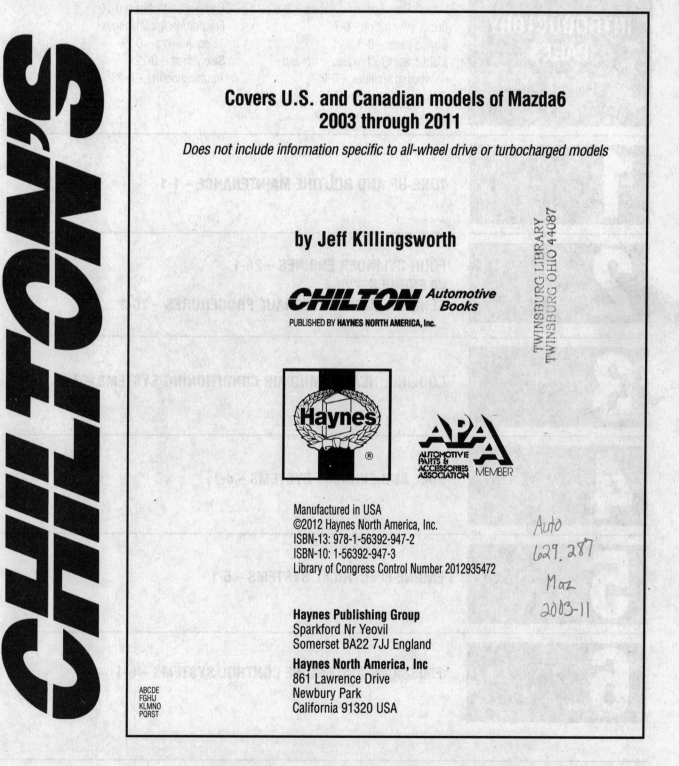

CHILTON'S

Covers U.S. and Canadian models of Mazda6
2003 through 2011

Does not include information specific to all-wheel drive or turbocharged models

by Jeff Killingsworth

CHILTON *Automotive Books*
PUBLISHED BY **HAYNES NORTH AMERICA, Inc.**

Haynes

APAA
AUTOMOTIVE
PARTS &
ACCESSORIES
ASSOCIATION MEMBER

Manufactured in USA
©2012 Haynes North America, Inc.
ISBN-13: 978-1-56392-947-2
ISBN-10: 1-56392-947-3
Library of Congress Control Number 2012935472

Haynes Publishing Group
Sparkford Nr Yeovil
Somerset BA22 7JJ England

Haynes North America, Inc
861 Lawrence Drive
Newbury Park
California 91320 USA

ABCDE
FGHIJ
KLMNO
PQRST

Contents

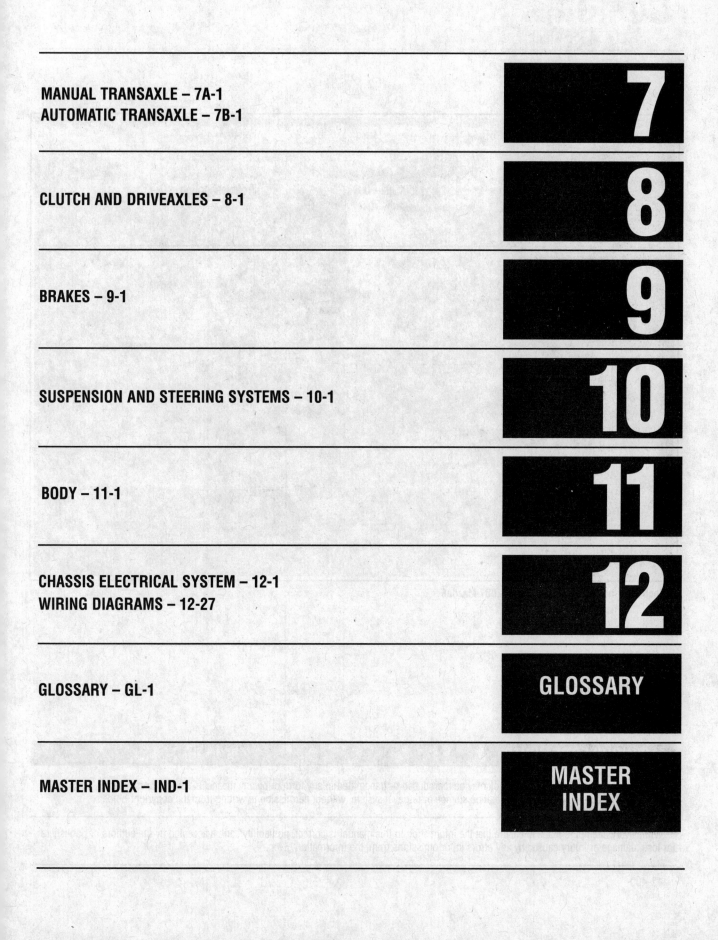

Mechanic and photographer with a 2007 Mazda6

ACKNOWLEDGEMENTS

While every attempt is made to ensure that the information in this manual is correct, no liability can be accepted by the authors or publishers for loss, damage or injury caused by any errors in, or omissions from, the information given.

About this manual

ITS PURPOSE

The purpose of this manual is to help you get the best value from your vehicle. It can do so in several ways. It can help you decide what work must be done, even if you choose to have it done by a dealer service department or a repair shop; it provides information and procedures for routine maintenance and servicing; and it offers diagnostic and repair procedures to follow when trouble occurs.

We hope you use the manual to tackle the work yourself. For many simpler jobs, doing it yourself may be quicker than arranging an appointment to get the vehicle into a shop and making the trips to leave it and pick it up. More importantly, a lot of money can be saved by avoiding the expense the shop must pass on to you to cover its labor and overhead costs. An added benefit is the sense of satisfaction and accomplishment that you feel after doing the job yourself.

USING THE MANUAL

The manual is divided into Chapters. Each Chapter is divided into numbered Sections. Each Section consists of consecutively numbered paragraphs.

At the beginning of each numbered Section you will be referred to any illustrations which apply to the procedures in that Section. The reference numbers used in illustration captions pinpoint the pertinent Section and the Step within that Section. That is, illustration 3.2 means the illustration refers to Section 3 and Step (or paragraph) 2 within that Section.

Procedures, once described in the text, are not normally repeated. When it's necessary to refer to another Chapter, the reference will be given as Chapter and Section number. Cross references given without use of the word "Chapter" apply to Sections and/or paragraphs in the same Chapter. For example, "see Section 8" means in the same Chapter.

References to the left or right side of the vehicle assume you are sitting in the driver's seat, facing forward.

Even though we have prepared this manual with extreme care, neither the publisher nor the author can accept responsibility for any errors in, or omissions from, the information given.

➡ NOTE

A *Note* provides information necessary to properly complete a procedure or information which will make the procedure easier to understand.

※ CAUTION

A *Caution* provides a special procedure or special steps which must be taken while completing the procedure where the Caution is found. Not heeding a Caution can result in damage to the assembly being worked on.

※ WARNING

A *Warning* provides a special procedure or special steps which must be taken while completing the procedure where the Warning is found. Not heeding a Warning can result in personal injury.

Introduction

This manual covers the Mazda6. There are several engines available: a 2.3L-DOHC, 16-valve (VVT) in-line four-cylinder engine (engine code L3); a 2.5L-DOHC, 16-valve (VVT) in-line four-cylinder engine (engine code L5); a 3.0L-DOHC, 24-valve (VVT) V6 engine (engine code AJ); and a 3.7L-DOHC, 24-valve (VVT) (engine code MZI).

The engine drives the front wheels through either a five- or six-speed manual or four-, five- or six-speed automatic transaxle via independent driveaxles.

The suspension is independent at all four wheels; coil spring/shock absorber assemblies are used at the front with parallel upper and lower control arms, and coil springs and telescopic shock absorbers at the rear with upper and lower control arms and trailing arms. The rack-and-pinion steering unit is mounted on the suspension crossmember.

The brakes are disc at the front and rear, with power assist standard. An Anti-lock Brake System (ABS) is standard on some models.

Vehicle identification numbers

Modifications are a continuing and unpublicized process in vehicle manufacturing. Since spare parts manuals and lists are compiled on a numerical basis, the individual vehicle numbers are essential to correctly identify the component required.

VEHICLE IDENTIFICATION NUMBER (VIN)

This very important identification number is stamped on a plate attached to the dashboard inside the windshield on the driver's side of the vehicle (see illustration). The VIN also appears on the Vehicle Certificate of Title and Registration. It contains information such as where and when the vehicle was manufactured, the model year and the body style.

The Vehicle Identification Number (VIN) is visible through the driver's side of the windshield

MANUFACTURER'S CERTIFICATION REGULATION LABEL

The Manufacturer's Certification Regulation label is attached to the driver's side door opening (see illustration). The label contains the name of the manufacturer, the month and year of production, the Gross Vehicle Weight Rating (GVWR), the Gross Axle Weight Rating (GAWR) and the certification statement.

VIN ENGINE CODE

Counting from the left, the engine code letter designation is the 8th character.

On all models covered by this manual the engine codes are:

C........ 2.3L four-cylinder engine (2008 and earlier models)
A........ 2.5L four-cylinder engine (Made in Mexico) (2009 and later models)

The Manufacturer's Certification Regulation label is located on the driver's door opening

H........ 2.5L four-cylinder engine (Made in Hiroshima) (2009 and later models)
D........ 3.0L V6 engine (2008 and earlier models)
B........ 3.7L V6 engine (2009 and later models)

VIN MODEL YEAR CODE

Counting from the left, the model year code letter designation is the 10th character.

On all models covered by this manual the model year codes are:

3 2003	8 2008
4 2004	9 2009
5 2005	A 2010
6 2006	B 2011
7 2007	

ENGINE NUMBER

On four-cylinder models, the engine identification number is stamped into a machined pad on the front side of the engine under the exhaust manifold.

On V6 models, the engine identification number is stamped into a machined pad on the left front end (driver's side) of the engine block (see illustration).

TRANSAXLE IDENTIFICATION

G35M-R, 5-speed manual transaxle (2008 and earlier four-cylinder models)
A65M-R, 5-speed manual transaxle (2008 and earlier V6 models)
G66M-R, 6-speed manual transaxle (2009 and later models)
FN4A-EL, 4-speed automatic transaxle (2006 and earlier four-cylinder models)
JA5A-EL, 5-speed automatic transaxle (2005 and earlier V6 models)
FS5A-EL, 5-speed automatic transaxle (2007 and later four-cylinder models and 2006 V6 models)
AW6A-EL and EI, 6-speed automatic transaxle (2007 and later V6 models)

Location of the engine identification number - V6 engine

Recall information

Vehicle recalls are carried out by the manufacturer in the rare event of a possible safety-related defect. The vehicle's registered owner is contacted at the address on file at the Department of Motor Vehicles and given the details of the recall. Remedial work is carried out free of charge at a dealer service department.

If you are the new owner of a used vehicle which was subject to a recall and you want to be sure that the work has been carried out, it's best to contact a dealer service department and ask about your individual vehicle - you'll need to furnish them your Vehicle Identification Number (VIN).

The table below is based on information provided by the National Highway Traffic Safety Administration (NHTSA), the body which oversees vehicle recalls in the United States. The recall database is updated constantly.

➡ **Note: This a partial list containing only the Mazda dealer recalls. There are additional aftermarket recalls available. For the latest information on vehicle recalls, check the NHTSA website at www.nhtsa.gov, or call the NHTSA hotline at 1-888-327-4236.**

Recall date	Recall campaign number	Model(s) affected	Concern
JUN 02, 2003	03V206000	2003 Mazda6	On some models, the socket holder in the fog lights is installed in the lamp casing using pressure. During operation of the fog light, the heat from the bulb can expand the socket holder. The expansion can force the socket holder rearward. After repeatedly being subject to this expansion, if the fog light is also subjected to vibration during vehicle operation, the socket holder with the bulb holder and the wiring harness may separate from the fog light casing. Should this occur, the bulb socket and the harness can drop inside the bumper and possibly but rarely, the heat generated by the bulb can cause the bumper to burn.
DEC 16, 2003	03V531000	2003 Mazda6	On certain passenger vehicles, the fuel sender unit (FSU) may have been improperly installed in the fuel tank, producing an inadequate seal, and fuel may leak. A fire could occur in the presence of an ignition source
DEC 09, 2004	04V582000	2004 Mazda6	On certain passenger vehicles, the right and/or left rear seat belts may not lock properly due to missing retaining pins on the housing. The locking mechanism of the seat belt retractor may malfunction, increasing the risk of death or serious injury to the rear seat passengers in the event of a crash. Passengers should not sit, and child seats should not be used, in the right or left rear seats until this defect has been corrected.

Recall date	Recall campaign number	Model(s) affected	Concern
SEP 26, 2007	03V207000	2003 Mazda6	Certain passenger vehicles fail to comply with requirements of federal motor vehicle safety standard No. 135, "passenger car brake systems". During production, the float in the fluid level sensor in the brake reservoir can be forced off of the guide rail during the filling of the master cylinder. Should this occur, it is possible that the float will not return to the guide rail and the brake fluid level warning indicator may not function.
AUG 08, 2008	08V412000	2007 and 2008 Mazda6	On some models with California emission specifications, the metal fuel tanks may have had the PVC protective coating on the outside of the fuel tank damaged during the assembly process, which may result in reduced corrosion resistance. This could lead to perforation of the fuel tank, causing fuel leakage. Fuel leakage in the presence of an ignition source could result in a fire.
FEB 03, 2009	09V043000	2009 Mazda6	The outer door handles may stick which may prevent the door from latching. This situation may allow the door to open while the vehicle is in motion. Driving the vehicle with the door unlatched could lead to an unbelted occupant being ejected and could result in injury or death.

Buying parts

Replacement parts are available from many sources, which generally fall into one of two categories - authorized dealer parts departments and independent retail auto parts stores. Our advice concerning these parts is as follows:

Retail auto parts stores: Good auto parts stores will stock frequently needed components which wear out relatively fast, such as clutch components, exhaust systems, brake parts, tune-up parts, etc. These stores often supply new or reconditioned parts on an exchange basis, which can save a considerable amount of money. Discount auto parts stores are often very good places to buy materials and parts needed for general vehicle maintenance such as oil, grease, filters, spark plugs, belts, touch-up paint, bulbs, etc. They also usually sell tools and general accessories, have convenient hours, charge lower prices and can often be found not far from home.

Authorized dealer parts department: This is the best source for parts which are unique to the vehicle and not generally available elsewhere (such as major engine parts, transmission parts, trim pieces, etc.).

Warranty information: If the vehicle is still covered under warranty, be sure that any replacement parts purchased - regardless of the source - do not invalidate the warranty!

To be sure of obtaining the correct parts, have engine and chassis numbers available and, if possible, take the old parts along for positive identification.

Maintenance techniques, tools and working facilities

MAINTENANCE TECHNIQUES

There are a number of techniques involved in maintenance and repair that will be referred to throughout this manual. Application of these techniques will enable the home mechanic to be more efficient, better organized and capable of performing the various tasks properly, which will ensure that the repair job is thorough and complete.

Fasteners

Fasteners are nuts, bolts, studs and screws used to hold two or more parts together. There are a few things to keep in mind when working with fasteners. Almost all of them use a locking device of some type, either a lockwasher, locknut, locking tab or thread adhesive. All threaded fasteners should be clean and straight, with undamaged threads and undamaged corners on the hex head where the wrench fits. Develop the habit of replacing all damaged nuts and bolts with new ones. Special locknuts with nylon or fiber inserts can only be used once. If they are removed, they lose their locking ability and must be replaced with new ones.

Rusted nuts and bolts should be treated with a penetrating fluid to ease removal and prevent breakage. Some mechanics use turpentine in a spout-type oil can, which works quite well. After applying the rust penetrant, let it work for a few minutes before trying to loosen the nut or bolt. Badly rusted fasteners may have to be chiseled or sawed off or removed with a special nut breaker, available at tool stores.

If a bolt or stud breaks off in an assembly, it can be drilled and removed with a special tool commonly available for this purpose. Most automotive machine shops can perform this task, as well as other repair procedures, such as the repair of threaded holes that have been stripped out.

Flat washers and lockwashers, when removed from an assembly, should always be replaced exactly as removed. Replace any damaged washers with new ones. Never use a lockwasher on any soft metal surface (such as aluminum), thin sheet metal or plastic.

Fastener sizes

For a number of reasons, automobile manufacturers are making wider and wider use of metric fasteners. Therefore, it is important to be able to tell the difference between standard (sometimes called U.S. or SAE) and metric hardware, since they cannot be interchanged.

All bolts, whether standard or metric, are sized according to diameter, thread pitch and length. For example, a standard 1/2 - 13 x 1 bolt is 1/2 inch in diameter, has 13 threads per inch and is 1 inch long. An M12 - 1.75 x 25 metric bolt is 12 mm in diameter, has a thread pitch of 1.75 mm (the distance between threads) and is 25 mm long. The two bolts are nearly identical, and easily confused, but they are not interchangeable.

In addition to the differences in diameter, thread pitch and length, metric and standard bolts can also be distinguished by examining the bolt heads. To begin with, the distance across the flats on a standard bolt head is measured in inches, while the same dimension on a metric bolt is sized in millimeters (the same is true for nuts). As a result, a standard wrench should not be used on a metric bolt and a metric wrench should not be used on a standard bolt. Also, most standard

bolts have slashes radiating out from the center of the head to denote the grade or strength of the bolt, which is an indication of the amount of torque that can be applied to it. The greater the number of slashes, the greater the strength of the bolt. Grades 0 through 5 are commonly used on automobiles. Metric bolts have a property class (grade) number, rather than a slash, molded into their heads to indicate bolt strength. In this case, the higher the number, the stronger the bolt. Property class numbers 8.8, 9.8 and 10.9 are commonly used on automobiles.

Strength markings can also be used to distinguish standard hex nuts from metric hex nuts. Many standard nuts have dots stamped into one side, while metric nuts are marked with a number. The greater the number of dots, or the higher the number, the greater the strength of the nut.

Metric studs are also marked on their ends according to property class (grade). Larger studs are numbered (the same as metric bolts), while smaller studs carry a geometric code to denote grade.

It should be noted that many fasteners, especially Grades 0 through 2, have no distinguishing marks on them. When such is the case, the only way to determine whether it is standard or metric is to measure the thread pitch or compare it to a known fastener of the same size.

Standard fasteners are often referred to as SAE, as opposed to metric. However, it should be noted that SAE technically refers to a non-metric fine thread fastener only. Coarse thread non-metric fasteners are referred to as USS sizes.

Since fasteners of the same size (both standard and metric) may have different strength ratings, be sure to reinstall any bolts, studs or nuts removed from your vehicle in their original locations. Also, when replacing a fastener with a new one, make sure that the new one has a strength rating equal to or greater than the original.

Tightening sequences and procedures

Most threaded fasteners should be tightened to a specific torque value (torque is the twisting force applied to a threaded component such as a nut or bolt). Overtightening the fastener can weaken it and cause it to break, while undertightening can cause it to eventually come loose. Bolts, screws and studs, depending on the material they are made of and their thread diameters, have specific torque values, many of which are noted in the Specifications at the end of each Chapter. Be sure to follow the torque recommendations closely. For fasteners not assigned a specific torque, a general torque value chart is presented here as a guide. These torque values are for dry (unlubricated) fasteners threaded into steel or cast iron (not aluminum). As was previously mentioned, the size and grade of a fastener determine the amount of torque that can safely be applied to it. The figures listed here are approximate for Grade 2 and Grade 3 fasteners. Higher grades can tolerate higher torque values.

Fasteners laid out in a pattern, such as cylinder head bolts, oil pan bolts, differential cover bolts, etc., must be loosened or tightened in sequence to avoid warping the component. This sequence will normally be shown in the appropriate Chapter. If a specific pattern is not given, the following procedures can be used to prevent warping.

Initially, the bolts or nuts should be assembled finger-tight only. Next, they should be tightened one full turn each, in a criss-cross or diagonal pattern. After each one has been tightened one full turn, return to the first one and tighten them all one-half turn, following the same

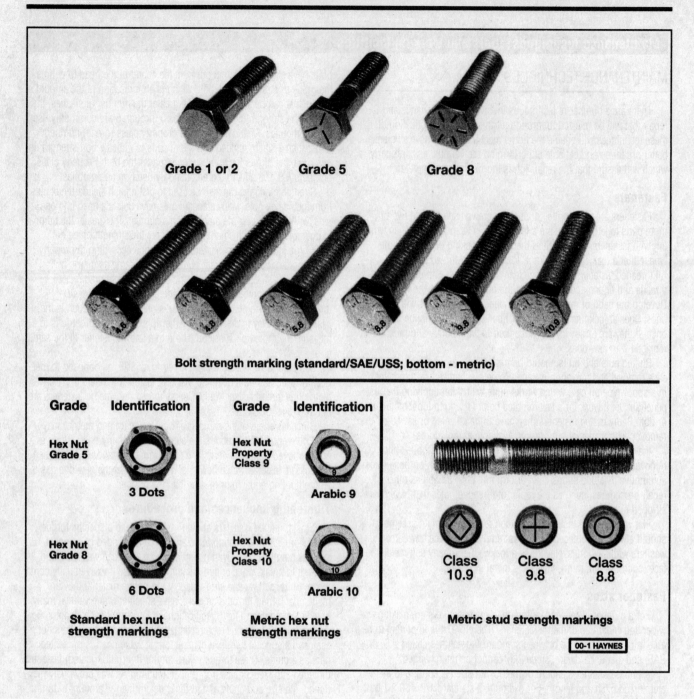

Grade 1 or 2   Grade 5   Grade 8

Bolt strength marking (standard/SAE/USS; bottom - metric)

Grade	Identification	Grade	Identification
Hex Nut Grade 5	3 Dots	Hex Nut Property Class 9	Arabic 9
Hex Nut Grade 8	6 Dots	Hex Nut Property Class 10	Arabic 10

Standard hex nut strength markings

Metric hex nut strength markings

Class 10.9   Class 9.8   Class 8.8

Metric stud strength markings

00-1 HAYNES

pattern. Finally, tighten each of them one-quarter turn at a time until each fastener has been tightened to the proper torque. To loosen and remove the fasteners, the procedure would be reversed.

Component disassembly

Component disassembly should be done with care and purpose to help ensure that the parts go back together properly. Always keep track of the sequence in which parts are removed. Make note of special characteristics or marks on parts that can be installed more than one way, such as a grooved thrust washer on a shaft. It is a good idea to lay the disassembled parts out on a clean surface in the order that they were removed. It may also be helpful to make sketches or take instant photos of components before removal.

When removing fasteners from a component, keep track of their locations. Sometimes threading a bolt back in a part, or putting the washers and nut back on a stud, can prevent mix-ups later. If nuts and bolts cannot be returned to their original locations, they should be kept in a compartmented box or a series of small boxes. A cupcake or muffin tin is ideal for this purpose, since each cavity can hold the bolts and nuts from a particular area (i.e. oil pan bolts, valve cover bolts, engine

Metric thread sizes

	Ft-lbs	Nm
M-6	6 to 9	9 to 12
M-8	14 to 21	19 to 28
M-10	28 to 40	38 to 54
M-12	50 to 71	68 to 96
M-14	80 to 140	109 to 154

Pipe thread sizes

1/8	5 to 8	7 to 10
1/4	12 to 18	17 to 24
3/8	22 to 33	30 to 44
1/2	25 to 35	34 to 47

U.S. thread sizes

1/4 - 20	6 to 9	9 to 12
5/16 - 18	12 to 18	17 to 24
5/16 - 24	14 to 20	19 to 27
3/8 - 16	22 to 32	30 to 43
3/8 - 24	27 to 38	37 to 51
7/16 - 14	40 to 55	55 to 74
7/16 - 20	40 to 60	55 to 81
1/2 - 13	55 to 80	75 to 108

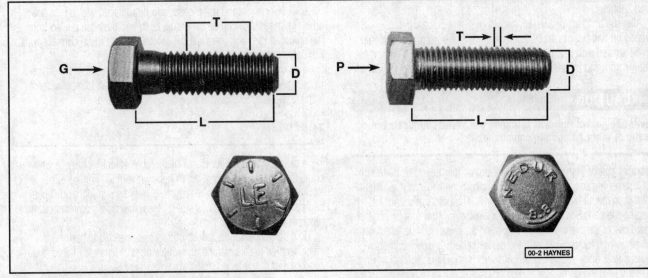

00-2 HAYNES

Standard (SAE and USS) bolt dimensions/grade marks

G   Grade marks (bolt strength)
L   Length (in inches)
T   Thread pitch (number of threads per inch)
D   Nominal diameter (in inches)

Metric bolt dimensions/grade marks

P   Property class (bolt strength)
L   Length (in millimeters)
T   Thread pitch (distance between threads in millimeters)
D   Diameter

mount bolts, etc.). A pan of this type is especially helpful when working on assemblies with very small parts, such as the carburetor, alternator, valve train or interior dash and trim pieces. The cavities can be marked with paint or tape to identify the contents.

Whenever wiring looms, harnesses or connectors are separated, it is a good idea to identify the two halves with numbered pieces of masking tape so they can be easily reconnected.

Gasket sealing surfaces

Throughout any vehicle, gaskets are used to seal the mating surfaces between two parts and keep lubricants, fluids, vacuum or pressure contained in an assembly.

Many times these gaskets are coated with a liquid or paste-type gasket sealing compound before assembly. Age, heat and pressure can sometimes cause the two parts to stick together so tightly that they are very difficult to separate. Often, the assembly can be loosened by striking it with a soft-face hammer near the mating surfaces. A regular hammer can be used if a block of wood is placed between the hammer and the part. Do not hammer on cast parts or parts that could be easily damaged. With any particularly stubborn part, always recheck to make sure that every fastener has been removed.

Avoid using a screwdriver or bar to pry apart an assembly, as they

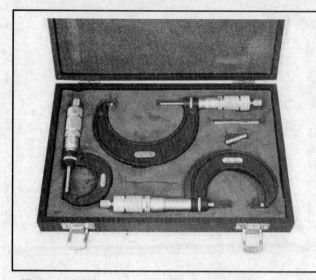

Micrometer set

Dial indicator set

can easily mar the gasket sealing surfaces of the parts, which must remain smooth. If prying is absolutely necessary, use an old broom handle, but keep in mind that extra clean up will be necessary if the wood splinters.

After the parts are separated, the old gasket must be carefully scraped off and the gasket surfaces cleaned. Stubborn gasket material can be soaked with rust penetrant or treated with a special chemical to soften it so it can be easily scraped off.

❋ CAUTION:

Never use gasket removal solutions or caustic chemicals on plastic or other composite components.

A scraper can be fashioned from a piece of copper tubing by flattening and sharpening one end. Copper is recommended because it is usually softer than the surfaces to be scraped, which reduces the chance of gouging the part. Some gaskets can be removed with a wire brush, but regardless of the method used, the mating surfaces must be left clean and smooth. If for some reason the gasket surface is gouged, then a gasket sealer thick enough to fill scratches will have to be used during reassembly of the components. For most applications, a non-drying (or semi-drying) gasket sealer should be used.

Hose removal tips

❋ WARNING:

If the vehicle is equipped with air conditioning, do not disconnect any of the A/C hoses without first having the system depressurized by a dealer service department or a service station.

Hose removal precautions closely parallel gasket removal precautions. Avoid scratching or gouging the surface that the hose mates against or the connection may leak. This is especially true for radiator hoses. Because of various chemical reactions, the rubber in hoses can bond itself to the metal spigot that the hose fits over. To remove a hose, first loosen the hose clamps that secure it to the spigot. Then, with slip-joint pliers, grab the hose at the clamp and rotate it around the spigot. Work it back and forth until it is completely free, then pull it off. Silicone or other lubricants will ease removal if they can be applied

between the hose and the outside of the spigot. Apply the same lubricant to the inside of the hose and the outside of the spigot to simplify installation.

As a last resort (and if the hose is to be replaced with a new one anyway), the rubber can be slit with a knife and the hose peeled from the spigot. If this must be done, be careful that the metal connection is not damaged.

If a hose clamp is broken or damaged, do not reuse it. Wire-type clamps usually weaken with age, so it is a good idea to replace them with screw-type clamps whenever a hose is removed.

TOOLS

A selection of good tools is a basic requirement for anyone who plans to maintain and repair his or her own vehicle. For the owner who has few tools, the initial investment might seem high, but when compared to the spiraling costs of professional auto maintenance and repair, it is a wise one.

To help the owner decide which tools are needed to perform the tasks detailed in this manual, the following tool lists are offered: *Maintenance and minor repair, Repair/overhaul and Special.*

The newcomer to practical mechanics should start off with the *maintenance and minor repair* tool kit, which is adequate for the simpler jobs performed on a vehicle. Then, as confidence and experience grow, the owner can tackle more difficult tasks, buying additional tools as they are needed. Eventually the basic kit will be expanded into the *repair and overhaul* tool set. Over a period of time, the experienced do-it-yourselfer will assemble a tool set complete enough for most repair and overhaul procedures and will add tools from the special category when it is felt that the expense is justified by the frequency of use.

Maintenance and minor repair tool kit

The tools in this list should be considered the minimum required for performance of routine maintenance, servicing and minor repair work. We recommend the purchase of combination wrenches (box-end and open-end combined in one wrench). While more expensive than open end wrenches, they offer the advantages of both types of wrench.

Combination wrench set (1/4-inch to 1 inch or 6 mm to 19 mm)
Adjustable wrench, 8 inch
Spark plug wrench with rubber insert

Spark plug gap adjusting tool
Feeler gauge set
Brake bleeder wrench
Standard screwdriver (5/16-inch x 6 inch)
Phillips screwdriver (No. 2 x 6 inch)
Combination pliers - 6 inch
Hacksaw and assortment of blades
Tire pressure gauge
Grease gun

Oil can
Fine emery cloth
Wire brush
Battery post and cable cleaning tool
Oil filter wrench
Funnel (medium size)
Safety goggles
Jackstands (2)
Drain pan

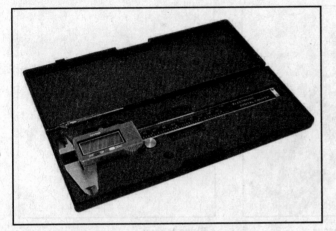

Dial caliper

Hand-operated vacuum pump

Timing light

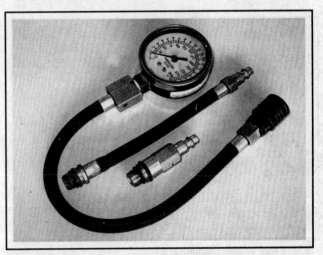

Compression gauge with spark plug hole adapter

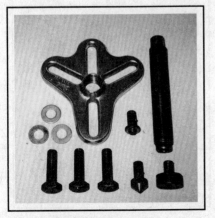

Damper/steering wheel puller

General purpose puller

Hydraulic lifter removal tool

➡ **Note: If basic tune-ups are going to be part of routine maintenance, it will be necessary to purchase a good quality stroboscopic timing light and combination tachometer/dwell meter. Although they are included in the list of special tools, it is mentioned here because they are absolutely necessary for tuning most vehicles properly.**

Repair and overhaul tool set

These tools are essential for anyone who plans to perform major repairs and are in addition to those in the maintenance and minor repair tool kit. Included is a comprehensive set of sockets which, though expensive, are invaluable because of their versatility, especially when various extensions and drives are available. We recommend the 1/2-inch drive over the 3/8-inch drive. Although the larger drive is bulky and more expensive, it has the capacity of accepting a very wide range of large sockets. Ideally, however, the mechanic should have a 3/8-inch drive set and a 1/2-inch drive set.

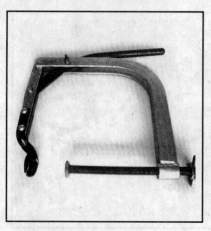

Valve spring compressor

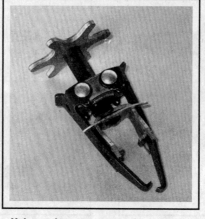

Valve spring compressor

Ridge reamer

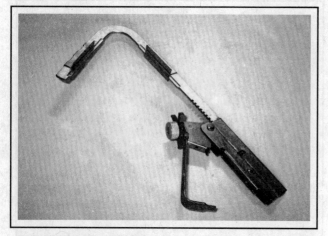

Piston ring groove cleaning tool

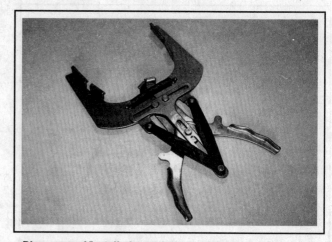

Ring removal/installation tool

Ring compressor

Cylinder hone

Brake hold-down spring tool

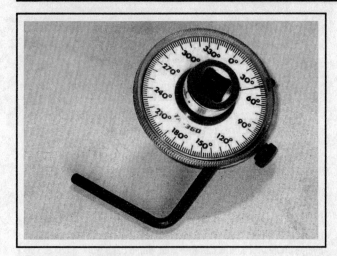

Torque angle gauge

Clutch plate alignment tool

Socket set(s)
Reversible ratchet
Extension - 10 inch
Universal joint
Torque wrench (same size drive as sockets)
Ball peen hammer - 8 ounce
Soft-face hammer (plastic/rubber)
Standard screwdriver (1/4-inch x 6 inch)
Standard screwdriver (stubby - 5/16-inch)
Phillips screwdriver (No. 3 x 8 inch)
Phillips screwdriver (stubby - No. 2)
Pliers - vise grip
Pliers - lineman's
Pliers - needle nose
Pliers - snap-ring (internal and external)
Cold chisel - 1/2-inch
Scribe
Scraper (made from flattened copper tubing)
Centerpunch
Pin punches (1/16, 1/8, 3/16-inch)
Steel rule/straightedge - 12 inch
Allen wrench set (1/8 to 3/8-inch or 4 mm to 10 mm)
A selection of files
Wire brush (large)
Jackstands (second set)
Jack (scissor or hydraulic type)

➡ **Note: Another tool which is often useful is an electric drill with a chuck capacity of 3/8-inch and a set of good quality drill bits.**

Special tools

The tools in this list include those which are not used regularly, are expensive to buy, or which need to be used in accordance with their manufacturer's instructions. Unless these tools will be used frequently, it is not very economical to purchase many of them. A consideration would be to split the cost and use between yourself and a friend or friends. In addition, most of these tools can be obtained from a tool rental shop on a temporary basis.

This list primarily contains only those tools and instruments widely available to the public, and not those special tools produced by the vehicle manufacturer for distribution to dealer service departments. Occasionally, references to the manufacturer's special tools are included in the text of this manual. Generally, an alternative method of doing the job without the special tool is offered. However, sometimes there is no alternative to their use. Where this is the case, and the tool cannot be purchased or borrowed, the work should be turned over to the dealer service department or an automotive repair shop.

Valve spring compressor
Piston ring groove cleaning tool
Piston ring compressor
Piston ring installation tool
Cylinder compression gauge
Cylinder ridge reamer
Cylinder surfacing hone
Cylinder bore gauge
Micrometers and/or dial calipers
Hydraulic lifter removal tool
Balljoint separator
Universal-type puller
Impact screwdriver
Dial indicator set
Stroboscopic timing light (inductive pick-up)
Hand operated vacuum/pressure pump
Tachometer/dwell meter
Universal electrical multimeter
Cable hoist
Brake spring removal and installation tools

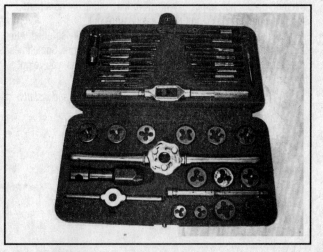

Tap and die set

Buying tools

For the do-it-yourselfer who is just starting to get involved in vehicle maintenance and repair, there are a number of options available when purchasing tools. If maintenance and minor repair is the extent of the work to be done, the purchase of individual tools is satisfactory. If, on the other hand, extensive work is planned, it would be a good idea to purchase a modest tool set from one of the large retail chain stores. A set can usually be bought at a substantial savings over the individual tool prices, and they often come with a tool box. As additional tools are needed, add-on sets, individual tools and a larger tool box can be purchased to expand the tool selection. Building a tool set gradually allows the cost of the tools to be spread over a longer period of time and gives the mechanic the freedom to choose only those tools that will actually be used.

Tool stores will often be the only source of some of the special tools that are needed, but regardless of where tools are bought, try to avoid cheap ones, especially when buying screwdrivers and sockets, because they won't last very long. The expense involved in replacing cheap tools will eventually be greater than the initial cost of quality tools.

Care and maintenance of tools

Good tools are expensive, so it makes sense to treat them with respect. Keep them clean and in usable condition and store them properly when not in use. Always wipe off any dirt, grease or metal chips before putting them away. Never leave tools lying around in the work area. Upon completion of a job, always check closely under the hood for tools that may have been left there so they won't get lost during a test drive.

Some tools, such as screwdrivers, pliers, wrenches and sockets, can be hung on a panel mounted on the garage or workshop wall, while others should be kept in a tool box or tray. Measuring instruments, gauges, meters, etc. must be carefully stored where they cannot be damaged by weather or impact from other tools.

When tools are used with care and stored properly, they will last a very long time. Even with the best of care, though, tools will wear out if used frequently. When a tool is damaged or worn out, replace it. Subsequent jobs will be safer and more enjoyable if you do.

HOW TO REPAIR DAMAGED THREADS

Sometimes, the internal threads of a nut or bolt hole can become stripped, usually from overtightening. Stripping threads is an all-too-common occurrence, especially when working with aluminum parts, because aluminum is so soft that it easily strips out.

Usually, external or internal threads are only partially stripped. After they've been cleaned up with a tap or die, they'll still work. Sometimes, however, threads are badly damaged. When this happens, you've got three choices:

1) *Drill and tap the hole to the next suitable oversize and install a larger diameter bolt, screw or stud.*

2) *Drill and tap the hole to accept a threaded plug, then drill and tap the plug to the original screw size. You can also buy a plug already threaded to the original size. Then you simply drill a hole to the specified size, then run the threaded plug into the hole with a bolt and jam nut. Once the plug is fully seated, remove the jam nut and bolt.*

3) *The third method uses a patented thread repair kit like Heli-Coil or Slimsert. These easy-to-use kits are designed to repair damaged threads in straight-through holes and blind holes. Both are available as kits which can handle a variety of sizes and thread patterns. Drill the hole, then tap it with the special included tap. Install the Heli-Coil and the hole is back to its original diameter and thread pitch.*

Regardless of which method you use, be sure to proceed calmly and carefully. A little impatience or carelessness during one of these relatively simple procedures can ruin your whole day's work and cost you a bundle if you wreck an expensive part.

WORKING FACILITIES

Not to be overlooked when discussing tools is the workshop. If anything more than routine maintenance is to be carried out, some sort of suitable work area is essential.

It is understood, and appreciated, that many home mechanics do not have a good workshop or garage available, and end up removing an engine or doing major repairs outside. It is recommended, however, that the overhaul or repair be completed under the cover of a roof.

A clean, flat workbench or table of comfortable working height is an absolute necessity. The workbench should be equipped with a vise that has a jaw opening of at least four inches.

As mentioned previously, some clean, dry storage space is also required for tools, as well as the lubricants, fluids, cleaning solvents, etc. which soon become necessary.

Sometimes waste oil and fluids, drained from the engine or cooling system during normal maintenance or repairs, present a disposal problem. To avoid pouring them on the ground or into a sewage system, pour the used fluids into large containers, seal them with caps and take them to an authorized disposal site or recycling center. Plastic jugs, such as old antifreeze containers, are ideal for this purpose.

Always keep a supply of old newspapers and clean rags available. Old towels are excellent for mopping up spills. Many mechanics use rolls of paper towels for most work because they are readily available and disposable. To help keep the area under the vehicle clean, a large cardboard box can be cut open and flattened to protect the garage or shop floor.

Whenever working over a painted surface, such as when leaning over a fender to service something under the hood, always cover it with an old blanket or bedspread to protect the finish. Vinyl covered pads, made especially for this purpose, are available at auto parts stores.

Jacking and towing

JACKING

❋❋ WARNING:

The jack supplied with the vehicle should only be used for changing a tire or placing jackstands under the frame. Never work under the vehicle or start the engine while this jack is being used as the only means of support.

The vehicle should be on level ground. Place the shift lever in Park, if you have an automatic, or Reverse if you have a manual transaxle. Block the wheel diagonally opposite the wheel being changed. Set the parking brake.

Remove the spare tire and jack from stowage. Remove the wheel cover and trim ring (if so equipped) with the tapered end of the lug nut

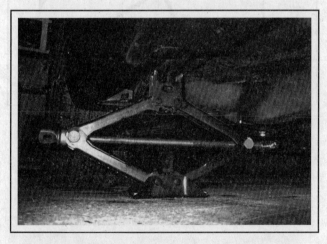

Place the jack between the raised welts on the rocker panel flange nearest the wheel to be changed

wrench by inserting and twisting the handle and then prying against the back of the wheel cover. Loosen, but do not remove, the lug nuts (one-half turn is sufficient).

Place the scissors-type jack under the vehicle and adjust the jack height until it engages with the proper jacking point. There is a front and rear jacking point on each side of the vehicle (see illustration).

Turn the jack handle clockwise until the tire clears the ground. Remove the lug nuts and pull the wheel off, then install the spare.

Install the lug nuts with the beveled edges facing in. Tighten them snugly. Don't attempt to tighten them completely until the vehicle is lowered or it could slip off the jack. Turn the jack handle counterclock-wise to lower the vehicle. Remove the jack and tighten the lug nuts in a diagonal pattern.

Stow the tire, jack and wrench. Unblock the wheels.

TOWING

These vehicles can be towed from the front with the front wheels off the ground, using a wheel lift type tow truck. If towed from the rear, the front wheels must be placed on a dolly. A sling-type tow truck cannot be used, as body damage will result. The best way to tow the vehicle is with a flat-bed car carrier.

In an emergency the vehicle can be towed a short distance with a cable or chain attached to one of the towing eyelets located under the front or rear bumpers. The driver must remain in the vehicle to operate the steering and brakes (remember that power steering and power brakes will not work with the engine off).

Booster battery (jump) starting

Observe these precautions when using a booster battery to start a vehicle:

a) *Before connecting the booster battery, make sure the ignition switch is in the Off position.*
b) *Turn off the lights, heater and other electrical loads.*
c) *Your eyes should be shielded. Safety goggles are a good idea.*
d) *Make sure the booster battery is the same voltage as the dead one in the vehicle.*
e) *The two vehicles MUST NOT TOUCH each other!*
f) *Make sure the transaxle is in Neutral (manual) or Park (automatic).*
g) *If the booster battery is not a maintenance-free type, remove the vent caps and lay a cloth over the vent holes.*

Connect the red jumper cable to the positive (+) terminals of each battery (see illustration).

Connect one end of the black jumper cable to the negative (-) terminal of the booster battery. The other end of this cable should be connected to a good ground on the vehicle to be started, such as a bolt or bracket on the body.

Start the engine using the booster battery, then, with the engine running at idle speed, disconnect the jumper cables in the reverse order of connection.

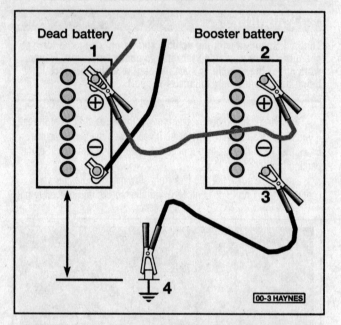

Make the booster battery cable connections in the numerical order shown (note that the negative cable of the booster battery is NOT attached to the negative terminal of the

Automotive chemicals and lubricants

A number of automotive chemicals and lubricants are available for use during vehicle maintenance and repair. They include a wide variety of products ranging from cleaning solvents and degreasers to lubricants and protective sprays for rubber, plastic and vinyl.

CLEANERS

Carburetor cleaner and choke cleaner is a strong solvent for gum, varnish and carbon. Most carburetor cleaners leave a dry-type lubricant film which will not harden or gum up. Because of this film it is not recommended for use on electrical components.

Brake system cleaner is used to remove brake dust, grease and brake fluid from the brake system, where clean surfaces are absolutely necessary. It leaves no residue and often eliminates brake squeal caused by contaminants.

Electrical cleaner removes oxidation, corrosion and carbon deposits from electrical contacts, restoring full current flow. It can also be used to clean spark plugs, carburetor jets, voltage regulators and other parts where an oil-free surface is desired.

Demoisturants remove water and moisture from electrical components such as alternators, voltage regulators, electrical connectors and fuse blocks. They are non-conductive and non-corrosive.

Degreasers are heavy-duty solvents used to remove grease from the outside of the engine and from chassis components. They can be sprayed or brushed on and, depending on the type, are rinsed off either with water or solvent.

LUBRICANTS

Motor oil is the lubricant formulated for use in engines. It normally contains a wide variety of additives to prevent corrosion and reduce foaming and wear. Motor oil comes in various weights (viscosity ratings) from 0 to 50. The recommended weight of the oil depends on the season, temperature and the demands on the engine. Light oil is used in cold climates and under light load conditions. Heavy oil is used in hot climates and where high loads are encountered. Multi-viscosity oils are designed to have characteristics of both light and heavy oils and are available in a number of weights from 0W-20 to 20W-50.

Gear oil is designed to be used in differentials, manual transmissions and other areas where high-temperature lubrication is required.

Chassis and wheel bearing grease is a heavy grease used where increased loads and friction are encountered, such as for wheel bearings, ball-joints, tie-rod ends and universal joints.

High-temperature wheel bearing grease is designed to withstand the extreme temperatures encountered by wheel bearings in disc brake equipped vehicles. It usually contains molybdenum disulfide (moly), which is a dry-type lubricant.

White grease is a heavy grease for metal-to-metal applications where water is a problem. White grease stays soft under both low and high temperatures (usually from -100 to +190-degrees F), and will not wash off or dilute in the presence of water.

Assembly lube is a special extreme pressure lubricant, usually containing moly, used to lubricate high-load parts (such as main and rod bearings and cam lobes) for initial start-up of a new engine. The assembly lube lubricates the parts without being squeezed out or washed away until the engine oiling system begins to function.

Silicone lubricants are used to protect rubber, plastic, vinyl and nylon parts.

Graphite lubricants are used where oils cannot be used due to contamination problems, such as in locks. The dry graphite will lubricate metal parts while remaining uncontaminated by dirt, water, oil or acids. It is electrically conductive and will not foul electrical contacts in locks such as the ignition switch.

Moly penetrants loosen and lubricate frozen, rusted and corroded fasteners and prevent future rusting or freezing.

Heat-sink grease is a special electrically non-conductive grease that is used for mounting electronic ignition modules where it is essential that heat is transferred away from the module.

SEALANTS

RTV sealant is one of the most widely used gasket compounds. Made from silicone, RTV is air curing, it seals, bonds, waterproofs, fills surface irregularities, remains flexible, doesn't shrink, is relatively easy to remove, and is used as a supplementary sealer with almost all low and medium temperature gaskets.

Anaerobic sealant is much like RTV in that it can be used either to seal gaskets or to form gaskets by itself. It remains flexible, is solvent resistant and fills surface imperfections. The difference between an anaerobic sealant and an RTV-type sealant is in the curing. RTV cures when exposed to air, while an anaerobic sealant cures only in the absence of air. This means that an anaerobic sealant cures only after the assembly of parts, sealing them together.

Thread and pipe sealant is used for sealing hydraulic and pneumatic fittings and vacuum lines. It is usually made from a Teflon compound, and comes in a spray, a paint-on liquid and as a wrap-around tape.

CHEMICALS

Anti-seize compound prevents seizing, galling, cold welding, rust and corrosion in fasteners. High-temperature anti-seize, usually made with copper and graphite lubricants, is used for exhaust system and exhaust manifold bolts.

Anaerobic locking compounds are used to keep fasteners from vibrating or working loose and cure only after installation, in the absence of air. Medium strength locking compound is used for small nuts, bolts and screws that may be removed later. High-strength locking compound is for large nuts, bolts and studs which aren't removed on a regular basis.

Oil additives range from viscosity index improvers to chemical treatments that claim to reduce internal engine friction. It should be noted that most oil manufacturers caution against using additives with their oils.

Gas additives perform several functions, depending on their chemical makeup. They usually contain solvents that help dissolve gum and varnish that build up on carburetor, fuel injection and intake parts. They also serve to break down carbon deposits that form on the inside surfaces of the combustion chambers. Some additives contain upper cylinder lubricants for valves and piston rings, and others contain chemicals to remove condensation from the gas tank.

MISCELLANEOUS

Brake fluid is specially formulated hydraulic fluid that can withstand the heat and pressure encountered in brake systems. Care must be taken so this fluid does not come in contact with painted surfaces or plastics. An opened container should always be resealed to prevent contamination by water or dirt.

Weatherstrip adhesive is used to bond weatherstripping around doors, windows and trunk lids. It is sometimes used to attach trim pieces.

Undercoating is a petroleum-based, tar-like substance that is designed to protect metal surfaces on the underside of the vehicle from corrosion. It also acts as a sound-deadening agent by insulating the bottom of the vehicle.

Waxes and polishes are used to help protect painted and plated surfaces from the weather. Different types of paint may require the use of different types of wax and polish. Some polishes utilize a chemical or abrasive cleaner to help remove the top layer of oxidized (dull) paint on older vehicles. In recent years many non-wax polishes that contain a wide variety of chemicals such as polymers and silicones have been introduced. These non-wax polishes are usually easier to apply and last longer than conventional waxes and polishes.

CONVERSION FACTORS

LENGTH (distance)

Inches (in)	X 25.4	= Millimeters (mm)	X 0.0394	= Inches (in)
Feet (ft)	X 0.305	= Meters (m)	X 3.281	= Feet (ft)
Miles	X 1.609	= Kilometers (km)	X 0.621	= Miles

VOLUME (capacity)

Cubic inches (cu in; in^3)	X 16.387	= Cubic centimeters (cc; cm^3)	X 0.061	= Cubic inches (cu in; in^3)
Imperial pints (Imp pt)	X 0.568	= Liters (l)	X 1.76	= Imperial pints (Imp pt)
Imperial quarts (Imp qt)	X 1.137	= Liters (l)	X 0.88	= Imperial quarts (Imp qt)
Imperial quarts (Imp qt)	X 1.201	= US quarts (US qt)	X 0.833	= Imperial quarts (Imp qt)
US quarts (US qt)	X 0.946	= Liters (l)	X 1.057	= US quarts (US qt)
Imperial gallons (Imp gal)	X 4.546	= Liters (l)	X 0.22	= Imperial gallons (Imp gal)
Imperial gallons (Imp gal)	X 1.201	= US gallons (US gal)	X 0.833	= Imperial gallons (Imp gal)
US gallons (US gal)	X 3.785	= Liters (l)	X 0.264	= US gallons (US gal)

MASS (weight)

Ounces (oz)	X 28.35	= Grams (g)	X 0.035	= Ounces (oz)
Pounds (lb)	X 0.454	= Kilograms (kg)	X 2.205	= Pounds (lb)

FORCE

Ounces-force (ozf; oz)	X 0.278	= Newtons (N)	X 3.6	= Ounces-force (ozf; oz)
Pounds-force (lbf; lb)	X 4.448	= Newtons (N)	X 0.225	= Pounds-force (lbf; lb)
Newtons (N)	X 0.1	= Kilograms-force (kgf; kg)	X 9.81	= Newtons (N)

PRESSURE

Pounds-force per square inch (psi; lbf/in^2; lb/in^2)	X 0.070	= Kilograms-force per square centimeter (kgf/cm^2; kg/cm^2)	X 14.223	= Pounds-force per square inch (psi; lbf/in^2; lb/in^2)
Pounds-force per square inch (psi; lbf/in^2; lb/in^2)	X 0.068	= Atmospheres (atm)	X 14.696	= Pounds-force per square inch (psi; lbf/in^2; lb/in^2)
Pounds-force per square inch (psi; lbf/in^2; lb/in^2)	X 0.069	= Bars	X 14.5	= Pounds-force per square inch (psi; lbf/in^2; lb/in^2)
Pounds-force per square inch (psi; lbf/in^2; lb/in^2)	X 6.895	= Kilopascals (kPa)	X 0.145	= Pounds-force per square inch (psi; lbf/in^2; lb/in^2)
Kilopascals (kPa)	X 0.01	= Kilograms-force per square centimeter (kgf/cm^2; kg/cm^2)	X 98.1	= Kilopascals (kPa)

TORQUE (moment of force)

Pounds-force inches (lbf in; lb in)	X 1.152	= Kilograms-force centimeter (kgf cm; kg cm)	X 0.868	= Pounds-force inches (lbf in; lb in)
Pounds-force inches (lbf in; lb in)	X 0.113	= Newton meters (Nm)	X 8.85	= Pounds-force inches (lbf in; lb in)
Pounds-force inches (lbf in; lb in)	X 0.083	= Pounds-force feet (lbf ft; lb ft)	X 12	= Pounds-force inches (lbf in; lb in)
Pounds-force feet (lbf ft; lb ft)	X 0.138	= Kilograms-force meters (kgf m; kg m)	X 7.233	= Pounds-force feet (lbf ft; lb ft)
Pounds-force feet (lbf ft; lb ft)	X 1.356	= Newton meters (Nm)	X 0.738	= Pounds-force feet (lbf ft; lb ft)
Newton meters (Nm)	X 0.102	= Kilograms-force meters (kgf m; kg m)	X 9.804	= Newton meters (Nm)

VACUUM

Inches mercury (in. Hg)	X 3.377	= Kilopascals (kPa)	X 0.2961	= Inches mercury
Inches mercury (in. Hg)	X 25.4	= Millimeters mercury (mm Hg)	X 0.0394	= Inches mercury

POWER

Horsepower (hp)	X 745.7	= Watts (W)	X 0.0013	= Horsepower (hp)

VELOCITY (speed)

Miles per hour (miles/hr; mph)	X 1.609	= Kilometers per hour (km/hr; kph)	X 0.621	= Miles per hour (miles/hr; mph)

FUEL CONSUMPTION *

Miles per gallon, Imperial (mpg)	X 0.354	= Kilometers per liter (km/l)	X 2.825	= Miles per gallon, Imperial (mpg)
Miles per gallon, US (mpg)	X 0.425	= Kilometers per liter (km/l)	X 2.352	= Miles per gallon, US (mpg)

TEMPERATURE

Degrees Fahrenheit = ($°C$ x 1.8) + 32   Degrees Celsius (Degrees Centigrade; $°C$) = ($°F$ - 32) x 0.56

*It is common practice to convert from miles per gallon (mpg) to liters/100 kilometers (l/100km), where mpg (Imperial) x l/100 km = 282 and mpg (US) x l/100 km = 235

FRACTION/DECIMAL/MILLIMETER EQUIVALENTS

DECIMALS TO MILLIMETERS

Decimal	mm	Decimal	mm
0.001	0.0254	0.500	12.7000
0.002	0.0508	0.510	12.9540
0.003	0.0762	0.520	13.2080
0.004	0.1016	0.530	13.4620
0.005	0.1270	0.540	13.7160
0.006	0.1524	0.550	13.9700
0.007	0.1778	0.560	14.2240
0.008	0.2032	0.570	14.4780
0.009	0.2286	0.580	14.7320
		0.590	14.9860
0.010	0.2540		
0.020	0.5080		
0.030	0.7620		
0.040	1.0160	0.600	15.2400
0.050	1.2700	0.610	15.4940
0.060	1.5240	0.620	15.7480
0.070	1.7780	0.630	16.0020
0.080	2.0320	0.640	16.2560
0.090	2.2860	0.650	16.5100
		0.660	16.7640
0.100	2.5400	0.670	17.0180
0.110	2.7940	0.680	17.2720
0.120	3.0480	0.690	17.5260
0.130	3.3020		
0.140	3.5560		
0.150	3.8100	0.700	17.7800
0.160	4.0640	0.710	18.0340
0.170	4.3180	0.720	18.2880
0.180	4.5720	0.730	18.5420
0.190	4.8260	0.740	18.7960
		0.750	19.0500
0.200	5.0800	0.760	19.3040
0.210	5.3340	0.770	19.5580
0.220	5.5880	0.780	19.8120
0.230	5.8420	0.790	20.0660
0.240	6.0960		
0.250	6.3500		
0.260	6.6040	0.800	20.3200
0.270	6.8580	0.810	20.5740
0.280	7.1120	0.820	21.8280
0.290	7.3660	0.830	21.0820
		0.840	21.3360
0.300	7.6200	0.850	21.5900
0.310	7.8740	0.860	21.8440
0.320	8.1280	0.870	22.0980
0.330	8.3820	0.880	22.3520
0.340	8.6360	0.890	22.6060
0.350	8.8900		
0.360	9.1440		
0.370	9.3980		
0.380	9.6520		
0.390	9.9060	0.900	22.8600
0.400	10.1600	0.910	23.1140
0.410	10.4140	0.920	23.3680
0.420	10.6680	0.930	23.6220
0.430	10.9220	0.940	23.8760
0.440	11.1760	0.950	24.1300
0.450	11.4300	0.960	24.3840
0.460	11.6840	0.970	24.6380
0.470	11.9380	0.980	24.8920
0.480	12.1920	0.990	25.1460
0.490	12.4460	1.000	25.4000

FRACTIONS TO DECIMALS TO MILLIMETERS

Fraction	Decimal	mm	Fraction	Decimal	mm
1/64	0.0156	0.3969	33/64	0.5156	13.0969
1/32	0.0312	0.7938	17/32	0.5312	13.4938
3/64	0.0469	1.1906	35/64	0.5469	13.8906
1/16	0.0625	1.5875	9/16	0.5625	14.2875
5/64	0.0781	1.9844	37/64	0.5781	14.6844
3/32	0.0938	2.3812	19/32	0.5938	15.0812
7/64	0.1094	2.7781	39/64	0.6094	15.4781
1/8	0.1250	3.1750	5/8	0.6250	15.8750
9/64	0.1406	3.5719	41/64	0.6406	16.2719
5/32	0.1562	3.9688	21/32	0.6562	16.6688
11/64	0.1719	4.3656	43/64	0.6719	17.0656
3/16	0.1875	4.7625	11/16	0.6875	17.4625
13/64	0.2031	5.1594	45/64	0.7031	17.8594
7/32	0.2188	5.5562	23/32	0.7188	18.2562
15/64	0.2344	5.9531	47/64	0.7344	18.6531
1/4	0.2500	6.3500	3/4	0.7500	19.0500
17/64	0.2656	6.7469	49/64	0.7656	19.4469
9/32	0.2812	7.1438	25/32	0.7812	19.8438
19/64	0.2969	7.5406	51/64	0.7969	20.2406
5/16	0.3125	7.9375	13/16	0.8125	20.6375
21/64	0.3281	8.3344	53/64	0.8281	21.0344
11/32	0.3438	8.7312	27/32	0.8438	21.4312
23/64	0.3594	9.1281	55/64	0.8594	21.8281
3/8	0.3750	9.5250	7/8	0.8750	22.2250
25/64	0.3906	9.9219	57/64	0.8906	22.6219
13/32	0.4062	10.3188	29/32	0.9062	23.0188
27/64	0.4219	10.7156	59/64	0.9219	23.4156
7/16	0.4375	11.1125	15/16	0.9375	23.8125
29/64	0.4531	11.5094	61/64	0.9531	24.2094
15/32	0.4688	11.9062	31/32	0.9688	24.6062
31/64	0.4844	12.3031	63/64	0.9844	25.0031
1/2	0.5000	12.7000	1	1.0000	25.4000

Regardless of how enthusiastic you may be about getting on with the job at hand, take the time to ensure that your safety is not jeopardized. A moment's lack of attention can result in an accident, as can failure to observe certain simple safety precautions. The possibility of an accident will always exist, and the following points should not be considered a comprehensive list of all dangers. Rather, they are intended to make you aware of the risks and to encourage a safety conscious approach to all work you carry out on your vehicle.

ESSENTIAL DOS AND DON'TS

DON'T rely on a jack when working under the vehicle. Always use approved jackstands to support the weight of the vehicle and place them under the recommended lift or support points.

DON'T attempt to loosen extremely tight fasteners (i.e. wheel lug nuts) while the vehicle is on a jack - it may fall.

DON'T start the engine without first making sure that the transmission is in Neutral (or Park where applicable) and the parking brake is set.

DON'T remove the radiator cap from a hot cooling system - let it cool or cover it with a cloth and release the pressure gradually.

DON'T attempt to drain the engine oil until you are sure it has cooled to the point that it will not burn you.

DON'T touch any part of the engine or exhaust system until it has cooled sufficiently to avoid burns.

DON'T siphon toxic liquids such as gasoline, antifreeze and brake fluid by mouth, or allow them to remain on your skin.

DON'T inhale brake lining dust - it is potentially hazardous (see Asbestos below).

DON'T allow spilled oil or grease to remain on the floor - wipe it up before someone slips on it.

DON'T use loose fitting wrenches or other tools which may slip and cause injury.

DON'T push on wrenches when loosening or tightening nuts or bolts. Always try to pull the wrench toward you. If the situation calls for pushing the wrench away, push with an open hand to avoid scraped knuckles if the wrench should slip.

DON'T attempt to lift a heavy component alone - get someone to help you.

DON'T rush or take unsafe shortcuts to finish a job.

DON'T allow children or animals in or around the vehicle while you are working on it.

DO wear eye protection when using power tools such as a drill, sander, bench grinder, etc. and when working under a vehicle.

DO keep loose clothing and long hair well out of the way of moving parts.

DO make sure that any hoist used has a safe working load rating adequate for the job.

DO get someone to check on you periodically when working alone on a vehicle.

DO carry out work in a logical sequence and make sure that everything is correctly assembled and tightened.

DO keep chemicals and fluids tightly capped and out of the reach of children and pets.

DO remember that your vehicle's safety affects that of yourself and others. If in doubt on any point, get professional advice.

STEERING, SUSPENSION AND BRAKES

These systems are essential to driving safety, so make sure you have a qualified shop or individual check your work. Also, compressed suspension springs can cause injury if released suddenly - be sure to use a spring compressor.

AIRBAGS

Airbags are explosive devices that can CAUSE injury if they deploy while you're working on the vehicle. Follow the manufacturer's instructions to disable the airbag whenever you're working in the vicinity of airbag components.

ASBESTOS

Certain friction, insulating, sealing, and other products - such as brake linings, brake bands, clutch linings, torque converters, gaskets, etc. - may contain asbestos or other hazardous friction material. Extreme care must be taken to avoid inhalation of dust from such products, since it is hazardous to health. If in doubt, assume that they do contain asbestos.

FIRE

Remember at all times that gasoline is highly flammable. Never smoke or have any kind of open flame around when working on a vehicle. But the risk does not end there. A spark caused by an electrical short circuit, by two metal surfaces contacting each other, or even by static electricity built up in your body under certain conditions, can ignite gasoline vapors, which in a confined space are highly explosive. Do not, under any circumstances, use gasoline for cleaning parts. Use an approved safety solvent.

Always disconnect the battery ground (-) cable at the battery before working on any part of the fuel system or electrical system. Never risk spilling fuel on a hot engine or exhaust component. It is strongly recommended that a fire extinguisher suitable for use on fuel and electrical fires be kept handy in the garage or workshop at all times. Never try to extinguish a fuel or electrical fire with water.

FUMES

Certain fumes are highly toxic and can quickly cause unconsciousness and even death if inhaled to any extent. Gasoline vapor falls into this category, as do the vapors from some cleaning solvents. Any draining or pouring of such volatile fluids should be done in a well ventilated area.

When using cleaning fluids and solvents, read the instructions on the container carefully. Never use materials from unmarked containers.

Never run the engine in an enclosed space, such as a garage. Exhaust fumes contain carbon monoxide, which is extremely poisonous. If you need to run the engine, always do so in the open air, or at least have the rear of the vehicle outside the work area.

THE BATTERY

Never create a spark or allow a bare light bulb near a battery. They normally give off a certain amount of hydrogen gas, which is highly explosive.

Always disconnect the battery ground (-) cable at the battery before working on the fuel or electrical systems.

If possible, loosen the filler caps or cover when charging the battery from an external source (this does not apply to sealed or maintenance-free batteries). Do not charge at an excessive rate or the battery may burst.

Take care when adding water to a non maintenance-free battery and when carrying a battery. The electrolyte, even when diluted, is very corrosive and should not be allowed to contact clothing or skin.

Always wear eye protection when cleaning the battery to prevent the caustic deposits from entering your eyes.

HOUSEHOLD CURRENT

When using an electric power tool, inspection light, etc., which operates on household current, always make sure that the tool is correctly connected to its plug and that, where necessary, it is properly grounded. Do not use such items in damp conditions and, again, do not create a spark or apply excessive heat in the vicinity of fuel or fuel vapor.

SECONDARY IGNITION SYSTEM VOLTAGE

A severe electric shock can result from touching certain parts of the ignition system (such as the spark plug wires) when the engine is running or being cranked, particularly if components are damp or the insulation is defective. In the case of an electronic ignition system, the secondary system voltage is much higher and could prove fatal.

HYDROFLUORIC ACID

This extremely corrosive acid is formed when certain types of synthetic rubber, found in some O-rings, oil seals, fuel hoses, etc. are exposed to temperatures above 750-degrees F (400-degrees C). The rubber changes into a charred or sticky substance containing the acid. *Once formed, the acid remains dangerous for years. If it gets onto the skin, it may be necessary to amputate the limb concerned.*

When dealing with a vehicle which has suffered a fire, or with components salvaged from such a vehicle, wear protective gloves and discard them after use.

Troubleshooting

CONTENTS

This section provides an easy reference guide to the more common problems which may occur during the operation of your vehicle. These problems and their possible causes are grouped under headings denoting various components or systems, such as Engine, Cooling system, etc. They also refer you to the chapter and/or section which deals with the problem.

Remember that successful troubleshooting is not a mysterious black art practiced only by professional mechanics. It is simply the result of the right knowledge combined with an intelligent, systematic approach to the problem. Always work by a process of elimination, starting with the simplest solution and working through to the most complex - and never overlook the obvious. Anyone can run the gas tank dry or leave the lights on overnight, so don't assume that you are exempt from such oversights.

Finally, always establish a clear idea of why a problem has occurred and take steps to ensure that it doesn't happen again. If the electrical system fails because of a poor connection, check the other connections in the system to make sure that they don't fail as well. If a particular fuse continues to blow, find out why - don't just replace one fuse after another. Remember, failure of a small component can often be indicative of potential failure or incorrect functioning of a more important component or system.

ENGINE

1   Engine will not rotate when attempting to start

1   Battery terminal connections loose or corroded (Chapter 1).
2   Battery discharged or faulty (Chapters 1 and 5).
3   Automatic transaxle not completely engaged in Park (Chapter 7) or clutch pedal not completely depressed (Chapter 6).
4   Broken, loose or disconnected wiring in the starting circuit (Chapters 5 and 12).
5   Starter motor pinion jammed in flywheel ring gear (Chapter 5).
6   Starter solenoid faulty (Chapter 5).
7   Starter motor faulty (Chapter 5).
8   Ignition switch faulty (Chapter 12).
9   Starter pinion or flywheel teeth worn or broken (Chapter 5).

2   Engine rotates but will not start

1   Fuel tank empty.
2   Battery discharged (engine rotates slowly) (Chapter 5).
3   Battery terminal connections loose or corroded (Chapter 1).
4   Leaking fuel injector(s), faulty fuel pump, pressure regulator, etc. (Chapter 4).
5   Broken timing chain (Chapter 2).
6   Ignition components damp or damaged (Chapter 5).
7   Worn, faulty or incorrectly-gapped spark plugs (Chapter 1).
8   Broken, loose or disconnected wiring in the starting circuit (Chapter 5).
9   Broken, loose or disconnected wires at the ignition coil or faulty coil (Chapter 5).
10 Defective crankshaft or camshaft sensor (Chapter 6).

3   Engine hard to start when cold

1   Battery discharged or low (Chapter 1).
2   Malfunctioning fuel system (Chapter 4).
3   Faulty coolant temperature sensor or intake air temperature sensor (Chapter 6).
4   Faulty ignition system (Chapter 5).

4   Engine hard to start when hot

1   Air filter clogged (Chapter 1).
2   Fuel not reaching the fuel injection system (Chapter 4).
3   Corroded battery connections (Chapter 1).
4   Faulty coolant temperature sensor or intake air temperature sensor (Chapter 6).

5   Starter motor noisy or excessively rough in engagement

1   Pinion or flywheel gear teeth worn or broken (Chapter 5).
2   Starter motor mounting bolts loose or missing (Chapter 5).

6   Engine starts but stops immediately

1   Insufficient fuel reaching the fuel injector(s) (Chapters 1 and 4).
2   Vacuum leak at the gasket between the intake manifold/plenum and throttle body (Chapter 4).

7   Oil puddle under engine

1   Oil pan gasket and/or oil pan drain bolt washer leaking (Chapter 2).
2   Oil pressure sending unit leaking (Chapter 2).
3   Valve cover leaking (Chapter 2).
4   Engine oil seals leaking (Chapter 2).
5   Oil pump housing leaking (Chapter 2).

8   Engine lopes while idling or idles erratically

1   Vacuum leakage (Chapters 2 and 4).
2   Leaking EGR valve (Chapter 6).
3   Air filter clogged (Chapter 1).
4   Malfunction in the fuel injection or engine control system (Chapters 4 and 6).
5   Leaking head gasket (Chapter 2).
6   Timing chain and/or sprockets worn (Chapter 2).
7   Camshaft lobes worn (Chapter 2).

9   Engine misses at idle speed

1   Spark plugs worn or not gapped properly (Chapter 1).
2   Faulty coil(s) (Chapter 1).
3   Vacuum leaks (Chapter 1).
4   Uneven or low compression (Chapter 2).
5   Problem with the fuel injection system (Chapter 4).

10   Engine misses throughout driving speed range

1   Fuel filter clogged and/or impurities in the fuel system (Chapters 1 and 4).
2   Low fuel pressure (Chapter 4).
3   Faulty or incorrectly gapped spark plugs (Chapter 1).
4   Faulty emission system components (Chapter 6).

5 Low or uneven cylinder compression pressures (Chapter 2).
6 Weak or faulty ignition system (Chapter 5).
7 Vacuum leak (Chapters 2 and 4).

11 Engine stumbles on acceleration

1 Spark plugs fouled (Chapter 1).
2 Problem with fuel injection or engine control system (Chapters 4 and 6).
3 Fuel filter clogged (Chapters 1 and 4).
4 Intake manifold air leak (Chapters 2 and 4).
5 Problem with the emissions control system (Chapter 6).

12 Engine surges while holding accelerator steady

1 Intake air leak (Chapter 4).
2 Fuel pump or fuel pressure regulator faulty (Chapter 4).
3 Problem with the fuel injection system (Chapter 4).
4 Problem with the emissions control system (Chapter 6).

13 Engine stalls

1 Fuel filter clogged and/or water and impurities in the fuel system (Chapters 1 and 4).
2 Faulty emissions system components (Chapter 6).
3 Faulty or incorrectly-gapped spark plugs (Chapter 1).
5 Vacuum leak in the fuel injection system, intake manifold or vacuum hoses (Chapters 2 and 4).

14 Engine lacks power

1 Obstructed exhaust system (Chapter 4).
2 Faulty or incorrectly-gapped spark plugs (Chapter 1).
3 Problem with the fuel injection system (Chapter 4).
4 Dirty air filter (Chapter 1).
5 Brakes binding (Chapter 9).
6 Automatic transaxle fluid level incorrect (Chapter 1).
7 Clutch slipping (Chapter 8).
8 Fuel filter clogged and/or impurities in the fuel system (Chapters 1 and 4).
9 Emission control system not functioning properly (Chapter 6).
10 Low or uneven cylinder compression pressures (Chapter 2).

15 Engine backfires

1 Emission control system not functioning properly (Chapter 6).
2 Problem with the fuel injection system (Chapter 4).
3 Vacuum leak at fuel injector(s), intake manifold or vacuum hoses (Chapters 2 and 4).
4 Valve clearances incorrectly set (four-cylinder engines) and/or valves sticking (Chapter 2A).

16 Pinging or knocking engine sounds during acceleration or uphill

1 Incorrect grade of fuel.
2 Fuel injection system faulty (Chapter 4).
3 Improper or damaged spark plugs or wires (Chapter 1).
4 Knock sensor defective (Chapter 6).
5 EGR valve not functioning (Chapter 6).
6 Vacuum leak (Chapters 2 and 4).

17 Engine runs with oil pressure light on

1 Low oil level (Chapter 1).
2 Idle rpm below specification (Chapter 1).
3 Short in wiring circuit (Chapter 12).
4 Faulty oil pressure sender (Chapter 2B).
5 Worn engine bearings and/or oil pump (Chapter 2).

18 Engine continues to run after switching off

1 Defective ignition switch (Chapter 12).
2 Faulty Powertrain Control Module.

ENGINE ELECTRICAL SYSTEMS

19 Battery will not hold a charge

1 Drivebelt or tensioner defective (Chapter 1).
2 Battery electrolyte level low (Chapter 1).
3 Battery terminals loose or corroded (Chapter 1).
4 Alternator not charging properly (Chapter 5).
5 Loose, broken or faulty wiring in the charging circuit (Chapter 5).
6 Short in vehicle wiring (Chapter 12).
7 Internally defective battery (Chapters 1 and 5).

20 Alternator light fails to go out

1 Faulty alternator or charging circuit (Chapter 5).
2 Drivebelt or tensioner defective (Chapter 1).

21 Alternator light fails to come on when key is turned on

1 Instrument cluster defective (Chapter 12).
2 Fault in the Smart Junction Box or wiring harness (Chapter 12).

FUEL SYSTEM

22 Excessive fuel consumption

1 Dirty air filter element (Chapter 1).
2 Emissions system not functioning properly (Chapter 6).
3 Fuel injection system not functioning properly (Chapter 4).
4 Low tire pressure or incorrect tire size (Chapter 1).

23 Fuel leakage and/or fuel odor

1 Leaking fuel line (Chapters 1 and 4).
2 Tank overfilled.
3 Evaporative emissions control system problem (Chapters 1 and 6).
4 Problem with the fuel injection system (Chapter 4).

COOLING SYSTEM

24 Overheating

1 Insufficient coolant in system (Chapter 1).

2   Water pump drivebelt defective or out of adjustment (Chapter 1).
3   Radiator core blocked or grille restricted (Chapter 3).
4   Thermostat faulty (Chapter 3).
5   Electric coolant fan inoperative or blades broken (Chapter 3).
6   Expansion tank cap not maintaining proper pressure (Chapter 3).

25   Overcooling

1   Faulty thermostat (Chapter 3).
2   Inaccurate temperature gauge sending unit (Chapter 3).

26   External coolant leakage

1   Deteriorated/damaged hoses; loose clamps (Chapters 1 and 3).
2   Water pump defective (Chapter 3).
3   Leakage from radiator core or coolant reservoir (Chapter 3).
4   Engine drain or water jacket core plugs leaking (Chapter 2).

27   Internal coolant leakage

1   Leaking cylinder head gasket (Chapter 2).
2   Cracked cylinder bore or cylinder head (Chapter 2).

28   Coolant loss

1   Too much coolant in reservoir (Chapter 1).
2   Coolant boiling away because of overheating (Chapter 3).
3   Internal or external leakage (Chapter 3).
4   Faulty radiator cap (Chapter 3).

29   Poor coolant circulation

1   Inoperative water pump (Chapter 3).
2   Restriction in cooling system (Chapters 1 and 3).
3   Drivebelt or tensioner defective (Chapter 1).
4   Thermostat sticking (Chapter 3).

CLUTCH

30   Pedal travels to floor - no pressure or very little resistance

1   Master or release cylinder faulty (Chapter 8).
2   Hose/pipe burst or leaking (Chapter 8).
3   Connections leaking (Chapter 8).
4   No fluid in reservoir (Chapter 8).
5   If fluid level in reservoir rises as pedal is depressed, master cylinder center valve seal is faulty (Chapter 8).
6   If there is fluid on dust seal at master cylinder, piston primary seal is leaking (Chapter 8).
7   Broken release bearing or fork (Chapter 8).
8   Faulty pressure plate diaphragm spring (Chapter 8).

31   Fluid in area of master cylinder dust cover and on pedal

Rear seal failure in master cylinder (Chapter 8).

32   Fluid on release cylinder

Release cylinder plunger seal faulty (Chapter 8).

33   Pedal feels spongy when depressed

Air in system (Chapter 8).

34   Unable to select gears

1   Faulty transaxle (Chapter 7).
2   Faulty clutch disc or pressure plate (Chapter 8).
3   Faulty release lever or release bearing (Chapter 8).
4   Faulty shift lever assembly or control cables (Chapter 8).

35   Clutch slips (engine speed increases with no increase in vehicle speed)

1   Clutch plate worn (Chapter 8).
2   Clutch plate is oil soaked by leaking rear main seal (Chapters 2 and 8).
3   Clutch plate not seated (Chapter 8).
4   Warped pressure plate or flywheel (Chapter 8).
5   Weak diaphragm springs (Chapter 8).
6   Clutch plate overheated. Allow to cool.

36   Grabbing (chattering) as clutch is engaged

1   Oil on clutch plate lining, burned or glazed facings (Chapter 8).
2   Worn or loose engine or transaxle mounts (Chapter 2).
3   Worn splines on clutch plate hub (Chapter 8).
4   Warped pressure plate or flywheel (Chapter 8).
5   Burned or smeared resin on flywheel or pressure plate (Chapter 8).

37   Transaxle rattling (clicking)

1   Release lever loose (Chapter 8).
2   Clutch plate damper spring failure (Chapter 8).

38   Noise in clutch area

1   Fork shaft improperly installed (Chapter 8).
2   Faulty bearing (Chapter 8).

39   Clutch pedal stays on floor

1   Clutch master cylinder piston binding in bore (Chapter 8).
2   Broken release bearing or fork (Chapter 8).

40   High pedal effort

1   Piston binding in bore (Chapter 8).
2   Pressure plate faulty (Chapter 8).
3   Incorrect size master or release cylinder (Chapter 8).

MANUAL TRANSAXLE

41   Knocking noise at low speeds

1   Worn driveaxle constant velocity (CV) joints (Chapter 8).
2   Worn side gear shaft counterbore in differential case (Chapter 7A).*

42   Noise most pronounced when turning

Differential gear noise (Chapter 7A).*

43   Clunk on acceleration or deceleration

1   Loose engine or transaxle mounts (Chapter 2).
2   Worn differential pinion shaft in case.*
3   Worn side gear shaft counterbore in differential case (Chapter 7A).*
4   Worn or damaged driveaxle inboard CV joints (Chapter 8).

44   Clicking noise in turns

Worn or damaged outboard CV joint (Chapter 8).

45   Vibration

1   Rough wheel bearing (Chapter 10).
2   Damaged driveaxle (Chapter 8).
3   Out-of-round tires (Chapter 1).
4   Tire out of balance (Chapters 1 and 10).
5   Worn CV joint (Chapter 8).

46   Noisy in neutral with engine running

1   Damaged input gear bearing (Chapter 7A).*
2   Damaged clutch release bearing (Chapter 8).

47   Noisy in one particular gear

1   Damaged or worn constant mesh gears (Chapter 7A).*
2   Damaged or worn synchronizers (Chapter 7A).*
3   Bent reverse fork (Chapter 7A).*
4   Damaged fourth speed gear or output gear (Chapter 7A).*
5   Worn or damaged reverse idler gear or idler bushing (Chapter 7A).*

48   Noisy in all gears

1   Insufficient lubricant (Chapter 7A).
2   Damaged or worn bearings (Chapter 7A).*
3   Worn or damaged input gear shaft and/or output gear shaft (Chapter 7A).*

49   Slips out of gear

1   Worn or improperly adjusted linkage (Chapter 7A).
2   Shift linkage does not work freely, binds (Chapter 7A).
3   Input gear bearing retainer broken or loose (Chapter 7A).*
4   Worn or bent shift fork (Chapter 7A).*

50   Leaks lubricant

1   Side gear shaft seals worn (Chapter 7).
2   Excessive amount of lubricant in transaxle (Chapters 1 and 7A).
3   Loose or broken input gear shaft bearing retainer (Chapter 7A).*
4   Input gear bearing retainer O-ring and/or lip seal damaged (Chapter 7A).*

51   Locked in gear

Lock pin or interlock pin missing (Chapter 7A).*

Although the corrective action necessary to remedy the symptoms described is beyond the scope of this manual, the above information should be helpful in isolating the cause of the condition so that the owner can communicate clearly with a professional mechanic.

AUTOMATIC TRANSAXLE

➡ **Note: Due to the complexity of the automatic transaxle, it is difficult for the home mechanic to properly diagnose and service this component. For problems other than the following, the vehicle should be taken to a dealer or transmission shop.**

52   Fluid leakage

1   Automatic transaxle fluid is a deep red color. Fluid leaks should not be confused with engine oil, which can easily be blown onto the transaxle by air flow.
2   To pinpoint a leak, first remove all built-up dirt and grime from the transaxle housing with degreasing agents and/or steam cleaning. Then drive the vehicle at low speeds so air flow will not blow the leak far from its source. Raise the vehicle and determine where the leak is coming from. Common areas of leakage are:

  a) *Dipstick tube (Chapters 1 and 7).*
  b) *Transaxle oil lines (Chapter 7).*
  c) *Speed sensor (Chapter 6).*
  d) *Driveaxle oil seals (Chapter 7).*

53   Transaxle fluid brown or has a burned smell

Transaxle fluid overheated (Chapter 1).

54   General shift mechanism problems

1   Chapter 7, Part B, deals with checking and adjusting the shift linkage on automatic transaxles. Common problems which may be attributed to poorly adjusted linkage are:

  a) *Engine starting in gears other than Park or Neutral.*
  b) *Indicator on shifter pointing to a gear other than the one actually being used.*
  c) *Vehicle moves when in Park.*

2   Refer to Chapter 7, Part B for the shift linkage adjustment procedure.

55   Transaxle slips, shifts roughly, is noisy or has no drive in forward or reverse gears

There are many probable causes for the above problems, but the home mechanic should be concerned with only one possibility - fluid level. Before taking the vehicle to a repair shop, check the level and condition of the fluid as described in Chapter 1. Correct the fluid level as necessary or change the fluid and filter if needed. If the problem persists, have a professional diagnose the cause.

DRIVEAXLES

56   Clicking noise in turns

Worn or damaged outboard CV joint (Chapter 8).

57 Shudder or vibration during acceleration

1 Excessive toe-in (Chapter 10).
2 Worn or damaged inboard or outboard CV joints (Chapter 8).
3 Sticking inboard CV joint assembly (Chapter 8).

58 Vibration at highway speeds

1 Out-of-balance front wheels and/or tires (Chapters 1 and 10).
2 Out-of-round front tires (Chapters 1 and 10).
3 Worn CV joint(s) (Chapter 8).

BRAKES

➡ **Note: Before assuming that a brake problem exists, make sure that:**

a) *The tires are in good condition and properly inflated (Chapter 1).*
b) *The front end alignment is correct.*
c) *The vehicle is not loaded with weight in an unequal manner.*

59 Vehicle pulls to one side during braking

1 Incorrect tire pressures (Chapter 1).
2 Front end out of alignment (have the front end aligned).
3 Front, or rear, tire sizes not matched to one another.
4 Restricted brake lines or hoses (Chapter 9).
5 Malfunctioning caliper assembly (Chapter 9).
6 Loose suspension parts (Chapter 10).
7 Excessive wear of pad material or disc on one side (Chapter 9).
8 Contamination (grease or brake fluid) of brake pad material or disc on one side (Chapter 9).

60 Noise (high-pitched squeal when the brakes are applied)

Brake pads worn out. Replace pads with new ones immediately (Chapter 9).

61 Brake roughness or chatter (pedal pulsates)

1 Excessive disc lateral runout (Chapter 9).
2 Uneven pad wear (Chapter 9).
3 Defective disc (Chapter 9).

62 Excessive brake pedal effort required to stop vehicle

1 Malfunctioning power brake booster (Chapter 9).
2 Partial system failure (Chapter 9).
3 Excessively worn pads (Chapter 9).
4 Piston in caliper stuck or sluggish (Chapter 9).
5 Brake pads contaminated with oil or grease (Chapter 9).
6 Brake disc grooved and/or glazed (Chapter 9).

63 Excessive brake pedal travel

1 Partial brake system failure (Chapter 9).
2 Insufficient fluid in master cylinder (Chapters 1 and 9).
3 Air trapped in system (Chapter 9).

64 Dragging brakes

1 Incorrect adjustment of brake light switch (Chapter 9).
2 Master cylinder pistons not returning correctly (Chapter 9).
3 Caliper piston stuck (Chapter 9).
4 Restricted brakes lines or hoses (Chapter 9).
5 Incorrect parking brake adjustment (Chapter 9).

65 Grabbing or uneven braking action

1 Malfunction of proportioning valve (Chapter 9).
2 Binding brake pedal mechanism (Chapter 9).
3 Contaminated brake linings (Chapter 9).

66 Brake pedal feels spongy when depressed

1 Air in hydraulic lines (Chapter 9).
2 Master cylinder mounting bolts loose (Chapter 9).
3 Master cylinder defective (Chapter 9).

67 Brake pedal travels to the floor with little resistance

1 Little or no fluid in the master cylinder reservoir caused by leaking caliper piston(s) (Chapter 9).
2 Loose, damaged or disconnected brake lines (Chapter 9).

68 Parking brake does not hold

Parking brake improperly adjusted (Chapter 9).

SUSPENSION AND STEERING SYSTEMS

➡ **Note: Before attempting to diagnose the suspension and steering systems, perform the following preliminary checks:**

a) *Tires for wrong pressure and uneven wear.*
b) *Steering universal joints from the column to the rack and pinion for loose connectors or wear.*
c) *Front and rear suspension and the rack-and-pinion assembly for loose or damaged parts.*
d) *Out-of-round or out-of-balance tires, bent rims and loose and/or rough wheel bearings.*

69 Vehicle pulls to one side

1 Mismatched or uneven tires (Chapter 10).
2 Broken or sagging springs (Chapter 10).
3 Wheel alignment incorrect. Have the wheels professionally aligned.
4 Front brake dragging (Chapter 9).

70 Abnormal or excessive tire wear

1 Wheel alignment out-of-specification. Have the wheels aligned.
2 Sagging or broken springs (Chapter 10).
3 Tire out-of-balance (Chapter 10).
4 Worn strut damper (Chapter 10).
5 Overloaded vehicle.
6 Tires not rotated regularly.

71 Wheel makes a thumping noise

1 Blister or bump on tire (Chapter 10).
2 Improper strut or shock absorber damper action (Chapter 10).

72 Shimmy, shake or vibration

1 Tire or wheel out-of-balance or out-of-round (Chapter 10).
2 Worn wheel bearings (Chapter 10).
3 Worn tie-rod ends (Chapter 10).
4 Worn balljoints (Chapters 1 and 10).
5 Excessive wheel runout (Chapter 10).
6 Blister or bump on tire (Chapter 10).

73 Hard steering

1 Lack of lubrication at balljoints and/or tie-rod ends (Chapter 10).
2 Wheel alignment out-of-specifications. Have the wheels professionally aligned.
3 Low tire pressure(s) (Chapter 1).
4 Worn steering gear (Chapter 10).

74 Poor returnability of steering to center

1 Worn balljoints or tie-rod ends (Chapter 10).
2 Worn steering gear assembly (Chapter 10).
3 Wheel alignment out-of-specifications. Have the wheels professionally aligned.

75 Abnormal noise at the front end

1 Worn balljoints or tie-rod ends (Chapter 10).
2 Damaged shock absorber mounting (Chapter 10).
3 Worn control arm bushings or tie-rod ends (Chapter 10).
4 Loose stabilizer bar (Chapter 10).
5 Loose wheel nuts (Chapter 1).
6 Loose suspension bolts (Chapter 10).

76 Wander or poor steering stability

1 Mismatched or uneven tires (Chapter 10).
2 Lack of lubrication at balljoints and tie-rod ends (Chapters 1 and 10).
3 Worn strut or shock absorber assemblies (Chapter 10).
4 Loose stabilizer bar (Chapter 10).
5 Broken or sagging springs (Chapter 10).
6 Wheels out of alignment. Have the wheels professionally aligned.

77 Erratic steering when braking

1 Wheel bearings worn (Chapter 10).
2 Broken or sagging springs (Chapter 10).
3 Leaking wheel cylinder or caliper (Chapter 10).
4 Excessive brake disc runout (Chapter 9).

78 Excessive pitching and/or rolling around corners or during braking

1 Loose stabilizer bar (Chapter 10).
2 Worn strut dampers or mountings (Chapter 10).
3 Broken or sagging springs (Chapter 10).
4 Overloaded vehicle.

79 Suspension bottoms

1 Overloaded vehicle.
2 Sagging springs (Chapter 10).

80 Cupped tires

1 Front wheel or rear wheel alignment out-of-specifications. Have the wheels professionally aligned.
2 Worn shock absorbers (Chapter 10).
3 Wheel bearings worn (Chapter 10).
4 Excessive tire or wheel runout (Chapter 10).
5 Worn balljoints (Chapter 10).

81 Excessive tire wear on outside edge

1 Inflation pressures incorrect (Chapter 1).
2 Excessive speed in turns.
3 Wheel alignment incorrect (excessive toe-in). Have professionally aligned.
4 Suspension arm bent or twisted (Chapter 10).

82 Excessive tire wear on inside edge

1 Inflation pressures incorrect (Chapter 1).
2 Wheel alignment incorrect (toe-out). Have professionally aligned.
3 Loose or damaged steering components (Chapter 10).

83 Tire tread worn in one place

1 Tires out-of-balance.
2 Damaged or buckled wheel. Inspect and replace if necessary.
3 Defective tire (Chapter 1).

84 Excessive play or looseness in steering system

1 Wheel bearing(s) worn (Chapter 10).
2 Tie-rod end loose (Chapter 10).
3 Steering gear loose (Chapter 10).
4 Worn or loose steering intermediate shaft U-joint (Chapter 10).

85 Rattling or clicking noise in steering gear

1 Steering gear loose (Chapter 10).
2 Steering gear defective.

Notes

Section

1

TUNE-UP AND ROUTINE MAINTENANCE

Typical engine compartment components (four-cylinder engine)

1	Automatic transaxle fluid dipstick	5	Air filter housing	9	Windshield washer fluid reservoir
2	Brake fluid reservoir	6	Radiator hose	10	Coolant expansion tank
3	Battery	7	Engine oil dipstick	11	Engine oil filler cap
4	Fuse/relay block	8	Drivebelt	12	Spark plugs (under ignition coils)

Typical engine compartment components (3.0L V6 engine)

1	Automatic transaxle fluid dipstick	6	Radiator hose	10	Windshield washer fluid reservoir
2	Brake fluid reservoir	7	Power steering fluid reservoir	11	Engine oil filler cap
3	Battery	8	Front cylinder bank spark plugs (under ignition coils)	12	Coolant expansion tank
4	Fuse/relay block				
5	Air filter housing	9	Engine oil dipstick		

Typical engine compartment underside components (3.0L V6 engine)

1	Engine oil filter	4	Engine oil drain plug	6	Exhaust system
2	Inner driveaxle boot	5	Automatic transaxle drain plug	7	Front disc brake caliper
3	Outer driveaxle boot				

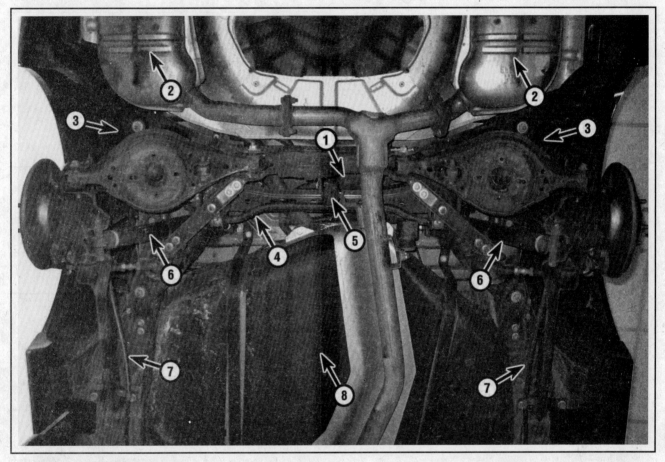

Typical rear underside components

1	EVAP canister	4	Stabilizer bar	7	Parking brake cables
2	Mufflers	5	Exhaust system hanger	8	Fuel tank
3	Coil springs	6	Shock absorbers		

1 Maintenance schedule

The maintenance intervals in this manual are provided with the assumption that you, not the dealer, will be doing the work. These are the minimum maintenance intervals recommended by the factory for vehicles that are driven daily. If you wish to keep your vehicle in peak condition at all times, you may wish to perform some of these procedures even more often. Because frequent maintenance enhances the efficiency, performance and resale value of your car, we encourage you to do so. If you drive in dusty areas, tow a trailer, idle or drive at low speeds for extended periods or drive for short distances (less than four miles) in below freezing temperatures, shorter intervals are also recommended.

When your vehicle is new, it should be serviced by a factory authorized dealer service department to protect the factory warranty. In many cases, the initial maintenance check is done at no cost to the owner.

EVERY 250 MILES OR WEEKLY, WHICHEVER COMES FIRST

Check the engine oil level (Section 4)
Check the engine coolant level (Section 4)
Check the brake and clutch fluid level (Section 4)
Check the windshield washer fluid level (Section 4)
Check the power steering fluid level (Section 4)
Check the automatic transaxle fluid level (Section 4)
Check the tires and tire pressures (Section 5)

EVERY 3000 MILES OR 3 MONTHS, WHICHEVER COMES FIRST

All items listed above plus:
Change the engine oil and oil filter (Section 6)

EVERY 7500 MILES OR 6 MONTHS, WHICHEVER COMES FIRST

All items listed above plus:
Inspect (and replace, if necessary) the windshield wiper blades (Section 7)
Check and service the battery (Section 8)
Check the cooling system (Section 9)
Rotate the tires (Section 10)
Check the seat belts (Section 11)

EVERY 15,000 MILES OR 12 MONTHS, WHICHEVER COMES FIRST

All items listed above plus:
Check all underhood hoses (Section 12)
Inspect the brake system (Section 13)*
Inspect the suspension, steering and driveaxle boots (Section 14)*
Check the fuel system (Section 15)

Check the manual transaxle lubricant level (Section 16)
Check (and replace, if necessary) the air filter (Section 17)*
Replace the cabin air filter (Section 18)

EVERY 30,000 MILES OR 24 MONTHS, WHICHEVER COMES FIRST

All items listed above plus:
Check the exhaust system (Section 19)
Service the cooling system (drain, flush and refill) (Section 20)
Change the brake fluid (Section 21)
Check/adjust the engine drivebelts (Section 22)

EVERY 60,000 MILES OR 48 MONTHS, WHICHEVER COMES FIRST

Replace the automatic transaxle fluid (Section 23)**
Replace the manual transaxle lubricant (Section 24)
Check (and replace, if necessary) the spark plugs (conventional, non-platinum or iridium type) (Section 25)

EVERY 75,000 MILES OR 60 MONTHS, WHICHEVER COMES FIRST

Check and, if necessary, adjust the valve clearances (Chapter 2A or 2B)

➡ **Note: This is only necessary if there is an abnormal amount of noise coming from the valve cover area of the engine.**

EVERY 100,000 MILES

Replace the spark plugs (platinum-tipped type) (Section 25)

This item is affected by "severe" operating conditions as described below. If your vehicle is operated under "severe" conditions, perform all maintenance indicated with an asterisk (*) at 3000 mile/3 month intervals. Severe conditions are indicated if you mainly operate your vehicle under one or more of the following conditions:

Operating in dusty areas
Towing a trailer
Idling for extended periods and/or low speed operation
Operating when outside temperatures remain below freezing and when most trips are less than 4 miles

** *If operated under one or more of the following conditions, change the manual or automatic transaxle fluid and differential lubricant every 30,000 miles:*

Operating in dusty areas
In heavy city traffic where the outside temperature regularly reaches 90-degrees F (32-degrees C) or higher
In hilly or mountainous terrain

2   Introduction

This Chapter is designed to help the home mechanic maintain the Mazda6 with the goals of maximum performance, economy, safety and reliability in mind.

Included is a master maintenance schedule, followed by procedures dealing specifically with each item on the schedule. Visual checks, adjustments, component replacement and other helpful items are included. Refer to the accompanying illustrations of the engine compartment and the underside of the vehicle for the locations of various components.

Servicing the vehicle, in accordance with the mileage/time maintenance schedule and the step-by-step procedures will result in a planned maintenance program that should produce a long and reliable service life. Keep in mind that it is a comprehensive plan, so maintaining some items but not others at the specified intervals will not produce the same results.

As you service the vehicle, you will discover that many of the procedures can - and should - be grouped together because of the nature of the particular procedure you're performing or because of the close proximity of two otherwise unrelated components to one another.

For example, if the vehicle is raised for chassis lubrication, you should inspect the exhaust, suspension, steering and fuel systems while you're under the vehicle. When you're rotating the tires, it makes good sense to check the brakes since the wheels are already removed. Finally, let's suppose you have to borrow or rent a torque wrench. Even if you only need it to tighten the spark plugs, you might as well check the torque of as many critical fasteners as time allows.

The first step in this maintenance program is to prepare yourself before the actual work begins. Read through all the procedures you're planning to do, then gather up all the parts and tools needed. If it looks like you might run into problems during a particular job, seek advice from a mechanic or an experienced do-it-yourselfer.

OWNER'S MANUAL AND VECI LABEL INFORMATION

Your vehicle owner's manual was written for your year and model and contains very specific information on component locations, specifications, fuse ratings, part numbers, etc. The Owner's Manual is an important resource for the do-it-yourselfer to have; if one was not supplied with your vehicle, it can generally be ordered from a dealer parts department.

Among other important information, the Vehicle Emissions Control Information (VECI) label contains specifications and procedures for applicable tune-up adjustments and, in some instances, spark plugs (see Chapter 6 for more information on the VECI label). The information on this label is the exact maintenance data recommended by the manufacturer. This data often varies by intended operating altitude, local emissions regulations, month of manufacture, etc.

This Chapter contains procedural details, safety information and more ambitious maintenance intervals than you might find in manufacturer's literature. However, you may also find procedures or specifications in your Owner's Manual or VECI label that differ with what's printed here. In these cases, the Owner's Manual or VECI label can be considered correct, since it is specific to your particular vehicle.

3   Tune-up general information

The term tune-up is used in this manual to represent a combination of individual operations rather than one specific procedure.

If, from the time the vehicle is new, the routine maintenance schedule is followed closely and frequent checks are made of fluid levels and high wear items, as suggested throughout this manual, the engine will be kept in relatively good running condition and the need for additional work will be minimized.

More likely than not, however, there will be times when the engine is running poorly due to lack of regular maintenance. This is even more likely if a used vehicle, which has not received regular and frequent maintenance checks, is purchased. In such cases, an engine tune-up will be needed outside of the regular routine maintenance intervals.

The first step in any tune-up or diagnostic procedure to help correct a poor running engine is a cylinder compression check. A compression check (see Chapter 2C) will help determine the condition of internal engine components and should be used as a guide for tune-up and repair procedures. If, for instance, a compression check indicates serious internal engine wear, a conventional tune-up will not improve the performance of the engine and would be a waste of time and money. Because of its importance, the compression check should be done by someone with the proper equipment and the knowledge to use it properly.

The following procedures are those most often needed to bring a generally poor running engine back into a proper state of tune.

MINOR TUNE-UP

Check all engine related fluids (Section 4)
Clean, inspect and test the battery (Section 8)
Check the cooling system (Section 9)
Check all underhood hoses (Section 12)
Check the fuel system (Section 15)
Check the air filter (Section 17)
Check the drivebelt (Section 22)

MAJOR TUNE-UP

All items listed under Minor tune-up, plus . . .

Replace the air filter (Section 17)
Replace the PCV valve (Chapter 6)
Replace the spark plugs (Section 25)

4   Fluid level checks (every 250 miles or weekly)

1   Fluids are an essential part of the lubrication, cooling, brake and windshield washer systems. Because the fluids gradually become depleted and/or contaminated during normal operation of the vehicle, they must be periodically replenished. See "Recommended lubricants and fluids" in this Chapter's Specifications before adding fluid to any of the following components.

➡ **Note: The vehicle must be on level ground when fluid levels are checked.**

ENGINE OIL

▶ **Refer to illustrations 4.2a, 4.2b and 4.4**

2   The oil level is checked with a dipstick, which is attached to the engine block (see illustrations). The dipstick extends through a metal tube down into the oil pan.

3   The oil level should be checked before the vehicle has been driven, or about 5 minutes after the engine has been shut off. If the oil is checked immediately after driving the vehicle, some of the oil will remain in the upper part of the engine, resulting in an inaccurate reading on the dipstick.

4   Pull the dipstick out of the tube and wipe all the oil from the end with a clean rag or paper towel. Insert the clean dipstick all the way back into the tube and pull it out again. Note the oil at the end of the dipstick. At its highest point, the level should be between the MIN and MAX marks on the dipstick (see illustration).

5   It takes about one quart of oil to raise the level from the MIN mark to the MAX mark on the dipstick. Do not allow the level to drop below the MIN mark or oil starvation may cause engine damage. Conversely, overfilling the engine (adding oil above the MAX mark) may cause oil fouled spark plugs, oil leaks or oil seal failures. Maintaining the oil level above the MAX mark can cause excessive oil consumption.

6   To add oil, remove the filler cap from the valve cover (see illustration 4.2a or 4.2b). After adding oil, wait a few minutes to allow the level to stabilize, then pull out the dipstick and check the level again. Add more oil if required. Install the filler cap and tighten it by hand only.

7   Checking the oil level is an important preventive maintenance step. A consistently low oil level indicates oil leakage through damaged seals, defective gaskets or past worn rings or valve guides. If the oil looks milky in color or has water droplets in it, the cylinder head gasket(s) may be blown or the head(s) or block may be cracked. The engine should be checked immediately. The condition of the oil should also be checked. Whenever you check the oil level, slide your thumb and index finger up the dipstick before wiping off the oil. If you see small dirt or metal particles clinging to the dipstick, the oil should be changed (see Section 6).

ENGINE COOLANT

▶ **Refer to illustrations 4.8 and 4.9**

⁑ WARNING:

Do not allow antifreeze to come in contact with your skin or painted surfaces of the vehicle. Flush contaminated areas immediately with plenty of water. Don't store new coolant or leave old coolant lying around where it's accessible to children or pets - they're attracted by its sweet smell. Ingestion of even a small amount of coolant can be fatal! Wipe up garage floor and drip pan spills immediately. Keep antifreeze containers covered and repair cooling system leaks as soon as they're noticed.

8   All vehicles covered by this manual are equipped with a pressurized coolant recovery system. A plastic expansion tank located at the right front corner of the engine compartment is connected by hoses

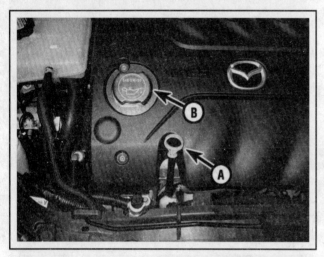

4.2a   Engine oil dipstick (A) and oil filler cap (B) locations - 3.0L V6

4.2b   Engine oil dipstick (A) and oil filler cap (B) locations - 2.5L four-cylinder engine

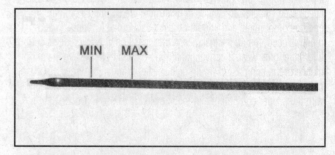

4.4   The oil level should be in the safe range - if it's below the MIN or ADD mark, add enough oil to bring it up to or near the MAX or FULL mark

4.8 The cooling system expansion tank is located at the right side of the engine compartment

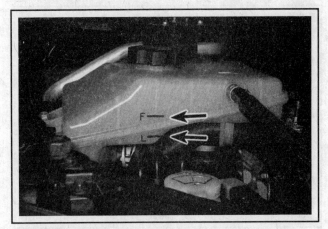

4.9 When the engine is cold, the coolant level should be between the "L" and "F" on the tank

to the cooling system (see illustration). As the engine heats up during operation, the expanding coolant fills the tank.

9   The coolant level in the tank should be checked regularly.

❊❊ WARNING:

Do not remove the expansion tank cap to check the coolant level when the engine is warm!

The level in the tank varies with the temperature of the engine. When the engine is cold, the coolant level should be at the "F" mark on the reservoir. If it isn't, remove the cap from the tank and add a 50/50 mixture of ethylene glycol-based antifreeze and water or FL-22 coolant (see illustration) depending on the year and engine model (refer to "Recommended lubricants and fluids" in this Chapter's Specifications or to your owner's manual).

10   Drive the vehicle, let the engine cool completely then recheck the coolant level. Don't use rust inhibitors or additives. If only a small amount of coolant is required to bring the system up to the proper level, water can be used. However, repeated additions of water will dilute the antifreeze and water solution. In order to maintain the proper ratio of antifreeze and water, always top up the coolant level with the correct mixture. An empty plastic milk jug or bleach bottle makes an excellent container for mixing coolant.

11   If the coolant level drops consistently, there may be a leak in the

system. Inspect the radiator, hoses, filler cap, drain plugs and water pump (see Section 9). If no leaks are noted, have the expansion tank cap pressure tested by a service station.

12   If you have to remove the expansion tank cap wait until the engine has cooled completely, then wrap a thick cloth around the cap and unscrew it slowly, stopping if you hear a hissing noise. If coolant or steam escapes, let the engine cool down longer, then remove the cap.

13   Check the condition of the coolant as well. If it's brown or rust colored, the system should be drained, flushed and refilled. Even if the coolant appears to be normal, the corrosion inhibitors wear out, so it must be replaced at the specified intervals.

BRAKE AND CLUTCH FLUID

▶ **Refer to illustrations 4.14 and 4.15**

14   The brake master cylinder is mounted on the front of the power booster unit in the engine compartment. The hydraulic clutch master cylinder used on manual transaxle vehicles is located next to the brake master cylinder (see illustration).

15   The brake master cylinder and the clutch master cylinder share a common reservoir. To check the fluid level of either system, simply look at the MAX and MIN marks on the brake fluid reservoir (see illustration).

4.14 The clutch master cylinder is located next to the brake master cylinder and the two share a common reservoir

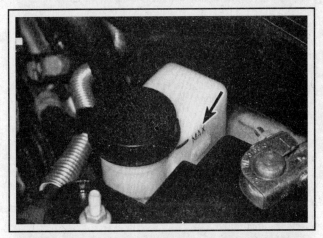

4.15 The brake fluid level should be kept between the MIN and MAX marks on the translucent plastic reservoir; the same reservoir contains the clutch fluid and is connected to the clutch master cylinder by a hose

4.22 The windshield/rear window washer fluid reservoir is located in the right front corner of the engine compartment

16 If the level is low, wipe the top of the reservoir cover with a clean rag to prevent contamination of the brake system before lifting the cover.

17 Add only the specified brake fluid to the reservoir (refer to *Recommended lubricants and fluids* in this Chapter's Specifications or to your owner's manual). Mixing different types of brake fluid can damage the system. Fill the brake master cylinder reservoir only to the MAX line.

✳ WARNING:

Use caution when filling the reservoir - brake fluid can harm your eyes and damage painted surfaces. Do not use brake fluid that is more than one year old or has been left open. Brake fluid absorbs moisture from the air. Excess moisture can cause a dangerous loss of braking.

18 While the reservoir cap is removed, inspect the master cylinder reservoir for contamination. If deposits, dirt particles or water droplets are present, the system should be drained and refilled.

19 After filling the reservoir to the proper level, make sure the lid is properly seated to prevent fluid leakage.

20 The fluid in the brake master cylinder will drop slightly as the brake pads at each wheel wear down during normal operation. If the master cylinder requires repeated replenishing to keep it at the proper level, this is an indication of leakage in the brake or clutch system, which should be corrected immediately. If the brake system shows an indication of leakage check all brake lines and connections, along with the calipers and booster (see Section 13 for more information). If the hydraulic clutch system shows an indication of leakage check all clutch lines and connections, along with the clutch release cylinder (see Chapter 8 for more information).

21 If, upon checking the brake or clutch master cylinder fluid level, you discover the reservoir empty or nearly empty, the systems should be bled (see Chapters 8 and 9).

WINDSHIELD WASHER FLUID

▶ **Refer to illustration 4.22**

22 Fluid for the windshield washer system is stored in a plastic reservoir located at the right front of the engine compartment (see illustration).

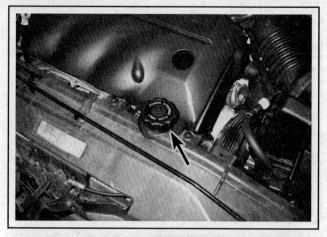

4.25 On models with a 3.0L V6 engine, the power steering fluid reservoir is located at the front of the engine compartment

23 In milder climates, plain water can be used in the reservoir, but it should be kept no more than 2/3 full to allow for expansion if the water freezes. In colder climates, use windshield washer system antifreeze, available at any auto parts store, to lower the freezing point of the fluid. Mix the antifreeze with water in accordance with the manufacturer's directions on the container.

✳ CAUTION:

Do not use cooling system antifreeze - it will damage the vehicle's paint.

POWER STEERING FLUID

▶ **Refer to illustrations 4.25 and 4.28**

24 Check the power steering fluid level periodically to avoid steering system problems, such as damage to the pump.

✳ CAUTION:

DO NOT hold the steering wheel against either stop (extreme left or right turn) for more than five seconds. If you do, the power steering pump could be damaged.

25 The power steering reservoir is located at either the right front corner of the engine compartment (four-cylinder models), the front of the engine compartment (3.0L V6 models) (see illustration), or the right rear corner of the engine compartment (3.7L V6 models). Four-cylinder models have MIN and MAX fluid level marks on the side of the reservoir. The fluid level can be seen without removing the reservoir cap. V6 models have a dipstick attached to the reservoir cap.

26 Park the vehicle on level ground and apply the parking brake.

27 Run the engine until it has reached normal operating temperature. With the engine at idle, turn the steering wheel back and forth about 10 times to get any air out of the steering system. Shut the engine off with the wheels in the straight-ahead position.

28 On four-cylinder models, note the fluid level on the side of the reservoir. It should be between the two marks. On V6 models remove

4.28 At normal operating temperature, the power steering fluid level should be between the HIGH (A) and LOW (B) marks

4.34a The automatic transaxle dipstick is located at the left rear corner of the engine compartment, near the brake master cylinder

the reservoir cap, wipe all the power steering fluid from the end of the dip stick with a clean rag or paper towel. Install the cap all the way and remove it again. Note the fluid at the end of the dipstick. At its highest point, the level should be between the HIGH and LOW marks on the dipstick (see illustration).

29 Add small amounts of fluid until the level is correct.

✲✲ CAUTION:

Do not overfill the reservoir. If too much fluid is added, remove the excess with a clean syringe or suction pump.

30 Check the power steering hoses and connections for leaks and wear.

AUTOMATIC TRANSAXLE FLUID

▸ **Refer to illustrations 4.34a and 4.34b**

31 The level of the automatic transaxle fluid should be carefully maintained. Low fluid level can lead to slipping or loss of drive, while overfilling can cause foaming, loss of fluid and transaxle damage.

32 The transaxle fluid level should only be checked when the transaxle is hot (at its normal operating temperature). If the vehicle has just been driven over 10 miles (15 miles in a frigid climate), and the fluid temperature is 160 to 175-degrees F, the transaxle is hot.

✲✲ CAUTION:

If the vehicle has just been driven for a long time at high speed or in city traffic in hot weather, or if it has been pulling a trailer, an accurate fluid level reading cannot be obtained. Allow the fluid to cool down for about 30 minutes.

33 If the vehicle has not just been driven, park the vehicle on level ground, set the parking brake and start the engine. While the engine is idling, depress the brake pedal and move the selector lever through all the gear ranges, beginning and ending in Park.

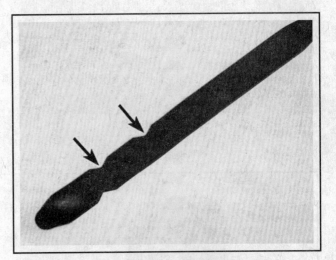

4.34b At operating temperature, the automatic transaxle fluid level should be between the notches, or in the cross-hatched area of the dipstick (depending on transaxle type)

34 With the engine still idling, remove the dipstick from its tube (see illustration). Check the level of the fluid on the dipstick (see illustration) and note its condition.

35 Wipe the fluid from the dipstick with a clean rag and reinsert it back into the filler tube until the cap seats.

36 Pull the dipstick out again and note the fluid level. The fluid level should be in the operating temperature range. If the level is at the low side of either range, add the specified automatic transmission fluid through the dipstick tube with a funnel.

37 Add just enough of the recommended fluid to fill the transaxle to the proper level. It takes about one pint to raise the level from the low mark to the high mark when the fluid is hot, so add the fluid a little at a time and keep checking the level until it is correct.

38 The condition of the fluid should also be checked along with the level. If the fluid at the end of the dipstick is black or a dark reddish brown color, or if it emits a burned smell, the fluid should be changed (see Section 23). If you are in doubt about the condition of the fluid, purchase some new fluid and compare the two for color and smell.

5 Tire and tire pressure checks (every 250 miles or weekly)

▶ Refer to illustrations 5.2, 5.3, 5.4a, 5.4b and 5.8

1   Periodic inspection of the tires may spare you the inconvenience of being stranded with a flat tire. It can also provide you with vital information regarding possible problems in the steering and suspension systems before major damage occurs.

2   The original tires on this vehicle are equipped with 1/2-inch wide bands that will appear when tread depth reaches 1/16-inch, at which point they can be considered worn out. Tread wear can be monitored with a simple, inexpensive device known as a tread depth indicator (see illustration).

3   Note any abnormal tread wear (see illustration). Tread pattern irregularities such as cupping, flat spots and more wear on one side than the other are indications of front end alignment and/or balance problems. If any of these conditions are noted, take the vehicle to a tire shop or service station to correct the problem.

4   Look closely for cuts, punctures and embedded nails or tacks. Sometimes a tire will hold air pressure for a short time or leak down very slowly after a nail has embedded itself in the tread. If a slow leak persists, check the valve stem core to make sure it is tight (see illustration). Examine the tread for an object that may have embedded itself in the tire or for a plug that may have begun to leak (radial tire punctures are repaired with a plug that is installed in a puncture). If a puncture is suspected, it can be easily verified by spraying a solution of soapy water onto the puncture area (see illustration). The soapy solution will bubble if there is a leak. Unless the puncture is unusually large, a tire shop or service station can usually repair the tire.

5   Carefully inspect the inner sidewall of each tire for evidence of brake fluid leakage. If you see any, inspect the brakes immediately.

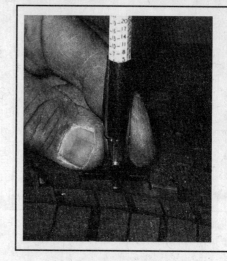

5.2 A tire tread depth indicator should be used to monitor tire wear - they are available at auto parts stores and service stations and cost very little

6   Correct air pressure adds miles to the life span of the tires, improves mileage and enhances overall ride quality. Tire pressure cannot be accurately estimated by looking at a tire, especially if it's a radial. A tire pressure gauge is essential. Keep an accurate gauge in the glove compartment. The pressure gauges attached to the nozzles of air hoses at gas stations are often inaccurate.

7   Always check tire pressure when the tires are cold. Cold, in this case, means the vehicle has not been driven over a mile in the three hours preceding a tire pressure check. A pressure rise of four to eight pounds is not uncommon once the tires are warm.

8   Unscrew the valve cap protruding from the wheel or hubcap and

UNDERINFLATION

CUPPING

OVERINFLATION

Cupping may be caused by:
- Underinflation and/or mechanical irregularities such as out-of-balance condition of wheel and/or tire, and bent or damaged wheel.
- Loose or worn steering tie-rod or steering idler arm.
- Loose, damaged or worn front suspension parts.

INCORRECT TOE-IN OR EXTREME CAMBER

FEATHERING DUE TO MISALIGNMENT

5.3 This chart will help you determine the condition of your tires, the probable cause(s) of abnormal wear and the corrective action necessary

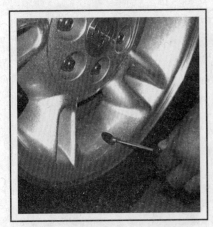

5.4a If a tire loses air on a steady basis, check the valve core first to make sure it's snug (special inexpensive wrenches are commonly available at auto parts stores)

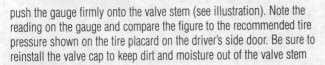

5.4b If the valve core is tight, raise the corner of the vehicle with the low tire and spray a soapy water solution onto the tread as the tire is turned slowly - slow leaks will cause small bubbles to appear

5.8 To extend the life of your tires, check the air pressure at least once a week with an accurate gauge (don't forget the spare!)

push the gauge firmly onto the valve stem (see illustration). Note the reading on the gauge and compare the figure to the recommended tire pressure shown on the tire placard on the driver's side door. Be sure to reinstall the valve cap to keep dirt and moisture out of the valve stem

mechanism. Check all four tires and, if necessary, add enough air to bring them up to the recommended pressure.

9 Don't forget to keep the spare tire inflated to the specified pressure (refer to the pressure molded into the tire sidewall).

6 Engine oil and filter change (every 3000 miles or 3 months)

▶ Refer to illustrations 6.2 and 6.7

✲✲ CAUTION:

On 2.5L engines, two different engine part manufacturers are used and the parts are not interchangeable. Use the 8th digit in the VIN number to determine which parts manufacturer you have; VIN A engine parts are made in Mexico and VIN H engine parts are made in Hiroshima.

1 Frequent oil changes are the most important preventive maintenance procedures that can be done by the home mechanic. As engine oil ages, it becomes diluted and contaminated, which leads to premature engine wear.

2 Make sure that you have all the necessary tools before you begin this procedure (see illustration). You should also have plenty of rags or newspapers handy for mopping up oil spills.

3 Access to the oil drain plug and filter will be improved if the vehicle can be lifted on a hoist, driven onto ramps or supported by jackstands.

✲✲ WARNING:

Do not work under a vehicle supported only by a jack - always use jackstands!

4 If you haven't changed the oil on this vehicle before, get under it and locate the oil drain plug and the oil filter. The exhaust components will be warm as you work, so note how they are routed to avoid touching them when you are under the vehicle.

5 Start the engine and allow it to reach normal operating temperature - oil and sludge will flow out more easily when warm. If new oil, a

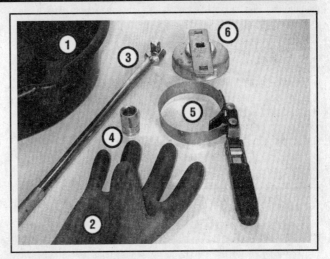

6.2 These tools are required when changing the engine oil and filter

1 **Drain pan** - It should be fairly shallow in depth, but wide in order to prevent spills
2 **Rubber gloves** - When removing the drain plug and filter, it is inevitable that you will get oil on your hands (the gloves will prevent burns)
3 **Breaker bar** - Sometimes the oil drain plug is pretty tight and a long breaker bar is needed to loosen it
4 **Socket** - To be used with the breaker bar or a ratchet (must be the correct size to fit the drain plug)
5 **Filter wrench** - This is a metal band-type wrench, which requires clearance around the filter to be effective
6 **Filter wrench** - This type fits on the bottom of the filter and can be turned with a ratchet or breaker bar (different size wrenches are available for different types of filters)

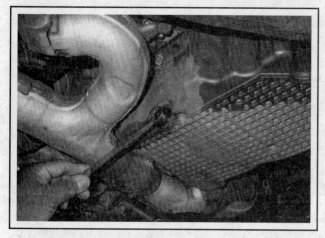

6.7 Use a proper size box-end wrench or socket to remove the oil drain plug and avoid rounding it off

6.20 Use an oil filter wrench to remove the filter (3.0L V6 engine shown)

filter or tools are needed, use the vehicle to go get them and warm up the engine/oil at the same time. Park on a level surface and shut off the engine when it's warmed up. Remove the oil filler cap from the valve cover.

6 Raise the vehicle and support it on jackstands. Make sure it is safely supported and remove the lower engine cover.

7 Being careful not to touch the hot exhaust components, position a drain pan under the plug in the bottom of the engine, then remove the plug (see illustration). It's a good idea to wear a rubber glove while unscrewing the plug the final few turns to avoid being scalded by hot oil.

8 It may be necessary to move the drain pan slightly as oil flow slows to a trickle. Inspect the old oil for the presence of metal particles.

9 After all the oil has drained, wipe off the drain plug with a clean rag. Any small metal particles clinging to the plug would immediately contaminate the new oil.

10 Clean the area around the drain plug opening, reinstall the plug and tighten it to the torque listed in this Chapter's Specifications.

CARTRIDGE TYPE FILTER

11 Move the drain pan into position under the oil filter cover.

12 Loosen the oil filter drain plug in the center of the oil filter cover, but do not remove it.

13 Loosen the oil filter cover one turn counterclockwise with a filter wrench.

14 Once the filter cover is loose, remove the filter cover drain plug and drain the engine oil from the filter housing.

➡ **Note: The oil will not drain quickly if the cover is not loosened.**

15 Use your hands to unscrew the cover and remove the cover and filter from the housing.

16 Using a clean rag, wipe off the mounting surface of the oil filter adapter. Also, make sure that the old O-ring is not stuck to the mounting surface.

17 Compare the old filter element with the new one to make sure they are the same type. Smear some clean engine oil on the new O-ring for the filter cover. Install the new filter then the oil filter cover with the new O-ring and screw it into place. Tighten the cover to the torque listed in this Chapter's Specifications.

18 Apply a small amount of clean oil to the filter cover drain plug

O-ring and tighten the filter cover drain plug to the torque listed in this Chapter's Specifications.

SPIN-ON TYPE FILTER

▶ **Refer to illustrations 6.20 and 6.23**

19 Move the drain pan into position under the oil filter.

20 Loosen the oil filter by turning it counterclockwise with a filter wrench (see illustration). Any standard filter wrench will work.

21 Once the filter is loose, use your hands to unscrew it from the block. Just as the filter is detached from the block, immediately tilt the open end up to prevent the oil inside the filter from spilling out.

22 Using a clean rag, wipe off the mounting surface on the block. Also, make sure that none of the old gasket remains stuck to the mounting surface. It can be removed with a scraper if necessary.

23 Compare the old filter with the new one to make sure they are the same type. Smear some engine oil on the rubber gasket of the new filter and screw it into place (see illustration). Overtightening the filter will damage the gasket, so don't use a filter wrench. Most filter manufacturers recommend tightening the filter by hand only. Normally they should

6.23 Lubricate the oil filter gasket with clean engine oil before installing the filter on the engine

be tightened 3/4-turn after the gasket contacts the block, but be sure to follow the directions on the filter or container.

ALL MODELS

24 Remove all tools and materials from under the vehicle, being careful not to spill the oil in the drain pan, then lower the vehicle.

25 Add four quarts of fresh oil to the engine. Wait a few minutes to allow the oil to drain into the pan, then check the level on the dipstick (see Section 4 if necessary). If the oil level is in the OK range, install the filler cap.

26 Start the engine and run it for about a minute. While the engine is running, look under the vehicle and check for leaks at the oil pan drain plug and around the oil filter. If either one is leaking, stop the engine and tighten the plug or filter slightly.

27 Wait a few minutes, then recheck the level on the dipstick. Add oil as necessary to bring the level into the OK range.

28 During the first few trips after an oil change, make it a point to check frequently for leaks and proper oil level.

29 The old oil drained from the engine cannot be reused in its present state and should be disposed of. Check with your local auto parts store, disposal facility or environmental agency to see if they will accept the oil for recycling. After the oil has cooled it can be drained into a container (capped plastic jugs, topped bottles, milk cartons, etc.) for transport to one of these disposal sites. Don't dispose of the oil by pouring it on the ground or down a drain!

---

7   Windshield wiper blade inspection and replacement (every 7500 miles or 6 months)

▶ **Refer to illustrations 7.4a and 7.4b**

1   The windshield wiper and blade assembly should be inspected periodically for damage, loose components and cracked or worn blade elements.

2   Road film can build up on the wiper blades and affect their efficiency, so they should be washed regularly with a mild detergent solution.

3   If the wiper blade elements are cracked, worn or warped, or no longer clean adequately, they should be replaced with new ones.

4   Lift the arm assembly away from the glass for clearance, press on the release lever, then slide the wiper blade assembly out of the hook in the end of the arm (see illustrations).

5   Attach the new wiper to the arm. Connection can be confirmed by an audible click.

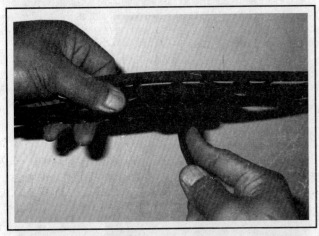

7.4a To release the blade holder, push the release pin . . .

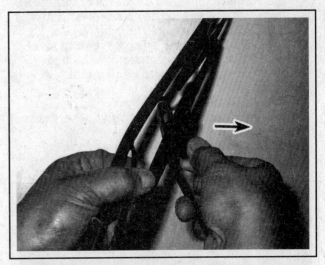

7.4b . . . and pull the wiper blade in the direction of the arrow to separate it from the arm

---

8   Battery check, maintenance and charging (every 7500 miles or 6 months)

▶ **Refer to illustrations 8.1, 8.6a, 8.6b, 8.7a, 8.7b and 8.8**

✳ WARNING:

Certain precautions must be followed when checking and servicing the battery. Hydrogen gas, which is highly flammable, is always present in the battery cells, so keep lighted tobacco and all other open flames and sparks away from the battery. The electrolyte inside the battery is actually diluted sulfuric acid, which will cause injury if splashed on your skin or in your eyes. It will also ruin clothes and painted surfaces. When removing the battery cables, always detach the negative cable first and hook it up last!

1   A routine preventive maintenance program for the battery in your vehicle is the only way to ensure quick and reliable starts. But before

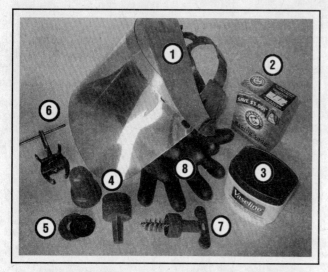

8.1 Tools and materials required for battery maintenance

1   Face shield/safety goggles - *When removing corrosion with a brush, the acidic particles can easily fly up into your eyes*

2   Baking soda - *A solution of baking soda and water can be used to neutralize corrosion*

3   Petroleum jelly - *A layer of this on the battery posts will help prevent corrosion*

4   Battery post/cable cleaner - *This cleaning tool will remove all traces of corrosion from the battery posts and cable clamps*

5   Treated felt washers - *Placing one of these on each post, directly under the cable clamps, will help prevent corrosion*

6   Puller - *Sometimes the cable clamps are very difficult to pull off the posts, even after the nut/bolt has been completely loosened. This tool pulls the clamp straight up and off the post without damage*

7   Battery post/cable cleaner - *Here is another cleaning tool which is a slightly different version of number 4 above, but it does the same thing*

8   Rubber gloves - *Another safety item to consider when servicing the battery; remember that's acid inside the battery*

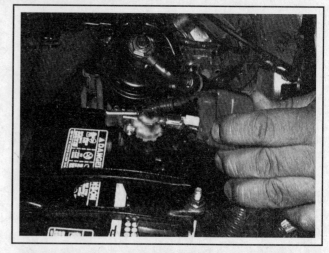

8.6a Battery terminal corrosion usually appears as light, fluffy powder

performing any battery maintenance, make sure that you have the proper equipment necessary to work safely around the battery (see illustration).

2   There are also several precautions that should be taken whenever battery maintenance is performed. Before servicing the battery, always turn the engine and all accessories off and disconnect the cables from the negative terminal of the battery (see Chapter 5).

3   The battery produces hydrogen gas, which is both flammable and explosive. Never create a spark, smoke or light a match around the battery. Always charge the battery in a ventilated area.

4   Electrolyte contains poisonous and corrosive sulfuric acid. Do not allow it to get in your eyes, on your skin on your clothes. Never ingest it. Wear protective safety glasses when working near the battery. Keep children away from the battery.

5   Note the external condition of the battery. If the positive terminal and cable clamp on your vehicle's battery is equipped with a rubber protector, make sure that it's not torn or damaged. It should completely cover the terminal. Look for any corroded or loose connections, cracks in the case or cover or loose hold-down clamps. Also check the entire length of each cable for cracks and frayed conductors.

6   If corrosion, which looks like white, fluffy deposits (see illustration) is evident, particularly around the terminals, the battery should be removed for cleaning. Loosen the cable clamp bolts with a wrench,

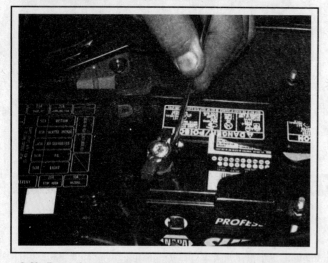

8.6b Removing a cable from the battery post with a wrench - sometimes a pair of special battery pliers are required for this procedure if corrosion has caused deterioration of the nut hex. Always remove the ground (-) cable first and hook it up last!

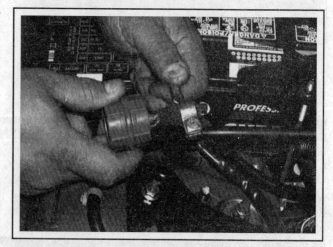

8.7a When cleaning the cable clamps, all corrosion must be removed

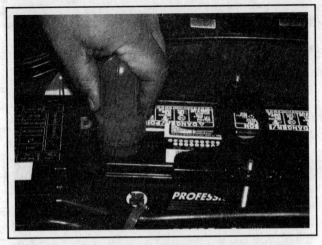

8.7b Regardless of the type of tool used to clean the battery posts, a clean, shiny surface should be the result

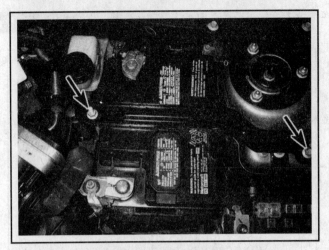

8.8 Make sure the battery hold-down fasteners are tight

being careful to remove the ground cable first, and slide them off the terminals (see illustration). Then disconnect the hold-down clamp bolt and nut, remove the clamp and lift the battery from the engine compartment.

7   Clean the cable clamps thoroughly with a battery brush or a terminal cleaner and a solution of warm water and baking soda (see illustration). Wash the terminals and the top of the battery case with the same solution but make sure that the solution doesn't get into the battery. When cleaning the cables, terminals and battery top, wear safety goggles and rubber gloves to prevent any solution from coming in contact with your eyes or hands. Wear old clothes too - even diluted, sulfuric acid splashed onto clothes will burn holes in them. If the terminals have been extensively corroded, clean them up with a terminal cleaner (see illustration). Thoroughly wash all cleaned areas with plain water.

8   Make sure that the battery tray is in good condition and the hold-down clamp fasteners are tight (see illustration). If the battery is removed from the tray, make sure no parts remain in the bottom of the tray when the battery is reinstalled. When reinstalling the hold-down clamp bolts, do not overtighten them.

9   Information on removing and installing the battery can be found in Chapter 5. If you disconnected the cable(s) from the negative and/or positive battery terminals, the powertrain control module (PCM) must relearn its idle and fuel trim strategy for optimum driveability and performance (see Chapter 5 for this procedure). Information on jump starting can be found at the front of this manual.

CLEANING

10   Corrosion on the hold-down components, battery case and surrounding areas can be removed with a solution of water and baking soda. Thoroughly rinse all cleaned areas with plain water.

11   Any metal parts of the vehicle damaged by corrosion should be covered with a zinc-based primer, then painted.

CHARGING

✳✳ WARNING:

When batteries are being charged, hydrogen gas, which is very explosive and flammable, is produced. Do not smoke or allow open flames near a charging or a recently charged battery. Wear eye protection when near the battery during charging. Also, make sure the charger is unplugged before connecting or disconnecting the battery from the charger.

12   Slow-rate charging is the best way to restore a battery that's discharged to the point where it will not start the engine. It's also a good way to maintain the battery charge in a vehicle that's only driven a few miles between starts. Maintaining the battery charge is particularly important in the winter when the battery must work harder to start the engine and electrical accessories that drain the battery are in greater use.

13   It's best to use a one or two-amp battery charger (sometimes called a "trickle" charger). They are the safest and put the least strain on the battery. They are also the least expensive. For a faster charge, you can use a higher amperage charger, but don't use one rated more than 1/10th the amp/hour rating of the battery. Rapid boost charges that claim to restore the power of the battery in one to two hours are hardest on the battery and can damage batteries not in good condition. This type of charging should only be used in emergency situations.

14   The average time necessary to charge a battery should be listed in the instructions that come with the charger. As a general rule, a trickle charger will charge a battery in 12 to 16 hours.

9   Cooling system check (every 7,500 miles or 6 months)

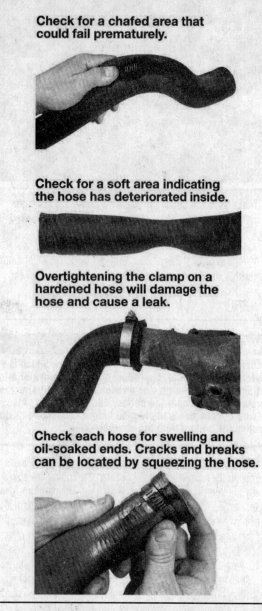

Check for a chafed area that could fail prematurely.

Check for a soft area indicating the hose has deteriorated inside.

Overtightening the clamp on a hardened hose will damage the hose and cause a leak.

Check each hose for swelling and oil-soaked ends. Cracks and breaks can be located by squeezing the hose.

9.4 Hoses, like drivebelts, have a habit of failing at the worst possible time - to prevent the inconvenience of a blown radiator or heater hose, inspect them carefully as shown here

▶ **Refer to illustration 9.4**

1   Many major engine failures can be caused by a faulty cooling system.

2   The engine must be cold for the cooling system check, so perform the following procedure before the vehicle is driven for the day or after it has been shut off for at least three hours.

3   Remove the pressure-relief cap from the expansion tank at the right side of the engine compartment. Clean the cap thoroughly, inside and out, with clean water. The presence of rust or corrosion in the expansion tank means the coolant should be changed (see Section 20). The coolant inside the expansion tank should be relatively clean and transparent. If it's rust colored, drain the system and refill it with new coolant.

4   Carefully check the radiator hoses and the smaller diameter heater hoses. Inspect each coolant hose along its entire length, replacing any hose which is cracked, swollen or deteriorated (see illustration). Cracks will show up better if the hose is squeezed. Pay close attention to hose clamps that secure the hoses to cooling system components. Hose clamps can pinch and puncture hoses, resulting in coolant leaks.

5   Make sure that all hose connections are tight. A leak in the cooling system will usually show up as white or rust colored deposits on the area adjoining the leak. If wire-type clamps are used on the hoses, it may be a good idea to replace them with screw-type clamps.

6   Clean the front of the radiator and air conditioning condenser with compressed air, if available, or a soft brush. Remove all bugs, leaves, etc. embedded in the radiator fins. Be extremely careful not to damage the cooling fins or cut your fingers on them.

7   If the coolant level has been dropping consistently and no leaks are detectable, have the expansion tank cap and cooling system pressure checked at a service station.

10   Tire rotation (every 7,500 miles or 6 months)

▶ **Refer to illustration 10.2**

1   The tires should be rotated at the specified intervals and whenever uneven wear is noticed. Since the vehicle will be raised and the

tires removed anyway, check the brakes also (see Section 13).

2   Radial tires must be rotated in a specific pattern (see illustration). Don't include the spare tire in the rotation pattern.

3   Refer to the information in *Jacking and towing* at the front of this

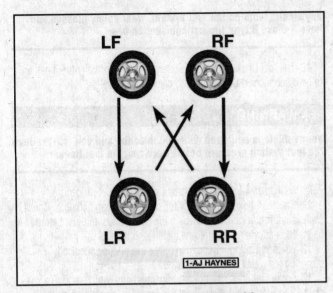

10.2a Tire rotation pattern for *non-directional* tires

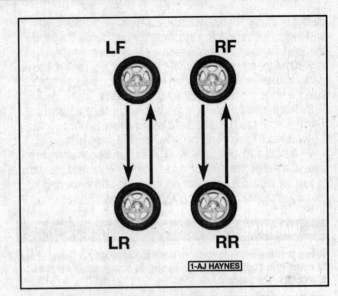

10.2b Tire rotation pattern for *directional* tires

manual for the proper procedure to follow when raising the vehicle and changing a tire. If the brakes must be checked, don't apply the parking brake as stated.

4   The vehicle must be raised on a hoist or supported on jackstands to get all four wheels off the ground. Make sure the vehicle is safely supported!

5   After the rotation procedure is finished, check and adjust the tire pressures as necessary and be sure to check the lug nut tightness.

11 Seat belt check (every 7,500 miles or 6 months)

1   Check seat belts, buckles, latch plates and guide loops for obvious damage and signs of wear.

2   See if the seat belt reminder light comes on when the key is turned to the Run or Start position. A chime should also sound.

3   The seat belts are designed to lock up during a sudden stop or impact, yet allow free movement during normal driving. Make sure the retractors return the belt against your chest while driving and rewind the belt fully when the buckle is unlatched.

4   If any of the above checks reveal problems with the seat belt system, replace parts as necessary.

12 Underhood hose check and replacement (every 15,000 miles or 12 months)

✳✳ WARNING:

Replacement of air conditioning hoses must be left to a dealer service department or air conditioning shop that has the equipment to depressurize the system safely. Never remove air conditioning components or hoses until the system has been depressurized.

GENERAL

1   High temperatures under the hood can cause deterioration of the rubber and plastic hoses used for engine, accessory and emission systems operation. Periodic inspection should be made for cracks, loose clamps, material hardening and leaks.

2   Information specific to the cooling system hoses can be found in Section 9.

3   Most (but not all) hoses are secured to the fittings with clamps. Where clamps are used, check to be sure they haven't lost their tension, allowing the hose to leak. If clamps aren't used, make sure the hose has not expanded and/or hardened where it slips over the fitting, allowing it to leak.

PCV SYSTEM HOSE

4   To reduce hydrocarbon emissions, crankcase blow-by gas is vented through the PCV valve in the valve cover to the intake manifold via a rubber hose on most models. The blow-by gases mix with incoming air in the intake manifold before being burned in the combustion chambers.

5   Check the PCV hose for cracks, leaks and other damage. Disconnect it from the valve cover and the intake manifold and check the inside for obstructions. If it's clogged, clean it out with solvent.

VACUUM HOSES

6   It's quite common for vacuum hoses, especially those in the emissions system, to be color coded or identified by colored stripes

molded into them. Various systems require hoses with different wall thickness, collapse resistance and temperature resistance. When replacing hoses, be sure the new ones are made of the same material.

7 Often the only effective way to check a hose is to remove it completely from the vehicle. If more than one hose is removed, be sure to label the hoses and fittings to ensure correct installation.

8 When checking vacuum hoses, be sure to include any plastic T-fittings in the check. Inspect the fittings for cracks and the hose where it fits over each fitting for distortion, which could cause leakage.

9 A small piece of vacuum hose (1/4-inch inside diameter) can be used as a stethoscope to detect vacuum leaks. Hold one end of the hose to your ear and probe around vacuum hoses and fittings, listening for the hissing sound characteristic of a vacuum leak.

❊❊ WARNING:

When probing with the vacuum hose stethoscope, be careful not to come into contact with moving engine components such as drivebelts, the cooling fan, etc.

FUEL HOSE

❊❊ WARNING:

Gasoline is flammable, so take extra precautions when you work on any part of the fuel system. Don't smoke or allow open flames or bare light bulbs near the work area, and don't work in a garage where a gas-type appliance (such as a water heater or clothes dryer) is present. Since fuel is carcinogenic, wear fuel-resistant gloves when there's a possibility of being exposed to fuel, and, if you spill any fuel on your skin, rinse it off immediately with soap and water. Mop up any spills immediately and do not store fuel-soaked rags where they could ignite. The fuel system is under constant pressure, so, if any fuel lines are to be disconnected, the fuel pressure in the system must be relieved first (see Chapter 4 for more information). When you perform

any kind of work on the fuel system, wear safety glasses and have a Class B type fire extinguisher on hand.

10 The fuel lines are usually under pressure, so if any fuel lines are to be disconnected be prepared to catch spilled fuel.

❊❊ WARNING:

Your vehicle is equipped with fuel injection and you must relieve the fuel system pressure before servicing the fuel lines.

Refer to Chapter 4 for the fuel system pressure relief procedure.

11 Check all flexible fuel lines for deterioration and chafing. Check especially for cracks in areas where the hose bends and just before fittings, such as where the fuel line attaches to the fuel rail.

12 When replacing a hose, use only hose that is specifically designed for your fuel injection system.

13 Some fuel lines use quick-connect fittings, which require a special tool to disconnect. See Chapter 4 for more information on these types of fittings.

METAL LINES

14 Sections of metal line are often used for fuel line that runs underneath the vehicle. Check carefully to make sure the line isn't bent, crimped or cracked.

15 If a section of metal fuel line must be replaced, use seamless steel tubing only, since copper and aluminum tubing do not have the strength necessary to withstand vibration caused by the engine.

16 Check the metal brake lines where they enter the master cylinder and brake proportioning unit (if used) for cracks in the lines and loose fittings. Any sign of brake fluid leakage calls for an immediate thorough inspection of the brake system.

13 Brake check (every 15,000 miles or 12 months)

❊❊ WARNING:

Dust created by the brake system is harmful to your health. Never blow it out with compressed air and don't inhale any of it. An approved filtering mask should be worn when working on brakes. Do not, under any circumstances, use petroleum-based solvents to clean brake parts. Use brake system cleaner only!

1 The brakes should be inspected every time the wheels are removed or whenever a defect is suspected. Indications of a potential brake system problem include the vehicle pulling to one side when the brake pedal is depressed, noises coming from the brakes when they are applied, excessive brake pedal travel, a pulsating pedal and leakage of fluid, usually seen on the inside of the tire or wheel.

➡ Note: It is normal for a vehicle equipped with an Anti-lock Brake System (ABS) to exhibit brake pedal pulsations during severe braking conditions.

DISC BRAKES

▶ **Refer to illustrations 13.5a and 13.5b**

2 Disc brakes can be visually checked without removing any parts except the wheels. Remove the hub caps (if applicable) and loosen the wheel lug nuts a quarter turn each.

3 Raise the vehicle and place it securely on jackstands.

❊❊ WARNING:

Never work under a vehicle that is supported only by a jack!

4 Remove the wheels. Now visible is the disc brake caliper which contains the pads. There is an outer brake pad and an inner pad. Both must be checked for wear.

5 Measure the thickness of the outer pad at each end of the caliper and the inner pad through the inspection hole in the caliper body (see

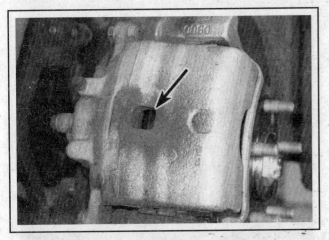

13.5a You will find an inspection hole like this in each caliper through which you can view the thickness of remaining friction material for the inner pad

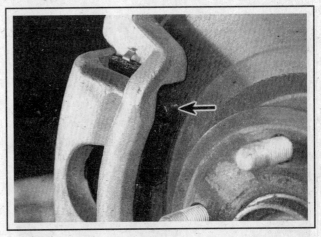

13.5b Be sure to check the thickness of the outer pad material, too

illustrations). Compare the measurement with the limit given in this Chapter's Specifications; if any brake pad thickness is less than specified, then all brake pads must be replaced (see Chapter 9).

6   If you're in doubt as to the exact pad thickness or quality, remove them for measurement and further inspection (see Chapter 9).

7   Check the disc for score marks, wear and burned spots. If any of these conditions exist, the disc should be removed for servicing or replacement (see Chapter 9).

8   Before installing the wheels, check all the brake lines and hoses for damage, wear, deformation, cracks, corrosion, leakage, bends and twists, particularly in the vicinity of the rubber hoses and calipers.

9   Install the wheels, lower the vehicle and tighten the wheel lug nuts to the torque given in this Chapter's Specifications.

PARKING BRAKE

10   Slowly pull up on the parking brake and count the number of clicks you hear until the handle is up as far as it will go. The adjustment is correct if you hear the specified number of clicks (see this Chapter's Specifications). If you hear more or fewer clicks, it's time to adjust the parking brake (see Chapter 9).

11   An alternative method of checking the parking brake is to park the vehicle on a steep hill with the engine running (so you can apply the brakes if necessary) with the parking brake set and the transaxle in Neutral. If the parking brake cannot prevent the vehicle from rolling, it needs adjustment (see Chapter 9).

14 Steering, suspension and driveaxle boot check (every 15,000 miles or 12 months)

➡ **Note: For detailed illustrations of the steering and suspension components, refer to Chapter 10.**

SHOCK ABSORBER CHECK

▶ **Refer to illustration 14.6**

1   Park the vehicle on level ground, turn the engine off and set the parking brake. Check the tire pressures.

2   Push down at one corner of the vehicle, then release it while noting the movement of the body. It should stop moving and come to rest in a level position within one or two bounces.

3   If the vehicle continues to move up-and-down or if it fails to return to its original position, a worn or weak shock absorber is probably the reason.

4   Repeat the above check at each of the three remaining corners of the vehicle.

5   Raise the vehicle and support it securely on jackstands.

6   Check the shock absorbers for evidence of fluid leakage (see illustration). A light film of fluid is no cause for concern. Make sure that

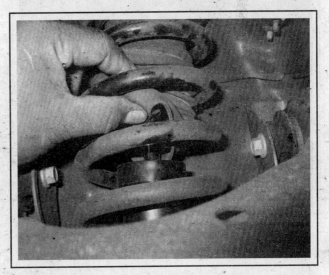

14.6 Check the shocks for leakage

14.11 To check a balljoint for wear, try to pry the control arm up and down to make sure there is no play in the balljoint (if there is, replace it)

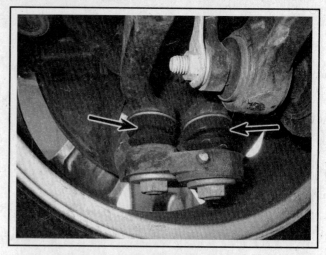

14.12 Check the balljoint boots for damage

any fluid noted is from the shocks and not from some other source. If leakage is noted, replace the shocks as a set.

7 Check the shocks to be sure that they are securely mounted and undamaged. Check the upper mounts for damage and wear. If damage or wear is noted, replace the shocks as a set (front or rear).

8 If the shocks must be replaced, refer to Chapter 10 for the procedure.

STEERING AND SUSPENSION CHECK

▶ Refer to illustrations 14.11 and 14.12

9 Check the tires for irregular wear patterns and proper inflation. See Section 5 for information regarding tire wear and Chapter 10 for information on wheel bearing replacement.

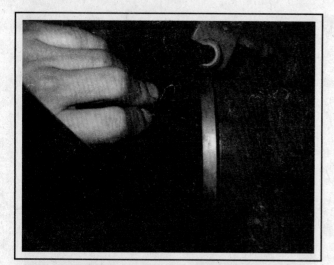

14.15 Flex the driveaxle boots by hand to check for cracks and/or leaking grease

10 Inspect the universal joint between the steering shaft and the steering gear housing. Check the steering gear housing for lubricant leakage. Make sure that the dust boots are not damaged and that the boot clamps are not loose. Check the tie-rod ends for excessive play. Look for loose bolts, broken or disconnected parts and deteriorated rubber bushings on all suspension and steering components. While an assistant turns the steering wheel from side to side, check the steering components for free movement, chafing and binding. If the steering components do not seem to be reacting with the movement of the steering wheel, try to determine where the slack is located.

11 Check the balljoints for wear by trying to move each control arm up and down with a prybar (see illustration) to ensure that its balljoint has no play. If any balljoint does have play, it's worn out. See Chapter 10 for the control arm replacement procedure (the balljoints aren't replaceable separately).

12 Inspect the balljoint boots for damage and leaking grease (see illustration).

13 At the rear of the vehicle, inspect the suspension arm bushings for deterioration. Additional information on suspension components can be found in Chapter 10.

DRIVEAXLE BOOT CHECK

▶ Refer to illustration 14.15

14 The driveaxle boots are very important because they prevent dirt, water and foreign material from entering and damaging the constant velocity (CV) joints. Oil and grease can cause the boot material to deteriorate prematurely, so it's a good idea to wash the boots with soap and water. Because it constantly pivots back and forth following the steering action of the front hub, the outer CV boot wears out sooner and should be inspected regularly.

15 Inspect the boots for tears and cracks as well as loose clamps (see illustration). If there is any evidence of cracks or leaking lubricant, they must be replaced as described in Chapter 8.

15 Fuel system check (every 15,000 miles or 12 months)

❋❋ WARNING:

Gasoline is flammable, so take extra precautions when you work on any part of the fuel system. Don't smoke or allow open flames or bare light bulbs near the work area, and don't work in a garage where a gas-type appliance (such as a water heater or clothes dryer) is present. Since fuel is carcinogenic, wear fuel-resistant gloves when there's a possibility of being exposed to fuel, and, if you spill any fuel on your skin, rinse it off immediately with soap and water. Mop up any spills immediately and do not store fuel-soaked rags where they could ignite. When you perform any kind of work on the fuel system, wear safety glasses and have a Class B type fire extinguisher on hand. The fuel system is under constant pressure, so, before any lines are disconnected, the fuel system pressure must be relieved (see Chapter 4).

1 If you smell gasoline while driving or after the vehicle has been sitting in the sun, inspect the fuel system immediately.

2 Remove the fuel filler cap and inspect if for damage and corrosion. The gasket should have an unbroken sealing imprint. If the gasket is damaged or corroded, install a new cap.

3 Inspect the fuel feed line for cracks. Make sure that the connections between the fuel lines and the fuel injection system and between the fuel lines and the fuel tank (inspect from below) are tight and dry.

❋❋ WARNING:

Your vehicle is fuel injected, so you must relieve the fuel system pressure before servicing fuel system components. The fuel system pressure relief procedure is outlined in Chapter 4.

4 Since some components of the fuel system - the fuel tank and part of the fuel feed line, for example - are underneath the vehicle, they can be inspected more easily with the vehicle raised on a hoist. If that's not possible, raise the vehicle and support it on jackstands.

5 With the vehicle raised and safely supported, inspect the gas tank and filler neck for punctures, cracks and other damage. The connection between the filler neck and the tank is particularly critical. Sometimes a rubber filler neck will leak because of loose clamps or deteriorated rubber. Inspect all fuel tank mounting brackets and straps to be sure that the tank is securely attached to the vehicle.

❋❋ WARNING:

Do not, under any circumstances, try to repair a fuel tank (except rubber components). A welding torch or any open flame can easily cause fuel vapors inside the tank to explode.

6 Carefully check all rubber hoses and metal lines leading away from the fuel tank. Check for loose connections, deteriorated hoses, crimped lines and other damage. Repair or replace damaged sections as necessary (see Chapter 4).

16 Manual transaxle lubricant level check (every 15,000 miles or 12 months)

1 The manual transaxle does not have a dipstick. To check the fluid level, raise the vehicle and support it securely on jackstands. On the front side of the transaxle housing there is a fill plug about half-way up on the transaxle case; it's the larger of the two hex-head bolts.

❋❋ CAUTION:

Do not remove the smaller hex-head bolt above the back-up light switch.

Remove the plug; if the lubricant level is correct, it should be up to the lower edge of the hole.

2 If the transaxle needs more lubricant (if the level is not up to the hole), use a syringe or a gear oil pump to add more. Stop filling the transaxle when the lubricant begins to run out of the hole.

3 Install the plug and tighten it to the torque listed in this Chapter's Specifications. Drive the vehicle a short distance, then check for leaks.

17 Air filter check and replacement (every 15,000 miles or 12 months)

▶ Refer to illustrations 17.1a and 17.1b

1 The air filter is located inside a housing at the left (driver's) side of the engine compartment. To remove the air filter, release the clamps that secure the two halves of the air filter housing together, then separate the cover halves and remove the air filter element (see illustrations).

17.1a Unlatch these clips . . .

17.1b . . . pull the cover out of the way and remove the filter element

2   Inspect the outer surface of the filter element. If it is dirty, replace it. If it is only moderately dusty, it can be reused by blowing it clean from the back to the front surface with compressed air. Because it is a pleated paper type filter, it cannot be washed or oiled. If it cannot be cleaned satisfactorily with compressed air, discard and replace it. While the cover is off, be careful not to drop anything down into the housing.

> ✳✳ **CAUTION:**
>
> **Never drive the vehicle with the air filter removed. Excessive engine wear could result and backfiring could even cause a fire under the hood.**

3   Wipe out the inside of the air filter housing.
4   Place the new filter into the housing, making sure it seats properly.
5   Make sure the top half of the housing is seated properly, then secure it with the clamps.

18   Cabin air filter replacement (every 15,000 miles or 12 months)

▸ **Refer to illustration 18.2 and 18.3**

1   Remove the glove box (see Chapter 11).
2   Lift up on the access door lower tabs, rotate the door out of the

upper catches and remove the door (see illustration).
3   Pull the filter from the housing (see illustration).
4   Installation is the reverse of removal.

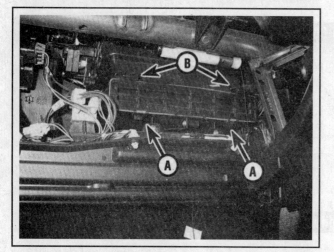

18.2   Release the lower clips (A), and rotate the cover up and out of the upper catches (B)

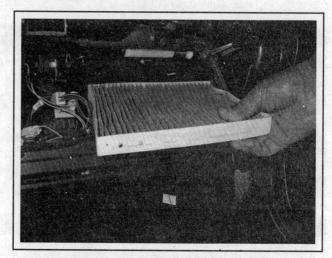

18.3   Pull the filter out of the housing

19   Exhaust system check (every 30,000 miles or 24 months)

▸ **Refer to illustration 19.2**

1   With the engine cold (at least three hours after the vehicle has been driven), check the complete exhaust system from the engine to

the end of the tailpipe. Ideally, the inspection should be done with the vehicle on a hoist to permit unrestricted access. If a hoist isn't available, raise the vehicle and support it securely on jackstands.
2   Check the exhaust pipes and connections for evidence of leaks,

severe corrosion and damage. Make sure that all brackets and hangers are in good condition and tight (see illustration).

3   At the same time, inspect the underside of the body for holes, corrosion, open seams, etc. which may allow exhaust gases to enter the passenger compartment. Seal all body openings with silicone or body putty.

4   Rattles and other noises can often be traced to the exhaust system, especially the mounts and hangers. Try to move the pipes, muffler and catalytic converter. If the components can come in contact with the body or suspension parts, secure the exhaust system with new mounts.

5   Check the running condition of the engine by inspecting inside the end of the tailpipe. The exhaust deposits here are an indication of engine state-of-tune. If the pipe is black and sooty or coated with white deposits, the engine may need a tune-up, including a thorough fuel system inspection and adjustment.

19.2 Be sure to check each exhaust system rubber hanger for damage

20   Cooling system servicing (draining, flushing and refilling) (every 30,000 miles or 24 months)

✱✱ WARNING:

Wait until the engine is completely cool before performing this procedure.

✱✱ WARNING:

Do not allow antifreeze to come in contact with your skin or painted surfaces of the vehicle. Rinse off spills immediately with plenty of water. Antifreeze is highly toxic if ingested. Never leave antifreeze lying around in an open container or in puddles on the floor; children and pets are attracted by its sweet smell and may drink it. Check with local authorities about disposing of used antifreeze. Many communities have collection centers which will see that antifreeze is disposed of safely. Never dump used antifreeze on the ground or pour it into drains.

✱✱ CAUTION:

Do not mix coolants of different colors. Doing so might damage the cooling system and/or the engine. The manufacturer specifies either a green colored coolant or a yellow colored coolant to be used in these systems. Read the warning label in the engine compartment for additional information.

➡ Note: Non-toxic antifreeze is now manufactured and available at local auto parts stores, but even this type must be disposed of properly.

1   Periodically, the cooling system should be drained, flushed and refilled to replenish the antifreeze mixture and prevent formation of rust and corrosion, which can impair the performance of the cooling system and cause engine damage. When the cooling system is serviced, all hoses and the expansion tank cap should be checked and replaced if necessary.

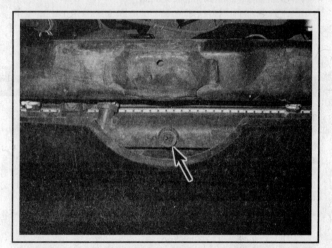

20.4 The radiator drain fitting is located at the bottom of the radiator

DRAINING

➡ **Refer to illustration 20.4**

2   Apply the parking brake and block the wheels. If the vehicle has just been driven, wait several hours to allow the engine to cool down before beginning this procedure.

3   Once the engine is completely cool, remove the expansion tank cap or, on models with a radiator cap, remove the radiator cap.

4   Move a large container under the radiator drain to catch the coolant and unscrew the drain plug (see illustration).

5   While the coolant is draining, check the condition of the radiator hoses, heater hoses and clamps (refer to Section 9 if necessary). Replace any damaged clamps or hoses.

FLUSHING

6 Fill the cooling system with clean water, following the *Refilling* procedure (see Step 12).

7 Start the engine and allow it to reach normal operating temperature, then rev up the engine a few times.

8 Turn the engine off and allow it to cool completely, then drain the system as described earlier.

9 Repeat Steps 6 through 8 until the water being drained is free of contaminants.

10 In severe cases of contamination or clogging of the radiator, remove the radiator (see Chapter 3) and have a radiator repair facility clean and repair it if necessary.

11 Many deposits can be removed by the chemical action of a cleaner available at auto parts stores. Follow the procedure outlined in the manufacturer's instructions.

➡ **Note: When the coolant is regularly drained and the system refilled with the correct antifreeze/water mixture, there should be no need to use chemical cleaners or descalers.**

REFILLING

12 Close and tighten the radiator drain.

13 Place the heater temperature control in the maximum heat position.

14 On 2005 and earlier models, slowly add new coolant (a 50/50 mixture of water and antifreeze). On 2006 and later models, look for the "FL22" mark. If the "FL22" mark is present, water should not be added to the system when replacing the coolant; "FL22" type engine coolant is shipped as a diluted solution.

15 On models with a radiator cap, add coolant until it is up to the bottom of the filler neck, then reinstall the cap. On all models, add coolant to the expansion tank until the level is at the MAX fill mark on the expansion tank. Install the expansion tank cap and run the engine at 2500 rpm for five minutes, then let idle for one minute.

> ✳ **CAUTION:**
>
> **If at any time the engine begins to overheat, or the coolant level falls below the MIN fill line on the expansion tank, turn off the engine, allow it to cool completely, then add coolant to the expansion tank to the MAX fill line.**

16 Turn the engine off and let it cool. Add more coolant mixture to bring the level to the MAX fill mark on the expansion tank.

17 Repeat Steps 15 and 16 if necessary.

18 Start the engine, allow it to reach normal operating temperature and check for leaks. Also, set the heater and blower controls to the maximum setting and check to see that the heater output from the air ducts is warm. This is a good indication that all air has been purged from the cooling system.

21 Brake fluid change (every 30,000 miles or 24 months)

> ✳ **WARNING:**
>
> **Brake fluid can harm your eyes and damage painted surfaces, so use extreme caution when handling or pouring it. Do not use brake fluid that has been standing open or is more than one year old. Brake fluid absorbs moisture from the air. Excess moisture can cause a dangerous loss of braking effectiveness.**

1 At the specified intervals, the brake fluid should be drained and replaced. Since the brake fluid may drip or splash when pouring it, place plenty of rags around the master cylinder to protect any surrounding painted surfaces.

2 Before beginning work, purchase the specified brake fluid (see *Recommended lubricants and fluids* in this Chapter's Specifications).

3 Remove the cap from the master cylinder reservoir.

4 Using a hand suction pump or similar device, withdraw the fluid from the master cylinder reservoir.

5 Add new fluid to the master cylinder until it rises to the base of the filler neck.

6 Bleed the brake system at all four brakes until new and uncontaminated fluid is expelled from the bleeder screw (see Chapter 9). Be sure to maintain the fluid level in the master cylinder as you perform the bleeding process. If you allow the master cylinder to run dry, air will enter the system.

7 Refill the master cylinder with fluid and check the operation of the brakes. The pedal should feel solid when depressed, with no sponginess.

> ✳ **WARNING:**
>
> **Do not operate the vehicle if you are in doubt about the effectiveness of the brake system.**

22 Drivebelt check and replacement (every 30,000 miles or 24 months)

ACCESSORY DRIVEBELT

1 A serpentine drivebelt is located at the front of the engine and plays an important role in the overall operation of the engine and its components. Due to its function and material make up, the belt is prone to wear and should be periodically inspected. The belt drives the alternator, power steering pump (all models except the 3.7L V6), water pump (four-cylinder models) and air conditioning compressor. Although the belt should be inspected at the recommended intervals, replacement may npt be necessary for more than 100,000 miles.

Check

◆ **Refer to illustrations 22.2 and 22.4**

2 Since the drivebelt is located very close to the right-hand side of the engine compartment, it is possible to gain better access by raising

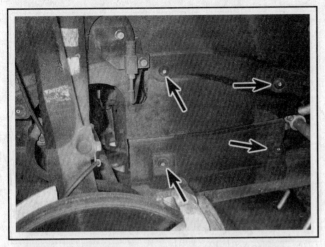

22.2 Remove fasteners from the front of the inner fender liner and pull it back for access (see Chapter 11), then remove this splash shield from the right fenderwell to gain access to the drivebelt tensioner (two rear pushpins not visible in this photo)

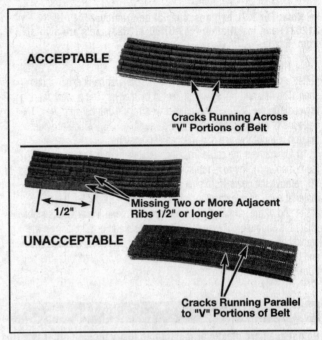

22.4 Small cracks in the underside of a V-ribbed belt are acceptable - lengthwise cracks, or missing pieces that cause the belt to make noise, are cause for replacement

the front of the vehicle and removing the right-hand wheel, then removing the splash shield in the right fenderwell (see illustration). Be sure to support the front of the vehicle securely on jackstands.

3   With the engine stopped, inspect the full length of the drivebelt for cracks and separation of the belt plies. It will be necessary to turn the engine (using a wrench or socket and bar on the crankshaft pulley bolt, working clockwise only) in order to move the belt from the pulleys so that the belt can be inspected thoroughly. Twist the belt between the pulleys so that both sides can be viewed. Also check for fraying, and glazing which gives the belt a shiny appearance. Check the pulleys for nicks, cracks, distortion and corrosion.

4   Note that it is not unusual for a ribbed belt to exhibit small cracks in the edges of the belt ribs, and unless these are extensive or very deep, belt replacement is not essential (see illustration).

Replacement

◆ Refer to illustration 22.6

5   Disconnect the cable from the negative terminal of the battery (see Chapter 5). Loosen the right front wheel lug nuts, then raise the front of the vehicle and support it on jackstands. Remove the right front wheel and the splash shield (see illustration 22.2).

6   Note how the drivebelt is routed, then remove the belt from the pulleys. On four-cylinder engines, use a wrench on the center of the pulley and turn the tensioner clockwise to release the drivebelt tension. On V6 engines, insert a 3/8-inch drive ratchet or breaker bar into the tensioner hole and pull the handle to release the drivebelt tension (see illustration). Once tension has been released, remove the belt from the pulleys.

7   Fit the new drivebelt onto the crankshaft, alternator, power steering pump, and air conditioning compressor pulleys, as applicable, then turn the tensioner back and locate the drivebelt on the pulley. Make sure that the drivebelt is correctly seated in all of the pulley grooves, then release the tensioner.

8   Install the splash shield and wheel, then lower the car to the ground. Tighten the lug nuts to the torque listed in this Chapter's Specifications.

22.6 To remove the drivebelt on a V6 model, insert a 3/8-inch drive ratchet or breaker bar into the square hole (A) and rotate the tensioner arm to relieve belt tension. (B) are the tensioner mounting bolts (typical 3.0L shown, other models similar)

WATER PUMP (3.0L V6 ENGINE) AND POWER STEERING PUMP (3.7L V6 ENGINE) DRIVEBELT REPLACEMENT

◆ Refer to illustration 22.10

➡ Note: On 2004 and earlier models, a spring loaded tensioner is used on the water pump drivebelt (see Steps 5 through 8 for replacement).

➡ Note: For 3.7L engines, special belt removal (#49-UN30 312521) and installation (#49-UN30 312523) tools are available from Mazda.

9 The water pump drivebelt on the 3.0L V6 engine is driven by a pulley attached to the left end of the front cylinder bank exhaust camshaft. The belt and pulley are protected by a cover. The power steering drivebelt on the 3.7L V6 engine is driven by the crankshaft pulley. The belts are of a unique design, called a "stretchy belt," which provides tension without the use of a mechanical tensioner.

10 Disconnect the cable from the negative terminal of the battery (see Chapter 5). If you're replacing the water pump drivebelt on a 3.0L V6, remove the cover from over the pulley. Insert a length of flexible material such as a leather or plastic strap under the belt at the pulley at the end of the camshaft or power steering pump. Have an assistant rotate the engine clockwise by using a socket and breaker bar on the crankshaft pulley bolt, while you feed the remover strap between the belt and the pulley (see illustration). Pull the strap quickly to force the belt from the pulley on the camshaft.

✳✳ CAUTION:

Do not use hard plastic or metal tools to pry the belt off; it is easily damaged.

➡ Note: If the belt is not going to be re-used, you can cut it off.

11 Water pump belt: Route the new belt under the water pump pulley, then over the pulley on the camshaft, and have your assistant rotate the engine again; the belt should pop over the pulley on the camshaft. Make sure the belt is positioned properly on both pulleys. Reinstall the cover and tighten the fasteners securely.

12 Power steering pump belt (3.7L V6 engine): Route the belt around

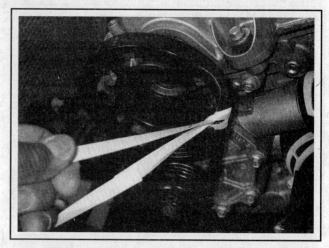

22.10 Removing the water pump belt on a 3.0L V6 engine. Warning: *While doing this, rotate the engine by hand only (do not use the starter)*

the crankshaft pulley, then around the back side of the power steering pump. Rotate the engine by hand to pop the belt onto the pulley.

ACCESSORY DRIVEBELT TENSIONER

13 On four-cylinder models, remove the two bolts securing the tensioner to the engine block and remove the tensioner.

14 On V6 models, remove the two bolts (3.0L engine) or three bolts (3.7L engine) securing the tensioner to the timing chain cover, then detach the tensioner from the cover (see illustration 22.6).

15 Installation is the reverse of removal. Be sure to tighten the tensioner bolt(s) to the torque listed in this Chapter's Specifications.

23 Automatic transaxle fluid change (every 60,000 miles or 48 months)

▸ Refer to illustrations 23.6 and 23.9

✳✳ WARNING:

Never work under a vehicle that is supported only by a jack!

23.6 Location of the transaxle drain plug

➡ Note: For transmission identification, refer to the "Vehicle Identification Numbers" information at the front of this manual.

1 The automatic transaxle fluid should be changed at the recommended intervals.

2 Before beginning work, purchase the specified transmission fluid (see *Recommended lubricants and fluids* in this Chapter's Specifications).

3 Other tools necessary for this job include jackstands to support the vehicle in a raised position, wrenches, a drain pan, newspapers and clean rags.

4 The fluid should be drained immediately after the vehicle has been driven. Hot fluid is more effective than cold fluid at removing built-up sediment.

✳✳ WARNING:

Fluid temperature can exceed 350-degrees F in a hot transaxle. Wear protective gloves.

5 After the vehicle has been driven to warm up the fluid, raise the front of the vehicle and support it securely on jackstands.

6 Place the drain pan under the drain plug in the transaxle pan and remove the drain plug (see illustration). Once the fluid has drained,

reinstall the drain plug and tighten it to the torque listed in this Chapter's Specifications.

7   Lower the vehicle.

8   Measure the amount of fluid drained and record this figure for reference when refilling.

9   On 2008 and earlier models equipped with the AW6A-EL 6-speed transaxle, remove the air filter housing (see Chapter 4) for access to the fill plug (see illustration). All other model are refilled through the dipstick tube.

10 With the engine off, add new fluid to the transaxle through the fill plug or dipstick tube until the fluid reaches the lowest notch on the dipstick. Start the engine, cycling the shifter through each gear position between additions). Check the fluid level and continue to add fluid until the level is correct on the dipstick.

11 Repeat Steps 6 through 10 two more times to flush any contaminated fluid from the torque converter.

12 Drive the vehicle a few miles until the fluid is up to normal operating temperature, then recheck the fluid level (see Section 4); it should be in the cross-hatched range (or in the range between the hot operation lines). If not, add fluid a little at a time (cycling the shifter through each gear position between additions) until the level is correct.

13 The old fluid drained from the transaxle cannot be reused in its present state and should be disposed of. Check with your local auto parts store, disposal facility or environmental agency to see if they will accept the fluid for recycling. After the fluid has cooled it can be drained

23.9 The fill plug on 2008 and earlier models with the AW6A-EL is located on the left side of the transaxle (air filter housing must be removed for access)

into a container (capped plastic jugs, topped bottles, milk cartons, etc.) for transport to one of these disposal sites. Don't dispose of the fluid by pouring it on the ground or down a drain!

24 Manual transaxle lubricant change (every 60,000 miles or 48 months)

1   This procedure should be performed after the vehicle has been driven so the lubricant will be warm and therefore flow out of the transaxle more easily.

2   Raise the vehicle and support it securely on jackstands. Position a drain pan under the transaxle. Remove the transaxle fill plug on the front of the case; it's about half-way up on the transaxle case and is the larger of the two hex-head bolts.

❋❋ CAUTION:

Do not remove the smaller hex-head bolt above the back-up light switch.

Remove the drain plug at the bottom of the case and allow the lubricant to drain into the pan.

3   After the lubricant has drained completely, reinstall the drain plug

and tighten it securely.

4   Using a hand pump, syringe or funnel, fill the transaxle with the specified lubricant until it is level with the lower edge of the filler hole. Using a new sealing washer, reinstall the fill plug and tighten it to the torque listed in this Chapter's Specifications.

5   Lower the vehicle.

6   Drive the vehicle for a short distance, then check the drain and fill plugs for leakage.

7   The old lubricant drained from the transaxle cannot be reused in its present state and should be disposed of. Check with your local auto parts store, disposal facility or environmental agency to see if they will accept the lubricant for recycling. After the lubricant has cooled it can be drained into a container (capped plastic jugs, topped bottles, milk cartons, etc.) for transport to one of these disposal sites. Don't dispose of the lubricant by pouring it on the ground or down a drain!

25 Spark plug check and replacement (see Maintenance schedule for service intervals)

▶ **Refer to illustrations 25.2, 25.5, 25.6, 25.8, 25.10a and 25.10b**

1   The spark plugs are located in the center of the valve cover(s). Access to the rear cylinder bank spark plugs on V6 models requires

removal of the upper intake manifold (see Chapter 2B).

2   In most cases, the tools necessary for spark plug replacement include a spark plug socket which fits onto a ratchet (spark plug sockets are padded inside to prevent damage to the porcelain insulators on the new plugs), various extensions and a gap gauge to check and adjust

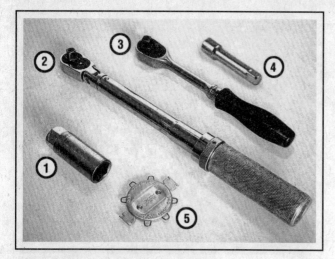

25.2 Tools required for changing spark plugs

1 **Spark plug socket** - *This will have special padding inside to protect the spark plug porcelain insulator*
2 **Torque wrench** - *Although not mandatory, use of this tool is the best way to ensure that the plugs are tightened properly*
3 **Ratchet** - *Standard hand tool to fit the plug socket*
4 **Extension** - *Depending on model and accessories, you may need special extensions and universal joints to reach one or more of the plugs*
5 **Spark plug gap gauge** - *This gauge for checking the gap comes in a variety of styles. Make sure the gap for your engine is included*

the gaps on the new plugs (see illustration). A torque wrench should be used to tighten the new plugs.

3 The best approach when replacing the spark plugs is to purchase the new ones in advance, adjust them to the proper gap and replace the plugs one at a time. When buying the new spark plugs, be sure to obtain the correct plug type for your particular engine. This information can be found in this Chapter's Specifications or in your owner's manual.

4 Allow the engine to cool completely before attempting to remove any of the plugs. These engines are equipped with aluminum cylinder heads, which can be damaged if the spark plugs are removed when the engine is hot. While you are waiting for the engine to cool, check the new plugs for defects and adjust the gaps.

5 The gap is checked by inserting the proper-thickness gauge between the electrodes at the tip of the plug (see illustration).

✳✳ CAUTION:

On 2.3L models, if the electrode does not have proper gap, the spark plug must be replaced.

The gap between the electrodes should be the same as the one specified on the *Emissions Control Information* label or in this Chapter's Specifications. The gauge should just slide between the electrodes with a slight amount of drag. If the gap is incorrect, use the adjuster on the gauge body to bend the curved side electrode slightly until the proper gap is obtained. If the side electrode is not exactly over the center electrode, bend it with the adjuster until it is. Check for cracks in the porcelain insulator (if any are found, the plug should not be used).

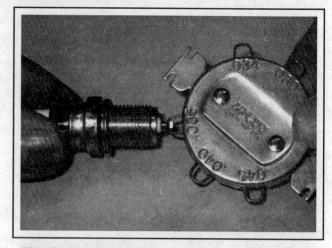

25.5 Using a wire-type thickness gauge to check the spark plug gap - if the wire does not slide between the electrodes with a slight drag, adjustment is required. Caution: *Do not force the gauge into the gap - the platinum or iridium coating could be scraped off*

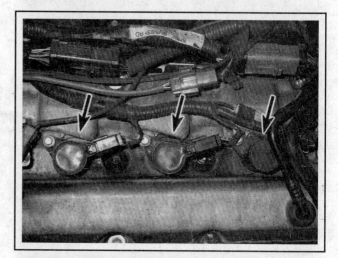

25.6 All models are equipped with individual coils which must be removed to access the spark plugs (V6 shown, front cylinder bank)

➡ **Note: We recommend using a wire-type thickness gauge when checking platinum- or iridium-type spark plugs. Other types of gauges may scrape the thin coating from the electrodes, thus dramatically shortening the life of the plugs.**

6 All models are equipped with individual ignition coils which must be removed first to access the spark plugs (see illustration).

7 If compressed air is available, use it to blow any dirt or foreign material away from the spark plug hole. The idea here is to eliminate the possibility of debris falling into the cylinder as the spark plug is removed.

8 Place the spark plug socket over the plug and remove it from the engine by turning it in a counterclockwise direction (see illustration).

9 Compare the spark plug to those shown in the photos located on the inside back cover of this book to get an indication of the general

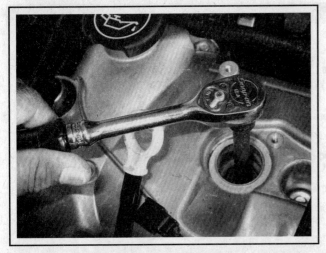

25.8 Use a ratchet and extension to remove the spark plugs

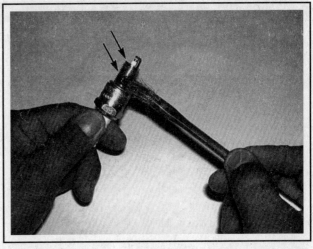

25.10a Apply a thin coat of anti-seize compound to the spark plug threads

running condition of the engine.

10 Apply a small amount of anti-seize compound to the spark plug threads (see illustration). Install one of the new plugs into the hole until you can no longer turn it with your fingers, then tighten it with a torque wrench (if available) or the ratchet. It is a good idea to slip a short length of rubber hose over the end of the plug to use as a tool to thread it into place (see illustration). The hose will grip the plug well enough to turn it, but will start to slip if the plug begins to cross-thread in the hole - this will prevent damaged threads and the accompanying repair costs.

11 Repeat the procedure for the remaining spark plugs.

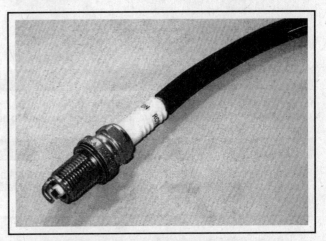

25.10b A length of snug-fitting rubber hose will save time and prevent damaged threads when installing the spark plugs (be careful not to get any near the lower threads)

Specifications

Recommended lubricants and fluids

➡ Note: Listed here are manufacturer recommendations at the time this manual was written. Manufacturers occasionally upgrade their fluid and lubricant specifications, so check with your local auto parts store for current recommendations.

Engine oil	
Type	API SM or ILSAC "certified for gasoline engines"
Viscosity	SAE 5W-20
Fuel	Unleaded gasoline, 87 octane
Automatic transaxle fluid	
4 and 5-speed	ATF M-V Automatic Transmission Fluid
6-speed	Mazda Genuine JWS3309 (T-IV) Automatic Transmission Fluid
Manual transaxle lubricant	
Type	API Service GL-4 or GL-5
Viscosity	SAE 75W-90 gear oil
Brake and clutch fluid	DOT 3 brake fluid
Engine coolant	
2006 and earlier models	50/50 mixture of ethylene-glycol based antifreeze and distilled water
2007 and later models	FL-22 premixed coolant.

✳✳ CAUTION:

On 2007 and later models, do not mix coolants. Doing so might damage the cooling system and/or the engine. The manufacturer specifies FL-22 coolant to be used in these systems, depending on what was originally installed in the vehicle.

✳✳ CAUTION:

The engine has aluminum parts that can be damaged by alcohol or methanol antifreeze. Do not use alcohol or methanol in the system. Use only ethylene-glycol based coolant. Use only soft (demineralized) water in the coolant mixture. Water that contains minerals will hamper the coolant's effectiveness.

Power steering system	MERCON V automatic transmission fluid or DEXRON III automatic transmission fluid

Capacities*

Engine oil (including filter)	
2.3L four-cylinder engine	4.5 quarts (4.3 liters)
2.5L four-cylinder engine	5.3 quarts (5.0 liters
3.0L V6 engine	6.0 quarts (5.7 liters)
3.7L V6 engine	5.5 quarts (5.2 liters)
Coolant	
2.3L four-cylinder engine	Up to 7.9 quarts (7.5 liters)
2.5L four-cylinder engine	Up to 9.9 quarts (9.4 liters)
3.0L V6 engine	Up to 9.0 quarts (8.5 liters)
3.7L V6 engine	Up to 10.0 quarts (9.5 liters)
Automatic transaxle (dry fill)**	
4-speed transmission (FN4A-EL)	Up to 7.6 quarts (7.2 liters)
5-speed transmission	
2004 and earlier models (JA5A-EL)	Up to 9.7 quarts (9.2 liters)
2005 through 2008 models (FS5A-EL)	Up to 8.6 quarts (8.14 liters)
2009 and later models (FS5A-EL)	Up to 5.3 quarts (5.0 liters)
6-speed transmission (AW6A-EL)	Up to 7.4 quarts (7.0 liters)

Capacities* (continued)

Manual transaxle

5-speed models

With four-cylinder engine (G35M-R)	Up to 3.3 quarts (2.87 liters)
With V6 engine (A65M-R)	Up to 2.4 quarts (2.3 liters)
6-speed models (G66M-R)	Up to 3.0 quarts (2.85 liters)

All capacities approximate. Add as necessary to bring up to appropriate level.

**Note: Since this is a dry-fill specification, the amount required during a routine fluid change will be substantially less. The best way to determine the amount of fluid to add during a routine fluid change is to measure the amount drained. Begin the refill procedure by initially adding 1/3 of the amount drained. Then, with the engine running, add 1/2-pint at a time (cycling the shifter through each gear position between additions) until the level is correct on the dipstick. It is important to not overfill the transaxle. You will, however, need to purchase a few extra quarts, since the fluid replacement procedure involves flushing the torque converter (see Section 23).

Ignition system

Spark plug type

2.3L four-cylinder engine

2003 and 2004	NGK ITR6F13 or equivalent
2005	NGK ITR5F13, ITR6F13 or equivalent
2006 and later	NGK ILTR5A-13G or equivalent
2.5L four-cylinder engines	NGK ILTR5A-13G or equivalent
3.0L V6 engine	Motorcraft AGSF 22FSCM or equivalent
3.7L V6 engine	Motorcraft AYSF-22FM or equivalent

Spark plug gap (replacement only)

Four-cylinder engines***

2.3L engine	0.049 to 0.053 inch (1.25 to 1.35 mm)
2.5L engine	0.049 to 0.057 inch (1.25 to 1.45 mm)
V6 engines	0.052 to 0.057 inch (1.30 to 1.45 mm)

Engine firing order

Four-cylinder engines	1-3-4-2
V6 engines	1-4-2-5-3-6

***If the electrode is worn or damaged, the spark plug must be replaced

Cylinder location - four cylinder engines

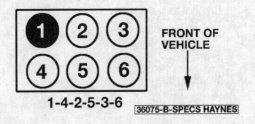

1-4-2-5-3-6

36075-B-SPECS HAYNES

Cylinder location - V6 engines

Clutch pedal

Freeplay

2007 and earlier models	0.20 to 0.59 inch (5 to 15 mm)
2008 and later models	0.04 to 0.11 inch (1 to 3 mm)

Height

2007 and earlier models	8.27 to 8.51 inches (210 to 216 mm)
2008 and later models	9.18 inch (233 mm)

Brakes

Disc brake pad lining thickness (minimum)	5/64 inch (2 mm)
Parking brake adjustment	3 to 5 clicks

Torque specifications

	Ft-lbs (unless otherwise indicated)	Nm

➡ **Note: One foot-pound (ft-lb) of torque is equivalent to 12 inch-pounds (in-lbs) of torque. Torque values below approximately 15 foot-pounds are expressed in inch-pounds, because most foot-pound torque wrenches are not accurate at these smaller values.**

	Ft-lbs	Nm
Engine oil drain plug		
2.3L four-cylinder engines	21	28
2.5L four-cylinder engines		
With washer	29	39
With rubber seal	21	28
3.0L V6 engine	21	28
3.7L V6 engine	20	27
Oil filter (cartridge type)		
Filter cover drain plug	97 in-lbs	11
Filter cover	26	35
Automatic transaxle drain plug		
All models except AW6A-EL	29	39
AW6A-EL	36	49
Automatic transaxle fill plug (AW6A-EL)	36	49
Manual transaxle drain and fill plugs	36	49
Spark plugs		
Four-cylinder engines	106 in-lbs	12
V6 engines	132 in-lbs	15
Drivebelt tensioner bolts		
Four-cylinder engines	18	24
3.0L V6 engine	22	30
3.7L V6 engine	106 in-lbs	12
Wheel lug nuts	87	118

Section

Reference to other Chapters

2A
FOUR-CYLINDER ENGINES

1 General information

HOW TO USE THIS CHAPTER

This Part of Chapter 2 is devoted to repair procedures possible while the engine is still installed in the vehicle. Since these procedures are based on the assumption that the engine is installed in the vehicle, if the engine has been removed from the vehicle and mounted on a stand, some of the preliminary steps outlined will not apply.

Information concerning engine/transaxle removal and installation and engine overhaul can be found in Part C of this Chapter.

ENGINE DESCRIPTION

❊❊ CAUTION:

On 2.5L engines, two different engine part manufacturers are used and the parts are not interchangeable. Use the 8th digit in the VIN number to determine which parts manufacturer you have; VIN A engine parts are made in Mexico and VIN H engine parts are made in Hiroshima.

These engines are sixteen-valve, double overhead camshaft (DOHC), four-cylinder, in-line type, mounted transversely at the front of the vehicle, with the transmission on the left-hand end. They incorporate an aluminum cylinder head and an aluminum cylinder block.

The two camshafts are driven by a timing chain, each operating eight valves via solid lifters. Each camshaft rotates in five bearings that are line-bored directly in the cylinder head and the (bolted-on) bearing caps. This means that the bearing caps are not available separately from the cylinder head, and must not be interchanged with caps from another engine.

These engines incorporate an aluminum timing chain cover and oil pan, and the crankshaft main caps are part of a one-piece lower block support. When working on these engines, note that Torx-type (both male and female heads) and hexagon socket (Allen head) fasteners are widely used. A good selection of sockets, with the necessary adapters, will be required, so that these can be unscrewed without damage and, on reassembly, tightened to the torque wrench settings specified.

LUBRICATION SYSTEM

The oil pump is driven via a chain from the front of the crankshaft, using the same sprocket that drives the timing chain. The pump forces oil through an externally mounted, full-flow, cartridge-type filter. From the filter, the oil is pumped into a main gallery in the cylinder block/crankcase, from where it is distributed to the crankshaft (main bearings) and cylinder head.

The connecting rod bearings are supplied with oil via internal drillings in the crankshaft. Each piston crown and connecting rod is cooled by a spray of oil.

The cylinder head is provided with two oil galleries, one on the intake side and one on the exhaust, to ensure constant oil supply to the camshaft bearings and lifters. A retaining valve (inserted into the cylinder head's top surface, in the middle, on the intake side) prevents these galleries from being drained when the engine is switched off. The valve incorporates a ventilation hole in its upper end, to allow air bubbles to escape from the system when the engine is restarted.

2 Repair operations possible with the engine in the vehicle

Many major repair operations can be accomplished without removing the engine from the vehicle.

Clean the engine compartment and the exterior of the engine with some type of degreaser before any work is done. It will make the job easier and help keep dirt out of the internal areas of the engine.

Depending on the components involved, it may be helpful to remove the hood to improve access to the engine as repairs are performed (refer to Chapter 11 if necessary). Cover the fenders to prevent damage to the paint. Special pads are available, but an old bedspread or blanket will also work.

If vacuum, exhaust, oil or coolant leaks develop, indicating a need for gasket or seal replacement, the repairs can generally be made with the engine in the vehicle. The intake and exhaust manifold gaskets, oil pan gasket, crankshaft oil seals and cylinder head gasket are all accessible with the engine in place.

Exterior engine components, such as the intake and exhaust manifolds, the oil pan, the oil pump, the water pump, the starter motor, the alternator and the fuel system components can be removed for repair with the engine in place.

Since the camshaft(s) and cylinder head can be removed without pulling the engine, valve component servicing can also be accomplished with the engine in the vehicle. Replacement of the timing chain and sprockets is also possible with the engine in the vehicle.

In extreme cases caused by a lack of necessary equipment, repair or replacement of piston rings, pistons, connecting rods and rod bearings is possible with the engine in the vehicle. However, this practice is not recommended because of the cleaning and preparation work that must be done to the components involved.

3 Top Dead Center (TDC) for number 1 piston - locating

▶ **Refer to illustrations 3.4, 3.5, 3.7a and 3.7b**

➡ **Note: You will need two special tools for this procedure: the camshaft positioning tool (303-465, or equivalent) and the timing pin (303-507).**

1 Disconnect the negative battery cable (see Chapter 5).
2 Remove the valve cover (see Section 4).

3 Using a wrench or socket on the crankshaft pulley bolt, rotate the crankshaft clockwise until the intake valves for no. 1 cylinder have opened and just closed again. The threaded hole in the crankshaft pulley should be near the corresponding hole in the timing chain cover (see illustration 8.10).

4 A TDC timing hole is located near the lower right front corner of the engine block (on the firewall side) to provide a means of accurately

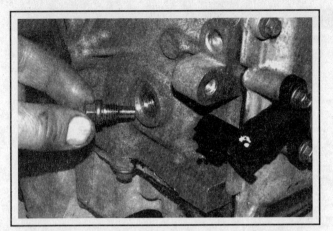

3.4 Remove the timing hole plug . . .

3.5 . . . and insert the timing pin tool

positioning the no. 1 cylinder at TDC. When you locate this hole, remove the timing pin plug (see illustration).

5 Screw in the timing pin (see illustration).

⚹⚹ CAUTION:

We don't recommend trying to fabricate a timing pin with a bolt because while you would be able to determine the correct bolt diameter and thread pitch, it is impossible to determine what the length of the bolt should be. These pins come in several lengths, depending on the engine family. There is no way to determine the correct pin length without comparing it to a factory or aftermarket tool designed to be used with this engine. Using a bolt of the wrong length could damage the engine. Also, never use the timing pin as a means to stop the engine from rotating - tool breakage and/or engine damage can result.

6 Turn the crankshaft slowly clockwise until the crankshaft counterweight comes into contact with the timing pin - in this position, the engine is set to TDC on no. 1 cylinder.

7 The camshafts each have a machined slot at the transaxle end of the engine. Both slots will be completely horizontal, and at the same

height as the cylinder head machined surface, when the engine is at TDC on the Number 1 cylinder. Manufacturer service tool 303-465 is used to check this position, and to positively locate the camshafts in position. Fortunately, a substitute tool can be made from a strip of metal 5 mm thick. While the strip's thickness is critical, its length and width are not, but should be approximately 180 to 230 mm long by 20 to 30 mm wide (see illustrations).

⚹⚹ CAUTION:

Never use the camshaft alignment tool as a means to stop the engine from rotating - engine damage can result.

8 Before rotating the crankshaft again, make sure that the tools are removed. Do not forget to install the blanking plug and tighten it securely.

9 Once no. 1 cylinder has been positioned at TDC on the compression stroke, TDC for any of the other cylinders can then be located by rotating the crankshaft clockwise 180-degrees at a time and following the firing order (see this Chapter's Specifications).

3.7a Turn the engine so that the camshaft end slots are aligned . . .

3.7b . . . then insert the metal strip into the slots to locate and set the shafts to TDC

4 Valve cover - removal and installation

REMOVAL

1   Disconnect the negative battery cable (see Chapter 5).

2   Remove the individual ignition coil assemblies from the spark plugs (see Chapter 5).

3   Disconnect the electrical connectors for the oil control valve, cylinder head temperature sensor and the camshaft position sensor.

4   Remove the bracket for the wiring harness on the valve cover stud, then set the harness aside.

5   Remove the engine oil dipstick.

6   Working progressively, unscrew the valve cover retaining fasteners, noting the (captive) spacer sleeve and rubber seal, then withdraw the cover.

7   Discard the cover gasket. This must be replaced whenever it is disturbed. Check that the sealing faces are undamaged and that the rubber seal at each bolt hole is serviceable. Replace any worn or damaged seals.

INSTALLATION

8   On installation, clean the cover and cylinder head gasket faces carefully, then install a new gasket onto the valve cover, ensuring that it is located correctly by the rubber seals and spacer sleeves.

9   At the top of the timing chain cover, apply a small bead of RTV sealant to the joints where the valve cover and timing cover meet the engine.

10 Install the cover to the cylinder head, ensuring as the cover is tightened that the gasket remains seated.

11 Working in a diagonal sequence from the center outwards, first tighten the cover bolts by hand only. Once all the bolts are hand-tight, go around once more in sequence, and tighten the bolts to the torque listed in this Chapter Specifications.

12 Reconnect the battery.

13 Run the engine and check for signs of oil leakage.

5 Valve clearances - check and adjustment

▶ **Refer to illustration 5.4**

➡ **Note: This procedure applies to all four-cylinder engines and 3.7L V6 engines.**

1   Disconnect the negative battery cable (see Chapter 5).

2   Remove all the spark plugs (see Chapter 1), then remove the valve cover (see Section 4).

3   Loosen the right front wheel lug nuts, raise the front of the vehicle and support it securely on jackstands, then remove the wheel. Remove the fender splash shield.

4   Using a wrench or socket on the crankshaft pulley bolt, rotate the crankshaft clockwise and check each lifter when its camshaft lobe is straight up, ensuring that the measurement is between the base circle of the camshaft lobe and the top of the lifter. Use feeler gauges to measure the clearances (see illustration).

5   The clearance must be checked between each camshaft lobe and the lifter it operates. Keep careful notes of the measurements recorded for each lifter.

6   If some measurements fall outside the recommended clearances in this Chapter's Specifications, the camshafts must be removed and the out-of-spec lifters removed (see Section 11). New lifters are available with various thicknesses to correct the valve clearances. Each lifter is marked with a thickness number. Only refer to the numbers after the decimal point. A "0.650" marking refers to an actual thickness of 3.650 mm.

7   To arrive at the desired thickness for new lifters: add the thickness of the original lifter (such as 0.650 mm) to the clearance you measured. Subtract the midrange figure for ideal clearance (see the Specifications)

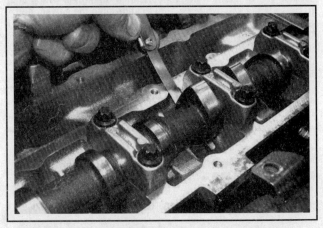

5.4 Check the valve clearances with a feeler gauge of the specified thickness. If the clearance is correct, you should feel a slight drag as the feeler gauge is slid between the lifter and the camshaft

from that number and you have the proper lifter thickness to order. Every thickness is not available, so choose the closest to your requirement.

8   Install the camshafts (see Section 11). Once the camshafts and timing chain have been installed, recheck the valve clearances.

9   The remainder of installation is the reverse of removal. Run the engine and check for oil leaks.

6 Intake manifold - removal and installation

Wait until the engine is completely cool before beginning the procedure.

REMOVAL

1 Relieve the fuel system pressure (see Chapter 4)

2 Disconnect the negative battery cable (see Chapter 5).

3 Disconnect the electrical connectors for the swirl control, throttle body, MAP sensor, and oil pressure sender.

➡ **Note: If you're removing the intake manifold plenum only to remove or service the cylinder head, it's not necessary to remove the throttle body from the intake manifold.**

4 Remove the air filter housing cover and the air duct between the cover and the throttle body (see Chapter 4).

5 Disconnect and plug the coolant hoses to the throttle body.

6 Release the harness clips and set aside the wiring harness at the top of the intake manifold.

7 If the coolant hose from the expansion tank will impede removal of the manifold, drain the coolant (see Chapter 1) and disconnect the hose.

8 Remove the fuel rail and injectors (see Chapter 4).

9 Raise the vehicle and support it securely on jackstands. Remove the lower engine cover fasteners and covers.

10 The intake manifold is secured with 8 bolts, one below and seven along the top.

➡ **Note: There are two sizes of bolts; make note of where the bolts were originally installed.**

Remove the bolts and pull the intake manifold away from the engine enough to access and disconnect the EGR pipe (if equipped) and the crankcase vent hose from the oil separator. Squeeze the two clips on the vent hose to release it.

INSTALLATION

11 There are individual gaskets for each of the four ports of the intake manifold. Using new manifold gaskets, install the intake manifold. Tighten the bolts and nuts in several stages, working from the center out, to the torque listed in this Chapter's Specifications.

12 Installation is otherwise the reverse of removal. If the cooling system was drained, refill it (see Chapter 1).

7 Exhaust manifold - removal and installation

Wait until the engine is completely cool before beginning the procedure.

➡ **Note: On 2.3L models, the catalytic converter is integral with the exhaust manifold, and they must be replaced as a unit (see Chapter 6).**

REMOVAL

1 Raise the vehicle and place it securely on jackstands.

2 When the engine has cooled, it will be helpful to soak the manifold heat-shield retaining nuts with penetrating oil to loosen any rust. Remove the heat shield. Apply penetrating oil to the exhaust manifold mounting bolts.

3 Disconnect the exhaust pipe from the exhaust manifold (see Chapter 4). Remove and discard the old flange gasket.

4 Unplug the electrical connector for the oxygen sensor and remove the oxygen sensor from the exhaust manifold (see Chapter 6).

5 Remove the exhaust manifold mounting nuts, then remove the exhaust manifold and the old manifold gasket.

6 Use a stud removal tool or two nuts tightened against each other to remove the old studs from the cylinder head.

INSPECTION

7 Inspect the exhaust manifold for cracks and any other obvious damage. If the manifold is cracked or damaged in any way, replace it.

8 Clean the mating surfaces of the manifold and cylinder head. Inspect the manifold for cracks.

Be very careful not to scratch or gouge the gasket surface. Any damage to the surface may cause an exhaust leak. Gasket removal solvents are available from auto parts stores and may prove helpful.

9 Using a straightedge and feeler gauge, inspect the exhaust manifold mating surface for warpage. Also check the exhaust manifold surface on the cylinder head. If the warpage on any surface exceeds the limits listed in this Chapter's Specifications, the exhaust manifold and/or cylinder head must be replaced or resurfaced at an automotive machine shop.

INSTALLATION

10 Install new exhaust studs in the cylinder head and install the manifold with a new gasket and new self-locking nuts.

➡ **Note: Coat the threads of the exhaust manifold studs with an anti-seize compound.**

Tighten the nuts in several stages, working from the center out, to the torque listed in this Chapter's Specifications.

11 The remainder of installation is the reverse of removal. Run the engine and check for exhaust leaks.

8 Crankshaft pulley - removal and installation

REMOVAL

♦ **Refer to illustration 8.4**

> ✳✳ **CAUTION:**
>
> **Once the crankshaft pulley is loosened, the crankshaft (timing) sprocket will be loosened as well. The engine is considered out-of-time at this point. The installation procedure in this Section must be followed exactly to re-time the engine properly. Severe engine damage may occur otherwise.**

1   Remove the drivebelt (see Chapter 1).
2   Remove the right-side driveaxle (see Chapter 8).
3   Set the engine to TDC using the camshaft and crankshaft locking tools (see Section 3).
4   The crankshaft must be held to prevent its rotation while the pulley bolt is unscrewed. A special tool to hold the crankshaft pulley is needed for this. The tool is available at most auto supply stores or equipment rental locations, but a suitable equivalent can be fabricated from a length of strap steel, bolts, washers and nuts (see illustration).

> ✳✳ **CAUTION:**
>
> **Use of a pry bar or similar tool can damage the crankshaft pulley.**

5   Insert the holding tool into the spaces in the front face of the pulley to hold it in place while turning the crankshaft pulley bolt with a large wrench or socket/breaker-bar combination.

> ✳✳ **CAUTION:**
>
> **Failure to hold the crankshaft pulley securely while removing the pulley bolt could result in engine damage. NEVER use the timing pin or the camshaft alignment tool as a means of locking the crankshaft - they are designed for calibration only. Engine damage could occur by using these tools for anything other than their intended purpose.**

6   Unscrew the pulley bolt and the holding tool.
7   Remove the pulley and, on 2.5L engines, the "diamond" washer behind it. Obtain a new pulley bolt and washer and, on 2.5L engines, a new diamond washer.

INSTALLATION

♦ **Refer to illustrations 8.10 and 8.19**

8   On 2.5L engines, install a new diamond washer onto the nose of the crankshaft.
9   Lightly coat the crankshaft front seal with clean engine oil, then install the crankshaft pulley.

➡ **Note: If the seal shows signs of leakage, you may want to replace it before installing the crankshaft pulley (see Section 10).**

Install a new crankshaft pulley bolt and washer and hand tighten only. Attempt to closely align the hole in the pulley with the threaded hole in the timing chain cover.

10   Install a crankshaft pulley alignment bolt (M6 x 18 mm) through the pulley and into the front engine cover (hand-tight only) (see illustration). Rotate the pulley as necessary to do this.

➡ **Note: This correctly aligns the pulley with the crankshaft.**

11   Insert the holding tool into the pulley and tighten the crankshaft pulley bolt to the torque listed in this Chapter's Specifications.
12   Remove the crankshaft pulley holding tool and the threaded crankshaft alignment bolt from the pulley and front engine cover.
13   Remove the timing pin from the cylinder block.
14   Remove the camshaft alignment tool.
15   Remove the spark plugs and rotate the engine clockwise two complete revolutions by turning the crankshaft pulley bolt with a wrench or large socket.

> ✳✳ **CAUTION:**
>
> **If you feel resistance at any point, stop and find out why. If the valve timing is incorrect, the valves may be contacting the pistons.**

16   Rotate the engine again to achieve TDC (see Section 3).

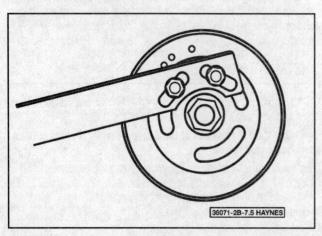

8.4 The crankshaft pulley holding tool installed

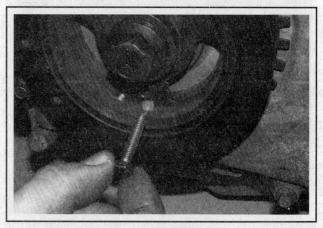

8.10 Install the M6 bolt to verify TDC

➡ **Note: Rotate the engine in the clockwise direction only.**

17 Install the timing pin into the cylinder block.

18 Install the crankshaft pulley alignment bolt (M6 x 18 mm). If it cannot be installed, the crankshaft pulley must be removed and aligned. Repeat Steps 8 through 18 until crankshaft pulley alignment is correct.

19 With the crankshaft pulley alignment bolt (M6 x 18 mm) installed, install the camshaft alignment tool and check the position of the camshafts (see illustration). If the tool cannot be installed, the engine timing must be corrected by repeating Steps 8 through 18.

20 The correct engine timing is achieved when the camshaft alignment tool, timing pin and the crankshaft pulley alignment bolt tool can be placed simultaneously.

21 Once correct engine timing is achieved, remove all the alignment tools and bolts and install the timing pin plug.

22 Reinstall all components removed previously.

8.19 The camshaft alignment tool installed

<h2>9   Timing chain cover, timing chain and tensioner - removal and installation</h2>

TIMING CHAIN COVER

Removal

1 Disconnect the negative battery cable (see Chapter 5).

2 Loosen the water pump pulley bolts, then remove the drivebelt, drivebelt idler pulley (see Chapter 1) and the water pump pulley (see Chapter 3).

3 Remove the crankshaft pulley (see Section 8). After this Step, the engine must remain at TDC with the valve cover removed.

4 Disconnect the Crankshaft Position (CKP) sensor electrical connector, then remove the sensor (see Chapter 6).

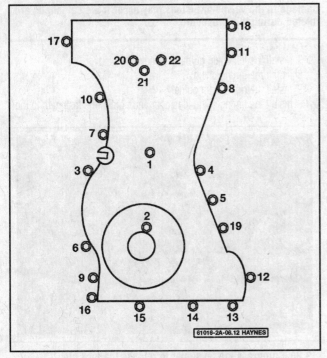

9.9 Timing chain cover bolt tightening sequence

➡ **Note: Unfortunately with these engines, anytime this sensor is removed, a new sensor must be installed. The new sensor is packaged with a special sensor alignment tool that is critical for installation.**

5 Support the engine from above with a support fixture (see Chapter 2C). Raise the engine enough to remove the right engine mount (see Section 17).

6 Disconnect the electrical connector to the power steering pressure switch. The switch is located on a high-pressure hose within the power steering system. Unbolt and set aside the power steering pump without disconnecting the hoses (see Chapter 10).

7 Remove the crankshaft front oil seal (see Section 10).

8 Remove the bolts and the timing cover.

Installation

▸ **Refer to illustration 9.9**

9 Installation is the reverse of removal, noting the following:

 a) Clean the mating surfaces of all sealant.

➡ **Note: Be careful not to gouge, or use any abrasives on, the mating surfaces.**

 b) Install the engine cover within four minutes of applying a 2.5 mm bead of RTV sealant.

 c) Tighten the bolts a little at a time, in sequence, to the torque listed in this Chapter's Specifications (see illustration).

 d) Install a new crankshaft front oil seal.

 e) Be sure to re-time the engine as described in Section 8 and also use a new crankshaft position sensor which includes the necessary alignment tool (see Chapter 6). Do not tighten the sensor mounting bolts until the installation tool is in place.

TIMING CHAIN AND TENSIONER

Removal

▸ **Refer to illustrations 9.11a and 9.11b**

10 Remove the timing chain cover (see Steps 1 through 8).

9.11a Compress the tensioner and insert the lock pin

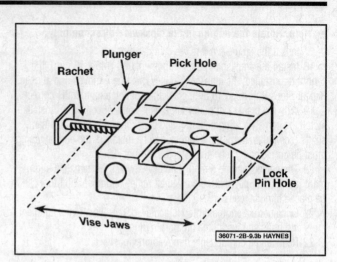

9.11b Timing chain tensioner reset details

11 Using a small screwdriver or pick, hold the chain tensioner ratchet arm away (UP) from the ratchet stem. Slowly compress the timing chain tensioner piston and place a pin (a drill bit or paper clip will work) into the hole to hold it in the compressed position (see illustration).

➡ **Note: The tensioner contacts the right-hand chain guide.**

※ **CAUTION:**

Compress the round plunger and the ratchet mechanism. The ratchet is next to the plunger and has square sides. If the ratchet needs to be reset, perform the following (see illustration):

a) *Remove the tensioner and place it lightly in a vise using the plunger and tensioner housing.*
b) *Place a pick-type tool in the hole closest to the ratchet to relieve the tension on the ratchet mechanism.*
c) *While holding the pick tool in place, move the ratchet back into the tensioner, then install a pin into the other hole to keep the plunger and ratchet compressed.*
d) *Remove the tensioner from the vise.*

12 Remove the two tensioner mounting bolts, then remove

the tensioner.

13 Remove the loose timing chain guide (right). Remove the timing chain.

14 The left chain guide and camshaft sprockets can now be removed if necessary.

Installation

▶ **Refer to illustrations 9.16 and 9.20**

15 Remove the camshaft alignment tool (if installed).

16 Loosen both camshaft sprocket bolts but don't remove them. Use a wrench on the hexagonal area of the camshaft to hold it while turning the camshaft sprocket bolt (see illustration).

※ **CAUTION:**

Damage to the valves or pistons may occur if the camshafts are rotated during this procedure.

17 Install the left chain guide (if removed).
18 Install the timing chain.
19 Install the right chain guide.
20 Install the timing chain tensioner and tighten the fasteners to the

9.16 Use a large wrench on the hex portion to hold the camshaft while removing/installing the sprocket bolt

9.20 Compress the tensioner to release the lock pin

torque listed in this Chapter's Specifications. Remove the pin to release the tensioner to engage the chain guide (see illustration).

21 Install the camshaft alignment tool.

22 Tighten the camshaft sprocket bolts to the torque listed in this Chapter's Specifications while holding the camshafts in place with a wrench.

⁕⁕ CAUTION:

Do not rely on the camshaft alignment tool to hold the camshafts while tightening the camshaft sprocket bolts. Tool and engine damage may occur.

---

23 Install the timing chain cover (see Step 9).

---

10 Crankshaft front oil seal - replacement

▶ **Refer to illustrations 10.5 and 10.6**

1 Remove the crankshaft pulley (see Section 8).

2 Use a screwdriver or hook tool to carefully pry out the seal.

➡ **Note: Be careful not to damage the timing chain cover bore where the seal is seated or the nose and sealing surface of the crankshaft.**

3 Another procedure for removing the seal is to drill a small hole on each side of the seal and place a self-tapping screw in each hole. Use these screws as a means of pulling the seal out without having to pry on it.

4 Wipe the sealing surfaces in the engine cover and on the crankshaft. Clean and coat them with clean engine oil.

5 Start installing the new seal by pressing it into the timing chain cover (see illustration).

6 Once started, use a seal driver or a suitable socket of the correct size to carefully drive the seal squarely into place (see illustration).

7 The seal should be flush with the engine cover and remain square when installed.

8 Coat the lip of the seal (where it contacts the crankshaft) with clean engine oil.

9 Install the crankshaft pulley (see Section 8).

10.5 Make certain that the oil seal is kept square as it is placed in the bore

10.6 A socket of the correct size can be used to install the new seal

---

11 Camshafts and lifters - removal, inspection and installation

➡ **Note: Whenever the camshafts are to be removed for a procedure, it's a good idea to check the valve clearances before disassembly (see Section 5), so any required new lifters can be ordered from a dealership.**

REMOVAL

▶ **Refer to illustrations 11.3 and 11.4**

1 Remove the timing chain (see Section 9).

➡ **Note: Before removing the timing chain, note the positions of the no. 1 cylinder cam lobes and the slots in the ends of the**

camshafts (for the alignment tool). When installing the camshafts, the lobes and the slots in the ends of the camshafts must be in the same positions.

2 Remove the camshaft sprockets.

➡ **Note: The camshaft phaser/sprocket on the intake camshaft should be marked with indelible ink so that it can be reinstalled on the intake camshaft in the same position.**

When loosening the camshaft sprocket bolts, place a wrench on the hexagonal area of the camshaft to prevent it from turning (see illustration 9.16).

3 All the camshaft bearing caps have a single-digit identifying number etched on them. The exhaust camshaft's bearing caps are numbered

11.3 Location of the camshaft bearing cap designations

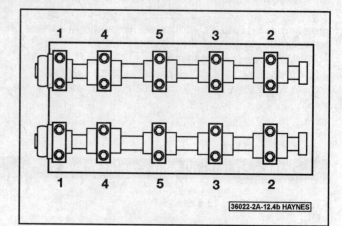

11.4 Camshaft bearing cap loosening sequence - loosen each pair of bolts on the designated bearing cap in sequence

in sequence from 0 (right-hand cap) to 4 (left-hand cap); the intake's are numbered from 5 (right-hand cap) to 9 (left-hand cap). Each cap must be installed with its numbered side facing the same direction (see illustration). If no marks are present, or they are hard to see, make your own - the bearing caps must be reinstalled in their original positions.

4   Working in the sequence shown, loosen the camshaft bearing cap bolts progressively by half a turn at a time (see illustration). Work only as described, to gradually and evenly release the pressure of the valve springs on the caps.

5   Withdraw the caps, noting their markings and the presence of the locating dowels, then remove the camshafts. The intake camshaft can be identified by the reference lobe for the camshaft position sensor; therefore, there is no need to mark the camshafts.

6   Obtain sixteen small, clean containers, and number them 1 to 16, or use a box with dividers in it. Using a rubber suction tool (such as a valve lapping tool), withdraw each lifter in turn and place them in the containers. Do not interchange the lifters (their thicknesses determine the valve clearance for each valve).

INSPECTION

▶ **Refer to illustrations 11.8 and 11.11**

7   With the camshafts and lifters removed, check each for signs of

obvious wear (scoring, pitting, etc) and for roundness and replace if necessary.

8   Measure the outside diameter of each lifter - take measurements at the top and bottom of each lifter, then a second set at right-angles to the first; if any measurement is significantly different from the others, the lifter is tapered or oval (as applicable) and must be replaced (see illustration). If the necessary equipment is available, measure the inside diameter of the corresponding cylinder head bore. No manufacturer's specifications were available at the time of writing; if the lifters or the cylinder head bores are excessively worn, new lifters and/or a new cylinder head may be required.

9   If the engine's valve components have sounded noisy, it may be just that the valve clearances need adjusting. Although this is part of the routine maintenance schedule in Chapter 1, the extended checking interval and the need for dismantling or special tools may result in the task being overlooked.

10 Visually examine the camshaft lobes for score marks, pitting, galling (wear due to rubbing) and evidence of overheating (blue, discolored areas). Look for flaking away of the hardened surface layer of each lobe. If any such signs are evident, replace the component concerned.

11 Examine the camshaft bearing journals and the cylinder head bearing surfaces for signs of obvious wear or pitting. If any such signs are evident, consult an automotive machine shop for advice. Also check that the bearing oilways in the cylinder head are clear (see illustration).

11.8 Measure the lifter outside diameter at several points

11.11 Check that the camshaft bearing oilways are not blocked with debris

12 Using a micrometer, measure the diameter of each journal at several points. If the diameter of any one journal is less than the specified value, replace the camshaft.

13 To check the bearing journal running clearance, remove the lifters, use a suitable solvent and a clean lint-free rag to carefully clean all bearing surfaces, then install the camshafts and bearing caps with a strand of Plastigage across each journal. Tighten the bearing cap bolts in the proper sequence (see illustration 11.23) to the specified torque setting (do not rotate the camshafts), then remove the bearing caps and use the scale provided to measure the width of the compressed strands. Scrape off the Plastigage with your fingernail or the edge of a credit card - don't scratch or nick the journals or bearing caps.

14 If the running clearance of any bearing is found to be worn to beyond the specified service limits, install a new camshaft and repeat the check; if the clearance is still excessive, the cylinder head must be replaced.

15 To check camshaft endplay, remove the lifters, clean the bearing surfaces carefully and install the camshafts and bearing caps. Tighten the bearing cap bolts to the specified torque wrench setting, then measure the endplay using a dial indicator mounted on the cylinder head so that its tip bears on the camshaft right-hand end.

16 Tap the camshaft fully towards the gauge, zero the gauge, then tap the camshaft fully away from the gauge and note the gauge reading. If the endplay measured is found to be at or beyond the specified service limit, install a new camshaft and repeat the check; if the clearance is still excessive, the cylinder head must be replaced.

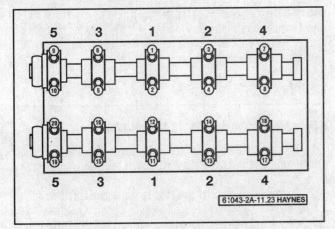

11.23 Camshaft bearing cap tightening sequence

INSTALLATION

▶ **Refer to illustration 11.23**

17 Confirm that the crankshaft is still positioned at TDC and that the timing pin is in place.

18 Liberally oil the cylinder head lifter bores and the lifters. Carefully install the lifters to the cylinder head, ensuring that each lifter is replaced to its original bore.

19 Liberally oil the camshaft bearing surfaces in the cylinder head, taking care not to get any on the camshaft cap mating surface.

20 Ensuring that each camshaft is in its original location, install the camshafts, locating each so that lobes for cylinder no. 1 are in the same position as noted in Step 1 and the slot in its left-hand end is parallel to, and just above, the cylinder head mating surface. Check that, as each camshaft is laid in position, the TDC setting tool will fit into the slot.

✳✳ CAUTION:

When the camshaft bearing caps are tightened, it is imperative that the camshafts do not rotate from their TDC positions.

21 Ensure that the locating dowels are pressed firmly into their recesses and check that all mating surfaces are completely clean, unmarked and free from oil.

22 Apply a little oil to the camshaft journals and lobes, then install each of the camshaft bearing caps to its previously-noted position, so that its numbered side faces outwards, to the front (exhaust) or to the rear (intake).

23 Ensuring that each cap is kept square to the cylinder head as it is evenly tightened down and working in the sequence shown, tighten the camshaft bearing cap bolts slowly and by one turn at a time, until each cap touches the cylinder head (see illustration). This is the Step 1 torque.

24 Next, using the same sequence, tighten the bearing cap bolts to the Step 2 torque listed in this Chapter's Specifications.

25 Tighten the bearing cap bolts to the Step 3 torque listed in this Chapter's Specifications.

26 Install the sprockets to the camshafts, tightening the retaining bolts loosely.

27 The remainder of the reassembly procedure, including replacement of the timing chain and setting the valve timing, is as described in Section 9.

28 Before installing the valve cover, check the valve clearances (see Section 5).

12 Cylinder head - removal and installation

✳✳ WARNING:

Wait until the engine is completely cool before beginning this procedure.

REMOVAL

1 Relieve the fuel pressure (see Chapter 4).

2 Disconnect the cable from the negative battery terminal (see Chapter 5).

3 Remove the intake duct from the air filter housing (see Chapter 4).

4 Remove the alternator and its air duct, if equipped (see Chapter 5).

5 Drain the cooling system (see Chapter 1).

6 Remove the coolant expansion tank (see Chapter 3).

7 Remove the timing chain (see Section 9).

8 Remove the camshafts (see Section 11).

➡ **Note: Whenever the camshafts are to be removed for a procedure, it's a good idea to check the valve clearances before disassembly, so any required new lifters can be ordered from a dealership.**

9 Disconnect the camshaft position sensor (see Chapter 6).

10 Disconnect the electrical connector then unbolt and remove the oil control valve from the cylinder head.

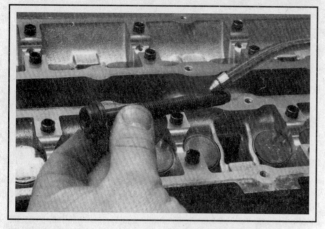

12.29 Apply a light coat of oil to the cylinder head bolt threads

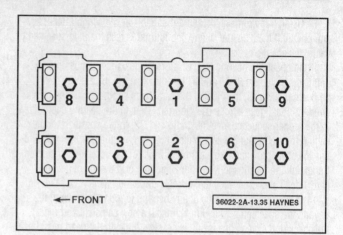

12.30a Cylinder head bolt tightening sequence

11 Remove the fuel rail and injectors (see Chapter 4).

12 Remove the thermostat housing from the cylinder head (see Chapter 3).

13 Remove the intake manifold (see Section 6).

14 Remove the exhaust manifold (see Section 7).

15 If an engine support fixture or hoist is being used to hold the engine up and it interferes with removal of the cylinder head, use a floor jack and block of wood to support the engine from below.

16 Loosen the ten cylinder head bolts progressively and by half a turn at a time, working in the reverse order of the tightening sequence (see illustration 12.30a).

✳✳ CAUTION:

The head bolts are torque-to-yield bolts that must be replaced with new ones on installation.

17 Lift the cylinder head from the engine compartment (see illustration).

18 If the head is stuck, be careful how you choose to free it. Remember that the cylinder head is made of aluminum alloy, which is easily damaged. Striking the head with tools carries the risk of damage, and the head is located on two dowels, so its movement will be limited. Do not, under any circumstances, pry the head between the mating surfaces, as this will certainly damage the sealing surfaces for the gasket, leading to leaks. Try rocking the head free, to break the seal, taking care not to damage any of the surrounding components.

19 Once the head has been removed, remove and discard the gasket. Check for the presence of locating dowels in the cylinder block and cylinder head. If dowels are present, make sure they are returned to their original locations after cleaning the components.

INSPECTION

20 The mating faces of the cylinder head and cylinder block must be perfectly clean before replacing the head. Use spray-on gasket remover and a hard plastic or wood scraper to remove all traces of gasket and carbon.

21 Take particular care during the cleaning operations, as aluminum alloy is easily damaged. Also, make sure that the carbon is not allowed to enter the oil and water passages - this is particularly important for the lubrication system, as carbon could block the oil supply to the engine's components.

22 To prevent carbon entering the gap between the pistons and bores, smear a little grease in the gap. After cleaning each piston, use a small brush to remove all traces of grease and carbon from the gap, then wipe away the remainder with a clean rag.

23 Check the mating surfaces of the cylinder block and the cylinder head for nicks, deep scratches and other damage. Also check the cylinder head gasket surface and the cylinder block gasket surface with a precision straight-edge and feeler gauges. If either surface exceeds the warpage limit listed in this Chapter's Specifications, the manufacturer states that the component out of specification must be replaced. If the gasket mating surface of your cylinder head or block is out of specification or is severely nicked or scratched, you may want to consult with an automotive machine shop for advice.

INSTALLATION

▶ **Refer to illustrations 12.29, 12.30a and 12.30b**

24 Wipe clean the mating surfaces of the cylinder head and cylinder block. If equipped, install the alignment dowels into their original locations.

25 The cylinder head bolt holes must be free from oil or water. This is most important, because a hydraulic lock in a cylinder head bolt hole can cause a fracture of the block casting when the bolt is tightened. Note the location of the cylinder head alignment dowels in the block.

26 Position a new gasket on the cylinder block surface, so that the "TOP" mark is facing up.

27 As the cylinder head is such a heavy and awkward assembly to install, it is helpful to make up a pair of guide studs from two 10 mm (thread size) studs approximately 90 mm long, with a screwdriver slot cut in one end - you can use two of the old cylinder head bolts with their heads cut off. Screw these guide studs, screwdriver slot upwards to permit removal, into the bolt holes at diagonally-opposite corners of the cylinder block surface; ensure that approximately 70 mm of stud protrudes above the gasket.

28 Install the cylinder head, sliding it down the guide studs (if used) and locating it on the dowels. Unscrew the guide studs (if used) when the head is in place.

29 Coat the threads with engine oil - do not apply more than a light film of oil (see illustration). Install the new cylinder head bolts and screw them in by hand only until finger-tight.

➡ **Note: New cylinder head bolts must be used.**

30 Working progressively and in the sequence shown, first tighten all the bolts to the specified Step 1 torque setting listed in this Chapter's Specifications (see illustration). On these engines there are five tightening stages, the final two using the angle torque method (see illustration).

31 Replacement of the other components removed is a reversal of removal.

32 Change the engine oil and filter and refill the cooling system (see Chapter 1).

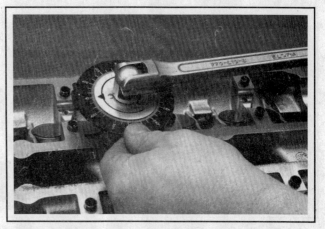

12.30b You can use a torque angle gauge, or you can carefully note the starting and stopping points of the wrench handle

13 Oil pan - removal and installation

REMOVAL

1   Raise the vehicle and support it securely on jackstands (see "Jacking and towing" at the front of this manual).

2   Drain the engine oil (see Chapter 1), then clean and install the engine oil drain plug, tightening it to the torque listed in the Chapter 1 Specifications. Remove and discard the oil filter, so that it can be replaced with the oil.

3   Remove the engine lower splash shield.

4   Remove the air filter housing (see Chapter 1).

5   On models with an automatic transaxle, remove the battery and battery tray (see Chapter 5).

6   The transaxle must be moved slightly back from the engine. Support the engine from above with an engine support fixture (connected to the left end of the engine, near the transaxle), and support the transaxle with a floor jack. Loosen the upper engine-to-transaxle mounting bolts and back them off about 0.20-inch (5 mm). Loosen the left-side engine-to-bellhousing bolts, then loosen the right-side bolts.

7   Remove the two oil pan-to-bellhousing bolts, and the one bellhousing-to-pan bolt. Also remove the timing chain cover-to-oil pan fasteners.

8   Use a screwdriver to pry between the engine and transaxle until the bellhousing has moved away from the block to the limit of the loosened bolts (about 0.20-inch [5 mm]).

9   Progressively unscrew the oil pan retaining bolts in a circular rotation, starting from the center out. Use a rubber mallet to loosen the oil pan seal, then lower the oil pan, turning it as necessary to clear the exhaust system. Unfortunately, the use of sealant can make removal of the oil pan more difficult. Be careful when prying between the mating surfaces, otherwise they will be damaged, resulting in leaks when finished. With care, a putty knife can be used to cut through the sealant.

INSTALLATION

10 Thoroughly clean and degrease the mating surfaces of the lower engine block/crankcase and oil pan, removing all traces of sealant, then use a clean rag to wipe out the oil pan.

11 Apply a 1/8-inch wide bead of sealant to the oil pan flange so that the bead is approximately 3/16-inch from the outside edge of the flange. Make sure the bead is around the inside edge of the bolt holes. Also apply sealant to the front flange of the oil pan where it meets the timing chain cover.

➡ **Note: The oil pan must be installed within 4 minutes of applying the sealant.**

12 Install the oil pan bolts, only tightening them finger tight at this time.

13 Install the timing chain cover-to-oil pan fasteners and tighten them to the torque listed in this Chapter's Specifications.

14 Tighten the oil pan-to engine block bolts, a little at a time, working from the center outwards in a criss-cross pattern, to the torque listed in this Chapter's Specifications.

15 Tighten the oil pan-to-bellhousing bolts and the transaxle-to-engine bolts, a little at a time to draw them together evenly, to the torque listed in this Chapter's Specifications.

16 Lower the vehicle to the ground. Before refilling the engine with oil, wait at least 1 hour for the sealant to cure, or whatever time is indicated by the sealant manufacturer. Trim off the excess sealant with a sharp knife. Install a new oil filter (see Chapter 1).

14 Oil pump - removal and installation

◗ **Refer to illustrations 14.4, 14.6 and 14.7**

➡ **Note: The oil pump is serviced as a complete unit without any sub-assembly or internal inspection.**

1   Drain the engine oil and remove the oil filter (see Chapter 1).

2   Remove the timing chain cover (see Section 9).

3   Remove the oil pan (see Section 13).

14.4 The oil pump pick-up tube is held by two mounting bolts (typical)

14.6 Using a holding tool on the oil pump drive sprocket to remove the retaining bolt

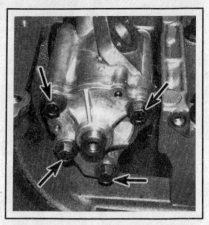

14.7 Remove the four mounting bolts for the oil pump

4   Remove the oil pick-up tube (see illustration).

5   Use a screwdriver to pry the end of the oil pump drive chain tensioner's spring from under the shouldered bolt. Remove the two bolts and the tensioner.

6   Remove the chain from the oil pump sprocket. While holding the oil pump drive sprocket with a suitable tool, remove the sprocket bolt from the oil pump, then remove the sprocket (see illustration).

7   Remove the oil pump mounting bolts, then remove the pump (see illustration).

8   Installation is the reverse of removal, noting the following points:

a) *Replace all gaskets with new ones.*

b) *Tighten the oil pump mounting bolts to the torque listed in this Chapter's Specifications in a criss-cross pattern.*

c) *After installing the oil pan, install a new oil filter and refill the crankcase with oil (see Chapter 1).*

d) *Be certain to check for any oil warning lights in the instrument panel after the vehicle has been started and idling.*

15 Flywheel/driveplate - removal, inspection and installation

REMOVAL

1   Remove the transaxle as described in Chapter 7A or 7B. Now is a good time to check components such as oil seals and replace them if necessary.

2   On manual transaxle models, remove the clutch as described in Chapter 8. Now is a good time to check or replace the clutch components and release bearing.

3   Use a center-punch or paint to make alignment marks on the flywheel/driveplate and crankshaft to make replacement easier - the bolt holes are slightly offset, and will only line up one way, but making a mark eliminates the guesswork (and the flywheel is heavy).

4   Hold the flywheel/driveplate stationary and unscrew the bolts. To prevent the flywheel/driveplate from turning, insert one of the transaxle mounting bolts into the cylinder block and have an assistant engage a wide-bladed screwdriver with the starter ring gear teeth while the flywheel or driveplate bolts are loosened.

5   Loosen and remove each bolt in turn and ensure that new replacements are obtained for reassembly. These bolts are subjected to severe stresses and so must be replaced, regardless of their apparent condition, whenever they are removed.

6   Remove the flywheel/driveplate. The flywheel is very heavy - do not drop it.

INSPECTION

7   Clean the flywheel to remove grease and oil. Inspect the surface for cracks, rivet grooves, burned areas and score marks. Light scoring can be removed with emery cloth. Check for cracked and broken ring gear teeth. Lay the flywheel on a flat surface and use a straight-edge to check for warpage.

8   Clean and inspect the mating surfaces of the flywheel/driveplate and the crankshaft. If the oil seal is leaking, replace it (see Section 16) before reinstalling the flywheel/driveplate. If the engine has high mileage, it may be worth installing a new seal as a matter of course, given the amount of work needed to access it.

9   While the flywheel/driveplate is removed, carefully clean its inboard face, particularly the recesses that serve as the reference points for the crankshaft speed/position sensor. Clean the sensor's tip and check that the sensor is securely fastened.

INSTALLATION

10 On installation, ensure that the engine/transaxle adapter plate is in place (where necessary), then install the flywheel/driveplate on the crankshaft so that all bolt holes align - it will fit only one way - check this using the marks made on removal. Install the new bolts, tightening them by hand.

11 Lock the flywheel/driveplate by the method used on disassembly. Working in a diagonal sequence to tighten them evenly and increasing to the final amount in two or three stages, tighten the new bolts to the torque listed in this Chapter's Specifications.

12 The remainder of installation is the reverse of removal

16 Rear main oil seal - replacement

▶ **Refer to illustration 16.9**

1   The one-piece rear main oil seal is pressed into the rear main oil seal carrier mounted at the rear of the block. Remove the transaxle (see Chapter 7A or 7B) and the flywheel/driveplate (see Section 15).

2   Remove the oil pan (see Section 13).

3   Unbolt the oil seal and carrier.

4   Clean the mating surface for the oil seal carrier on the cylinder

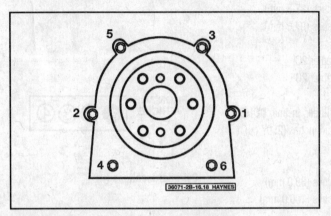

16.9 Rear oil seal carrier tightening sequence

block and the crankshaft. Carefully remove and polish any burrs or raised edges on the crankshaft that may have caused the seal to fail.

5   Lightly coat the inside lip of the new seal with clean engine oil. Use a thin (but durable) two-inch wide plastic strip (or a two-liter plastic beverage bottle cut to size) around the inside circumference of the seal to act as a liner for installation. A manufacturer tool (#303-328) for this purpose also works well.

6   With the plastic seal liner or tool in place, carefully move the new carrier (with seal factory-installed) into position by sliding it onto the contact surface of the crankshaft.

7   Install the oil seal carrier bolts and finger tighten them while holding the carrier in place. Align the bottom of the seal carrier precisely with the bottom edge of the engine block to ensure that the surfaces are flush before tightening the carrier mounting bolts.

✳✳ CAUTION:

The oil pan may leak if the two surfaces are not perfectly flush.

8   Carefully remove the plastic liner or tool so that the new seal contacts the crankshaft mating surface correctly.

9   Tighten the oil seal carrier in the proper sequence (see illustration) to the torque listed in this Chapter's Specifications.

10   The remainder of installation is the reverse of removal.

17 Engine mounts - check and replacement

1   Engine mounts seldom require attention, but broken or deteriorated mounts should be replaced immediately or the added strain placed on the driveline components may cause damage or wear.

CHECK

2   During the check, the engine must be raised slightly to remove the weight from the mounts.

3   Raise the vehicle and support it securely on jackstands, then position a jack under the engine oil pan. Place a large wood block between the jack head and the oil pan to prevent oil pan damage, then carefully raise the engine just enough to take the weight off the mounts.

✳✳ WARNING:

DO NOT place any part of your body under the engine when it's supported only by a jack!

4   Check the mounts to see if the rubber is cracked, hardened or separated from the bushing in the center of the mount.

5   Check for relative movement between the mount and the engine or chassis. Use a large screwdriver or prybar to attempt to move the mounts. If movement is noted, lower the engine and tighten the mount fasteners.

REPLACEMENT

▶ **Refer to illustration 17.8**

➡ **Note: Refer to Chapter 7 for information on the transaxle mounts.**

6   Disconnect the cable from the negative terminal of the battery

(see Chapter 5), then raise the vehicle and support it securely on jackstands (if not already done).

7   Place a floor jack under the engine with a wood block between the jack head and oil pan and raise the engine slightly to relieve the weight from the mounts.

8   Remove the fasteners and detach the mount from the frame and engine (see illustration).

✳✳ CAUTION:

Do not disconnect more than one mount at a time, except during engine removal.

9   Installation is the reverse of removal. Use thread-locking compound on the mount bolts and be sure to tighten them securely.

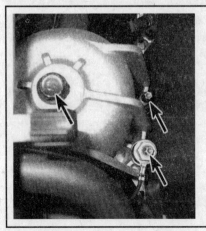

17.8 Remove the fasteners and lift the engine mount upper bracket off the engine mount

Specifications

General

2.3L engine

Engine type	Four cylinder, in-line DOHC
Displacement	137.9 cubic inches (2261 cc)
Engine VIN code	C
Firing order	1-3-4-2
Bore	3.44 inches (87.5 mm)
Stroke	3.70 inches (94.0 mm)
Compression ratio	9.7:1
Compression pressure	See Chapter 2C
Oil pressure	See Chapter 2C

2.5L engine

Engine type	Four-cylinder, in-line, DOHC
Displacement	153 cubic inches (2507 cc)
Engine VIN code	A or H
Firing order	1-3-4-2
Bore	3.50 inches (89.0 mm)
Stroke	3.94 inches (100.0 mm)
Compression ratio	9.7:1
Compression pressure	See Chapter 2C
Oil pressure	See Chapter 2C

FRONT OF VEHICLE

Cylinder locations

Camshafts

Lobe height	
Intake	1.671 inches (42.44 mm)
Exhaust	1.621 inches (41.18 mm)
Bearing journal diameter	0.9827 to 0.9834 inch (24.96 to 24.98 mm)
Endplay	
2.3L engine	0.003 to 0.009 inch (0.08 to 0.23 mm)
2.5L engine	0.004 to 0.009 inch (0.10 to 0.23 mm)

Valve clearances (cold)

Intake	0.009 to 0.011 inch (0.23 to 0.28 mm)
Exhaust	0.011 to 0.012 inch (0.28 to 0.30 mm)

Warpage limits

Cylinder head gasket surfaces (head and block)	0.002 inch (0.05 mm)
Exhaust manifold	0.030 inch (0.76 mm)

Torque specifications   Ft-lbs (unless otherwise indicated)   Nm

➡ **Note:** One foot-pound (ft-lb) of torque is equivalent to 12 inch-pounds (in-lbs) of torque. Torque values below approximately 15 foot-pounds are expressed in inch-pounds, because most foot-pound torque wrenches are not accurate at these smaller values.

	Ft-lbs (unless otherwise indicated)	Nm
Camshaft bearing cap bolts (in sequence - see illustration 11.23)		
Step 1	Hand tighten all bolts	
Step 2	45 to 79 in-lbs	5 to 9
Step 3	132 to 144 in-lbs	15 to 16
Camshaft sprocket bolt		
Exhaust camshaft	52	71
Intake camshaft (variable valve timing actuator)	55	75
Crankshaft pulley bolt		
Step 1	72	98
Step 2	Tighten an additional 90-degrees (1/4 turn)	
Cylinder head bolts (in sequence - see illustration 12.30a)		
Step 1	44 in-lbs	5
Step 2	120 to 150 in-lbs	13.5 to 17
Step 3	33	45
Step 4	Tighten an additional 90-degrees (1/4 turn)	
Step 5	Tighten an additional 90-degrees (1/4 turn)	
Valve cover bolts	80 in-lbs	9
Exhaust manifold/catalytic converter nuts (2.3L engine)	41	56
Exhaust manifold nuts (2.5L engine)	35	47
Flywheel/driveplate bolts		
Step 1	37	50
Step 2	59	80
Step 3	83	111
Intake manifold bolts	15	20
Crankshaft rear oil seal and retainer	89 in-lbs	10
Oil control valve (OCV) bolt	89 in-lbs	10
Oil pan-to-bellhousing bolts	35	47
Timing chain cover-to-oil pan bolts	89 in-lbs	10
Oil pan-to-engine block bolts	15	20
Oil pick-up pipe bolts	89 in-lbs	10
Oil pump-to-cylinder block bolts		
Step 1	89 in-lbs	10
Step 2	15	20
Oil pump sprocket bolt	18	24
Oil pump chain tensioner and guide bolts	89 in-lbs	10
Timing chain cover		
8 mm bolts	71 in-lbs	8
13 mm bolts	35	47
Timing chain guide bolts	89 in-lbs	10
Timing chain tensioner bolts	89 in-lbs	10
Transaxle-to-engine bolts	35	47

Notes

Section

Reference to other Chapters

Valve clearances (3.7L V6 engine) - check and adjustment - See Chapter 2A

2B

V6 ENGINES

1   General information

This Part of Chapter 2 covers in-vehicle repairs for the 3.0L and 3.7L Double Overhead Camshaft (DOHC) V6 engines. These engines feature aluminum engine blocks and aluminum cylinder heads with dual overhead camshafts and four valves per cylinder.

Information on engine removal and installation, as well as general overhaul procedures, is in Part C of Chapter 2.

The following repair procedures are based on the assumption that the engine is installed in the vehicle. If the engine has been removed and mounted on a stand, many of the Steps in this Part of Chapter 2 will not apply. Some procedures on the 3.7L engine do, however, require engine removal.

In this Chapter, "left" and "right" are used to describe locations on the vehicle. These directions are in relation to the vehicle overall from the position of sitting in the driver's seat. However, for simplicity in describing the cylinder banks of the V6 engine, they are termed "front" (closest to the radiator) and "rear" (closest to the firewall).

2   Repair operations possible with the engine in the vehicle

Many major repairs can be done without removing the engine from the vehicle. Clean the engine compartment and the exterior of the engine with a pressure washer or degreaser solvent before doing any work. Cleaning the engine and engine compartment will make repairs easier and help to keep dirt out of the engine.

It may help to remove the hood for better access to the engine. Refer to Chapter 11, if necessary.

If the engine has vacuum, exhaust, oil, or coolant leaks that indicate the need for gasket replacement, repairs to the 3.0L engine can usually be done with the engine in the vehicle. The intake and exhaust manifold gaskets, the timing chain cover gasket, the oil pan gasket, crankshaft oil seals, and cylinder head gaskets are all accessible with the engine in the vehicle.

Exterior engine components, such as the intake and exhaust manifolds, the oil pan (3.0L V6), the water pump, the starter motor, the alternator, and many fuel system components also can be serviced with the engine installed. On 3.7L engines, the oil pan, timing chain cover, timing chain, camshaft and cylinder head procedures must be performed with the engine removed from the vehicle.

On 3.0L V6 engines, the timing chain and sprockets also can be replaced without removing the engine, although clearance is very limited.

3   Top Dead Center (TDC) for number one piston - locating

1   Top Dead Center (TDC) is the highest point in the cylinder that each piston reaches as it travels upward when the crankshaft turns. Each piston reaches TDC on the compression stroke and on the exhaust stroke, but TDC usually refers to piston position on the compression stroke.

2   Positioning one or more pistons at TDC is an essential part of several procedures such as rocker arm removal, valve adjustment, and timing chain replacement. These engines do not have TDC marks on the crankshaft pulley or front cover. The timing chain procedure in Section 9 describes setting the engine at TDC for cylinder Number 1.

3   After the number one piston is at TDC on the compression stroke, TDC for any of the remaining cylinders can be located by turning the crankshaft and following the firing order (refer to the Specifications). Divide the crankshaft pulley into three equal sections with chalk marks at three points, each indicating 120-degrees of crankshaft rotation, and a corresponding mark on the timing chain cover, next to the TDC mark for cylinder number 1. For example, rotating the engine 120-degrees past TDC for number 1 piston will place the engine at TDC for cylinder number 4. Refer to the firing order for the remaining cylinder numbers.

4   Valve covers - removal and installation

➡ **Note: the number and location of stud-bolts and standard bolts used to secure the valve covers may vary, depending on the year and build date of the vehicle. Keep track of the stud locations for reassembly.**

1   Remove the engine access cover, if equipped.

FRONT VALVE COVER

▶ **Refer to illustrations 4.2, 4.7a, 4.7b, 4.9, 4.10a, 4.10b, 4.14a, 4.14b and 4.14c**

2   Disconnect the crankcase ventilation tube (see illustration).

3   Remove the ignition coils (see Chapter 5). Remove the air filter housing and duct (see Chapter 4).

4   Disconnect the wiring harness from the valve cover and position it off to the side. On 3.7L engines, remove the engine oil dipstick and tube.

4.2 Disconnect the crankcase ventilation tube from the front valve cover

4.7a Remove and discard the old valve cover gasket - it must be replaced during assembly to prevent leakage

4.7b Remove and discard the spark plug tube seals from the valve cover (3.0L engine)

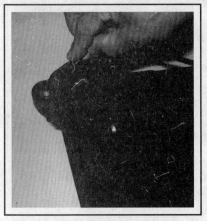

4.9 Press the new gasket into the groove in the valve cover, making sure it isn't twisted

4.10a Apply a 5/16-inch bead of RTV sealant to the seams of the timing chain cover/cylinder head . . .

4.10b . . . and, on 3.0L engines, the camshaft seal retainer/cylinder head

5   Disconnect the VCT electrical connector and oxygen sensor connector.

6   Loosen the valve cover bolts/nuts gradually and evenly until all are loose. Follow the reverse of the tightening sequence (see illustration 4.14a, 4.14b or 4.14c). Remove the valve cover fasteners and lift the valve cover off the engine.

7   Remove and discard the valve cover gaskets and spark plug tube seals (see illustrations). Install new gaskets and seals during reassembly.

➡ Note: The spark plug tube seals can be re-used if they are in good condition and were not leaking.

8   Inspect the valve cover and cylinder head sealing surfaces for nicks or other damage. Clean the sealing surfaces with brake system cleaner.

9   Install a new valve cover gasket, making sure the gasket is properly seated in the groove (see illustration). Press the corner sections of the gasket in first, then the areas around the bolt holes, and finally the sections in between. If there is evidence of damage to the spark plug tube seals, replace these and the seal that surrounds the VCT solenoid.

10 Apply a 5/16-inch bead of RTV sealant at the locations shown (see illustrations).

11 Lower the valve cover into position, making sure that the gaskets stay in place. Install the cover fasteners and tighten them gradually and

evenly to the torque listed in this Chapter's Specifications.

12 Reconnect the wiring harness to the bracket studs.

13 Reconnect the crankcase ventilation tube to the valve cover.

14 Tighten the valve cover bolts to the torque listed in this Chapter's

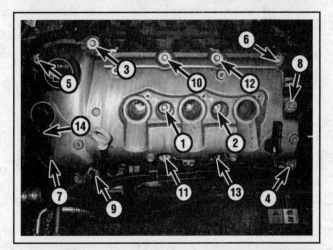

4.14a Valve cover bolt tightening sequence for the left (front) valve cover (3.0L V6 engine)

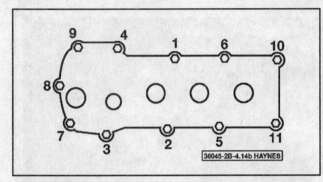

4.14b Valve cover bolt tightening sequence for the left (front) valve cover (3.7L V6 engine, early production - 11 bolts)

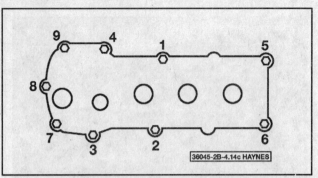

4.14c Valve cover bolt tightening sequence for the left (front) valve cover (3.7L V6 engine, late production - 9 bolts)

4.22a Remove the bolts and studs from the rear valve cover

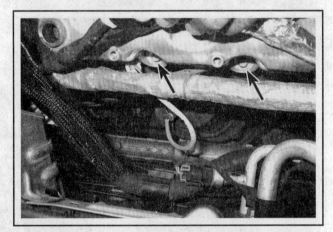

4.22b Raise the wiring harness at the rear of the rear cover to access the rear bolts

Specifications. Follow the correct torque sequence (see illustrations).

15 The remainder of installation is the reverse of removal.

REAR VALVE COVER

▶ **Refer to illustrations 4.22a, 4.22b, 4.27a, 4.27b and 4.27c**

16 Remove the power steering fluid reservoir (see Chapter 10), the lower cowl cover (see Chapter 11), and the windshield washer fluid reservoir (see Chapter 1).

17 Remove the upper intake manifold (see Section 5), then remove the ignition coils from the top of the valve cover (see Chapter 5).

18 Disconnect the oxygen sensor connector and position the wiring harness off to the side.

19 Remove the radio/ignition interference capacitor from the stud on the valve cover (if equipped).

20 Disconnect the crankcase ventilation tube.

21 On 3.7L engines, remove the bolts securing the air conditioning refrigerant pipe and move the pipe aside to clear the valve cover.

❋❋ WARNING:

Do not disconnect the refrigerant line/hose connections.

22 Loosen the valve cover fasteners gradually and evenly, until all fasteners are loose (see illustrations). Follow the reverse of the tightening sequence (see illustration 4.27a, 4.27b or 4.27c). Then, unscrew and remove the fasteners. Keep track of the stud locations for reassembly. Lift the valve cover off the cylinder head.

23 Remove and discard the valve cover gasket and inspect the spark plug tube seals (see illustrations 4.7a, 4.7b and 4.9). Install new gaskets and seals during reassembly.

➡ **Note: The spark plug tube seals can be re-used if they are in good condition and were not leaking.**

24 Inspect the valve cover and cylinder head sealing surfaces for nicks or other damage. Clean the sealing surfaces with brake system cleaner.

25 Install a new valve cover gasket, making sure the gasket is properly seated in the groove (see Steps 7 through 10). Press the corner sections of the gasket in first, then the areas around the bolt holes, and

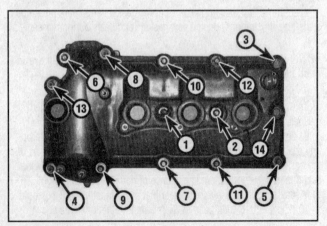

4.27a Valve cover bolt tightening sequence for the right (rear) valve cover (3.0L V6 engine)

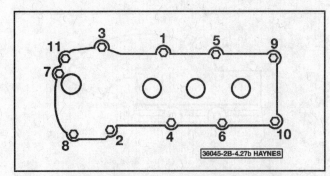

4.27b Valve cover bolt tightening sequence for the right (rear) valve cover (3.7L V6 engine, early production - 11 bolts)

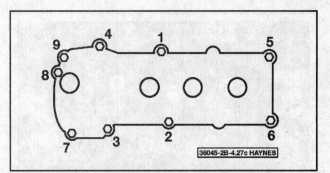

4.27c Valve cover bolt tightening sequence for the right (rear) valve cover (3.7L V6 engine, late production - 9 bolts)

finally the sections in between. If there is evidence of damage to the spark plug tube seals, replace these and the seal that surrounds the VCT solenoid.

26 Apply a 5/16-inch bead of RTV sealant to the head-to-front cover joints and the cam seal retainer (see illustrations 4.10a and 4.10b).

27 Install the valve cover fasteners and tighten them gradually and

evenly to the torque listed in this Chapter's Specifications. Follow the correct torque sequence (see illustrations).

28 Reinstall all wiring harnesses and brackets.

29 Reinstall the ignition coils (see Chapter 5).

30 Install the upper intake manifold (see Section 5).

31 The remainder of installation is the reverse of removal.

5   Intake manifold - removal and installation

UPPER INTAKE MANIFOLD

✳ WARNING:

If you are going to be removing the lower intake manifold, relieve the fuel system pressure before proceeding (see Chapter 4).

Removal

▶ **Refer to illustrations 5.5 and 5.12**

1   Disconnect the cable from the negative battery terminal (see Chapter 5).

2   Remove the air filter housing and the intake duct (see Chapter 4).

3   Remove the engine cover, if equipped.

4   Disconnect the connector at the electronic throttle body, and any coolant hoses or other connectors at the throttle body.

5   On 3.0L engines, disconnect the MAP sensor connector, the EGR

valve electrical connector and the EGR pipe (see illustration).

6   Disconnect the EVAP hose, brake booster vacuum hose and PCV hose.

7   On 3.7L engines, disconnect the heated PCV valve connector.

8   Disconnect the vacuum lines and electrical connectors from the upper intake manifold. Be sure to mark them with tape to insure correct reassembly.

9   Remove the wire harness bracket nuts and position the wiring harness off to the side. On 3.7L engines, remove the manifold brace, near the throttle body end of the manifold.

10   Remove the mounting bolt from the upper manifold brace(s). On some models, there is both a long brace and a short brace (near the throttle body).

11   Loosen the upper intake manifold bolts. Follow the opposite of the tightening sequence (see illustration 5.15a or 5.15b).

➡ **Note: The bolts are captive and come out with the manifold.**

12   Remove and discard the upper intake-to-lower intake manifold gaskets (see illustration).

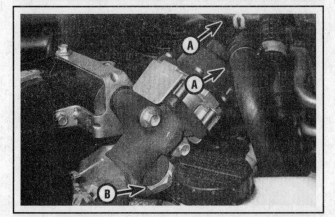

5.5 At the left end of the manifold, disconnect the hoses (A) and the EGR pipe (B)

5.12 Remove the gaskets from the upper intake manifold

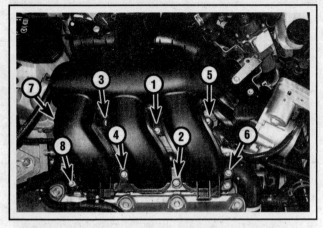

5.15a Upper intake manifold bolt TIGHTENING sequence (3.0L V6 engine)

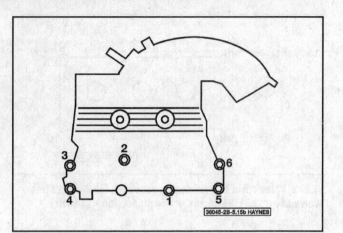

5.15b Upper intake manifold bolt TIGHTENING sequence (3.7L V6 engine)

Installation

▶ **Refer to illustrations 5.15a and 5.15b**

13 If the gasket was leaking, check the mating surfaces for warpage. Check carefully around the mounting points of components such as the EGR pipe. Replace the manifold if it is cracked or badly warped.

14 Install new gaskets. If the mating surfaces are clean and flat, new gaskets will ensure the joint is sealed. Don't use any kind of sealant on any part of the fuel system or intake manifold.

15 Locate the upper manifold on the lower manifold and install the fasteners. Tighten the fasteners in three or four steps, in the sequence shown (see illustrations), to the torque listed in this Chapter's Specifications.

16 Install the remaining parts in the reverse order of removal.

17 Reconnect the battery. After you're done, the Powertrain Control Module (PCM) must relearn its idle and fuel trim strategy for optimum driveability and performance (see Chapter 5).

18 When the engine is fully warm, check for fuel and vacuum leaks. Road test the vehicle and check for proper operation of all components.

LOWER INTAKE MANIFOLD

Removal

➡ **Note: Allow the engine to cool completely before beginning this procedure.**

19 Relieve the fuel system pressure (see Chapter 4).

20 Disconnect the cable from the negative battery terminal (see Chapter 5).

21 On 3.7L V6 engines, drain the cooling system (see Chapter 1).

22 Remove the upper intake manifold (see Steps 1 through 12).

23 Disconnect the fuel line from the fuel rail (see Chapter 4).

24 Disconnect the fuel injection electrical connectors from the fuel injectors (see Chapter 4). Move the injector wiring harness out of the way. On 3.7L engines, remove the fuel rail and injectors (on 3.0L engines, the fuel rail and injectors will come off with the two lower intake manifolds).

25 On 3.7L engines, remove the four bolts securing the thermostat housing to the lower intake manifold (see Chapter 3). The coolant hoses can remain on the thermostat housing.

26 Loosen the lower manifold bolts gradually and evenly in the reverse of the tightening sequence until all are loose (see illustrations 5.31a or 5.31b), then remove the bolts.

27 Lift the lower intake manifold(s) from the engine. Remove and discard the manifold gaskets. If you're working on a 3.0L engine, remove the fuel rail and injectors from the manifold (see Chapter 4).

28 Carefully clean all gasket material from the manifold and cylinder head mating surfaces. Don't nick, scratch or gouge the sealing surfaces.

※※ **CAUTION:**

Be very careful when scraping on aluminum engine parts. Aluminum is soft and gouges easily. Severely gouged parts may require replacement.

Inspect all parts for cracks or other damage. If the manifold gaskets were leaking, check the mating surfaces for warpage.

Installation

▶ **Refer to illustrations 5.31a and 5.31b**

29 Install new lower intake manifold gaskets on the cylinder heads.

30 Place the lower manifold(s) into position on the cylinder heads. Make sure the gaskets are not dislodged.

➡ **Note: On 3.0L V6 engines, assemble the fuel rail and injectors to the manifolds, installing the fuel rail bolts loosely. After the intake manifold bolts have been tightened in the next Step, tighten the fuel rail bolts.**

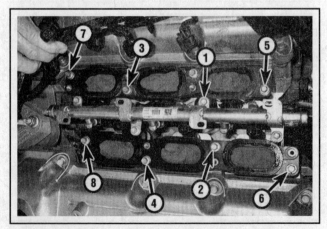

5.31a Lower intake manifold bolt TIGHTENING sequence (3.0L V6 engine)

31 Install the lower manifold bolts. Tighten the bolts gradually and evenly, in the sequence shown (see illustrations), to the torque listed in this Chapter's Specifications.

32 The remainder of installation is the reverse of removal. Tighten the fasteners to the torque listed in this Chapter's Specifications.

33 On 3.7L V6 engines, change the engine oil and filter, then refill and bleed the cooling system (see Chapter 1).

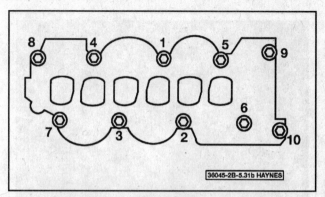

5.31b Lower intake manifold bolt TIGHTENING sequence (3.7L V6 engine)

6 Exhaust manifolds - removal and installation

➡ Note: Before beginning this procedure, allow the engine to cool completely, and apply penetrating oil to the manifold and converter fasteners.

➡ Note: Most models have a catalytic converter that is an integral part of the exhaust manifold.

FRONT EXHAUST MANIFOLD

▶ Refer to illustrations 6.4, 6.5 and 6.6

❊❊ WARNING:

The engine and exhaust system must be completely cool before performing this procedure.

1 Disconnect the cable from the negative battery terminal (see Chapter 5).

2 Disconnect the electrical connector for the upstream and downstream oxygen sensors (see Chapter 6).

3 Raise the front of the vehicle and support it securely on jackstands.

6.4 Disconnect the exhaust crossover pipe

4 From below, disconnect the crossover pipe (see illustration).

5 Remove the heat shield over the front exhaust manifold (see illustration).

6 Remove and discard the six nuts securing the exhaust manifold (see illustration). Remove and discard the manifold gasket.

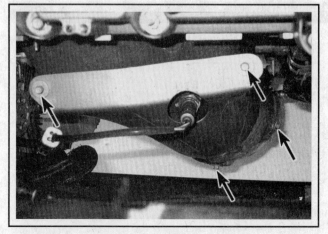

6.5 Front exhaust heat shield bolts

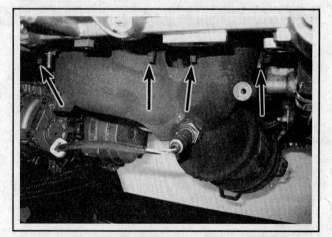

6.6 Remove the front exhaust mounting nuts from the studs (four of six shown)

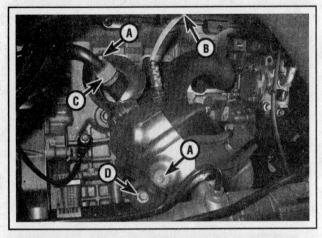

6.18 Remove the rear exhaust heat shield bolts (A), then disconnect the oxygen sensor connector (B) and the EGR pipe (C). Remove the catalytic converter brace bolt (D) (3.0L V6 engine)

7 Remove the exhaust manifold.

8 Using a stud holding tool (available at auto parts stores) or a pair of nuts tightened together over a stud, extract the exhaust manifold studs and discard them.

9 Using a scraper, remove all old gasket material and carbon deposits from the manifold and cylinder head mating surfaces.

❋❋ CAUTION:

Be very careful when scraping on aluminum engine parts such as the cylinder heads. Aluminum is soft and gouges easily. Severely gouged parts may require replacement.

If the gasket was leaking, check the manifold for warpage and have it resurfaced if necessary.

10 Install new exhaust manifold studs with light oil on the threads, then install a new manifold gasket over the studs. Install the manifold and new self-locking nuts.

11 Tighten the nuts, starting with the center fasteners and working towards the ends, to the torque listed in this Chapter's Specifications.

12 The remainder of installation is the reverse of removal.

REAR EXHAUST MANIFOLD

▶ **Refer to illustration 6.18**

❋❋ WARNING:

The engine and exhaust system must be completely cool before performing this procedure.

13 Disconnect the cable from the negative battery terminal (see Chapter 5).

14 On 3.0L engines, remove the EGR pipe from the exhaust manifold (see Chapter 6).

15 Disconnect the connector to the rear bank oxygen sensor.

16 On 3.7L engines, remove the rear-bank catalytic converter (see Chapter 6).

17 Remove the nuts from the exhaust manifold flange and separate the crossover pipe from the manifold (see Chapter 4).

18 Remove the six exhaust manifold mounting nuts and remove the manifold from the engine (see illustration). Remove and discard the manifold gasket.

19 Using a stud holding tool (available at auto parts stores) or a pair of new nuts tightened together over a stud, extract the exhaust manifold studs and discard them.

20 Using a scraper, remove all gasket material and carbon deposits from the exhaust manifold and cylinder head mating surfaces.

❋❋ CAUTION:

Be very careful when scraping on aluminum engine parts. Aluminum is soft and gouges easily. Severely gouged parts may require replacement.

If the gasket was leaking, check the manifold for warpage and have it resurfaced if necessary.

21 Install new exhaust manifold studs with light oil on the threads, then install a new manifold gasket over the studs. Install the manifold and new self-locking nuts.

22 Tighten the nuts, starting with the center fasteners and working towards the ends, to the torque listed in this Chapter's Specifications.

23 The remainder of installation is the reverse of removal.

7 Crankshaft pulley and front oil seal - removal and installation

7.5 Use a two-pin spanner to hold the pulley while removing the bolt

REMOVAL

▶ **Refer to illustrations 7.5 and 7.6**

1 Disconnect the cable from the negative battery terminal (see Chapter 5).

2 Loosen the right front wheel lug nuts. Raise the front of the vehicle and support it securely on jackstands, then remove the wheel.

3 Remove the fender splash shield.

4 Remove the drivebelt (see Chapter 1).

5 Use a two-pin spanner to hold the crankshaft pulley while removing the crankshaft pulley retaining bolt (see illustration).

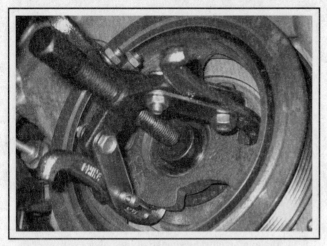

7.6 Remove the crankshaft pulley with a three-jaw puller

7.10 Using a pulley installation tool, rotate the nut to drive the pulley onto the nose of the crankshaft

6 Using a three-jaw puller, remove the crankshaft pulley (see illustration).

✻ CAUTION:

Be sure to use the proper adapter on the end of the crankshaft to prevent damage to the threads or end of the crankshaft. Also, the jaws of the puller must grasp the hub of the pulley, not the outer diameter.

7 Using a seal puller, remove the seal from the timing chain cover. Note the depth at which the seal fits in the front cover and the orientation of the sealing lip so that the new seal will be installed in the same direction and to the same depth.

INSTALLATION

▶ **Refer to illustration 7.10**

8 Inspect the front cover and the pulley seal surface for nicks, burrs, or other roughness that could damage the new seal. Correct as necessary.

9 Lubricate the new seal with clean engine oil and install it in the engine timing chain cover with a suitable seal driver which draws the seal in slowly. Be sure that the lip of the seal faces inward. If a seal driver is unavailable, carefully tap the seal into place with a large socket and hammer until it's flush with the timing chain cover surface.

10 On 3.0L engines, apply RTV sealant to the keyway and inner bore of the pulley and lubricate the outer sealing surface of the pulley with clean engine oil. The pulley should be installed and tightened within four minutes of applying the sealant. Align the pulley keyway with the crankshaft key and install the pulley with a suitable pulley installation tool available at auto parts stores (see illustration).

11 Install and tighten the pulley bolt to the torque listed in this Chapter's Specifications.

➡ **Note: The manufacturer suggests that a new pulley bolt be installed.**

12 Reinstall the remaining parts in the reverse order of removal. Tighten the wheel lug nuts to the torque listed in the Chapter 1 Specifications.

13 Reconnect the battery, then start the engine and check for oil leaks.

8   Timing chain cover - removal and installation

✻ WARNING:

Wait until the engine is completely cool before beginning this procedure.

➡ **Note: On 3.0L engines, the timing chain cover can be removed with the engine in the vehicle. On 3.7L engines, the engine must be removed to perform this procedure (see Chapter 2C); ignore the steps which don't apply.**

REMOVAL

▶ **Refer to illustrations 8.10, 8.11, 8.13a, 8.13b, 8.13c and 8.14**

1 Relieve the fuel system pressure (see Chapter 4).

2 Disconnect the cable from the negative battery terminal (see Chapter 5).

3 Loosen the right front wheel lug nuts. Raise the front of the vehicle and support it securely on jackstands, then remove the wheel.

4 Remove the drivebelt (see Chapter 1).

8.10 Disconnect the camshaft position sensor connector (A) and the sensor mounting bolt (B)

8.11 The engine must be supported from above with a support fixture and chains

5   Remove the drivebelt tensioner and two idler pulleys from the front cover.

6   Remove the valve covers (see Section 4).

7   Remove the alternator and alternator mounting bracket (see Chapter 5).

8   Remove the crankshaft pulley (see Section 7).

9   Remove the power steering pump (see Chapter 10).

10 Disconnect the crankshaft position sensor. Remove the camshaft position sensors in front of each cylinder head (see illustration).

11 Support the engine from above with a hoist or engine support fixture, using chains fastened to the engine lift brackets (see illustration).

12 Disconnect the electrical connectors at the air conditioning compressor, then loosen the compressor mounting bolts and move the compressor aside as required for access to the engine cover. Remove the compressor bracket from the front cover.

※※ WARNING:

The air conditioning system is under high pressure. Do not disconnect the hoses from the compressor.

Remove or disconnect any remaining wires, hoses, clamps, or brackets that will interfere with engine cover removal.

13 3.0L engine: Loosen the timing chain cover fasteners gradually and evenly, then remove the fasteners. Start with the oil pan-to-cover bolts, then the other bolts and studs (see illustrations). Remove the timing chain cover.

➡ Note: Take a digital photo or draw a sketch of the timing chain cover and fasteners. Identify the location of all stud bolts for installation in their original locations.

14 3.7L engine: Remove the cover bolts (see illustration 8.22) and install six of them into the threaded holes in the cover (see illustration). Tightening the bolts evenly a few turns will push the cover from the engine without damage.

※※ CAUTION:

Make sure all of the timing chain cover bolts are removed before attempting to remove the cover.

15 Remove and discard the cover-to-cylinder block gaskets.

8.13a Remove the cover fasteners - note the locations of all studs and bolts for installation reference

8.13b Front cover fasteners (seen from above)

8.13c Front cover fasteners (seen from below)

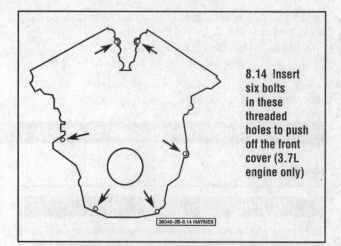

8.14 Insert six bolts in these threaded holes to push off the front cover (3.7L engine only)

INSTALLATION

♦ **Refer to illustrations 8.18, 8.21 and 8.22**

16 Inspect and clean all sealing surfaces of the timing chain cover and the block.

☀ CAUTION:

Be very careful when scraping on aluminum engine parts. Aluminum is soft and gouges easily. Severely gouged parts may require replacement.

17 Replace the crankshaft seal in the front cover (see Section 7).

18 Apply a bead of RTV sealant approximately 1/8-inch wide at the locations shown (see illustration).

19 Install new front cover gaskets into the grooves on the cover. On 3.7L engines, install two dowel pins (bolts with heads cut off) into holes 21 and 22 in the engine block (see illustration 8.22).

20 Install the timing chain cover and cover fasteners. Make sure the fasteners are in their original locations. Tighten the fasteners by hand until the cover is contacting the block and cylinder heads around its entire periphery.

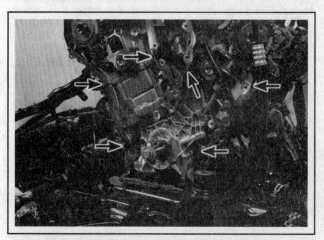

8.18 Apply a bead of RTV sealant at the locations shown

21 3.0L engine: Following the correct sequence (see illustration), tighten the bolts to the torque listed in this Chapter's Specifications.

22 3.7L engine: Install bolts 1 through 9 and remove the locating pins (see illustration). Install the rest of the bolts and tighten in sequence to the torque steps listed in this Chapter's Specifications. Install the engine mount.

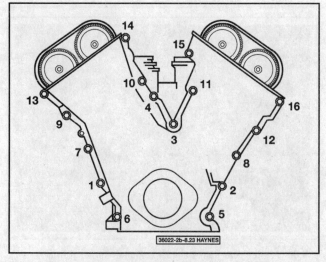

8.21 Timing chain cover bolt tightening sequence (3.0L engine)

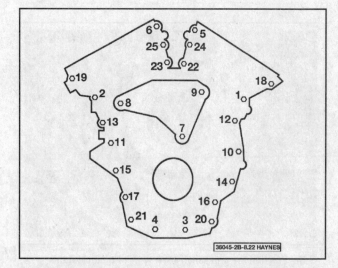

8.22 Timing chain cover bolt tightening sequence (3.7L engine)

23 Install the drivebelt and tensioner. Tighten the tensioner pulley to the torque listed in this Chapter's Specifications.
24 Install the crankshaft pulley (see Section 7).
25 Connect the wiring harness connectors to the camshaft and crankshaft position sensors.
26 Install the power steering pump and hoses (see Chapter 10).
27 Reinstall the remaining parts in the reverse order of removal.
28 Reconnect the battery, then start the engine and check for leaks.

9 Timing chains, tensioners, and chain guides - removal, inspection, and installation

REMOVAL

> ❋❋ **CAUTION:**
>
> **The timing system is complex. Severe engine damage will occur if you make any mistakes. Do not attempt this procedure unless you are highly experienced with this type of repair. If you are at all unsure of your abilities, consult an expert. Double-check all your work and be sure everything is correct before you attempt to start the engine.**

9.1 The trigger wheel must be installed in the original orientation; on 3.0L engines, align this slot with the keyway

3.0L engine

▶ Refer to illustrations 9.1, 9.3a, 9.3b, 9.3c, 9.3d, 9.4a, 9.4b, 9.5, 9.10 and 9.11

1 Remove the timing chain cover (see Section 8). Slide the crankshaft position sensor trigger wheel off the crankshaft.

> ❋❋ **CAUTION:**
>
> **The pulse (trigger) wheel has slots for more than one engine. Note the exact position of the pulse wheel to insure correct reassembly. On 3.0L engines, the slot marked in orange and stamped "30 RFF" must align over the crankshaft/pulley key (see illustration).**

2 Remove the spark plugs (see Chapter 1). 3.0L engines have two timing chains; the front most chain drives the camshaft sprockets on the rear cylinder head, while the chain closest to the block drives the camshafts for the front cylinder head.
3 Install the crankshaft pulley retaining bolt. Use a wrench on the bolt to turn the crankshaft clockwise and place the crankshaft keyway at the 11 o'clock position. TDC number 1 is the starting position and the ending position for this procedure. Verify TDC by observing the index marks on the front of the camshaft sprockets (see illustrations). If not properly aligned, turn the crankshaft exactly one full turn and again position the crankshaft keyway at 11 o'clock.

> ❋❋ **CAUTION:**
>
> **Turning the crankshaft counterclockwise can cause the timing chains to bind and damage the chains, sprockets and tensioners. Only turn the crankshaft clockwise.**

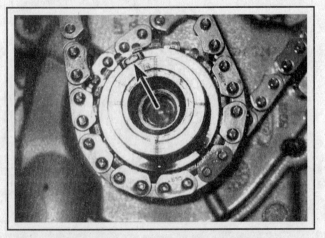

9.3a Position the crankshaft keyway at 11 o'clock; if the engine is at TDC for the number one piston . . .

9.3b . . . the rear bank exhaust camshaft sprocket timing marks will be positioned like this . . .

9.3c . . . the rear bank intake camshaft sprocket timing marks will be positioned like this . . .

9.3d . . . and the front bank camshaft sprocket timing marks will be positioned like this - intake at left, exhaust at right (3.0L engine)

4   Recheck the marks on the sprockets. If there are no marks on the chain links, mark the links directly above the camshaft sprocket marks. Continue to turn the crankshaft clockwise until the keyway is at the 3 o'clock position, which will set the camshafts on the rear cylinder head in their neutral position (see illustrations). This ensures that the valves in the rear cylinder head will not contact the pistons. Remove the mounting bolts for the VCT assembly on the rear cylinder head.

5   Remove the two bolts securing the timing chain tensioner for the rear chain. Remove the tensioner, then remove the tensioner arm (see illustration). Mark all parts that will be reused so they can be reinstalled in their original locations.

6   Lift the rear timing chain from the cam sprockets and remove the chain.

7   Remove the mounting bolts for the chain guide/VCT assembly on the rear cylinder head.

8   Slide the sprocket for the rear timing chain off the crankshaft.

9   Rotate the crankshaft 600-degrees (1-2/3 turns) clockwise, until the keyway is in the 11 o'clock position, setting the camshafts in the front cylinder head in their neutral position (see illustration 9.3d).

9.4a Crankshaft keyway positioned at 3 o'clock for Neutral position of rear bank camshafts (3.0L engine)

9.4b Position of rear bank camshaft timing marks and colored links for Neutral position (3.0L engine)

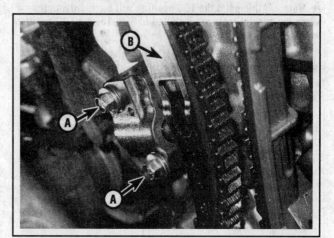

9.5 Remove the bolts (A) securing the rear timing chain tensioner and remove the tensioner, then slide the tensioner arm (B) off its pivot (3.0L engine)

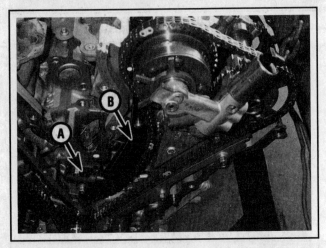

9.10 Remove the front timing chain tensioner (A) and the tensioner arm (B)

9.11 Remove the these bolts to remove the VCT assembly (3.0L engines - front shown, rear similar)

10 Remove the front timing chain tensioner mounting bolts. Remove the tensioner and tensioner arm (see illustration).

11 Lift the front timing chain off the sprockets and remove the chain. On 2009 and earlier models, remove the VCT assembly from the front cylinder head (see illustration).

12 If necessary, slide the crankshaft sprocket for the front timing chain off the crankshaft. If you are removing the intake phaser/sprocket(s), insert a 3/8-inch-drive ratchet and extension in the hole at the back of the camshaft while loosening the phaser bolt(s).

3.7L engine

▸ Refer to illustration 9.13

➡ **Note: Two special camshaft holding tools (manufacturer tool no. 303-1248) are required for this procedure.**

➡ **Note: Since the water pump on this engine is located behind the timing chain and components, it makes sense to replace the water pump while it is easily accessed during a timing chain replacement procedure.**

13 Remove the timing chain cover (see Section 8). Reinstall the crankshaft sprocket bolt and set the engine to TDC for cylinder number 1 (see illustration).

➡ **Note: At this point the TDC position will be approximate; when the special tools are installed in Step 15, the TDC position will be exact.**

14 3.7L engines have three timing chains: The long primary chain drives the intake cam VCT sprocket on each intake camshaft and the water pump, while a smaller chain on each head drives the exhaust camshafts.

15 Install the special camshaft holding tools (manufacturer tool no. 303-1248) on each cylinder head to lock the camshafts in the TDC position.

16 Remove the VCT assembly mounting bolts from the rear cylinder head, then the front cylinder head (see illustration 9.13).

17 Remove the bolts and the primary timing chain tensioner and tensioner arm. Remove the lower chain guide from the front cylinder bank. Mark the chain links opposite the timing marks on the camshafts (if not already marked), and remove the primary timing chain.

18 Remove the upper chain guide from the front cylinder bank. If necessary, remove the crankshaft sprocket.

19 If the secondary timing chains and camshaft sprockets are to be removed for inspection or another procedure, compress the tensioner(s)

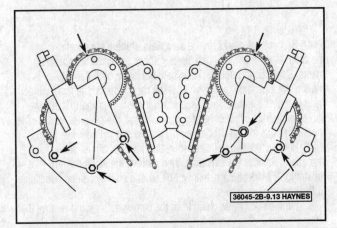

9.13 The position of the intake cam sprocket marks when the engine is set to TDC compression for cylinder no. 1 (upper arrows) on 3.7L engines - lower arrows indicate the VCT assembly mounting bolts

and insert a pin into the hole in the tensioner to hold the tensioner in the retracted position. Unscrew the bolts for the intake (VCT) and exhaust camshaft sprockets, then remove both sprockets and the chain as an assembly.

❋❋ **CAUTION:**

Make sure the camshaft holding tool is in place and prevents the camshafts from turning while unscrewing the bolts. New bolts must be used for reassembly.

20 Remove the bolts and the secondary chain tensioners.

➡ **Note: The camshaft holding tool must be loosened and tilted (toward the flywheel end of the engine) to access the rearmost bolt of the tensioner.**

INSPECTION

➡ **Note: Do not mix parts from the front and rear timing chains and tensioners, and on 3.7L engines, keep the primary and secondary tensioners separate.**

21 Clean all parts with clean solvent. Dry with compressed air, if available.

22 Inspect the chain tensioners and tensioner arms for excessive wear or other damage.

23 Inspect the timing chain guides for deep grooves, excessive wear, or other damage.

24 Inspect the timing chain for excessive wear or damage.

25 Inspect the camshaft and crankshaft sprockets for chipped or broken teeth, excessive wear, or damage.

26 Replace any component that is in questionable condition.

INSTALLATION

✴ CAUTION:

Before starting the engine, carefully rotate the crankshaft by hand through at least two full revolutions (use a socket and breaker bar on the crankshaft pulley center bolt). If you feel any resistance, STOP! There is something wrong - most likely, valves are contacting the pistons. You must find the problem before proceeding. Check your work and see if any updated repair information is available.

➡ Note: The installation procedure is very much the reverse of the removal procedure, but refer to both the Removal and Installation Steps to ensure that you understand.

3.0L engine

27 The timing chain tensioners must be fully compressed and locked in place before chain installation. To prepare the chain tensioners for installation:

a) Insert a small pick into the hole in the tensioner and release the pawl mechanism.

b) Using a soft-jawed vise, compress the plunger into the tensioner housing until the plunger is bottomed in its bore.

c) Insert a 1/16-inch drill bit or a straightened paper clip into the small hole above the pawl mechanism to hold the plunger in place.

d) Repeat this procedure for the other tensioner.

28 If removed, install the crankshaft sprocket for the front timing chain. Make sure the crankshaft keyway is still at 11 o'clock.

29 Look at the index marks on the sprockets of the front bank intake and exhaust camshafts. The marks should be at 9 o'clock (intake) and at 12 o'clock (exhaust) in relation to the top of the cylinder head (see illustration 9.3d).

✴ CAUTION:

The timing chains have three links that are a different color than the rest of the links. When installed, the colored links on the chain must be aligned with the index marks on the camshaft and crankshaft sprockets.

➡ Note: If you are installing new timing chains and the colored links are not visible, mark the chain as follows:

a) Lay the chain on a flat surface in a circular shape. Select any link and mark it with a permanent marker.

b) Count 29 links counterclockwise and mark that link.

c) Continue counting (counterclockwise) and mark the 42nd link.

30 Install the front timing chain guide/VCT assembly. Tighten the

mounting bolts to the torque listed in this Chapter's Specifications.

31 Install the front timing chain around the camshaft and crankshaft sprockets. Make sure the index marks on the sprockets are aligned with the colored (or marked) links of the chain.

32 Install the front tensioner arm over its pivot dowel. Seat the tensioner arm firmly on the cylinder head and block.

33 Install the front timing chain tensioner. Be sure the tensioner plunger is fully compressed and locked in place. Tighten the tensioner mounting bolts to the torque listed in this Chapter's Specifications. Verify that the colored (or marked) links of the timing chain are still aligned with the index marks on the camshaft and crankshaft sprockets, and the crankshaft keyway is at 11 o'clock. If not, remove the timing chain and repeat the installation procedure.

34 Install the crankshaft sprocket for the rear timing chain on the crankshaft.

35 Rotate the crankshaft clockwise until the crankshaft keyway is in the 3 o'clock position. This will correctly position the pistons for installation of the rear timing chain.

36 Install the rear timing chain guide/VCT assembly. Tighten the mounting bolts to the torque listed in this Chapter's Specifications.

37 Double-check the position of the rear camshafts so the index marks on the sprockets are at (approximately) 3 o'clock (intake) and at 12 o'clock (exhaust) in relation to the top of the cylinder head (see illustration 9.4b).

✴ CAUTION:

The timing chains have three links that are a different color than the rest of the links. When installed, the colored (or marked) links on the chain must be aligned with the index marks on the camshaft and crankshaft sprockets.

38 Install the rear timing chain around the camshaft and crankshaft sprockets. Make sure the colored (or marked) links of the chain are aligned with the index marks on the front of the camshaft and crankshaft sprockets.

39 Install the rear tensioner arm over its pivot dowel. Seat the tensioner arm firmly on the cylinder head and block.

40 Install the rear timing chain tensioner. Be sure the tensioner plunger is fully compressed and locked in place. Tighten the tensioner mounting bolts to the torque listed in this Chapter's Specifications. Verify that the colored (or marked) links of the timing chain are still aligned with the index marks on the camshaft and crankshaft sprockets, and the crankshaft keyway is at 3 o'clock. If not, remove the timing chain and repeat the installation procedure.

41 Remove the drill bits or wires (locking pins) from the timing chain tensioners.

42 Rotate the crankshaft counterclockwise back to the 11 o'clock position (the no. 1 TDC position). Verify the timing marks on the camshaft sprockets and the crankshaft sprocket line up with the colored links (see illustrations 9.3a, 9.3b, 9.3c, 9.3d and 9.4b).

43 Install the crankshaft position sensor pulse (trigger) wheel on the crankshaft.

✴ CAUTION:

Make sure the pulse wheel is installed with the crankshaft key in the slot marked "30 RFF" (see illustration 9.1).

44 Rotate the engine by hand at least two revolutions and verify that there is no binding.

45 Install the timing chain cover (see Section 8).

46 Reinstall the remaining parts in the reverse order of removal.

47 Fill the crankcase with the recommended oil (see Chapter 1).

48 Reconnect the battery (see Chapter 5), then start the engine and check for leaks.

3.7L engine

▶ **Refer to illustration 9.51**

49 Install the primary timing chain guide for the rear (right) cylinder bank and tighten the bolts to the torque listed in this Chapter's Specifications.

50 Tilt the rear (right) cylinder bank camshaft holding tool to the rear and install the secondary timing chain tensioner, tightening the bolts to the torque listed in this Chapter's Specifications. Don't remove the lock pin from the tensioner yet.

51 Install the secondary timing chains onto the camshaft sprockets. The colored links on the chain must align with the marks/camshaft keyway slots in the sprockets (see illustration).

52 Install the sprockets/VCT actuator (phaser)/secondary timing chain onto the rear camshafts. When installing the camshaft sprocket bolts, NEW bolts must be used. Tighten the bolts to the torque listed in this Chapter's Specifications.

53 Tilt the front (left) cylinder bank camshaft holding tool to the rear and install the secondary timing chain tensioner, tightening the bolts to the torque listed in this Chapter's Specifications. Don't remove the lock pin from the tensioner yet.

54 Install the sprockets/VCT actuator (phaser)/secondary timing chain (with the marks aligned as shown in illustration 9.51) onto the front camshafts. When installing the camshaft sprocket bolts, NEW bolts must be used. Tighten the bolts to the torque listed in this Chapter's Specifications. Remove the lock pin from the tensioner.

55 Install the crankshaft sprocket.

56 Install the primary timing chain onto the crankshaft sprocket and the VCT sprockets, making sure the colored links (or marks) on the chain align with the marks on the sprockets.

➡ **Note: At TDC compression for cylinder no. 1, the crankshaft sprocket keyway will be in approximately the 11 o'clock position and the timing mark on the crankshaft sprocket will be in approximately the 4 o'clock position.**

57 Install the upper chain guide on the front (left) cylinder bank, tightening the bolts to the torque listed in this Chapter's Specifications.

58 Install the lower chain guide for the front cylinder bank, tightening the bolts to the torque listed in this Chapter's Specifications.

59 Install the primary timing chain tensioner arm to the rear cylinder bank.

60 Place the timing chain tensioner in a soft-jawed vise, with the jaws bearing on the tensioner body and the plunger. Swing the lever on the tensioner counterclockwise, then tighten the vise until the tensioner plunger has been retracted. Swing the lever clockwise, aligning the hole in the lever with the hole in the tensioner body, then install a lock pin made of heavy wire or a drill bit or small Allen wrench. Remove the tensioner from the vise.

61 Install the primary timing chain tensioner, tightening the bolts to the torque listed in this Chapter's Specifications.

➡ **Note: It might be necessary to rotate the crankshaft slightly to create a little slack in the chain to enable the tensioner to be installed.**

Remove the lock pin from the tensioner.

62 Recheck the timing marks to make sure they are all in proper alignment.

63 Check the seals on the VCT housing, replacing them if necessary.

64 Install the VCT housings, making sure the dowels engage completely with their corresponding holes in the cylinder head, then install the bolts and tighten them a little at a time to the torque listed in this Chapter's Specifications.

65 Remove the camshaft holding tools, then rotate the engine by hand at least two revolutions and verify that there is no binding.

66 Install the timing chain cover (see Section 8).

67 Reinstall the engine/transaxle. Refill the engine with oil (install a new filter) and coolant (see Chapter 1).

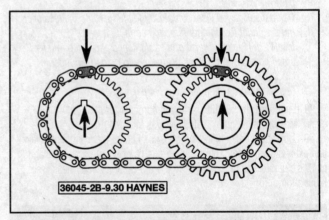

36045-2B-9.30 HAYNES

9.51 Align the secondary timing chain colored links with the keyways of the sprockets (3.7L engine)

10 Camshafts and valvetrain - removal inspection, and installation

3.0L ENGINE

Removal

Rear bank cylinder head

♦ **Refer to illustration 10.6**

1 Remove the timing chain for the rear cylinder bank (see Section 9).

2 Note the location of each camshaft cap. Use a marker on each cap or notes on paper or cardboard if they're not marked. Do not mix any of the camshaft caps.

3 Working in the order opposite that of the tightening sequence (see illustration 10.31), gradually loosen the bolts that secure the camshaft bearing caps to the cylinder head, then remove the camshaft caps. It may be necessary to tap the caps lightly with a soft-faced mallet to loosen them from the locating dowels.

❊❊ CAUTION:

The camshaft bearing caps and cylinder heads are numbered to identify the locations of the caps. The caps must be installed in their original locations. Keep all parts from each camshaft together; never mix parts from one camshaft with those for another.

4 Mark the intake and exhaust camshafts to prevent reinstalling them in the wrong locations, then lift the camshafts straight up and out of the cylinder head.

5 Mark the positions of the rocker arms so they can be reinstalled in their original locations, then remove the rocker arms.

6 Place the rocker arms in a suitable container so they can be separated and identified (see illustration).

7 Lift the hydraulic lash adjusters from their bores in the cylinder head. Identify and separate the adjusters so they can be reinstalled in their original locations.

Front bank cylinder head

8 To place the front bank camshafts in the neutral position, turn the crankshaft 1-2/3 turns (clockwise) until the crankshaft keyway is at 11 o'clock (see illustration 9.3a).

9 Remove the timing chain for the front cylinder bank (see Section 9). Also remove the water pump pulley and oil seal retainer from the rear of the exhaust camshaft.

➡ **Note: Refer to Chapter 3, Section 8 for the pulley removal procedure.**

10 Repeat Steps 3 to 7 to remove the front (left side) camshafts, rocker arms and lash adjusters. Be sure to loosen the bearing caps on the front camshafts in the order opposite that of the tightening sequence (see illustration 10.25).

Inspection

♦ **Refer to illustrations 10.11, 10.13, 10.14, 10.15a, 10.15b, 10.16, 10.17 and 10.18**

11 Check each hydraulic lash adjuster for excessive wear, scoring, pitting, or an out-of-round condition (see illustration). Replace as necessary.

12 Measure the outside diameter of each adjuster at the top and bottom of the adjuster. Then take a second set of measurements at a right angle to the first. If any measurement is significantly different from the others, the adjuster is tapered or out of round and must be replaced. If the necessary equipment is available, measure the diameter of the lash adjuster and the inside diameter of the corresponding cylinder head bore. Subtract the diameter of the lash adjuster from the bore diameter to obtain the oil clearance. Compare the measurements obtained to those given in this Chapter's Specifications. If the adjusters or the cylinder head bores are excessively worn, new adjusters or a new cylinder head, or both, may be required. If the valve train is noisy, particularly if the noise persists after a cold start, you can suspect a faulty hydraulic adjuster.

10.6 Place all the parts in a container so they can be separated and identified for installation in their original locations (3.0L shown)

10.11 Inspect the lash adjusters for signs of excessive wear or damage, such as pitting, scoring or signs of overheating (bluing or discoloration), where the tip contacts the rocker arm (1) and the side surfaces that contact the bore in the cylinder head (2) (3.0L models)

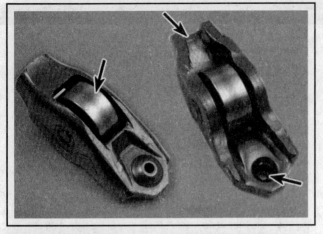

10.13 Check the roller surface (left arrow) of the rocker arm and the areas where the valve stem and lash adjuster contact the rocker arm (right arrows) (3.0L models)

10.14 Check the cam lobes for pitting, excessive wear, and scoring. If scoring is excessive, as shown here, replace the camshaft

10.15a Measure the camshaft lobe height (greatest dimension) . . .

10.15b . . . and subtract the camshaft lobe base circle diameter (smallest dimension) to obtain the lobe lift specification

10.16 Measure each journal diameter with a micrometer. If any journal is less than the specified minimum, replace the camshaft

13 Inspect the rocker arms for signs of wear or damage. The areas of wear are the tip that contacts the valve stem, the socket that contacts the lash adjuster and the roller that contacts the camshaft (see illustration).

14 Examine the camshaft lobes for scoring, pitting, galling (wear due to rubbing), and evidence of overheating (blue, discolored areas). Look for flaking of the hardened surface layer of each lobe (see illustration). If any such wear is evident, replace the camshaft.

15 Calculate the camshaft lobe lift by measuring the lobe height and the diameter of the base circle of the lobe (see illustrations). Subtract the base circle measurement from the lobe height to determine the lobe lift. If the lobe lift is less than that listed in this Chapter's Specifications the camshaft lobe is worn and should be replaced.

16 Inspect the camshaft bearing journals and the cylinder head bearing surfaces for pitting or excessive wear. If any such wear is evident, replace the component concerned. Using a micrometer, measure the diameter of each camshaft bearing journal at several points (see illustration). If the diameter of any journal is less than specified, replace the camshaft.

17 To check the bearing journal oil clearance, remove the rocker arms and hydraulic lash adjusters (if not already done), use a suitable solvent and a clean lint-free rag to clean all bearing surfaces, then install the camshafts and bearing caps with a piece of Plastigage across each journal (see illustration). Tighten the bearing cap bolts to the specified torque. Don't rotate the camshafts.

18 Remove the bearing caps and measure the width of the flattened Plastigage with the Plastigage scale (see illustration). Scrape off the Plastigage with your fingernail or the edge of a credit card. Don't scratch or nick the journals or bearing caps.

19 If the oil clearance of any bearing is worn beyond the specified service limit, install a new camshaft and repeat the check. If the clearance is still excessive, replace the cylinder head.

20 To check camshaft endplay, clean the bearing surfaces and install the camshafts (without the lash adjusters or rocker arms) and bearing caps. Tighten the bearing cap bolts to the specified torque, then measure the endplay using a dial indicator mounted on the cylinder head so that its tip bears on the camshaft end.

21 Lightly but firmly tap the camshaft fully toward the gauge, zero the gauge, then tap the camshaft fully away from the gauge and note the gauge reading. If the measured endplay is at or beyond the specified service limit, install a new camshaft thrust cap and repeat the check. If the clearance is still excessive, the camshaft or the cylinder head must be replaced.

10.17 Lay a strip of Plastigage on each camshaft journal, in line with the camshaft

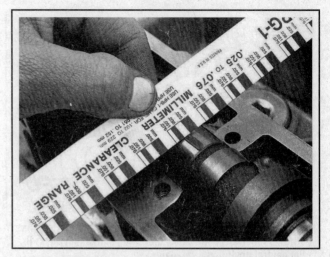

10.18 Compare the width of the crushed Plastigage to the scale on the package to determine the journal oil clearance

Installation

Front bank cylinder head

◗ Refer to illustration 10.25

22 Make sure the crankshaft keyway is at the 11 o'clock position (see illustration 9.3a).

23 Lubricate the rocker arms and hydraulic lash adjusters with engine assembly lubricant or fresh engine oil. Install the adjusters into their original bores, then install the rocker arms in their correct locations.

24 Similarly lubricate the camshafts and install them in their correct locations.

25 Install the camshaft bearing caps in their correct locations. Install the cap bolts and tighten by hand until snug. Install the camshaft thrust caps and bolts. Tighten the bolts in four to five steps, following the sequence shown (see illustration), to the torque listed in this Chapter's Specifications.

26 Install the seal retainer with a new seal over the left end of the exhaust camshaft. Tighten the bolts to the torque listed in this Chapter's Specifications.

27 Install the front timing chain sprocket on the crankshaft. Install the front timing chain (see Section 9). Install the water pump pulley onto the left end of the exhaust camshaft.

➡ **Note: Refer to Chapter 3, Section 8 for the pulley installation procedure.**

Rear bank cylinder head

◗ Refer to illustration 10.31

28 Turn the crankshaft clockwise and position the crankshaft keyway at the 3 o'clock position.

29 Lubricate the rocker arms and hydraulic lash adjusters with engine assembly lubricant or fresh engine oil. Install the adjusters into their original bores, then install the rocker arms in their correct locations.

30 Similarly lubricate the camshafts and install them in their correct locations.

31 Install the camshaft bearing caps in their correct locations. Install the cap bolts and tighten by hand until snug, then install the camshaft thrust caps and bolts. Tighten the bolts in four to five steps, following the sequence shown (see illustration) to the torque listed in this Chapter's Specifications.

32 Install the rear timing chain (see Section 9).

33 Install the timing chain cover (see Section 8).

34 Reinstall the remaining parts in the reverse order of removal.

35 Fill the crankcase with the recommended oil (see Chapter 1); fill the power steering reservoir with the correct fluid and refill the cooling system.

36 Reconnect the battery, then start the engine and check for leaks.

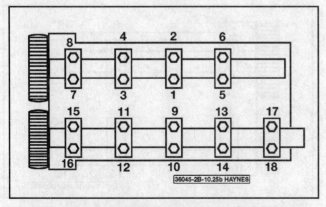

10.25 Front bank camshaft bearing cap tightening sequence (2009 and later 3.0L models)

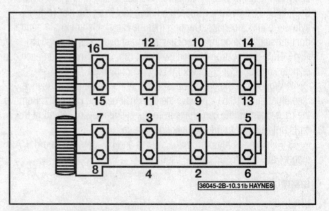

10.31 Rear bank camshaft bearing cap tightening sequence (2009 and later 3.0L models)

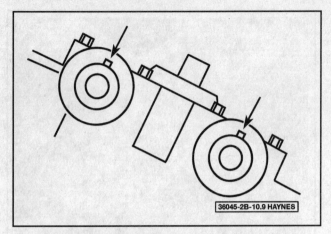

10.37 Front (left) bank camshaft timing marks (keyways) in the neutral position (3.7L engine)

3.7L ENGINE

➡ **Note: This procedure can only be performed with the engine removed (see Chapter 2C).**

➡ **Note: Two special camshaft holding tools (manufacturer tool no. 303-1248) are required for this procedure.**

➡ **Note: Before removing the camshafts, check the valve clearances as described in Chapter 2A, Section 5 (but refer to this Chapter's Specifications).**

Removal

▶ **Refer to illustrations 10.37 and 10.40**

37 Remove the primary timing chain and the front (left) cylinder bank VCT assembly/camshaft sprockets/secondary timing chain (see Section 9), then remove the camshaft holding tool from the front (left) cylinder bank camshafts. Confirm that the camshafts are in the neutral positions after the holding tool has been removed (see illustration).

38 Note the location of each camshaft cap. Make a mark on each cap if they're not marked.

39 Working in the order opposite that of the tightening sequence (see illustration 10.49), remove the camshaft bearing cap bolts. Remove the caps, then lift the camshafts from the cylinder head. Lay all of the parts out in order to prevent mixing them up.

40 Remove the primary timing chain and the rear (right) cylinder bank VCT assembly/camshaft sprockets/secondary timing chain (see Section 9). Remove the camshaft holding tool from the rear (right) cylinder bank camshafts. Confirm that the camshafts are in the neutral positions after the holding tool has been removed (see illustration).

41 Note the location of each camshaft cap. Use a marker on each cap or notes on paper or cardboard if they're not marked.

42 Working in the order opposite that of the tightening sequence (see illustration 10.51), remove the camshaft bearing cap bolts. Remove the caps, then lift the camshafts from the cylinder head. Lay all of the parts out in order to prevent mixing them up.

43 Remove the lifters from their bores and lay them out in order. A magnet or suction cup can be used.

Inspection

Lifters

44 Inspect the contact and sliding surfaces of each lifter for wear and scratches.

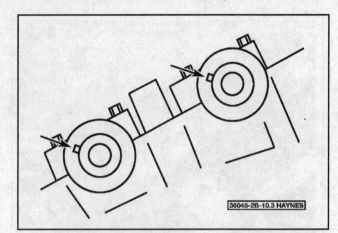

10.40 Rear (right) bank camshaft timing marks (keyways) in the neutral position (3.7L engine)

➡ **Note: If the lifter face is worn, be sure to check the corresponding camshaft lobe carefully.**

45 Verify that each lifter moves up and down freely in its bore.

Camshafts

46 Inspect the camshafts as described in Steps 14 through 21.

Installation

▶ **Refer to illustrations 10.49 and 10.51**

47 Turn the crankshaft counterclockwise to place the keyway in the 9 o'clock position.

✷✷ CAUTION:

The crankshaft must remain in this position until the camshafts are installed and the valve clearances are checked and, if necessary, adjusted.

48 Lubricate the camshafts and bearing saddles in the cylinder head for the front (left) cylinder bank with clean engine oil or camshaft installation lube. Set the camshafts in the cylinder head, making sure they are in their neutral positions (see illustration 10.37).

49 Lubricate the friction surfaces of the camshaft bearing caps with clean engine oil or camshaft installation lube and install them in their proper positions. Install the bolts and tighten them, in the proper

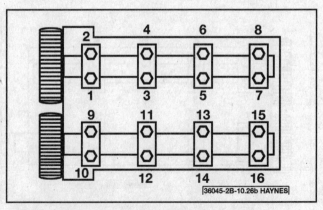

10.49 Front (left) bank camshaft bearing cap tightening sequence (3.7L engine)

sequence (see illustration), to the torque listed in this Chapter's Specifications.

50 Lubricate the camshafts and bearing saddles in the cylinder head for the rear (right) cylinder bank with clean engine oil or camshaft installation lube. Set the camshafts in the cylinder head, making sure they are in their neutral positions (see illustration 10.40).

51 Lubricate the friction surfaces of the camshaft bearing caps with clean engine oil or camshaft installation lube and install them in their proper positions. Install the bolts and tighten them, in the proper sequence (see illustration), to the torque listed in this Chapter's Specifications.

52 Check and if necessary, adjust the valve clearances as described in Chapter 2A, Section 5.

➡ **Note: Since the crankshaft is in its neutral position, the camshafts can be turned without the danger of the valves contacting the pistons. Insert a bolt into the front of the camshaft to turn it.**

53 Return the camshafts to their positions shown in illustrations 10.37 and 10.40, then install the camshaft holding tools.

54 Install the secondary timing chains, VCT actuator and camshaft sprockets as described in Section 9.

55 Turn the crankshaft clockwise 60-degrees until the keyway is in

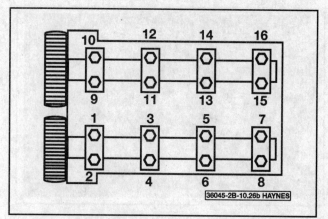

10.51 Rear (right) bank camshaft bearing cap tightening sequence (3.7L engine)

the 11 o'clock position.

56 Install the primary timing chain and timing chain cover (see Section 9).

11 Cylinder heads - removal and installation

※ WARNING:

Wait until the engine is completely cool before beginning this procedure.

➡ **Note: On 3.7L V6 engines, this procedure can only be performed with the engine removed (see Chapter 2C). Ignore the steps which don't apply.**

REMOVAL

1   Relieve the fuel system pressure (see Chapter 4), then disconnect the cable from the negative battery terminal (see Chapter 5).

2   Drain the cooling system (see Chapter 1).

3   Remove the upper and lower intake manifolds (see Section 5).

4   With the vehicle raised and supported properly, disconnect the front oxygen sensors and the catalytic converters (see Chapter 4).

5   Disconnect the CHT sensor, catalytic converter monitor sensor, and camshaft position sensors (see Chapter 6).

6   Remove the camshafts from the cylinder head to be removed (see Section 10).

7   Where applicable, disconnect bolts or clips that secure wiring harnesses or ground straps to the cylinder heads.

8   Remove the exhaust manifold(s) (see Section 6).

9   Remove any additional components that might interfere with cylinder head removal, referring to the appropriate Chapters of this manual.

10 Remove the hoses and any electrical connectors from the coolant bypass tube. Remove the two fasteners securing the coolant bypass tube, then remove the tube.

11 Loosen each cylinder head bolt, one turn at a time, following the reverse order of the tightening sequence (see illustrations 11.20a or 11.20b and 11.20c). When all cylinder head bolts are loose, remove and discard the bolts. New torque-to-yield cylinder head bolts must be used during installation.

12 Remove the cylinder head from the engine block and place it on a workbench.

※ CAUTION:

If the cylinder head sticks to the block, pry only on a casting protrusion to prevent damaging the mating surfaces.

Remove and discard the cylinder head gasket.

INSTALLATION

▸ **Refer to illustrations 11.20a, 11.20b and 11.20c**

13 The mating surfaces of the cylinder head and the block must be perfectly clean before installing the cylinder head. Clean the surfaces with a scraper, but be careful not to gouge the aluminum.

※ CAUTION:

Be very careful when scraping on aluminum engine parts. Aluminum is soft and gouges easily. Severely gouged parts may require replacement.

14 Check the mating surfaces of the block and the cylinder head for nicks, deep scratches, and other damage. If slight, they can be removed carefully with a file; if excessive, machining may be the only alternative to replacement.

15 If you suspect warpage of the cylinder head gasket surface, use a straightedge to check it for distortion. If the gasket mating surface of your cylinder head or block is out of specification or is severely nicked or scratched, consult an automotive machine shop for advice.

16 Clean the mating surfaces of the cylinder head and block with a clean shop towel and brake system cleaner

17 Ensure that the two locating dowels are in position in the cylinder

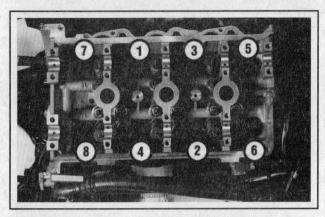

11.20a Cylinder head bolt TIGHTENING sequence (3.0L engines)

11.20b Cylinder head bolt TIGHTENING sequence (3.7L engines)

11.20c An angle gauge takes the guesswork out of tightening the torque-to-yield cylinder head bolts

block and that all cylinder head bolt holes are free of oil, corrosion, or other contamination.

18 Install new cylinder head gaskets on the block, over the locating dowels.

19 Carefully install the cylinder heads. Use caution when lowering the cylinder heads onto the cylinder block to prevent damage to the cylinder heads or block. Make sure the cylinder heads fit properly over the locating dowels in the block.

20 Install *new* cylinder head bolts and tighten them by hand until snug.

> ✳ **CAUTION:**
>
> **The cylinder head bolts are the torque-to-yield type and are stretched during tightening. Therefore, the original bolts must be discarded and new bolts installed during assembly.**

Tighten the cylinder head bolts in the sequence shown to the torque and angle of rotation listed in this Chapter's Specifications (see illustrations).

➡ **Note: The method used for the cylinder head bolt tightening procedure is referred to as the "torque angle" or "torque-to-yield" method; follow the procedure exactly. Tighten the bolts using a torque wrench, then use a breaker bar and a special torque angle adapter (available at auto parts stores) to tighten the bolts the required angle.**

21 Install the remaining parts in the reverse order of removal. Tighten fasteners to the torque values listed in this Chapter's Specifications.

22 Change the engine oil and filter, then fill and bleed the cooling system (see Chapter 1).

23 Start the engine and check for leaks.

12 Oil pan - removal and installation

➡ **Note: On 3.7L engines, the procedure can only be performed with the engine removed (see Chapter 2C). In the Steps below, it is assumed that the 3.7L engine has been removed; ignore the steps which don't apply.**

REMOVAL

▸ **Refer to illustrations 12.8 and 12.10**

1 Disconnect the cable from the negative battery terminal (see Chapter 5).

2 Raise the vehicle and support it securely on jackstands.

3 Drain the engine oil (see Chapter 1). Reinstall the oil drain plug and tighten it to the torque listed in the Chapter 1 Specifications, using a new sealing washer.

4 Remove the oil filter (see Chapter 1).

5 Disconnect the oxygen sensor connector(s) (see Chapter 6).

6 Remove the crossover and flexible exhaust pipe and converter assembly from the vehicle (see Chapter 4).

7 Remove the driveplate access cover. On 3.7L engines, remove the nut and stud from the alternator.

8 Remove the bolts that secure the oil pan to the transaxle (see illustration).

9 On 3.7L engines, remove the timing chain cover (see Section 8), the flywheel/driveplate (see Section 15), and the timing ring for the crankshaft position sensor. Mount the engine to an engine stand.

➡ **Note: Bolt only at the bellhousing flange, not the oil pan.**

10 Remove the oil pan fasteners and remove the oil pan (see illustra-

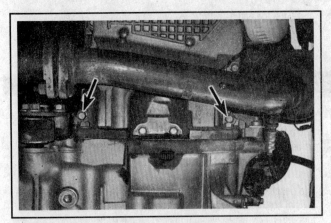

12.8 Remove these bolts that secure the oil pan to the transaxle

12.10 Oil pan bolts on the rear side of the pan (not all seen here)

tion). Note the location of any stud bolts. On 3.7L engines, install two of the original oil pan bolts in the two threaded holes at the front and rear of the pan. Tighten the bolts to push the pan evenly away from the block.

11 Remove and discard the oil pan gasket. If necessary, remove the fasteners that secure the oil screen and pick-up tube and remove the screen and tube assembly.

12 Thoroughly clean the oil pan and cylinder block mating surfaces using lacquer thinner or acetone. The surfaces must be free of any residue that will keep the sealant from adhering properly. Clean the oil pan inside and out with solvent and dry with compressed air. Use RTV sealant remover rather than scraping the pan or block surfaces.

INSTALLATION

13 If removed, install a new O-ring seal onto the oil pick-up tube. Install the tube and screen assembly and tighten the retaining fasteners to the torque listed in this Chapter's Specifications. Use a new self-locking nut to secure the pick-up tube support bracket. Tighten the nut to the torque listed in this Chapter's Specifications.

14 On 3.0L engines, install a new gasket on the oil pan. Apply a 1/8-inch bead of RTV sealant to the oil pan gasket in the area of the timing

chain cover-to-cylinder block parting line.

15 On 3.0L engines, install the pan bolts and tighten by hand. Be sure to install any stud bolts in the locations noted during removal. Install the oil pan-to-transaxle bolts. Firmly push the oil pan against the transaxle and tighten the pan-to-transaxle bolts snugly, then, tighten the oil pan bolts gradually and evenly, to the torque listed in this Chapter's Specifications.

16 On 3.7L engines, apply a 1/8-inch bead of RTV to the oil pan flange and install the pan with only the four corner bolts hand-tight. Align the pan to the boss under the alternator and hold a straightedge to align the pan flush to the rear face of the block. Work quickly to install the rest of the bolts, tightening them a little at a time, in a criss-cross pattern, to the torque listed in this Chapter's Specifications.

17 The remainder of installation is the reverse of removal, noting the following points:

a) Tighten all fasteners to the torque values listed in this Chapter's Specifications.
b) Always replace any self-locking nuts disturbed on removal.
c) Fill the engine with fresh engine oil and install a new oil filter (see Chapter 1).
d) Start the engine and check for leaks.

13 Oil pump - removal, inspection and installation

➡ **Note: On 3.7L engines, the procedure can only be performed with the engine removed (see Chapter 2C). In the Steps below, it is assumed that the 3.7L engine has been removed; ignore the steps which don't apply.**

REMOVAL

1 Remove the oil pan and the oil screen/pick-up tube assembly (see Section 12).

2 Remove the timing chain cover (see Section 8), timing chains and crankshaft sprockets (see Section 9).

3 Loosen each of the four oil pump mounting bolts one turn (three bolts on 3.7L engines), then gradually and evenly loosen each bolt in several steps. When all bolts are loose, remove the bolts and oil pump. On 3.7L engines, rotate the oil pump housing clockwise to separate it from the oil pickup tube.

INSPECTION

4 Remove the oil pump cover from the oil pump body.

5 Note any identification marks on the rotors and withdraw the rotors from the pump body.

6 Thoroughly clean and dry the components.

7 Inspect the rotors for obvious wear or damage. If either rotor, the pump body or the cover is scored or damaged, the complete oil pump assembly must be replaced.

8 If the oil pump components are in acceptable condition, dip the rotors in clean engine oil and install them into the pump body, with any identification marks positioned as noted during disassembly.

9 Install the cover and tighten the screws securely.

INSTALLATION

10 Rotate the oil pump inner rotor so it aligns with the flats on the crankshaft. Install the oil pump over the crankshaft and fit it firmly against the cylinder block. On 3.7L engines, rotate the pump assembly counterclockwise to seat it against the oil pickup tube's O-ring.

11 Install the oil pump bolts and tighten by hand until snug. Tighten the bolts gradually and evenly, in a criss-cross pattern, to the torque

listed in this Chapter's Specifications.

12 Install the remainder of the components in the reverse order of removal.

13 Fill the engine with fresh engine oil and install a new oil filter (see Chapter 1).

14 Start the engine and check for leaks.

14 Rear main oil seal - replacement

1 The one-piece rear main oil seal is pressed into a rear main oil seal carrier mounted at the rear of the block. Remove the transaxle (see Chapter 7).

2 Use a seal-removal tool or screwdriver to remove the rear seal.

✳✳ CAUTION:

Be careful not to scratch the crankshaft seal surface.

3 On 3.7L engines, remove the CKP sensor (see Chapter 6).

4 Clean the mating surface for the oil seal carrier on the cylinder block and the crankshaft. Carefully remove and polish any burrs or raised edges on the crankshaft that may have caused the seal to fail.

5 Lightly coat the inside lip of the new seal with clean engine oil. Use a thin (but durable) two-inch wide plastic strip (or a two-liter plastic beverage bottle cut to size) around the inside circumference of the seal to act as a liner for installation.

6 With the plastic seal liner in place, carefully move the new seal into position by sliding it onto the contact surface of the crankshaft. A special seal installer can be used. On 3.0L engines, use manufacturer tool #303-178, which, when tightened on the studs, will force the seal evenly into place. On 3.7L engines, use manufacturer tool #49 W011 101 and a small hammer to tap the seal in place on the block.

7 Carefully remove the plastic liner or tool so that the new seal contacts the crankshaft mating surface correctly.

8 Be sure to check for signs of oil leakage when the engine is operable.

15 Flywheel/driveplate - removal and installation

This procedure is essentially the same as the flywheel/driveplate removal procedure for the four-cylinder engine. Refer to Chapter 2A and follow the procedure outlined there. However, use the bolt torque listed in this Chapter's Specifications.

➡ **Note: On 3.7L engines, the bolt pattern of the driveplate will only align one way with the crankshaft flange.**

16 Engine mounts - inspection and replacement

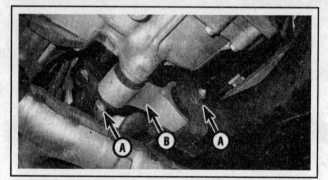

16.1a Remove the two bolts (A) and the roll restrictor (B) from the frame bracket

16.1b Remove the engine mount bracket nuts (A), the bracket-to-mount bolt (B) and the mount bolts (C)

16.1c Remove the transaxle mount bracket-to-mount through bolt (A), the bracket-to-transaxle nuts (B) and bolt (C)

▶ **Refer to illustrations 16.1a. 16.1b and 16.1c**

This procedure is essentially the same as for the four cylinder engine. The engine must be fully supported when removing/installing engine mounts. Refer to Chapter 2A and follow the procedure outlined there but refer to the illustrations for this Section.

Specifications

General

3.0L V6 engine

Engine type	Double overhead cam (DOHC) V6
Displacement	182 cubic inches
Engine VIN code	D
Bore	3.50 inches (89.0 mm)
Stroke	3.13 inches (79.5 mm)
Firing order	1-4-2-5-3-6
Compression ratio	10.0:1
Compression pressure	See Chapter 2C
Oil pressure	See Chapter 2C

3.7L V6 engine

Engine type	Double overhead cam (DOHC) V6
Displacement	227 cubic inches
Engine VIN code	B
Bore	3.75 inches (95.5 mm)
Stroke	3.41 inches (86.7 mm)
Firing order	1-4-2-5-3-6
Compression ratio	10.3:1
Compression pressure	See Chapter 2C
Oil pressure	See Chapter 2C

1-4-2-5-3-6

36075-B-SPECS HAYNES

Cylinder location diagram

Camshafts

3.0L V6 engine

Lobe lift (intake and exhaust)	0.189 inch (4.79 mm)
Journal diameter	1.060 to 1.061 inches (26.936 to 26.962 mm)
Bearing inside diameter	1.062 to 1.063 inches (26.987 to 27.012 mm)
Journal-to-bearing oil clearance	
Standard	0.001 to 0.003 inch (0.025 to 0.076 mm)
Service limit	0.0047 inch (0.121 mm)
Endplay	
Standard	0.001 to 0.0064 inch (0.025 to 0.165 mm)
Service limit	0.0075 inch (0.190 mm)

3.7L V6 engine

Lobe lift (intake and exhaust)	0.38 inch (9.68 mm)
Journal diameter	
First journal	1.2202 to 1.2209 inches (30.993 to 31.013 mm)
Others	1.021 to 1.022 inches (25.937 to 25.963 mm)
Bearing inside diameter	
First journal	1.221 to 1.222 inches (31.0375 to 31.0625 mm)
Others	1.023 to 1.024 inches (25.987 to 26.012 mm)
Journal-to-bearing oil clearance (maximum)	
First journal	0.0027 inch (0.070 mm)
Others	0.0030 inch (0.075 mm)
Endplay	
Standard	0.001 to 0.0066 inch (0.025 to 0.170 mm)
Service limit	0.0075 inch (0.190 mm)

Specifications (continued)

Hydraulic lash adjuster (3.0L V6 only)

Diameter	0.6290 to 0.6294 inch (15.988 to 16.000 mm)
Lash adjuster-to-bore clearance	
Standard	0.0007 to 0.0027 inch (0.018 to 0.069 mm)
Minimum	0.0006 inch (0.016 mm)

Valve clearances (3.7L V6 engine only) - engine cold

Intake	0.006 to 0.010 inch (0.15 to 0.25 mm)
Exhaust	0.012 to 0.015 inch (0.30 to 0.40 mm)

Warpage limits

Head gasket surface warpage limit	
3.0L V6	0.0031 inch (0.08 mm)
3.7L V6	
End-to-end	0.003 inch (0.076 mm)
Side-to-side	0.002 inch (0.050 mm)

Torque specifications

	Ft-lbs (unless otherwise indicated)	Nm

➡ **Note:** One foot-pound (ft-lb) of torque is equivalent to 12 inch-pounds (in-lbs) of torque. Torque values below approximately 15 foot-pounds are expressed in inch-pounds, because most foot-pound torque wrenches are not accurate at these smaller values.

	Ft-lbs (unless otherwise indicated)	Nm
Camshaft bearing cap bolts	89 in-lbs	10
Camshaft oil seal retainer bolts (3.0L V6 engine)	89 in-lbs	10
Camshaft sprocket bolt		
Step 1	30	40
Step 2	Loosen one full turn (360-degrees)	
Step 3	89 in-lbs	10
Step 4	Tighten an additional 90-degrees	
Crankshaft pulley bolt		
Step 1		
3.0L engine	88.5	120
3.7L engine	103	140
Step 2	Loosen one full turn (360-degrees)	
Step 3	37	50
Step 4	Tighten an additional 90-degrees	
Cylinder head bolts		
3.0L engine (in sequence - see illustration 11.20a)		
Step 1	28	38
Step 2	Tighten an additional 90-degrees	
Step 3	Loosen one full turn (360-degrees)	
Step 4	28	38
Step 5	Tighten an additional 90-degrees	
Step 6	Tighten an additional 90-degrees	

Torque specifications (continued)	Ft-lbs (unless otherwise indicated)	Nm
Cylinder head bolts (continued)		
3.7L engine		
Main bolts (in sequence - see illustration 11.20b)		
Step 1	15	20
Step 2	26	35
Step 3	Tighten an additional 90-degrees	
Step 4	Tighten an additional 90-degrees	
Step 5	Tighten an additional 90-degrees	
M6 bolt (at front of cylinder head)	89 in-lbs	10
Drivebelt tensioner bolt	18	24
Driveplate-to-crankshaft bolts	59	80
Exhaust manifold/catalytic converter nuts		
3.0L V6	18	24
3.7L V6		
Step 1	15	20
Step 2	18	24
Exhaust manifold heat shield		
Black color bolts	18	24
Silver color bolts	109 in-lbs	12
Flywheel-to-crankshaft bolts		
2008 and earlier models	60	81
2009 and later models	82	111
Intake manifold assembly (in sequence - see illustrations in Section 5)		
Upper intake manifold bolts	89 in-lbs	10
Lower intake manifold bolts	89 in-lbs	10
Oil pan bolts		
3.0L V6 engine		
To engine block	18	24
To transaxle	35	47
3.7L V6 engine		
Step 1, bolts 10 ,11, 13, 14	27 in-lbs	3
Step 2	Loosen 1/2-turn (180-degrees)	
Step 3	Align oil pan with rear of cylinder block	
Step 4, bolts 10 ,11, 13, 14	27 in-lbs	3
Step 5, bolts 1 through 14	18	24
Step 6, bolts 15 and 16	89 in-lbs	10
Oil pump screen cover and tube bolts	89 in-lbs	10
Oil pump-to-engine block bolts	89 in-lbs	10
Oil pan baffle bolts		
Step 1		
Smaller nuts	44 in-lbs	5
Larger nuts	132 in-lbs	15
Step 2	Tighten all 8 nuts an additional 45-degrees	
Timing chain cover bolts		
3.0L engines (in sequence - see illustration 8.21)	18	24

Torque specifications (continued)   Ft-lbs (unless otherwise indicated)   Nm

Timing chain cover bolts (continued)

3.7L engines (in sequence - see illustration 8.22)

	Ft-lbs	Nm
Step 1, bolts 1 through 6	89 in-lbs	10
Step 2, bolts 7 through 9	133 in-lbs	15
Step 3, bolts 1 through 6	18	24
Step 4, bolts 7 through 9	55	75
Step 5, bolts 10 through 25	89 in-lbs	10
Step 6, bolts 10 through 25	18	24

Timing chain guides

	Ft-lbs	Nm
3.0L V6 engine	18	24
3.7L V6 engine	89 in-lbs	10

Timing chain tensioner arm bolts

	Ft-lbs	Nm
3.0L V6 engine	18	24
3.7L V6 engine	89 in-lbs 10	

Timing chain tensioner bolts

	Ft-lbs	Nm
3.0L V6 engine	18	24
3.7L V6 engine	89 in-lbs	10

Valve cover bolts (in sequence - see illustrations in Section 4)   89 in-lbs   10

Variable Camshaft Timing (VCT)

Actuator bolt

	Ft-lbs	Nm
Step 1	30	40
Step 2	Tighten an additional 90-degrees	
Assembly (housing)	18	24
Solenoid	89 in-lbs	10

➡ **Refer to Chapter 2, Part C for additional torque specifications**

Section

Reference to other Chapters

CHECK ENGINE light on - See Chapter 6

2C

GENERAL ENGINE OVERHAUL PROCEDURES

1 General information - engine overhaul

▶ **Refer to illustrations 1.1, 1.2, 1.3, 1.4, 1.5 and 1.6**

Included in this portion of Chapter 2 are general information and diagnostic testing procedures for determining the overall mechanical condition of your engine.

The information ranges from advice concerning preparation for an overhaul and the purchase of replacement parts and/or components to detailed, step-by-step procedures covering removal and installation.

The following Sections have been written to help you determine whether your engine needs to be overhauled and how to remove and install it once you've determined it needs to be rebuilt. For information concerning in-vehicle engine repair, see Chapter 2A or 2B.

It's not always easy to determine when, or if, an engine should be completely overhauled, because a number of factors must be considered.

High mileage is not necessarily an indication that an overhaul is needed, while low mileage doesn't preclude the need for an overhaul. Frequency of servicing is probably the most important consideration. An engine that's had regular and frequent oil and filter changes, as well as other required maintenance, will most likely give many thousands of miles of reliable service. Conversely, a neglected engine may require an overhaul very early in its service life.

Excessive oil consumption is an indication that piston rings, valve seals and/or valve guides are in need of attention. Make sure that oil leaks aren't responsible before deciding that the rings and/or guides are bad. Perform a cylinder compression check to determine the extent of the work required (see Section 3). Also check the vacuum readings under various conditions (see Section 4).

Check the oil pressure with a gauge installed in place of the oil pressure sending unit and compare it to this Chapter's Specifications (see Section 2). If it's extremely low, the bearings and/or oil pump are probably worn out.

Loss of power, rough running, knocking or metallic engine noises, excessive valve train noise and high fuel consumption rates may also point to the need for an overhaul, especially if they're all present at the same time. If a complete tune-up doesn't remedy the situation, major mechanical work is the only solution.

An engine overhaul involves restoring the internal parts to the specifications of a new engine. During an overhaul, the piston rings are replaced and the cylinder walls are reconditioned (rebored and/or honed) (see illustrations 1.1 and 1.2). If a rebore is done by an automotive machine shop, new oversize pistons will also be installed. The main bearings and connecting rod bearings are generally replaced with new ones and, if necessary, the crankshaft may be reground to restore the journals (see illustration 1.3). Generally, the valves are serviced as well, since they're usually in less-than-perfect condition at this point. While the engine is being overhauled, other components, such as the starter and alternator, can be rebuilt as well. The end result should be a like-new engine that will give many trouble-free miles.

➡ **Note: Critical cooling system components such as the hoses, drivebelts, thermostat and water pump should be replaced with new parts when an engine is overhauled. The radiator should be checked carefully to ensure that it isn't clogged or leaking (see Chapter 3). If you purchase a rebuilt engine or short block, some rebuilders will not warranty their engines unless the radiator has been professionally flushed. Also, we don't recommend overhauling the oil pump - always install a new one when an engine is rebuilt.**

1.1 An engine block being bored. An engine rebuilder will use special machinery to recondition the cylinder bores

1.2 If the cylinders are bored, the machine shop will normally hone the engine on a machine like this

1.3 A crankshaft having a main bearing journal ground

1.4 A machinist checks for a bent connecting rod, using specialized equipment

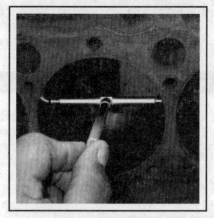

1.5 A bore gauge being used to check the main bearing bore

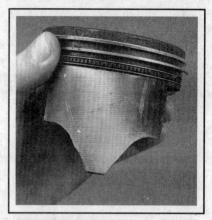

1.6 Uneven piston wear like this indicates a bent connecting rod

Overhauling the internal components on today's engines is a difficult and time-consuming task that requires a significant amount of specialty tools and is best left to a professional engine rebuilder (see illustrations 1.4, 1.5 and 1.6). A competent engine rebuilder will handle the inspection of your old parts and offer advice concerning the reconditioning or replacement of the original engine. Never purchase parts or have machine work done on other components until the block has been thoroughly inspected by a professional machine shop. As a general rule, time is the primary cost of an overhaul, especially since the vehicle may be tied up for a minimum of two weeks or more. Be aware that some engine builders only have the capability to rebuild the engine you bring them while other rebuilders have a large inventory of rebuilt exchange engines in stock. Also be aware that many machine shops could take as much as two weeks time to completely rebuild your engine depending on shop workload. Sometimes it makes more sense to simply exchange your engine for another engine that's already rebuilt to save time.

2 Oil pressure check

▶ **Refer to illustrations 2.2 and 2.3**

1   Low engine oil pressure can be a sign of an engine in need of rebuilding. A low oil pressure indicator (often called an "idiot light") is not a test of the oiling system. Such indicators only come on when the oil pressure is dangerously low. Even a factory oil pressure gauge in the instrument panel is only a relative indication, although much better for driver information than a warning light. A better test is with a mechanical (not electrical) oil pressure gauge.

2   Locate the oil pressure sending unit on the engine block:

a) *On four-cylinder engines, the oil pressure sending unit is located on the front of the engine block, threaded into the oil filter adapter.*

b) *On V6 engines, the sending unit is located near the oil filter housing behind the air conditioning compressor, on the front side of the block (see illustration).*

3   Unscrew the oil pressure sending unit and screw in the hose for your oil pressure gauge (see illustration). If necessary, install an adapter fitting. Use Teflon tape or thread sealant on the threads of the adapter and/or the fitting on the end of your gauge's hose.

2.2 On V6 engines the oil pressure sending unit is located on the front of the engine block behind the air conditioning compressor (3.0L V6 shown)

2.3 The oil pressure can be checked by removing the sending unit and installing a pressure gauge in its place

4   Connect an accurate tachometer to the engine, according to the tachometer manufacturer's instructions.

5   Check the oil pressure with the engine running (normal operating temperature) at the specified engine speed, and compare it to this Chapter's Specifications. If it's extremely low, the bearings and/or oil pump are probably worn out.

3   Cylinder compression check

▶ **Refer to illustration 3.6**

1   A compression check will tell you what mechanical condition the upper end of your engine (pistons, rings, valves, head gaskets) is in. Specifically, it can tell you if the compression is down due to leakage caused by worn piston rings, defective valves and seats or a blown head gasket.

➡ **Note: The engine must be at normal operating temperature and the battery must be fully charged for this check.**

2   Begin by cleaning the area around the ignition coils before you remove them (compressed air should be used, if available). The idea is to prevent dirt from getting into the cylinders as the compression check is being done.

3   Remove all of the spark plugs from the engine (see Chapter 1).

4   Remove the air intake duct from the throttle body, then block the throttle wide open.

5   Remove the fuel pump relay (see Chapter 4, Section 2).

6   Install a compression gauge in the spark plug hole (see illustration).

7   Crank the engine over at least seven compression strokes and watch the gauge. The compression should build up quickly in a healthy engine. Low compression on the first stroke, followed by gradually increasing pressure on successive strokes, indicates worn piston rings. A low compression reading on the first stroke, which doesn't build up during successive strokes, indicates leaking valves or a blown head gasket (a cracked head could also be the cause). Deposits on the undersides of the valve heads can also cause low compression. Record the highest gauge reading obtained.

8   Repeat the procedure for the remaining cylinders and compare the results to this Chapter's Specifications.

9   Add some engine oil (about three squirts from a plunger-type oil can) to each cylinder, through the spark plug hole, and repeat the test.

10 If the compression increases after the oil is added, the piston rings are definitely worn. If the compression doesn't increase significantly, the leakage is occurring at the valves or head gasket. Leakage past the valves may be caused by burned valve seats and/or faces or warped, cracked or bent valves.

11 If two adjacent cylinders have equally low compression, there's a strong possibility that the head gasket between them is blown. The appearance of coolant in the combustion chambers or the crankcase would verify this condition.

12 If one cylinder is slightly lower than the others, and the engine has a slightly rough idle, a worn lobe on the camshaft could be the cause.

13 If the compression is unusually high, the combustion chambers are probably coated with carbon deposits. If that's the case, the cylinder head(s) should be removed and decarbonized.

14 If compression is way down or varies greatly between cylinders, it would be a good idea to have a leak-down test performed by an automotive repair shop. This test will pinpoint exactly where the leakage is occurring and how severe it is.

15 After performing the test, don't forget to unblock the throttle plate.

3.6 Use a compression gauge with a threaded fitting for the spark plug hole, not the type that requires hand pressure to maintain the seal

4   Vacuum gauge diagnostic checks

▶ **Refer to illustrations 4.4 and 4.6**

1   A vacuum gauge provides inexpensive but valuable information about what is going on in the engine. You can check for worn rings or cylinder walls, leaking head or intake manifold gaskets, restricted exhaust, stuck or burned valves, weak valve springs, improper ignition or valve timing and ignition problems.

2   Unfortunately, vacuum gauge readings are easy to misinterpret, so they should be used in conjunction with other tests to confirm the diagnosis.

3   Both the absolute readings and the rate of needle movement are important for accurate interpretation. Most gauges measure vacuum in inches of mercury (in-Hg). The following references to vacuum assume the diagnosis is being performed at sea level. As elevation increases (or atmospheric pressure decreases), the reading will decrease. For every 1,000-foot increase in elevation above approximately 2000 feet, the gauge readings will decrease about one inch of mercury.

4   Connect the vacuum gauge directly to the intake manifold vacuum, not to ported (throttle body) vacuum (see illustration). Be sure no hoses are left disconnected during the test or false readings will result.

5   Before you begin the test, allow the engine to warm up completely. Block the wheels and set the parking brake. With the transmission in Park, start the engine and allow it to run at normal idle speed.

Keep your hands and the vacuum gauge clear of the fans and drivebelts.

6   Read the vacuum gauge; an average, healthy engine should normally produce about 17 to 22 in-Hg with a fairly steady needle (see illustration). Refer to the following vacuum gauge readings and what they indicate about the engine's condition:

7   A low steady reading usually indicates a leaking gasket between the intake manifold and cylinder head(s) or throttle body, a leaky vacuum hose, late ignition timing or incorrect camshaft timing. Check ignition timing with a timing light and eliminate all other possible causes, utilizing the tests provided in this Chapter before you remove the timing belt cover to check the timing marks.

8   If the reading is three to eight inches below normal and it fluctuates at that low reading, suspect an intake manifold gasket leak at an intake port or a faulty fuel injector.

9   If the needle has regular drops of about two-to-four inches at a steady rate, the valves are probably leaking. Perform a compression check or leak-down test to confirm this.

10   An irregular drop or down-flick of the needle can be caused by a

4.4 A simple vacuum gauge can be handy in diagnosing engine condition and performance

sticking valve or an ignition misfire. Perform a compression check or leak-down test and read the spark plugs.

11   A rapid vibration of about four in-Hg variation at idle combined

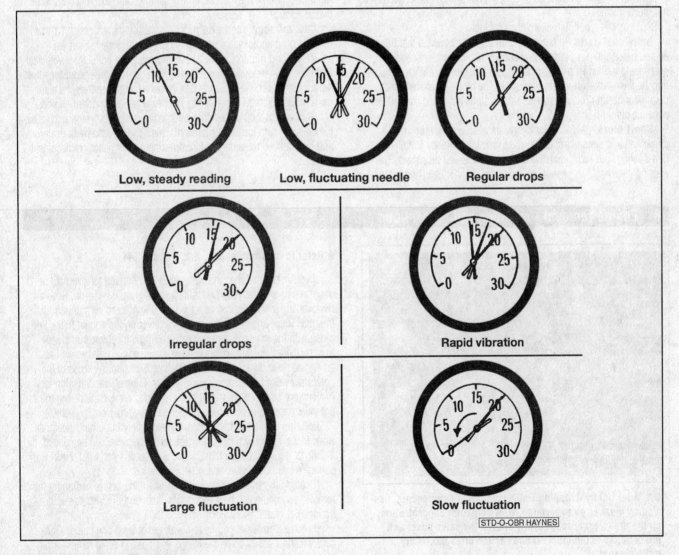

Low, steady reading   Low, fluctuating needle   Regular drops

Irregular drops   Rapid vibration

Large fluctuation   Slow fluctuation

STD-O-OBR HAYNES

4.6 Typical vacuum gauge readings

with exhaust smoke indicates worn valve guides. Perform a leak-down test to confirm this. If the rapid vibration occurs with an increase in engine speed, check for a leaking intake manifold gasket or head gasket, weak valve springs, burned valves or ignition misfire.

12 A slight fluctuation, say one inch up and down, may mean ignition problems. Check all the usual tune-up items and, if necessary, run the engine on an ignition analyzer.

13 If there is a large fluctuation, perform a compression or leakdown test to look for a weak or dead cylinder or a blown head gasket.

14 If the needle moves slowly through a wide range, check for a clogged PCV system, incorrect idle fuel mixture, throttle body or intake manifold gasket leaks.

15 Check for a slow return after revving the engine by quickly snapping the throttle open until the engine reaches about 2,500 rpm and let it shut. Normally the reading should drop to near zero, rise above normal idle reading (about 5 in-Hg over) and then return to the previous idle reading. If the vacuum returns slowly and doesn't peak when the throttle is snapped shut, the rings may be worn. If there is a long delay, look for a restricted exhaust system (often the muffler or catalytic converter). An easy way to check this is to temporarily disconnect the exhaust ahead of the suspected part and redo the test.

5 Engine rebuilding alternatives

The do-it-yourselfer is faced with a number of options when purchasing a rebuilt engine. The major considerations are cost, warranty, parts availability and the time required for the rebuilder to complete the project. The decision to replace the engine block, piston/connecting rod assemblies and crankshaft depends on the final inspection results of your engine. Only then can you make a cost effective decision whether to have your engine overhauled or simply purchase an exchange engine for your vehicle.

Some of the rebuilding alternatives include:

Individual parts - If the inspection procedures reveal that the engine block and most engine components are in reusable condition, purchasing individual parts and having a rebuilder rebuild your engine may be the most economical alternative. The block, crankshaft and piston/connecting rod assemblies should all be inspected carefully by a machine shop first.

Short block - A short block consists of an engine block with a crankshaft and piston/connecting rod assemblies already installed. All new bearings are incorporated and all clearances will be correct. The existing camshafts, valve train components, cylinder head and external parts can be bolted to the short block with little or no machine shop work necessary.

Long block - A long block consists of a short block plus an oil pump, oil pan, cylinder head, valve cover, camshaft and valve train components, timing sprockets and belt or gears and timing cover. All components are installed with new bearings, seals and gaskets incorporated throughout. The installation of manifolds and external parts is all that's necessary.

Low mileage used engines - Some companies now offer low mileage used engines that are a very cost effective way to get your vehicle up and running again. These engines often come from vehicles that have been in totaled in accidents or come from other countries that have a higher vehicle turn over rate. A low mileage used engine also usually has a similar warranty like the newly remanufactured engines.

Give careful thought to which alternative is best for you and discuss the situation with local automotive machine shops, auto parts dealers and experienced rebuilders before ordering or purchasing replacement parts.

6 Engine removal - methods and precautions

6.1 After tightly wrapping water-vulnerable components, use a spray cleaner on everything, with particular concentration on the greasiest areas, usually around the valve cover and lower edges of the block. If one section dries out, apply more cleaner

♦ **Refer to illustrations 6.1, 6.2, 6.3 and 6.4**

If you've decided that an engine must be removed for overhaul or major repair work, several preliminary steps should be taken. Read all removal and installation procedures carefully prior to committing to this job. These engines are removed by lowering the engine to the floor, along with the transmission, and then raising the vehicle sufficiently to slide the assembly out; this will require a vehicle hoist as well as an engine hoist. Make sure the engine hoist is rated in excess of the combined weight of the engine and transmission. A transmission jack is also very helpful. Safety is of primary importance, considering the potential hazards involvved in removing the engine from the vehicle.

Locating a suitable place to work is extremely important. Adequate work space, along with storage space for the vehicle, will be needed. If a shop or garage isn't available, at the very least a flat, level, clean work surface made of concrete or asphalt is required.

Cleaning the engine compartment and engine before beginning the removal procedure will help keep tools clean and organized (see illustrations 6.1 and 6.2).

If you're a novice at engine removal, get at least one helper. One person cannot easily do all the things you need to do to remove a big heavy engine and transmission assembly from the engine compartment.

6.2 Depending on how dirty the engine is, let the cleaner soak in according to the directions and then hose off the grime and cleaner. Get the rinse water down into every area you can get at; then dry important components with a hair dryer or paper towels

6.3 Get an engine stand sturdy enough to firmly support the engine while you're working on it. Stay away from three-wheeled models: they have a tendency to tip over more easily, so get a four-wheeled unit

Also helpful is to seek advice and assistance from someone who's experienced in engine removal.

Plan the operation ahead of time. Arrange for or obtain all of the tools and equipment you'll need prior to beginning the job (see illustrations 6.3 and 6.4). Some of the equipment necessary to perform engine removal and installation safely and with relative ease are (in addition to a vehicle hoist and an engine hoist) a heavy duty floor jack (preferably fitted with a transmission jack head adapter), complete sets of wrenches and sockets as described in the front of this manual, wooden blocks, plenty of rags and cleaning solvent for mopping up spilled oil, coolant and gasoline.

Plan for the vehicle to be out of use for quite a while. A machine shop can do the work that is beyond the scope of the home mechanic. Machine shops often have a busy schedule, so before removing the engine, consult the shop for an estimate of how long it will take to rebuild or repair the components that may need work.

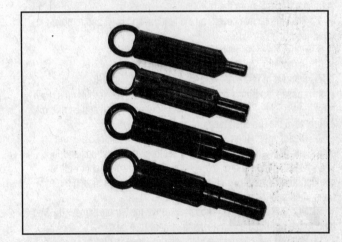

6.4 A clutch alignment tool is necessary if you plan to install a rebuilt engine mated to a manual transaxle

7 Engine - removal and installation

✳✳ WARNING:

The models covered by this manual are equipped with Supplemental Restraint systems (SRS), more commonly known as airbags. Always disable the airbag system before working in the vicinity of airbag system components to avoid the possibility of accidental deployment of the airbag, which could cause personal injury (see Chapter 12).

✳✳ WARNING:

Gasoline is extremely flammable, so take extra precautions when you work on any part of the fuel system. Don't smoke or allow open flames or bare light bulbs near the work area, and don't work in a garage where a gas-type appliance (such as a water heater or clothes dryer) is present. Since gasoline is carcinogenic, wear fuel-resistant gloves when there's a possibility of being exposed to fuel, and, if you spill any fuel on your skin, rinse it off immediately with soap and water. Mop up any spills immediately and dvo not store fuel-soaked rags where they could ignite. The fuel system is under constant pressure, so, if any fuel lines are to be disconnected, the fuel pressure in the system must be relieved first (see Chapter 4 for more information). When you perform any kind of work on the fuel system, wear safety glasses and have a Class B type fire extinguisher on hand.

✱✱ WARNING:

The engine must be completely cool before beginning this procedure.

➡ **Note: Engine removal on these models is a difficult job, especially for the do-it-yourself mechanic working at home. Because of the vehicle's design, the manufacturer states that the engine and transaxle have to be removed as a unit from the bottom of the vehicle, not the top. With a floor jack and jackstands, the vehicle can't be raised high enough and supported safely enough for the engine/transaxle assembly to slide out from underneath. The manufacturer recommends that removal of the engine/transaxle assembly only be performed on a vehicle hoist.**

REMOVAL

1   Have the air conditioning system discharged by an automotive air conditioning technician.

2   Park the vehicle on a frame-contact type vehicle hoist. The pads of the hoist arms must contact the body welt along each side of the vehicle.

3   Relieve the fuel system pressure (see Chapter 4), then disconnect the negative cable from the battery.

4   Place protective covers on the fenders and cowl and remove the hood (see Chapter 11).

5   Remove the air filter housing (see Chapter 4).

6   Remove the cowl panels (see Chapter 11).

7   Remove the battery and battery tray (see Chapter 5).

8   Loosen the front wheel lug nuts and the driveaxle/hub nuts, then raise the vehicle on the hoist. Drain the cooling system and engine oil and remove the drivebelt (see Chapter 1).

9   Clearly label, then disconnect all vacuum lines, coolant and emissions hoses, wiring harness connectors, ground straps and fuel lines. Masking tape and/or a touch up paint applicator work well for marking items (see illustration). Take instant photos or sketch the locations of components and brackets.

10   On 2009 and later V6 models, remove the wiring harness-to-body bolt, to the right of the engine compartment fuse box.

11   Remove the alternator and the starter (see Chapter 5).

12   Remove the power steering pump (see Chapter 10).

13   Remove the engine cooling fan, radiator support (2008 and earlier models) and the radiator (see Chapter 3).

14   Disconnect the shift cable(s) from the transaxle (see Chapter 7A or 7B). Also disconnect any wiring harness connectors from the transaxle.

15   Remove the air conditioning compressor (see Chapter 3).

16   Detach the steering column shaft from the steering gear (see Chapter 10).

17   If equipped with a manual transaxle, disconnect the clutch release cylinder from the transaxle (see Chapter 8).

18   Detach the exhaust pipe(s) from the exhaust manifold(s) (see Chapter 4).

19   Detach all wiring harnesses and hoses from between the engine/transaxle and the chassis. Be sure to mark all connectors to facilitate reassembly.

20   Remove the driveaxles (see Chapter 8).

21   Detach the stabilizer bar links from the bar, separate the lower control arms from the steering knuckles and detach the shock absorber damper forks from the front lower control arms. Also detach the tie-rod ends from the steering knuckles (see Chapter 10).

22   On automatic transaxle models, mark the relationship of the torque converter to the driveplate, then remove the torque converter-to-driveplate nuts (see Chapter 7B).

23   Remove the roll restrictor between the lower rear part of the engine and the subframe.

24   Attach a lifting sling or chain to the engine. Position an engine hoist and connect the sling to it. If no lifting hooks or brackets are present, you'll have to fasten the chains or slings to some substantial part of the engine - ones that are strong enough to take the weight, but in locations that will provide good balance. Take up the slack until there is slight tension on the sling or chain. Position the chain on the hoist so it balances the engine and the transaxle level with the vehicle.

25   Mark the position of each corner of the subframe to the chassis. Support the subframe with two floor jacks, then remove the fasteners and lower the subframe. Remove it from underneath the vehicle.

26   Remove the transaxle mount and the engine mount.

27   Recheck to be sure nothing except the mounts are still connecting the engine to the vehicle or to the transaxle. Disconnect and label anything still remaining.

28   Slowly lower the engine/transaxle from the vehicle.

29   Once the powertrain is on the floor, disconnect the engine lifting hoist and raise the vehicle hoist.

30   Reconnect the chain or sling and raise the engine/transaxle with the hoist. Support the transaxle with a jack (preferably one with a transmission jack head adapter). Separate the engine from the transaxle (see Chapter 7).

31   Remove the flywheel/driveplate and mount the engine on a stand.

INSTALLATION

➡ **Note: The manufacturer recommends replacing all subframe and suspension fasteners with new ones whenever they are loosened or removed.**

32   Installation is the reverse of removal, noting the following points:

  a) *Check the engine/transaxle mounts. If they're worn or damaged, replace them.*

  b) *Attach the transaxle to the engine following the procedure described in Chapter 7.*

  c) *Add coolant, oil, power steering and transmission fluids as needed (see Chapter 1).*

  d) *Align the subframe reference marks before tightening the bolts.*

  e) *Tighten the subframe mounting fasteners to the torque listed in the Chapter 10 Specifications.*

  f) *Reconnect the negative battery cable (see Chapter 5).*

  g) *Run the engine and check for proper operation and leaks. Shut off the engine and recheck fluid levels.*

  h) *Have the air conditioning system re-charged and leak tested by the shop that discharged it.*

8 Engine overhaul - disassembly sequence

1   It's much easier to remove the external components if it's mounted on a portable engine stand. A stand can often be rented quite cheaply from an equipment rental yard. Before the engine is mounted on a stand, the flywheel/driveplate should be removed from the engine.

2   If a stand isn't available, it's possible to remove the external engine components with it blocked up on the floor. Be extra careful not to tip or drop the engine when working without a stand.

3   If you're going to obtain a rebuilt engine, all external components must come off first, to be transferred to the replacement engine. These components include:

Clutch and flywheel (models with manual transaxle)
Driveplate (models with automatic transaxle)
Crankshaft position sensor ring
Emissions-related components
Engine mounts and mount brackets
Intake/exhaust manifolds

Fuel injection components
Oil filter
Ignition coils and spark plugs
Thermostat and housing assembly
Water pump

➡ **Note: When removing the external components from the engine, pay close attention to details that may be helpful or important during installation. Note the installed position of gaskets, seals, spacers, pins, brackets, washers, bolts and other small items.**

4   If you're going to obtain a short block (assembled engine block, crankshaft, pistons and connecting rods), remove the timing chain, cylinder head, oil pan, oil pump pick-up tube, oil pump and water pump from your engine so that you can turn in your old short block to the rebuilder as a core. See *Engine rebuilding alternatives* for additional information regarding the different possibilities to be considered.

9 Pistons and connecting rods - removal and installation

REMOVAL

▶ **Refer to illustrations 9.1, 9.3 and 9.4**

➡ **Note: Prior to removing the piston/connecting rod assemblies, remove the cylinder head and oil pan (see Chapter 2A).**

1   Use your fingernail to feel if a ridge has formed at the upper limit of ring travel (about 1/4-inch down from the top of each cylinder). If carbon deposits or cylinder wear have produced ridges, they must be completely removed with a special tool (see illustration). Follow the manufacturer's instructions provided with the tool. Failure to remove the ridges before attempting to remove the piston/connecting rod assemblies may result in piston breakage.

2   After the cylinder ridges have been removed, turn the engine so the crankshaft is facing up. On four-cylinder engines, remove the balance shaft assembly (see Section 13). On 3.7L V6 engines, remove the main bearing cap support brace.

3   Before the main bearing caps or main-bearing support bridge and connecting rods are removed, check the connecting rod endplay with feeler gauges. Slide them between the first connecting rod and the crankshaft throw until the play is removed (see illustration). Repeat this procedure for each connecting rod. The endplay is equal to the thickness of the feeler gauge(s). Check with an automotive machine shop for the endplay service limit (a typical end play limit should measure between 0.005 to 0.015 inch [0.127 to 0.381 mm]). If the play exceeds the service limit, new connecting rods will be required. If new rods (or a new crankshaft) are installed, the endplay may fall under the minimum allowable. If it does, the rods will have to be machined to restore it. If necessary, consult an automotive machine shop for advice.

9.1 Before you try to remove the pistons, use a ridge reamer to remove the raised material (ridge) from the top of the cylinders

9.3 Checking the connecting rod endplay (side clearance)

9.4 If the connecting rods and caps are not marked, use permanent ink or paint to mark the caps to the rods by cylinder number (for example, this would be the No. 4 connecting rod)

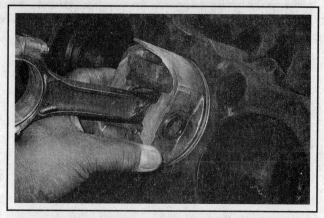

9.13 Install the piston ring into the cylinder then push it down into position using a piston so the ring will be square in the cylinder

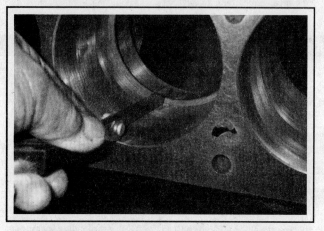

9.14 With the ring square in the cylinder, measure the ring end gap with a feeler gauge

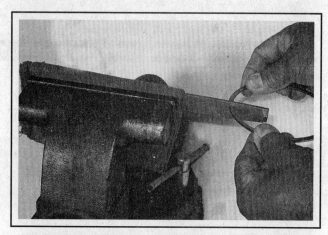

9.15 If the ring end gap is too small, clamp a file in a vise as shown and file the piston ring ends - be sure to remove all raised material

4   Check the connecting rods and caps for identification marks. If they aren't plainly marked, use paint or marker to clearly identify each rod and cap (1, 2, 3, etc., depending on the cylinder they're associated with) (see illustration).

5   Loosen each of the connecting rod cap bolts 1/2-turn at a time until they can be removed by hand.

➡ **Note: New connecting rod cap bolts must be used when reassembling the engine, but save the old bolts for use when checking the connecting rod bearing oil clearance.**

6   Remove the number one connecting rod cap and bearing insert. Don't drop the bearing insert out of the cap.

7   Remove the bearing insert and push the connecting rod/piston assembly out through the top of the engine. Use a wooden or plastic hammer handle to push on the upper bearing surface in the connecting rod. If resistance is felt, double-check to make sure that all of the ridge was removed from the cylinder.

8   Repeat the procedure for the remaining cylinders.

9   After removal, reassemble the connecting rod caps and bearing inserts in their respective connecting rods and install the cap bolts finger tight. Leaving the old bearing inserts in place until reassembly will help prevent the connecting rod bearing surfaces from being accidentally nicked or gouged.

10   The pistons and connecting rods are now ready for inspection and overhaul at an automotive machine shop.

PISTON RING INSTALLATION

▶ **Refer to illustrations 9.13, 9.14, 9.15, 9.19a, 9.19b and 9.22**

11   Before installing the new piston rings, the ring end gaps must be checked. It's assumed that the piston ring side clearance has been checked and verified correct.

12   Lay out the piston/connecting rod assemblies and the new ring sets so the ring sets will be matched with the same piston and cylinder during the end gap measurement and engine assembly.

13   Insert the top (number one) ring into the first cylinder and square it up with the cylinder walls by pushing it in with the top of the piston (see illustration). The ring should be near the bottom of the cylinder, at the lower limit of ring travel.

14   To measure the end gap, slip feeler gauges between the ends of the ring until a gauge equal to the gap width is found (see illustration). The feeler gauge should slide between the ring ends with a slight amount of drag. A typical ring gap should fall between 0.010 and 0.020 inch (0.25 to 0.50 mm) for compression rings and up to 0.030 inch (0.76 mm) for the oil ring steel rails. If the gap is larger or smaller than specified, double-check to make sure you have the correct rings before proceeding.

15   If the gap is too small, it must be enlarged or the ring ends may

9.19a Installing the spacer/expander in the oil ring groove

9.19b DO NOT use a piston ring installation tool when installing the oil control side rails

come in contact with each other during engine operation, which can cause serious damage to the engine. If necessary, increase the end gaps by filing the ring ends very carefully with a fine file. Mount the file in a vise equipped with soft jaws, slip the ring over the file with the ends contacting the file face and slowly move the ring to remove material from the ends. When performing this operation, file only by pushing the ring from the outside end of the file towards the vise (see illustration).

16 Excess end gap isn't critical unless it's greater than 0.040 inch (1.01 mm). Again, double-check to make sure you have the correct ring type.

17 Repeat the procedure for each ring that will be installed in the first cylinder and for each ring in the remaining cylinders. Remember to keep rings, pistons and cylinders matched up.

18 Once the ring end gaps have been checked/corrected, the rings can be installed on the pistons.

19 The oil control ring (lowest one on the piston) is usually installed first. It's composed of three separate components. Slip the spacer/expander into the groove (see illustration). If an anti-rotation tang is used, make sure it's inserted into the drilled hole in the ring groove. Next, install the upper side rail in the same manner (see illustration). Don't use a piston ring installation tool on the oil ring side rails, as they may be damaged. Instead, place one end of the side rail into the groove between the spacer/expander and the ring land, hold it firmly in place and slide a finger around the piston while pushing the rail into the groove. Finally, install the lower side rail.

20 After the three oil ring components have been installed, check to make sure that both the upper and lower side rails can be rotated smoothly inside the ring grooves.

21 The number two (middle) ring is installed next. It's usually stamped with a mark which must face up, toward the top of the piston. Do not mix up the top and middle rings, as they have different cross-sections.

➡ **Note: Always follow the instructions printed on the ring package or box - different manufacturers may require different approaches.**

22 Use a piston ring installation tool and make sure the identification mark is facing the top of the piston, then slip the ring into the middle groove on the piston (see illustration). Don't expand the ring any more than necessary to slide it over the piston.

23 Install the number one (top) ring in the same manner. Make sure the mark is facing up. Be careful not to confuse the number one and number two rings.

24 Repeat the procedure for the remaining pistons and rings.

9.22 Use a piston ring installation tool to install the number 2 and the number 1 (top) rings - be sure the directional mark on the piston ring(s) is facing toward the top of the piston

INSTALLATION

25 Before installing the piston/connecting rod assemblies, the cylinder walls must be perfectly clean, the top edge of each cylinder bore must be chamfered, and the crankshaft must be in place.

26 Remove the cap from the end of the number one connecting rod (refer to the marks made during removal). Remove the original bearing inserts and wipe the bearing surfaces of the connecting rod and cap with a clean, lint-free cloth. They must be kept spotlessly clean.

Connecting rod bearing oil clearance check

▶ **Refer to illustrations 9.30, 9.35, 9.37 and 9.41**

27 Clean the back side of the new upper bearing insert, then lay it in place in the connecting rod.

28 Make sure the tab on the bearing fits into the recess in the rod. Don't hammer the bearing insert into place and be very careful not to nick or gouge the bearing face. Don't lubricate the bearing at this time.

29 Clean the back side of the other bearing insert and install it in the rod cap. Again, make sure the tab on the bearing fits into the recess in the cap, and don't apply any lubricant. It's critically important that the mating surfaces of the bearing and connecting rod are perfectly clean and oil free when they're assembled.

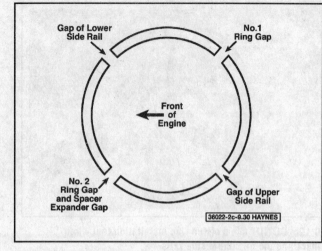

9.30 Position the piston ring end gaps as shown

9.35 Use a plastic or wooden hammer handle to push the piston into the cylinder

30 Position the piston ring gaps at 90-degree intervals around the piston as shown (see illustration).

31 Lubricate the piston and rings with clean engine oil and attach a piston ring compressor to the piston. Leave the skirt protruding about 1/4-inch to guide the piston into the cylinder. The rings must be compressed until they're flush with the piston.

32 Rotate the crankshaft until the number one connecting rod journal is at BDC (bottom dead center) and apply a liberal coat of engine oil to the cylinder walls.

33 With the mark on top of the piston facing the front (timing belt or chain end) of the engine, gently insert the piston/connecting rod assembly into the number one cylinder bore and rest the bottom edge of the ring compressor on the engine block.

34 Tap the top edge of the ring compressor to make sure it's contacting the block around its entire circumference.

35 Gently tap on the top of the piston with the end of a wooden or plastic hammer handle (see illustration) while guiding the end of the connecting rod into place on the crankshaft journal. The piston rings may try to pop out of the ring compressor just before entering the cylinder bore, so keep some downward pressure on the ring compressor. Work slowly, and if any resistance is felt as the piston enters the cylinder, stop immediately. Find out what's hanging up and fix it before

proceeding. Do not, for any reason, force the piston into the cylinder - you might break a ring and/or the piston.

36 Once the piston/connecting rod assembly is installed, the connecting rod bearing oil clearance must be checked before the rod cap is permanently installed.

37 Cut a piece of the appropriate size Plastigage slightly shorter than the width of the connecting rod bearing and lay it in place on the number one connecting rod journal, parallel with the journal axis (see illustration).

38 Clean the connecting rod cap bearing face and install the rod cap. Make sure the mating mark on the cap is on the same side as the mark on the connecting rod (see illustration 9.4).

39 Install the old rod bolts, at this time, and tighten them to the torque listed in this Chapter's Specifications.

➡ **Note: Use a thin-wall socket to avoid erroneous torque readings that can result if the socket is wedged between the rod cap and the bolt head. If the socket tends to wedge itself between the fastener and the cap, lift up on it slightly until it no longer contacts the cap. DO NOT rotate the crankshaft at any time during this operation.**

40 Remove the fasteners and detach the rod cap, being very careful not to disturb the Plastigage.

41 Compare the width of the crushed Plastigage to the scale printed on the Plastigage envelope to obtain the oil clearance (see illustration).

9.37 Place Plastigage on each connecting rod bearing journal parallel to the crankshaft centerline

9.41 Use the scale on the Plastigage package to determine the bearing oil clearance - be sure to measure the widest part of the Plastigage and use the correct scale; it comes with both standard and metric scales

The connecting rod oil clearance is usually about 0.001 to 0.002 inch (0.025 to 0.05 mm). Consult an automotive machine shop for the clearance specified for the rod bearings on your engine. One the covered vehicles, code numbers on the block and crankshaft are used to select the proper bearings, using a chart at a dealership service/parts department.

42 If the clearance is not as specified, the bearing inserts may be the wrong size (which means different ones will be required). Before deciding that different inserts are needed, make sure that no dirt or oil was between the bearing inserts and the connecting rod or cap when the clearance was measured. Also, recheck the journal diameter. If the Plastigage was wider at one end than the other, the journal may be tapered. If the clearance still exceeds the limit specified, the bearing will have to be replaced with an undersize bearing.

✳✳ CAUTION:

When installing a new crankshaft always use a standard size bearing.

Final installation

43 Carefully scrape all traces of the Plastigage material off the rod journal and/or bearing face. Be very careful not to scratch the bearing - use your fingernail or the edge of a plastic card.

44 Make sure the bearing faces are perfectly clean, then apply a uniform layer of clean moly-base grease or engine assembly lube to both of them. You'll have to push the piston into the cylinder to expose the face of the bearing insert in the connecting rod.

45 Slide the connecting rod back into place on the journal, install the rod cap, install the new bolts and tighten them to the torque listed in this Chapter's Specifications.

✳✳ CAUTION:

Install new connecting rod cap bolts. Do NOT reuse old bolts - they have stretched and cannot be reused.

Again, work up to the torque in three steps.

46 Repeat the entire procedure for the remaining pistons/connecting rods.

47 The important points to remember are:
  a) Keep the back sides of the bearing inserts and the insides of the connecting rods and caps perfectly clean when assembling them.
  b) Make sure you have the correct piston/rod assembly for each cylinder.
  c) The mark on the piston must face the front (timing belt end [four-cylinder engine] or timing chain [V6 engine] end) of the engine.
  d) Lubricate the cylinder walls liberally with clean oil.
  e) Lubricate the bearing faces when installing the rod caps after the oil clearance has been checked.

48 After all the piston/connecting rod assemblies have been correctly installed, rotate the crankshaft a number of times by hand to check for any obvious binding.

49 Check the connecting rod endplay (see Step 3). If it was correct before disassembly and the original crankshaft and rods were reinstalled, it should still be correct. If new rods or a new crankshaft were installed, the endplay may be inadequate. If so, the rods will have to be removed and taken to an automotive machine shop for resizing.

10 Crankshaft - removal and installation

REMOVAL

▶ **Refer to illustrations 10.1 and 10.3**

➡ **Note: The crankshaft can be removed only after the engine has been removed from the vehicle. It's assumed that the flywheel or driveplate, crankshaft pulley, timing chain, oil pan, oil pump body, oil filter and piston/connecting rod assemblies have already been removed. The rear main oil seal retainer must be unbolted and separated from the block before proceeding with crankshaft removal.**

1 Before the crankshaft is removed, measure the endplay. Mount a dial indicator with the indicator in line with the crankshaft and just touching the end of the crankshaft as shown (see illustration).

10.1 Checking crankshaft endplay with a dial indicator

ENGINE BEARING ANALYSIS

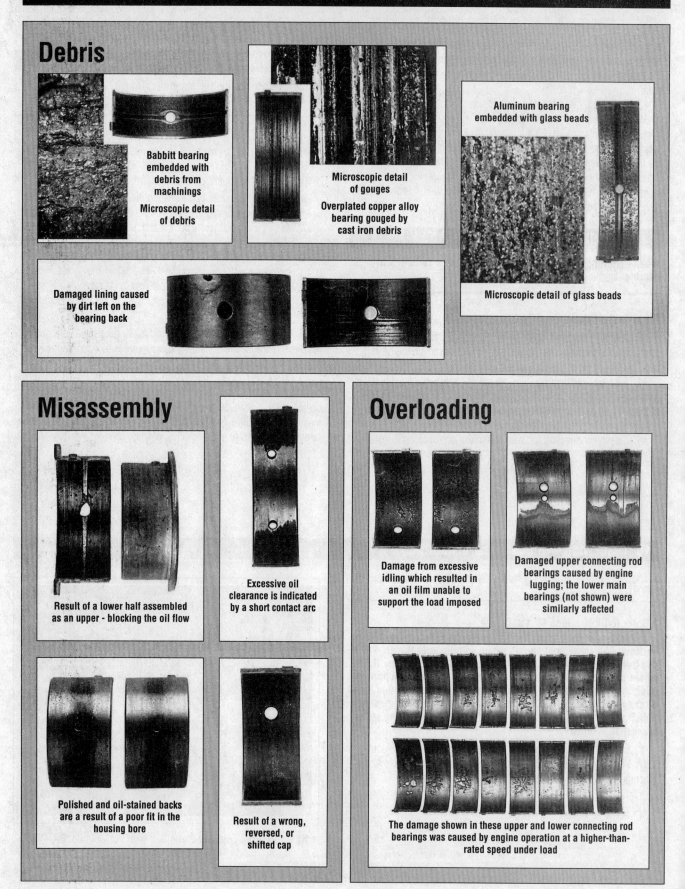

Debris

Babbitt bearing embedded with debris from machinings

Microscopic detail of debris

Microscopic detail of gouges

Overplated copper alloy bearing gouged by cast iron debris

Aluminum bearing embedded with glass beads

Microscopic detail of glass beads

Damaged lining caused by dirt left on the bearing back

Misassembly

Result of a lower half assembled as an upper - blocking the oil flow

Excessive oil clearance is indicated by a short contact arc

Polished and oil-stained backs are a result of a poor fit in the housing bore

Result of a wrong, reversed, or shifted cap

Overloading

Damage from excessive idling which resulted in an oil film unable to support the load imposed

Damaged upper connecting rod bearings caused by engine lugging; the lower main bearings (not shown) were similarly affected

The damage shown in these upper and lower connecting rod bearings was caused by engine operation at a higher-than-rated speed under load

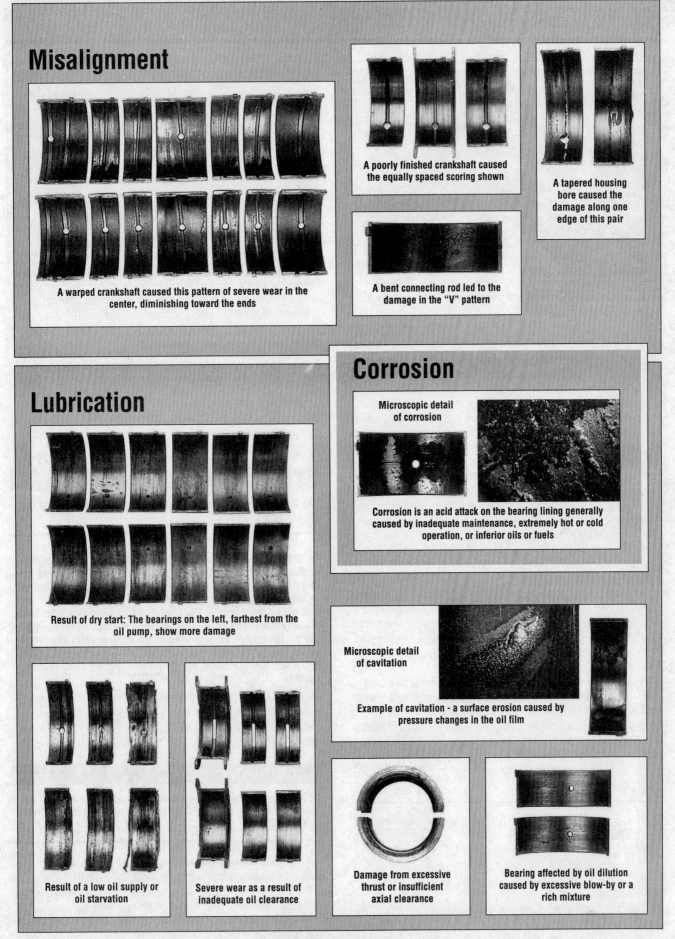

Misalignment

A warped crankshaft caused this pattern of severe wear in the center, diminishing toward the ends

A poorly finished crankshaft caused the equally spaced scoring shown

A bent connecting rod led to the damage in the "V" pattern

A tapered housing bore caused the damage along one edge of this pair

Lubrication

Result of dry start: The bearings on the left, farthest from the oil pump, show more damage

Result of a low oil supply or oil starvation

Severe wear as a result of inadequate oil clearance

Corrosion

Microscopic detail of corrosion

Corrosion is an acid attack on the bearing lining generally caused by inadequate maintenance, extremely hot or cold operation, or inferior oils or fuels

Microscopic detail of cavitation

Example of cavitation - a surface erosion caused by pressure changes in the oil film

Damage from excessive thrust or insufficient axial clearance

Bearing affected by oil dilution caused by excessive blow-by or a rich mixture

10.3 Checking the crankshaft endplay with feeler gauges at the thrust bearing journal

10.17 Place the Plastigage onto the crankshaft bearing journal as shown

2   Pry the crankshaft all the way to the rear and zero the dial indicator. Next, pry the crankshaft to the front as far as possible and check the reading on the dial indicator. The distance traveled is the endplay. A typical crankshaft endplay will fall between 0.003 to 0.010 inch (0.076 to 0.254 mm). If it is greater than that, check the crankshaft thrust surfaces for wear after it's removed. If no wear is evident, new main bearings should correct the endplay.

3   If a dial indicator isn't available, feeler gauges can be used. Gently pry the crankshaft all the way to the front of the engine. Slip feeler gauges between the crankshaft and the front face of the thrust bearing or washer to determine the clearance (see illustration).

4   Loosen the main bearing cap beam bolts (four-cylinder engines), lower cylinder block bolts (3.0L V6 engine) or main bearing cap support brace and main bearing cap bolts (3.7L V6 engine) 1/4-turn at a time each, until they can be removed by hand. Loosen the bolts in the reverse of the tightening sequence (see illustrations 10.19a, 10.19b or 10.19c and 10.19d).

5   On four-cylinder engines, remove the main bearing cap support beam. On 3.0L V6 engines, gently tap the lower cylinder block with a soft-face hammer around its perimeter and pull the lower cylinder block straight up and off the cylinder block. On 3.7L V6 engines, remove the main bearing caps. Try not to drop the bearing inserts if they come out with the assembly.

6   Carefully lift the crankshaft out of the engine. It may be a good idea to have an assistant available, since the crankshaft is quite heavy and awkward to handle. With the bearing inserts in place inside the engine block and main bearing caps or lower cylinder block, reinstall the main bearing caps or lower cylinder block onto the engine block and tighten the bolts finger tight.

INSTALLATION

7   Crankshaft installation is the first step in engine reassembly. It's assumed at this point that the engine block and crankshaft have been cleaned, inspected and repaired or reconditioned.

8   Position the engine block with the bottom facing up.

9   Remove the bolts and lift off the support beam, main bearing caps or lower cylinder block, as applicable.

10 If they're still in place, remove the original bearing inserts. Wipe the bearing surfaces of the block and main bearing cap assembly with a clean, lint-free cloth. They must be kept spotlessly clean. This is critical for determining the correct bearing oil clearance.

Main bearing oil clearance check

▶ **Refer to illustrations 10.17, 10.19a, 10.19b, 10.19c, 10.19d and 10.21**

11 Without mixing them up, clean the back sides of the new upper main bearing inserts (with grooves and oil holes) and lay one in each main bearing saddle in the engine block. Each upper bearing (engine block) has an oil groove and oil hole in it.

✳✳ CAUTION:

The oil holes in the block must line up with the oil holes in the upper bearing inserts.

➡ **Note:** The thrust bearing on four-cylinder engines is located on the engine block number 3 (center) journal. The flanged thrust bearing on 3.0L V6 engines is located on the 4th journal on the lower cylinder block, and there is a thrust washer at the rear of the rear (number four) main saddle on the cylinder block. The thrust washers on 3.7L V6 engines are located on the 4th journal (two upper on each side of the main saddle, one lower on the rear of the main bearing cap). The grooves on shim-type thrust washers must face the crankshaft (not the main bearing saddle).

Clean the back sides of the lower main bearing inserts and lay them in the corresponding location in the main bearing caps or the lower cylinder block. Make sure the tab on the bearing insert fits into its corresponding recess.

✳✳ CAUTION:

Do not hammer the bearing insert into place and don't nick or gouge the bearing faces. DO NOT apply any lubrication at this time.

12 Clean the faces of the bearing inserts in the block and the crankshaft main bearing journals with a clean, lint-free cloth.

13 Check or clean the oil holes in the crankshaft, as any dirt here can go only one way - straight through the new bearings.

14 Once you're certain the crankshaft is clean, carefully lay it in position in the cylinder block.

15 Before the crankshaft can be permanently installed, the main

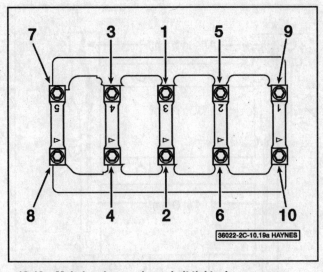

10.19a Main bearing cap beam bolt tightening sequence (four-cylinder engines)

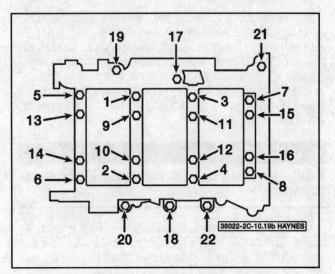

10.19b Lower cylinder block bolt tightening sequence (3.0L V6 engines)

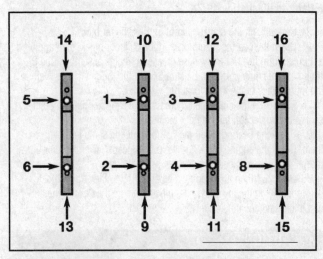

10.19c Main bearing cap bolt tightening sequence (3.7L V6 engines)

bearing oil clearance must be checked.

16 Cut several strips of the appropriate size of Plastigage. They must be slightly shorter than the width of the main bearing journal.

17 Place one piece on each crankshaft main bearing journal, parallel with the journal axis as shown (see illustration).

18 Clean the faces of the bearing inserts in the main bearing caps or the lower cylinder block. Hold the bearing inserts in place and install the caps or the lower cylinder block onto the crankshaft and cylinder block. DO NOT disturb the Plastigage.

19 Apply clean engine oil to all bolt threads prior to installation, then install all bolts finger-tight. Tighten the bolts in the sequence shown (see illustrations) progressing in steps, to the torque listed in this Chapter's Specifications. DO NOT rotate the crankshaft at any time during this operation.

20 Remove the bolts in the reverse order of the tightening sequence and carefully lift the caps or the lower cylinder block straight up and off the block. Do not disturb the Plastigage or rotate the crankshaft.

21 Compare the width of the crushed Plastigage on each journal to the scale printed on the Plastigage envelope to determine the main bearing oil clearance (see illustration). Check with an automotive machine shop for the oil clearance for your engine.

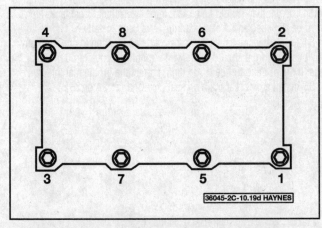

10.19d Main bearing cap support brace, bolt tightening sequence (3.7L V6 engines)

10.21 Use the scale on the Plastigage package to determine the bearing oil clearance - be sure to measure the widest part of the Plastigage and use the correct scale; it comes with both standard and metric scales

22 If the clearance is not as specified, the bearing inserts may be the wrong size (which means different ones will be required). Before deciding if different inserts are needed, make sure that no dirt or oil was between the bearing inserts and the cap assembly or block when the clearance was measured. If the Plastigage was wider at one end than the other, the crankshaft journal may be tapered. If the clearance still exceeds the limit specified, the bearing insert(s) will have to be replaced with an undersize bearing insert(s).

❊❊ CAUTION:

When installing a new crankshaft always install a standard bearing insert set.

23 Carefully scrape all traces of the Plastigage material off the main bearing journals and/or the bearing insert faces. Be sure to remove all residue from the oil holes. Use your fingernail or the edge of a plastic card - don't nick or scratch the bearing faces.

Final installation

▸ **Refer to illustration 10.28**

24 Carefully lift the crankshaft out of the cylinder block.
25 Clean the bearing insert faces in the cylinder block, then apply a thin, uniform layer of moly-base grease or engine assembly lube to each of the bearing surfaces. Be sure to coat the thrust faces as well as the journal face of the thrust bearing.
26 Make sure the crankshaft journals are clean, then lay the crankshaft back in place in the cylinder block.
27 Clean the bearing insert faces and apply the same lubricant to them. Clean the engine block and the bearing caps/lower cylinder block thoroughly. The surfaces must be free of oil residue.
28 On 3.0L V6 engines, apply a bead of RTV to the engine block before installing the lower cylinder block. Be sure the bead is the correct thickness (see illustration).

❊❊ CAUTION:

You have only four minutes to install the lower block mounting bolts and studs. If it takes longer, the lower block will have to be removed, cleaned of all sealant, and the installation procedure repeated.

29 On V6 engines, install the lower cylinder block onto the crankshaft and cylinder block.
30 On four-cylinder engines, install the main bearing caps in their proper locations, with the arrows on the caps facing the front of the engine.
31 Prior to installation, apply clean engine oil to all bolt threads wiping off any excess, then install all bolts finger-tight.

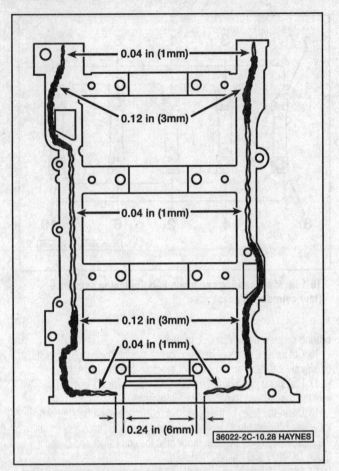

10.28 3.0L V6 engine: Apply RTV sealant to the cylinder block mating surface - make sure the bead of sealant is the correct diameter

32 Tighten the lower cylinder block (3.0L V6 engines), main bearing cap beam (four-cylinder engine) or cap (3.7L V6 engine) bolts, following the correct sequence (see illustrations 10.19a, 10.19b or 10.19c) to the torque listed in this Chapter's Specifications. On 3.7L V6 engines, install the main bearing cap support brace, tightening the bolts in the proper sequence to the torque listed in this Chapter's Specifications (see illustration 10.19d).
33 Recheck the crankshaft endplay with a feeler gauge or a dial indicator. The endplay should be correct if the crankshaft thrust faces aren't worn or damaged and if new bearings have been installed.
34 Rotate the crankshaft a number of times by hand to check for any obvious binding. It should rotate with a running torque of 50 in-lbs or less. If the running torque is too high, correct the problem at this time.
35 Install a new rear main oil seal (see Chapter 2A or 2B).

11 Engine overhaul - reassembly sequence

1   Before beginning engine reassembly, make sure you have all the necessary new parts, gaskets and seals as well as the following items on hand:

Common hand tools
A 1/2-inch drive torque wrench
New engine oil
Gasket sealant
Thread locking compound

2   If you obtained a short block it will be necessary to install the cylinder head, the oil pump and pick-up tube, the oil pan, the water pump, the timing belt and timing cover, and the valve cover (see Chapter 2A or 2B). In order to save time and avoid problems, the external components must be installed in the following general order:

Thermostat and housing cover
Water pump
Intake and exhaust manifolds
Fuel injection components
Emission control components
Spark plugs
Ignition coils
Oil filter
Engine mounts and mount brackets
Clutch and flywheel (manual transaxle)
Driveplate (automatic transaxle)

12 Balance shaft assembly (four-cylinder engines) - removal and installation

1   The balance shaft assembly is bolted to the crankshaft main bearing support beam. A gear on the crankshaft meshes with a gear on the balance shaft assembly. When the engine is operating, the assembly smoothes engine vibrations.

2   The balancer is a precision-machined assembly; there are no serviceable parts inside and it should not be disassembled. If the backlash is out of Specification (see Steps 5 through 8), the assembly must be replaced as a complete unit.

REMOVAL

3   Position the crankshaft at TDC (see Chapter 2A). Remove the four mounting bolts.

4   With the engine turned crankshaft-side-up on the engine stand, lift the assembly straight up from the engine.

INSPECTION

▶ **Refer to illustration 12.6**

5   When the balance shaft assembly is in place, the backlash

between the drive gear (on the crankshaft) and the driven gear on the assembly can be checked. Remove the timing peg.

6   Attach a 5 mm Allen wrench to the top of the driveshaft with the long end of the wrench pointing straight up. Secure a dial-indicator fixture to the engine so that the tip of the indicator is against the top of the wrench (see illustration).

7   Use a pry tool against the crankshaft front counterweight to apply thrust pressure, while turning the crankshaft back-and-forth. Record the measurements of the dial-indicator. Measurements should be taken at the following degrees of engine rotation: 10, 30, 100, 190 and 210 degrees. Compare your results with the allowable range of backlash given in this Chapter's Specifications.

8   If the backlash is out of range, the assembly must be replaced.

INSTALLATION

▶ **Refer to illustration 12.9**

9   When installing the balance shaft assembly, the engine must set to TDC for cylinder number 1. Before installing the assembly, rotate the assembly to align the timing marks on both shafts of the assembly (see

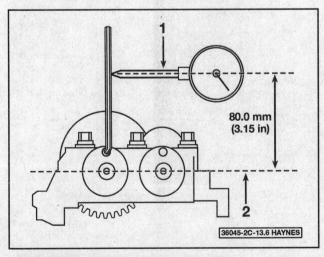

12.6 Method of checking the backlash in the balancer assembly

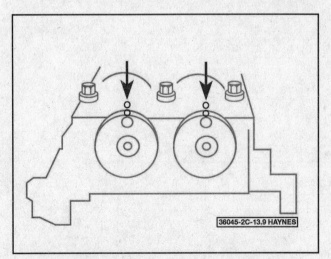

12.9 Remove/install the balance shaft assembly bolts only when the crank is at TDC and these balancer dots align

illustration). Bolt the assembly to the engine and recheck that the timing marks are still aligned and that the crankshaft has not moved. Tighten the bolts in a criss-cross pattern to the torque listed in this Chapter's Specifications.

13 Initial start-up and break-in after overhaul

✳✳ WARNING:

Have a fire extinguisher handy when starting the engine for the first time.

1   Once the engine has been installed in the vehicle, double-check the engine oil and coolant levels.

2   With the spark plugs out of the engine and the fuel pump disabled (see Chapter 4, Section 3), crank the engine until oil pressure registers on the gauge or the light goes out.

3   Install the spark plugs, hook up the plug wires and restore the ignition system and fuel pump functions.

4   Start the engine. It may take a few moments for the fuel system to build up pressure, but the engine should start without a great deal of effort.

5   After the engine starts, it should be allowed to warm up to normal

10 The crankshaft timing peg should remain installed to keep the engine at TDC until installation of the timing chain and sprockets is completed.

operating temperature. While the engine is warming up, make a thorough check for fuel, oil and coolant leaks.

6   Shut the engine off and recheck the engine oil and coolant levels.

7   Drive the vehicle to an area with minimum traffic, accelerate from 30 to 50 mph, then allow the vehicle to slow to 30 mph with the throttle closed. Repeat the procedure 10 or 12 times. This will load the piston rings and cause them to seat properly against the cylinder walls. Check again for oil and coolant leaks.

8   Drive the vehicle gently for the first 500 miles (no sustained high speeds) and keep a constant check on the oil level. It is not unusual for an engine to use oil during the break-in period.

9   At approximately 500 to 600 miles, change the oil and filter.

10 For the next few hundred miles, drive the vehicle normally. Do not pamper it or abuse it.

11 After 2,000 miles, change the oil and filter again and consider the engine broken in.

Specifications

General

Cylinder compression

Lowest cylinder must be within	70% of the highest cylinder
Maximum difference between cylinders	15% of the adjacent cylinders

Oil pressure

Four-cylinder engines, warm, at 3000 rpm

2003 through 2005	57.3 to 94.1 psi (395 to 649 kPa)
2006 through 2008	33.9 to 75.5 psi (234 to 521 kPa)
2009 and later	57.3 to 94.1 psi (395 to 649 kPa)
3.0L V6 engine, warm, at 1500 rpm	20 to 45 psi (138 to 310 kPa)
3.7L V6 engine, warm, at 2000 rpm	45 to 90 psi (310 to 621 kPa)
Balance shaft assembly backlash (four-cylinder engines)	0.00019 to 0.0039 inch (0.005 to 0.099 mm)

Torque specifications — Ft-lbs (unless otherwise indicated)   Nm

➡ **Note: One foot-pound (ft-lb) of torque is equivalent to 12 inch-pounds (in-lbs) of torque. Torque values below approximately 15 foot-pounds are expressed in inch-pounds, because most foot-pound torque wrenches are not accurate at these smaller values.**

Balance shaft assembly mounting bolts (four-cylinder engines)

	Ft-lbs	Nm
Step 1	18	24
Step 2	37	50

Connecting rod bolts

Four-cylinder engines

	Ft-lbs	Nm
Step 1	21	28
Step 2	Tighten an additional 90 degrees	

3.0L V6 engine

	Ft-lbs	Nm
Step 1	17	23
Step 2	32	43
Step 3	Tighten an additional 100 degrees	

3.7L V6 engine   Not available

Main bearing bolts

2.3L four-cylinder engine

110 mm length bolt (Plastic region type)

	Ft-lbs	Nm
Step 1	33	45
Step 3	Tighten an additional 180 degrees	

104 mm length bolts (Elastic region type)

	Ft-lbs	Nm
Step 1	61 in-lbs	7
Step 2	19	26
Step 3	30	40
Step 4	44 in-lbs	5
Step 5	Loosen all bolts two turns	
Step 6	61 in-lbs	7
Step 7	16	22
Step 8	Tighten an additional 90 degrees	

2.5L four-cylinder engine

	Ft-lbs	Nm
Step 1	44 in-lbs	5
Step 2	18	24
Step 3	Tighten an additional 90 degrees	

➡ **Note: One foot-pound (ft-lb) of torque is equivalent to 12 inch-pounds (in-lbs) of torque. Torque values below approximately 15 foot-pounds are expressed in inch-pounds, because most foot-pound torque wrenches are not accurate at these smaller values.**

Main bearing bolts (continued)
    3.0L V6 engine (lower block)

	Ft-lbs	Nm
Step 1, bolts 1 through 8	18	24
Step 2, bolts 9 through 16	30	40
Step 3, bolts 1 through 16	Tighten an additional 90 degrees	
Step 4, bolts 17 through 22 (side bolts)	18	24
3.7L V6 engine	Not available	

Section

Reference to other Chapters

3

COOLING, HEATING AND AIR CONDITIONING SYSTEMS

1 General information

☀ WARNING:

Do not allow antifreeze to come in contact with your skin or painted surfaces of the vehicle. Rinse off spills immediately with plenty of water. Antifreeze is highly toxic if ingested. Never leave antifreeze lying around in an open container or in puddles on the floor; children and pets are attracted by it's sweet smell and may drink it. Check with local authorities about disposing of used antifreeze. Many communities have collection centers which will see that antifreeze is disposed of safely. Never dump used antifreeze on the ground or pour it into drains.

ENGINE COOLING SYSTEM

All modern vehicles employ a pressurized engine cooling system with thermostatically controlled coolant circulation. The cooling system consists of a radiator, an expansion tank or coolant reservoir, a pressure cap (located on the expansion tank or radiator), a thermostat, a cooling fan, and a water pump.

The water pump circulates coolant through the engine. The coolant flows around each cylinder and around the intake and exhaust ports, near the spark plug areas and in close proximity to the exhaust valve guides.

A thermostat controls engine coolant temperature. During warm up, the closed thermostat prevents coolant from circulating through the radiator. As the engine nears normal operating temperature, the thermostat opens and allows hot coolant to travel through the radiator, where it's cooled before returning to the engine.

HEATING SYSTEM

The heating system consists of a blower fan and heater core located in a housing under the dash, the hoses connecting the heater core to the engine cooling system and the heater/air conditioning control head on the dashboard. Hot engine coolant is circulated through the heater core. When the heater mode is activated, a flap door in the housing opens to expose the heater core to the passenger compartment through air ducts. A fan switch on the control head activates the blower motor, which forces air through the core, heating the air.

AIR CONDITIONING SYSTEM

The air conditioning system consists of a condenser mounted in front of the radiator, an evaporator mounted adjacent to the heater core, a compressor mounted on the engine, a receiver-drier or accumulator and the plumbing connecting all of the above components.

A blower fan forces the warmer air of the passenger compartment through the evaporator core (sort of a radiator-in-reverse), transferring the heat from the air to the refrigerant. The liquid refrigerant boils off into low pressure vapor, taking the heat with it when it leaves the evaporator.

2 Troubleshooting

COOLANT LEAKS

◆ **Refer to illustration 2.2**

1   A coolant leak can develop anywhere in the cooling system, but the most common causes are:
   a) *A loose or weak hose clamp*
   b) *A defective hose*
   c) *A faulty pressure cap*
   d) *A damaged radiator*
   e) *A bad heater core*
   f) *A faulty water pump*
   g) *A leaking gasket at any joint that carries coolant*

2   Coolant leaks aren't always easy to find. Sometimes they can only be detected when the cooling system is under pressure. Here's where a cooling system pressure tester comes in handy. After the engine has cooled completely, the tester is attached in place of the pressure cap, then pumped up to the pressure value equal to that of the pressure cap rating (see illustration). Now, leaks that only exist when the engine is fully warmed up will become apparent. The tester can be left connected to locate a nagging slow leak.

COOLANT LEVEL DROPS, BUT NO EXTERNAL LEAKS

◆ **Refer to illustrations 2.5a and 2.5b**

3   If you find it necessary to keep adding coolant, but there are no

2.2 The cooling system pressure tester is connected in place of the pressure cap, then pumped up to pressurize the system

external leaks, the probable causes include:
   a) *A blown head gasket*
   b) *A leaking intake manifold gasket (only on engines that have coolant passages in the manifold)*
   c) *A cracked cylinder head or cylinder block*

4   Any of the above problems will also usually result in contamination of the engine oil, which will cause it to take on a milkshake-like appearance. A bad head gasket or cracked head or block can also result in engine oil contaminating the cooling system.

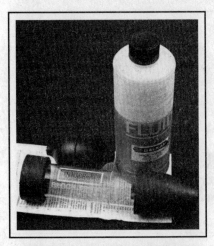

2.5a The combustion leak detector consists of a bulb, syringe and test fluid

2.5b Place the tester over the cooling system filler neck and use the bulb to draw a sample into the tester

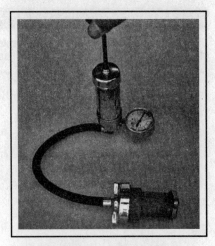

2.8 Checking the cooling system pressure cap with a cooling system pressure tester

5   Combustion leak detectors (also known as block testers) are available at most auto parts stores. These work by detecting exhaust gases in the cooling system, which indicates a compression leak from a cylinder into the coolant. The tester consists of a large bulb-type syringe and bottle of test fluid (see illustration). A measured amount of the fluid is added to the syringe. The syringe is placed over the cooling system filler neck and, with the engine running, the bulb is squeezed and a sample of the gases present in the cooling system are drawn up through the test fluid (see illustration). If any combustion gases are present in the sample taken, the test fluid will change color.

6   If the test indicates combustion gas is present in the cooling system, you can be sure that the engine has a blown head gasket or a crack in the cylinder head or block, and will require disassembly to repair.

PRESSURE CAP

▶ **Refer to illustration 2.8**

> ⁂ **WARNING:**

Wait until the engine is completely cool before beginning this check.

7   The cooling system is sealed by a spring-loaded cap, which raises the boiling point of the coolant. If the cap's seal or spring are worn out, the coolant can boil and escape past the cap. With the engine completely cool, remove the cap and check the seal; if it's cracked, hardened or deteriorated in any way, replace it with a new one.

8   Even if the seal is good, the spring might not be; this can be checked with a cooling system pressure tester (see illustration). If the cap can't hold a pressure within approximately 1-1/2 lbs of its rated pressure (which is marked on the cap), replace it with a new one.

9   The cap is also equipped with a vacuum relief spring. When the engine cools off, a vacuum is created in the cooling system. The vacuum relief spring allows air back into the system, which will equalize the pressure and prevent damage to the radiator (the radiator tanks could collapse if the vacuum is great enough). If, after turning the engine off and allowing it to cool down you notice any of the cooling system hoses collapsing, replace the pressure cap with a new one.

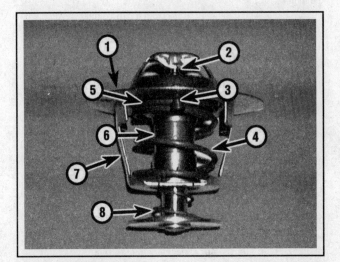

2.10 Typical thermostat:

1	Flange	5	Valve seat
2	Piston	6	Valve
3	Jiggle valve	7	Frame
4	Main coil spring	8	Secondary coil spring

THERMOSTAT

▶ **Refer to illustration 2.10**

10   Before assuming the thermostat (see illustration) is responsible for a cooling system problem, check the coolant level (see Chapter 1), drive-belt tension (see Chapter 1) and temperature gauge (or light) operation.

11   If the engine takes a long time to warm up (as indicated by the temperature gauge or heater operation), the thermostat is probably stuck open. Replace the thermostat with a new one.

12   If the engine runs hot or overheats, a thorough test of the thermostat should be performed.

13   Definitive testing of the thermostat can only be made when it is removed from the vehicle. If the thermostat is stuck in the open position at room temperature, it is faulty and must be replaced.

14 To test a thermostat, suspend the (closed) thermostat on a length of string or wire in a pot of cold water.

15 Heat the water on a stove while observing thermostat. The thermostat should fully open before the water boils.

16 If the thermostat doesn't open and close as specified, or sticks in any position, replace it.

COOLING FAN

Electric cooling fan

17 If the engine is overheating and the cooling fan is not coming on when the engine temperature rises to an excessive level, unplug the fan motor electrical connector(s) and connect the motor directly to the battery with fused jumper wires. If the fan motor doesn't come on, replace the motor.

18 If the radiator fan motor is okay, but it isn't coming on when the engine gets hot, the fan relay might be defective. A relay is used to control a circuit by turning it on and off in response to a control decision by the Powertrain Control Module (PCM). These control circuits are fairly complex, and checking them should be left to a qualified automotive technician. Sometimes, the control system can be fixed by simply identifying and replacing a bad relay.

19 Locate the fan relays in the engine compartment fuse/relay box.

20 Test the relay (see Chapter 12).

21 If the relay is okay, check all wiring and connections to the fan motor. Refer to the wiring diagrams at the end of Chapter 12. If no obvious problems are found, the problem could be the Engine Coolant Temperature (ECT) sensor or the Powertrain Control Module (PCM). Have the cooling fan system and circuit diagnosed by a dealer service department or repair shop with the proper diagnostic equipment.

➡ **Note: These models are equipped with a cooling fan motor resistor. Have the resistor checked if the fan motor does not respond to the speed variations signaled by the PCM.**

Belt-driven cooling fan

22 Disconnect the cable from the negative terminal of the battery and rock the fan back and forth by hand to check for excessive bearing play.

23 With the engine cold (and not running), turn the fan blades by hand. The fan should turn freely.

24 Visually inspect for substantial fluid leakage from the clutch assembly. If problems are noted, replace the clutch assembly.

25 With the engine completely warmed up, turn off the ignition switch and disconnect the negative battery cable from the battery. Turn the fan by hand. Some drag should be evident. If the fan turns easily, replace the fan clutch.

WATER PUMP

26 A failure in the water pump can cause serious engine damage due to overheating.

Drivebelt-driven water pump

▸ **Refer to illustration 2.28**

27 There are two ways to check the operation of the water pump

2.28 The water pump weep hole is generally located on the underside of the pump

while it's installed on the engine. If the pump is found to be defective, it should be replaced with a new or rebuilt unit.

28 Water pumps are equipped with weep (or vent) holes (see illustration). If a failure occurs in the pump seal, coolant will leak from the hole.

29 If the water pump shaft bearings fail, there may be a howling sound at the pump while it's running. Shaft wear can be felt with the drivebelt removed if the water pump pulley is rocked up and down (with the engine off). Don't mistake drivebelt slippage, which causes a squealing sound, for water pump bearing failure.

Timing chain or timing belt-driven water pump

30 Water pumps driven by the timing chain or timing belt are located underneath the timing chain or timing belt cover.

31 Checking the water pump is limited because of where it is located. However, some basic checks can be made before deciding to remove the water pump. If the pump is found to be defective, it should be replaced with a new or rebuilt unit.

32 One sign that the water pump may be failing is that the heater (climate control) may not work well. Warm the engine to normal operating temperature, confirm that the coolant level is correct, then run the heater and check for hot air coming from the ducts.

33 Check for noises coming from the water pump area. If the water pump impeller shaft or bearings are failing, there may be a howling sound at the pump while the engine is running.

➡ **Note: Be careful not to mistake drivebelt noise (squealing) for water pump bearing or shaft failure.**

34 It you suspect water pump failure due to noise, wear can be confirmed by feeling for play at the pump shaft. This can be done by rocking the drive sprocket on the pump shaft up and down. To do this you will need to remove the tension on the timing chain or belt as well as access the water pump.

All water pumps

35 In rare cases or on high-mileage vehicles, another sign of water pump failure may be the presence of coolant in the engine oil. This condition will adversely affect the engine in varying degrees.

➡ **Note: Finding coolant in the engine oil could indicate other serious issues besides a failed water pump, such as a blown head gasket or a cracked cylinder head or block.**

36 Even a pump that exhibits no outward signs of a problem, such

as noise or leakage, can still be due for replacement. Removal for close examination is the only sure way to tell. Sometimes the fins on the back of the impeller can corrode to the point that cooling efficiency is diminished significantly.

HEATER SYSTEM

37 Little can go wrong with a heater. If the fan motor will run at all speeds, the electrical part of the system is okay. The three basic heater problems fall into the following general categories:

a) Not enough heat
b) Heat all the time
c) No heat

38 If there's not enough heat, the control valve or door is stuck in a partially open position, the coolant coming from the engine isn't hot enough, or the heater core is restricted. If the coolant isn't hot enough, the thermostat in the engine cooling system is stuck open, allowing coolant to pass through the engine so rapidly that it doesn't heat up quickly enough. If the vehicle is equipped with a temperature gauge instead of a warning light, watch to see if the engine temperature rises to the normal operating range after driving for a reasonable distance.

39 If there's heat all the time, the control valve or the door is stuck wide open.

40 If there's no heat, coolant is probably not reaching the heater core, or the heater core is plugged. The likely cause is a collapsed or plugged hose, core, or a frozen heater control valve. If the heater is the type that flows coolant all the time, the cause is a stuck door or a broken or kinked control cable.

AIR CONDITIONING SYSTEM

41 If the cool air output is inadequate:

a) Inspect the condenser coils and fins to make sure they're clear
b) Check the compressor clutch for slippage.
c) Check the blower motor for proper operation.
d) Inspect the blower discharge passage for obstructions.
e) Check the system air intake filter for clogging.

42 If the system provides intermittent cooling air:

a) Check the circuit breaker, blower switch and blower motor for a malfunction.

b) Make sure the compressor clutch isn't slipping.
c) Inspect the plenum door to make sure it's operating properly.
d) Inspect the evaporator to make sure it isn't clogged.
e) If the unit is icing up, it may be caused by excessive moisture in the system, incorrect super heat switch adjustment or low thermostat adjustment.

43 If the system provides no cooling air:

a) Inspect the compressor drivebelt. Make sure it's not loose or broken.
b) Make sure the compressor clutch engages. If it doesn't, check for a blown fuse.
c) Inspect the wire harness for broken or disconnected wires.
d) If the compressor clutch doesn't engage, bridge the terminals of the A/C pressure switch(es) with a jumper wire; if the clutch now engages, and the system is properly charged, the pressure switch is bad.
e) Make sure the blower motor is not disconnected or burned out.
f) Make sure the compressor isn't partially or completely seized.
g) Inspect the refrigerant lines for leaks.
h) Check the components for leaks.
i) Inspect the receiver-drier/accumulator or expansion valve/tube for clogged screens.

44 If the system is noisy:

a) Look for loose panels in the passenger compartment.
b) Inspect the compressor drivebelt. It may be loose or worn.
c) Check the compressor mounting bolts. They should be tight.
d) Listen carefully to the compressor. It may be worn out.
e) Listen to the idler pulley and bearing and the clutch. Either may be defective.
f) The winding in the compressor clutch coil or solenoid may be defective.
g) The compressor oil level may be low.
h) The blower motor fan bushing or the motor itself may be worn out.
i) If there is an excessive charge in the system, you'll hear a rumbling noise in the high pressure line, a thumping noise in the compressor, or see bubbles or cloudiness in the sight glass.
j) If there's a low charge in the system, you might hear hissing in the evaporator case at the expansion valve, or see bubbles or cloudiness in the sight glass.

---

3   Air conditioning and heating system - check and maintenance

AIR CONDITIONING SYSTEM

▶ Refer to illustration 3.1

✳✳ WARNING:

The air conditioning system is under high pressure. Do not loosen any hose fittings or remove any components until after the system has been discharged. Air conditioning refrigerant should be properly discharged into an EPA-approved recovery/recycling unit at a dealer service department or an automotive air conditioning repair facility. Always wear eye protection when disconnecting air conditioning system fittings.

✳✳ CAUTION 1:

All models covered by this manual use environmentally friendly R-134a. This refrigerant (and its appropriate refrigerant oils) are not compatible with R-12 refrigerant system components and must never be mixed or the components will be damaged.

✳✳ CAUTION 2:

When replacing entire components, additional refrigerant oil should be added equal to the amount that is removed with the component being replaced. Be sure to read the can before adding any oil to the system, to make sure it is compatible with the R-134a system.

1   The following maintenance checks should be performed on a regular basis to ensure that the air conditioning continues to operate at peak efficiency.

a) *Inspect the condition of the compressor drivebelt. If it is worn or deteriorated, replace it (see Chapter 1).*

b) *Check the drivebelt tension (see Chapter 1).*

c) *Inspect the system hoses. Look for cracks, bubbles, hardening and deterioration. Inspect the hoses and all fittings for oil bubbles or seepage. If there is any evidence of wear, damage or leakage, replace the hose(s).*

d) *Inspect the condenser fins for leaves, bugs and any other foreign material that may have embedded itself in the fins. Use a fin comb or compressed air to remove debris from the condenser.*

e) *Make sure the system has the correct refrigerant charge.*

f) *If you hear water sloshing around in the dash area or have water dripping on the carpet, check the evaporator housing drain tube (see illustration) and insert a piece of wire into the opening to check for blockage.*

2   It's a good idea to operate the system for about ten minutes at least once a month. This is particularly important during the winter months because long term non-use can cause hardening, and subsequent failure, of the seals. Note that using the Defrost function operates the compressor.

3   If the air conditioning system is not working properly, proceed to Step 6 and perform the general checks outlined below.

4   Because of the complexity of the air conditioning system and the special equipment necessary to service it, in-depth troubleshooting and repairs beyond checking the refrigerant charge and the compressor clutch operation are not included in this manual. However, simple checks and component replacement procedures are provided in this Chapter.

5   The most common cause of poor cooling is simply a low system refrigerant charge. If a noticeable drop in system cooling ability occurs, one of the following quick checks will help you determine if the refrigerant level is low.

Checking the refrigerant charge

▶ **Refer to illustration 3.9**

6   Warm the engine up to normal operating temperature.

7   Place the air conditioning temperature selector at the coldest setting and put the blower at the highest setting.

8   After the system reaches operating temperature, feel the larger pipe exiting the evaporator at the firewall. The outlet pipe should be cold (the tubing that leads back to the compressor). If the evaporator outlet pipe is warm, the system probably needs a charge.

9   Insert a thermometer in the center air distribution duct (see illustration) while operating the air conditioning system at its maximum setting - the temperature of the output air should be 35 to 40 degrees F below the ambient air temperature (down to approximately 40 degrees F). If the ambient (outside) air temperature is very high, say 110 degrees F, the duct air temperature may be as high as 60 degrees F, but generally the air conditioning is 35 to 40 degrees F cooler than the ambient air.

10 Further inspection or testing of the system requires special tools and techniques and is beyond the scope of the home mechanic.

Adding refrigerant

▶ **Refer to illustrations 3.11 and 3.13**

※ CAUTION:

Make sure any refrigerant, refrigerant oil or replacement component you purchase is designated as compatible with R-134a systems.

11 Purchase an R-134a automotive charging kit at an auto parts store (see illustration). A charging kit includes a can of refrigerant, a tap valve and a short section of hose that can be attached between the tap valve and the system low side service valve.

※ CAUTION:

Never add more than one can of refrigerant to the system. If more refrigerant than that is required, the system should be evacuated and leak tested.

12 Back off the valve handle on the charging kit and screw the kit onto the refrigerant can, making sure first that the O-ring or rubber seal inside the threaded portion of the kit is in place.

3.1 Evaporator drain hose is located on the passenger's side of the firewall

3.9 Insert a thermometer in the center vent, turn on the air conditioning system and wait for it to cool down; depending on the humidity, the output air should be 35 to 40 degrees cooler than the ambient air temperature

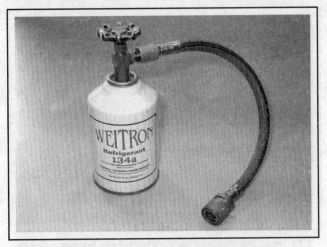

3.11 R-134a automotive air conditioning charging kit

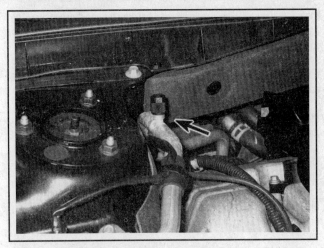

3.13 Location of the low-side charging port

use with the piercing valve in the UP position, to prevent inadvertently piercing the can on the next use.

HEATING SYSTEMS

19 If the carpet under the heater core is damp, or if antifreeze vapor or steam is coming through the vents, the heater core is leaking. Remove it (see Section 12) and install a new unit (most radiator shops will not repair a leaking heater core).

20 If the air coming out of the heater vents isn't hot, the problem could stem from any of the following causes:

a) *The thermostat is stuck open, preventing the engine coolant from warming up enough to carry heat to the heater core. Replace the thermostat (see Section 4).*

b) *There is a blockage in the system, preventing the flow of coolant through the heater core. Feel both heater hoses at the firewall. They should be hot. If one of them is cold, there is an obstruction in one of the hoses or in the heater core, or the heater control valve is shut. Detach the hoses and back flush the heater core with a water hose. If the heater core is clear but circulation is impeded, remove the two hoses and flush them out with a water hose.*

c) *If flushing fails to remove the blockage from the heater core, the core must be replaced (see Section 12).*

ELIMINATING AIR CONDITIONING ODORS

▶ **Refer to illustration 3.24**

21 Unpleasant odors that often develop in air conditioning systems are caused by the growth of a fungus, usually on the surface of the evaporator core. The warm, humid environment there is a perfect breeding ground for mildew to develop.

22 The evaporator core on most vehicles is difficult to access, and factory dealerships have a lengthy, expensive process for eliminating the fungus by opening up the evaporator case and using a powerful disinfectant and rinse on the core until the fungus is gone. You can service your own system at home, but it takes something much stronger than basic household germ-killers or deodorizers.

23 Aerosol disinfectants for automotive air conditioning systems are available in most auto parts stores, but remember when shopping for

---

※ **WARNING:**

Wear protective eyewear when dealing with pressurized refrigerant cans.

13 Remove the dust cap from the low-side charging port and attach the hose's quick-connect fitting to the port (see illustration).

※ **WARNING:**

DO NOT hook the charging kit hose to the system high side! The fittings on the charging kit are designed to fit only on the low side of the system.

14 Warm up the engine and turn On the air conditioning. Keep the charging kit hose away from the fan and other moving parts.

➡ **Note: The charging process requires the compressor to be running. If the clutch cycles off, you can put the air conditioning switch on High and leave the car doors open to keep the clutch on and compressor working. The compressor can be kept on during the charging by removing the connector from the pressure switch and bridging it with a paper clip or jumper wire during the procedure.**

15 Turn the valve handle on the kit until the stem pierces the can, then back the handle out to release the refrigerant. You should be able to hear the rush of gas. Keep the can upright at all times, but shake it occasionally. Allow stabilization time between each addition.

➡ **Note: The charging process will go faster if you wrap the can with a hot-water-soaked rag to keep the can from freezing up.**

16 If you have an accurate thermometer, you can place it in the center air conditioning duct inside the vehicle and keep track of the output air temperature. A charged system that is working properly should cool down to approximately 40 degrees F. If the ambient (outside) air temperature is very high, say 110 degrees F, the duct air temperature may be as high as 60 degrees F, but generally the air conditioning is 35 to 40 degrees F cooler than the ambient air.

17 When the can is empty, turn the valve handle to the closed position and release the connection from the low-side port. Reinstall the dust cap.

18 Remove the charging kit from the can and store the kit for future

them that the most effective treatments are also the most expensive. The basic procedure for using these sprays is to start by running the system in the RECIRC mode for ten minutes with the blower on its highest speed. Use the highest heat mode to dry out the system and keep the compressor from engaging by disconnecting the wiring connector at the compressor.

24 The disinfectant can usually comes with a long spray hose. Insert the nozzle into an intake port inside the cabin, and spray according to the manufacturer's recommendations (see illustration). Try to cover the whole surface of the evaporator core, by aiming the spray up, down and sideways. Follow the manufacturer's recommendations for the length of spray and waiting time between applications.

25 Once the evaporator has been cleaned, the best way to prevent the mildew from coming back again is to make sure your evaporator housing drain tube is clear (see illustration 3.1).

AUTOMATIC HEATING AND AIR CONDITIONING SYSTEMS

26 Some vehicles are equipped with an optional automatic climate control system. This system has its own computer that receives inputs from various sensors in the heating and air conditioning system. This computer, like the PCM, has self-diagnostic capabilities to help pinpoint

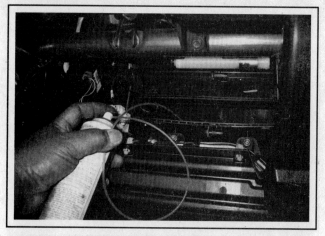

3.24 Insert the nozzle of the disinfectant can into the return-air intake behind the glove box

problems or faults within the system. Vehicles equipped with automatic heating and air conditioning systems are very complex and considered beyond the scope of the home mechanic. Vehicles equipped with automatic heating and air conditioning systems should be taken to dealer service department or other qualified facility for repair.

4 Thermostat - replacement

❄❄ WARNING:

Wait until the engine is completely cool before performing this procedure.

REMOVAL

▶ **Refer to illustrations 4.4a and 4.4b**

1 Disconnect the cable from the negative battery terminal (see Chapter 5).

2 Drain the cooling system (see Chapter 1). If the coolant is relatively new and still in good condition, save it and reuse it.

3 Follow the lower radiator hose to the engine to locate the thermostat housing.

4 Loosen the hose clamp, then detach the hose from the fitting (see illustrations). If it's stuck, grasp it near the end with a pair of adjustable pliers, twist it to break the seal, then pull it off. If the hose is old or if it has deteriorated, cut it off and install a new one.

5 If the outer surface of the thermostat housing cover, which mates with the hose, is already corroded, pitted, or otherwise deteriorated, it might be damaged even more by hose removal. If it is, replace the thermostat housing cover.

Four-cylinder models

6 Remove the engine drivebelt (see Chapter 1) and the power steering pump (see Chapter 10).

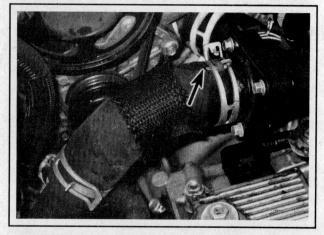

4.4a Remove the spring clamp from the radiator hose at the thermostat housing cover (V6 engine shown)

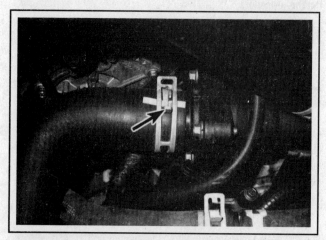

4.4b Disconnect the radiator hose from the thermostat housing cover (four-cylinder engine shown)

4.10 Thermostat housing cover mounting fasteners (3.0L V6 shown, 3.7L V6 similar)

4.11 Remove the thermostat from the housing, but note that the jiggle valve on the thermostat is located in the 12 o'clock position

7   Remove the bypass hose from the thermostat housing (if equipped).

8   Remove the thermostat housing bolts, then detach the housing.

➡ **Note: The thermostat and housing can't be disassembled, and must be replaced as a unit.**

V6 models

▶ **Refer to illustrations 4.10 and 4.11**

9   On 3.7L V6 engines, remove the battery and battery tray (see Chapter 5).

10 Remove the fasteners and detach the thermostat housing cover (see illustration). If the cover is stuck, tap it with a soft-face hammer to jar it loose. Be prepared for some coolant to spill as the gasket seal is broken.

11 Note how it's installed, which end is facing up, or out, then remove O-ring and the thermostat (see illustration).

INSTALLATION

12 Clean the sealing surfaces. Also inspect the hoses, replacing them as necessary.

Four-cylinder models

13 Install the thermostat housing, using a new molded gasket. Reconnect the radiator hose, then install the housing and tighten the bolts to the torque listed in this Chapter's Specifications. Reconnect the heater hose.

V6 models

▶ **Refer to illustration 4.14a and 4.14b**

14 Install the thermostat in the housing, spring-end first, then install a new rubber gasket or O-ring to the thermostat housing (see illustrations). Make sure that you install the thermostat with the jiggle valve at 12 o'clock (see illustration 4.11).

15 Install the thermostat housing cover and bolts, then tighten the bolts to the torque listed in this Chapter's Specifications.

16 Reattach the lower radiator hose to the thermostat housing cover. Make sure that the hose clamp is still tight. If it isn't, replace it.

All models

17 Refill the cooling system and bleed the air from the system (see Chapter 1).

18 Start the engine and allow it to reach normal operating temperature, then check for leaks and proper thermostat operation.

4.14a Install the new thermostat into the housing

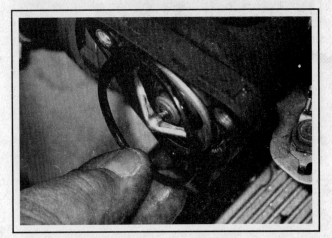

4.14b Install the O-ring seal

5   Engine cooling fans - replacement

❈❈ WARNING:

To avoid possible injury or damage, DO NOT operate the engine with a damaged fan. Do not attempt to repair fan blades - replace a damaged fan with a new one.

➡ **Note: Always be sure to check for blown fuses before attempting to diagnose an electrical circuit problem.**

1   If the engine is overheating and the cooling fan is not coming on when the engine temperature rises to an excessive level, see Section 2. Check the fan relays in the underhood fuse/relay box.

2   If the relays are okay, check all wiring and connections to the fan motor. Refer to the wiring diagrams at the end of Chapter 12. If no obvious problems are found, the problem could be the Engine Coolant Temperature (ECT) sensor, the fan control module (3.0L engines) or the Powertrain Control Module (PCM). Have the cooling fan system and circuit diagnosed by a dealer service department or repair shop with the proper diagnostic equipment.

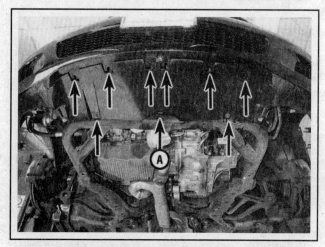

5.6 Remove the splash shield plastic mounting clip (A) and remaining fasteners below the radiator

5.9 Typical 3.0L engine fan shroud details

1   *Left side fan shroud mounting fastener*
2   *Power steering reservoir mounting fasteners*
3   *Fan control module mounting fasteners*
4   *Automatic transaxle cooler line mounting fastener*

REMOVAL

◆ **Refer to illustration 5.6**

❈❈ WARNING:

Wait until the engine is completely cool before performing this procedure.

❈❈ WARNING:

These models have an airbag sensor mounted near the radiator support bracket. It will be necessary to disarm the system prior to performing any work around the radiator, fans or other components in this area (see Chapter 12).

3   Disconnect the cable from the negative battery terminal (see Chapter 5).

4   Disconnect the fan motor electrical connector(s).

5   Detach the wire harness clips from the fan shroud and move the harness away from the shroud.

6   Raise the vehicle and support it securely on jackstands. Remove the lower splash shield under the radiator (see illustration).

7   Drain the cooling system (see Chapter 1). If the coolant is relatively new and still in good condition, save it and reuse it. Detach the upper radiator hose from the radiator.

8   Disconnect the expansion tank hose from the tank.

2008 and earlier models

◆ **Refer to illustrations 5.9, 5.12, 5.14a, 5.14b and 5.15**

9   On 3.0L engines, remove the power steering reservoir mounting nuts, set the reservoir to the side and disconnect the electrical connectors to the fan-control electronic module (see illustration).

5.12 Bumper reinforcement mounting fasteners - left side shown, right side identical (energy-absorbing foam insert removed)

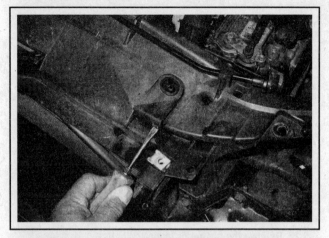

5.14a Pry the radiator upper mount cover out from the radiator support

10 Remove the front bumper cover (see Chapter 11).

11 Remove the headlight housings (see Chapter 12).

12 Remove the front bumper energy-absorbing foam insert, reinforcement mounting bolts and reinforcement (see illustration).

13 Remove the condenser line support bracket mounting bolt and move the bracket to the side.

14 Remove the radiator mount covers and radiator mount insulators (see illustrations).

15 Remove the radiator support mounting bolts (see illustration) and radiator support.

16 Support the radiator and condenser with wire or rope.

17 Detach the transaxle cooling lines attached to the fan shroud (see illustration 5.9).

18 Remove the shroud mounting bolts and lift out the fan/shroud assembly.

2009 and later models

▸ Refer to illustrations 5.23 and 5.24

19 Remove the air filter housing and inlet air assembly (see Chapter 4) then disconnect the fan motor electrical connector(s).

20 Remove the upper radiator hose (see Chapter 1).

21 Remove the lower radiator hose mounting clip to the fan shroud.

22 Remove the lower radiator hose mounting bracket-to-crossmember bolt.

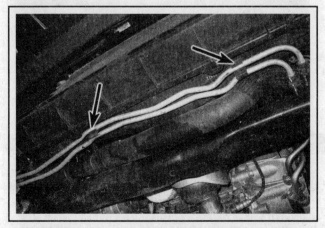

5.23 Release the transaxle fluid cooler lines from the clips

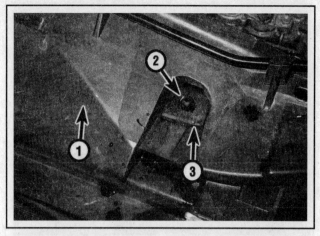

5.14b Typical 3.0L engine upper radiator mount details

1 Radiator support	3 Upper rubber mount
2 Radiator mount locating pin	

5.15 Radiator support mounting bolt location (left side shown, right side identical)

23 On automatic transaxle-equipped vehicles, disconnect the clips securing the transaxle cooling lines to the fan shroud (see illustration).

24 Release the two large clips at the top of the fan shroud and lift the fan/shroud assembly from the vehicle (see illustration).

5.24 On 2009 and later models, release the clip on each side and pull the fan/shroud up and out

5.25 Use a flat-bladed screwdriver and drive the locking washer off the fan motor shaft

5.26 Remove the fan motor mounting bolts

All models

▶ **Refer to illustrations 5.25 and 5.26**

25 To detach the fan blade from the motor, remove the nut or retaining clip from the motor shaft (see illustration). Remove the fan blade from the motor.

26 To detach the motor from the shroud, remove the retaining bolts (see illustration).

INSTALLATION

27 Installation is the reverse of removal.

➡ **Note: When reinstalling the fan assembly, make sure the rubber air shields around the shroud are still in place - without them, the cooling system may not work efficiently.**

28 Reconnect the battery, refill the cooling system and bleed the air from the system (see Chapter 1).

29 Start the engine and allow it to reach normal operating temperature, then check for leaks and proper operation.

6 Coolant expansion tank - removal and installation

▶ **Refer to illustration 6.3**

✳✳ WARNING:

Wait until the engine is completely cool before beginning this procedure.

1 Drain the cooling system (see Chapter 1).
2 Remove the fasteners securing the expansion tank to the fender.
3 Lift the tank up enough to disconnect the hoses (see illustration).
4 Clean out the tank with soapy water and a brush to remove any deposits inside. Inspect the reservoir carefully for cracks. If you find a crack, replace the reservoir.
5 Installation is the reverse of removal.

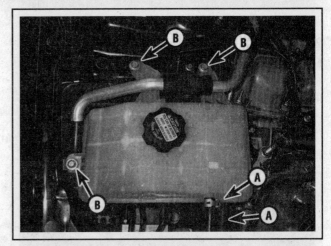

6.3 Disconnect the expansion tank hoses (A), then remove the mounting fasteners (B)

7 Radiator - removal and installation

✳✳ WARNING:

Wait until the engine is completely cool before beginning this procedure.

✳✳ WARNING:

These models have an airbag sensor mounted near the radiator support. It will be necessary to disarm the airbag system prior to performing any work around the radiator, fans or other components in this area (see Chapter 12)

REMOVAL

1 Disconnect the cable from the negative battery terminal (see Chapter 5).

2 Raise the vehicle and place it securely on jackstands. Remove the lower splash shield (see illustration 5.6).

3 Drain the cooling system (see Chapter 1). If the coolant is relatively new and in good condition, save it and reuse it. Detach the radiator hose from the bottom of the radiator.

4 If you're working on a vehicle equipped with an automatic transaxle, disconnect the transaxle cooler lines from the radiator. Use a drip pan to catch spilled fluid and plug the lines and fittings.

2008 and earlier models

5 Remove the radiator support and cooling fan/shroud assembly (see Section 5).

6 On four-cylinder models, remove the upper radiator hose.

7 On V6 models, remove the power steering reservoir mounting nuts and set the reservoir to the side.

8 Remove the coolant reservoir hose (if equipped).

9 Remove the radiator mounting bolts and carefully lift out the radiator. Don't spill coolant on the vehicle or scratch the paint. Make sure the rubber radiator insulators that fit on the bottom of the radiator and into the sockets in the body remain in place in the body for proper reinstallation of the radiator.

2009 and later models

◗ **Refer to illustration 7.16**

10 Remove the air filter housing and inlet air assembly (see Chapter 4), then disconnect the fan motor electrical connector(s).

11 Remove the cooling fan/shroud assembly from the radiator (see Section 5).

12 Remove the front bumper cover (see Chapter 11).

13 Remove the radiator hoses (see Chapter 1).

14 Remove the coolant reservoir hose.

15 Press each of the upper radiator mount covers down and towards the front of the vehicle to remove the covers. Once the covers are out, remove the upper rubber mounts.

16 From the front side of the radiator, squeeze the radiator-to-radiator support locking tabs together and pull the radiator and condenser forward (see illustration). Lift the condenser up a few inches and out to separate it from the radiator brackets, then set the condenser back into the opening.

7.16 Release the clips at each side securing the radiator to the radiator support

17 Carefully lift out the radiator. Don't spill coolant on the vehicle or scratch the paint. Make sure the rubber radiator insulators that fit on the bottom of the radiator and into the sockets in the body remain in place in the body for proper reinstallation of the radiator.

INSTALLATION

18 Remove bugs and dirt from the radiator with compressed air and a soft brush. Don't bend the cooling fins. Inspect the radiator for leaks and damage. If it needs repair, have a radiator shop or a dealer service department do the work.

19 Inspect the rubber insulators in the lower crossmember for cracks and deterioration. Make sure that they're free of dirt and gravel. When installing the radiator, make sure that it's correctly seated on the insulators before fastening the top brackets.

20 Installation is otherwise the reverse of removal. After installation, fill the cooling system with the correct mixture of antifreeze and water, then bleed the air from the system (see Chapter 1).

21 Start the engine and check for leaks. Allow the engine to reach normal operating temperature, indicated by the upper radiator hose becoming hot. Recheck the coolant level and add more if required.

22 On automatic transaxle-equipped vehicles, check and add transaxle fluid as needed.

8	Water pump - replacement

✳✳ WARNING:

Wait until the engine is completely cool before beginning this procedure.

REMOVAL

1 Disconnect the cable from the negative battery terminal (see Chapter 5).

2 Drain the cooling system (see Chapter 1).

Four-cylinder models

◗ **Refer to illustration 8.7, 8.8 and 8.9**

3 Loosen the water pump pulley bolts.

4 Remove the drivebelt (see Chapter 1).

5 Loosen the right front wheel lug nuts. Raise the vehicle and support it securely on jackstands.

6 Remove the right front wheel and the fender splash shield (see Chapter 11).

8.7 Remove the bolts and separate the water pump pulley from the pump

8.8 Remove the water pump bolts

8.9 Clean the water pump bolt threads, the threaded holes in the housing and the pump mating surface of the housing

8.11 Two water pump bolts (not visible in this photo) are accessible only after the drive pulley is removed from the end of the exhaust camshaft with special tools (3.0L V6 engine)

7   Remove the water pump pulley (see illustration).

8   Remove the bolts attaching the water pump to the engine block and remove the pump from the engine (see illustration). If the water pump is stuck, gently tap it with a soft-faced hammer to break the seal.

9   Clean the bolt threads and the threaded holes in the engine (see illustration), removing all corrosion and sealant. Remove all traces of old gasket material from the sealing surfaces.

3.0L V6 models

▶ **Refer to illustration and 8.11**

10   Remove the water pump drivebelt (see Chapter 1). Several special tools are required to remove the water pump pulley from the camshaft for access to the water pump bolts (manufacturer tool numbers: 303-456, 303-457, and 303-009).

11   Leave the water pump-to-thermostat housing hose connected to the pump, but disconnect it from the thermostat housing. Disconnect the other water pump hoses, then remove the water pump mounting bolts (see illustration) and remove the pump.

12   Clean all the gasket and O-ring surfaces on the pump and the housing.

3.7L V6 models

▶ **Refer to illustration 8.13**

13   The water pump is mounted to the front of the block but is driven by the timing chain and thus not accessible without removing the engine and timing chain (see Chapters 2B and 2C). Remove the pump mounting bolts (see illustration) and remove the pump.

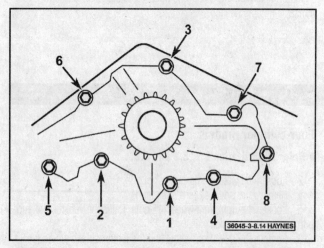

8.13 Water pump bolt locations and tightening sequence (3.7L V6 engine)

INSTALLATION

14 Compare the new pump to the old one to make sure that they're identical.

15 Apply a thin film of RTV sealant to hold the new gasket in place during installation. O-rings should be coated with clean coolant.

❊❊ CAUTION:

Make sure that the gasket is correctly positioned on the water pump and the mating surfaces are clean and free of old gasket material.

Carefully mate the pump to the water pump housing.

16 Install the water pump bolts and tighten them to the torque listed in this Chapter's Specifications.

17 The remainder of installation is the reverse of removal, noting the following points:

a) *On 3.0L V6 engines, a special tool (manufacturer tool number 211-185) is required to reinstall the water pump pulley to the camshaft.*

b) *Refill and bleed the cooling system (see Chapter 1).*

c) *Operate the engine to check for leaks.*

9 Coolant temperature sending unit - replacement

The coolant temperature indicator system consists of a warning light or a temperature gauge on the dash and a coolant temperature sending unit mounted on the engine. The Cylinder Head Temperature (CHT) sensor (3.7L V6 models) and Engine Coolant Temperature (ECT) sensor (four-cylinder and 3.0L V6 models) are information sensors for the Powertrain Control Module (PCM), and also function as the coolant temperature sending unit for the temperature gauge. Information on the CHT and ECT sensors can be found in Chapter 6.

10 Blower motor resistor/transistor and blower motor - replacement

❊❊ WARNING:

The models covered by this manual are equipped with Supplemental Restraint Systems (SRS), more commonly known as airbags. Always disable the airbag system before working in the vicinity of any airbag system component to avoid the possibility of accidental deployment of the airbag, which could cause personal injury (see Chapter 12).

BLOWER MOTOR RESISTOR/TRANSISTOR

1 Remove the lower trim panel from below the glove box (see Chapter 11).

2008 and earlier models

2 Remove the glove box (see Chapter 11).

3 Disconnect the electrical connector from the blower motor resistor.

4 Remove the blower motor resistor mounting screws and remove the resistor from the evaporator housing.

5 Installation is the reverse of removal.

2009 and later models

▶ **Refer to illustration 10.6**

6 Disconnect the electrical connector from the blower motor resistor (see illustration).

7 On models with manual air conditioning, depress the tab located at the top of the resistor, slide the resistor to the right and remove it from the evaporator housing.

10.6 Unplug the blower motor resistor connector, then remove the mounting screws

8 On models with automatic air conditioning, depress the tab located at the top of the transistor, slide the transistor to the right and remove it from the evaporator housing.

9 Installation is the reverse of removal.

BLOWER MOTOR

▶ **Refer to illustration 10.11**

10 Remove the lower trim panel from below the glovebox (see Chapter 11).

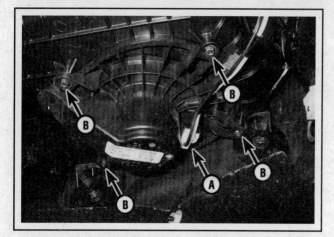

10.11 Location of the blower motor electrical connector (A) and the blower motor mounting screws (B)

11 Disconnect the blower motor electrical connector (see illustration).

12 Remove the blower motor mounting screws and remove the blower motor.

13 Installation is the reverse of removal.

11 Heater/air conditioner control assembly - removal and installation

✳✳ WARNING:

The models covered by this manual are equipped with Supplemental Restraint Systems (SRS), more commonly known as airbags. Always disable the airbag system before working in the vicinity of any airbag system component to avoid the possibility of accidental deployment of the airbag, which could cause personal injury (see Chapter 12).

1 Disconnect the cable from the negative battery terminal (see Chapter 5).

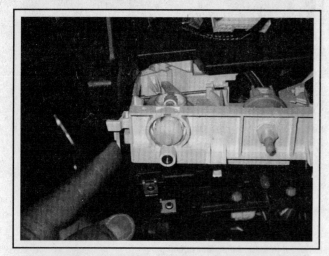

11.5 Push the locking tabs in on each side of the control unit and pull the unit out from the instrument panel

2 Remove the center console (see Chapter 11).

3 Remove the shift lever knob and shift panel (see Chapter 7).

4 Use a plastic trim tool to pry the center trim panel assembly from the instrument panel (see Chapter 12), if necessary, disconnect any electrical connectors.

2008 AND EARLIER MODELS

Manual A/C models

▸ Refer to illustration 11.5

5 Depress the locking tabs on each side of the control unit and pull the unit forward (see illustration).

6 Disconnect the electrical connectors at the module and the control cables.

7 Remove the control unit from the instrument panel.

8 Installation is the reverse of removal.

Automatic A/C models

9 Remove the heater/air conditioner control assembly retaining screws on the back of the center trim panel.

10 Installation is the reverse of removal.

2009 AND LATER MODELS

11 Remove the heater/air conditioner control assembly retaining screws and pull the unit forward.

12 Disconnect the electrical connectors to the module.

13 Installation is the reverse of removal.

12 Heater core - replacement

▶ Refer to illustrations 12.3 and 12.5

❈❈ WARNING:

The air conditioning system is under high pressure. DO NOT loosen any fittings or remove any components until after the system has been discharged. Air conditioning refrigerant must be properly discharged into an EPA-approved container at a dealer service department or an automotive air conditioning repair facility. Always wear eye protection when disconnecting air conditioning system fittings.

❈❈ WARNING:

The models covered by this manual are equipped with Supplemental Restraint Systems (SRS), more commonly known as airbags. Always disarm the airbag system before working in the vicinity of any airbag system component to avoid the possibility of accidental deployment of the airbag, which could cause personal injury (see Chapter 12).

❈❈ WARNING:

Wait until the engine is completely cool before beginning this procedure.

➡ **Note:** This is a difficult procedure for the home mechanic, involving numerous hard-to-find fasteners, clips and electrical connectors.

1 Have the air conditioning system discharged by an automotive air conditioning technician (see **Warning** above).

2 Disconnect the cable from the negative battery terminal (see Chapter 5).

3 Drain the cooling system (see Chapter 1). Disconnect the heater hoses from the heater core inlet and outlet pipes at the firewall and disconnect the thermal expansion valve and the two refrigerant pipes (see illustration).

4 Remove the instrument panel (see Chapter 11). On V6 models, remove the lower cowl grille panel to access some HVAC unit fasteners.

5 Tag and disconnect the cables (if equipped) and electrical connectors from the HVAC unit. Remove the mounting fasteners (see illustration).

6 The heater core is in the center of the HVAC unit, below the A/C housing. Remove the heater core cover screws and pull the heater core out of the housing.

➡ **Note:** On 2009 and later models, remove the heater core coolant pipe mounting screws, remove the coolant pipes and O-rings from the heater core, then remove the heater core.

7 Installation is the reverse of removal. Don't forget to reconnect the heater core inlet and outlet hoses at the firewall. Use a new gasket where the two air conditioning pipes meet the expansion valve at the firewall.

8 Refill and bleed the cooling system (see Chapter 1). Have the system evacuated, recharged and leak tested by the shop that discharged it.

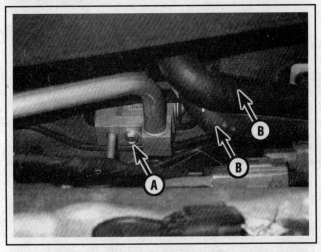

12.3 Remove the nut securing the expansion valve and pipes to the firewall (A), then remove the two heater core hoses (B)

12.5 Remove the fasteners securing the HVAC housing from the firewall (not all fasteners visible here)

13 Air conditioning compressor - removal and installation

※※ WARNING:

The air conditioning system is under high pressure. DO NOT loosen any fittings or remove any components until after the system has been discharged. Air conditioning refrigerant must be properly discharged into an EPA-approved container at a dealer service department or an automotive air conditioning repair facility. Always wear eye protection when disconnecting air conditioning system fittings.

※※ CAUTION:

If the compressor is being replaced due to failure, the rest of the system should be flushed by a technician to remove particles or contaminants.

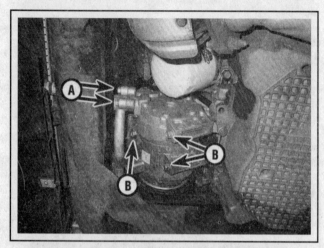

13.7 Remove the bolts (A) securing the refrigerant pipes to the compressor and the compressor mounting bolts (B)

REMOVAL

▶ **Refer to illustration 13.7**

1 Have the air conditioning system discharged by an automotive air conditioning technician (see **Warning** above).

2 Loosen the right front wheel lug nuts. Raise the vehicle and secure it on jackstands. Remove the right front wheel.

3 Remove the right front fender splash shield and the splash shield under the radiator.

4 Remove the drivebelt (see Chapter 1).

5 Disconnect the electrical connector from the compressor clutch field coil.

6 On 3.0L V6 engines, remove the front catalytic converter (see Chapter 6).

7 Disconnect the compressor inlet and outlet line manifold from the compressor (see illustration). Remove and discard the old O-rings.

8 Remove the compressor mounting bolts (see illustration 13.7) and remove the compressor.

INSTALLATION

9 If a new compressor is being installed, follow the directions that came with the compressor regarding the draining of excess oil prior to installation.

10 The clutch may have to be transferred from the original to the new compressor.

11 Before reconnecting the inlet and outlet lines to the compressor, replace all manifold O-rings and lubricate them with refrigerant oil.

12 Installation is otherwise the reverse of removal.

13 Have the system evacuated, recharged and leak tested by the shop that discharged it.

14 Air conditioning condenser - removal and installation

※※ WARNING:

The air conditioning system is under high pressure. DO NOT loosen any fittings or remove any components until after the system has been discharged. Air conditioning refrigerant must be properly discharged into an EPA-approved container at a dealer service department or an automotive air conditioning repair facility. Always wear eye protection when disconnecting air conditioning system fittings.

1 Have the air conditioning system discharged by an automotive air conditioning technician (see **Warning** above).

2008 AND EARLIER MODELS

2 Remove the radiator support (see Section 5).

2009 AND LATER MODELS

3 Drain the engine coolant (see Chapter 1).

4 Remove the air filter housing and inlet air assembly (see Chapter 4) then disconnect the fan motor electrical connector(s).

5 Remove the cooling fan/shroud assembly from the radiator (see Section 5).

6 Remove the throttle body (see Chapter 4) with all coolant hoses attached and set it to the side.

7 Remove the radiator (see Section 7).

ALL MODELS

8 Disconnect the refrigerant inlet and outlet pipes from the condenser. Remove the bolt or nut securing the pipes to the block that is part of the condenser. Cap the lines to prevent contamination. The

refrigerant pipe block is retained by a bolt and a rivet that must be drilled out.

9   Remove the condenser mounting bolts and remove the condenser. If you're going to reinstall the same condenser, store it with the line fittings facing up to prevent oil from draining out.

10 If you're going to install a new condenser, pour one ounce of refrigerant oil of the correct type into it prior to installation.

11 Before reconnecting the refrigerant lines to the condenser, be sure to coat a pair of new O-rings with refrigerant oil, install them in the refrigerant line fittings and tighten the condenser inlet and outlet nuts to the torque listed in this Chapter's Specifications.

12 Installation is otherwise the reverse of removal.

13 Have the system evacuated, recharged and leak tested by the shop that discharged it.

15 Air conditioning pressure cycling switch - replacement

※※ WARNING:

The air conditioning system is under high pressure. DO NOT loosen any fittings or remove any components until after the system has been discharged. Air conditioning refrigerant must be properly discharged into an EPA-approved container at a dealer service department or an automotive air conditioning repair facility. Always wear eye protection when disconnecting air conditioning system fittings.

1   The pressure cycling switch is located on the hard line. The pressure cycling switch detects low refrigerant line pressure, and switches

15.5 Pressure switch details (2008 and earlier models)

1	Pressure switch electrical connector	2	Back up wrench placement
		3	Pressure switch

the A/C system off, then back on again to provide higher pressure. If the pressure increases too high, the pressure cut-off switch, located in the high pressure side of the system, shuts the system off.

2   Have the air conditioning system discharged by an automotive air conditioning technician (see **Warning** above).

3   Disconnect the battery (see Chapter 5).

2008 AND EARLIER MODELS

▸ **Refer to illustration 15.5**

4   Remove the passenger's side headlight assembly (see Chapter 12).

5   Unplug the electrical connector from the pressure cycling switch (see illustration).

6   Using two wrenches, loosen then remove the pressure cycling switch.

2009 AND LATER MODELS

7   Unplug the electrical connector from the pressure cycling switch.

8   Locate and unscrew the pressure cycling switch.

ALL MODELS

9   Lubricate the switch O-ring with clean refrigerant oil of the correct type.

10 Using two wrenches, screw the new switch into place until hand tight, then tighten it securely.

11 Reconnect the electrical connector.

12 Have the system evacuated, recharged and leak tested by the shop that discharged it.

16 Air conditioning thermostatic expansion valve (TXV) - general information and replacement

※※ WARNING:

The air conditioning system is under high pressure. DO NOT loosen any hose fittings or remove any components until the system has been discharged. Air conditioning refrigerant must be properly discharged into an EPA-approved recovery/recycling unit by a dealer service department or an automotive air conditioning repair facility. Always wear eye protection when disconnecting air conditioning system fittings.

There are several ways that air conditioning systems convert the high-pressure liquid refrigerant from the compressor to lower-pressure

vapor. The conversion takes place at the air conditioning evaporator; the evaporator is chilled as the refrigerant passes through, cooling the airflow through the evaporator for delivery to the vents. The conversion is usually accomplished by a sudden change in the tubing size. Many vehicles have a removable controlled orifice in one of the AC pipes at the firewall.

The models covered by this manual use a thermostatic expansion valve (TXV) that accomplishes the same purpose as a controlled orifice. To remove the TXV, have the air conditioning system discharged by a licensed air conditioning technician, then disconnect the refrigerant lines from the TXV at the firewall. Remove the two bolts securing the valve, then remove the valve.

Specifications

General

Expansion tank cap pressure rating	14 to 18 psi (93 to 123 kPa)
Cooling system capacity	See Chapter 1
Refrigerant type	R-134a
Refrigerant capacity	Refer to HVAC specification tag

Torque specifications — Ft-lbs (unless otherwise indicated) — Nm

➡ **Note:** One foot-pound (ft-lb) of torque is equivalent to 12 inch-pounds (in-lbs) of torque. Torque values below approximately 15 foot-pounds are expressed in inch-pounds, because most foot-pound torque wrenches are not accurate at these smaller values.

	Ft-lbs (unless otherwise indicated)	Nm
Air conditioning compressor inlet and		
outlet bolts/nuts	16	22
Condenser inlet and outlet bolts/nuts	53 in-lbs	6
Coolant inlet pipe bolts	89 in-lbs	10
Thermostat housing cover bolts	89 in-lbs	10
Water pump fasteners		
Four-cylinder and 3.7L V6 engines	89 in-lbs	10
3.0L V6 engine		
Step 1	89 in-lbs	10
Step 2	Tighten an additional 85 degrees	
Water pump pulley bolts	15	20

Section

4

FUEL AND EXHAUST SYSTEMS

1   General information

FUEL SYSTEM WARNINGS

Gasoline is extremely flammable and repairing fuel system components can be dangerous. Consider your automotive repair knowledge and experience before attempting repairs which may be better suited for a professional mechanic.

- *Don't smoke or allow open flames or bare light bulbs near the work area*
- *Don't work in a garage with a gas-type appliance (water heater, clothes dryer)*
- *Use fuel-resistant gloves. If any fuel spills on your skin, wash it off immediately with soap and water*
- *Clean up spills immediately*
- *Do not store fuel-soaked rags where they could ignite*
- *Prior to disconnecting any fuel line, you must relieve the fuel pressure (see Section 3)*
- *Wear safety glasses*
- *Have a proper fire extinguisher on hand*

FUEL SYSTEM

The fuel system consists of the fuel tank, electric fuel pump/fuel level sending unit (located in the fuel tank), fuel rail and fuel injectors. The fuel injection system is a multi-port system; multi-port fuel injection uses timed impulses to inject the fuel directly into the intake port of each cylinder. The Powertrain Control Module (PCM) controls the injectors. The PCM monitors various engine parameters and delivers the exact amount of fuel required into the intake ports.

Fuel is circulated from the fuel pump to the fuel rail through fuel lines running along the underside of the vehicle. Various sections of the fuel line are either rigid metal or nylon, or flexible fuel hose. The various sections of the fuel hose are connected either by quick-connect fittings or threaded metal fittings.

EXHAUST SYSTEM

The exhaust system consists of the exhaust manifold(s), catalytic converter(s), muffler(s), tailpipe and all connecting pipes, flanges and clamps. The catalytic converters are an emission control device added to the exhaust system to reduce pollutants.

Fuel system components (3.0L V6 engine)

1	Engine compartment fuse and relay box (fuel pump fuse and relay)	3	Air intake duct	6	Fuel injectors (under upper intake manifold)
2	Air filter housing	4	Throttle body		
		5	Upper intake manifold		

2 Troubleshooting

FUEL PUMP

▶ **Refer to illustrations 2.2a and 2.2b**

1   The fuel pump is located inside the fuel tank. Sit inside the vehicle with the windows closed, turn the ignition key to ON (not START) and listen for the sound of the fuel pump as it's briefly activated. You will only hear the sound for a second or two, but that sound tells you that the pump is working. Alternatively, have an assistant listen at the fuel filler cap.

2   If the pump does not come on, check the fuel pump fuse and relay (see illustrations). If the fuse and relay are okay, check the wiring back to the fuel pump. If the fuse, relay and wiring are okay, the fuel pump is probably defective. If the pump runs continuously with the ignition key in the ON position, the Powertrain Control Module (PCM) is probably defective. Have the PCM checked by a professional mechanic.

FUEL INJECTION SYSTEM

▶ **Refer to illustration 2.9**

➡ **Note: The following procedure is based on the assumption that the fuel pump is working and the fuel pressure is adequate (see Section 4).**

3   Check all electrical connectors that are related to the system. Check the ground wire connections for tightness.

4   Verify that the battery is fully charged (see Chapter 5).

5   Inspect the air filter element (see Chapter 1).

6   Check all fuses related to the fuel system (see Chapter 12).

7   Check the air induction system between the throttle body and the intake manifold for air leaks. Also inspect the condition of all vacuum hoses connected to the intake manifold and to the throttle body.

8   Remove the air intake duct from the throttle body and look for dirt, carbon, varnish, or other residue in the throttle body, particularly around the throttle plate. If it's dirty, clean it with carb cleaner, a toothbrush and a clean shop towel.

9   With the engine running, place an automotive stethoscope against each injector, one at a time, and listen for a clicking sound that indi-

2.2a The fuel pump fuse is located in the engine compartment fuse box (the location of the fuse and relay may vary with model and year - refer to the guide on the underside of the fuse box cover in your owner's manual)

cates operation (see illustration).

✳✳ WARNING:

Stay clear of the drivebelt and any rotating or hot components.

10 If you can hear the injectors operating, but the engine is misfiring, the electrical circuits are functioning correctly, but the injectors might be dirty or clogged. Try a commercial injector cleaning product (available at auto parts stores). If cleaning the injectors doesn't help, replace the injectors.

11 If an injector is not operating (it makes no sound), disconnect the injector electrical connector and measure the resistance across the injector terminals with an ohmmeter. Compare this measurement to the other injectors. If the resistance of the non-operational injector is quite different from the other injectors, replace it.

12 If the injector is not operating, but the resistance reading is within the range of resistance of the other injectors, the PCM or the circuit between the PCM and the injector might be faulty.

2.2b On 2008 and earlier models, the fuel pump relay is located in the interior fuse/relay box. On 2009 and later models, it's located in the underhood fuse/relay box. On 3.7L V6 models, there's an additional relay behind the rear seat back and quarter trim panel

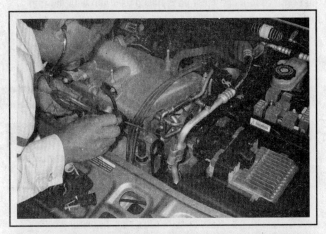

2.9 An automotive stethoscope is used to listen to the fuel injectors in operation

3 Fuel pressure relief procedure

1 Remove the fuel filler cap to relieve any pressure built-up in the fuel tank.

2 Unplug the electrical connector from the fuel pump (see illustration 7.4a).

3 Attempt to start the engine; it should immediately stall. Crank the engine several more times to ensure the fuel system has been completely relieved. Disconnect the cable from the negative terminal of the battery before working on the fuel system.

4 It's a good idea to cover any fuel connection to be disassembled with rags to absorb the residual fuel that may leak out. Properly dispose of the rags.

4 Fuel pressure - check

♦ **Refer to illustration 4.2**

➡ **Note: The following procedure assumes that the fuel pump is receiving voltage and runs.**

1 Relieve the fuel system pressure (see Section 3), then disconnect the cable from the negative battery terminal (see Chapter 5). Remove the upper engine cover, pull the cover up from each side and lift the cover off the mounting posts in the center of the cover.

2 Disconnect the fuel supply line to the fuel rail (see the "Disconnecting Fuel Line Fittings" chart), then use an adapter to connect the fuel pressure gauge between the fuel line and the fuel rail (see illustration).

3 Reconnect the battery. Start the engine and allow it to idle. Note the gauge reading as soon as the pressure stabilizes, and compare it with the pressure listed in this Chapter's Specifications.

4 If the fuel pressure is not within specifications, check the following:

a) Check for a restriction in the fuel system (kinked fuel line, plugged fuel pump inlet strainer or clogged fuel filter). If no restrictions are found, replace the fuel pump module (see Section 7).

➡ **Note: At the time of writing, the fuel strainer and filter are not replaceable and must be replaced as a unit with the fuel pump module.**

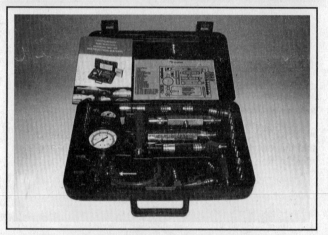

4.2 This fuel pressure testing kit contains all the necessary fittings and adapters, along with the fuel pressure gauge, to test most automotive systems

b) If the fuel pressure is higher than specified, replace the fuel pump module (see Section 7).

5 Turn off the engine. Fuel pressure should not fall more than 8 psi over five minutes. If it does, the problem could be a leaky fuel injector, fuel line leak, or faulty fuel pump module.

6 Relieve the fuel system pressure (see Section 3), then disconnect the fuel pressure gauge.

7 Reconnect the fuel line to the fuel rail.

8 Reconnect the battery (see Chapter 5). Turn the ignition key to the On position and check for fuel leaks.

5 Fuel lines and fittings - general information and disconnection

1 Relieve the fuel pressure before servicing fuel lines or fittings (see Section 3), then disconnect the cable from the negative battery terminal (see Chapter 5) before proceeding.

2 The fuel supply line connects the fuel pump in the fuel tank to the fuel rail on the engine. The Evaporative Emission (EVAP) system lines connect the fuel tank to the EVAP canister and connect the canister to the intake manifold.

3 Whenever you're working under the vehicle, be sure to inspect all fuel and evaporative emission lines for leaks, kinks, dents and other damage. Always replace a damaged fuel or EVAP line immediately.

4 If you find signs of dirt in the lines during disassembly, disconnect all lines and blow them out with compressed air. Inspect the fuel strainer on the fuel pump pick-up unit for damage and deterioration.

Disconnecting Fuel Line Fittings

Two-tab type fitting; depress both tabs with your fingers, then pull the fuel line and the fitting apart

On this type of fitting, depress the two buttons on opposite sides of the fitting, then pull it off the fuel line

Threaded fuel line fitting; hold the stationary portion of the line or component (A) while loosening the tube nut (B) with a flare-nut wrench

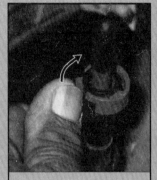

Plastic collar-type fitting; rotate the outer part of the fitting

Metal collar quick-connect fitting; pull the end of the retainer off the fuel line and disengage the other end from the female side of the fitting . . .

. . . insert a fuel line separator tool into the female side of the fitting, push it into the fitting and pull the fuel line off the pipe

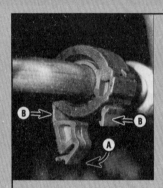

Some fittings are secured by lock tabs. Release the lock tab (A) and rotate it to the fully-opened position, squeeze the two smaller lock tabs (B) . . .

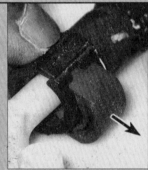

. . . then push the retainer out and pull the fuel line off the pipe

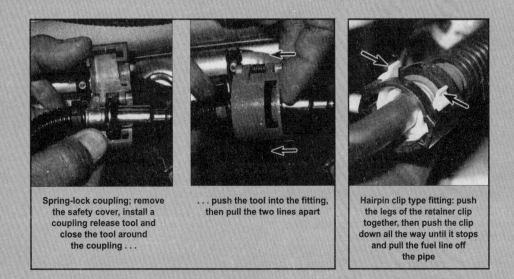

Spring-lock coupling; remove the safety cover, install a coupling release tool and close the tool around the coupling . . .

. . . push the tool into the fitting, then pull the two lines apart

Hairpin clip type fitting: push the legs of the retainer clip together, then push the clip down all the way until it stops and pull the fuel line off the pipe

STEEL TUBING

5   It is critical that the fuel lines be replaced with lines of equivalent type and specification.

6   Some steel fuel lines have threaded fittings. When loosening these fittings, hold the stationary fitting with a wrench while turning the tube nut.

PLASTIC TUBING

7   When replacing fuel system plastic tubing, use only original equipment replacement plastic tubing.

✳ CAUTION:

When removing or installing plastic fuel line tubing, be careful not to bend or twist it too much, which can damage it. Also, plastic fuel tubing is NOT heat resistant, so keep it away from excessive heat.

FLEXIBLE HOSES

8   When replacing fuel system flexible hoses, use only original equipment replacements.

9   Don't route fuel hoses (or metal lines) within four inches of the exhaust system or within ten inches of the catalytic converter. Make sure that no rubber hoses are installed directly against the vehicle, particularly in places where there is any vibration. If allowed to touch some vibrating part of the vehicle, a hose can easily become chafed and it might start leaking. A good rule of thumb is to maintain a minimum of 1/4-inch clearance around a hose (or metal line) to prevent contact with the vehicle underbody.

6   Exhaust system servicing - general information

▶ **Refer to illustration 6.1**

✳ WARNING:

Allow exhaust system components to cool before inspection or repair. Also, when working under the vehicle, make sure it is securely supported on jackstands.

1   The exhaust system consists of the exhaust manifolds, catalytic converter, muffler, tailpipe and all connecting pipes, flanges and clamps. The exhaust system is isolated from the vehicle body and from chassis components by a series of rubber hangers (see illustration). Periodically inspect these hangers for cracks or other signs of deterioration, replacing them as necessary.

2   Conduct regular inspections of the exhaust system to keep it safe and quiet. Look for any damaged or bent parts, open seams, holes, loose connections, excessive corrosion or other defects which could allow exhaust fumes to enter the vehicle. Do not repair deteriorated exhaust system components; replace them with new parts.

3   If the exhaust system components are extremely corroded, or rusted together, a cutting torch is the most convenient tool for removal. Consult a properly-equipped repair shop. If a cutting torch is not available, you can use a hacksaw, or if you have compressed air, there are special pneumatic cutting chisels that can also be used. Wear safety goggles to protect your eyes from metal chips and wear work gloves to protect your hands.

4   Here are some simple guidelines to follow when repairing the exhaust system:

   a) Work from the back to the front when removing exhaust system components.

   b) Apply penetrating oil to the exhaust system component fasteners to make them easier to remove.

   c) Use new gaskets, hangers and clamps.

   d) Apply anti-seize compound to the threads of all exhaust system fasteners during reassembly.

   e) Be sure to allow sufficient clearance between newly installed parts and all points on the underbody to avoid overheating the floor pan and possibly damaging the interior carpet and insulation. Pay particularly close attention to the catalytic converter and heat shield.

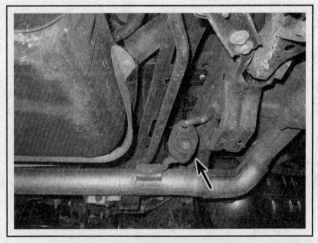

6.1 A typical exhaust system hanger. Inspect regularly and replace at the first sign of damage or deterioration

7   Fuel pump module - removal and installation

♦ Refer to illustrations 7.3, 7.4a, 7.4b, 7.5 and 7.6

⁂ **WARNING:**

Gasoline is extremely flammable. See *Fuel system warnings* in Section 1.

➡ **Note: The fuel pump module includes the fuel pump, the fuel level sending unit, a fuel filter and, on mechanical returnless pumps, a fuel pressure regulator. The fuel level sending unit on 2008 and earlier models is the only component separately serviceable.**

1   Relieve the fuel system pressure (see Section 3). Disconnect the cable from the negative battery terminal (see Chapter 5).
2   Remove the rear seat cushion (see Chapter 11).
3   Remove the fuel pump access cover screws (see illustration).
4   Disconnect the electrical connector (see illustration) and the fuel supply line quick-connect fitting from the fuel pump module (see illustration).
5   On 2008 and earlier locking cap/ring type models, tap the fuel tank module lock ring counterclockwise with a hammer and brass punch (to avoid sparks) (see illustration).
6   On other 2008 and earlier models, remove the fuel tank module mounting plate fasteners and plate (see illustration).
7   On 2009 and later models, use special service tool # 49 F042 001 to unscrew the fuel pump cap or locking ring.
8   Carefully pull the fuel pump module out of the tank. Angle it as necessary to protect the fuel level sensor float arm.
9   Inspect the O-ring and replace it if it shows any sign of deterioration.
10 Installation is the reverse of removal.

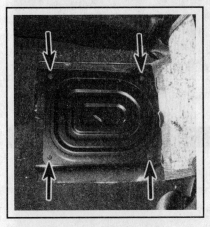

7.3 Fuel pump module access over screws

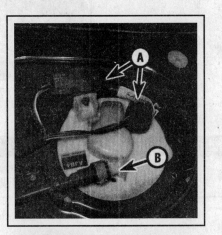

7.4a Typical fuel pump module electrical connector (A) and fuel supply line quick-connect fitting (B)

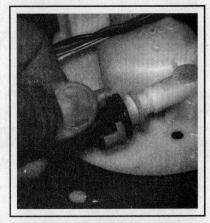

7.4b Open the quick connect fitting lock, then push the line in and pull the line off of the module

7.5 Use a brass punch and a hammer to loosen and unscrew the fuel pump module lock ring

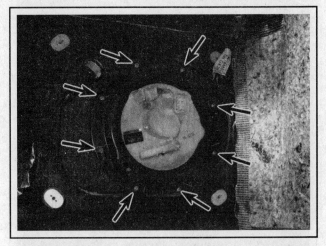

7.6 Remove the fuel pump module lock plate mounting screws

8 Fuel tank - removal and installation

▶ Refer to illustration 8.9

✷✷ WARNING:

Gasoline is extremely flammable. See *Fuel system warnings* in Section 1.

➥ Note: The following procedure is much easier to perform if the fuel tank is empty.

1 Remove the fuel tank filler cap to relieve fuel tank pressure.

2 Relieve the fuel system pressure (see Section 3).

3 Disconnect the cable from the negative battery terminal (see Chapter 5).

4 Disconnect the electrical connector and fuel supply line quick-connect fitting from the fuel pump module (see Section 7).

5 Raise the rear of the vehicle and support it securely on jackstands.

6 Remove the exhaust pipe (see Section 6).

7 Loosen the hose clamps and disconnect the fuel filler neck hose and EVAP system hoses from the tank.

8 Remove the splash shield (if equipped).

9 Support the fuel tank securely, then remove the fuel tank retaining strap bolts (see illustration). Remove the straps and carefully lower the fuel tank.

10 Installation is the reverse of removal. Be sure to tighten the fuel tank strap bolts securely.

11 Reconnect the cable to the negative battery terminal (see Chapter 5), then start the engine and check for fuel leaks.

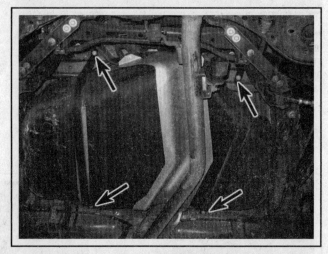

8.9 Fuel tank strap mounting fastener locations

9 Air filter housing - removal and installation

AIR INTAKE DUCT

▶ Refer to illustration 9.1

1 Disconnect the PCV fresh air hose from the air intake duct (see illustration).

2 Loosen the clamps at the air filter housing and the throttle body and remove the air intake duct.

3 Installation is the reverse of removal.

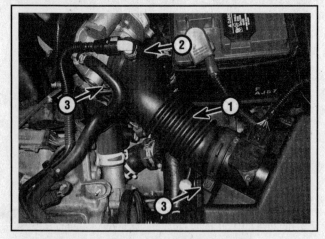

9.1 Air intake duct details (3.0L V6 shown, other models similar)

1 Air intake duct   *3 Hose clamps*
2 PCV fresh air hose

AIR FILTER HOUSING

▶ Refer to illustration 9.6

4 Remove the air intake duct (see Steps 1 and 2).

5 Disconnect the electrical connector from the MAF sensor (see Chapter 6) and remove the housing cover.

6 Disconnect any vacuum lines and electrical connectors (see illustration). Remove the air filter housing from the grommets and remove the housing from the vehicle.

7 Inspect the condition of the filter housing mounting grommets. If they're cracked, torn or deteriorated, replace them.

8 Installation is the reverse of removal.

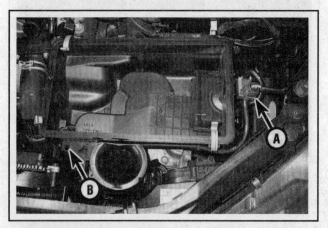

9.6 Disconnect any electrical connectors (A) and vacuum lines (B) mounted to the housing

10 Throttle body - removal and installation

▶ **Refer to illustration 10.3**

❋❋ WARNING:

Wait until the engine is completely cool before beginning this procedure.

1 Disconnect the cable from the negative battery terminal (see Chapter 5).

2 Remove the air intake duct (see Section 9).

3 Disconnect the electrical connector from the throttle body (see illustration).

4 Clamp-off and disconnect the coolant hoses from the throttle body.

5 Remove the throttle body mounting fasteners and detach the throttle body from the intake manifold. Discard the gasket; it should be replaced with a new one. Cover the intake manifold opening with a clean shop towel.

6 Installation is the reverse of removal. Be sure to use a new gasket and tighten the throttle body fasteners to the torque listed in this Chapter's Specifications.

10.3 Throttle body details (3.0L V6 engine shown)

1	Electrical connector (pull out the locking tab to release)	2	Coolant hoses
		3	Throttle body mounting fasteners

11 Fuel rail and injectors - removal and installation

❋❋ WARNING:

Gasoline is extremely flammable. See *Fuel system warnings* in Section 1.

1 Relieve the fuel system pressure (see Section 3).

2 Disconnect the cable from the negative battery terminal (see Chapter 5).

FOUR-CYLINDER MODELS

3 Disconnect the fuel supply line quick-connect fitting from the fuel rail (see the "Disconnecting Fuel Line Fittings" chart).

4 Disconnect the two wiring harness retainers from the fuel rail and remove the fuel rail insulator.

5 Disconnect the electrical connectors for all wiring that shares the harness with the fuel injectors, then disconnect the four fuel injector electrical connectors. Using a trim removal tool, disengage the two pin-type retainers that secure the wiring harness and harness insulator to the fuel rail, then push the harness aside.

6 Remove the fuel rail mounting fasteners, then remove both fuel rails and their injectors as an assembly.

7 Remove each fuel injector retaining clip with a pair of needle-nose pliers and remove the injector from its bore in the fuel rail. Remove and discard the upper and lower injector O-rings. Repeat this procedure for each injector.

➡ **Note: Even if you only removed the fuel rail assembly to replace a single injector or a leaking O-ring, it's a good idea to remove all of the injectors from the fuel rail and replace all of the O-rings at the same time.**

8 Coat the new upper O-rings with clean engine oil and slide them into place on each of the fuel injectors. Coat the new lower O-rings with clean engine oil and install them on the lower ends of the injectors.

9 Coat the outside surface of each upper O-ring with clean engine oil, then insert each injector into its bore in the fuel rail. Install the isolators with new seals on the injectors, if equipped.

10 Install the injectors and fuel rail assembly on the intake manifold. Tighten the fuel rail mounting fasteners securely.

11 The remainder of installation is the reverse of removal.

12 Reconnect the cable to the negative battery terminal (see Chapter 5).

13 Turn the ignition switch to ON (but don't operate the starter).This activates the fuel pump for about two seconds, which builds up fuel pressure in the fuel lines and the fuel rail. Repeat this step two or three times, then check the fuel lines, fuel rails and injectors for fuel leaks.

V6 MODELS

▶ **Refer to illustrations 11.16, 11.18, 11.20, 11.21 and 11.24**

14 Remove the upper intake manifold (see Chapter 2B).

15 Disconnect the fuel supply line at the fuel rail (see the "Disconnecting Fuel Line Fittings" chart).

11.16 Disconnect the injector electrical connectors (A, three not visible in this photo), then detach the harness retainers (B) from the fuel rail (3.0L V6 model shown)

11.18 Lower intake manifold bolt tightening sequence and fuel rail mounting bolts (3.0L V6 models)

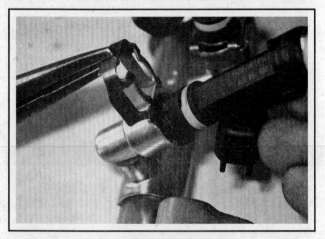

11.20 Before removing the injector retaining clips, note how they're installed to ensure that they're correctly reinstalled

11.21 Injector O-rings

16 Disconnect the electrical connector from each fuel injector (see illustration).

17 Detach the three pin-type retainers from the fuel rail, push the wiring harness aside and remove the other three injector electrical connectors.

18 On 3.0L models, remove the eight lower intake manifold bolts in the reverse of the tightening sequence (see illustration), then remove the two lower intake manifolds and the fuel rail and injectors as a single assembly. Remove the fuel rail mounting bolts and pull the two lower intake manifolds off the injectors.

19 On 3.7L models, remove the four fuel rail mounting bolts, then remove the fuel rail and injectors as a single assembly.

20 Release the fuel injector retaining clip (see illustration) and remove each injector from its bore in the fuel rail.

21 Remove the upper and lower injector O-rings (see illustration) from each injector and discard them.

➡ **Note: Even if you only removed the fuel rail assembly to replace a single injector or a leaking O-ring, it's a good idea to remove all of the injectors from the fuel rail and replace all of the O-rings at the same time.**

22 Coat the new upper O-rings with clean engine oil and slide them into place on each of the fuel injectors. Coat the new lower O-rings with

clean engine oil and install them on the lower ends of the injectors.

23 Coat the outside surface of each upper O-ring with clean engine oil, then insert each injector into its bore in the fuel rail. Secure the injectors to the fuel rail with the injector retaining clips.

24 On 3.0L models, remove the intake manifold gaskets and install new ones (see illustration).

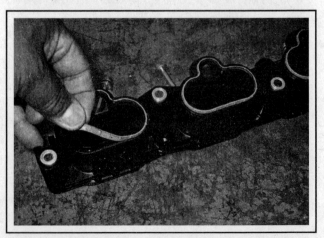

11.24 Remove and inspect the intake manifold gaskets

25 On 3.0L models, install the intake manifolds on the injectors, then attach the fuel rail assembly to the intake manifolds, tightening the bolts by hand. Install the fuel rail and intake manifolds as a single assembly. Be sure to tighten the intake manifold bolts in the correct sequence (see illustration 11.18) to the torque listed in this Chapter's Specifications.

26 Tighten the fuel rail bolts securely. The remainder of installation is the reverse of removal.

27 Reconnect the cable to the negative battery terminal (see Chapter 5).

28 Turn the ignition switch to ON (but don't operate the starter). This activates the fuel pump for about two seconds, which builds up fuel pressure in the fuel lines and the fuel rail. Repeat this step two or three times, then check the fuel lines, fuel rails and injectors for fuel leaks.

Specifications

Fuel system pressure (approximate)	
Four cylinder models	54.4 to 65.2 psi (375 to 450 kPa)
V6 models	62.4 to 73.9 psi (430 to 510 kPa)

Torque specifications

➡ **Note: One foot-pound (ft-lb) of torque is equivalent to 12 inch-pounds (in-lbs) of torque. Torque values below approximately 15 foot-pounds are expressed in inch-pounds, because most foot-pound torque wrenches are not accurate at these smaller values.**

Throttle body mounting fasteners	89 in-lbs	10 Nm
Intake manifold bolts (3.0L V6 models)	89 in-lbs	10 Nm

Section

5

ENGINE ELECTRICAL SYSTEMS

1 General information and precautions

GENERAL INFORMATION

Ignition system

The electronic ignition system consists of the Crankshaft Position (CKP) sensor, the Camshaft Position (CMP) sensor, the Knock Sensor (KS), the Powertrain Control Module (PCM), the ignition switch, the battery, the individual ignition coils or a coil pack, and the spark plugs. For more information on the CKP, CMP and KS sensors, as well as the PCM, refer to Chapter 6.

Charging system

The charging system includes the alternator (with an integral voltage regulator), the Powertrain Control Module (PCM), the Body Control Module (BCM), a charge indicator light on the dash, the battery, a fuse or fusible link and the wiring connecting all of these components. The charging system supplies electrical power for the ignition system, the lights, the radio, etc. The alternator is driven by a drivebelt.

Starting system

The starting system consists of the battery, the ignition switch, the starter relay, the Powertrain Control Module (PCM), the Body Control Module (BCM), the Transmission Range (TR) switch, the starter motor

and solenoid assembly, and the wiring connecting all of the components.

PRECAUTIONS

Always observe the following precautions when working on the electrical system:

a) Be extremely careful when servicing engine electrical components. They are easily damaged if checked, connected or handled improperly.

b) Never leave the ignition switched on for long periods of time when the engine is not running.

c) Never disconnect the battery cables while the engine is running.

d) Maintain correct polarity when connecting battery cables from another vehicle during jump starting - see the "Booster battery (jump) starting" Section at the front of this manual.

e) Always disconnect the cable from the negative battery terminal before working on the electrical system, but read the battery disconnection procedure first (see Section 3).

It's also a good idea to review the safety-related information regarding the engine electrical systems located in the "Safety first!" Section at the front of this manual before beginning any operation included in this Chapter.

Electrical system components (3.0L V6 shown, others similar)

1	Battery	4	Alternator
2	Engine compartment fuse and relay panel	5	Starter motor (under air filter housing - 3.0L V6 engine)
3	Ignition coils (back coils under upper intake manifold)	6	Starter motor (under battery tray - 3.7L V6 engine)

2 Troubleshooting

IGNITION SYSTEM

1   If a malfunction occurs in the ignition system, do not immediately assume that any particular part is causing the problem. First, check the following items:

a) *Make sure that the cable clamps at the battery terminals are clean and tight.*
b) *Test the condition of the battery (see Steps 21 through 24). If it doesn't pass all the tests, replace it.*
c) *Check the ignition coil or coil pack connections.*
d) *Check any relevant fuses in the engine compartment fuse and relay box (see Chapter 12). If they're burned, determine the cause and repair the circuit.*

Check

▶ **Refer to illustration 2.3**

✳ WARNING:

Because of the high voltage generated by the ignition system, use extreme care when performing a procedure involving ignition components.

➡ **Note 1: The ignition system components on these vehicles are difficult to diagnose. In the event of ignition system failure that you can't diagnose, have the vehicle tested at a dealer service department or other qualified auto repair facility.**

➡ **Note 2: You'll need a spark tester for the following test. Spark testers are available at most auto supply stores.**

2   If the engine turns over but won't start, verify that there is sufficient ignition voltage to fire the spark plugs as follows.

3   On models with a coil-over-plug type ignition system, remove a coil and install the tester between the boot at the lower end of the coil and the spark plug (see illustration). On models with spark plug wires, disconnect a spark plug wire from a spark plug and install the tester between the spark plug wire boot and the spark plug.

4   Crank the engine and note whether or not the tester flashes.

✳ CAUTION:

Do NOT crank the engine or allow it to run for more than five seconds; running the engine for more than five seconds may set a Diagnostic Trouble Code (DTC) for a cylinder misfire.

Models with a coil-over-plug type ignition system

5   If the tester flashes during cranking, the coil is delivering sufficient voltage to the spark plug to fire it. Repeat this test for each cylinder to verify that the other coils are OK.

6   If the tester doesn't flash, remove a coil from another cylinder and swap it for the one being tested. If the tester now flashes, you know that the original coil is bad. If the tester still doesn't flash, the PCM or wiring harness is probably defective. Have the PCM checked out by a dealer service department or other qualified repair shop (testing the PCM is beyond the scope of the do-it-yourselfer because it requires expensive special tools).

7   If the tester flashes during cranking but a misfire code (related to the cylinder being tested) has been stored, the spark plug could be fouled or defective.

Models with spark plug wires

8   If the tester flashes during cranking, sufficient voltage is reaching the spark plug to fire it.

9   Repeat this test on the remaining cylinders.

10   Proceed on this basis until you have verified that there's a good spark from each spark plug wire. If there is, then you have verified that the coils in the coil pack are functioning correctly and that the spark plug wires are OK.

11   If there is no spark from a spark plug wire, then either the coil is bad, the plug wire is bad or a connection at one end of the plug wire is loose. Assuming that you're using new plug wires or known good wires, then the coil is probably defective. Also inspect the coil pack electrical connector. Make sure that it's clean, tight and in good condition.

12   If all the coils are firing correctly, but the engine misfires, then one or more of the plugs might be fouled. Remove and check the spark plugs or install new ones (see Chapter 1).

13   No further testing of the ignition system is possible without special tools. If the problem persists, have the ignition system tested by a dealer service department or other qualified repair shop.

CHARGING SYSTEM

14   If a malfunction occurs in the charging system, do not automatically assume the alternator is causing the problem. First check the following items:

a) *Check the drivebelt tension and condition, as described in Chapter 1. Replace it if it's worn or deteriorated.*
b) *Make sure the alternator mounting bolts are tight.*
c) *Inspect the alternator wiring harness and the connectors at the alternator and voltage regulator. They must be in good condition, tight and have no corrosion.*
d) *Check the fusible link (if equipped) or main fuse in the underhood fuse/relay box. If it is burned, determine the cause, repair the circuit and replace the link or fuse (the vehicle will not start and/or the accessories will not work if the fusible link or main fuse is blown).*
e) *Start the engine and check the alternator for abnormal noises (a shrieking or squealing sound indicates a bad bearing).*
f) *Check the battery. Make sure it's fully charged and in good condition (one bad cell in a battery can cause overcharging by the alternator).*

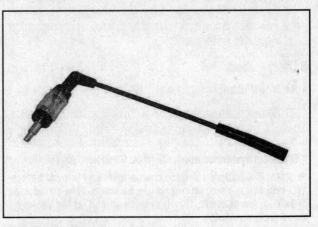

2.3 Spark tester

2.21 To test the open circuit voltage of the battery, touch the black probe of the voltmeter to the negative terminal and the red probe to the positive terminal of the battery; a fully charged battery should be at least 12.6 volts

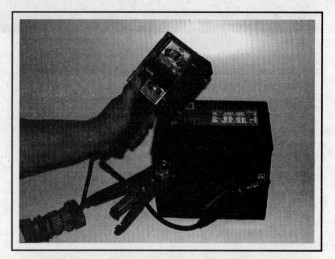

2.23 Connect a battery load tester to the battery and check the battery condition under load following the tool manufacturer's instructions

g) *Disconnect the battery cables (negative first, then positive). Inspect the battery posts and the cable clamps for corrosion. Clean them thoroughly if necessary (see Chapter 1). Reconnect the cables (positive first, negative last).*

Alternator - check

15 Use a voltmeter to check the battery voltage with the engine off. It should be at least 12.6 volts (see illustration 2.21).

16 Start the engine and check the battery voltage again. It should now be approximately 13.5 to 15 volts.

17 If the voltage reading is more or less than the specified charging voltage, the voltage regulator is probably defective, which will require replacement of the alternator (the voltage regulator is not replaceable separately). Remove the alternator and have it bench tested (most auto parts stores will do this for you).

18 The charging system (battery) light on the instrument cluster lights up when the ignition key is turned to ON, but it should go out when the engine starts.

19 If the charging system light stays on after the engine has been started, there is a problem with the charging system. Before replacing the alternator, check the battery condition, alternator belt tension and electrical cable connections.

20 If replacing the alternator doesn't restore voltage to the specified range, have the charging system tested by a dealer service department or other qualified repair shop.

Battery - check

▶ **Refer to illustrations 2.21 and 2.23**

21 Check the battery state of charge. Visually inspect the indicator eye on the top of the battery (if equipped with one); if the indicator eye is black in color, charge the battery as described in Chapter 1. Next perform an open circuit voltage test using a digital voltmeter.

➡ **Note: The battery's surface charge must be removed before accurate voltage measurements can be made. Turn on the high beams for ten seconds, then turn them off and let the vehicle stand for two minutes.**

With the engine and all accessories Off, touch the negative probe of the

voltmeter to the negative terminal of the battery and the positive probe to the positive terminal of the battery (see illustration). The battery voltage should be 12.6 volts or slightly above. If the battery is less than the specified voltage, charge the battery before proceeding to the next test. Do not proceed with the battery load test unless the battery charge is correct.

22 Disconnect the negative battery cable, then the positive cable from the battery.

23 Perform a battery load test. An accurate check of the battery condition can only be performed with a load tester (see illustration). This test evaluates the ability of the battery to operate the starter and other accessories during periods of high current draw. Connect the load tester to the battery terminals. Load test the battery according to the tool manufacturer's instructions. This tool increases the load demand (current draw) on the battery.

24 Maintain the load on the battery for 15 seconds and observe that the battery voltage does not drop below 9.6 volts. If the battery condition is weak or defective, the tool will indicate this condition immediately.

➡ **Note: Cold temperatures will cause the minimum voltage reading to drop slightly. Follow the chart given in the manufacturer's instructions to compensate for cold climates. Minimum load voltage for freezing temperatures (32 degrees F) should be approximately 9.1 volts.**

STARTING SYSTEM

The starter rotates, but the engine doesn't

25 Remove the starter (see Section 8). Check the overrunning clutch and bench test the starter to make sure the drive mechanism extends fully for proper engagement with the flywheel ring gear. If it doesn't, replace the starter.

26 Check the flywheel ring gear for missing teeth and other damage. With the ignition turned off, rotate the flywheel so you can check the entire ring gear.

The starter is noisy

27 If the solenoid is making a chattering noise, first check the battery

(see Steps 21 through 24). If the battery is okay, check the cables and connections.

28 If you hear a grinding, crashing metallic sound when you turn the key to Start, check for loose starter mounting bolts. If they're tight, remove the starter and inspect the teeth on the starter pinion gear and flywheel ring gear. Look for missing or damaged teeth.

29 If the starter sounds fine when you first turn the key to Start, but then stops rotating the engine and emits a zinging sound, the problem is probably a defective starter drive that's not staying engaged with the ring gear. Replace the starter.

The starter rotates slowly

30 Check the battery (see Steps 21 through 24).

31 If the battery is okay, verify all connections (at the battery, the starter solenoid and motor) are clean, corrosion-free and tight. Make sure the cables aren't frayed or damaged.

32 Check that the starter mounting bolts are tight so it grounds properly. Also check the pinion gear and flywheel ring gear for evidence of a mechanical bind (galling, deformed gear teeth or other damage).

The starter does not rotate at all

33 Check the battery (see Steps 21 through 24).

34 If the battery is okay, verify all connections (at the battery, the starter solenoid and motor) are clean, corrosion-free and tight. Make sure the cables aren't frayed or damaged.

35 Check all of the fuses in the underhood fuse/relay box.

36 Check that the starter mounting bolts are tight so it grounds properly.

37 Check for voltage at the starter solenoid "S" terminal when the ignition key is turned to the start position. If voltage is present, replace the starter/solenoid assembly. If no voltage is present, the problem could be the starter relay, the Transmission Range (TR) switch (see Chapter 6) or clutch start switch (see Chapter 8), or with an electrical connector somewhere in the circuit (see the wiring diagrams at the end of Chapter 12). Also, on many modern vehicles, the Powertrain Control Module (PCM) and the Body Control Module (BCM) control the voltage signal to the starter solenoid; on such vehicles a special scan tool is required for diagnosis.

3   Battery - disconnection

※ CAUTION:

Always disconnect the cable from the negative battery terminal FIRST and hook it up LAST or the battery may be shorted by the tool being used to loosen the cable clamps.

Some systems on the vehicle require battery power to be available at all times, either to maintain continuous operation (alarm system, power door locks, etc.), or to maintain control unit memory (radio station presets, Powertrain Control Module and other control units). When the battery is disconnected, the power that maintains these systems is cut. So, before you disconnect the battery, please note that on a vehicle with power door locks, it's a wise precaution to remove the key from the ignition and to keep it with you, so that it does not get locked inside if the power door locks should engage accidentally when the battery is reconnected!

Devices known as "memory-savers" can be used to avoid some of these problems. Precise details vary according to the device used. The typical memory saver is plugged into the cigarette lighter and is connected to a spare battery. Then the vehicle battery can be disconnected from the electrical system. The memory saver will provide sufficient current to maintain audio unit security codes, PCM memory, etc. and will provide power to always hot circuits such as the clock and radio memory circuits.

※ WARNING 1:

Some memory savers deliver a considerable amount of current in order to keep vehicle systems operational after the main battery is disconnected. If you're using a memory saver, make sure that the circuit concerned is actually open before servicing it.

※ WARNING 2:

If you're going to work near any of the airbag system components, the battery MUST be disconnected and a memory saver must NOT be used. If a memory saver is used, power will be supplied to the airbag, which means that it could accidentally deploy and cause serious personal injury.

To disconnect the battery for service procedures requiring power to be cut from the vehicle, loosen the cable end bolt and disconnect the cable from the negative battery terminal. Isolate the cable end to prevent it from coming into accidental contact with the battery terminal.

4 Battery and battery tray - removal and installation

▶ **Refer to illustrations 4.1 and 4.4**

1   Disconnect the cable from the negative battery terminal first, then disconnect the cable from the positive battery terminal (see illustration).

2   Remove the battery hold-down clamp.

3   Lift out the battery. Be careful - it's heavy.

➡ **Note:** Battery straps and handlers are available at most auto parts stores for reasonable prices. They make it easier to remove and carry the battery.

4   Remove the battery tray mounting fasteners and remove the tray (see illustration).

5   If you are replacing the battery, make sure you get one that's identical, with the same dimensions, amperage rating, cold cranking rating, etc. Also, be sure to remove the heat shield from the old battery and install it on the new battery.

6   Installation is the reverse of removal. Be sure to connect the positive cable first and the negative cable last.

4.1 Typical battery details - 2008 and earlier models

1	Negative battery cable	4	Hold-down bolt
2	Positive battery cable	5	Battery hold-down clamp
3	Hold-down nut/J-bolt		

4.4 Typical battery tray mounting fastener locations

5 Battery cables - replacement

1   When removing the cables, always disconnect the cable from the negative battery terminal first and hook it up last, or you might accidentally short out the battery with the tool you're using to loosen the cable clamps. Even if you're only replacing the cable for the positive terminal, be sure to disconnect the negative cable from the battery first.

2   Disconnect the old cables from the battery, then trace each of them to their opposite ends and disconnect them. Be sure to note the routing of each cable before disconnecting it to ensure correct installation.

3   If you are replacing any of the old cables, take them with you when buying new cables. It is vitally important that you replace the cables with identical parts.

4   Clean the threads of the solenoid or ground connection with a wire brush to remove rust and corrosion. Apply a light coat of battery terminal corrosion inhibitor or petroleum jelly to the threads to prevent future corrosion.

5   Attach the cable to the solenoid or ground connection and tighten the mounting nut/bolt securely.

6   Before connecting a new cable to the battery, make sure that it reaches the battery post without having to be stretched.

7   Connect the cable to the positive battery terminal first, then connect the ground cable to the negative battery terminal.

6 Ignition coils - replacement

▶ **Refer to illustrations 6.4 and 6.6**

1   Disconnect the cable from the negative battery terminal (see Section 3).

2   Remove the upper engine cover, pull the cover up from each side and lift the cover off the mounting posts in the center of the cover.

3   On V6 engines, remove the upper intake manifold (see Chapter 2B).

6.4 Ignition coil details (3.0L V6 engine shown, others similar)

1 Electrical connector   *2 Mounting fastener*

4 Disconnect the electrical connector from the ignition coil (see illustration).
5 Remove the mounting fastener from the ignition coil.

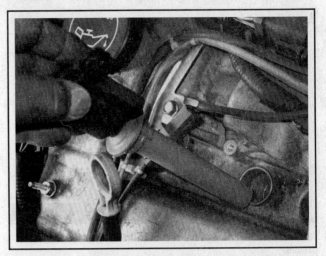

6.6 Remove the coil assembly from the spark plug tube

6 Grasp the coil firmly and pull it off the spark plug (see illustration).
7 Installation is the reverse of removal.

7 Alternator - removal and installation

1 Disconnect the cable from the negative battery terminal (see Section 3).
2 Loosen the right front wheel lug nuts. Raise the front of the vehicle and place it securely on jackstands. Remove the right front wheel.
3 Remove the splash shield screws and pushpins and remove the splash shield (see Chapter 11, Section 10).
4 Remove the upper engine cover, pull the cover up from each side and lift the cover off the mounting posts in the center of the cover.
5 Remove the drivebelt (see Chapter 1).

2.3L FOUR-CYLINDER MODELS

6 Remove the alternator upper air duct bracket mounting bolt and air duct mounting bolts, then remove the upper duct.
7 Disconnect the alternator B+ terminal nut and electrical connector.
8 Remove the alternator mounting fasteners.
9 Remove the alternator and heat shield from the vehicle as an assembly.
10 Remove the heat shield mounting fasteners and remove the heat shield from the alternator.

2.5L FOUR-CYLINDER MODELS

11 Remove the alternator duct mounting nut and duct. Remove the duct mounting bracket bolts from the front of the alternator and remove the bracket.

➡ **Note: Remove the air conditioning line bracket and move the line out of the way. Do not disconnect the air conditioning line.**

12 Disconnect the alternator B+ terminal nut and electrical connector.
13 Remove the three alternator mounting bolts and remove the alternator.

3.0L V6 MODELS

▶ **Refer to illustration 7.15**

14 Remove the rear exhaust manifold and exhaust pipe (see Chapter 2B).
15 Disconnect the alternator B+ terminal nut and electrical connector (see illustration).
16 Remove the alternator mounting bolts and remove the alternator.

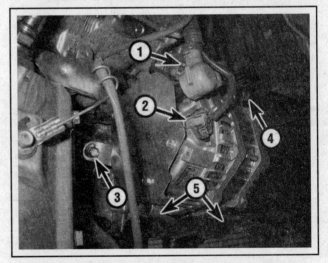

7.15 Alternator details (3.0L V6 shown, others similar)

1 B+ terminal nut (under cover)	3 Shield mounting bolt
	4 Upper mounting bolt
2 Alternator electrical connector	5 Lower mounting bolts

3.7L V6 MODELS

17 Drain the engine coolant (see Chapter 1).

18 Remove the air filter housing fresh air duct (see Chapter 4).

19 Remove the cooling fan assembly (see Chapter 3).

20 Remove the air conditioning compressor (see Chapter 3) without disconnecting the lines to the compressor, and secure it out of the way.

21 Disconnect the alternator B+ terminal nut and electrical connector.

22 Loosen the alternator lower mounting bolt.

23 Remove the alternator upper mounting bolt and lift the alternator off of the lower bolt and out of the vehicle.

❈❈ CAUTION:

Take care not to damage the radiator fins during the removal process.

ALL MODELS

24 If you're replacing the alternator, take the old one with you when purchasing the replacement unit. Make sure that the new/rebuilt unit looks identical to the old alternator. Look at the electrical terminals on the backside of the alternator. They should be the same in number, size and location as the terminals on the old alternator. Finally, look at the identification numbers. They will be stamped into the housing or printed on a tag attached to the housing. Make sure that the ID numbers are the same on both alternators.

25 Many new/rebuilt alternators DO NOT have a pulley installed, so you might have to swap the pulley from the old unit to the new/rebuilt one. When buying an alternator, find out the store's policy regarding pulley swaps. Some stores perform this service free of charge. If your local auto parts store doesn't offer this service, you'll have to purchase a puller for removing the pulley and do it yourself.

26 Installation is the reverse of removal. Be sure to tighten the alternator mounting bolts securely.

27 Reconnect the cable to the negative terminal of the battery. Check the charging voltage (see Section 2) to verify that the alternator is operating correctly.

---

8   Starter motor - removal and installation

FOUR-CYLINDER MODELS

▶ **Refer to illustration 8.6**

1 Detach the cable from the negative terminal of the battery (see Section 3).

2 Remove the air filter housing (see Chapter 4).

3 Raise the vehicle and support it securely on jackstands. Remove the underbody cover.

4 Remove the wiring harness bracket fasteners and bracket.

5 Disconnect the starter motor solenoid wire nut and the starter motor battery cable nut, and disconnect both wires from the starter

➡ **Note: On 2.5L engines, remove the Manifold Absolute Pressure (MAP) sensor (see Chapter 6).**

6 Remove the starter mounting studs and remove the starter (see illustration).

➡ **Note: The end of the starter uses an insulator/gasket between the motor and the block that must be replaced if damaged.**

7 Installation is the reverse of removal. Be sure to tighten the starter mounting stud and bolt securely.

V6 MODELS

▶ **Refer to illustrations 8.10 and 8.11**

8 Remove the battery and the battery tray (see Section 4). If you're

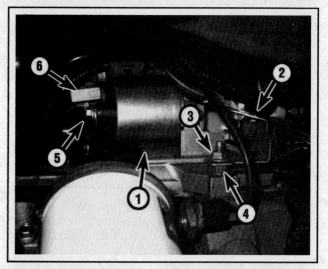

8.6 Starter motor details (2.3L four-cylinder shown, 2.5L four-cylinder similar)

1	Starter motor	4	Starter lower mounting stud
2	Wiring harness bracket		(upper stud not visible)
3	Wiring harness bracket	5	Starter motor (B) battery
	lower mounting nut (upper		terminal
	nut not visible)	6	Starter solenoid (S) terminal

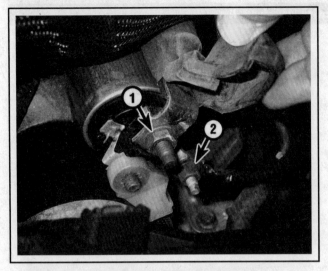

8.10 Starter motor details (3.0L V6 model shown)

1 Starter motor battery   *2 Starter solenoid terminal*
terminal

working on a model with a 3.0L V6 engine, also remove the air filter housing (see Chapter 4).

9 Remove the transaxle selector cable bracket mounting bolts and position the bracket, with cables still attached, out of the way.

8.11 Starter motor mounting bolt (other bolt not visible) (3.0L V6 model shown)

10 Remove the starter motor solenoid wire nut and the starter motor battery cable nut, then disconnect both wires from the starter motor (see illustration).

11 Remove the starter motor mounting fasteners (see illustration) and remove the starter motor.

12 Installation is the reverse of removal.

Torque specifications	Ft-lbs (unless otherwise indicated)	Nm
Front suspension		
Alternator mounting bolts		
2.3L engines	33	45
All other engines	37	50
Starter mounting bolts	33	45

Section

6

EMISSIONS AND ENGINE CONTROL SYSTEMS

1　General information

➡ **Note: There are two different parts manufacturers; one in Mexico and one in Hiroshima. These parts are not interchangeable, and will not operate correctly if used in the wrong application. Check the "Vehicle identification numbers" Section at the beginning of this manual to verify which manufacturer's parts are in your vehicle.**

To prevent pollution of the atmosphere from incompletely burned and evaporating gases, and to maintain good driveability and fuel economy, a number of emission control systems are incorporated. They include the:

CATALYTIC CONVERTER

A catalytic converter is an emission control device in the exhaust system that reduces certain pollutants in the exhaust gas stream. There are two types of converters: oxidation converters and reduction converters.

Oxidation converters contain a monolithic substrate (a ceramic honeycomb) coated with the semi-precious metals platinum and palladium. An oxidation catalyst reduces unburned hydrocarbons (HC) and carbon monoxide (CO) by adding oxygen to the exhaust stream as it passes through the substrate, which, in the presence of high temperature and the catalyst materials, converts the HC and CO to water vapor (H_2O) and carbon dioxide (CO_2).

Reduction converters contain a monolithic substrate coated with platinum and rhodium. A reduction catalyst reduces oxides of nitrogen (NOx) by removing oxygen, which in the presence of high temperature and the catalyst material produces nitrogen (N) and carbon dioxide (CO_2).

Catalytic converters that combine both types of catalysts in one assembly are known as "three-way catalysts" or TWCs. A TWC can reduce all three pollutants.

EVAPORATIVE EMISSIONS CONTROL (EVAP) SYSTEM

The Evaporative Emissions Control (EVAP) system prevents fuel system vapors (which contain unburned hydrocarbons) from escaping into the atmosphere. On warm days, vapors trapped inside the fuel tank expand until the pressure reaches a certain threshold. Then the fuel vapors are routed from the fuel tank through the fuel vapor vent valve and the fuel vapor control valve to the EVAP canister, where they're stored temporarily until the next time the vehicle is operated. When the conditions are right (engine warmed up, vehicle up to speed, moderate or heavy load on the engine, etc.) the PCM opens the canister purge valve, which allows fuel vapors to be drawn from the canister into the intake manifold. Once in the intake manifold, the fuel vapors mix with incoming air before being drawn through the intake ports into the combustion chambers where they're burned up with the rest of the air/fuel mixture. The EVAP system is complex and virtually impossible to troubleshoot without the right tools and training.

EXHAUST GAS RECIRCULATION (EGR) SYSTEM

The EGR system reduces oxides of nitrogen by recirculating exhaust gases from the exhaust manifold, through the EGR valve and intake manifold, then back to the combustion chambers, where it mixes with the incoming air/fuel mixture before being consumed. These recirculated exhaust gases dilute the incoming air/fuel mixture, which cools the combustion chambers, thereby reducing NOx emissions.

The EGR system consists of the Powertrain Control Module (PCM), the EGR valve, the EGR valve position sensor and various other information sensors that the PCM uses to determine when to open the EGR valve. The degree to which the EGR valve is opened is referred to as "EGR valve lift." The PCM is programmed to produce the ideal EGR valve lift for varying operating conditions. The EGR valve position sensor, which is an integral part of the EGR valve, detects the amount of EGR valve lift and sends this information to the PCM. The PCM then compares it with the appropriate EGR valve lift for the operating conditions. The PCM increases current flow to the EGR valve to increase valve lift and reduces the current to reduce the amount of lift. If EGR flow is inappropriate to the operating conditions (idle, cold engine, etc.) the PCM simply cuts the current to the EGR valve and the valve closes.

SECONDARY AIR INJECTION (AIR) SYSTEM

Some models are equipped with a secondary air injection (AIR) system. The secondary air injection system is used to reduce tailpipe emissions on initial engine start-up. The system uses an electric motor/pump assembly, relay, vacuum valve/solenoid, air shut-off valve, check valves and tubing to inject fresh air directly into the exhaust manifolds. The fresh air (oxygen) reacts with the exhaust gas in the catalytic converter to reduce HC and CO levels. The air pump and solenoid are controlled by the PCM through the AIR relay. During initial start-up, the PCM energizes the AIR relay, the relay supplies battery voltage to the air pump and the vacuum valve/solenoid, engine vacuum is applied to the air shut-off valve which opens and allows air to flow through the tubing into the exhaust manifolds. The PCM will operate the air pump until closed loop operation is reached (approximately four minutes). During normal operation, the check valves prevent exhaust backflow into the system.

POWERTRAIN CONTROL MODULE (PCM)

The Powertrain Control Module (PCM) is the brain of the engine management system. It also controls a wide variety of other vehicle systems. In order to program the new PCM, the dealer needs the vehicle as well as the new PCM. If you're planning to replace the PCM with a new one, there is no point in trying to do so at home because you won't be able to program it yourself.

POSITIVE CRANKCASE VENTILATION (PCV) SYSTEM

The Positive Crankcase Ventilation (PCV) system reduces hydrocarbon emissions by scavenging crankcase vapors, which are rich in unburned hydrocarbons. A PCV valve or orifice regulates the flow of gases into the intake manifold in proportion to the amount of intake vacuum available.

The PCV system generally consists of the fresh air inlet hose, the PCV valve or orifice and the crankcase ventilation hose (or PCV hose). The fresh air inlet hose connects the air intake duct to a pipe on the valve cover. The crankcase ventilation hose (or PCV hose) connects the PCV valve or orifice in the valve cover to the intake manifold.

Emissions and engine control system components

1 Accelerator Pedal Position (APP) sensor (at the top of accelerator pedal assembly)

2 Camshaft Position (CMP) sensor, front cylinder head (right end of head, near intake camshaft)

3 Camshaft Position (CMP) sensor, rear cylinder head (right end of head, near intake camshaft)

4 Crankshaft Position (CKP) sensor (lower right rear corner of block, near crankshaft pulley)

5 Engine Coolant Temperature (ECT) sensor (on coolant passage at left end of engine, behind water pump)

6 Knock sensor (on lower left rear side of engine block)

7 Mass Air Flow/Intake Air Temperature (MAF/IAT) sensor

8 Upstream and downstream oxygen sensor, front cylinder head (exhaust manifold/catalyst and exhaust pipe)

9 Upstream and downstream oxygen sensor, rear cylinder head (exhaust manifold/catalyst)

10 Power Steering Pressure (PSP) switch (on underside of power steering pump)

11 Transmission Control Module (TCM) with integral TR sensor, 6-speed automatic (on top of transaxle, at selector shaft)

12 Powertrain Control Module (PCM) (behind and below the battery box)

13 Front catalytic converter (integral component of front exhaust manifold)

14 Rear catalytic converter (integral component of rear exhaust manifold)

15 EVAP canister purge solenoid valve (lower right rear corner of engine compartment, below lower cowl cover)

16 Exhaust Gas Recirculation (EGR) valve

17 Positive Crankcase Ventilation (PCV) valve (on left end of rear valve cover)

Information Sensors

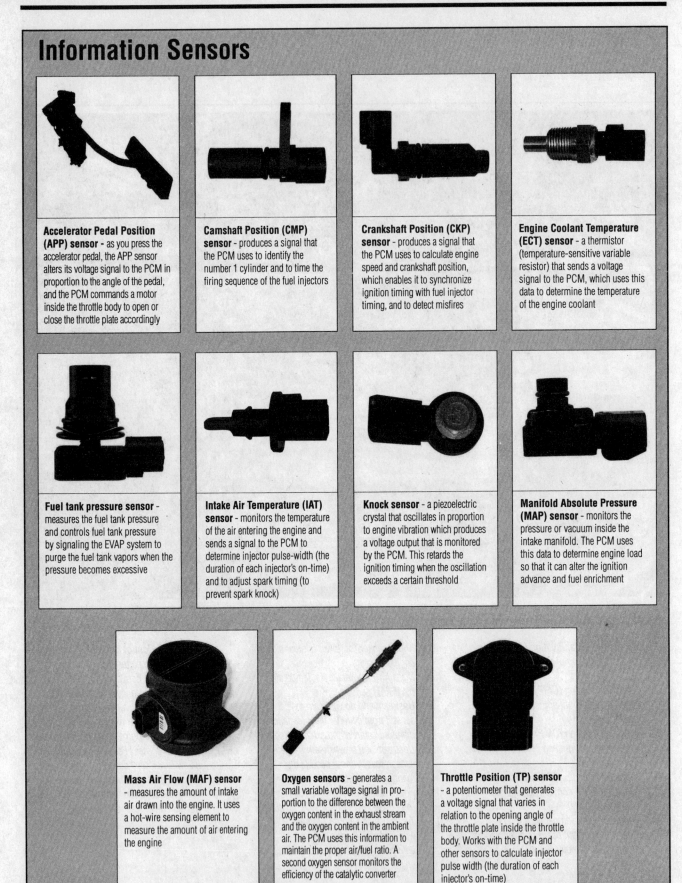

Accelerator Pedal Position (APP) sensor - as you press the accelerator pedal, the APP sensor alters its voltage signal to the PCM in proportion to the angle of the pedal, and the PCM commands a motor inside the throttle body to open or close the throttle plate accordingly

Camshaft Position (CMP) sensor - produces a signal that the PCM uses to identify the number 1 cylinder and to time the firing sequence of the fuel injectors

Crankshaft Position (CKP) sensor - produces a signal that the PCM uses to calculate engine speed and crankshaft position, which enables it to synchronize ignition timing with fuel injector timing, and to detect misfires

Engine Coolant Temperature (ECT) sensor - a thermistor (temperature-sensitive variable resistor) that sends a voltage signal to the PCM, which uses this data to determine the temperature of the engine coolant

Fuel tank pressure sensor - measures the fuel tank pressure and controls fuel tank pressure by signaling the EVAP system to purge the fuel tank vapors when the pressure becomes excessive

Intake Air Temperature (IAT) sensor - monitors the temperature of the air entering the engine and sends a signal to the PCM to determine injector pulse-width (the duration of each injector's on-time) and to adjust spark timing (to prevent spark knock)

Knock sensor - a piezoelectric crystal that oscillates in proportion to engine vibration which produces a voltage output that is monitored by the PCM. This retards the ignition timing when the oscillation exceeds a certain threshold

Manifold Absolute Pressure (MAP) sensor - monitors the pressure or vacuum inside the intake manifold. The PCM uses this data to determine engine load so that it can alter the ignition advance and fuel enrichment

Mass Air Flow (MAF) sensor - measures the amount of intake air drawn into the engine. It uses a hot-wire sensing element to measure the amount of air entering the engine

Oxygen sensors - generates a small variable voltage signal in proportion to the difference between the oxygen content in the exhaust stream and the oxygen content in the ambient air. The PCM uses this information to maintain the proper air/fuel ratio. A second oxygen sensor monitors the efficiency of the catalytic converter

Throttle Position (TP) sensor - a potentiometer that generates a voltage signal that varies in relation to the opening angle of the throttle plate inside the throttle body. Works with the PCM and other sensors to calculate injector pulse width (the duration of each injector's on-time)

Photos courtesy of Wells Manufacturing, except APP and MAF sensors.

2   On Board Diagnosis (OBD) system

GENERAL DESCRIPTION

1   All models are equipped with the second generation OBD-II system. This system consists of an on-board computer known as the Powertrain Control Module (PCM), and information sensors, which monitor various functions of the engine and send data to the PCM. This system incorporates a series of diagnostic monitors that detect and identify fuel injection and emissions control system faults and store the information in the computer memory. This system also tests sensors and output actuators, diagnoses drive cycles, freezes data and clears codes.

2   The PCM is the brain of the electronically controlled fuel and emissions system. It receives data from a number of sensors and other electronic components (switches, relays, etc.). Based on the information it receives, the PCM generates output signals to control various relays, solenoids (fuel injectors) and other actuators. The PCM is specifically calibrated to optimize the emissions, fuel economy and driveability of the vehicle.

3   It isn't a good idea to attempt diagnosis or replacement of the PCM or emission control components at home while the vehicle is under warranty. Because of a federally-mandated warranty which cov- ers the emissions system components and because any owner-induced damage to the PCM, the sensors and/or the control devices may void this warranty, take the vehicle to a dealer service department if the PCM or a system component malfunctions.

SCAN TOOL INFORMATION

▶ Refer to illustrations 2.4a and 2.4b

4   Because extracting the Diagnostic Trouble Codes (DTCs) from an engine management system is now the first step in troubleshooting many computer-controlled systems and components, a code reader, at the very least, will be required (see illustration). More powerful scan tools can also perform many of the diagnostics once associated with expensive factory scan tools (see illustration). If you're planning to obtain a generic scan tool for your vehicle, make sure that it's compatible with OBD-II systems. If you don't plan to purchase a code reader or scan tool and don't have access to one, you can have the codes extracted by a dealer service department or an independent repair shop.

➡ Note: Some auto parts stores even provide this service.

2.4a Simple code readers are an economical way to extract trouble codes when the CHECK ENGINE light comes on

2.4b Hand-held scan tools like these can extract computer codes and also perform diagnostics

3   Obtaining and clearing Diagnostic Trouble Codes (DTCs)

All models covered by this manual are equipped with on-board diagnostics. When the PCM recognizes a malfunction in a monitored emission or engine control system, component or circuit, it turns on the Malfunction Indicator Light (MIL) on the dash. The PCM will continue to display the MIL until the problem is fixed and the Diagnostic Trouble Code (DTC) is cleared from the PCM's memory. You'll need a scan tool to access any DTCs stored in the PCM.

Before outputting any DTCs stored in the PCM, thoroughly inspect ALL electrical connectors and hoses. Make sure that all electrical connections are tight, clean and free of corrosion. And make sure that all hoses are correctly connected, fit tightly and are in good condition (no cracks or tears).

ACCESSING THE DTCS

▶ **Refer to illustration 3.1**

1   The Diagnostic Trouble Codes (DTCs) can only be accessed with a code reader or scan tool. Professional scan tools are expensive, but relatively inexpensive generic code readers or scan tools (see illustrations 2.4a and 2.4b) are available at most auto parts stores. Simply plug the connector of the scan tool into the diagnostic connector (see illustration). Then follow the instructions included with the scan tool to extract the DTCs.

2   Once you have outputted all of the stored DTCs, look them up on the accompanying DTC chart.

3   After troubleshooting the source of each DTC, make any necessary repairs or replace the defective component(s).

Clearing the DTCs

4   Clear the DTCs with the code reader or scan tool in accordance with the instructions provided by the tool's manufacturer.

DIAGNOSTIC TROUBLE CODES

5   The accompanying tables are a list of the Diagnostic Trouble Codes (DTCs) that can be accessed by a do-it-yourselfer working at home (there are many, many more DTCs available to professional mechanics with proprietary scan tools and software, but those codes cannot be accessed by a generic scan tool). If, after you have checked and repaired the connectors, wire harness and vacuum hoses (if applicable) for an emission-related system, component or circuit, the problem persists, have the vehicle checked by a dealer service department or other qualified repair shop.

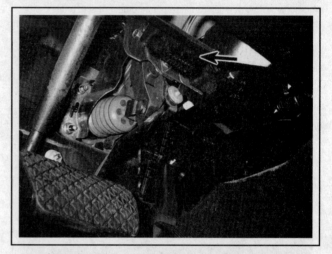

3.1 The Data Link Connector (DLC) is located under the lower edge of the dash, to the left of the steering column

OBD-II TROUBLE CODES

➡ **Note: Not all trouble codes apply to all models.**

Code	Probable cause
P0010	Intake camshaft position actuator, open circuit (Bank 1)
P0010	Variable valve timing actuator circuit open (RH), 3.7L engines
P0011	Intake camshaft position timing, over-advanced (Bank 1)
P0012	Intake camshaft position timing, over-retarded (Bank 1)
P0016	Crankshaft position-to-camshaft position correlation (Bank 1)
P0018	Crankshaft position-to-camshaft position correlation (Bank 2)
P0020	Intake camshaft position actuator, open circuit (Bank 2)

Code	Probable cause
P0021	Intake camshaft position timing over-advanced (Bank 2)
P0022	Intake camshaft position timing over-retarded (Bank 2)
P0030	Oxygen sensor heater control circuit (Bank 1, Sensor 1)
P0031	Oxygen sensor (A/F) heater control circuit problem
P0032	Oxygen sensor (A/F) heater control circuit low input
P0037	Oxygen sensor heater control circuit high input
P0038	Oxygen sensor heater control circuit problem
P0040	Oxygen sensor signals swapped (Bank 1, Sensor 1/Bank 2, Sensor 1)
P0041	Oxygen sensor signals swapped (Bank 1, Sensor 2/Bank 2, Sensor 2)
P0050	Oxygen sensor heater control circuit (Bank 2, Sensor 1)
P0053	Oxygen sensor heater resistance (Bank 1, Sensor 1)
P0054	Oxygen sensor heater resistance (Bank 1, Sensor 2)
P0055	Oxygen sensor heater resistance (Bank 1, Sensor 3)
P0059	Oxygen sensor heater resistance (Bank 2, Sensor 1)
P0060	Oxygen sensor heater resistance (Bank 2, Sensor 2)
P0068	Manifold Absolute Pressure (MAP) sensor/Mass Air Flow (MAF) sensor-to-throttle position correlation
P0069	Manifold Absolute Pressure (MAP) sensor/Mass Air Flow (MAF) sensor-to-atmospheric pressure correlation
P0097	Intake Air Temperature (IAT) sensor 2 circuit, low voltage
P0098	Intake Air Temperature (IAT) sensor 2 circuit, high voltage
P0101	MAF sensor circuit range or performance problem
P0102	MAF/Mass or volume air flow A circuit, low voltage
P0103	MAF/Mass or volume air flow A circuit, high voltage
P0104	Mass Air Flow (MAF) sensor A circuit, intermittent or erratic signal
P0106	Manifold Absolute Pressure (MAP) sensor circuit, range or performance problem
P0107	Manifold Absolute Pressure (MAP) sensor circuit, low voltage
P0108	Manifold Absolute Pressure (MAP) sensor circuit, high voltage
P0109	Manifold Absolute Pressure (MAP) sensor circuit, intermittent signal

OBD-II TROUBLE CODES (CONTINUED)

➡ Note: Not all trouble codes apply to all models.

Code	Probable cause
P0111	Intake Air Temperature (IAT) sensor circuit, range or performance problem
P0112	Intake Air Temperature (IAT) sensor circuit, low voltage
P0113	Intake Air Temperature (IAT) sensor circuit, high voltage
P0114	Intake Air Temperature (IAT) sensor circuit, intermittent or erratic signal
P0116	Engine Coolant Temperature (ECT) sensor circuit, range or performance problem
P0117	Engine Coolant Temperature (ECT) sensor circuit, low voltage
P0118	Engine Coolant Temperature (ECT) sensor circuit, high voltage
P0119	Engine Coolant Temperature (ECT) sensor circuit, intermittent or erratic signal
P0121	Throttle Position (TP) sensor A circuit, range or performance problem
P0122	Throttle Position (TP) sensor A circuit, low voltage
P0123	Throttle Position (TP) sensor A circuit, high voltage
P0125	Insufficient coolant temperature for closed loop fuel control
P0126	Thermostat stuck open
P0128	Coolant temperature below coolant thermostat's regulating temperature
P0130	Oxygen sensor circuit malfunction (Bank 1, Sensor 1)
P0131	Oxygen sensor circuit low input
P0132	Oxygen sensor circuit, high voltage (Bank 1, Sensor 1)
P0133	Oxygen sensor circuit, slow response (Bank 1, Sensor 1)
P0134	Oxygen sensor circuit, no activity detected (Bank 1, Sensor 1)
P0135	Oxygen sensor heater circuit malfunction (Bank 1, Sensor 1)
P0137	Oxygen sensor circuit low input
P0138	Oxygen sensor circuit, high voltage (Bank 1, Sensor 2)
P0139	Oxygen sensor circuit, slow response (Bank 1, Sensor 2)
P013A	Oxygen sensor slow response, rich to lean (Bank 1, Sensor 2)
P013C	Oxygen sensor slow response, rich to lean (Bank 2, Sensor 2)

Code	Probable cause
P013E	Oxygen sensor delayed response, rich to lean (Bank 1, Sensor 2)
P0140	Oxygen sensor circuit, no activity detected
P0141	Oxygen sensor heater circuit
P0144	Oxygen sensor circuit, high voltage (Bank 1, Sensor 3)
P0147	Oxygen sensor heater circuit malfunction (Bank 1, Sensor 3)
P0148	Fuel delivery error
P014A	Oxygen sensor delayed response, rich to lean (Bank 2, Sensor 2)
P0150	Oxygen sensor circuit malfunction (Bank 2, Sensor 1)
P0151	Oxygen sensor circuit, low voltage
P0152	Oxygen sensor circuit, high voltage (Bank 2, Sensor 1)
P0153	Oxygen sensor circuit, slow response (Bank 2, Sensor 1)
P0154	Oxygen sensor circuit, no activity detected (Bank 2, Sensor 1)
P0155	Oxygen sensor heater circuit malfunction (Bank 2, Sensor 1)
P0158	Oxygen sensor circuit, high voltage (Bank 2, Sensor 2)
P0159	Oxygen sensor circuit, slow response (Bank 2, Sensor 2)
P0161	Oxygen sensor heater circuit malfunction (Bank 2, Sensor 2)
P0171	System too lean (Bank 1)
P0172	System too rich (Bank 1)
P0174	System too lean (Bank 2)
P0175	System too rich (Bank 2)
P0180	Fuel temperature sensor circuit malfunction
P0181	Fuel temperature sensor circuit, range or performance problem
P0182	Fuel temperature sensor circuit, low voltage
P0183	Fuel temperature sensor circuit, high voltage
P0191	Fuel rail pressure sensor circuit, range or performance problem
P0192	Fuel rail pressure sensor circuit, low voltage
P0193	Fuel rail pressure sensor circuit, high voltage

OBD-II TROUBLE CODES (CONTINUED)

➡ **Note: Not all trouble codes apply to all models.**

Code	Probable cause
P0196	Engine Oil Temperature (EOT) sensor circuit, range or performance problem
P0197	Engine Oil Temperature (EOT) sensor circuit, low voltage
P0198	Engine Oil Temperature (EOT) sensor circuit, high voltage
P0201	Injector open circuit, cylinder 1
P0202	Injector open circuit, cylinder 2
P0203	Injector open circuit, cylinder 3
P0204	Injector open circuit, cylinder 4
P0205	Injector open circuit, cylinder 5
P0206	Injector open circuit, cylinder 6
P0217	Engine coolant over-temperature condition
P0218	Transaxle fluid temperature over-temperature condition
P0219	Engine over-speed condition
P0221	Throttle Position (TP) sensor circuit, range or performance problem
P0222	Throttle Position (TP) sensor circuit, low voltage
P0223	Throttle Position (TP) sensor circuit, high voltage
P0230	Fuel pump primary circuit malfunction
P0231	Fuel pump secondary circuit, low voltage
P0232	Fuel pump secondary circuit, high voltage
P025A	Fuel pump module control circuit open
P025B	Fuel pump module control circuit range or performance problem
P0297	Vehicle over-speed condition
P0298	Engine oil over-temperature condition
P0300	Random misfire detected
P0301	Cylinder 1 misfire
P0302	Cylinder 2 misfire

Code	Probable cause
P0303	Cylinder 3 misfire
P0304	Cylinder 4 misfire
P0305	Cylinder 5 misfire
P0306	Cylinder 6 misfire
P0315	Crankshaft position system variation not learned
P0316	Misfire detected on start-up (first 1000 revolutions)
P0320	Ignition/distributor engine speed input circuit
P0325	Knock sensor 1 circuit malfunction (Bank 1)
P0326	Knock sensor 1 circuit, range or performance problem (Bank 1)
P0327	Knock sensor circuit low input
P0328	Knock sensor circuit high input
P0330	Knock sensor 2 circuit malfunction (Bank 2)
P0331	Knock sensor 2 circuit, range or performance problem (Bank 2)
P0335	Crankshaft Position (CKP) sensor circuit, range or performance problem
P0340	Camshaft Position (CMP) sensor circuit malfunction (Bank 1 or single sensor)
P0341	Camshaft Position (CMP) sensor circuit, range or performance problem (Bank 1 or single sensor)
P0344	Camshaft Position (CMP) sensor circuit, intermittent signal (Bank 1 or single sensor)
P0345	Camshaft Position (CMP) sensor circuit malfunction (Bank 2)
P0346	Camshaft Position (CMP) sensor circuit, range or performance problem (Bank 2)
P0349	Camshaft Position (CMP) sensor circuit, intermittent signal (Bank 2)
P0350	Ignition coil primary/secondary circuit malfunction
P0351	Ignition coil A primary/secondary circuit malfunction
P0352	Ignition coil B primary/secondary circuit malfunction
P0353	Ignition coil C primary/secondary circuit malfunction
P0354	Ignition coil D primary/secondary circuit malfunction
P0355	Ignition coil E primary/secondary circuit malfunction
P0356	Ignition coil F primary/secondary circuit malfunction

OBD-II TROUBLE CODES (CONTINUED)

➡ **Note: Not all trouble codes apply to all models.**

Code	Probable cause
P0400	Exhaust Gas Recirculation (EGR) system flow
P0401	Exhaust Gas Recirculation (EGR) system, insufficient flow detected
P0402	Exhaust Gas Recirculation (EGR) system, excessive flow detected
P0403	Exhaust Gas Recirculation (EGR) system control circuit malfunction
P0405	Exhaust Gas Recirculation (EGR) system, differential pressure feedback sensor circuit, low voltage
P0406	Exhaust Gas Recirculation (EGR) system, differential pressure feedback sensor circuit, high voltage
P0410	Secondary Air Injection (AIR) system
P0412	Secondary Air Injection (AIR) system, switching valve circuit malfunction
P0420	Catalyst system efficiency below threshold (Bank 1)
P0421	Catalyst system efficiency below threshold
P0430	Catalyst system efficiency below threshold (Bank 2)
P0442	Evaporative Emission (EVAP) system, small leak detected
P0443	Evaporative Emission (EVAP) system, purge control valve circuit malfunction
P0446	Evaporative Emission (EVAP) system, vent control circuit malfunction
P0451	Evaporative Emission (EVAP) system, pressure sensor range or performance problem
P0452	Evaporative Emission (EVAP) system, pressure sensor, low voltage
P0453	Evaporative Emission (EVAP) system, pressure sensor, high voltage
P0454	Evaporative Emission (EVAP) system, pressure sensor, intermittent signal
P0455	Evaporative Emission (EVAP) system, gross leak detected/no flow
P0456	Evaporative Emission (EVAP) system, very small leak detected
P0457	Evaporative Emission (EVAP) system, leak detected (fuel cap loose or off)
P0460	Fuel level sensor circuit malfunction
P0461	Fuel level sensor circuit, range or performance problem
P0462	Fuel level sensor circuit, low voltage
P0463	Fuel level sensor circuit, high voltage

Code	Probable cause
P0480	Fan 1 control circuit malfunction
P0481	Fan 2 control circuit malfunction
P0483	Fan performance
P0491	Secondary Air Injection (AIR) system, insufficient flow (Bank 1)
P0500	Vehicle Speed Sensor (VSS)
P0503	Vehicle Speed Sensor (VSS), intermittent, erratic or high signal
P0505	Idle Air Control (IAC) system
P0506	Idle Air Control (IAC) system, rpm lower than expected
P0507	Idle Air Control (IAC) system, rpm higher than expected
P050A	Cold start idle air control performance problem
P050B	Cold start ignition timing performance problem
P050E	Cold start engine exhaust temperature out of range
P0511	Idle Air Control (IAC) system circuit malfunction
P0512	Starter request circuit malfunction
P0528	Fan speed sensor circuit, no signal
P052A	Cold start camshaft position timing over-advanced (Bank 1)
P052B	Cold start camshaft position timing over-retarded (Bank 1)
P052C	Cold start camshaft position timing over-advanced (Bank 2)
P052D	Cold start camshaft position timing over-retarded (Bank 2)
P0532	Air conditioning refrigerant pressure sensor circuit, low voltage
P0533	Air conditioning refrigerant pressure sensor circuit, high voltage
P0534	Air conditioning refrigerant charge loss
P0537	Air conditioning evaporator temperature sensor circuit, low voltage
P0538	A/C evaporator temperature sensor circuit, high voltage
P053A	Positive Crankcase Ventilation (PCV) heater control circuit open
P0550	Power Steering Pressure (PSP) sensor circuit, problem
P0552	Power Steering Pressure (PSP) sensor circuit, low voltage

OBD-II TROUBLE CODES (CONTINUED)

➡ **Note: Not all trouble codes apply to all models.**

Code	Probable cause
P0553	Power Steering Pressure (PSP) sensor circuit, high voltage
P0562	System voltage low
P0563	System voltage high
P0571	Brake switch circuit malfunction
P0572	Brake switch circuit, low voltage
P0573	Brake switch circuit, high voltage
P0579	Cruise control multifunction input circuit, ranger or performance problem
P0581	Cruise control multifunction input circuit, high voltage
P0600	Serial communication link
P0601	Powertrain Control Module (PCM), memory checksum error
P0602	Powertrain Control Module (PCM) programming error
P0603	Powertrain Control Module (PCM), Keep Alive Memory (KAM) error
P0604	Powertrain Control Module (PCM), Random Access Memory (RAM) error
P0605	Powertrain Control Module (PCM), Read Only Memory (ROM) error
P0606	Powertrain Control Module (PCM) processor
P0607	Powertrain Control Module (PCM) performance
P060A	Internal control module monitoring processor performance problem
P060B	Internal control module analog/digital processing performance
P060C	Internal control module main processor performance problem
P060D	Internal control module accelerator pedal position performance problem
P0610	Powertrain Control Module (PCM) options error
P061B	Internal control module torque calculation performance problem
P061C	Internal control module engine rpm performance problem
P061D	Internal control module engine air mass performance problem
P061F	Internal control module throttle valve actuator controller performance problem

Code	Probable cause
P0620	Alternator control circuit malfunction
P0622	Alternator field terminal, circuit malfunction
P0625	Alternator field terminal, low circuit voltage
P0626	Alternator field terminal, high circuit voltage
P0627	Fuel pump, open control circuit
P062C	Internal control module vehicle speed performance
P062F	Internal control module EEPROM error
P0638	Throttle valve actuator control circuit performance problem
P0642	Sensor reference voltage (VREF) circuit below VREF minimum voltage
P0643	Sensor reference voltage (VREF) circuit, high voltage
P0645	Air conditioning clutch relay control circuit malfunction
P064D	Internal control module oxygen sensor processor performance (RH)
P064D	Internal control module oxygen sensor processor performance (Bank 1)
P064E	Internal control module oxygen sensor processor performance (Bank 2)
P0657	Actuator supply voltage, open circuit
P065B	Alternator control circuit range or performance problem
P0660	Intake Manifold Tuning Valve (IMTV) control circuit, open circuit (Bank 1)
P0661	Variable intake air solenoid valve circuit, low input
P0662	Variable intake air solenoid valve circuit, high input
P0663	Intake Manifold Tuning Valve (IMTV) control circuit, open circuit (Bank 2)
P0685	Powertrain Control Module (PCM) power relay control circuit open
P0689	Powertrain Control Module (PCM) power relay sense circuit, low voltage
P068A	Powertrain Control Module (PCM) power relay de-engaged-too early
P068B	Internal control module Volatile Random Access Memory (NVRAM) error
P0690	Powertrain Control Module (PCM) power relay sense circuit, high voltage
P0703	Brake switch input circuit malfunction
P0704	Clutch switch input circuit malfunction

OBD-II TROUBLE CODES (CONTINUED)

➡ **Note: Not all trouble codes apply to all models.**

Code	Probable cause
P0705	Transmission Range (TR) sensor circuit (PRNDL) input problem
P0706	Transmission Range (TR) sensor circuit, range or performance problem
P0707	Transmission Range (TR) sensor circuit, low voltage
P0708	Transmission range sensor circuit, high voltage
P0711	Transmission fluid temperature sensor circuit, range or performance problem
P0712	Transmission fluid temperature sensor circuit, low input
P0713	Transmission fluid temperature sensor circuit, high input
P0715	Input/turbine speed sensor circuit malfunction
P0716	Input/turbine speed sensor circuit, range or performance problem
P0717	Input/turbine speed sensor circuit, no signal
P0720	Output Shaft Speed (OSS) sensor circuit malfunction
P0721	Output Shaft Speed (OSS) sensor circuit, range or performance problem
P0722	No signal from Output Shaft Speed (OSS) sensor
P0723	Output Shaft Speed (OSS) sensor circuit, intermittent signal
P0729	Gear 6 incorrect ratio
P0730	Incorrect gear ratio
P0731	Incorrect gear ratio, first gear
P0732	Incorrect gear ratio, second gear
P0733	Incorrect gear ratio, third gear
P0734	Incorrect gear ratio, fourth gear
P0735	Incorrect gear ratio, fifth gear
P0736	Incorrect gear ratio, reverse gear
P0741	Torque converter clutch, circuit performance problem or stuck in Off position
P0742	Torque converter clutch circuit, stuck in On position
P0744	Torque converter clutch circuit, intermittent

Code	Probable cause
P0745	Pressure control solenoid malfunction
P0751	Shift solenoid A, performance problem or stuck in Off position
P0752	Shift solenoid A, stuck in On position
P0753	Shift solenoid A, electrical problem
P0756	Shift solenoid B, performance problem or stuck in Off position
P0757	Shift solenoid B, stuck in On position
P0758	Shift solenoid B, electrical problem
P0761	Shift solenoid C, performance problem or stuck in Off position
P0762	Shift solenoid C, stuck in On position
P0763	Shift solenoid C, electrical problem
P0766	Shift solenoid D, performance problem or stuck in Off position
P0767	Shift solenoid D, stuck in On position
P0768	Shift solenoid D, electrical problem
P0771	Shift solenoid E, performance problem or stuck in Off position
P0772	Shift solenoid E, stuck in On position
P0773	Shift solenoid E, electrical problem
P0777	Pressure control solenoid "B" stuck On
P0778	Pressure control solenoid "B" electrical
P0780	Shift malfunction
P0791	Intermediate shaft speed sensor circuit malfunction
P0812	Reverse input circuit malfunction
P0815	Upshift switch circuit malfunction
P0817	Starter disable circuit malfunction
P0830	Clutch pedal switch circuit malfunction
P0840	Transmission fluid pressure sensor circuit malfunction
P0841	Transmission fluid pressure sensor/switch "A" circuit range/performance problem
P0850	Neutral switch input circuit problem

OBD-II TROUBLE CODES (CONTINUED)

➡ **Note: Not all trouble codes apply to all models.**

Code	Probable cause
P0882	Transmission control module (TCM) power input signal low
P0894	Transmission component slipping
P0961	Pressure control (PC) solenoid A - control circuit range/performance problem
P0962	Pressure control (PC) solenoid A - control circuit low
P0963	Pressure control (PC) solenoid A - control circuit high
P0973	Shift solenoid (SS) A - control circuit low
P0974	Shift solenoid (SS) A - control circuit high
P0976	Shift solenoid (SS) B - control circuit low
P0977	Shift solenoid (SS) B - control circuit high
P0978	Shift solenoid (SS) C - control circuit range/performance problem
P0979	Shift solenoid (SS) C - control circuit low
P0980	Shift solenoid (SS) C - control circuit high
P0981	Shift solenoid (SS) D - control circuit range/performance problem
P0982	Shift solenoid (SS) D - control circuit low
P0983	Shift solenoid (SS) D - control circuit high
P0984	Shift solenoid (SS) E - control circuit range/performance problem
P0985	Shift solenoid (SS) E - control circuit low
P0986	Shift solenoid (SS) E - control circuit high
P0997	Shift solenoid (SS) F - control circuit range/performance problem
P0998	Shift solenoid (SS) F - control circuit low
P0999	Shift solenoid (SS) F - control circuit high

4   Accelerator Pedal Position (APP) sensor - replacement

▶ **Refer to illustration 4.2**

➡ **Note: Replacing the APP sensor is difficult. The APP sensor is located at the upper end of the accelerator pedal assembly, between the brake pedal assembly and the housing for the heater core and air conditioning evaporator.**

1   Remove the knee bolster trim panel and the knee bolster (see Chapter 11, Section 24).

2   Using a flashlight and mirror, disconnect the electrical connector from the upper end of the APP sensor assembly (see illustration).

3   Remove the accelerator pedal/APP sensor assembly mounting nuts and remove the assembly.

4   Installation is the reverse of removal.

4.2 APP sensor electrical connector (A) and mounting nuts (B) (instrument panel and heater core/air conditioning evaporator housing removed for clarity)

5   Camshaft Position (CMP) sensor - replacement

1   Disconnect the cable from the negative battery terminal (see Chapter 5).

FOUR-CYLINDER MODELS

➡ **Note: The CMP sensor is located at the left front corner of the valve cover, above the left end of the intake camshaft.**

2   Disconnect the CMP sensor electrical connector.

3   Remove the CMP sensor mounting bolt and remove the CMP sensor.

4   Inspect the condition of the CMP sensor O-ring. If it's cracked, torn or deteriorated, replace it.

5   Installation is the reverse of removal.

V6 MODELS

▶ **Refer to illustrations 5.8a and 5.8b**

➡ **Note: V6 engines have two CMP sensors; one on either the right end (3.0L engines) or the left end (3.7L engines) of each cylinder head.**

6   On 3.0L engines, if you're removing the CMP sensor from the front cylinder head, detach the wiring harness clip from the valve cover stud and set it aside. If you're removing the CMP sensor from the rear cylinder head, it may be necessary to remove the coolant reservoir (see Chapter 3) and set it aside.

➡ **Note: It is not necessary to disconnect the coolant lines to the reservoir.**

7   On 3.7L engines, remove the air intake duct and air filter housing (see Chapter 4).

➡ **Note: On 3.7L engines, the front cylinder head CMP is hidden behind the harness bracket; it will be necessary to remove the bracket mounting bolts and the bracket.**

8   Disconnect the CMP sensor electrical connector (see illustrations).

9   Remove the CMP sensor mounting bolt and remove the sensor.

10   Remove the CMP sensor O-ring and inspect its condition. If it's cracked, torn or otherwise deteriorated, replace it.

11   Lubricate the sensor O-ring with clean engine oil. Installation is otherwise the reverse of removal.

5.8a The CMP sensor for the front cylinder head is located on the right end of the head (3.0L V6 engine)

5.8b The CMP sensor for the rear cylinder head is located on the right end of the head (3.0L V6 engine)

6   Crankshaft Position (CKP) sensor - replacement

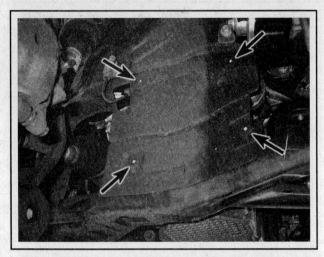

6.2a CKP sensor access panel retainers (front)

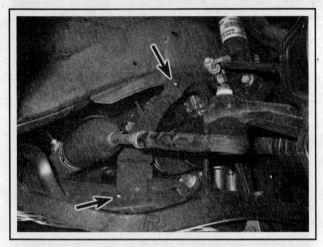

6.2b CKP sensor access panel retainers (rear) (four-cylinder and 3.0L V6 models)

6.5 CKP sensor details (four-cylinder models):

1 Electrical connector	3 CKP sensor
2 Mounting bolts	

▶ Refer to illustrations 6.2a and 6.2b

➡ **Note: On some models, replacing the CKP sensor might set a Diagnostic Trouble Code (DTC). If it does, and if you have a generic scan tool that can clear codes, erase the code and see if it reappears. If it does, have a dealer service department perform a Misfire Monitor Neutral Profile Correction procedure with a factory scan tool.**

1   Disconnect the cable from the negative battery terminal (see Chapter 5).

2   On all except 3.7L V6 models, loosen the right front wheel lug nuts, raise the front of the vehicle and place it securely on jackstands. Remove the right front wheel, then remove the small access panel below the larger fender splash shield (see illustrations).

3   On 3.7L V6 models, raise the front of the vehicle and place it securely on jackstands. Remove the engine under cover.

FOUR-CYLINDER MODELS

Removal

▶ Refer to illustration 6.5

➡ **Note: The CKP sensor is located at the lower rear corner of the timing chain cover, behind the crankshaft pulley.**

4   Place the No. 1 cylinder at Top Dead Center (TDC) (see Chapter 2A).

5   Disconnect the electrical connector from the CKP sensor (see illustration), unscrew the CKP sensor mounting bolts and remove the sensor.

Installation

▶ Refer to illustrations 6.6 and 6.9

➡ **Note: If you're installing a new CKP sensor, the new sensor comes with a special alignment jig that, according to the manufacturer, is available only with a new sensor. You might, however, be able to find an aftermarket tool that does the same thing. If, on the other hand, you removed the CKP sensor simply to access some other component, like the timing chain, use the alternate method of aligning the CKP sensor included here.**

6   Install a 6 mm x 18 mm (0.23 x 0.7 inch) bolt in the threaded

6.6 Insert the correct size bolt into the threaded hole in the pulley and timing chain cover

hole provided in the crankshaft pulley (see illustration) and screw it into the timing chain cover.

7   Install the CKP sensor but don't tighten the sensor mounting bolts.

8   *If you're installing a new CKP sensor,* align the sensor with the special alignment jig (included with the new sensor) in accordance with the manufacturer's instructions. With the alignment jig in place, tighten the CKP sensor bolts securely, then remove the alignment jig.

9   *If you're installing the old CKP sensor,* look at the sensor trigger wheel, or timing plate, that's mounted on the backside of the crankshaft pulley. Note the small teeth that stick out from the circumference of the timing plate. At about ten o'clock there is a blank spot on the edge of the timing plate, where there are no teeth. From this blank area, count five teeth in a counterclockwise direction, then, using a straightedge, draw a straight line from the center of this fifth tooth through the center of the crankshaft pulley (see illustration). Position the centerline of the CKP sensor with the line that you made, then tighten the sensor bolts securely.

10   Remove the crankshaft pulley bolt installed in Step 6, then remove the special timing tool and install the cylinder block plug (see Chapter 2A).

11   Installation is otherwise the reverse of removal.

V6 MODELS

3.0L engine

▶ **Refer to illustration 6.12**

12   Disconnect the electrical connector from the CKP sensor (see illustration).

13   Unscrew the CKP sensor mounting bolt and remove the CKP sensor.

14   Remove and inspect the sensor O-ring. If it's cut, torn or otherwise deteriorated, replace it.

15   Lubricate the sensor O-ring with clean engine oil. Installation is otherwise the reverse of removal.

3.7L engine

➡ **Note: The CKP sensor is located on the left front side of the engine block, near the transaxle.**

16   Remove the upstream and downstream oxygen sensors from the catalytic converter for the front cylinder head (see Section 12), then remove the catalyst for the front cylinder head (see Section 18).

17   Remove the CKP sensor heat shield mounting bolt and nut and remove the heat shield.

18   Remove the rubber grommet cover.

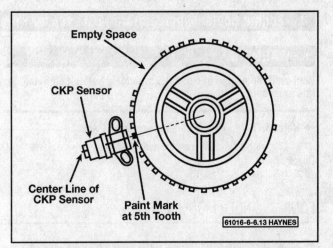

6.9 CKP sensor alignment details (four-cylinder models)

6.12 On 3.0L V6 models, the CKP sensor is located at the lower rear edge of the timing chain cover, behind the crankshaft pulley

19   Loosen the CKP sensor mounting bolt completely and remove the sensor and bolt together.

➡ **Note: The sensor mounting bolt and sensor are one piece and the bolt can't be removed from the sensor.**

20   Disconnect the CKP sensor electrical connector from the sensor.

21   Connect the CKP sensor electrical connector to the sensor, then install the sensor. Installation is otherwise the reverse of removal.

---

7   Cylinder Head Temperature (CHT) sensor (3.7L V6 models only) - replacement

❄ **WARNING:**

Wait until the engine has cooled completely before beginning this procedure.

➡ **Note: Only 2009 and later 3.7L V6 models are equipped with a CHT sensor. The CHT sensor is located in the valley below the lower intake manifold, and is screwed into the rear cylinder head.**

1   Disconnect the cable from the negative battery terminal (see Chapter 5).

2   Remove the lower intake manifold (see Chapter 2B).

3   Disconnect the CHT sensor electrical connector.

4   Unscrew and remove the CHT sensor.

5   Installation is the reverse of removal. Tighten the sensor to the torque listed in this Chapter's Specifications.

8 Engine Coolant Temperature (ECT) sensor - replacement

※※ **WARNING:**

Wait until the engine has cooled completely before beginning this procedure.

➡ Note: 3.7L V6 engines do not have an ECT sensor.

1 Disconnect the cable from the negative battery terminal (see Chapter 5).

2 Drain the engine coolant (see Chapter 1).

FOUR-CYLINDER MODELS

➡ **Note: There are two different parts manufacturers; one in Mexico and one in Hiroshima. These parts are not interchangeable, and will not operate correctly if used in the wrong application. Check the "Vehicle identification numbers" Section at the beginning of this manual to verify which manufacturer's parts are in your vehicle.**

3 Remove the battery and battery tray (see Chapter 5).

8.7 The ECT sensor is located at the left end of the engine (3.0L V6 engine)

4 Pull back the rubber weather cover from the ECT sensor electrical connector (if equipped) and disconnect the connector.

5 Unscrew the ECT sensor from the cylinder head.

6 Installation is the reverse of removal.

3.0L V6 MODELS

◗ **Refer to illustrations 8.7 and 8.8**

7 Disconnect the electrical connector from the ECT sensor (see illustration).

8 To remove the ECT sensor, pull out the locking tab, rotate the sensor counterclockwise, then pull it out of the coolant passage (see illustration).

9 Remove and inspect the sensor O-ring. If it's cut, torn, damaged or otherwise deteriorated, replace it.

10 To install the ECT sensor, insert it into the coolant passage, then turn it clockwise until the locking tab snaps into place. Installation is otherwise the reverse of removal.

11 Refill the cooling system (see Chapter 1).

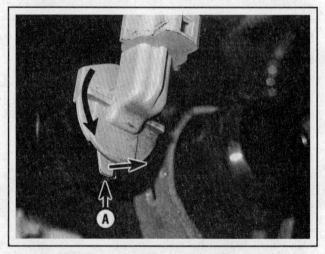

8.8 Pull out the locking tab (A), rotate the sensor counterclockwise, then pull it out of the coolant passage

9 Knock sensor - replacement

FOUR-CYLINDER MODELS

➡ **Note: The knock sensor is located on the front side of the block, behind the intake manifold runners.**

1 Disconnect the cable from the negative battery terminal (see Chapter 5).

2 Remove the intake manifold (see Chapter 2A).

3 Disconnect the electrical connector from the knock sensor.

4 Remove the knock sensor retaining bolt and remove the knock sensor.

5 Installation is the reverse of removal. Tighten the knock sensor retaining bolt to the torque listed in this Chapter's Specifications.

V6 MODELS

3.0L models

◗ **Refer to illustration 9.8**

6 Disconnect the cable from the negative battery terminal (see Chapter 5).

7   Raise the vehicle and place it securely on jackstands. Remove the engine compartment under cover.

8   Disconnect the knock sensor electrical connector (see illustration).

9   Remove the knock sensor retaining bolt and remove the knock sensor.

10 Installation is the reverse of removal. Tighten the knock sensor retaining bolt to the torque listed in this Chapter's Specifications.

3.7L models

➡ **Note: 3.7L engines have two knock sensors, both of which are located in the valley between the cylinder heads.**

11 Remove the upper intake manifold (see Chapter 2B).

12 Remove the lower intake manifold (see Chapter 2B).

13 Disconnect the knock sensor electrical connector(s).

14 Remove the knock sensor retaining bolt(s) and remove the knock sensor(s).

15 Installation is the reverse of removal. Tighten the knock sensor retaining bolt(s) to the torque listed in this Chapter's Specifications.

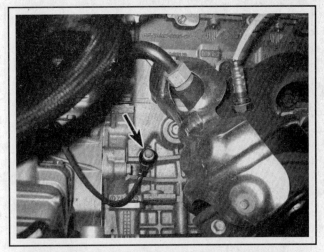

9.8 The knock sensor is located on the left rear side of the engine block (3.0L V6 engines)

10 Manifold Absolute Pressure (MAP) sensor (four-cylinder models only) - replacement

➡ **Note: The MAP sensor is located on the front left side of the intake manifold.**

1   Disconnect the cable from the negative battery terminal (see Chapter 5).

2   Disconnect the electrical connector from the MAP sensor.

3   Remove the MAP sensor retaining bolt and remove the sensor.

4   Installation is the reverse of removal.

11 Mass Air Flow/Intake Air Temperature (MAF/IAT) sensor - replacement

▶ **Refer to illustration 11.2**

1   Remove the air intake duct (see Chapter 4, Section 9).

2   Disconnect the electrical connector from the MAF/IAT sensor (see illustration).

3   Remove the MAF/IAT sensor mounting fasteners and remove the sensor from the air filter housing.

4   Installation is the reverse of removal.

11.2 The MAF/IAT sensor is located on the air filter housing cover (3.0L V6 engine shown, other engines similar)

12 Oxygen sensors - replacement

➡ **Note: Because it is installed in the exhaust manifold or pipe, both of which contract when cool, an oxygen sensor might be very difficult to loosen when the engine is cold. Rather than risk damage to the sensor or its mounting threads, start and run the engine for a minute or two, then shut it off. Be careful not to burn yourself during the following procedure.**

1   Be particularly careful when servicing an oxygen sensor:

a) *Oxygen sensors have a permanently attached pigtail and an electrical connector that cannot be removed. Damaging or removing the pigtail or electrical connector will render the sensor useless.*

b) *Keep grease, dirt and other contaminants away from the electrical connector and the louvered end of the sensor.*

12.4a Front cylinder head exhaust manifold oxygen sensor locations (3.0L V6 engine shown, 3.7L V6 similar)

    A   *Upstream oxygen sensor*
    B   *Downstream oxygen sensor*

12.4b Rear cylinder head exhaust manifold, oxygen sensor locations (3.0L V6 engine shown, 3.7L V6 similar)

    A   *Upstream oxygen sensor*
    B   *Downstream oxygen sensor*

c) Do not use cleaning solvents of any kind on an oxygen sensor.

d) Oxygen sensors are extremely delicate. Do not drop a sensor or handle it roughly.

e) Make sure that the silicone boot on the sensor is installed in the correct position. Otherwise, the boot might melt and it might prevent the sensor from operating correctly.

REPLACEMENT

▶ **Refer to illustrations 12.4a, 12.4b and 12.5**

➡ **Note: This procedure applies to upstream and downstream oxygen sensors.**

➡ **Note: The upstream sensor is installed in the upper part of the exhaust manifold/catalytic converter assembly. There is an upstream sensor in each exhaust manifold on V6 models.**

➡ **Note: The downstream oxygen sensor is located in the lower end of the exhaust manifold/catalytic converter assembly or on the short section of exhaust pipe, just below the catalyst. There is a downstream oxygen sensor in each exhaust pipe on V6 models.**

2   Disconnect the cable from the negative battery terminal (see Chapter 5).

3   To access downstream sensors and the upstream sensor on the exhaust manifold for the rear cylinder head on V6 models, raise the front of the vehicle and place it securely on jackstands. Remove the engine under cover.

4   Locate the oxygen sensor (see illustrations), then trace the sensor's electrical lead to its electrical connector and disconnect the con-

nector. Disengage any harness clips.

5   Using a wrench or an oxygen sensor socket, unscrew the sensor (see illustration).

6   If you're going to install the old sensor, apply anti-seize compound to the threads of the sensor to facilitate future removal. If you're going to install a new oxygen sensor, it's not necessary to apply anti-seize compound to the threads; the threads on new sensors already have anti-seize compound on them.

7   Installation is the reverse of removal. Tighten the oxygen sensor to the torque listed in this Chapter's Specifications.

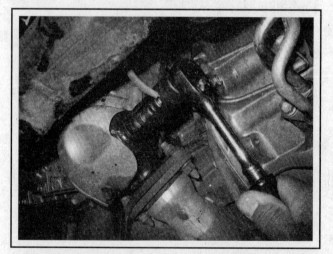

12.5 Use a wrench or an oxygen sensor socket to remove the oxygen sensor

13 Power Steering Pressure (PSP) switch - replacement

◆ **Refer to illustration 13.3**

➡ **Note: The PSP switch is located on top of the power steering pump.**

1   On V6 models, raise the front of the vehicle and place it securely on jackstands. Remove the engine under cover.

2   Siphon a small amount of power steering fluid from the power steering reservoir, or be prepared to catch spilled power steering fluid when you unscrew the PSP switch.

3   Disconnect the electrical connector from the PSP switch (see illustration).

➡ **Note: On V6 models, it may be necessary to remove the power steering pump for access to the switch (see Chapter 10).**

4   Using a deep socket, unscrew the PSP switch.

5   Installation is the reverse of removal. Refill the power steering system as necessary (see Chapter 1).

13.3 Typical location of the Power Steering Pressure (PSP) switch (3.0L V6 engine shown, 3.7L V6 similar)

14 Throttle Position (TP) sensor - replacement

The TP sensor is an integral component of the electronic throttle body, and is not separately serviceable. If you need to replace the TP sensor, you must replace the throttle body (see Chapter 4).

15 Transmission Range (TR) sensor - removal and installation

JA5A-EL (5-SPEED) TRANSAXLE

➡ **Note: This procedure requires a special alignment tool (SST #49 L019 013) to align the TR sensor during installation.**

➡ **Note: The TR sensor is located on the lower left front side of the transaxle.**

Removal

1   Place the shift lever in NEUTRAL, raise the vehicle and support it securely on jackstands. Remove the underbody cover.

2   Disconnect the electrical connector from the TR sensor.

3   Pry the end of the shift cable off the ball stud on the manual control lever.

4   Remove the manual control lever nut and lock washer and remove the manual control lever.

❋❋ CAUTION:

To protect the internal shift mechanism from damage, use an appropriate tool to immobilize the manual control lever and prevent it from turning while loosening the nut.

5   Remove the TR sensor mounting bolts and remove the sensor.

Installation

6   Install the TR sensor and loosely install the sensor mounting bolts. Before tightening the mounting bolts, install the special alignment tool (SST #49 L019 013) to align the sensor, then tighten the mounting bolts.

7   Install the manual lever, lock washer and nut and tighten it securely.

❋❋ CAUTION:

To protect the internal shift mechanism from damage, use an appropriate tool to immobilize the manual lever and prevent it from turning while tightening the nut.

8   Before reconnecting the shift cable to the manual control lever, verify that the manual lever is in the DRIVE position. When the manual lever is in the DRIVE position, the marks on the manual control lever will line up with the marks on the TR sensor.

9   Reconnect the electrical connector to the TR sensor.

10 The remainder of installation is the reverse of removal. After lowering the vehicle, verify that the engine will only start in PARK or NEUTRAL.

AW6A-EL (6-SPEED) TRANSAXLE

Removal

◆ **Refer to illustration 15.12**

➡ **Note: On this transaxle, the TR sensor is an integral component of the Transaxle Control Module (TCM) and is not separately serviceable. If you need to replace the TR sensor, you must replace the TCM. The TCM cannot be replaced at home, because the replacement unit must be programmed with a factory scan tool before it will operate properly. The following pro-**

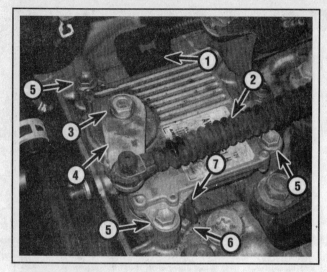

15.12 Transaxle Control Module (TCM) details (six-speed transaxle):

1	Electrical connector	5	TCM mounting bolts
2	Shift cable	6	Transaxle case notch
3	Manual control lever nut	7	Coupler component
4	Manual control lever		connector

cedure assumes that you are simply removing the current TCM unit from the old transaxle and installing it on a replacement transaxle.

➡ **Note: The TCM is located on top of the transaxle.**

11 Place the shift lever in NEUTRAL, then remove the air filter housing (see Chapter 4).

12 Disconnect the electrical connector from the TCM (see illustration).

13 Using a trim removal tool or a screwdriver, carefully pry the end of the shift cable off the ball stud on the manual control lever.

14 Remove the manual control lever nut and remove the lever.

15 Remove the TCM mounting bolts and remove the TCM.

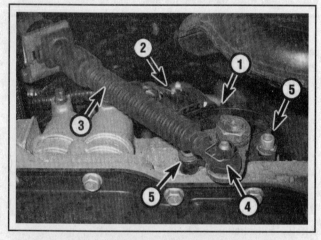

15.25 Transmission Range (TR) sensor details (FN4A-EL [4-speed] and FS5A-EL [5-speed] transaxles):

1	Transmission range sensor	4	Retaining clip
2	Sensor electrical connector	5	Mounting bolts
3	Selector cable		

15.16 TCM manual control lever NEUTRAL position alignment marks (6-speed transaxle)

Installation

➧ **Refer to illustration 15.16**

16 Before installing the TCM, verify that the manual control lever is in the NEUTRAL position by aligning the mark on the control lever with the stationary mark on the TCM (see illustration).

17 Install the TCM, making sure the coupler component connector is in line with the notch in the case (see illustration 15.12). Tighten the TCM mounting bolts securely.

18 Install the manual control lever, then install the lever nut and tighten it securely.

19 Reconnect the electrical connector to the TCM.

20 Reconnect the shift cable to the ball stud on the manual control lever.

21 The remainder of installation is the reverse of removal. Verify that the engine will only start in PARK or NEUTRAL.

FN4A-EL (4-SPEED) AND FS5A-EL (5-SPEED) TRANSAXLES

➡ **Note: This procedure requires an ohmmeter to align the TR sensor during installation.**

➡ **Note: The TR sensor is located on the lower left front side of the transaxle.**

Removal

➧ **Refer to illustration 15.25**

22 Disconnect the cable from the negative battery terminal (see Chapter 5).

23 Remove the air filter housing (see Chapter 4).

24 Place the shift lever in NEUTRAL, raise the vehicle and support it securely on jackstands. Remove the underbody cover.

25 Disconnect the electrical connector from the TR sensor (see illustration).

26 Remove the selector cable-to-manual shift lever retaining clip, then pull the end of the shift cable off the ball stud on the manual control lever.

27 Remove the manual control lever nut and lock washer and remove the manual control lever.

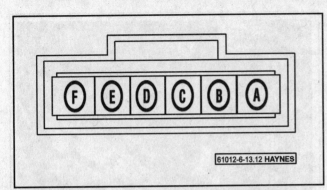

15.30 Transmission range sensor terminal pin locations (FN4A-EL [4-speed] and FS5A-EL [5-speed] transaxles)

✻✻ CAUTION:

To protect the internal shift mechanism from damage, use an appropriate tool to immobilize the manual control lever and prevent it from turning while loosening the nut.

28 Remove the TR sensor mounting bolts and remove the sensor.

Installation

▶ **Refer to illustration 15.30**

29 With the shift lever in the NEUTRAL position, find the groove in the manual shift lever - it should be around the eleven o'clock position.

30 Connect the leads of the ohmmeter to pins B and C on the TR sensor (see illustration), then find the protrusion in the switch where it mounts to the manual shaft. Rotate the protrusion until the resistance reads 750 ohms.

31 Slide the switch on to the manual shaft, making sure the protrusion fits into the groove on the shaft and loosely install the sensor mounting bolts.

32 Before tightening the mounting bolts completely, check the resistance again - it should be at 750 ohms. Tighten the mounting bolts. If the resistance is incorrect, readjust the switch.

33 Install the manual lever, lock washer and nut and tighten it securely.

✻✻ CAUTION:

To protect the internal shift mechanism from damage, use an appropriate tool to immobilize the manual lever and prevent it from turning while tightening the nut.

34 Before reconnecting the shift cable to the manual control lever, verify that the manual lever is in the DRIVE position. When the manual lever is in the DRIVE position, the marks on the manual control lever will line up with the marks on the TR sensor.

35 Reconnect the electrical connector to the TR sensor.

36 The remainder of installation is the reverse of removal. After lowering the vehicle, verify that the engine will only start in PARK or NEUTRAL.

16 Vehicle Speed Sensor (VSS) - replacement

MANUAL TRANSAXLE

➡ **Note: The VSS is located on the right rear corner of the transaxle, above the inner CV joint for the right driveaxle.**

1 Raise the vehicle and place it securely on jackstands. Remove the engine under cover.

2 Disconnect the electrical connector from the VSS.

3 Remove the VSS mounting bolt and remove the VSS.

4 Remove and discard the old VSS O-ring. Use a new O-ring on installation.

5 Installation is the reverse of removal.

AUTOMATIC TRANSAXLE (ALL EXCEPT AW6A-EL [6-SPEED] TRANSAXLE)

➡ **Note: The speed sensors on the 6-speed automatic transaxle are integral components of the transaxle assembly and cannot be replaced at home.**

➡ **Note: There are three speed sensors: the Intermediate Shaft Speed (ISS) sensor, the Turbine Shaft Speed (TSS) sensor and the Output Shaft Speed (OSS) sensor. The ISS and TSS sensors are located on top of the transaxle. The TSS sensor is the forward unit; the ISS sensor is the rear unit. The OSS sensor is located near the lower left rear corner of the transaxle. The following procedure applies to all three sensors.**

6 If you're replacing the OSS sensor, raise the vehicle and place it securely on jackstands. Remove the engine under cover.

7 Disconnect the electrical connector from the sensor.

8 Remove the sensor mounting bolt and remove the sensor.

9 Remove and discard the old sensor O-ring. Use a new O-ring on installation.

10 Installation is the reverse of removal.

17 Powertrain Control Module (PCM) - removal and installation

✻✻ CAUTION:

To avoid electrostatic discharge damage to the PCM, handle the PCM only by its case. Do not touch the electrical terminals during removal and installation. If available, ground yourself to the vehicle with an anti-static ground strap, available at computer supply stores.

➡ **Note: This procedure applies only to disconnecting, removing and installing the PCM that is already installed in your vehicle. If the PCM is defective and has to be replaced, it must be programmed with new software and calibrations. This procedure requires the use of a Mazda scan tool and Mazda's latest PCM-configuration software, so you WILL NOT BE ABLE TO REPLACE THE PCM AT HOME.**

1 Disconnect the battery (see Chapter 5).

2008 AND EARLIER MODELS

▶ **Refer to illustration 17.3**

2 Remove the PCM cover mounting fasteners and cover.
3 Disconnect the electrical connectors from the PCM (see illustration), and remove the PCM.
4 Installation is the reverse of removal.

2009 AND LATER MODELS

Four-cylinder models

5 Remove the battery and battery tray (see Chapter 5).
6 Depress the PCM upper cover tabs and separate the upper cover from the lower cover.
7 Remove the lower cover mounting nuts and cover.
8 Disconnect the electrical connectors from the PCM.
9 Slide the PCM from the studs and remove the PCM.
10 Installation is the reverse of removal.

V6 models

11 Remove the battery and battery tray (see Chapter 5).
12 Remove and disconnect any clips or connectors that are in the way of the PCM.

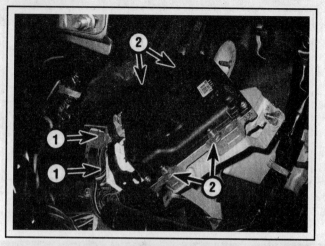

17.3 Powertrain Control Module (PCM) details:

1 Electrical connectors
2 PCM mounting bolts (lower bolts not visible)

13 Loosen the PCM mounting bracket nuts.
14 Disconnect the electrical connectors from the PCM.
15 Remove the PCM-to-bracket mounting nuts and slide the PCM out of the bracket.
16 Installation is the reverse of removal.

18 Catalytic converter (3.7L V6 models only) - replacement

❋❋ WARNING:

Wait until the engine has cooled completely before beginning this procedure.

➡ **Note: On all engines except the 3.7L V6, the catalytic converters are integral components of the exhaust manifolds and cannot be serviced separately. Refer to the exhaust manifold removal and installation procedures in Chapter 2A or 2B for replacement.**

➡ **Note: The catalytic converter is located under the vehicle.**

1 Raise the vehicle and place it securely on jackstands.
2 Locate the downstream oxygen sensor on the upper central part of the catalyst, trace the sensor to its electrical connector and disconnect it. Unscrew and remove the downstream oxygen sensor from the catalyst (see Section 12).
3 Remove the nuts and bolts that secure the flange at the front end of the catalyst to the exhaust down pipe. If the threads are severely damaged or rusted, apply some penetrant to the threads and wait awhile before loosening them.
4 Loosen the fasteners on the clamp that secures the rear end of the catalyst to the exhaust system. If the threads are severely damaged or rusted, apply some penetrant to the threads and wait awhile before loosening them.
5 Remove the heat shields and remove the catalytic converter.
6 Remove and discard the old gasket between the exhaust down pipe and the catalyst mounting flange.
7 Installation is the reverse of removal. Use a new gasket and, if necessary, new fasteners.

19 Evaporative Emissions Control (EVAP) system - component replacement

EVAP CANISTER PURGE VALVE

▶ **Refer to illustrations 19.3a and 19.3b**

➡ **Note: The EVAP canister purge valve is located at the end of the cylinder head (four-cylinder models), the right rear corner of the engine compartment (3.0L V6 models) or the left rear corner of the engine compartment (3.7L V6 models).**

1 Disconnect the cable from the negative battery terminal (see Chapter 5).
2 On V6 models, remove the lower cowl trim panel (see Chapter 11).
3 Disconnect the electrical connector from the canister purge valve (see illustrations).
4 Disconnect the EVAP line quick-connect fittings (see Chapter 4 for information on quick-connect fittings).

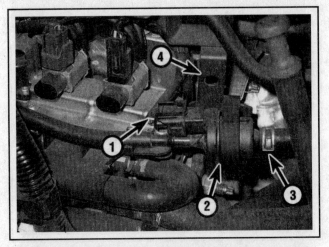

19.3a The EVAP canister purge valve is located near the end of the cylinder head on four-cylinder models

1 EVAP canister purge solenoid electrical connector
2 Retaining clip
3 Fuel vapor hose and clamp
4 Mounting bracket

5 Remove the purge valve and mounting bracket as a single assembly, then depress the lock tab and slide the purge valve off the mounting bracket.

6 Installation is the reverse of removal.

EVAP CANISTER

▶ **Refer to illustration 19.9**

➡ **Note: The EVAP canister is located under the vehicle, on the underside of the spare tire well.**

7 Disconnect the cable from the negative battery terminal (see Chapter 5).

8 Raise the vehicle and support it securely on jackstands.

9 Disconnect the electrical connector and the vapor hose quick-connect fitting from the EVAP canister vent solenoid (see illustration).

10 Disconnect the two EVAP line quick-connect fittings from the EVAP canister (see Chapter 4 for information on quick-connect fittings).

11 Remove the mounting fasteners that secure the canister and remove the canister.

12 Installation is the reverse of removal.

EVAP CANISTER VENT SOLENOID AND DUST SEPARATOR ASSEMBLY

➡ **Note: The EVAP canister vent solenoid is mounted on the EVAP canister.**

19.3b The EVAP canister purge valve is located in the right rear corner of the engine compartment, at the right shock tower (3.0L engines) or the left rear corner (3.7L engines)

13 Remove the EVAP canister (see Steps 7 through 11).

14 Release the two lock tabs and remove the EVAP canister vent solenoid heat shield from the canister by pushing it straight down.

15 Loosen the hose clamp and disconnect the fuel vapor hose from the vent solenoid.

16 Release the lock tab and detach the vent solenoid and dust separator assembly from the EVAP canister.

17 Installation is the reverse of removal.

19.9 Typical EVAP canister details:

1 EVAP canister vent solenoid and dust separator electrical connector
2 Fuel vapor hose
3 Fuel vapor hose quick-connect fitting
4 Fuel vapor hose quick-connect fitting
5 EVAP canister mounting nuts
6 EVAP canister mounting bolts
7 Heat shield for EVAP canister vent solenoid and dust separator
8 Fuel vapor hose

20 Exhaust Gas Recirculation (EGR) valve - replacement

FOUR-CYLINDER MODELS

▶ Refer to illustration 20.4

➡ Note: The EGR valve is located at the left end of the cylinder head, behind the throttle body.

   1 Disconnect the cable from the negative battery terminal (see Chapter 5).

   2 Drain the cooling system (see Chapter 1).

➡ Note: On 2.5L models, remove the upper radiator hose.

   3 Remove the air cleaner duct and housing (see Chapter 4).

   4 Disconnect the electrical connector from the EGR valve (see illustration).

   5 On 2.3L engines, release the coolant hose clamp and disconnect the upper radiator hose from the coolant outlet passage.

   6 Release the clamp and disconnect the coolant hose from the EGR valve.

   7 Remove the two EGR valve mounting bolts and remove the EGR valve.

   8 Remove and discard the EGR valve gasket, then clean the gasket mating surfaces of the cylinder head and the EGR valve.

   9 Installation is the reverse of removal. Use a new EGR valve gasket, and tighten the EGR valve mounting bolts securely.

   10 Refill the cooling system (see Chapter 1).

3.0L V6 MODELS

▶ Refer to illustrations 20.12 and 20.13

➡ Note: The EGR valve is located at the left end of the intake manifold, behind the throttle body.

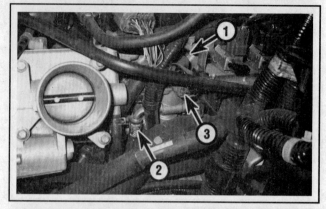

20.4 EGR valve details (2.3L four-cylinder models):

1	*EGR valve*	*3*	*EGR coolant hose*
2	*EGR electrical connector*		

   11 Disconnect the cable from the negative battery terminal (see Chapter 5).

   12 Disconnect the electrical connector and vacuum hose from the EGR valve (see illustration).

   13 Unscrew the tube nut fitting (see illustration) and disconnect the EGR pipe from the EGR valve.

   14 Remove the EGR valve mounting bolts and remove the EGR valve.

   15 Remove and discard the EGR valve gasket, then clean the gasket mating surfaces of the intake manifold and the EGR valve.

   16 Installation is the reverse of removal. Use a new EGR valve gasket, and tighten the EGR valve mounting nuts securely.

20.12 EGR valve electrical connector (3.0L V6 models)

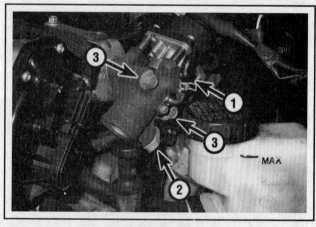

20.13 EGR valve mounting details (3.0L V6 models):

1	*EGR boost vacuum hose*	*3*	*EGR valve mounting bolts*
2	*EGR tube nut fitting*		

21 Positive Crankcase Ventilation (PCV) valve - replacement

FOUR-CYLINDER MODELS

➡ Note: The PCV valve is located on the crankcase vent oil separator, which is located on the front side of the engine block, under the intake manifold.

   1 Remove the intake manifold (see Chapter 2A).

   2 Loosen the hose clamp and disconnect the PCV hose from the PCV valve.

   3 Using a small screwdriver, carefully push the PCV valve retaining ring up, over the locking tab.

4   Pull the PCV valve out of the crankcase vent oil separator.

5   Installation is the reverse of removal.

V6 MODELS

▶ Refer to illustrations 21.6 and 21.10

➡ Note: According to the manufacturer, the PCV valve must be replaced if it's removed.

3.0L V6 engines

➡ Note: On 3.0L engines, the PCV valve is located at the left rear corner of the valve cover for the rear cylinder head.

6   Disconnect the PCV hose (see illustration).

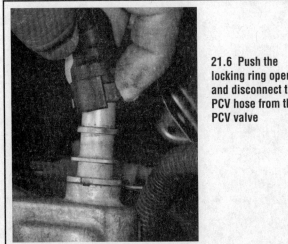

21.6 Push the locking ring open and disconnect the PCV hose from the PCV valve

3.7L engines

➡ Note: On 3.7L engines, the PCV valve is located on the rear valve cover.

7   Disconnect the negative battery cable (see Chapter 5).

8   Move the power steering reservoir to the side (see Chapter 10).

9   Using pliers, squeeze the PCV hose clamps, then slide the clamps back and remove the hose.

All engines

10 Turn the PCV valve counterclockwise and remove it from the valve cover (see illustration). The PCV valve must be replaced every time it is removed, because the locking mechanism of the PCV valve is damaged by removal.

11 Install the new PCV valve.

12 The remainder of installation is the reverse of removal.

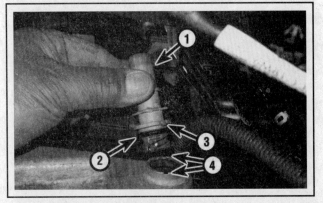

21.10 PCV valve details (3.0L V6 models):

1	PCV valve	3	Locking tab (opposite tab not visible)
2	O-ring	4	Valve cover notches

22 Variable Valve Timing (VVT) system - description

1   The VVT system controls intake valve timing to increase engine torque in the low and mid-speed range and to increase horsepower in the high-speed range.

2   The VVT system consists of the PCM-controlled Oil Control Valve (OCV), which is mounted on top of the cylinder head, and the VVT actuator or camshaft phaser/sprocket, which is mounted on the front end of the intake camshaft.

3   The PCM-controlled OCV varies the oil pressure in the VVT actuator, which continually varies the timing of the intake cam in relation to the fixed timing of the exhaust cam.

4   Refer to Chapter 2 for component replacement procedures for the VVT actuator or camshaft phaser/sprocket.

OIL CONTROL VALVE (OCV) REPLACEMENT

▶ Refer to illustration 22.7

➡ Note: V6 models have two OCVs, one in each cylinder head.

5   Disconnect the cable from the negative battery terminal (see Chapter 5).

6   Remove the upper engine cover, pull the cover up from each side and lift the cover off the mounting posts in the center of the cover.

7   Disconnect the electrical connector from the OCV (see illustration).

8   Remove the valve cover (see Chapter 2).

9   Remove the camshaft timing oil control valve mounting bolt from the cylinder head and remove the oil control valve from the cylinder head.

10 Installation is the reverse of removal.

22.7 Front cylinder head oil control valve location, rear cylinder head similar (3.0L engine shown)

Torque specifications	Ft-lbs (unless otherwise indicated)	Nm

➡ **Note: One foot-pound (ft-lb) of torque is equivalent to 12 inch-pounds (in-lbs) of torque. Torque values below approximately 15 foot-pounds are expressed in inch-pounds, because most foot-pound torque wrenches are not accurate at these smaller values.**

Cylinder Head Temperature (CHT) sensor (3.7L V6 engine)	89 in-lbs	10
Knock sensor mounting bolt(s)		
Four-cylinder models	12 to 17	16 to 23
3.0L V6 models	15 to 21	21 to 28
3.7L V6 models	12 to 17	17 to 23
Oxygen sensors		
Four-cylinder models	22 to 36	29 to 49
3.0L V6 models	22 to 36	29 to 49
3.7L V6 models	30 to 40	41 to 54

Section

7A

MANUAL
TRANSAXLE

1   General information

The vehicles covered by this manual are equipped with either a 5-speed or 6-speed manual transaxle or a 4-, 5- or 6-speed automatic transaxle. This Part of Chapter 7 contains information on the manual transaxle. Service procedures for the automatic transaxle are contained in Part B.

The transaxle is contained in a cast-aluminum alloy casing bolted to the engine's left-hand end, and consists of the gearbox and final drive differential. The transaxle unit type is stamped on a plate attached to the transaxle.

TRANSAXLE OVERHAUL

Because of the complexity of the assembly, possible unavailability of replacement parts and special tools necessary, internal repair procedures for the transaxle are not recommended for the home mechanic. The bulk of the information in this Chapter is devoted to removal and installation procedures.

2   Shift lever - removal and installation

1   Apply the parking brake. Place the shift lever in Neutral. Unscrew the shift knob from the lever.

2   Remove the center console (see Chapter 11).

3   Working through the openings in the shifter housing, use a small screwdriver to pry the shift cable and selector cable from the ball-studs on the shift lever assembly.

4   Remove the four nuts securing the shift lever and remove the shifter.

5   Installation is the reverse of removal

➡ **Note: See Section 4 for selector cable adjustment.**

3   Shift cables - replacement and adjustment

✳✳ WARNING:

These models are equipped with a Supplemental Restraint System (SRS), more commonly known as airbags. Always disable the airbag system before working in the vicinity of any airbag system component to avoid the possibility of accidental deployment of the airbag(s), which could cause personal injury (see Chapter 12). Do not use a memory saving device to preserve the PCM or radio memory when working on or near airbag system components.

✳✳ WARNING:

The air conditioning system is under high pressure. DO NOT loosen any fittings or remove any components until after the system has been discharged. Air conditioning refrigerant must be properly discharged into an EPA-approved container at a dealer service department or an automotive air conditioning repair facility. Always wear eye protection when disconnecting air conditioning system fittings.

➡ **Note: This is a difficult procedure for the home mechanic, since replacement of the cables requires removal of the instrument panel and the HVAC module under the instrument panel.**

REPLACEMENT

1   Have the air conditioning system discharged by an automotive air conditioning technician (see **Warning** above).

2   If the vehicle has just been driven, wait several hours to allow the engine to cool down before beginning this procedure. Disconnect both the negative and positive cables from the battery (see Chapter 5). Wait at least two minutes before proceeding.

3   Remove the battery and battery tray (see Chapter 5).

4   Remove the center console (see Chapter 11)

5   Remove the heater core/evaporator core housing (see Chapter 3).

6   Remove the shift lever and disconnect the shift cables from the shift lever (see Section 2).

7   On 2008 and earlier models, remove the clips securing the shift linkage cables to the shift lever arms at the transaxle. Do not damage the spring clips.

➡ **Note: The spring clips can be rotated for easier removal if the cable end is lifted to take pressure from the clips.**

8   On 2009 and later models, use a small screwdriver to pry the shift cable and selector cable from the ball studs on the shift lever arms at the transaxle.

9   Release the cable housing ends at the transaxle from the transaxle support bracket, taking care not to damage the plastic flanges of the cable housing.

10 Disconnect and remove the airbag module from the floor of the vehicle, then remove the insulation pad (see Chapter 12). Release the two clips securing the airbag module harness and push the harness forward.

11 Remove the fasteners securing the transmission cable plate/grommet where the cable goes through the floor.

12 Pull the shift cables through the floor from the inside.

➡ **Note: The grommet is integral to the cable assembly.**

13 Installation is the reverse of removal. Be sure to adjust the new cable after installation (see Steps 15 through 21).

14 Refill and bleed the cooling system (see Chapter 1). Have the system evacuated, recharged and leak tested by the shop that discharged it.

ADJUSTMENT

▶ **Refer to illustration 3.16**

15 With the parking brake set, remove the gearshift knob and center console trim panel (see Chapter 11).

16 Slide the safety lock away from the shifter ball stud (see illustration).

17 Slide the cable lock away from the selector cable end fitting.

18 Place the shift lever in the center position. The lever and the transaxle should now be in the Neutral position.

19 Push the cable lock onto the cable.

20 Slide the safety lock over the primary shift cable lock.

21 Install the center console trim panel and the gearshift knob.

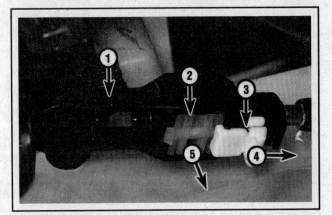

3.16 Selector cable adjustment details

1	Selector cable	4	Safety lock unlock direction
2	Lock piece	5	Lock piece unlock direction
3	Safety lock		

4 Driveaxle oil seals - replacement

1   Oil leaks frequently occur due to wear of the driveaxle oil seals. Replacement of these seals is relatively easy, since the repair can be performed without removing the transaxle from the vehicle.

2   Driveaxle oil seals are located at the sides of the transaxle, where the driveaxles are attached. If leakage at the seal is suspected, raise the vehicle and support it securely on jackstands. If the seal is leaking, lubricant will be found on the sides of the transaxle, below the seals.

3   Remove the driveaxles (see Chapter 8).

4   Use a screwdriver or prybar to carefully pry the oil seal out of the transaxle bore.

5   If the oil seal cannot be removed with a screwdriver or prybar, a special oil seal removal tool (available at auto parts stores) will be required.

6   Using a large section of pipe or a large deep socket (slightly smaller than the outside diameter of the seal) as a drift, install the new oil seal. Drive it into the bore squarely and make sure it's completely seated. Coat the seal lip with transaxle lubricant.

7   Install the driveaxle(s). Be careful not to damage the lip of the new seal with the inboard splines of the driveaxle.

5 Manual transaxle - removal and installation

REMOVAL

1   Disconnect the cables from the battery and remove the battery and battery tray (see Chapter 5).

2   Remove the air filter housing and duct (see Chapter 4).

3   Disconnect the electrical connectors for the back-up light switch.

4   Disconnect the shift cables from the transaxle shift arms (see Section 3).

5   Remove the transaxle front and rear wire harness brackets from the transaxle.

6   Disconnect the electrical connector for the vehicle speed sensor (see Chapter 6).

7   Attach an engine support fixture to the lifting hook at the transaxle end of the engine. If no hook is provided, use a bolt of the proper size and thread pitch to attach the support fixture chain to a hole at the end of the cylinder head.

➡ **Note: Engine support fixtures can be obtained at most equipment rental yards and some auto parts stores.**

8   Remove the upper engine-to-transmission mounting bolts.

9   Loosen the driveaxle/hub nuts and the wheel lug nuts, raise the front of the vehicle and support it securely on jackstands. Remove the wheels.

10 Remove the splash shield screws and pushpins and remove the splash shields (see Chapter 11, Section 10).

11 Disconnect the exhaust system from the manifold(s) the exhaust hangers and remove the front section of exhaust system (see Chapter 4).

12 Disconnect the clutch release cylinder and line from the transaxle and remove the clutch cable mounting bracket bolts (see Chapter 8).

13 Remove the steering gear (see Chapter 10).

14 Remove the transaxle mounts and brackets.

15 Remove the rear mount through-bolt.

16 Remove the starter (see Chapter 5).

17 Remove the driveaxles (see Chapter 8).

18 Drain the transaxle lubricant (see Chapter 1).

19 Remove the four bolts securing the transaxle support insulator bracket, then remove the bracket.

➡ **Note: On models with the A65M-R transaxles, remove the stud from the transaxle side mount.**

20 Remove the subframe bracket mounting bolts and brackets (see Chapter 2C, Section 7).

21 Remove the suspension subframe (see Chapter 2C, Section 7).

22 Remove the longitudinal crossmember and the engine roll restrictor (see Chapter 2A or 2B).

23 Support the transaxle with a jack - preferably a transmission

jack made for this purpose (available at most tool rental yards). Safety chains will help steady the transaxle on the jack.

24 Remove the remaining bolts securing the transaxle to the engine.

25 Move the transaxle away from the engine to disengage it from the engine block dowel pins. Carefully lower the transmission jack to the floor and remove the transaxle.

➡ **Note: It may be necessary to lean the engine towards the transaxle side to increase the clearance and make the removal easier.**

INSTALLATION

26 Lubricate the input shaft with a light coat of high-temperature grease. With the transaxle secured to the jack, raise it into position behind the engine and carefully slide it forward, engaging the input shaft with the clutch. Do not use excessive force to install the transaxle - if the input shaft won't slide into place, readjust the angle of the transaxle or turn the input shaft so the splines engage properly with the clutch.

27 Once the transaxle is flush with the engine, install the transaxle-to-engine bolts. Tighten the bolts to the torque listed in this Chapter's Specifications.

✶✶ CAUTION:

Don't use the bolts to force the transaxle and engine together.

28 The remainder of installation is the reverse of removal, noting the following points:

a) *Tighten the suspension crossmember mounting bolts to the torque values listed in this Chapter's Specifications.*

b) *Tighten the driveaxle/hub nuts to the torque value listed in the Chapter 8 Specifications.*

c) *Tighten the starter mounting bolts to the torque value listed in the Chapter 5 Specifications.*

d) *Tighten the wheel lug nuts to the torque listed in the Chapter 1 Specifications.*

e) *Fill the transaxle with the correct type and amount of transaxle fluid as described in Chapter 1.*

6   Manual transaxle overhaul - general information

1   Overhauling a manual transaxle is a difficult job for the do-it-yourselfer. It involves the disassembly and reassembly of many small parts. Numerous clearances must be precisely measured and, if necessary, changed with select-fit spacers and snap-rings. As a result, if transaxle problems arise, it can be removed and installed by a competent do-it-yourselfer, but overhaul should be left to a transmission repair shop. Rebuilt transaxles may be available - check with your dealer parts department and auto parts stores. At any rate, the time and money involved in an overhaul is almost sure to exceed the cost of a rebuilt unit.

2   Nevertheless, it's not impossible for an inexperienced mechanic to rebuild a transaxle if the special tools are available and the job is done in a deliberate step-by-step manner so nothing is overlooked.

3   The tools necessary for an overhaul include internal and external snap-ring pliers, a bearing puller, a slide hammer, a set of pin punches, a dial indicator and possibly a hydraulic press. In addition, a large, sturdy workbench and a vise or transaxle stand will be required.

4   During disassembly of the transaxle, make careful notes of how each piece comes off, where it fits in relation to other pieces and what holds it in place.

5   Before taking the transaxle apart for repair, it will help if you have some idea what area of the transaxle is malfunctioning. Certain problems can be closely tied to specific areas in the transaxle, which can make component examination and replacement easier. Refer to the *Troubleshooting* Section at the front of this manual for information regarding possible sources of trouble.

7   Transaxle mount - replacement

1   Insert a large screwdriver or prybar between the mount and the transaxle and pry up.

2   The transaxle should not move excessively away from the mount. If it does, replace the mount.

3   Remove the battery and battery tray (see Chapter 5).

4   Remove the air filter housing (see Chapter 4)

5   Unbolt and set aside the underhood fuse/relay box (see Chapter 12).

6   Supporting the transaxle with a floor jack, remove the nuts and bolts and remove the mount. It may be necessary to raise the transaxle slightly to provide enough clearance to remove the mount.

7   Disconnect the two clips securing the clutch hydraulic hose (one metal U-clip, one plastic clip on the transmission mount).

8   Remove the remaining mount bolts.

9   Installation is the reverse of removal.

➡ **Note: Install all of the mount fasteners before tightening any of them.**

Specifications

General

Transaxle oil type	See Chapter 1
Transaxle oil capacity	See Chapter 1

Torque specifications	Ft-lbs	Nm

➡ **Note:** One foot-pound (ft-lb) of torque is equivalent to 12 inch-pounds (in-lbs) of torque. Torque values below approximately 15 foot-pounds are expressed in inch-pounds, because most foot-pound torque wrenches are not accurate at these smaller values.

	Ft-lbs	Nm
Transaxle-to-engine mounting bolts	35	47
Transaxle drain plug and fill plugs		
G66M-R and G35M-R	36	49
A65M-R	25	34
Crossmember-to-subframe nuts	100	136
Crossmember bracket		
Bolts	85	115
Nuts	100	136
Rear mount through bolts/nuts	75	102
Shifter assembly mounting bolts	16	22
Clutch release cylinder mounting bolts	16	22

Notes

Notes

Section

Reference to other Chapters

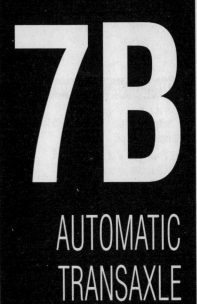

7B

AUTOMATIC
TRANSAXLE

1 General information

All information on the automatic 4-speed (FN4A-EL), the 5-speed (JA5A-EL, FS5A-EL) and 6-speed (AW6A-EL) transaxles are included in this Part of Chapter 7. Information for the manual transaxles can be found in Part A of this Chapter.

Because of the complexity of the automatic transaxles and the specialized equipment necessary to perform most service operations, this Chapter contains only those procedures related to general diagnosis, routine maintenance, adjustment and removal and installation.

If the transaxle requires major repair work, it should be left to a dealer service department or an automotive or transmission repair shop. Once properly diagnosed you can, however, remove and install the transaxle yourself and save the expense, even if the repair work is done by a transmission shop.

2 Diagnosis - general

1 Automatic transaxle malfunctions may be caused by five general conditions:

   a) *Poor engine performance*
   b) *Improper adjustments*
   c) *Hydraulic malfunctions*
   d) *Mechanical malfunctions*
   e) *Malfunctions in the computer or its signal network*

2 Diagnosis of these problems should always begin with a check of the easily repaired items: fluid level and condition (see Chapter 1), shift cable adjustment and shift lever installation. Next, perform a road test to determine if the problem has been corrected or if more diagnosis is necessary. If the problem persists after the preliminary tests and corrections are completed, additional diagnosis should be performed by a dealer service department or other qualified transmission repair shop. On modern electronically controlled automatic transaxles, a scan tool is helpful in retrieving trouble codes relating to the transaxle. Refer to the "Troubleshooting" Section at the front of this manual for information on symptoms of transaxle problems.

PRELIMINARY CHECKS

3 Drive the vehicle to warm the transaxle to normal operating temperature.

4 Check the fluid level as described in Chapter 1:

   a) *If the fluid level is unusually low, add enough fluid to bring the level within the designated area of the dipstick, then check for external leaks (see following).*
   b) *If the fluid level is abnormally high, drain off the excess, then check the drained fluid for contamination by coolant. The presence of engine coolant in the automatic transmission fluid indicates that a failure has occurred in the internal radiator oil cooler walls that separate the coolant from the transmission fluid (see Chapter 3).*
   c) *If the fluid is foaming, drain it and refill the transaxle, then check for coolant in the fluid, or a high fluid level.*

5 Check the engine idle speed.

➡ **Note: If the engine is malfunctioning, do not proceed with the preliminary checks until it has been repaired and runs normally.**

6 Check and adjust the shift cable, if necessary (see Section 4).

7 If hard shifting is experienced, inspect the shift cable under the steering column and at the manual lever on the transaxle (see Section 4).

FLUID LEAK DIAGNOSIS

8 Most fluid leaks are easy to locate visually. Repair usually consists of replacing a seal or gasket. If a leak is difficult to find, the following procedure may help.

9 Identify the fluid. Make sure it's transmission fluid and not engine oil or brake fluid (automatic transmission fluid is a deep red color).

10 Try to pinpoint the source of the leak. Drive the vehicle several miles, then park it over a large sheet of cardboard. After a minute or two, you should be able to locate the leak by determining the source of the fluid dripping onto the cardboard.

11 Make a careful visual inspection of the suspected component and the area immediately around it. Pay particular attention to gasket mating surfaces. A mirror is often helpful for finding leaks in areas that are hard to see.

12 If the leak still cannot be found, clean the suspected area thoroughly with a degreaser or solvent, then dry it thoroughly.

13 Drive the vehicle for several miles at normal operating temperature and varying speeds. After driving the vehicle, visually inspect the suspected component again.

14 Once the leak has been located, the cause must be determined before it can be properly repaired. If a gasket is replaced but the sealing flange is bent, the new gasket will not stop the leak. The bent flange must be straightened.

15 Before attempting to repair a leak, check to make sure that the following conditions are corrected or they may cause another leak.

➡ **Note: Some of the following conditions cannot be fixed without highly specialized tools and expertise. Such problems must be referred to a qualified transmission shop or a dealer service department.**

Gasket leaks

16 Check the pan periodically. Make sure the bolts are tight, no bolts are missing, the gasket is in good condition and the pan is flat (dents in the pan may indicate damage to the valve body inside).

17 If the pan gasket is leaking, the fluid level or the fluid pressure may be too high, the vent may be plugged, the pan bolts may be too tight, the pan sealing flange may be warped, the sealing surface of the transaxle housing may be damaged, the gasket may be damaged or the transaxle casting may be cracked or porous. If sealant instead of gasket material has been used to form a seal between the pan and the transaxle housing, it may be the wrong type of sealant.

Seal leaks

18 If a transaxle seal is leaking, the fluid level or pressure may be too high, the vent may be plugged, the seal bore may be damaged, the seal itself may be damaged or improperly installed, the surface of the shaft protruding through the seal may be damaged or a loose bearing may be causing excessive shaft movement.

19 Make sure the dipstick tube seal is in good condition and the tube is properly seated. Periodically check the area around the sensors for leakage. If transmission fluid is evident, check the seals for damage.

Case leaks

20 If the case itself appears to be leaking, the casting is porous and will have to be repaired or replaced.

21 Make sure the oil cooler hose fittings are tight and in good condition.

Fluid comes out vent pipe or fill tube

22 If this condition occurs the possible causes are: the transaxle is overfilled; there is coolant in the fluid; the case is porous; the dipstick is incorrect; the vent is plugged or the drain-back holes are plugged.

3   Shift lever - replacement

❋ WARNING:

These models are equipped with a Supplemental Restraint System (SRS), more commonly known as airbags. Always disable the airbag system before working in the vicinity of any airbag system component to avoid the possibility of accidental deployment of the airbag(s), which could cause personal injury (see Chapter 12).

❋ WARNING:

Do not use a memory saving device to preserve the PCM or radio memory when working on or near airbag system components.

SHIFT KNOB

▶ **Refer to illustration 3.1**

1   Unscrew the shift knob from the shift lever assembly and remove the knob (see illustration).

2   Installation is the reverse of removal.

SHIFT LEVER ASSEMBLY

▶ **Refer to illustrations 3.5, 3.6 and 3.8**

3   Disconnect the cable from the negative battery terminal (see Chapter 5). Wait at least two minutes before proceeding.

4   Remove the floor console indicator panel (see Chapter 11).

5   Remove the interlock cable from the shift lever (see illustration).

6   Pull back the catch at the bottom of the cable housing. Pry the cable housing up and out of the bracket on the shift assembly (see illustration) and slide the cable end off of the lever.

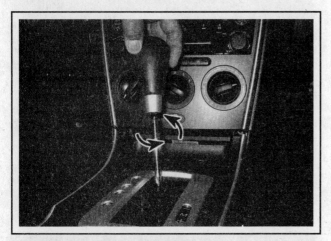

3.1 Unscrew the shift knob to remove it

3.5 Remove the interlock cable lock pin (A), then the cable end (B) from the lever and the cable housing (C) from the lever base

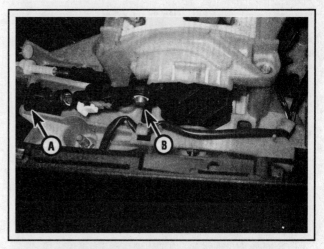

3.6 Pry the shift cable (A) from the bracket and slide the cable end (B) from the shift lever

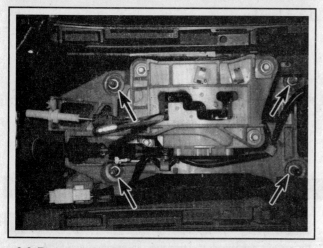

3.8 To remove the shifter assembly, remove the four mounting nuts

7 Disconnect any electrical connectors at the shift assembly.

8 Remove the four mounting nuts and remove the shift assembly from the floor (see illustration).

9 Installation is the reverse of removal. The shift cable should be adjusted anytime it has been disconnected (see Section 4).

4 Shift cable - replacement and adjustment

✳✳ WARNING:

The models covered by this manual are equipped with Supplemental Restraint Systems (SRS), more commonly known as airbags. Always disarm the airbag system before working in the vicinity of any airbag system component to avoid the possibility of accidental deployment of the airbag, which could cause personal injury (see Chapter 12). Do not use a memory saving device to preserve the PCM or radio memory when working on or near airbag system components.

✳✳ WARNING:

The air conditioning system is under high pressure. DO NOT loosen any fittings or remove any components until after the system has been discharged. Air conditioning refrigerant must be properly discharged into an EPA-approved container at a dealer service department or an automotive air conditioning repair facility. Always wear eye protection when disconnecting air conditioning system fittings.

➡ Note: This is a difficult procedure for the home mechanic, since replacement of the cables requires removal of the instrument panel and the HVAC housing under the instrument panel.

REPLACEMENT

▶ Refer to illustrations 4.9 and 4.10

1 Have the air conditioning system discharged by an automotive air conditioning technician (see **Warning** above).

2 If the vehicle has just been driven, wait several hours to allow the engine to cool down before beginning this procedure. Disconnect both the negative and positive cables from the battery (see Chapter 5). Wait at least two minutes before proceeding.

3 Remove the battery and battery tray (see Chapter 5).

4 Remove the center console (see Chapter 11).

5 Remove the heater core/evaporator core housing (see Chapter 3).

6 Disconnect and remove the airbag module ahead of the console area of the floor, then remove the insulation pad (see Chapter 12). Release the two clips securing the airbag module harness and push the harness forward.

7 Disconnect the cable from the shift assembly on the floor and release the clips securing the cable housing end (see Section 3).

8 Remove the insulation from the floor area under the center of the instrument panel to access the fasteners securing the cable grommet to the floorpan. Remove the fasteners securing the transaxle cable plate/grommet.

9 To disconnect the shift cable at the transaxle control arm, lift the cable end to release pressure on the spring clip, then rotate the clip for removal. On some models, the cable end is released by squeezing two clips and pulling the cable from the ball-stud (see illustration).

✳✳ CAUTION:

Take care not to damage the spring clip.

4.9 On models without a spring clip, pry the cable end from the ballstud on the shift control lever

10 Release the clips to remove the cable housing end from the mounting bracket on the transaxle, without damaging the plastic groove that holds the cable end (see illustration).

11 Disconnect any cable retainers along the length of the cable.

12 Pull the shift cable through the floor from the inside.

➡ **Note: The grommet is integral to the cable assembly.**

13 Installation is the reverse of removal. Adjust the new cable after installation (see Steps 15 through 23).

14 Refill and bleed the cooling system (see Chapter 1). Have the system evacuated, recharged and leak tested by the shop that discharged it.

ADJUSTMENT

▶ **Refer to illustration 4.21**

15 Set the parking brake, then disconnect the cable from the negative battery terminal (see Chapter 5).

16 Remove the air filter housing (see Chapter 4).

17 Place the shifter in Drive.

18 Remove the cable eye from the control arm on the transaxle.

19 Manually move the shift arm at the transaxle to Drive, then to the Park position.

20 Move the shift arm at the transaxle three clicks clockwise for four and five-speed transaxles, or three clicks counterclockwise for six-speed transaxles. The shift arm should now be in the Drive position.

21 The interior end of the shift cable is equipped with an adjuster mechanism. Slide the safety lock back and move the lock piece outwards (see illustration).

22 Press the lock piece into the cable and slide the safety lock into place. The safety lock should snap firmly onto the end of the cable.

23 After installing any remaining components, apply the parking brake, and operate the vehicle in each range to verify the adjustment is correct.

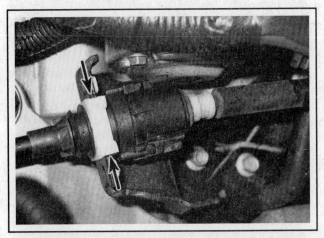

4.10 Squeeze the tabs to remove the cable from the bracket on the transaxle

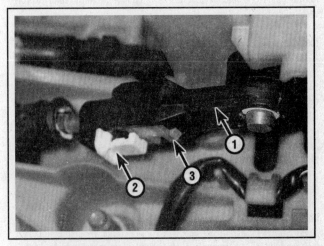

4.21 Shift select cable details:

1	Shift select cable	3	Lock piece
2	Safety lock		

5 Automatic transaxle - removal and installation

REMOVAL

▶ **Refer to illustrations 5.7 and 5.25**

1 Disconnect the cables from the battery and remove the battery and battery tray (see Chapter 5).

2 Remove the air filter housing and duct (see Chapter 4).

3 Disconnect the TCM harness electrical connector at the transmission range sensor. Also disconnect the ground straps and remove the bolts holding the electrical harness to the transaxle.

4 Disconnect the shift cable from the transaxle shift control arm (see Section 4). Remove the transaxle cable mount fasteners and mount.

5 Remove the transaxle front and rear wire harness brackets from the transaxle.

6 Disconnect the electrical connectors for the vehicle speed sensor and at the TCM (see Chapter 6).

7 Attach an engine support fixture to the lifting hook at the transaxle end of the engine (see illustration). On V6 engines, the upper intake manifold must be removed (see Chapter 2B). If no hook is provided,

5.7 Use an overhead support fixture to secure the engine while the transaxle and subframe are removed - note the chain locations

use a bolt of the proper size and thread pitch to attach the support fixture chain to a hole at the end of the cylinder head.

➡ **Note: Engine support fixtures can be obtained at most equipment rental yards and some auto parts stores.**

8 Remove the upper engine-to-transaxle mounting bolts.

9 Loosen the driveaxle/hub nuts and the wheel lug nuts, raise the front of the vehicle and support it securely on jackstands or a lift. Remove the wheels.

10 Disconnect the shift cable from the transaxle, and remove the bolts securing the shift cable brackets.

11 Remove the EGR valve (see Chapter 6).

12 Remove the steering gear, linkage, power steering hoses and brackets (see Chapter 10) and wire the steering gear out of the way.

13 On 6-speed models, remove the cowl panel (see Chapter 11) and the windshield wiper assembly (see Chapter 12).

14 Disconnect the flexible exhaust pipe sections and the Y-pipe. Remove the right-side exhaust heat shield and remove the catalytic converter (see Chapter 4).

15 Remove the heat shield over the roll restrictor, then unbolt the roll restrictor.

16 Remove the driveaxles (see Chapter 8).

17 Remove the splash aprons from the left and right fenderwells.

18 Place a block of wood above the lower control arm to protect the outer CV joint on the left side. Remove the left steering knuckle (see Chapter 10).

19 Remove the starter (see Chapter 5).

20 Drain the transaxle lubricant (see Chapter 1). Disconnect and plug the transmission fluid hoses.

21 Remove the bolts securing the transaxle support insulator brackets, then remove the brackets.

22 Remove the front suspension subframe (see Chapter 2C, Section 7).

23 Support the transaxle with a jack - preferably a transmission jack made for this purpose (available at most tool rental yards). Safety chains will help steady the transaxle on the jack.

24 Disconnect the oxygen sensors (see Chapter 6).

25 Remove the torque converter cover and mark the relationship of the torque converter to the driveplate (see illustration). Remove the converter mounting nuts.

26 Remove the remaining bolts securing the transaxle to the engine.

27 Move the transaxle away from the engine to disengage it from the engine block dowel pins. Carefully lower the transmission jack to the floor and remove the transaxle.

5.25 Mark the relationship of the torque converter to the driveplate

INSTALLATION

28 Installation of is the reverse of removal, noting the following points:

a) As the torque converter is reinstalled, ensure that the drive tangs at the center of the torque converter hub engage with the recesses in the automatic transaxle fluid pump inner gear. This can be confirmed by turning the torque converter while pushing it towards the transaxle. If it isn't fully engaged, it will clunk into place.

b) When installing the transaxle, make sure the matchmarks you made on the torque converter and driveplate line up.

c) Install all of the driveplate-to-torque converter nuts before tightening any of them.

d) Tighten the driveplate-to-torque converter nuts to the specified torque.

e) Tighten the transaxle mounting bolts to the specified torque.

f) Tighten the suspension crossmember mounting bolts to the torque values listed in this Chapter's Specifications.

g) Tighten the driveaxle/hub nuts to the torque value listed in the Chapter 8 Specifications.

h) Tighten the wheel lug nuts to the torque listed in the Chapter 1 Specifications.

i) Fill the transaxle with the correct type and amount of automatic transmission fluid as described in Chapter 1.

j) On completion, adjust the shift cable as described in Section 4.

6 Automatic transaxle overhaul - general information

In the event of a problem occurring, it will be necessary to establish whether the fault is electrical, mechanical or hydraulic in nature, before repair work can be contemplated. Diagnosis requires detailed knowledge of the transaxle's operation and construction, as well as access to specialized test equipment, and so is deemed to be beyond the scope of this manual. It is therefore essential that problems with the automatic transaxle are referred to a dealer service department or other qualified repair facility for assessment.

Note that a faulty transaxle should not be removed before the vehicle has been diagnosed by a knowledgeable technician equipped with the proper tools, as troubleshooting must be performed with the transaxle installed in the vehicle.

Specifications

General

Fluid type and capacity	See Chapter 1

Torque specifications

	Ft-lbs (unless otherwise indicated)	Nm

➡ **Note: One foot-pound (ft-lb) of torque is equivalent to 12 inch-pounds (in-lbs) of torque. Torque values below approximately 15 foot-pounds are expressed in inch-pounds, because most foot-pound torque wrenches are not accurate at these smaller values.**

Crossmember mounting bolts	35	47
Fluid pan bolts	115 in-lbs	13
Torque converter-to-driveplate nuts	27	37
Transaxle-to-engine mounting bolts		
3.0L V6	30	40
Four-cylinder and 3.7L V6	35	47

Notes

Section

8

CLUTCH AND DRIVELINE

1   General information

The information in this Chapter deals with the components from the rear of the engine to the drive wheels, except for the transaxle, which is dealt with in the previous Chapter.

Since nearly all the procedures covered in this Chapter involve

working under the vehicle, make sure it's securely supported on sturdy jackstands or on a hoist where the vehicle can be easily raised and lowered.

2   Clutch - description and check

1   All vehicles with a manual transaxle have a single dry plate, diaphragm-spring type clutch. The clutch disc has a splined hub which allows it to slide along the splines of the transaxle input shaft. The clutch and pressure plate are held in contact by spring pressure exerted by the diaphragm in the pressure plate.

2   The clutch release system is operated by hydraulic pressure. The hydraulic release system consists of the clutch pedal, a master cylinder and a shared common reservoir with the brake master cylinder, a release (or slave) cylinder and the hydraulic line connecting the two components.

3   When the clutch pedal is depressed, a pushrod pushes against brake fluid inside the master cylinder, applying hydraulic pressure to the release cylinder, which pushes the release bearing against the diaphragm fingers of the clutch pressure plate.

4   Terminology can be a problem when discussing the clutch components because common names are in some cases different from those used by the manufacturer. For example, the driven plate is also called the clutch plate or disc, the clutch release bearing is sometimes called a throwout bearing, the release cylinder is sometimes called the slave cylinder.

5   Unless you're replacing components with obvious damage, perform these preliminary checks to diagnose clutch problems:

a) *The first check should be of the fluid level in the clutch master cylinder. If the fluid level is low, add fluid as necessary and inspect the hydraulic system for leaks. If the master cylinder reservoir is dry, bleed the system (see Section 5) and recheck the clutch operation.*

b) *To check clutch spin-down time, run the engine at normal idle speed with the transaxle in Neutral (clutch pedal up - engaged). Disengage the clutch (pedal down), wait several seconds and shift the transaxle into Reverse. No grinding noise should be heard. A grinding noise would most likely indicate a bad pressure plate or clutch disc.*

c) *To check for complete clutch release, run the engine (with the parking brake applied to prevent vehicle movement) and hold the clutch pedal approximately 1/2-inch from the floor. Shift the transaxle between 1st gear and Reverse several times. If the shift is rough, component failure is indicated.*

d) *Visually inspect the pivot bushing at the top of the clutch pedal to make sure there's no binding or excessive play.*

3   Clutch master cylinder - removal and installation

REMOVAL

1   Remove the upper engine cover, pull the cover up from each side and lift the cover off the mounting posts in the center of the cover.

2   Remove the battery and battery tray (see Chapter 5).

3   On 2010 models, remove the cowl panel (see Chapter 11).

4   On 2010 models, remove the PCM and the PCM bracket (see Chapter 6).

5   Clamp a pair of locking pliers onto the clutch fluid feed hose, a couple of inches downstream of the brake fluid reservoir (the clutch master cylinder is supplied with fluid from the brake fluid reservoir). The pliers should be just tight enough to prevent fluid flow when the hose is disconnected. Disconnect the reservoir hose from the clutch master cylinder.

6   Using a flare-nut wrench, disconnect the hydraulic line fitting at the cylinder. Have rags handy, as some fluid will be lost as the line is removed. Cap or plug the ends of the line to prevent fluid leakage and the entry of contaminants.

7   Remove the two nuts (one on the engine side and one on the inside) that secure the clutch master cylinder to the firewall.

8   Detach the cylinder from the firewall.

✳ CAUTION:

Don't allow brake fluid to come into contact with the paint, as it will damage the finish.

INSTALLATION

9   Place the master cylinder in position on the firewall, insert the clutch pedal rod into the cylinder and install the interior mounting nut finger tight.

10   Connect the hydraulic line fitting to the clutch master cylinder and tighten it finger tight (since the cylinder is still a bit loose, it'll be easier to start the threads into the cylinder).

11   Tighten the engine-side mounting nut to the torque listed in this Chapter's Specifications, then tighten the hydraulic line fitting securely.

12   Attach the fluid feed hose from the reservoir to the clutch master cylinder and tighten the hose clamp. Remove the locking pliers.

13   Working under the dash, tighten the remaining mounting nut. Reinstall the PCM (see Chapter 6).

14   Fill the reservoir with brake fluid conforming to DOT 3 specifications and bleed the clutch system (see Section 5).

4 Clutch release cylinder - removal and installation

REMOVAL

1 Raise the front of the vehicle and place it securely on jackstands.
2 Remove the splash shield screws and pushpins and remove the splash shield (see Chapter 11, Section 10).
3 Disconnect the hydraulic line at the release cylinder using a flare-nut wrench. Have a small can and rags handy, as some fluid will be spilled as the line is removed. Plug the line to prevent excessive fluid loss and contamination.
4 Remove the release cylinder mounting bolts.
5 Remove the release cylinder.

INSTALLATION

6 Connect the hydraulic line fitting to the release cylinder, using your fingers only at this time (since the cylinder is still a bit loose, it'll be easier to start the threads into the cylinder).
7 Tighten the mounting bolts to the torque listed in this Chapter's Specifications.
8 Tighten the hydraulic fitting securely, using a flare-nut wrench.
9 Check the fluid level in the brake fluid reservoir, adding brake fluid conforming to DOT 3 specifications until the level is correct.
10 Bleed the system (see Section 5), then recheck the brake fluid level.

5 Clutch hydraulic system - bleeding

1 Bleed the hydraulic system whenever any part of the system has been removed or the fluid level has fallen so low that air has been drawn into the master cylinder. The bleeding procedure is very similar to bleeding a brake system.
2 Raise the front of the vehicle and place it securely on jackstands.
3 Remove the splash shield screws and pushpins and remove the splash shield (see Chapter 11, Section 10).
4 Fill the brake master cylinder reservoir with new brake fluid conforming to DOT 3 specifications.

✳ CAUTION:

Do not re-use any of the fluid coming from the system during the bleeding operation or use fluid which has been inside an open container for an extended period of time.

5 Have an assistant depress the clutch pedal and hold it. Open the bleeder valve on the release cylinder, allowing fluid and any air to escape. Close the bleeder valve when the flow of fluid (and bubbles) ceases. Once closed, have your assistant release the pedal.
6 Continue this process until all air is evacuated from the system, indicated by a solid stream of fluid being ejected from the bleeder valve each time with no air bubbles. Keep a close watch on the fluid level inside the brake master cylinder reservoir - if the level drops too far, air will get into the system and you'll have to start all over again.

➡ **Note: Wash the area with water to remove any excess brake fluid.**

7 Check the brake fluid level again, and add some, if necessary, to bring it to the appropriate level. Check carefully for proper operation before placing the vehicle into normal service.

6 Clutch components - removal, inspection and installation

✳ WARNING:

Dust produced by clutch wear is hazardous to your health. DO NOT blow it out with compressed air and DO NOT inhale it. DO NOT use gasoline or petroleum-based solvents to remove the dust. Brake system cleaner should be used to flush the dust into a drain pan. After the clutch components are wiped clean with a rag, dispose of the contaminated rags and cleaner in a covered, marked container.

REMOVAL

▶ **Refer to illustration 6.5**

1 Access to the clutch components is normally accomplished by removing the transaxle, leaving the engine in the vehicle. If the engine is being removed for major overhaul, check the clutch for wear and replace worn components as necessary. However, the relatively low cost of the clutch components compared to the time and trouble spent gaining access to them warrants their replacement anytime the engine or transaxle is removed, unless they are new or in near-perfect condition. The following procedures are based on the assumption the engine will stay in place.
2 Remove the transaxle from the vehicle (see Chapter 7A).
3 The clutch fork and release bearing can remain attached to the transaxle housing for the time being.
4 To support the clutch disc during removal, install a clutch alignment tool through the clutch disc hub.
5 Carefully inspect the flywheel and pressure plate for indexing marks. The marks are usually an X, an O or a white letter. If they cannot

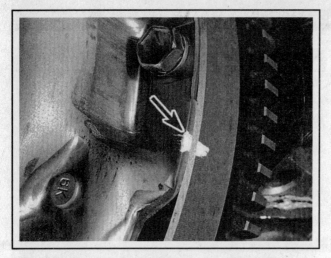

6.5 Mark the relationship of the pressure plate to the flywheel (if you're planning to re-use the old pressure plate)

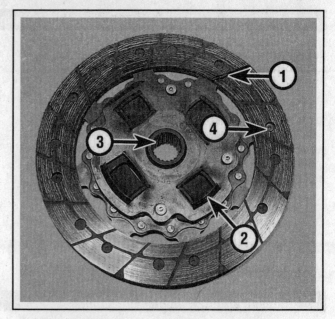

6.9 The clutch disc

1   *Lining* - this will wear down in use
2   *Springs or dampers* - check for cracking and deformation
3   *Splined hub* - the splines must not be worn and should slide smoothly on the transaxle input shaft splines
4   *Rivets* - these secure the lining and will damage the flywheel or pressure plate if allowed to contact the surfaces

be found, scribe or paint marks yourself so the pressure plate and the flywheel will be in the same alignment during installation (see illustration).

6   Turning each bolt a little at a time, loosen the pressure plate-to-flywheel bolts. Work in a criss-cross pattern until all spring pressure is relieved. Then hold the pressure plate securely and completely remove the bolts, followed by the pressure plate and clutch disc.

INSPECTION

▶ **Refer to illustrations 6.9, 6.11a and 6.11b**

7   Ordinarily, when a problem occurs in the clutch, it can be attributed to wear of the clutch driven plate assembly (clutch disc). However, all components should be inspected at this time.

8   Inspect the flywheel for cracks, heat checking, grooves and other obvious defects. If the imperfections are slight, a machine shop can machine the surface flat and smooth, which is highly recommended regardless of the surface appearance. Refer to Chapter 2 for the flywheel removal and installation procedure.

9   Inspect the lining on the clutch disc. There should be at least 1/16-inch of lining above the rivet heads. Check for loose rivets, distortion, cracks, broken springs and other obvious damage (see illustration). As mentioned above, ordinarily the clutch disc is routinely

replaced, so if in doubt about the condition, replace it with a new one.

10 The release bearing should also be replaced along with the clutch disc (see Section 7).

11 Check the machined surfaces and the diaphragm spring fingers of the pressure plate (see illustrations). If the surface is grooved or otherwise damaged, replace the pressure plate. Also check for obvious damage, distortion, cracking, etc. Light glazing can be removed with emery cloth or sandpaper. If a new pressure plate is required, new and re-manufactured units are available.

12 Check the pilot bearing in the end of the crankshaft for excessive wear, scoring, dryness, roughness and any other obvious damage. If any of these conditions are noted, replace the bearing.

13 Removal can be accomplished with a slide hammer and puller attachment, which are available at most auto parts stores or tool rental yards. Refer to Chapter 2 for the flywheel removal procedure (it must be removed before the pilot bearing is removed).

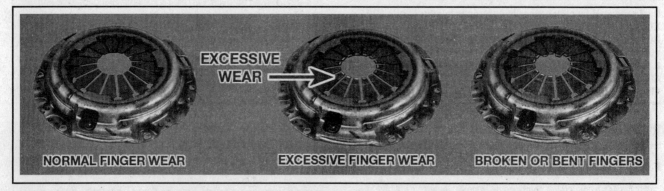

6.11a Replace the pressure plate if excessive wear or damage are noted

6.11b Inspect the pressure plate surface for excessive score marks, cracks and signs of overheating

6.16 Center the clutch disc in the pressure plate with a clutch alignment tool

INSTALLATION

▶ **Refer to illustration 6.16**

14 To install a new pilot bearing, lightly lubricate the outside surface with grease, then drive it into the recess with a bearing driver or a socket. Install the flywheel (see Chapter 2).

15 Before installation, clean the flywheel and pressure plate machined surfaces with brake cleaner, lacquer thinner or acetone. It's important that no oil or grease is on these surfaces or the lining of the clutch disc. Handle the parts only with clean hands.

16 Position the clutch disc and pressure plate against the flywheel with the clutch held in place with an alignment tool (see illustration). Make sure the disc is installed properly (most replacement clutch discs will be marked "flywheel side" or something similar - if not marked,

install the clutch disc with the damper springs toward the transaxle).

17 Tighten the pressure plate-to-flywheel bolts only finger tight, working around the pressure plate.

18 Center the clutch disc by ensuring the alignment tool extends through the splined hub and into the pilot bearing in the crankshaft. Wiggle the tool up, down or side-to-side as needed to center the disc. Tighten the pressure plate-to-flywheel bolts a little at a time, working in a criss-cross pattern to prevent distorting the cover. After all of the bolts are snug, tighten them to the torque listed in this Chapter's Specifications. Remove the alignment tool.

19 Using high-temperature grease, lubricate the inner groove of the release bearing (see Section 7). Also place a small amount of grease on the release lever contact areas and the transaxle input shaft bearing retainer.

20 Install the clutch release bearing (see Section 7).

21 Install the transaxle and all components removed previously.

---

7   Clutch release bearing and lever - removal, inspection and installation

❋❋ WARNING:

Dust produced by clutch wear is hazardous to your health. DO NOT blow it out with compressed air and DO NOT inhale it. DO NOT use gasoline or petroleum-based solvents to remove the dust. Brake system cleaner should be used to flush the dust into a drain pan. After the clutch components are wiped clean with a rag, dispose of the contaminated rags and cleaner in a covered, marked container.

REMOVAL

1 Remove the transaxle (see Chapter 7A).

2 Pull the clutch release fork off the ballstud and slide the release bearing off the input shaft along with the release fork.

INSPECTION

▶ **Refer to illustration 7.4**

3 Wipe off the bearing with a clean rag and inspect it for damage, wear and cracks. Don't immerse the bearing in solvent - it's sealed for

life and immersion in solvent will ruin it.

4 Hold the center of the bearing and rotate the outer portion while

7.4 To check the bearing, hold it by the outer race and rotate the inner race while applying pressure; if the bearing doesn't turn smoothly or if it is noisy, replace the bearing

applying pressure (see illustration). If the bearing doesn't turn smoothly or if it's noisy or rough, replace it.

➡ **Note: Considering the difficulty involved with replacing the release bearing, we recommend replacing the release bearing whenever the clutch components are replaced.**

---

8   Driveaxles - removal and installation

⁕⁕ **WARNING:**

Wait until the engine is completely cool before beginning this procedure.

REMOVAL

♦ **Refer to illustrations 8.1 and 8.11**

1   Remove the wheel cover or hub cap. Break the driveaxle/hub nut loose with a socket and large breaker bar (see illustration).

➡ **Note: If your socket is too big to fit through the opening in the wheel, loosen the nut after removing the wheel (use a long prybar braced across the wheel studs to prevent the hub from turning).**

2   Loosen the wheel lug nuts, raise the vehicle and support it securely on jackstands. Remove the wheel. Remove the pushpins securing the splash apron in the fenderwell.

3   Separate the lower control arms from the steering knuckle (see Chapter 10).

4   Remove the brake caliper and wire it aside, so that the flexible brake hose is not under tension (see Chapter 9).

5   Disconnect the brake hose tab that secures the brake hose to the steering knuckle.

6   Remove the driveaxle/hub nut from the axle and discard it. Remove the wheel speed sensor and set it aside.

7   Detach the damper fork from the lower control arm (see Chapter 10, Section 2).

8   Use a tool such as a hub driver to push the outboard end of the driveaxle from the steering knuckle.

INSTALLATION

5   Lightly lubricate the friction surfaces of the release bearing, ballstud and input shaft bearing retainer with high-temperature grease.

6   Install the release lever and bearing onto the input shaft.

7   The remainder of installation is the reverse of removal.

9   Swing the knuckle/hub assembly out (away from the vehicle) until the end of the driveaxle is free of the hub.

➡ **Note: If the driveaxle splines stick in the hub, tap on the inner end of the driveaxle with a brass or plastic hammer.**

Support the outer end of the driveaxle with a piece of wire to avoid unnecessary strain on the inner CV joint.

10   If you're removing the right driveaxle, carefully pry the inner CV joint off the intermediate shaft using a large screwdriver or prybar positioned between the CV joint housing and the intermediate shaft bearing support.

11   If you're removing the left driveaxle, pry the inner CV joint out of the transaxle using a large screwdriver or prybar positioned between the transaxle and the CV joint housing (see illustration). Be careful not to damage the differential seal.

12   Support the CV joints and carefully remove the driveaxle from the vehicle.

INSTALLATION

13   Pry the old spring clip from the inner end of the driveaxle (left side) or outer end of the intermediate shaft (right side) and install a new one. Lubricate the differential or intermediate shaft seal with multi-purpose grease and raise the driveaxle into position while supporting the CV joints.

➡ **Note: Position the spring clip with the opening facing down; this will ease insertion of the driveaxle and prevent damage to the clip.**

14   Push the splined end of the inner CV joint into the differential side gear (left side) or onto the intermediate shaft (right side) and make sure the spring clip locks in its groove.

8.1 Loosen the driveaxle/hub nut with a long breaker bar

8.11 Carefully pry the inner end of the driveaxle from the transaxle

➡ Note: The inner driveaxle end must go through the damper fork before the inner driveaxle end goes into the transaxle.

15 Apply a light coat of multi-purpose grease to the outer CV joint splines, pull out on the steering knuckle assembly and install the stub axle into the hub.

16 Reconnect the lower control arms to the steering knuckle and tighten the fasteners to the torque listed in the Chapter 10 Specifications.

17 Reconnect the damper fork to the lower control arm, using new fasteners.

18 Install a new driveaxle/hub nut. Tighten the hub nut securely, but don't try to tighten it to the actual torque specification until you've lowered the vehicle to the ground.

➡ Note: If your socket is too big to fit through the wheel opening, use the method described in the Step 1 Note to prevent the hub from turning.

19 Grasp the inner CV joint housing (not the driveaxle) and pull out to make sure the driveaxle has seated securely in the transaxle or on the intermediate shaft.

20 Install the wheel and lug nuts, then lower the vehicle. Tighten the lug nuts to the torque listed in the Chapter 1 Specifications.

21 Tighten the driveaxle/hub nut to the torque listed in this Chapter's Specifications. Install the hub cap or wheel cover.

INTERMEDIATE SHAFT

Removal

◆ Refer to illustration 8.26

22 Remove the right side wheel cover or hub cap. Break the hub nut loose with a socket and large breaker bar.

➡ Note: If your socket is too big to fit through the opening in the wheel, loosen the nut after removing the wheel (use a long prybar braced across the wheel studs to prevent the hub from turning).

23 Loosen the wheel lug nuts, raise the vehicle and support it securely on jackstands. Remove the wheel.

24 Remove the right driveaxle (see Steps 1 through 12).

25 Remove the bolts and nuts securing the catalytic converter support bracket.

26 Remove the bearing-support mounting bolts (see illustration) and slide the intermediate shaft out of the transaxle. Be careful not to damage the differential seal when pulling the shaft out.

27 Check the support bearing for smooth operation by turning the shaft while holding the bearing. If you feel any roughness, take the intermediate shaft to an automotive machine shop or other qualified repair facility to have a new bearing installed.

Installation

28 Lubricate the lips of the transaxle seal with multi-purpose grease. Carefully guide the intermediate shaft into the transaxle side gear, then install the mounting nuts for the bearing support. Tighten the nuts to the torque listed in this Chapter's Specifications.

29 The remainder of installation is the reverse of removal.

8.26 Remove the bolts securing the intermediate shaft bearing support

9   Driveaxle boot - replacement

➡ Note: If the CV joints are worn, indicating the need for an overhaul (usually due to torn boots), explore all options before beginning the job. Complete rebuilt driveaxles are available on an exchange basis, which eliminates much time and work.

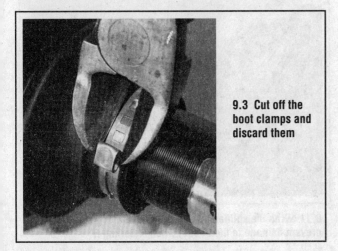

9.3 Cut off the boot clamps and discard them

➡ Note: Some auto parts stores carry split type replacement boots, which can be installed without removing the driveaxle from the vehicle. This is a convenient alternative; however, the driveaxle should be removed and the CV joint disassembled and cleaned to ensure the joint is free from contaminants such as moisture and dirt which will accelerate CV joint wear.

➡ Note: Models equipped with ABS are equipped with ABS sensor rings on the outer CV joints. Be sure to inspect the sensor rings for chipped or missing teeth. Replace the sensor ring if necessary.

1   Remove the driveaxle (see Section 8).

2   Mount the driveaxle in a vise. The jaws of the vise should be lined with wood or rags to prevent damage to the driveaxle.

INNER CV JOINT AND BOOT

Removal

◆ Refer to illustrations 9.3, 9.4, 9.5, 9.6a, 9.6b and 9.7

3   Remove the boot clamps (see illustration).

9.4 Mark the relationship of the tri-pod assembly to the outer race

9.5 Make marks on the tri-pod and the driveaxle to ensure that they are properly reassembled

9.6a Spread the ends of the stop-ring apart and slide it towards the center of the shaft . . .

9.6b . . . then slide the tri-pod assembly back and remove the retainer clip

9.7 Drive the tri-pod joint from the axleshaft with a brass punch and hammer - make sure you don't damage the bearing surfaces or the splines on the shaft

4   Pull the boot back from the inner CV joint and slide the joint housing off. Mark the relationship of the tri-pod to the outer race (see illustration).

5   Mark the tri-pod and axleshaft to ensure that they are reassembled properly (see illustration).

6   Spread the ends of the stop-ring apart, slide it towards the center of the shaft, then remove the retainer clip from the end of the axleshaft (see illustrations).

7   Use a hammer and a brass punch to drive the tri-pod joint from the driveaxle (see illustration).

8   Remove the stop-ring from the axleshaft and discard it.

Inspection

9   Clean the old grease from the outer race and the tri-pod bearing assembly. Carefully disassemble each section of the tri-pod assembly, one at a time so as not to mix up the parts. Clean the needle bearings with solvent.

10 Inspect the rollers, tri-pod, bearings and outer race for scoring, pitting or other signs of abnormal wear, which will warrant the replacement of the inner CV joint.

Reassembly

▶ **Refer to illustrations 9.11, 9.14, 9.16, 9.17a, 9.17b, 9.17c, 9.17d and 9.17e**

11 Slide the clamps and boot onto the axleshaft. It's a good idea to

9.11 Wrap the splined area of the axleshaft with tape to prevent damage to the boot(s) when installing it

9.14 Pack the outer race with CV joint grease and slide it over the tri-pod assembly - make sure the match marks on the CV joint housing and tri-pod line up

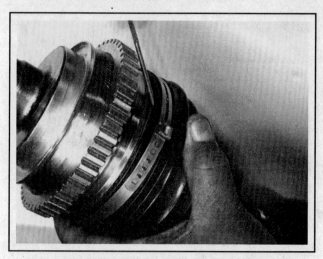

9.16 Equalize the pressure inside the boot by inserting a small, dull screwdriver between the boot and the outer race

9.17a To install new fold-over type clamps, bend the tang down . . .

9.17b . . . and flatten the tabs to hold it in place

wrap the axleshaft splines with tape to prevent damaging the boot (see illustration).

12 Install a new stop-ring on the axleshaft, but don't seat it in its groove; position it on the shaft past the groove.

13 Place the tri-pod on the shaft (making sure the marks are aligned) and install a new bearing retainer clip. Slide the tri-pod up against the retainer clip and seat the stop-ring in its groove.

14 Apply CV joint grease to the tri-pod assembly, the inside of the joint housing and the inside of the boot (see illustration).

15 Slide the boot into place.

16 Position the CV joint mid-way through its travel, then equalize the pressure in the boot (see illustration).

17 Tighten the boot clamps (see illustrations).

18 Install the driveaxle assembly (see Section 8).

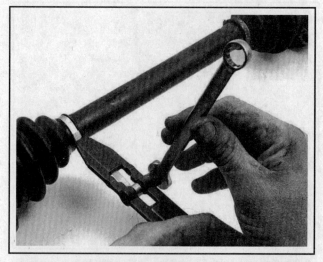

9.17c To install band-type clamps you'll need a special tool; install the band with its end pointing in the direction of axle rotation and tighten it securely. Pivot the tool up 90-degrees and tap the center of the clip with a center punch . . .

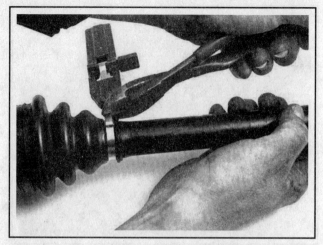

9.17d . . . then bend the end of the clamp back over the clip and cut off the excess

9.17e If you're installing crimp-type boot clamps, you'll need a pair of special crimping pliers (available at most auto parts stores)

OUTER CV JOINT AND BOOT

Removal

▶ **Refer to illustration 9.20**

19 Remove the boot clamps (see illustration 9.3).

20 Strike the edge of the CV joint housing sharply with a soft-face hammer to dislodge the outer CV joint from the axleshaft (see illustration). Remove and discard the bearing retainer clip from the axleshaft.

21 Slide the outer CV joint boot off the axleshaft.

Inspection

22 Thoroughly clean all components with solvent until the old CV grease is completely removed. Inspect the bearing surfaces of the inner tri-pods and housings for cracks, pitting, scoring, and other signs of wear. If any part of the outer CV joint is worn, you must replace the entire driveaxle assembly (inner CV joint, axleshaft and outer CV joint).

9.20 Strike the edge of the CV joint housing sharply with a soft-faced hammer to dislodge the CV joint from the shaft

9.25a Pack the outer CV joint assembly with CV joint grease . . .

9.25b . . . then apply grease to the inside of the boot . . .

Reassembly

▶ **Refer to illustrations 9.25a, 9.25b and 9.25c**

23 Slide a new sealing boot clamp and sealing boot onto the axle-shaft. It's a good idea to wrap the axleshaft splines with tape to prevent damaging the boot (see illustration 9.11).

24 Place a new bearing retainer clip onto the axleshaft.

25 Place half the grease provided in the sealing boot kit into the outer CV joint assembly housing (see illustration). Put the remaining grease into the sealing boot (see illustrations).

26 Align the splines on the axleshaft with the splines on the outer CV joint assembly and, using a soft-faced hammer, gently drive the CV joint onto the axleshaft until the CV joint is seated to the axleshaft.

27 Position the CV joint boot over the joint housing, then equalize the pressure in the boot (see illustration 9.16).

28 Tighten the boot clamps (see illustrations 9.17a through 9.17e).

29 Install the driveaxle (see Section 8)

9.25c . . . until the level is up to the end of the axle

Specifications

| Clutch fluid type | See Chapter 1 | |

Torque specifications	Ft-lbs	Nm
Clutch		
Clutch master cylinder mounting nuts	16	22
Clutch pressure plate-to-flywheel bolts	21	28
Clutch release cylinder mounting bolts	16	22
Driveaxles		
Brake hose-to-knuckle bolt	17	23
Driveaxle/hub nut	185	251

Section

Reference to other Chapters

9

BRAKES

GENERAL

The vehicles covered by this manual are equipped with hydraulically operated front and rear brake systems. Both front and rear brakes are disc-type and are self-adjusting.

HYDRAULIC SYSTEM

The hydraulic system consists of two separate circuits. The master cylinder has separate reservoirs for the two circuits, and, in the event of a leak or failure in one hydraulic circuit, the other circuit will remain operative and a warning indicator will light up on the instrument panel when a substantial amount of brake fluid is lost, showing that a failure has occurred.

POWER BRAKE BOOSTER

The power brake booster uses engine manifold vacuum to provide assistance to the brakes. It is mounted on the firewall in the engine compartment, directly behind the master cylinder.

PARKING BRAKE

Control cables are routed to the rear brakes, where they operate actuators in the brake calipers.

SERVICE

After completing any operation involving disassembly of any part of the brake system, always test drive the vehicle to check for proper braking performance before resuming normal driving. When testing the brakes, perform the tests on a clean, dry, flat surface. Conditions other than these can lead to inaccurate test results.

Test the brakes at various speeds with both light and heavy pedal pressure. The vehicle should stop evenly without pulling to one side or the other. Under hard braking, the ABS system may engage, resulting in brake pedal pulsation. This is considered normal operation.

Tires, vehicle load and wheel alignment are factors which also affect braking performance.

PRECAUTIONS

There are some general cautions and warnings involving the brake system on this vehicle:

a) *Use only brake fluid conforming to DOT 3 specifications.*

b) *The brake pads and linings contain fibers which are hazardous to your health if inhaled. Whenever you work on brake system components, clean all parts with brake system cleaner. Do not allow the fine dust to become airborne. Also, wear an approved filtering mask.*

c) *Safety should be paramount whenever any servicing of the brake components is performed. Do not use parts or fasteners which are not in perfect condition, and be sure that all clearances and torque specifications are adhered to. If you are at all unsure about a certain procedure, seek professional advice. Upon completion of any brake system work, test the brakes carefully in a controlled area before putting the vehicle into normal service. If a problem is suspected in the brake system, don't drive the vehicle until it's fixed.*

d) *Used brake fluid is considered a hazardous waste and it must be disposed of in accordance with federal, state and local laws.* **DO NOT pour it down the sink, into septic tanks or storm drains, or on the ground.**

e) *Clean up any spilled brake fluid immediately and then wash the area with large amounts of water. This is especially true for any finished or painted surfaces.*

2 Troubleshooting

PROBABLE CAUSE	CORRECTIVE ACTION

No brakes - pedal travels to floor

1 Low fluid level 2 Air in system	1 and 2 Low fluid level and air in the system are symptoms of another problem a leak somewhere in the hydraulic system. Locate and repair the leak
3 Defective seals in master cylinder	3 Replace master cylinder
4 Fluid overheated and vaporized due to heavy braking	4 Bleed hydraulic system (temporary fix). Replace brake fluid (proper fix)

Brake pedal slowly travels to floor under braking or at a stop

1 Defective seals in master cylinder	1 Replace master cylinder
2 Leak in a hose, line, caliper or wheel cylinder	2 Locate and repair leak
3 Air in hydraulic system	3 Bleed the system, inspect system for a leak

Brake pedal feels spongy when depressed

1 Air in hydraulic system	1 Bleed the system, inspect system for a leak
2 Master cylinder or power booster loose	2 Tighten fasteners
3 Brake fluid overheated (beginning to boil)	3 Bleed the system (temporary fix). Replace the brake fluid (proper fix)
4 Deteriorated brake hoses (ballooning under pressure)	4 Inspect hoses, replace as necessary (it's a good idea to replace all of them if one hose shows signs of deterioration)

Brake pedal feels hard when depressed and/or excessive effort required to stop vehicle

1 Power booster faulty	1 Replace booster
2 Engine not producing sufficient vacuum, or hose to booster clogged, collapsed or cracked	2 Check vacuum to booster with a vacuum gauge. Replace hose if cracked or clogged, repair engine if vacuum is extremely low
3 Brake linings contaminated by grease or brake fluid	3 Locate and repair source of contamination, replace brake pads or shoes
4 Brake linings glazed	4 Replace brake pads or shoes, check discs and drums for glazing, service as necessary
5 Caliper piston(s) or wheel cylinder(s) binding or frozen	5 Replace calipers or wheel cylinders
6 Brakes wet	6 Apply pedal to boil-off water (this should only be a momentary problem)
7 Kinked, clogged or internally split brake hose or line	7 Inspect lines and hoses, replace as necessary

Excessive brake pedal travel (but will pump up)

1 Drum brakes out of adjustment	1 Adjust brakes
2 Air in hydraulic system	2 Bleed system, inspect system for a leak

Excessive brake pedal travel (but will not pump up)

1 Master cylinder pushrod misadjusted	1 Adjust pushrod
2 Master cylinder seals defective	2 Replace master cylinder
3 Brake linings worn out	3 Inspect brakes, replace pads and/or shoes
4 Hydraulic system leak	4 Locate and repair leak

Troubleshooting (continued)

PROBABLE CAUSE	CORRECTIVE ACTION

Brake pedal doesn't return

1 Brake pedal binding	1 Inspect pivot bushing and pushrod, repair or lubricate
2 Defective master cylinder	2 Replace master cylinder

Brake pedal pulsates during brake application

1 Brake drums out-of-round	1 Have drums machined by an automotive machine shop
2 Excessive brake disc runout or disc surfaces out-of-parallel	2 Have discs machined by an automotive machine shop
3 Loose or worn wheel bearings	3 Adjust or replace wheel bearings
4 Loose lug nuts	4 Tighten lug nuts

Brakes slow to release

1 Malfunctioning power booster	1 Replace booster
2 Pedal linkage binding	2 Inspect pedal pivot bushing and pushrod, repair/lubricate
3 Malfunctioning proportioning valve	3 Replace proportioning valve
4 Sticking caliper or wheel cylinder	4 Repair or replace calipers or wheel cylinders
5 Kinked or internally split brake hose	5 Locate and replace faulty brake hose

Brakes grab (one or more wheels)

1 Grease or brake fluid on brake lining	1 Locate and repair cause of contamination, replace lining
2 Brake lining glazed	2 Replace lining, deglaze disc or drum

Vehicle pulls to one side during braking

1 Grease or brake fluid on brake lining	1 Locate and repair cause of contamination, replace lining
2 Brake lining glazed	2 Deglaze or replace lining, deglaze disc or drum
3 Restricted brake line or hose	3 Repair line or replace hose
4 Tire pressures incorrect	4 Adjust tire pressures
5 Caliper or wheel cylinder sticking	5 Repair or replace calipers or wheel cylinders
6 Wheels out of alignment	6 Have wheels aligned
7 Weak suspension spring	7 Replace springs
8 Weak or broken shock absorber	8 Replace shock absorbers

PROBABLE CAUSE	CORRECTIVE ACTION

Brakes drag (indicated by sluggish engine performance or wheels being very hot after driving)

1 Brake pedal pushrod incorrectly adjusted	1 Adjust pushrod
2 Master cylinder pushrod (between booster and master cylinder) incorrectly adjusted	2 Adjust pushrod
3 Obstructed compensating port in master cylinder	3 Replace master cylinder
4 Master cylinder piston seized in bore	4 Replace master cylinder
5 Contaminated fluid causing swollen seals throughout system	5 Flush system, replace all hydraulic components
6 Clogged brake lines or internally split brake hose(s)	6 Flush hydraulic system, replace defective hose(s)
7 Sticking caliper(s) or wheel cylinder(s)	7 Replace calipers or wheel cylinders
8 Parking brake not releasing	8 Inspect parking brake linkage and parking brake mechanism, repair as required
9 Improper shoe-to-drum clearance	9 Adjust brake shoes
10 Faulty proportioning valve	10 Replace proportioning valve

Brakes fade (due to excessive heat)

1 Brake linings excessively worn or glazed	1 Deglaze or replace brake pads and/or shoes
2 Excessive use of brakes	2 Downshift into a lower gear, maintain a constant slower speed (going down hills)
3 Vehicle overloaded	3 Reduce load
4 Brake drums or discs worn too thin	4 Measure drum diameter and disc thickness, replace drums or discs as required
5 Contaminated brake fluid	5 Flush system, replace fluid
6 Brakes drag	6 Repair cause of dragging brakes
7 Driver resting left foot on brake pedal	7 Don't ride the brakes

Brakes noisy (high-pitched squeal)

1 Glazed lining	1 Deglaze or replace lining
2 Contaminated lining (brake fluid, grease, etc.)	2 Repair source of contamination, replace linings
3 Weak or broken brake shoe hold-down or return spring	3 Replace springs
4 Rivets securing lining to shoe or backing plate loose	4 Replace shoes or pads
5 Excessive dust buildup on brake linings	5 Wash brakes off with brake system cleaner
6 Brake drums worn too thin	6 Measure diameter of drums, replace if necessary
7 Wear indicator on disc brake pads contacting disc	7 Replace brake pads
8 Anti-squeal shims missing or installed improperly	8 Install shims correctly

➡ **Note: Other remedies for quieting squealing brakes include the application of an anti-squeal compound to the backing plates of the brake pads, and lightly chamfering the edges of the brake pads with a file. The latter method should only be performed with the brake pads thoroughly wetted with brake system cleaner, so as not to allow any brake dust to become airborne.**

Brakes noisy (scraping sound)

1 Brake pads or shoes worn out; rivets, backing plate or brake shoe metal contacting disc or drum	1 Replace linings, have discs and/or drums machined (or replace)

PROBABLE CAUSE	CORRECTIVE ACTION

Brakes chatter

1 Worn brake lining	1 Inspect brakes, replace shoes or pads as necessary
2 Glazed or scored discs or drums	2 Deglaze discs or drums with sandpaper (if glazing is severe, machining will be required)
3 Drums or discs heat checked	3 Check discs and/or drums for hard spots, heat checking, etc. Have discs/drums machined or replace them
4 Disc runout or drum out-of-round excessive	4 Measure disc runout and/or drum out-of-round, have discs or drums machined or replace them
5 Loose or worn wheel bearings	5 Adjust or replace wheel bearings
6 Loose or bent brake backing plate (drum brakes)	6 Tighten or replace backing plate
7 Grooves worn in discs or drums	7 Have discs or drums machined, if within limits (if not, replace them)
8 Brake linings contaminated (brake fluid, grease, etc.)	8 Locate and repair source of contamination, replace pads or shoes
9 Excessive dust buildup on linings	9 Wash brakes with brake system cleaner
10 Surface finish on discs or drums too rough after machining (especially on vehicles with sliding calipers)	10 Have discs or drums properly machined
11 Brake pads or shoes glazed	11 Deglaze or replace brake pads or shoes

Brake pads or shoes click

1 Shoe support pads on brake backing plate grooved or excessively worn	1 Replace brake backing plate
2 Brake pads loose in caliper	2 Loose pad retainers or anti-rattle clips
3 Also see items listed under Brakes chatter	

Brakes make groaning noise at end of stop

1 Brake pads and/or shoes worn out	1 Replace pads and/or shoes
2 Brake linings contaminated (brake fluid, grease, etc.)	2 Locate and repair cause of contamination, replace brake pads or shoes
3 Brake linings glazed	3 Deglaze or replace brake pads or shoes
4 Excessive dust buildup on linings	4 Wash brakes with brake system cleaner
5 Scored or heat-checked discs or drums	5 Inspect discs/drums, have machined if within limits (if not, replace discs or drums)
6 Broken or missing brake shoe attaching hardware	6 Inspect drum brakes, replace missing hardware

Rear brakes lock up under light brake application

1 Tire pressures too high	1 Adjust tire pressures
2 Tires excessively worn	2 Replace tires
3 Defective proportioning valve	3 Replace proportioning valve

PROBABLE CAUSE	CORRECTIVE ACTION

Brake warning light on instrument panel comes on (or stays on)

1 Low fluid level in master cylinder reservoir (reservoirs with fluid level sensor)	1 Add fluid, inspect system for leak, check the thickness of the brake pads and shoes
2 Failure in one half of the hydraulic system	2 Inspect hydraulic system for a leak
3 Piston in pressure differential warning valve not centered	3 Center piston by bleeding one circuit or the other (close bleeder valve as soon as the light goes out)
4 Defective pressure differential valve or warning switch	4 Replace valve or switch
5 Air in the hydraulic system	5 Bleed the system, check for leaks
6 Brake pads worn out (vehicles with electric wear sensors - small probes that fit into the brake pads and ground out on the disc when the pads get thin)	6 Replace brake pads (and sensors)

Brakes do not self adjust

Disc brakes

1 Defective caliper piston seals	1 Replace calipers. Also, possible contaminated fluid causing soft or swollen seals (flush system and fill with new fluid if in doubt)
2 Corroded caliper piston(s)	2 Same as above

Drum brakes

1 Adjuster screw frozen	1 Remove adjuster, disassemble, clean and lubricate with high-temperature grease
2 Adjuster lever does not contact star wheel or is binding	2 Inspect drum brakes, assemble correctly or clean or replace parts as required
3 Adjusters mixed up (installed on wrong wheels after brake job)	3 Reassemble correctly
4 Adjuster cable broken or installed incorrectly (cable-type adjusters)	4 Install new cable or assemble correctly

Rapid brake lining wear

1 Driver resting left foot on brake pedal	1 Don't ride the brakes
2 Surface finish on discs or drums too rough	2 Have discs or drums properly machined
3 Also see Brakes drag	

3 Anti-lock Brake System (ABS), Traction Control System (TCS) and Dynamic Stability Control (DSC) - general information

1   The Anti-lock Brake System (ABS), Traction Control System (TCS) and Dynamic Stability Control (DSC) are designed to help maintain vehicle steerability, directional stability and optimum deceleration under severe braking or maneuvering conditions and on most road surfaces. The ABS system is primarily designed to prevent wheel lockup during heavy or panic braking situations. It works by monitoring the rotational speed of each wheel and controlling the brake line pressure to each wheel when engaged. Data provided by the ABS wheel speed sensors is shared with the Traction Control and Dynamic Stability Control. This very sophisticated system helps with traction control, over/understeering and acceleration control under all driving conditions. Overall, these systems aid in vehicle control and handling.

COMPONENTS

Actuator assembly

2   The actuator assembly is mounted in the engine compartment and consists of an electric hydraulic pump and solenoid valves.

a) The electric pump provides hydraulic pressure to charge the reservoirs in the actuator, which supplies pressure to the braking system. The pump and reservoirs are housed in the actuator assembly.

b) The solenoid valves modulate brake line pressure during ABS and DSC operation.

Wheel speed sensors

3   There is a wheel speed sensor for each wheel. Each sensor generates a signal in the form of a low-voltage electrical current or a frequency when the wheel is turning. A variable signal is generated as a result of a square-toothed ring (tone-ring, exciter-ring, reluctor, etc.) that rotates very close to the sensor. The signal is directly proportional to the wheel speed and is interpreted by an electronic module (computer).

4   The front sensors are mounted to the top of the wheel bearing assemblies.

5   The rear sensors are mounted in the rear trailing link.

ABS/TCS/DSC computer

6   The ABS/TCS/DSC computer is mounted with the actuator and is the brain of these systems. The function of the computer is to accept and process information received from the wheel speed sensors to control the hydraulic line pressure, avoiding wheel lock up or wheel spin. The computer also constantly monitors the system, even under normal driving conditions, to find faults within the system.

DIAGNOSIS AND REPAIR

7   If a dashboard warning light comes on and stays on while the vehicle is in operation, the ABS, TCS or DSC system requires attention. Although special electronic diagnostic testing tools are necessary to properly diagnose the system, you can perform a few preliminary checks before taking the vehicle to a dealer service department.

  a) *Check the brake fluid level in the reservoir.*
  b) *Verify that the computer electrical connectors are securely connected.*
  c) *Check the electrical connectors at the hydraulic control unit.*
  d) *Check the fuses.*
  e) *Follow the wiring harness to each wheel and verify that all connections are secure and that the wiring is undamaged.*

8   If the above preliminary checks do not rectify the problem, the vehicle should be diagnosed by a dealer service department or other qualified repair shop. Due to the complexity of this system, all actual repair work must be done by a qualified automotive technician.

❋ WARNING:

Do NOT try to repair an ABS/TSC/DSC wiring harness. These systems are sensitive to even the smallest changes in resistance. Repairing the harness could alter resistance values and cause the system to malfunction. If the wiring harness is damaged in any way, it must be replaced.

❋ CAUTION:

Make sure the ignition is turned off before unplugging or reattaching any electrical connections.

WHEEL SPEED SENSOR - REMOVAL AND INSTALLATION

9   Loosen the wheel lug nuts, raise the vehicle and support it securely on jackstands. Remove the wheel.

10   Make sure the ignition key is turned to the Off position.

11   Trace the wiring back from the sensor, detaching all brackets and clips while noting its correct routing, then disconnect the electrical connector.

12   Remove the mounting bolt and carefully pull the sensor out from the knuckle.

13   Installation is the reverse of the removal procedure. Tighten the mounting bolt securely.

14   Install the wheel and lug nuts, tightening them securely. Lower the vehicle and tighten the lug nuts to the torque listed in the Chapter 1 Specifications.

4   Disc brake pads - replacement

▶ **Refer to illustrations 4.5, 4.6a through 4.6m and 4.7a through 4.7k**

❋ WARNING:

Disc brake pads must be replaced on both front or both rear wheels at the same time - never replace the pads on only one wheel. Also, the dust created by the brake system is harmful to your health. Never blow it out with compressed air and don't inhale any of it. An approved filtering mask should be worn when working on the brakes. Do not, under any circumstances, use petroleum-based solvents to clean brake parts. Use brake system cleaner only!

1   Remove the cap from the brake fluid reservoir.

2   Loosen the wheel lug nuts, raise the vehicle and support it securely on jackstands. Block the wheels at the opposite end.

3   Remove the wheels. Work on one brake assembly at a time, using the assembled brake for reference if necessary.

4   Inspect the brake disc carefully (see Section 6). If machining is necessary, remove the disc (see Section 6), at which time the pads can be removed as well.

4.5 Always wash the brakes with brake cleaner before disassembling anything

5   Before disassembling the brake, wash it thoroughly with brake system cleaner and allow it to dry (see illustration). Position a drain pan

4.6a Depress the piston into the bottom of its bore in the caliper with a large C-clamp to make room for the new pads - make sure the fluid in the master cylinder reservoir doesn't overflow

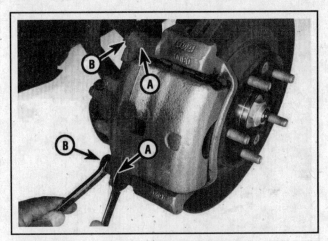

4.6b Using two wrenches, hold the guide pin (A) while loosening the caliper mounting bolt (B) - 2006 and later models shown (on 2005 and earlier models, remove the upper slide pin)

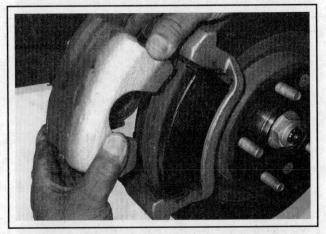

4.6c Pull the caliper from the caliper mounting bracket (on 2005 and earlier models, pivot the caliper down, then slide the caliper off the lower pin)

4.6d Secure the caliper to the suspension with a length of stiff wire

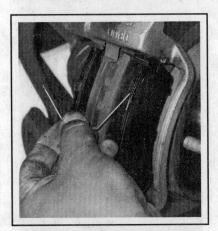

4.6e Remove the brake pad retraction springs from the pads

4.6f Remove the inner brake pad

4.6g Remove the outer brake pad

under the brake to catch the residue - DO NOT use compressed air to blow off the brake dust.

6   For the front brake pad replacement sequence, follow the accom-

panying photos (illustrations 4.6a through 4.6m) for the actual pad replacement procedure. Be sure to stay in order and read the caption under each illustration, then proceed to Step 8.

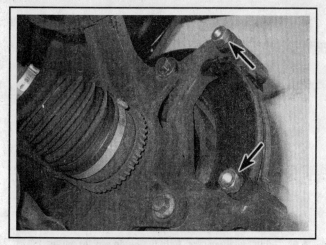

4.6h Remove the two caliper guide pins (2006 and later models) . . .

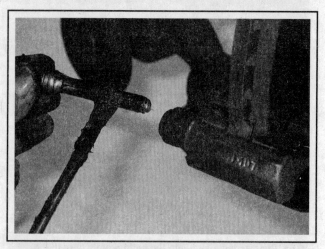

4.6i . . . and clean them, then apply a coat of high-temperature grease to the pins and reinstall them. On 2005 and earlier models, do the same with the lower mounting pin and the upper bolt

4.6j Remove the pad slide clips, clean them and lubricate the wear points with high-temp brake grease, then reinstall on the caliper mounting bracket

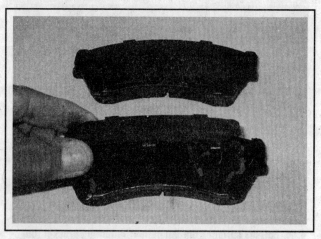

4.6k Snap the two stainless-steel shims to the back of each pad, then apply anti-squeal compound to the outboard side of the shims

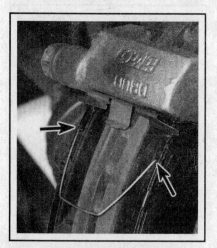

4.6l Place the pads in the caliper mounting bracket and install the upper and lower pad retraction springs

4.6m Install the caliper and tighten the caliper mounting bolt(s) to the torque listed in this Chapter's Specifications

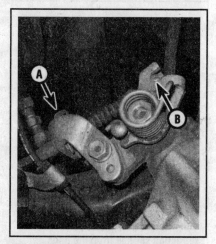

4.7a Pull the clip (A) on the parking brake cable, then detach the cable from the lever (B)

4.7b Hold the caliper guide pins with one wrench while loosening the caliper mounting bolts

4.7c Remove the caliper and use needle-nose pliers to rotate the piston clockwise while pushing it back in the caliper - make sure the fluid in the master cylinder reservoir doesn't overflow

4.7d One of the notches must be at the bottom position to align with the pin on the inner pad

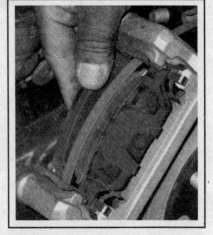

4.7e Remove the inner brake pad

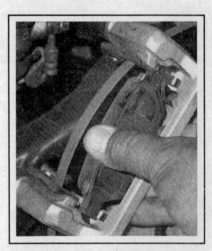

4.7f Remove the outer brake pad

4.7g Remove the slide clips, clean them and lubricate the pad contact areas with high-temp brake grease

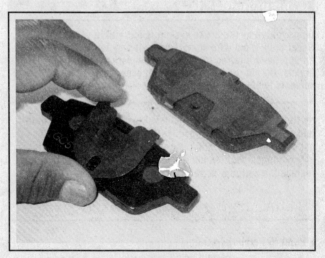

4.7h Attach the shims to the outside of each pad - the longer shim goes on the outer pad - then apply anti-squeal compound to the backs of the shims

4.7i Pull out the caliper guide pins and clean them, then apply a coat of high-temperature grease to the pins and reinstall the pins in the caliper bracket

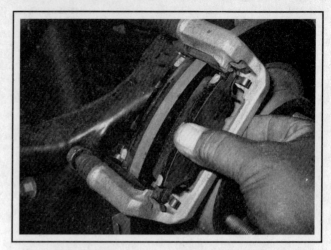

4.7j Install the pads

7   For the rear brake pad replacement sequence, follow Steps 1 through 5 and see illustrations 4.7a through 4.7k.

8   When reinstalling the caliper, be sure to tighten the mounting bolts to the torque listed in this Chapter's Specifications. After the job has been completed, firmly depress the brake pedal a few times to bring the pads into contact with the disc. Check the level of the brake fluid, adding some if necessary. Check the operation of the brakes carefully before placing the vehicle into normal service.

4.7k Install the caliper, tighten the caliper mounting bolts and reattach the parking brake cable. Check the operation of the parking brake, adjusting it if necessary (see Section 11)

5   Disc brake caliper - removal and installation

✳✳ WARNING:

Dust created by the brake system is harmful to your health. Never blow it out with compressed air and don't inhale any of it. An approved filtering mask should be worn when working on the brakes. Do not, under any circumstances, use petroleum-based solvents to clean brake parts. Use brake system cleaner only.

➡ **Note:** If replacement is indicated (usually because of fluid leakage), it is recommended that the calipers be replaced, not overhauled. New and factory rebuilt units are available on an exchange basis, which makes this job quite easy. Always replace the calipers in pairs - never replace just one of them.

REMOVAL

▸ **Refer to illustration 5.2**

1   Loosen the wheel lug nuts, raise the vehicle (front or rear) and place it securely on jackstands. Remove the wheels.
2   Remove the banjo fitting bolt and disconnect the brake hose from

the caliper (see illustration). Discard the sealing washers from each side of the hose fitting. Plug the brake hose to keep contaminants out of the

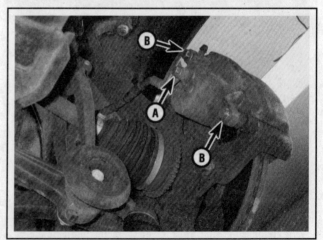

5.2 Remove the brake line banjo bolt (A), then remove the caliper mounting bolts (B)

brake system and to prevent losing any more brake fluid than is necessary.

➡ **Note: If the caliper is being removed for access to another component, don't disconnect the hose.**

3   Refer to illustration 4.6b (front) or 4.7b (rear) for the caliper removal procedure. If the caliper is being removed just to access another component, use a piece of wire to securely hang it out of the way (see illustration 4.6d).

❋❋ **CAUTION:**

Do not let the caliper hang by the brake hose.

---

4   If you are replacing a rear caliper, disconnect the parking brake

cable from the caliper by removing the retaining clip (see illustration 4.7a).

INSTALLATION

5   Install the caliper by reversing the removal procedure, tightening the mounting bolts to the torque listed in this Chapter's Specifications. Be sure to use new sealing washers and tighten the banjo fitting bolt to the torque listed in this Chapter's Specifications.

6   Bleed the brake system (see Section 9). Make sure there are no leaks from the hose connections. Test the brakes carefully before returning the vehicle to normal service.

7   If you removed or replaced a rear caliper, check and, if necessary, adjust the parking brake (see Section 11).

---

6   Brake disc - inspection, removal and installation

INSPECTION

▶ **Refer to illustrations 6.3, 6.4a, 6.4b, 6.5a and 6.5b**

1   Loosen the wheel lug nuts, raise the vehicle and support it securely on jackstands.

2   Remove the brake caliper (see Section 5). It isn't necessary to disconnect the brake hose. After removing the caliper bolts, suspend the caliper out of the way with a piece of wire (see illustration 4.6d).

3   Visually inspect the disc surface for score marks and other damage. Light scratches and shallow grooves are normal after use and may not always be detrimental to brake operation, but deep scoring requires disc removal and refinishing by an automotive machine shop. Be sure to check both sides of the disc (see illustration). If pulsating has been noticed during application of the brakes, suspect disc runout.

4   To check disc runout, reinstall the lug nuts (inverted) and place a dial indicator at a point about 1/2-inch from the outer edge of the disc (see illustration). Set the indicator to zero and turn the disc. The indicator reading should not exceed the specified allowable runout limit. If it does, the disc should be refinished by an automotive machine shop.

6.3   The brake pads on this vehicle were obviously neglected, as they wore down completely and cut deep grooves into the disc - wear this severe means the disc must be replaced

6.4a   To check disc runout, mount a dial indicator as shown and rotate the disc

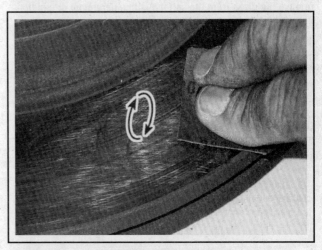

6.4b   Using a swirling motion, remove the glaze from the disc surface with sandpaper or emery cloth

6.5a The minimum thickness dimension is cast into the front or back side of the disc

6.5b Use a micrometer to measure disc thickness

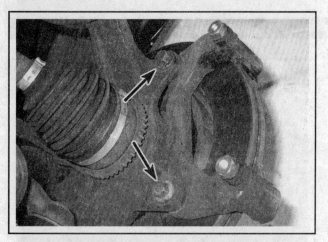

6.6a Caliper mounting bracket-to-knuckle bolts

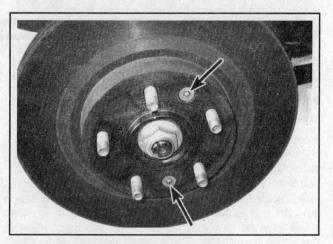

6.6b Two screws secure the disc to the hub

➡ Note: The discs should be resurfaced regardless of the dial indicator reading, as this will impart a smooth finish and ensure a perfectly flat surface, eliminating any brake pedal pulsation or other undesirable symptoms related to questionable discs. At the very least, if you elect not to have the discs resurfaced, remove the glaze from the surface with emery cloth or sandpaper, using a swirling motion (see illustration).

5   It's absolutely critical that the disc not be machined to a thickness under the specified minimum thickness. The minimum (or discard) thickness is cast or stamped into the inside of the disc (see illustration). The disc thickness can be checked with a micrometer (see illustration).

REMOVAL

▶ **Refer to illustrations 6.6a and 6.6b**

6   Remove the caliper mounting bracket (see illustration). Also remove the lug nuts, if they were reinstalled for the runout check. Remove the two screws that secure the disc to the hub, then remove the disc (see illustration).

INSTALLATION

7   While the disc is off, wire-brush the backside of the center portion that contacts the wheel hub. Also clean off any rust or dirt on the hub face.

8   Apply small dots of high-temperature anti-seize around the circumference of the hub, and around the raised center portion.

9   Place the disc in position over the threaded studs. Install the disc retaining screws, tightening them securely.

10   Install the caliper mounting bracket and caliper, tightening the bolts to the torque values listed in this Chapter's Specifications.

11   Install the wheel, then lower the vehicle to the ground. Tighten the lug nuts to the torque listed in the Chapter 1 Specifications. Depress the brake pedal a few times to bring the brake pads into contact with the disc. Bleeding won't be necessary unless the brake hose was disconnected from the caliper. Check the operation of the brakes carefully before driving the vehicle.

12   If new or resurfaced rear discs are being installed, check the operation of the parking brake and adjust it if necessary (see Section 11).

13   Check the operation of the brakes carefully before driving the vehicle.

7 Master cylinder - removal and installation

REMOVAL

▶ **Refer to illustrations 7.5 and 7.7**

➡ **Note: The master cylinder is located in the engine compartment, mounted to the power brake booster.**

1   Remove the battery and battery tray (see Chapter 5).
2   Remove as much fluid as you can from the reservoir with a syringe, such as an old turkey baster.

✴✴ WARNING:

If a baster is used, never again use it for the preparation of food.

3   Place rags under the fluid fittings and prepare caps or plastic bags to cover the ends of the lines once they are disconnected.

✴✴ CAUTION:

Brake fluid will damage paint. Cover all body parts and be careful not to spill fluid during this procedure.

4   On manual transaxle models, disconnect the clutch master cylinder supply hose from the brake fluid reservoir and pinch it shut with a clamp.
5   Loosen the fittings at the ends of the brake lines where they enter the master cylinder (see illustration). To prevent rounding off the corners on these nuts, the use of a flare-nut wrench, which wraps around the nut, is preferred. Pull the brake lines slightly away from the master cylinder and plug the ends to prevent contamination.
6   Disconnect the electrical connector at the brake fluid level switch on the master cylinder reservoir, then remove the nuts attaching the master cylinder to the power booster. Pull the master cylinder off the studs and out of the engine compartment. Again, be careful not to spill the fluid as this is done.
7   If a new master cylinder is being installed, remove the reservoir

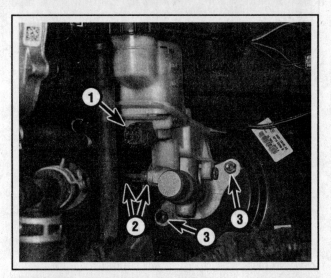

7.5 Master cylinder mounting details

1	Fluid level warning switch connector	2	Brake line fittings
		3	Mounting nuts

from the old master cylinder and transfer it to the new master cylinder.

➡ **Note: Be sure to install new seals when transferring the reservoir (see illustration).**

INSTALLATION

▶ **Refer to illustrations 7.9 and 7.14**

8   Bench bleed the new master cylinder before installing it. Mount the master cylinder in a vise, with the jaws of the vise clamping on the mounting flange.
9   Attach a pair of master cylinder bleeder tubes to the outlet ports of the master cylinder (see illustration).
10 Fill the reservoir with brake fluid of the recommended type (see Chapter 1).

7.7 After the reservoir has been removed, replace the O-rings with new ones

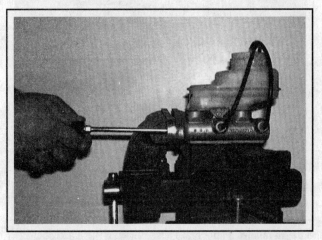

7.9 The best way to bleed air from the master cylinder before installing it on the vehicle is with a pair of bleeder tubes that direct brake fluid into the reservoir during bleeding

7.14 Install a new O-ring onto the master cylinder sleeve

11 Slowly push the pistons into the master cylinder (a large Phillips screwdriver can be used for this) - air will be expelled from the pressure chambers and into the reservoir. Because the tubes are submerged in fluid, air can't be drawn back into the master cylinder when you release the pistons.

12 Repeat the procedure until no more air bubbles are present.

13 Remove the bleed tubes, one at a time, and install plugs in the open ports to prevent fluid leakage and air from entering. Install the reservoir cap.

14 Install the master cylinder over the studs on the power brake booster and tighten the attaching nuts only finger tight at this time.

➡ Note: Be sure to install a new O-ring into the sleeve of the master cylinder (see illustration).

15 Thread the brake line fittings into the master cylinder. Since the master cylinder is still a bit loose, it can be moved slightly in order for the fittings to thread in easily. Do not strip the threads as the fittings are tightened.

16 Tighten the mounting nuts to the torque listed in this Chapter's Specifications, then tighten the brake line fittings securely.

17 Fill the master cylinder reservoir with fluid, then bleed the master cylinder and the brake system (see Section 9). To bleed the cylinder on the vehicle, have an assistant depress the brake pedal and hold the pedal to the floor. Loosen the fitting to allow air and fluid to escape. Repeat this procedure on both fittings until the fluid is clear of air bubbles.

✳ CAUTION:

Have plenty of rags on hand to catch the fluid - brake fluid will ruin painted surfaces. After the bleeding procedure is completed, rinse the area under the master cylinder with clean water.

---

18 Test the operation of the brake system carefully before placing the vehicle into normal service.

✳ WARNING

Do not operate the vehicle if you are in doubt about the effectiveness of the brake system. It is possible for air to become trapped in the anti-lock brake system hydraulic control unit, so, if the pedal continues to feel spongy after repeated bleedings or the BRAKE or ANTI-LOCK light stays on, have the vehicle towed to a dealer service department or other qualified shop to be bled with the aid of a scan tool.

---

8   Brake hoses and lines - inspection and replacement

1   About every six months, with the vehicle raised and placed securely on jackstands, the flexible hoses which connect the steel brake lines with the front and rear brake assemblies should be inspected for cracks, chafing of the outer cover, leaks, blisters and other damage. These are important and vulnerable parts of the brake system and inspection should be complete. A light and mirror will be needed for a thorough check. If a hose exhibits any of the above defects, replace it with a new one.

FLEXIBLE HOSES

▶ Refer to illustrations 8.3a and 8.3b

2   Clean all dirt away from the ends of the hose.

3   To remove a brake hose, unscrew the tube nut with a flare-nut wrench, if available, to prevent rounding-off the corners of the nut, then remove the bolt(s) or clip(s) securing the hose to the body (and any suspension components) (see illustrations).

4   Disconnect the hose from the caliper, discarding the sealing washers on either side of the fitting.

5   Using new sealing washers, attach the new brake hose to the caliper. Tighten the banjo fitting bolt to the torque listed in this Chapter's Specifications.

6   Reverse the removal procedure to install the hose, making sure it isn't twisted.

7   Carefully check to make sure the suspension or steering components don't make contact with the hose. Have an assistant push down

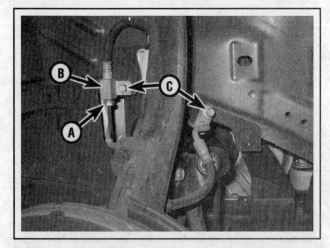

8.3a To remove a front brake hose, unscrew the brake line fitting (A) while holding the fitting block (B) with another wrench, remove the mounting bolts (C), then unscrew the banjo bolt (see illustration 5.2) and detach the hose from the caliper

on the vehicle and also turn the steering wheel lock-to-lock during inspection.

8   Bleed the brake system (see Section 9).

METAL BRAKE LINES

9   When replacing brake lines, be sure to use the correct parts. Don't use copper tubing for any brake system components. Purchase steel brake lines from a dealer parts department or auto parts store.

10 Prefabricated brake line, with the tube ends already flared and fittings installed, is available at auto parts stores and dealer parts departments. These lines can be bent to the proper shapes using a tubing bender.

11 When installing the new line make sure it's well supported in the brackets and has plenty of clearance between moving or hot components.

12 After installation, check the master cylinder fluid level and add fluid as necessary. Bleed the brake system (see Section 9) and test the brakes carefully before placing the vehicle into normal operation.

8.3b To remove a rear brake hose, unscrew the brake line fitting (A) while holding the bracket with a pair of pliers, remove the clip (B), then unscrew the banjo bolt and detach the hose from the caliper

9   Brake hydraulic system - bleeding

▶ **Refer to illustration 9.8**

✳✳ WARNING:

If air has found its way into the hydraulic control unit, the system must be bled with the use of a scan tool. If the brake pedal feels spongy even after bleeding the brakes, or the ABS light on the instrument panel does not go off, or if you have any doubts whatsoever about the effectiveness of the brake system, have the vehicle towed to a dealer service department or other repair shop equipped with the necessary tools for bleeding the system.

✳✳ WARNING:

Wear eye protection when bleeding the brake system. If the fluid comes in contact with your eyes, immediately rinse them with water and seek medical attention.

➡ **Note: Bleeding the brake system is necessary to remove any air that's trapped in the system when it's opened during removal and installation of a hose, line, caliper, wheel cylinder or master cylinder.**

1   It will probably be necessary to bleed the system at all four brakes if air has entered the system due to low fluid-level, or if the brake lines have been disconnected at the master cylinder.

2   If a brake line was disconnected only at a wheel, then only that caliper or wheel cylinder must be bled.

3   If a brake line is disconnected at a fitting located between the master cylinder and any of the brakes, that part of the system served by the disconnected line must be bled.

4   Remove any residual vacuum (or hydraulic pressure) from the brake power booster by applying the brake several times with the engine off.

5   Remove the master cylinder reservoir cap and fill the reservoir with brake fluid. Reinstall the cap.

➡ **Note: Check the fluid level often during the bleeding operation and add fluid as necessary to prevent the fluid level from falling low enough to allow air bubbles into the master cylinder.**

6   Have an assistant on hand, as well as a supply of new brake fluid, an empty clear plastic container, a length of plastic, rubber or vinyl tubing to fit over the bleeder valve and a wrench to open and close the bleeder valve.

7   Beginning at the right rear wheel, loosen the bleeder screw slightly, then tighten it to a point where it's snug but can still be loosened quickly and easily.

8   Place one end of the tubing over the bleeder screw fitting and submerge the other end in brake fluid in the container (see illustration).

9   Have the assistant slowly depress the brake pedal and hold it in the depressed position.

10 While the pedal is held depressed, open the bleeder screw just enough to allow a flow of fluid to leave the valve. Watch for air bubbles to exit the submerged end of the tube. When the fluid flow slows after a couple of seconds, tighten the screw and have your assistant release the pedal.

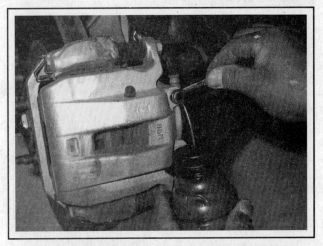

9.8 When bleeding the brakes, a hose is connected to the bleed screw at the caliper and submerged in brake fluid - air will be seen as bubbles in the tube and container (all air must be expelled before moving to the next wheel)

11 Repeat Steps 9 and 10 until no more air is seen leaving the tube, then tighten the bleeder screw and proceed to the left rear wheel, the right front wheel and the left front wheel, in that order, and perform the same procedure. Be sure to check the fluid in the master cylinder reservoir frequently.

12 Never use old brake fluid. It contains moisture which can boil, rendering the brake system inoperative.

13 Refill the master cylinder with fluid at the end of the operation.

14 Check the operation of the brakes. The pedal should feel solid when depressed, with no sponginess. If necessary, repeat the entire process.

❈❈ WARNING:

Do not operate the vehicle if you are in doubt about the effectiveness of the brake system. It is possible for air to become trapped in the anti-lock brake system hydraulic control unit, so, if the pedal continues to feel spongy after repeated bleedings or the BRAKE or ANTI-LOCK light stays on, have the vehicle towed to a dealer service department or other qualified shop to be bled with the aid of a scan tool.

10 Power brake booster - check, removal and installation

OPERATING CHECK

1 Depress the brake pedal several times with the engine off and make sure that there is no change in the pedal reserve distance.

2 Depress the pedal and start the engine. If the pedal goes down slightly, operation is normal.

AIRTIGHTNESS CHECK

3 Start the engine and turn it off after one or two minutes. Depress the brake pedal several times slowly. If the pedal goes down farther the first time but gradually rises after the second or third depression, the booster is airtight.

4 Depress the brake pedal while the engine is running, then stop the engine with the pedal depressed. If there is no change in the pedal reserve travel after holding the pedal for 30 seconds, the booster is airtight.

REMOVAL AND INSTALLATION

▶ **Refer to illustration 10.13**

5 Disassembly of the power unit requires special tools and is not ordinarily performed by the home mechanic. If a problem develops, it's recommended that a new or factory rebuilt unit be installed.

6 Remove the air filter housing (see Chapter 4), the battery and the battery tray (see Chapter 5).

7 Remove the windshield wiper motor (see Chapter 12) and the lower cowl panel (see Chapter 1).

8 Remove the master cylinder (see Section 7).

9 Remove the Powertrain Contol Module (PCM) and its bracket (see Chapter 6).

10 On 3.7L V6 models, remove the EVAP purge solenoid (see Chapter 6).

11 Disconnect the vacuum hose where it attaches to the power brake booster.

12 Under the instrument panel, remove the retaining pin and washer, then disconnect the pushrod from the brake pedal arm.

13 Remove the nuts attaching the booster to the firewall (see illustration).

14 Carefully lift the booster unit away from the firewall and out of the engine compartment.

15 To install the booster, place it into position and tighten the retaining nuts to the torque listed in this Chapter's Specifications. Connect the pushrod to the brake pedal.

➡ **Note: If the booster-to-firewall gasket has been damaged, replace it with a new gasket.**

16 Install the master cylinder. Reconnect the vacuum hose.

17 Carefully test the operation of the brakes before placing the vehicle in normal service.

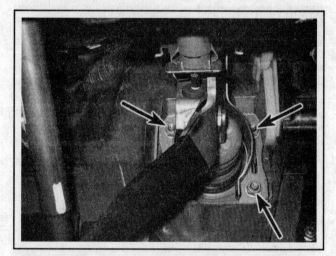

10.13 To detach the power brake booster from the firewall, remove the four nuts (one nut not visible here)

11 Parking brake - adjustment

♦ **Refer to illustrations 11.2 and 11.3**

1   Release the parking brake lever.

2   On 2008 and earlier models, use a plastic trim tool to remove the rear access panel of the floor console, taking care not to damage the panel (see illustration). On 2009 and later models, pry up the center console center section and lift it up and around the parking brake lever (see Chapter 11).

3   Adjust the nut so that the exposed threads equal 0.59 inch/15 mm (see illustration). When the parking brake cables are old, they may have stretched and require more threads showing on the adjuster.

4   Verify the parking brake is actually holding the vehicle when applied. Raise and support the rear of the vehicle and block the front wheels. You can rotate the rear tires by hand to check for proper cable adjustment.

5   Pull the handle up two clicks. This should apply noticeable drag on the rear brakes. At four clicks, the rear brakes should be locked.

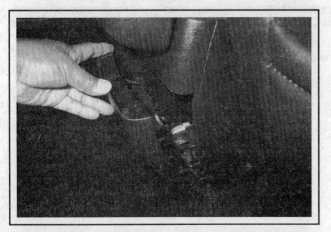

11.2 Pry the rear console cover off to access the parking brake adjuster

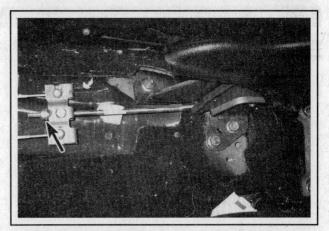

11.3 Turn the adjusting nut until the exposed threads measure 0.59 inch (15 mm)

12 Brake light switch - replacement

♦ **Refer to illustration 12.1**

1   Disconnect the electrical connector at the switch, then rotate the switch 45-degrees clockwise and remove it (see illustration).

2   The brake light switch is self-adjusting.

➡ **Note: Do not press on the brake pedal during installation of the switch.**

Insert the switch into its holder and push it into its bracket, then rotate the switch 45-degrees counterclockwise to lock it in place.

3   Connect the switch electrical connector.

4   Confirm that the brake lights work properly before placing the vehicle into normal service.

12.1 Disconnect the electrical connector (A), then rotate the switch (B) 45-degrees clockwise to remove it

Specifications

General

Brake fluid type	See Chapter 1

Disc brakes

Minimum pad lining thickness	See Chapter 1
Disc lateral runout limit	0.004 inch (0.10 mm)
Disc minimum thickness	Cast into disc

Torque specifications	Ft-lbs (unless otherwise indicated)	Nm

➡ **Note: One foot-pound (ft-lb) of torque is equivalent to 12 inch-pounds (in-lbs) of torque. Torque values below approximately 15 foot-pounds are expressed in inch-pounds, because most foot-pound torque wrenches are not accurate at these smaller values.**

Brake line banjo bolt	18	24
Caliper mounting bolts		
Front		
2005 and earlier models	37	50
2006 and later models	22	29
Rear		
2005 and earlier models	30	40
2006 and later models	19	25
Caliper mounting bracket bolts		
Front	66	89
Rear	44	59
Master cylinder mounting nuts		
2005 and earlier models	140 in-lbs	15
2006 and later models	18	24
Power brake booster mounting nuts	17	23
Wheel lug nuts	See Chapter 1	

Section

10

SUSPENSION AND STEERING SYSTEMS

1.1 Front suspension and steering components (2008 and earlier models)

1	Upper control arm	5	Stabilizer bar	9	Damper fork
2	Steering knuckle	6	Steering gear boot	10	Shock absorber
3	Tie-rod end	7	Lower control arm (front)	11	Coil spring
4	Lower control arm (rear)	8	Damper weight	12	Crossmember support bracket

1 General information

▶ **Refer to illustrations 1.1 and 1.2**

The front suspension is made up of two lower control arms on 2008 and earlier models, one lower control arm with a transverse member on 2009 and later models and an upper control arm, a steering knuckle/

hub assembly, coil-over shock absorbers and a stabilizer bar (see illustration).

The rear suspension employs a trailing arm, upper and lower control arms, a coil spring and shock absorber per side, and an adjustable toe-

1.2 Typical rear suspension components

1	Trailing arm	4	Shock absorber	6	Coil spring
2	Upper suspension arm	5	Stabilizer bar	7	Lower suspension arm
3	Toe adjuster link				

link that permits toe setting adjustment for each rear wheel (see illustration).

The rack-and-pinion steering gear is located behind the engine/transaxle assembly on the front suspension subframe and actuates the tie-rods, which are attached to the steering knuckles. The inner ends of the tie-rods are protected by rubber boots which should be inspected periodically for secure attachment, tears and leaking lubricant (which would indicate a failed rack seal).

The power assist system consists of a belt-driven pump and associated lines and hoses. The fluid level in the power steering pump reservoir should be checked periodically (see Chapter 1).

The steering wheel operates the steering shaft, which actuates the steering gear through universal joints. Looseness in the steering can be caused by wear in the steering shaft universal joints, the steering gear, the tie-rod ends and loose retaining bolts.

PRECAUTIONS

Frequently, when working on the suspension or steering system components, you may come across fasteners which seem impossible to loosen. These fasteners on the underside of the vehicle are continually subjected to water, road grime, mud, etc., and can become rusted or frozen, making them extremely difficult to remove. In order to unscrew these stubborn fasteners without damaging them (or other components), be sure to use lots of penetrating oil and allow it to soak in for a while. Using a wire brush to clean exposed threads will also ease removal of the nut or bolt and prevent damage to the threads. Sometimes a sharp blow with a hammer and punch will break the bond between a nut and bolt threads, but care must be taken to prevent the punch from slipping off the fastener and ruining the threads. Heating the stuck fastener and surrounding area with a torch sometimes helps too, but isn't recommended because of the obvious dangers associated with fire. Long breaker bars and extension, or cheater, pipes will increase leverage, but never use an extension pipe on a ratchet - the ratcheting mechanism could be damaged. Sometimes tightening the nut or bolt first will help to break it loose. Fasteners that require drastic measures to remove should always be replaced with new ones.

Since most of the procedures dealt with in this Chapter involve jacking up the vehicle and working underneath it, a good pair of jackstands will be needed. A hydraulic floor jack is the preferred type of jack to lift the vehicle, and it can also be used to support certain components during various operations.

> **⁂ WARNING:**
>
> **Never, under any circumstances, rely on a jack to support the vehicle while working on it. Whenever any of the suspension or steering fasteners are loosened or removed they must be inspected and, if necessary, replaced with new ones of the same part number or of original equipment quality and design. Torque specifications must be followed for proper reassembly and component retention. Never attempt to heat or straighten any suspension or steering components. Instead, replace any bent or damaged part with a new one.**

2 Shock absorber/coil spring assembly (front) - removal, inspection and installation

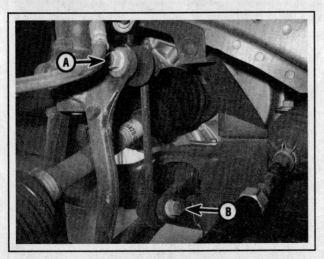

2.3 Disconnect the stabilizer bar link from the damper fork (A). If you're removing the stabilizer bar, disconnect the link from the bar (B)

2.5 Remove the bolt and flag-nut securing the damper fork to the lower control arm

> **⁂ CAUTION:**
>
> **The manufacturer recommends replacing all fasteners with new ones during installation.**

REMOVAL

▶ **Refer to illustrations 2.3, 2.5, 2.6 and 2.7**

1   Loosen the wheel lug nuts, raise the vehicle and support it securely on jackstands. Remove the wheel.

2   Unbolt the brake hose bracket from the shock absorber. Remove the ABS speed sensor and detach the wiring harness by removing the clamp bracket bolt.

3   Detach the stabilizer bar link from the damper fork (see illustration). If the ballstud spins, hold it with an Allen wrench placed in the center of the stud while loosening the nut.

4   Support the steering knuckle with a floor jack.

5   Remove the bolt and flag nut securing the damper fork to lower control arm (see illustration).

6   Remove the pinch-bolt securing the damper fork to the bottom of the shock absorber (see illustration). Tap the fork with a hammer, if necessary, to remove it from the shock body.

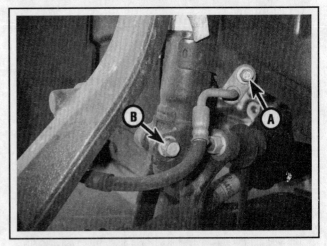

2.6 Remove the brake hose mounting bolt (A), then the damper fork-to-shock absorber pinch bolt (B)

7   In the engine compartment, mark the relationship of the outer mounting stud to the body. Support the shock absorber/coil spring assembly, then remove the three upper mounting nuts (see illustration).

8   Lower the knuckle to allow room to remove the shock absorber/ coil spring assembly, but be careful not to overextend the inner CV joint.

INSPECTION

9   Check the shock body for leaking fluid, dents, cracks and other obvious damage which would warrant replacement.

10 Check the coil spring for chips or cracks in the spring coating (this will cause premature spring failure due to corrosion). Inspect the spring seat for cuts, hardness and general deterioration.

11 If any undesirable conditions exist, proceed to the shock absorber/coil spring disassembly procedure (see Section 3).

INSTALLATION

12 Guide the assembly up into the fenderwell, align the previously made matchmarks and insert the upper mounting studs through the holes in the body. Once the studs protrude, install the new nuts so the shock won't fall back through. This is most easily accomplished with the help of an assistant, as the strut is quite heavy and awkward.

13 Push the damper fork onto the bottom of the shock body. Install a new pinch-bolt but do not tighten it at this time. Be sure to align the bolt with the notch on the shock.

14 Align the bottom of the damper fork so that the new bolt can be inserted to secure it to the lower control arm.

15 Use the jack to position the steering knuckle to approximate the

2.7 Mark the relationship of the outer mounting stud to the body, then remove the upper mounting nuts

normal ride height, then tighten the damper fork-to-shock pinch bolt and the damper fork-to-lower control arm bolt to the torque listed in this Chapter's Specifications.

16 Connect the stabilizer bar link to the damper fork. Tighten the nut to the torque listed in this Chapter's Specifications. The remainder of installation is the reverse of removal.

17 Install the wheel and lug nuts, then lower the vehicle and tighten the lug nuts to the torque listed in the Chapter 1 Specifications.

18 Tighten the upper mounting nuts to the torque listed in this Chapter's Specifications.

19 Drive the vehicle to an alignment shop to have the front end alignment checked and, if necessary, adjusted.

---

3   Shock absorber/coil spring assembly (front) - replacement

▶ **Refer to illustrations 3.3, 3.4, 3.5a, 3.5b, 3.5c, 3.5d and 3.9**

☀ WARNING:

Before attempting to disassemble the shock absorber/coil spring assembly, a tool to hold the coil spring in compression must be obtained. Do not attempt to use makeshift methods. Uncontrolled release of the spring could cause damage and personal injury or even death. Use a high-quality spring compressor, and carefully follow the tool manufacturer's instructions provided with it. After removing the coil spring with the compressor still installed, place it in a safe, isolated area.

1   If the front suspension shock absorber/coil springs exhibit signs of wear (leaking fluid, loss of damping capability, sagging or cracked coil springs), then they should be disassembled and overhauled as necessary. The shock absorbers themselves cannot be serviced, and should be replaced if faulty; the springs and related components can be replaced individually. To maintain balanced characteristics on both sides of the vehicle, the components on both sides should be replaced at the same time.

2   Remove the assembly (see Section 2), clean away all external dirt, then mount it in a vise.

3.3 Make sure the spring compressor tool is on securely

3   Install the coil spring compressor tools (ensuring that they are fully engaged), and compress the spring until all tension is relieved from the upper mount (see illustration).

3.4 Loosen and remove the piston rod nut

3.5a Remove the upper mount and spring seat . . .

3.5b . . . then carefully remove the spring . . .

3.5c . . . followed by the boot . . .

3.5d . . . and the bump stop

4 Hold the shock absorber piston rod with an Allen key and unscrew the thrust bearing retaining nut with a box-end wrench (see illustration).

5 Withdraw the top mount, upper spring seat and spring, followed by the boot and the bump stop (see illustrations).

6 If a new spring is to be installed, the original spring must now be carefully released from the compressor. If it is to be re-used, the spring can be left in compression.

7 With the strut assembly now completely disassembled, examine all the components for wear and damage, and check the bearing for smoothness of operation. Replace components as necessary.

8 Examine the shock for signs of fluid leakage. Check the piston rod for signs of pitting along its entire length, and check the shock body for signs of damage. Test the operation of the shock, while holding it in an upright position, by moving the piston through a full stroke, then through short strokes of 2 to 4 inches. In both cases, the resistance felt should be smooth and continuous. If the resistance is jerky or uneven, or if there is any visible sign of wear or damage, replacement is necessary.

9 Installation is the reverse of removal, noting the following points:

a) The coil springs must be installed with the paint mark at the bottom.
b) Make sure that the coil spring ends are correctly located in the upper and lower seats before releasing the compressor (see illustration).
c) Tighten the piston rod nut to the specified torque.

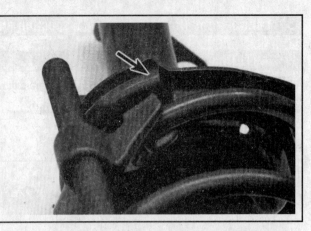

3.9 When installing the spring, make sure the ends fit into the recessed portion of the seats

4   Stabilizer bar and bushings (front) - removal and installation

REMOVAL

▶ **Refer to illustration 4.7**

1 Loosen the front wheel lug nuts. Raise the front of the vehicle and support it securely on jackstands. Apply the parking brake and block the rear wheels to keep the vehicle from rolling off the stands. Remove the front wheels.

2 Detach the stabilizer bar links from the bar (see illustration 2.3). If the ballstud turns with the nut, use an Allen wrench to hold the stud.

3 Disconnect the steering shaft from the steering gear (see Chapter 10).

✳✳ CAUTION:

Don't allow the steering wheel to turn after the steering shaft is disconnected - the airbag clockspring could be damaged.

4 Disconnect the tie-rod ends from the steering knuckles (see Section 14), then remove the steering gear mounting bolts (see Section 16).

5 Detach the exhaust pipe(s) from the exhaust manifold(s).

6 Support the rear of the subframe with a floor jack. Loosen the front subframe mounting fasteners and remove the rear subframe fasteners, then lower the rear of the subframe with the jack.

7 Unbolt the stabilizer bar bushing clamps (see illustration). Guide the stabilizer bar out from between the subframe and the body.

8 While the stabilizer bar is off the vehicle, slide off the retainer bushings and inspect them. If they're cracked, worn or deteriorated, replace them.

9 Clean the bushing area of the stabilizer bar with a stiff wire brush to remove any rust or dirt.

INSTALLATION

10 Lubricate the inside and outside of the new bushing with vegetable oil (used in cooking) to simplify reassembly.

✳✳ CAUTION:

Don't use petroleum or mineral-based lubricants or brake fluid - they will lead to deterioration of the bushings.

The slits of the bushings must face the rear of the vehicle.

11 Installation is the reverse of removal. Tighten the fasteners to the torque values listed in this Chapter's Specifications.

4.7 Stabilizer bar bushing clamp mounting fasteners

5   Control arms (front) - removal, inspection and installation

---

✳✳ CAUTION:

All suspension bolts should be replaced with new fasteners during assembly.

REMOVAL

2008 and earlier models
Lower arms

1   Loosen the wheel lug nuts on the side to be disassembled. Raise the front of the vehicle, support it securely on jackstands and remove the wheel.

Rear lower arm

2   Disconnect the steering shaft from the steering gear (see Chapter 10).

✳✳ CAUTION:

Don't allow the steering wheel to turn after the steering shaft is disconnected - the airbag clockspring could be damaged.

---

3   Disconnect the tie-rod ends from the steering knuckles (see Section 14), then remove the steering gear mounting bolts (see Section 16).

4   Detach the exhaust pipe(s) from the exhaust manifold(s).

5   Support the rear of the subframe with a floor jack. Loosen the front subframe mounting fasteners and remove the rear subframe fasteners, then lower the rear of the subframe with the jack.

Either lower arm

▶ **Refer to illustrations 5.6a and 5.6b**

6   Loosen the lower arm-to-balljoint nut (see illustrations). Position

a block of wood under the outer CV joint of the driveaxle to prevent damage to the joint when the balljoint at the steering knuckle is disconnected. Using a balljoint removal tool, separate the balljoint.

7   If you're removing the front lower arm, remove the damper fork mounting bolt at the front lower control arm.

8   Remove the arm-to-subframe mounting bolt.

9   Remove the lower control arm.

2009 and later models
Lower arm

➡ **Note: On 3.7L V6 models, when working on the right side, it will be necessary to remove the front exhaust pipe (see Chapter 4).**

10   Remove the ABS sensor and brake hose bracket (see Chapter 9).

11   Remove the stabilizer control link upper nut (see Section 4).

12   Remove the control arm-to-knuckle nuts.

13   Remove the lower arm-to-subframe through bolt nut.

14   Remove the subframe support bracket mounting nut and bolts.

15   Support the subframe using a jack, loosen the subframe mounting bolts and lower the subframe to access the bolts at the rear of the arm.

➡ **Note: Remove any mounting brackets for hoses that may be connected to the subframe.**

16   Remove the lower arm rear mounting bolts and front through bolt, then remove the arm from the subframe.

Upper arm

▶ **Refer to illustration 5.19**

17   The upper control arm is attached to the top of the steering knuckle with a balljoint, and to two positions on the chassis with pivot bolts.

18   Unbolt the wheel speed sensor and the three upper strut-to-body nuts (see Section 2).

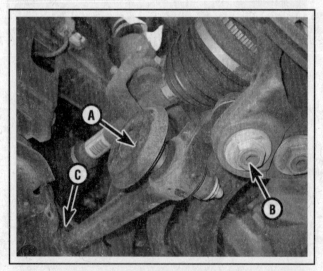

5.6a Front lower control arm details (2008 and earlier models)

A Damper fork bolt/nut	C Pivot bolt
B Balljoint nut	

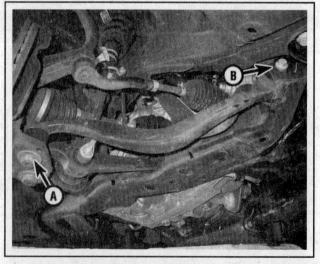

5.6b Rear lower control arm details (2008 and earlier models)

A Balljoint nut	B Pivot bolt

19 Disconnect the balljoint at the top of the steering knuckle, then remove the inner arm mounting bolts and the upper arm (see illustration).

Transverse member (2009 and later models)

20 Remove the transverse member mounting nuts.
21 Remove the transverse member from the subframe.

INSPECTION

22 Check the control arm for distortion and the bushings for wear, replacing parts as necessary. Do not attempt to straighten a bent control arm.

INSTALLATION

23 Installation is the reverse of removal. Tighten all of the fasteners to the torque values listed in this Chapter's Specifications.

➡ **Note: Before tightening the control arm fasteners, raise the outer end of the control arm with a floor jack to simulate normal ride height. On upper control arms, install the pivot bolts loosely, then install a 0.25-inch drill bit through the two holes in the chassis just below the bushing. This will set the proper height for tightening of the pivot bolts.**

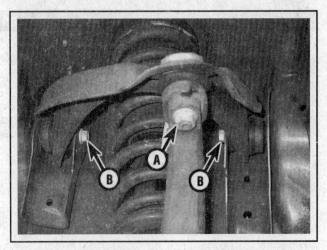

5.19 Remove the nut (A) and separate the balljoint, then remove the two pivot bolts (B)

24 Install the wheel and lug nuts, lower the vehicle and tighten the lug nuts to the torque listed in the Chapter 1 Specifications.
25 It's a good idea to have the front wheel alignment checked and, if necessary, adjusted after this job has been performed.

6   Steering knuckle and hub - removal and installation

✳ WARNING:

Dust created by the brake system is harmful to your health. Never blow it out with compressed air and don't inhale any of it. Do not, under any circumstances, use petroleum-based solvents to clean brake parts. Use brake system cleaner only.

✳ CAUTION:

All suspension bolts should be replaced with new fasteners during assembly.

REMOVAL

1   Remove the wheel cover and loosen, but don't remove, the driveaxle/hub nut. Loosen the wheel lug nuts, raise the vehicle and support it securely on jackstands, then remove the wheel.
2   Remove the brake caliper (don't disconnect the hose), the caliper mounting bracket and the brake disc (see Chapter 9). Disconnect the brake hose from the strut. Hang the caliper from the coil spring with a piece of wire - don't let it hang by the brake hose.
3   Remove the ABS wheel speed sensor and remove the harness bolt (see Chapter 9).
4   Separate the tie-rod end from the steering knuckle arm (see Section 14).
5   Place a block of wood above the lower control arm to prevent damage to the inner CV joint. Separate the two lower control arm balljoints from the steering knuckle (see Section 5).
6   Remove the driveaxle/hub nut and push the driveaxle from the hub (see Chapter 8). Support the end of the driveaxle with a piece of wire.

7   Separate the upper control arm balljoint from the steering knuckle (see Section 5).

INSTALLATION

8   Guide the knuckle and hub assembly into position, inserting the driveaxle into the hub.
9   Connect the balljoints to the knuckle and tighten the nuts to the torque listed in this Chapter's Specifications.

✳ CAUTION:

All suspension bolts should be replaced with new ones during assembly.

10 Attach the tie-rod end to the steering knuckle arm (see Section 14). Tighten the nut to the torque listed in this Chapter's Specifications.

➡ **Note: Before tightening the control arm fasteners, raise the outer end of the control arm with a floor jack to simulate normal ride height.**

11 Place the brake disc on the hub, install the two disc-locating bolts, and install the caliper (see Chapter 9).
12 Install the driveaxle/hub nut and tighten it securely, but not completely yet.
13 Install the wheel and lug nuts. Lower the vehicle and tighten the lug nuts to the torque listed in the Chapter 1 Specifications.
14 Tighten the driveaxle/hub nut to the torque listed in the Chapter 8 Specifications. Install the wheel cover.
15 Have the front-end alignment checked and, if necessary, adjusted.

7 Hub and bearing assembly (front) - removal and installation

Due to the special tools and expertise required to press the hub and bearing from the steering knuckle, this job should be left to a professional mechanic. However, the steering knuckle and hub may be removed and the assembly taken to an automotive machine shop or other qualified repair facility equipped with the necessary tools. See Section 6 for the steering knuckle and hub removal procedure.

8 Shock absorber (rear) - removal and installation

▶ **Refer to illustrations 8.3 and 8.4**

1 Loosen the wheel lug nuts, raise the rear of the vehicle and support it securely on jackstands. Block the front wheels to prevent the vehicle from rolling. Remove the wheel.

2 Support the trailing arm with a floor jack, then remove the upper control arm (see Section 9).

3 Remove the lower shock mounting bolt (see illustration).

4 Remove the three bolts securing the upper shock mount to the body (see illustration).

5 Maneuver the shock out of the vehicle. If new shocks are to be installed, swap the bracket to the top of the new shock.

6 Installation is the reverse of removal.

✳✳ CAUTION:

New shock absorbers are gas-filled and come compressed and retained with a fiberglass strap. Do NOT remove the strap until the shock is installed.

7 Raise the trailing arm with a floor jack to simulate normal ride height, then tighten the mounting fasteners to the torque listed in this Chapter's Specifications.

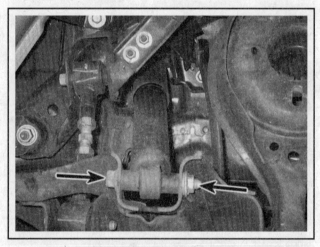

8.3 Remove the rear shock lower mounting nut and bolt

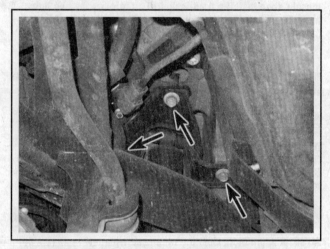

8.4 Remove the three shock mount-to-body bolts (two of three bolts visible)

9 Suspension arms (rear) - removal and installation

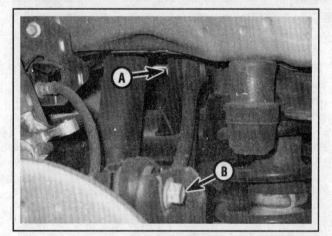

9.3 Rear upper control arm inner pivot bolt (A) and arm-to-trailing arm bolt (B)

➥ **Note: Any rear suspension fasteners should only be tightened with the hub raised to simulate normal ride height. This can be done by supporting the trailing arm with a floor jack.**

1 Loosen the wheel lug nuts, raise the rear of the vehicle and support it securely on jackstands. Block the front wheels to prevent the vehicle from rolling. Remove the wheel.

UPPER SUSPENSION ARM

▶ **Refer to illustration 9.3**

2 Support the rear lower control arm with a floor jack, then remove the lower shock absorber mounting bolt (see Section 8).

3 Raise the lower control arm with a floor jack. Remove the outboard bolt securing the upper arm to the trailing arm (see illustration).

4 Lower the jack to remove tension from the upper arm, and move the shock absorber as needed to remove the upper arm.

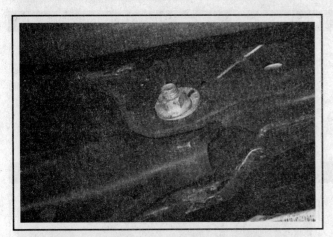

9.8 Mark the position of the cam to the subframe, then remove the lower control arm inner pivot bolt

5   Remove the pivot bolt from the inner end of the arm. Remove the arm.

6   Installation is the reverse of removal. Tighten the fasteners to the torque listed in this Chapter's Specifications.

LOWER SUSPENSION ARM

▶ **Refer to illustration 9.8**

7   Remove the rear coil spring (see Sec-tion 10).

8   Mark the position of the cam adjuster bolt to the subframe, then remove the cam adjuster bolt and nut (see illustration). Remove the arm from the vehicle.

9   Installation is the reverse of removal. When installing the cam adjuster bolt, align the matchmarks and install a new nut. Tighten the fasteners to the torque listed in this Chapter's Specifications.

TRAILING ARM

10   If a new arm is being installed, remove the caliper dust shield and the four bolts on the inboard side of the trailing arm and remove the wheel spindle. If the arm is to be reused, leave the wheel spindle bolted in place.

11   Unbolt the brake hose and brake line brackets from the trailing arm. Unbolt the parking brake cable brackets from the caliper and trailing arm (see Chapter 9).

12   Remove the ABS wheel speed sensor and unbolt the harness brackets from the trailing arm.

13   Support the lower control arm with a floor jack positioned underneath the coil spring pocket.

✳✳ WARNING:

The jack must remain in this position until the trailing arm is reinstalled.

14   Remove the lower shock absorber bolt (see Section 8).

15   Remove the outboard toe-link bolt and remove the trailing arm.

16   Remove the outboard bolt at the upper arm, and the outboard bolts at the lower arm.

17   Remove the two front trailing arm mounting bolts.

18   Inspect the trailing arm pivot bushing for signs of deterioration. If it is in need of replacement, take the trailing arm to an automotive machine shop to have the bushing replaced.

19   Installation is the reverse of removal, noting the following points:

a) Tighten all fasteners to the proper torque specifications.
b) It won't be necessary to bleed the brakes unless a hydraulic fitting was loosened.
c) Have the rear wheel alignment checked and, if necessary, adjusted.

10 Coil spring (rear) - removal and installation

✳✳ WARNING:

Always replace the springs as a set - never replace just one of them.

1   Loosen the wheel lug nuts, raise the vehicle and support it securely on jackstands. Block the front wheels to prevent the vehicle from rolling. Remove the wheel.

2   Support the lower control arm with a floor jack positioned underneath the coil spring pocket.

3   Support the trailing arm with another floor jack.

➡ **Note: If you don't have another floor jack, remove the caliper and hang it out of the way with a length of wire (see Chapter 9).**

4   Disconnect the stabilizer bar link.

5   Remove the lower control arm outboard bolt.

6   Lower the trailing arm slowly with the floor jack until the coil spring is extended.

✳✳ WARNING:

The spring is under considerable pressure. Use a chain and bolts to secure the bottom of the spring to the lower arm until it can be safely removed.

7   Mark the position of the coil spring to the spring insulators.

8   Check the spring for cracks and chips, replacing the springs as a set if any defects are found. Also check the upper insulator for damage and deterioration, replacing it if necessary.

9   Installation is the reverse of removal. Be sure to position the lower end of the coil spring in the depressed area of the trailing arm. Tighten all fasteners to the proper torque specifications.

11 Hub and bearing assembly (rear) - removal and installation

1   Raise and support the rear of the vehicle and remove the wheel speed sensor (see Chapter 9).

2   Unbolt and set aside the caliper and caliper mounting bracket. Do not let the caliper hang by the rubber brake hose; wire the caliper to the spring or shock absorber with mechanic's wire.

3   Remove the brake disc (see Chapter 9).

4   Pry off the grease cap with a screwdriver, tapping it with a small hammer if necessary.

5   Remove the hub nut and slide the hub and bearing assembly from the wheel spindle.

6   Installation is the reverse of removal. Tighten all fasteners to the proper torque specifications. Use a new hub nut.

12 Steering wheel - removal and installation

※ WARNING:

These models are equipped with a Supplemental Restraint System (SRS), more commonly known as airbags. Always disable the airbag system before working in the vicinity of any airbag system component to avoid the possibility of accidental deployment of the airbag(s), which could cause personal injury (see Chapter 12).

※ WARNING:

Do not use a memory saving device to preserve the PCM or radio memory when working on or near airbag system components.

REMOVAL

▶ Refer to illustrations 12.3, 12.4 and 12.6

1   Turn the ignition key to Off, then disconnect the cable from the negative terminal of the battery. Wait at least two minutes before proceeding.

2   Turn the steering wheel so the wheels are pointing straight ahead and remove the key.

3   Use a small screwdriver to remove the plastic covers for the airbag module mounting bolts (see illustration) from each side of the steering wheel, then remove the bolts. Gently pull the airbag module away from the wheel on the side you have released, then repeat this Step on the other side of the wheel.

4   Pry up the connector locks and disconnect the airbag module electrical connectors (see illustration).

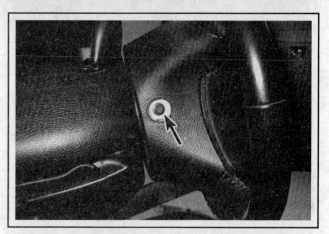

12.3 Remove the airbag module bolts through the holes on each side of the steering wheel to release the airbag

5   Remove the airbag and set the airbag module in a safe, isolated area.

※ WARNING:

Carry the airbag module with the trim side facing away from you, and set the steering wheel/airbag module down with the trim side facing up. Don't place anything on top of the steering wheel/airbag module.

6   Make match marks on the wheel and the steering shaft, then

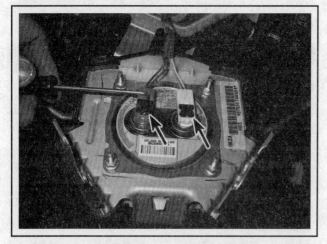

12.4 Pry up the locking tabs, then disconnect the airbag connectors

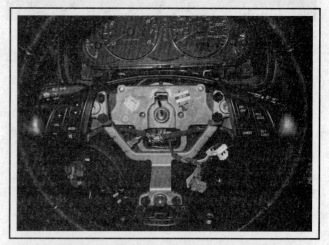

12.6 Mark the position of the steering wheel to the shaft, then use a socket to loosen the steering wheel nut

remove the steering wheel mounting nut (see illustration). Rock the wheel lightly to remove it from the shaft.

7   Feed the wires and connectors through the steering wheel as you remove it.

8   Tape the clockspring so that it cannot rotate.

✶✶ CAUTION:

Do not rotate the steering shaft at any time while the wheel and airbag are removed or the clockspring could be damaged.

---

9   To remove the clockspring, remove the steering column covers (see Chapter 11), unplug its connectors and remove the mounting screws.

INSTALLATION

10   If the clockspring was removed, install it now, then center it (even if it was not removed, but if the inner rotor has turned, it must be centered).

  a) *Rotate the inner rotor of the clockspring counterclockwise until you feel resistance.*

✶✶ CAUTION:

Don't apply too much force.

---

  b) *Turn the rotor clockwise approximately 2 to 2-1/4 turns, placing the electrical connector in the 12 o'clock position.*

11   To install the wheel, feed the wiring and airbag connectors through the wheel and place the steering wheel on the steering shaft, aligning the match marks made in Step 6.

12   Tighten the steering wheel nut to the torque listed in this Chapter's Specifications.

13   The remainder of installation is the reverse of removal.

✶✶ CAUTION:

Make sure the connectors fit correctly on the airbag module (with the safety tabs still UP). When connecting the two airbag connectors, follow the color-coding. The orange connector goes to the orange connection on the airbag. Do not push the connectors on if the clips are down. After the clips are secured, push the airbag module down toward the wheel until the retaining clips lock.

---

13   Steering column - removal and installation

✶✶ WARNING:

These models are equipped with a Supplemental Restraint System (SRS), more commonly known as airbags. Always disable the airbag system before working in the vicinity of any airbag system component to avoid the possibility of accidental deployment of the airbag(s), which could cause personal injury (see Chapter 12).

✶✶ WARNING:

Do not use a memory saving device to preserve the PCM or radio memory when working on or near airbag system components.

REMOVAL

▶ **Refer to illustrations 13.6, 13.7 and 13.8**

1   Park the vehicle with the wheels pointing straight ahead. Disconnect the cable from the negative terminal of the battery (see Chapter 5).

2   Remove the steering wheel (see Section 12)

3   Remove the steering column covers, then tape the airbag clockspring to prevent it from turning.

✶✶ WARNING:

If this is not done, the airbag clockspring could be damaged. Remove the instrument panel lower trim panel and steering column reinforcement panel (see Chapter 11).

---

4   Remove the clockspring (see Section 12).

5   Disconnect the electrical connectors for the multi-function switch (see Chapter 12).

6   Remove the fasteners securing the cover at the firewall (see illustration).

7   Mark the relationship of the U-joint to the intermediate shaft, then remove and discard the pinch bolt (see illustration).

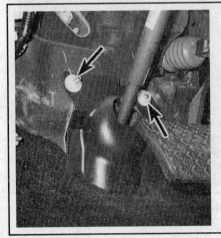

13.6 Remove the two nuts and the cover over the U-joint at the firewall

13.7 Mark the U-joint-to-intermediate shaft, then remove the pinch bolt

8 Remove the steering column mounting fasteners (see illustration). Lower the column and pull it to the rear, making sure nothing is still connected, then remove the column.

INSTALLATION

9 Guide the steering column into position, engaging the U-joint with the bottom of the steering shaft. Install the steering column mounting fasteners and tighten them to the torque listed in this Chapter's Specifications.

➡ **Note: An assistant will be very helpful in this procedure.**

10 Connect the U-joint to the intermediate shaft. Install a new intermediate shaft pinch bolt, tightening it to the torque listed in this Chapter's Specifications.

11 The remainder of installation is the reverse of removal.

13.8 Remove the four nuts securing the steering column

14 Tie-rod ends - removal and installation

REMOVAL

▶ **Refer to illustrations 14.2a, 14.2b and 14.4**

1 Loosen the front wheel lug nuts. Apply the parking brake, raise the front of the vehicle and support it securely on jackstands. Remove the front wheel.

2 Hold the tie-rod with a pair of locking pliers or wrench and loosen the jam nut enough to mark the position of the tie-rod end in relation to the threads (see illustrations).

3 Remove the cotter pin and loosen (but don't remove) the nut on the tie-rod end stud.

4 Disconnect the tie-rod end from the steering knuckle arm with a puller (see illustration). Remove the nut and detach the tie-rod end.

5 Unscrew the tie-rod end from the tie-rod.

INSTALLATION

6 Thread the tie-rod end on to the marked position and insert the stud into the steering knuckle arm. Tighten the jam nut securely.

7 Install the nut on the stud and tighten it to the torque listed in this

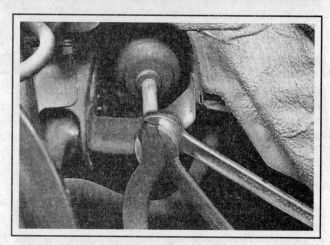

14.2a Loosen the jam nut . . .

Chapter's Specifications. Install a new cotter pin.

8 Install the wheel and lug nuts. Lower the vehicle and tighten the lug nuts to the torque listed in the Chapter 1 Specifications.

9 Have the alignment checked and, if necessary, adjusted.

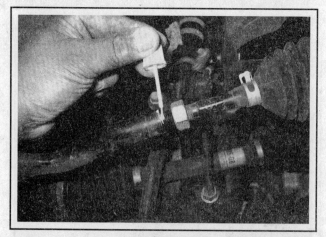

14.2b . . . then mark the position of the tie-rod end in relation to the threads

14.4 Disconnect the tie-rod end from the steering knuckle arm with a puller

15 Steering gear boots - replacement

▶ Refer to illustration 15.3

1   Loosen the lug nuts, raise the vehicle and support it securely on jackstands. Remove the wheel.

2   Remove the tie-rod end and jam nut (see Section 14).

3   Remove the outer steering gear boot clamp with a pair of pliers (see illustration). Cut off the inner boot clamp with a pair of diagonal cutters. Slide off the boot.

4   Before installing the new boot, wrap the threads and serrations on the end of the steering rod with a layer of tape so the small end of the new boot isn't damaged.

5   Slide the new boot into position on the steering gear until it seats in the groove in the steering rod and install new clamps.

6   Remove the tape and install the tie-rod end (see Section 14).

7   Install the wheel and lug nuts. Lower the vehicle and tighten the lug nuts to the torque listed in the Chapter 1 Specifications.

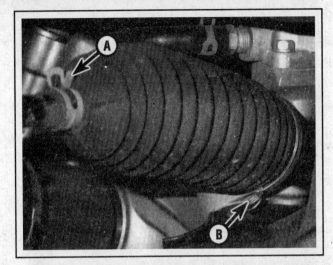

15.3 The outer ends of the steering gear boots are secured by band-type clamps (A); they're easily released with a pair of pliers. The inner ends of the steering gear boots are retained by boot clamps which must be cut off and discarded (B)

16 Steering gear - removal and installation

❋❋ WARNING:

These models are equipped with airbags. Always disable the airbag system before working in the vicinity of airbag system components (see Chapter 12). Make sure the steering column shaft is not turned while the steering gear is removed or you could damage the airbag system clockspring. To prevent the shaft from turning, turn the ignition key to the lock position before beginning work, and run the seat belt through the steering wheel and clip it into its latch.

REMOVAL

▶ Refer to illustrations 16.6 and 16.10

1   Disconnect the cable from the negative terminal of the battery (see Chapter 5).

2   From inside the vehicle under the instrument panel, remove and discard the intermediate shaft pinch bolt (see Section 13).

3   Loosen the front wheel lug nuts. Raise the vehicle and place it securely on jackstands. Remove both front wheels.

4   Detach the tie-rod ends from the steering knuckles (see Section 14).

5   Remove the front portion of the exhaust system (see Chapter 4).

6   Place a drain pan under the steering gear and detach the power steering pressure and return lines (see illustration). Cap the ends to prevent excessive fluid loss and contamination

➡ **Note: Some models have a sheetmetal shield that must be removed for access to the fittings.**

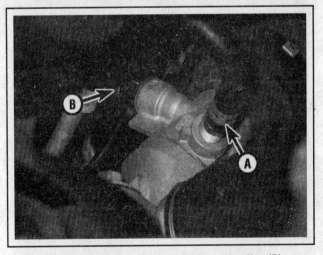

16.6 Steering gear return hose (A) and pressure line (B)

7   Support the rear of the subframe with a floor jack.

8   Remove the crossmember support bracket mounting nut and bolts from each side, then remove the brackets (see illustration 1.1).

9   Loosen the front subframe mounting fasteners and remove the rear subframe fasteners, then lower the rear of the subframe with the jack approximately 3 inches.

➡ **Note: If this is not enough room to remove the steering gear, the engine will need to be supported (see Chapter 2C) and the crossmember removed.**

10 Remove the three steering gear mounting bolts (see illustration).
11 Remove the steering gear.

INSTALLATION

12 Installation is the reverse of removal, noting the following points:

a) *When connecting the steering gear input shaft to the intermediate shaft U-joint, align the matchmarks and install a new pinch bolt.*

b) *Use new subframe mounting fasteners.*

c) *Use a new banjo bolt and sealing washers for the power steering pressure line.*

d) *Tighten all fasteners to the torque values listed in this Chapter's Specifications.*

e) *Tighten the lug nuts to the torque listed in the Chapter 1 Specifications.*

f) *Fill the power steering reservoir with the recommended fluid (see Chapter 1). Bleed the power steering system (see Section 18).*

g) *Have the front end alignment checked and, if necessary, adjusted.*

16.10 Left-side steering gear front mounting bolt

17 Power steering pump - removal and installation

REMOVAL

1 Disconnect the cable from the negative battery terminal (see Chapter 5).
2 Using a large syringe or suction gun, siphon as much fluid out of the power steering fluid reservoir as possible. Place a drain pan under the vehicle to catch any fluid that spills out when the hoses are disconnected. On models with a remote fluid reservoir, remove the power steering fluid reservoir.
3 Remove the drivebelt (see Chapter 1).

Four-cylinder models

4 Disconnect the electrical connector at the power steering pump.
5 Unscrew and remove the bolt securing the high pressure fluid line support bracket.
6 Disconnect the supply and pressure hoses from the power steering pump.
7 Unscrew and remove the mounting bolts, and withdraw the power steering pump from the engine.

V6 models

3.0L models

▶ **Refer to illustration 17.14**

8 Loosen the right front wheel lug nuts, raise the front of the vehicle, support it securely on jackstands and remove the wheel.
9 Remove the lower splash shields.
10 Remove the engine oil dipstick, dipstick tube mounting fastener and the tube.
11 Remove the A/C compressor mounting bolts (see Chapter 3) and tie the compressor to the side, using wire or rope.
12 Remove the front side exhaust manifold (see Chapter 2B).
13 Disconnect the electrical connector at the power steering pump.

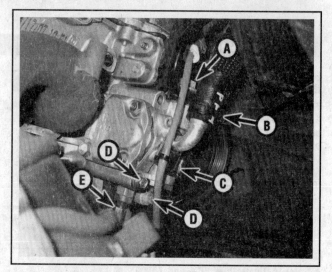

17.14 Typical power steering pump details (3.0L V6 engine)

A	Pressure line banjo bolt	D	Mounting bolts (upper bolt
B	Supply hose		not visible)
C	Oxygen sensor harness clip	E	Electrical connector

14 Disconnect the supply and pressure hoses from the power steering pump (see illustration).
15 Remove the mounting bolts, and withdraw the power steering pump from the bracket.
16 Remove the bracket-to-engine mounting bolts.
17 Remove the bracket, then remove the power steering pump.

3.7L models

18 Remove the power steering reservoir mounting bolt and set the reservoir to the side.

19 Remove the windshield wiper arms, cowl assembly and wiper motor (see Chapter 11).

20 Loosen the right front wheel lug nuts, raise the front of the vehicle, support it securely on jackstands and remove the wheel.

21 Remove the lower splash shields.

22 Disconnect the electrical connector at the power steering pump.

23 Disconnect the supply and pressure hoses from the power steering pump.

24 Remove the mounting bolts, and withdraw the power steering pump from the bracket.

INSTALLATION

25 Installation is the reverse of removal, noting the following points:

a) *The banjo bolt and sealing washers on the high-pressure line should be replaced.*

b) *Tighten the mounting bolts and banjo bolt to the torque listed in this Chapter's Specifications.*

c) *Fill the power steering reservoir with the recommended fluid (see Chapter 1). Bleed the power steering system (see Section 18).*

18 Power steering system - bleeding

1 The power steering system must be bled whenever a line is disconnected. Bubbles can be seen in power steering fluid that has air in it and the fluid will often have a tan or milky appearance. Low fluid level can cause air to mix with the fluid, resulting in a noisy pump as well as foaming of the fluid.

2 Open the hood and check the fluid level in the reservoir, add-ing the specified fluid necessary to bring it up to the proper level (see Chapter 1).

3 Start the engine and slowly turn the steering wheel several times from left-to-right and back again. Do not turn the wheel completely from lock-to-lock. Check the fluid level, topping it up as necessary until it remains steady and no more bubbles are visible.

19 Wheels and tires - general information

▶ **Refer to illustration 19.1**

1 All vehicles covered by this manual are equipped with metric-sized fiberglass or steel belted radial tires (see illustration). Use of other size or type of tires may affect the ride and handling of the vehicle. Don't mix different types of tires, such as radials and bias belted, on the same vehicle as handling may be seriously affected. It's recommended that tires be replaced in pairs on the same axle, but if only one tire is being replaced, be sure it's the same size, structure and tread design as the other.

2 Because tire pressure has a substantial effect on handling and wear, the pressure on all tires should be checked at least once a month or before any extended trips (see Chapter 1).

3 Wheels must be replaced if they are bent, dented, leak air, have elongated bolt holes, are heavily rusted, out of vertical symmetry or if the lug nuts won't stay tight. Wheel repairs that use welding or peening are not recommended.

4 Tire and wheel balance is important in the overall handling, brak-ing and performance of the vehicle. Unbalanced wheels can adversely affect handling and ride characteristics as well as tire life. Whenever a tire is installed on a wheel, the tire and wheel should be balanced by a shop with the proper equipment.

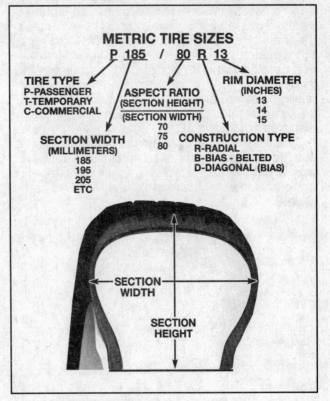

19.1 Metric tire size code

20 Wheel alignment - general information

▶ **Refer to illustration 20.1**

A wheel alignment refers to the adjustments made to the wheels so they are in proper angular relationship to the suspension and the ground. Wheels that are out of proper alignment not only affect vehicle control, but also increase tire wear. The front end angles normally measured are camber, caster and toe-in (see illustration). Toe-in and camber are adjustable; if the caster is not correct, check for bent components. Rear toe-in is also adjustable.

Getting the proper wheel alignment is a very exacting process, one in which complicated and expensive machines are necessary to perform the job properly. Because of this, you should have a technician with the proper equipment perform these tasks. We will, however, use this space to give you a basic idea of what is involved with a wheel alignment so you can better understand the process and deal intelligently with the shop that does the work.

Toe-in is the turning in of the wheels. The purpose of a toe specification is to ensure parallel rolling of the wheels. In a vehicle with zero toe-in, the distance between the front edges of the wheels will be the same as the distance between the rear edges of the wheels. The actual amount of toe-in is normally only a fraction of an inch. On the front end, toe-in is controlled by the tie-rod end position on the tie-rod. On the rear end, it's controlled by a threaded toe-link. Incorrect toe-in will cause the tires to wear improperly by making them scrub against the road surface.

Camber is the tilting of the wheels from vertical when viewed from one end of the vehicle. When the wheels tilt out at the top, the camber is said to be positive (+). When the wheels tilt in at the top the camber is negative (-). The amount of tilt is measured in degrees from vertical and this measurement is called the camber angle. This angle affects the amount of tire tread which contacts the road and compensates for changes in the suspension geometry when the vehicle is cornering or traveling over an undulating surface. On the front end it is not adjustable. On the rear end it's adjusted by cam bolts on the inner ends of the lower control arms.

Caster is the tilting of the front steering axis from the vertical. A tilt toward the rear is positive caster and a tilt toward the front is negative caster. On the front end, caster can only be adjusted by installing a new upper control arm with offset bushings. On the rear end, caster isn't adjustable.

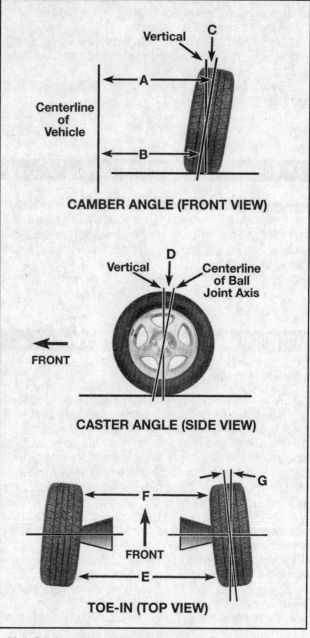

CAMBER ANGLE (FRONT VIEW)

CASTER ANGLE (SIDE VIEW)

TOE-IN (TOP VIEW)

20.1 Camber, caster and toe-in angles

A minus B = C (degrees camber)
D = degrees caster
E minus F = toe-in (measured in inches)
G = toe-in (expressed in degrees)

Torque specifications	Ft-lbs	Nm
Front suspension		
Upper control arm		
Arm-to-chassis pivot bolts	41	56
Balljoint-to-knuckle nut	35	47
Lower control arms		
Balljoint-to-knuckle nut (2008 and earlier models)	140	190
Front lower arm		
2008 and earlier models		
Through bolt-to-subframe	80	108
Damper fork-to-front lower control arm bolt	76	103
2009 and later models		
Arm-to-knuckle nuts	126	171
Front through bolt	100	136
Rear bolts	81	110
Rear lower arm-to-subframe bolt (2008 and earlier models)	80	108
Stabilizer bar		
Bushing clamp nuts	35	47
Link nuts	27	37
Shock absorber/coil spring assembly		
Upper mounting nuts	22	30
Damper fork pinch bolt	40	54
Damper fork-to-front lower control arm bolt	76	103
Shock absorber piston rod-to-upper mount nut	30	40
Subframe		
Subframe mounting nuts	111	150
Subframe mounting bolts	76	103
Subframe support bracket		
Mounting bolts	80	108
Mounting nut	100	136
Transverse member nuts (2009 and later)	55	75
Rear suspension		
Shock absorber		
Bracket-to-body bolts	35	47
Upper and lower mounting bolt/nut	76	103
Rear stabilizer bar		
Bracket bolts	35	47
Link nuts	31	42
Upper control arm	74	100
Lower control arm	76	103
Trailing arm-to-body bolts	81	110
Toe link		
Inner bolt	92	125
Outer bolt	81	110

Torque specifications	Ft-lbs	Nm
Steering		
Power steering pump mounting bolts	18	24
Power steering pressure line banjo bolts		
2.3L, 2.5L and 3.0L V6 models	26	35
3.7L V6 models	35	47
Steering shaft-to-gear U-joint pinch bolt	18	24
Steering column mounting nuts	15	20
Steering wheel nut	26	35
Steering gear mounting bolts	70	95
Tie-rod end-to-steering knuckle nut	35	47

Section

11

BODY

1 General information

WARNING:

The models covered by this manual are equipped with Supplemental Restraint Systems (SRS), more commonly known as airbags. Always disable the airbag system before working in the vicinity of any airbag system components to avoid the possibility of accidental deployment of the airbags, which could cause personal injury (see Chapter 12).

Certain body components are particularly vulnerable to accident damage and can be unbolted and repaired or replaced. Among these parts are the hood, doors, tailgate, liftgate, bumpers and front fenders.

Only general body maintenance practices and body panel repair procedures within the scope of the do-it-yourselfer are included in this Chapter.

2 Repair minor paint scratches

No matter how hard you try to keep your vehicle looking like new, it will inevitably be scratched, chipped or dented at some point. If the metal is actually dented, seek the advice of a professional. But you can fix minor scratches and chips yourself. Buy a touch-up paint kit from a

dealer service department or an auto parts store. To ensure that you get the right color, you'll need to have the specific make, model and year of your vehicle and, ideally, the paint code, which is located on a special metal plate under the hood or in the door jamb.

Make sure the damaged area is perfectly clean and rust free. If the touch-up kit has a wire brush, use it to clean the scratch or chip. Or use fine steel wool wrapped around the end of a pencil. Clean the scratched or chipped surface only, not the good paint surrounding it. Rinse the area with water and allow it to dry thoroughly

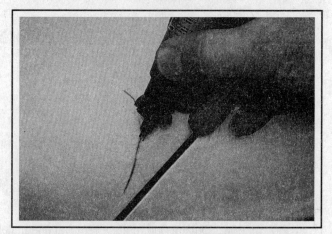

Thoroughly mix the paint, then apply a small amount with the touch-up kit brush or a very fine artist's brush. Brush in one direction as you fill the scratch area. Do not build up the paint higher than the surrounding paint

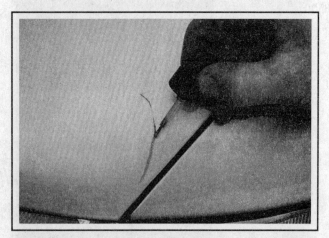

If the vehicle has a two-coat finish, apply the clear coat after the color coat has dried

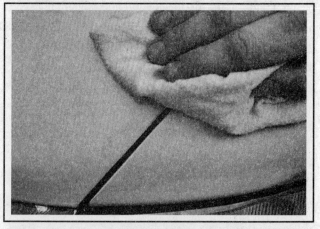

Wait a few days for the paint to dry thoroughly, then rub out the repainted area with a polishing compound to blend the new paint with the surrounding area. When you're happy with your work, wash and polish the area

PLASTIC BODY PANELS

The following repair procedures are for minor scratches and gouges. Repair of more serious damage should be left to a dealer service department or qualified auto body shop. Below is a list of the equipment and materials necessary to perform the following repair procedures on plastic body panels.

Wax, grease and silicone removing solvent
Cloth-backed body tape
Sanding discs
Drill motor with three-inch disc holder
Hand sanding block
Rubber squeegees
Sandpaper
Non-porous mixing palette
Wood paddle or putty knife
Curved-tooth body file
Flexible parts repair material

Flexible panels (bumper trim)

1   Remove the damaged panel, if necessary or desirable. In most cases, repairs can be carried out with the panel installed.

2   Clean the area(s) to be repaired with a wax, grease and silicone removing solvent applied with a water-dampened cloth.

3   If the damage is structural, that is, if it extends through the panel, clean the backside of the panel area to be repaired as well. Wipe dry.

4   Sand the rear surface about 1-1/2 inches beyond the break.

5   Cut two pieces of fiberglass cloth large enough to overlap the break by about 1-1/2 inches. Cut only to the required length.

6   Mix the adhesive from the repair kit according to the instructions included with the kit, and apply a layer of the mixture approximately 1/8-inch thick on the backside of the panel. Overlap the break by at least 1-1/2 inches.

7   Apply one piece of fiberglass cloth to the adhesive and cover the cloth with additional adhesive. Apply a second piece of fiberglass cloth to the adhesive and immediately cover the cloth with additional adhesive in sufficient quantity to fill the weave.

8   Allow the repair to cure for 20 to 30 minutes at 60-degrees to 80-degrees F.

9   If necessary, trim the excess repair material at the edge.

10   Remove all of the paint film over and around the area(s) to be repaired. The repair material should not overlap the painted surface.

11   With a drill motor and a sanding disc (or a rotary file), cut a "V" along the break line approximately 1/2-inch wide. Remove all dust and loose particles from the repair area.

12   Mix and apply the repair material. Apply a light coat first over the damaged area; then continue applying material until it reaches a level slightly higher than the surrounding finish.

13   Cure the mixture for 20 to 30 minutes at 60-degrees to 80-degrees F.

14   Roughly establish the contour of the area being repaired with a body file. If low areas or pits remain, mix and apply additional adhesive.

15   Block sand the damaged area with sandpaper to establish the actual contour of the surrounding surface.

16   If desired, the repaired area can be temporarily protected with several light coats of primer. Because of the special paints and techniques required for flexible body panels, it is recommended that the vehicle be taken to a paint shop for completion of the body repair.

STEEL BODY PANELS

♦ **See photo sequence**

Repair of dents

17   When repairing dents, the first job is to pull the dent out until the affected area is as close as possible to its original shape. There is no point in trying to restore the original shape completely as the metal in the damaged area will have stretched on impact and cannot be restored to its original contours. It is better to bring the level of the dent up to a point that is about 1/8-inch below the level of the surrounding metal. In cases where the dent is very shallow, it is not worth trying to pull it out at all.

18   If the backside of the dent is accessible, it can be hammered out gently from behind using a soft-face hammer. While doing this, hold a block of wood firmly against the opposite side of the metal to absorb the hammer blows and prevent the metal from being stretched.

19   If the dent is in a section of the body which has double layers, or some other factor makes it inaccessible from behind, a different technique is required. Drill several small holes through the metal inside the damaged area, particularly in the deeper sections. Screw long, self-tapping screws into the holes just enough for them to get a good grip in the metal. Now pulling on the protruding heads of the screws with locking pliers can pull out the dent.

20   The next stage of repair is the removal of paint from the damaged area and from an inch or so of the surrounding metal. This is easily done with a wire brush or sanding disk in a drill motor, although it can be done just as effectively by hand with sandpaper. To complete the preparation for filling, score the surface of the bare metal with a screwdriver or the tang of a file or drill small holes in the affected area. This will provide a good grip for the filler material. To complete the repair, see the Section on filling and painting.

Repair of rust holes or gashes

21   Remove all paint from the affected area and from an inch or so of the surrounding metal using a sanding disk or wire brush mounted in a drill motor. If these are not available, a few sheets of sandpaper will do the job just as effectively.

22   With the paint removed, you will be able to determine the severity of the corrosion and decide whether to replace the whole panel, if possible, or repair the affected area. New body panels are not as expensive as most people think and it is often quicker to install a new panel than to repair large areas of rust.

23   Remove all trim pieces from the affected area except those which will act as a guide to the original shape of the damaged body, such as headlight shells, etc. Using metal snips or a hacksaw blade, remove all loose metal and any other metal that is badly affected by rust. Hammer the edges of the hole in to create a slight depression for the filler material.

24   Wire-brush the affected area to remove the powdery rust from the surface of the metal. If the back of the rusted area is accessible, treat it with rust inhibiting paint.

25   Before filling is done, block the hole in some way. This can be done with sheet metal riveted or screwed into place, or by stuffing the hole with wire mesh.

26   Once the hole is blocked off, the affected area can be filled and painted. See the following subsection on filling and painting.

These photos illustrate a method of repairing simple dents. They are intended to supplement Body repair - minor damage in this Chapter and should not be used as the sole instructions for body repair on these vehicles.

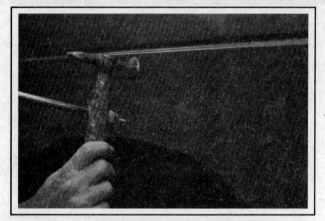

1 If you can't access the backside of the body panel to hammer out the dent, pull it out with a slide-hammer-type dent puller. Tap with a hammer near the edge of the dent to help 'pop' the metal back to its original shape, about 1/8-inch below the surface of the surrounding metal

2 Using coarse-grit sandpaper, remove the paint down to the bare metal. Clean the repair area with wax/silicone remover.

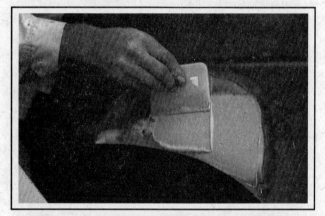

3 Following label instructions, mix up a batch of plastic filler and hardener, then quickly press it into the metal with a plastic applicator. Work the filler until it matches the original contour and is slightly above the surrounding metal

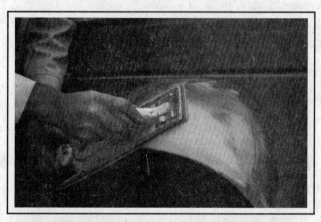

4 Let the filler harden until you can just dent it with your fingernail. File, then sand the filler down until it's smooth and even. Work down to finer grits of sandpaper - always using a board or block - ending up with 360 or 400 grit

5 When the area is smooth to the touch, clean the area and mask around it. Apply several layers of primer to the area. A professional-type spray gun is being used here, but aerosol spray primer works fine

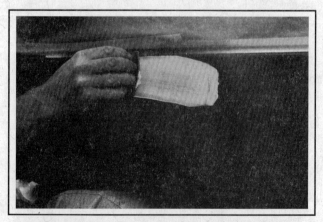

6 Fill imperfections or scratches with glazing compound. Sand with 360 or 400-grit and re-spray. Finish sand the primer with 600 grit, clean thoroughly, then apply the finish coat. Don't attempt to rub out or wax the repair area until the paint has dried completely (at least two weeks)

Filling and painting

27 Many types of body fillers are available, but generally speaking, body repair kits which contain filler paste and a tube of resin hardener are best for this type of repair work. A wide, flexible plastic or nylon applicator will be necessary for imparting a smooth and contoured finish to the surface of the filler material. Mix up a small amount of filler on a clean piece of wood or cardboard (use the hardener sparingly). Follow the manufacturer's instructions on the package, otherwise the filler will set incorrectly.

28 Using the applicator, apply the filler paste to the prepared area. Draw the applicator across the surface of the filler to achieve the desired contour and to level the filler surface. As soon as a contour that approximates the original one is achieved, stop working the paste. If you continue, the paste will begin to stick to the applicator. Continue to add thin layers of paste at 20-minute intervals until the level of the filler is just above the surrounding metal.

29 Once the filler has hardened, the excess can be removed with a body file. From then on, progressively finer grades of sandpaper should be used, starting with a 180-grit paper and finishing with 600-grit wet-or-dry paper. Always wrap the sandpaper around a flat rubber or wooden block, otherwise the surface of the filler will not be completely flat. During the sanding of the filler surface, the wet-or-dry paper should be periodically rinsed in water. This will ensure that a very smooth finish is produced in the final stage.

30 At this point, the repair area should be surrounded by a ring of bare metal, which in turn should be encircled by the finely feathered edge of good paint. Rinse the repair area with clean water until all of the dust produced by the sanding operation is gone.

31 Spray the entire area with a light coat of primer. This will reveal any imperfections in the surface of the filler. Repair the imperfections with fresh filler paste or glaze filler and once more smooth the surface with sandpaper. Repeat this spray-and-repair procedure until you are satisfied that the surface of the filler and the feathered edge of the paint are perfect. Rinse the area with clean water and allow it to dry completely.

32 The repair area is now ready for painting. Spray painting must be carried out in a warm, dry, windless and dust free atmosphere. These conditions can be created if you have access to a large indoor work area, but if you are forced to work in the open, you will have to pick the day very carefully. If you are working indoors, dousing the floor in the work area with water will help settle the dust that would otherwise be in the air. If the repair area is confined to one body panel, mask off the surrounding panels. This will help minimize the effects of a slight mismatch in paint color. Trim pieces such as chrome strips, door handles, etc., will also need to be masked off or removed. Use masking tape and several thickness of newspaper for the masking operations.

33 Before spraying, shake the paint can thoroughly, then spray a test area until the spray painting technique is mastered. Cover the repair area with a thick coat of primer. The thickness should be built up using several thin layers of primer rather than one thick one. Using 600-grit wet-or-dry sandpaper, rub down the surface of the primer until it is very smooth. While doing this, the work area should be thoroughly rinsed with water and the wet-or-dry sandpaper periodically rinsed as well. Allow the primer to dry before spraying additional coats.

34 Spray on the top coat, again building up the thickness by using several thin layers of paint. Begin spraying in the center of the repair area and then, using a circular motion, work out until the whole repair area and about two inches of the surrounding original paint is covered. Remove all masking material 10 to 15 minutes after spraying on the final coat of paint. Allow the new paint at least two weeks to harden, then use a very fine rubbing compound to blend the edges of the new paint into the existing paint. Finally, apply a coat of wax

4 Body repair - major damage

1 Major damage must be repaired by an auto body shop specifically equipped to perform body and frame repairs. These shops have the specialized equipment required to do the job properly.

2 If the damage is extensive, the frame must be checked for proper alignment or the vehicle's handling characteristics may be adversely affected and other components may wear at an accelerated rate.

3 Due to the fact that all of the major body components (hood, fenders, etc.) are separate and replaceable units, any seriously damaged components should be replaced rather than repaired. Sometimes the components can be found in a wrecking yard that specializes in used vehicle components, often at considerable savings over the cost of new parts.

5 Upholstery, carpets and vinyl trim - maintenance

UPHOLSTERY AND CARPETS

1 Every three months remove the floormats and clean the interior of the vehicle (more frequently if necessary). Use a stiff whiskbroom to brush the carpeting and loosen dirt and dust, then vacuum the upholstery and carpets thoroughly, especially along seams and crevices.

2 Dirt and stains can be removed from carpeting with basic household or automotive carpet shampoos available in spray cans. Follow the directions and vacuum again, then use a stiff brush to bring back the "nap" of the carpet.

3 Most interiors have cloth or vinyl upholstery, either of which can be cleaned and maintained with a number of material-specific cleaners or shampoos available in auto supply stores. Follow the directions on the product for usage, and always spot-test any upholstery cleaner on an inconspicuous area (bottom edge of a backseat cushion) to ensure that it doesn't cause a color shift in the material.

4 After cleaning, vinyl upholstery should be treated with a protectant.

➡ **Note: Make sure the protectant container indicates the product can be used on seats - some products may make a seat too slippery.**

✳ **CAUTION:**

Do not use protectant on vinyl-covered steering wheels.

5   Leather upholstery requires special care. It should be cleaned regularly with saddlesoap or leather cleaner. Never use alcohol, gasoline, nail polish remover or thinner to clean leather upholstery.

6   After cleaning, regularly treat leather upholstery with a leather conditioner, rubbed in with a soft cotton cloth. Never use car wax on leather upholstery.

7   In areas where the interior of the vehicle is subject to bright sunlight, cover leather seating areas of the seats with a sheet if the vehicle is to be left out for any length of time.

VINYL TRIM

8   Don't clean vinyl trim with detergents, caustic soap or petroleum-based cleaners. Plain soap and water works just fine, with a soft brush to clean dirt that may be ingrained. Wash the vinyl as frequently as the rest of the vehicle.

9   After cleaning, application of a high-quality rubber and vinyl protectant will help prevent oxidation and cracks. The protectant can also be applied to weather-stripping, vacuum lines and rubber hoses, which often fail as a result of chemical degradation, and to the tires.

6   Fastener and trim removal

▶ **Refer to illustration 6.4**

1   There is a variety of plastic fasteners used to hold trim panels, splash shields and other parts in place in addition to typical screws, nuts and bolts. Once you are familiar with them, they can usually be removed without too much difficulty.

2   The proper tools and approach can prevent added time and expense to a project by minimizing the number of broken fasteners and/or parts.

3   The following illustration shows various types of fasteners that are typically used on most vehicles and how to remove and install them (see illustration). Replacement fasteners are commonly found at most auto parts stores, if necessary.

4   Trim panels are typically made of plastic and their flexibility can

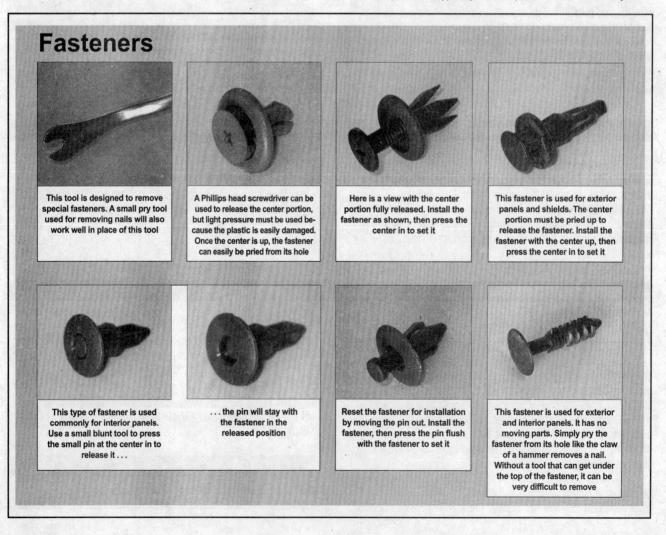

Fasteners

This tool is designed to remove special fasteners. A small pry tool used for removing nails will also work well in place of this tool

A Phillips head screwdriver can be used to release the center portion, but light pressure must be used because the plastic is easily damaged. Once the center is up, the fastener can easily be pried from its hole

Here is a view with the center portion fully released. Install the fastener as shown, then press the center in to set it

This fastener is used for exterior panels and shields. The center portion must be pried up to release the fastener. Install the fastener with the center up, then press the center in to set it

This type of fastener is used commonly for interior panels. Use a small blunt tool to press the small pin at the center in to release it . . .

. . . the pin will stay with the fastener in the released position

Reset the fastener for installation by moving the pin out. Install the fastener, then press the pin flush with the fastener to set it

This fastener is used for exterior and interior panels. It has no moving parts. Simply pry the fastener from its hole like the claw of a hammer removes a nail. Without a tool that can get under the top of the fastener, it can be very difficult to remove

help during removal. The key to their removal is to use a tool to pry the panel near its retainers to release it without damaging surrounding areas or breaking-off any retainers. The retainers will usually snap out of their designated slot or hole after force is applied to them. Stiff plastic tools designed for prying on trim panels are available at most auto parts stores (see illustration). Tools that are tapered and wrapped in protective tape, such as a screwdriver or small pry tool, are also very effective when used with care.

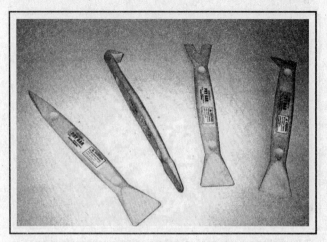

6.4 These small plastic pry tools are ideal for prying off trim panels

7   Hood - removal, installation and adjustment

➡ **Note: The hood is awkward to remove and install; at least two people should perform this procedure.**

REMOVAL AND INSTALLATION

▶ **Refer to illustrations 7.2 and 7.3**

1   Open the hood, then place blankets or pads over the fenders and cowl area of the body. This will protect the body and paint as the hood is lifted off.

2   Make marks around the hood hinge to ensure proper alignment during installation (see illustration).

3   Have an assistant support one side of the hood. Grasp the lower corner of the hood and use your shoulder to brace the hood (see illustra-

tion). Take turns removing the hinge-to-hood bolts and lift off the hood.

4   Installation is the reverse of removal. Align the hinge bolts with the marks made in Step 2.

ADJUSTMENT

▶ **Refer to illustrations 7.8a and 7.8b**

5   Fore-and-aft and side-to-side adjustment of the hood is done by moving the hinges after loosening the hinge-to-body bolts.

6   Loosen the bolts and move the hood into correct alignment. Move it only a little at a time. Tighten the hinge bolts and carefully lower the hood to check the position.

7   The hood can also be adjusted vertically so that it's flush with the fenders.

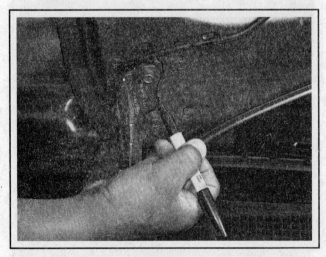

7.2 Draw alignment marks around the hood hinges to ensure proper alignment of the hood when it's reinstalled

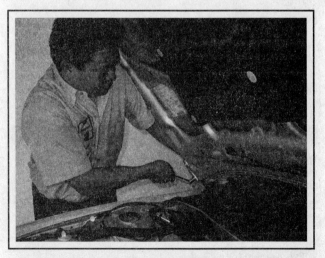

7.3 Support the hood with your shoulder while removing the hood bolts

7.8a There are two vertical height adjustment cushions on the underside of the hood . . .

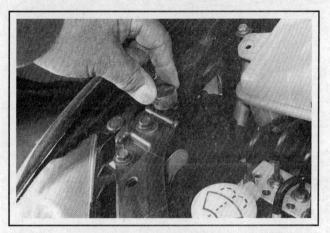

7.8b . . . and two on small brackets adjacent to the front fenders

8   Turn each cushion clockwise to lower the hood or counterclockwise to raise the hood (see illustrations).

9   The hood latch assembly, as well as the hinges, should be periodically lubricated with white, lithium-base grease to prevent binding and wear.

8   Hood latch and release cable - removal and installation

8.2 Hood latch mounting bolts (1) and front airbag crash sensor (2)

WARNING:

The models covered by this manual are equipped with Supplemental Restraint Systems (SRS), more commonly known as airbags. Always disable the airbag system before working in the vicinity of any airbag system component to avoid the possibility of accidental deployment of the airbag, which could cause personal injury (see Chapter 12).

HOOD LATCH

▶ **Refer to illustration 8.2**

1   Disconnect the cable from the negative battery terminal (see Chapter 5).

2   Scribe a line around the latch to aid alignment when installing, then remove the retaining bolts securing the hood latch to the radiator support (see illustration). Remove the latch.

CAUTION:

The front airbag crash sensor is mounted with the hood latch mounting bolt; do not strike or drop the sensor, as damage or airbag deployment may result (see Chapter 12).

3   Lift the cable from the bracket to release it from the latch assembly, then disengage the cable end plug from the latch (see illustration 8.10b).

4   Installation is the reverse of removal.

RELEASE CABLE

▶ **Refer to illustrations 8.10a and 8.10b**

5   Working in the engine compartment, remove the hood latch and disconnect the hood release cable from the latch (see Steps 1 through 3).

6   Remove the front bumper cover (see Section 9).

7   Remove the headlight housing (see Chapter 12).

8   Loosen the wheel lug nuts. Raise the vehicle and place it securely

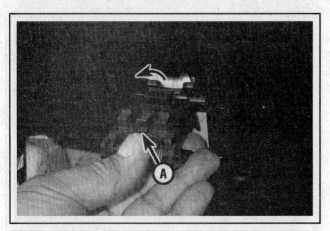

8.10a Depress the locking tab (A), then remove the release handle from the instrument panel

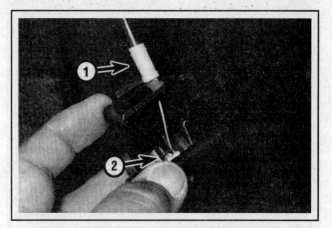

8.10b Hood release cable retainer (1) and end plug (2)

on jackstands. Remove the left front wheel. Remove the inner fender splash shield (see Section 10).

9   Detach the release cable clips from the fender and the wiring harness.

10   Working inside the vehicle, pull the release handle down, then

use a small screwdriver to press the locking tab down. With the tab released, slide the handle up and out of the instrument panel (see illustrations). Disengage the release cable from the release handle and pull the release cable through the firewall.

11   Installation is the reverse of removal.

9   Bumper covers - removal and installation

➡ **Note: Refer to Section 6 for fastener and trim removal.**

FRONT BUMPER COVER

▶ **Refer to illustrations 9.3a, 9.3b, 9.4 and 9.5**

1   Disconnect the cable from the negative battery terminal (see Chapter 5).

2   Loosen the front wheel lug nuts, raise the vehicle and support it securely on jackstands. Remove the front wheels.

3   Remove the splash shield mounting fasteners (see illustrations) and remove the splash shields.

4   Remove the bumper cover upper mounting fasteners from the radiator support (see illustration).

➡ **Note: On 2009 and later models, the rubber hood stops must be removed.**

9.3a Inner fender/splash shield-to-bumper cover fastener locations (2008 and earlier models shown, later models similar)

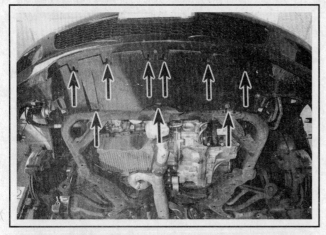

9.3b Lower splash shield-to-bumper cover fastener locations (2008 and earlier models shown, later models similar)

9.4 Bumper cover upper mounting fastener locations

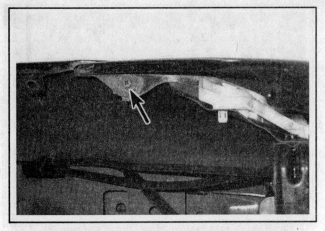

9.5 Bumper cover-to-fender fastener location (right side shown, left side identical)

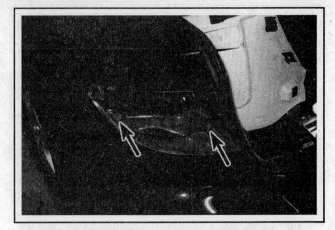

9.11 Rear bumper cover, upper corner fastener locations (left corner shown)

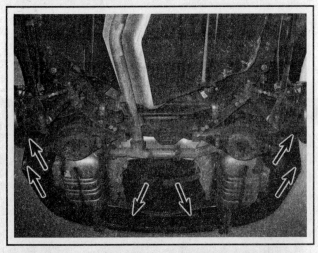

9.13a Rear wheel well splash shield pin-type retainers and rear bumper cover lower mounting fasteners

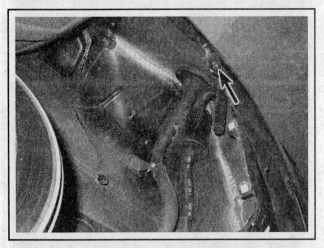

9.13b Rear bumper cover, corner mounting screw location

5 Pull the inner fenderwell back and remove the bumper cover-to-fender mounting fastener (see illustration).

6 Disconnect the electrical connectors to the marker lights and fog lamps, if equipped.

7 Disengage the bumper cover mounting tabs along the upper rear edges of the bumper cover from their corresponding slots in the lower edge of the front fenders by pulling the bumper cover outwards, starting from the fender side and working towards the middle of the cover.

8 Using a flashlight, perform a final inspection and verify that the bumper cover is completely detached, all electrical connectors are disconnected and all wiring harnesses are safely out of the way.

9 With the aid of an assistant, remove the front bumper cover.

10 Installation is the reverse of removal.

REAR BUMPER COVER

▶ **Refer to illustrations 9.11, 9.13a and 9.13b**

11 Remove the taillight housing assemblies (see Chapter 12) and remove the bumper cover mounting fasteners (see illustration).

12 Loosen the rear wheel lug nuts, raise the vehicle and support it securely on jackstands. Remove the rear wheels.

13 Remove the mounting fasteners from the underside of the rear bumper cover and the rear part of the wheel wells (see illustrations).

14 Using a flashlight, do a final inspection and verify that the bumper cover is completely detached, all electrical connectors are disconnected and all wiring harnesses are safely out of the way.

15 With the aid of an assistant, remove the rear bumper cover.

➡ **Note: On 2009 and later models, the bumper cover ends at the fenderwell must be pulled outwards to disengage the mounting clips from the bracket.**

16 Installation is the reverse of removal. Get help from an assistant when putting the bumper cover back into position.

10 Front fender - removal and installation

▶ Refer to illustrations 10.3, 10.5, 10.6, 10.7, 10.8, 10.9a
and 10.9b

➡ Note: Refer to Section 6 for fastener and trim removal.

   1 Remove the headlight housing (see Chapter 12).
   2 Loosen the front wheel lug nuts. Raise the vehicle, support it
securely on jackstands and remove the front wheel.
   3 Remove the fasteners that secure the inner fender splash shield
(see illustration) and remove the splash shield.
   4 Remove the front bumper cover (see Section 9).
   5 Disconnect the electrical connector from the front sidemarker
light, remove the front bracket fasteners (see illustration) and remove
the bumper cover mounting bracket.
   6 Remove the two lower fender bolts (see illustration).

➡ Note: On 2009 and later models, the lower bolts are under a
side molding; remove the plastic push-pins and pry the molding
from the lower end of the fender to access the bolts.

   7 Carefully pry back the rocker panel to disconnect the rocker
panel-to-fender fasteners (see illustration).

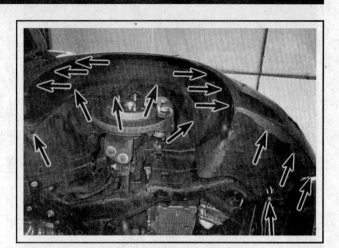

10.3 Inner fender splash shield pin-type fasteners

   8 Open the front door, then remove the upper rear fender bolt from
inside the doorjamb (see illustration).

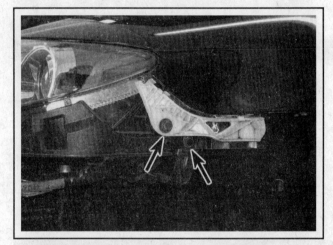

10.5 Bumper cover mounting bracket and fender front
mounting bolt

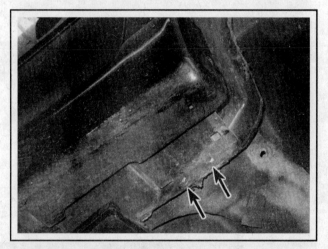

10.6 Front fender lower bolts

10.7 Carefully pry the rocker panel back to release the
mounting clips

10.8 Upper rear fender bolt (inside door opening)

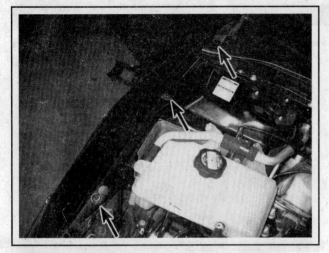

10.9a Front fender upper mounting bolts

10.9b Inner rear fender bolt

9 Remove the upper fender bolts and the inner rear fender bolt (see illustrations), then lift off the fender. It's a good idea to have an assistant support the fender while it's being moved away from the vehicle to pre-vent damage to the surrounding body panels.

10 Installation is the reverse of removal. Check the alignment of the fender to the hood and front edge of the door before tightening the bolts.

11 Radiator grille - removal and installation

2008 AND EARLIER MODELS

1 Remove the bumper cover upper fasteners (see illustration 9.4).
2 Pull the grille forward slightly and remove the fasteners on the back side of the grille.
3 Press the clips at the bottom of the grille down and pull the grille outwards.
4 Installation is the reverse of removal.

2009 AND LATER MODELS

5 Remove the front bumper cover (see Section 9).
6 Remove the grille-to-bumper cover fasteners and remove the grille.
7 Installation is the reverse of removal.

12 Cowl panels - removal and installation

12.2 Remove these screws to remove the trim

➡ **Note: Refer to Section 6 for fastener and trim removal techniques.**

UPPER COWL PANEL

❖ **Refer to illustrations 12.2 and 12.3**

1 Remove the wiper arms (see Chapter 12, Section 18).
2 Two small trim pieces fill the gap between the windshield and the front fenders. Both of them must be removed before you can remove the upper cowl panel. Remove the two screws (see illustration) from each trim piece and remove the trim.

3   Remove the screws, pin-type retainers and any retainer clips from the upper cowl panel (see illustration).

➡ **Note: On 2009 and later models, the upper panel is one piece, with one end locked on the end of the windshield and the other end held in place by plastic pin-type retainers.**

4   Remove the upper cowl panel.
5   Installation is the reverse of removal.

LOWER COWL PANEL

➧ **Refer to illustration 12.8**

6   Remove the upper cowl panel (see Steps 1 through 4).

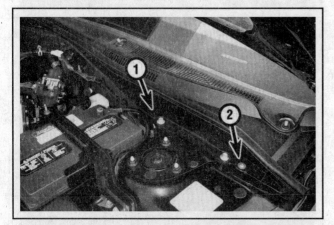

12.3 Upper cowl panel details (left side shown, right side similar):

1   Screws   *2   Pin-type retainers*

7   Remove the windshield wiper motor and linkage assembly (see Chapter 12, Section 18).

8   Remove the lower cowl panel support bracket mounting bolts and bracket (see illustration).

9   Remove the lower cowl panel mounting bolts (see illustration 12.8) and remove the lower cowl panel.

10 Installation is the reverse of removal.

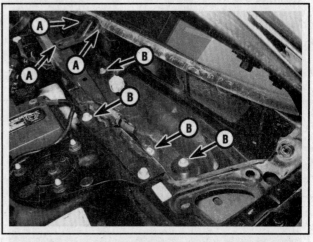

12.8 Remove the cowl panel support bracket mounting bolts (A) and the lower cowl panel mounting bolts (B). Remove the cowl panel (left side shown, right side similar)

13 Door and liftgate trim panels - removal and installation

⁂ CAUTION:

Wear gloves when working inside the door openings to protect against sharp metal edges.

➡ **Note: Refer to Section 6 for fastener and trim removal.**

1   Disconnect the cable from the negative battery terminal (see Chapter 5).

FRONT AND REAR DOORS

➧ **Refer to illustrations 13.2a, 13.2b, 13.3, 13.4a, 13.4b and 13.5**

2   Remove the trim cover from the inside door handle bezel and remove the screw from the bezel (see illustration). Pull out the bezel and disconnect the electrical connector (see illustration).

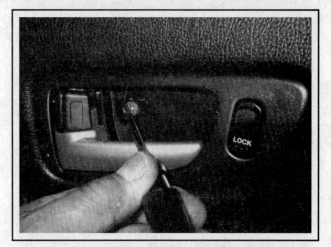

13.2a Remove the trim cover from the inside door handle and remove the screw

13.2b Pull out the inside door handle bezel and disconnect the electrical connector

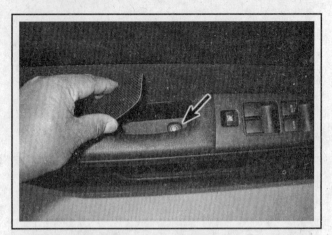

13.3 Armrest mounting fastener location

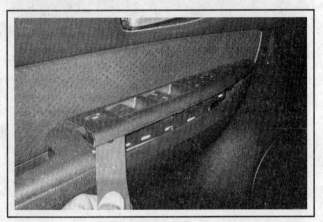

13.4a Pry the back end of the power window switch (the front end has a mounting clip that hooks under the armrest)

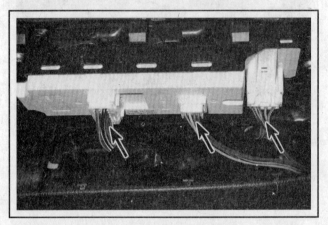

13.4b Disconnect the electrical connectors to the switch

3   Remove the small trim panel inside the armrest, then remove the screw that secures the larger trim panel to the armrest (see illustration).

4   Carefully pry the back end of the power window switch, lift up the panel and disconnect the electrical connectors from the power window switch (see illustrations).

5   To detach the door trim panel from its mounting clips, work your way around the outside of the trim panel, carefully prying loose the clips with a suitable door trim removal tool (see illustration), then pull off the panel and disconnect any electrical connectors.

6   Installation is the reverse of removal.

LIFTGATE

▶ **Refer to illustrations 13.8a, 13.8b and 13.10**

7   Open the liftgate.

8   Carefully pry out the clips and remove the upper trim panels and side trim panels from the back door (see illustrations).

9   Carefully pry out the recess for the handle at the bottom of the

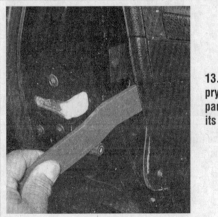

13.5 Carefully pry the door trim panel loose from its mounting clips

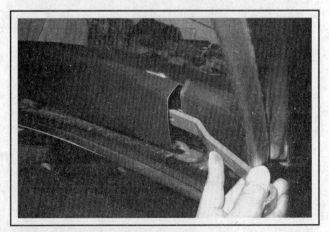

13.8a Carefully pry out the upper trim panel

13.8b Rotate the strap hangers on the side trim panels to the 3 o'clock position, and pry the panels off the liftgate

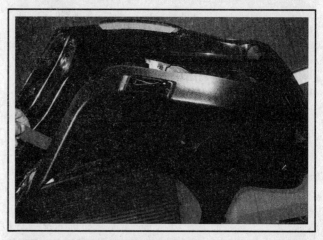

13.10 Work your way around the edges of the trim panel and carefully pry loose the clips

liftgate, then remove the plastic fasteners at each end of the liftgate panel.

10 Detach the liftgate trim panel from its mounting clips, working your way around the edges of the trim panel, carefully prying loose the clips with a suitable door trim removal tool (see illustration), then pull off the panel.

11 Prior to installation of the liftgate trim panel, be sure to reinstall any clips in the panel which may have come out during removal.

12 Press the panel(s) into place until the clips are seated, then install the recess into the bottom of the liftgate.

13 The remainder of installation is the reverse of removal.

14 Door - removal, installation and adjustment

❉❉ WARNING:

The models covered by this manual are equipped with Supplemental Restraint Systems (SRS), more commonly known as airbags. Always disable the airbag system before working in the vicinity of any airbag system component to avoid the possibility of accidental deployment of the airbag, which could cause personal injury (see Chapter 12).

REMOVAL AND INSTALLATION

▶ **Refer to illustrations 14.4 and 14.5**

➡ **Note: The door is heavy and somewhat awkward to remove and install - at least two people should perform this procedure.**

➡ **Note: This procedure applies to front and rear doors.**

1 Raise the window completely in the door.

2 Disconnect the cable from the negative battery terminal (see Chapter 5).

3 Open the door all the way and support it with a jack or blocks covered with rags to prevent damaging the outer surface.

4 Pull off the rubber conduit (see illustration) that protects the door's wiring harness, then disconnect the connector.

5 Remove the door stop strut mounting bolt (see illustration).

14.4 Door assembly details:

1   *Wiring harness rubber conduit*
2   *Door hinge mounting bolts*

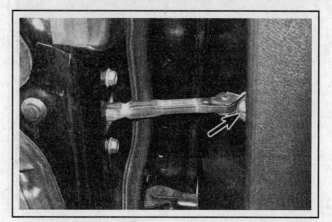

14.5 Door stop strut bolt

6 Mark around the door hinges with a pen or a scribe to facilitate realignment during reassembly.

7 With an assistant holding the door to steady it, remove the hinge-to-door bolts (see illustration 14.4) and lift off the door.

➡ **Note: On some models, it may be necessary to remove the front fender to gain access to the upper hinge (see Chapter 10).**

8 Installation is the reverse of removal.

ADJUSTMENT

▶ **Refer to illustration 14.12**

9 Correct door-to-body alignment is a critical part of a well-functioning door assembly. First check the door hinge pins for excessive play. Fully open the door and lift up and down on the door without lifting the body. If a door has 1/16-inch or more excessive play, replace the hinges.

10 If you need to adjust or replace the hinges for a front door, remove the front fender (see Section 10).

11 Make door-to-body alignment adjustments by loosening the hinge-to-body bolts or hinge-to-door bolts and moving the door. When body alignment is correct, the top of each door is parallel with the roof section, the front door is flush with the fender, the rear door is flush with the rear quarter panel and the bottom of each door is aligned with the lower rocker panel. If you're unable to adjust the door correctly, you might be able to obtain body alignment shims that are inserted behind the hinges to correctly align the door.

14.12 Adjust the door latch striker by loosening the mounting screws and gently tapping the striker in the desired direction

12 To adjust the door-closed position, scribe a line or mark around the striker plate to provide a reference point, then verify that the door latch is contacting the center of the striker. If not, adjust the up and down position first. To move the striker, tap it gently with a small hammer (see illustration).

13 Once the door latch is contacting the center of the striker, adjust the latch striker sideways position, so that the door panel is flush with the center pillar or rear quarter panel and provides positive engagement with the latch mechanism.

15 Door latch, lock cylinder and handles - removal and installation

1 Remove the door window glass (see Section 16).

2 Disconnect the cable from the negative battery terminal (see Chapter 5).

3 Remove the door trim panel (see Section 13).

OUTSIDE DOOR HANDLE

▶ **Refer to illustrations 15.4, 15.5, 15.6, 15.7 and 15.8**

4 Remove the outside handle access hole cover and mounting screw (see illustration).

➡ **Note: On 2009 and later models, there is a stop that prevents the screw from being removed.**

5 Rotate the latch rod and lock rod clips back and disconnect the rods from the outer handle (see illustration).

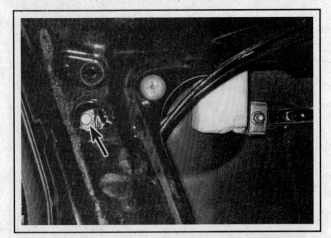

15.4 Outside door handle cover retaining screw location (trim cap removed)

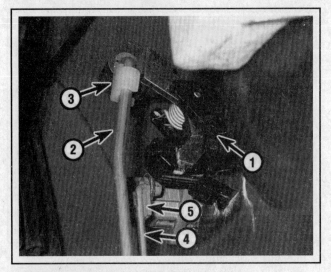

15.5 Outside door handle details

1 Outside door handle
2 Door latch rod
3 Door latch rod mounting clip
4 Door lock rod
5 Door lock rod mounting clip

15.6 Remove the outside door handle cover

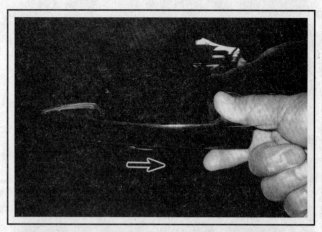

15.7 To disengage the outside door handle lever from the handle reinforcement inside the door, pull it out of the door and to the rear

6   Pull the handle outwards and on 2008 and earlier models, remove the cover from the outside handle (see illustration).
7   Pull the handle out and to the rear to disengage it from the handle reinforcement inside the door (see illustration).
8   Remove the outside handle support mounting bolt from inside the door and remove the support (see illustration).
9   Remove and inspect the outside door handle seals. If the seals are cracked, torn or otherwise deteriorated, replace them.
10 Installation is the reverse of removal.

INSIDE DOOR HANDLE

▶ **Refer to illustrations 15.11 and 15.12**

11 Pull the locking tab back, then slide the shaft up (see illustration) and detach the handle assembly from the door module.
12 Disconnect the door lock cable from the inside door handle cable (see illustration).
13 Installation is the reverse of removal.

DOOR LATCH

▶ **Refer to illustrations 15.16 and 15.19**

14 Remove the outside door handle (see Steps 4 through 9).

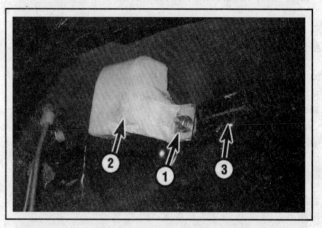

15.8 Outside door handle reinforcement details

1   Reinforcement mounting nut   3   Door handle reinforcement
2   Sound pad

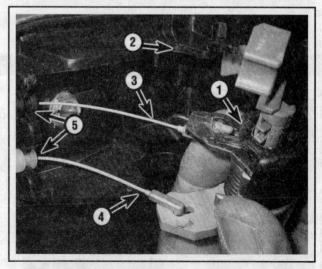

15.12 Inside door handle details

1   Inside door handle   4   Inside door handle cable
2   Door module   5   Cable mounting bracket
3   Door lock cable

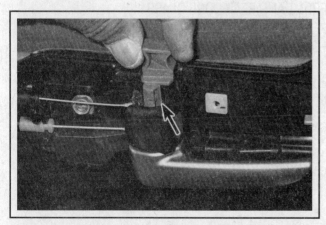

15.11 Pull the tab outwards and pull the shaft up

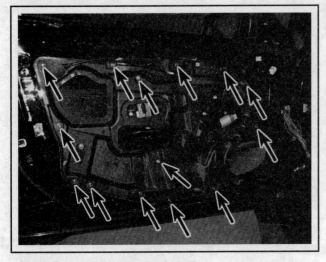

15.16 Door module mounting fasteners

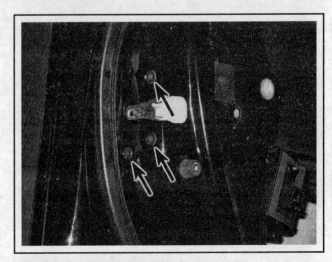

15.19 Door latch mounting fasteners

15 Disconnect the inside door handle and cables (see Steps 11 and 12).

16 Remove the door module mounting screws (see illustration) and remove the module.

➡ **Note: The door module will have the power window motor and window regulator attached.**

17 Disconnect the harness connector from the latch lock actuator (if not done when the door module was removed).

18 Disconnect the lock rod and latch rod from the door latch (see illustration 15.5).

19 Remove the door latch mounting screws and guide the latch assembly from the door (see illustration).

20 Installation is the reverse of removal.

DOOR LOCK CYLINDER

2008 and earlier models

21 Remove the door latch (see Steps 14 through 19).

22 Rotate the lock cylinder counterclockwise until the tab fits into the notch opening.

23 Pull the key lock cylinder out through the door

24 Installation is otherwise the reverse of removal.

2009 and later models

25 Remove the outside door handle (see Steps 4 through 9).

26 Remove the access plug from the end of the door.

27 Working from the inside of the door, remove the key lock rod clip and disconnect the rod from the key cylinder.

28 Working from the end of the door, loosen the screw through the access hole.

➡ **Note: There is a stop that prevents the screw from being removed.**

29 Press the release tab on the inside of the door handle and remove the lock cylinder from the door.

30 Separate the exterior trim cap from the key lock cylinder using a small screwdriver to disengage the tabs and separate the lock cylinder.

31 Installation is otherwise the reverse of removal.

16 Door window glass - removal and installation

16.5 Remove the access cover(s), then remove the window glass-to-regulator mounting bolts

FRONT AND REAR DOOR GLASS

▶ **Refer to illustration 16.5**

1 Lower the window until! the top of the glass, measured at the back of the window is 8.3 inches (2008 and earlier models) or 3.1 inches (2009 and later models) from the top of the door panel.

2 Disconnect the cable from the negative battery terminal (see Chapter 5).

3 Remove the door trim panel (see Section 13).

4 On 2009 and later models, remove the front door speaker (see Chapter 12).

5 Remove the access hole cover(s) (see illustration).

➡ **Note: 2009 and later models have two small access hole covers.**

6   Working through the access holes, remove the window mounting screws. Lift the door glass up, then rotate the front of the window down and tilt it outward to remove it through the window opening.

➡ **Note: If the door window regulator motor is broken or disconnected, you'll have to remove it (see Section 17) and move the window glass manually.**

7   Installation is the reverse of removal. Work through the speaker access hole to align the glass edge with the glass run channel.

LIFTGATE GLASS

8   Replacement of the liftgate glass requires the use of special fast-setting adhesive/caulk materials and some specialized tools and techniques. These operations should be left to a dealer service department or a shop specializing in glass work.

INITIALIZATION PROCEDURE

9   Turn the ignition key to ON.

10   Press the switch of each window and fully open the window glass.

11   Pull the switch of each window to the UP position to close the window glass and hold the power window control switch until the window glass stalls for two seconds at the top of its travel, then release the switch.

12   Test the operation of the power window by activating the power window switch in the one-touch up-mode. If the window doesn't operate correctly, repeat this procedure.

---

17   Door window regulator and motor - removal and installation

POWER WINDOW MOTOR

▶ **Refer to illustrations 17.4 and 17.5**

1   Disconnect the cable from the negative battery terminal (see Chapter 5).

2   Remove the door trim panel (see Section 13).

3   Disconnect the electrical connector from the regulator motor.

4   Secure the window in place with tape (see illustration).

5   Remove the three regulator motor mounting screws (see illustration), then remove the motor.

6   Installation is the reverse of removal.

REGULATOR ASSEMBLY

▶ **Refer to illustrations 17.11, 17.12 and 17.14**

7   Remove the door trim panel (see Section 13).

8   Remove the front door speaker (see Chapter 12, Section 11).

9   Remove the door glass (see Section 16).

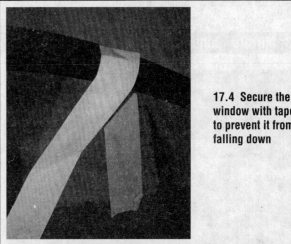

17.4 Secure the window with tape to prevent it from falling down

10   If equipped with power windows, remove the power window motor (see Steps 1 through 5).

11   Remove the regulator mounting nuts (see illustration).

17.5 Power window regulator motor mounting screws

17.11 Widow regulator mounting nut locations

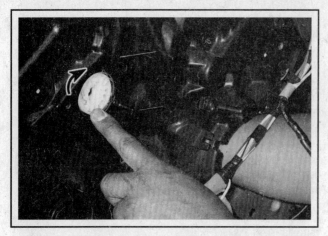

17.12 Rotate the regulator drum hub clockwise to disengage the locking tabs from the door module

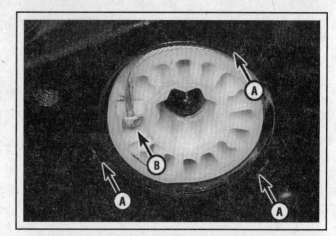

17.14 Lock the regulator drum hub into the door module (A), making sure the cable (B) does not un-spool

12 Insert one hand through the speaker hole, rotate the window regulator drum housing clockwise from the inside and disconnect the tabs from the door module (see illustration).
13 Remove the window regulator through the speaker hole.
14 Install the regulator through the speaker hole and lock the drum

housing into the door module (see illustration). Make sure the cable does not un-spool from the drum housing when installing the regulator assembly.
15 Tighten the regulator mounting nuts/bolts securely.
16 The remainder of installation is the reverse of removal.

18 Mirrors - removal and installation

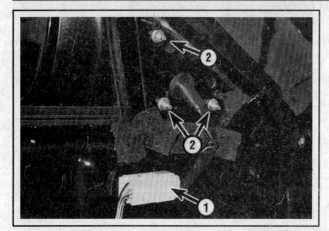

18.3 Mirror electrical connector (1) and mounting fasteners (2)

▶ Refer to illustration 18.3

1 Remove the door trim panel (see Section 13).
2 Remove the front door mirror trim panel. If the trim panel is equipped with a speaker, disconnect the speaker electrical connector (see Chapter 12).
3 Disconnect the electrical connector from the mirror (see illustration).
4 Remove the mirror mounting fasteners and remove the mirror (see illustration 18.3).
5 Installation is the reverse of removal.

19 Trunk lid - removal and installation

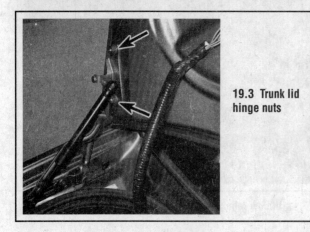

19.3 Trunk lid hinge nuts

TRUNK LID

▶ Refer to illustration 19.3

➡ Note: The trunk lid is heavy and awkward to remove and install - at least two people should perform this procedure.

1 Disconnect the cable from the negative battery terminal (see Chapter 5).
2 Follow the wiring harness rubber conduit from the trunk lid to the body. From inside the trunk disconnect the harness connector and remove the conduit and harness from the body.
3 With an assistant helping you to support the trunk lid, remove the nuts from the trunk lid hinges (see illustration) and remove the trunk lid.
4 Installation is the reverse of removal.

TRUNK LID SUPPORT STRUTS

▶ **Refer to illustration 19.5**

5   Using a screwdriver, pry the support struts stay bands (see illustration).

6   Have an assistant hold the trunk lid, then pull the support strut(s) from the ball stud at each end of the strut.

7   Installation is the reverse of removal.

➡ **Note: If the old support strut is being reused, snap the stay bands back on to the ends of the support struts.**

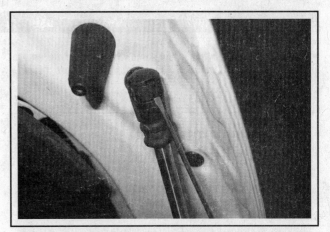

19.5 Use a small screwdriver to pry up the stay band at each strut end, just enough to remove the strut from the ballstud

20 Trunk lid key lock cylinder and latch - removal and installation

▶ **Refer to illustrations 20.2, 20.3 and 20.8**

1   Disconnect the cable from the negative battery terminal (see Chapter 5).

2   Remove the trunk lid trim panel (see illustration).

KEY LOCK CYLINDER

3   Rotate the trunk lid actuator rod mounting clip and disconnect the rod from the trunk lid key lock cylinder assembly (see illustration).

4   Disconnect the electrical connector from the lock cylinder (if equipped).

5   Remove the mounting nuts and maneuver the lock cylinder out from the trunk lid.

6   Installation is the reverse of removal.

20.2 Trunk lid trim panel pin-type fasteners

LATCH

7   Disconnect the actuator rod from the trunk lid lock cylinder (see illustration 20.3).

8   Disconnect the electrical connector from the trunk lid latch (see illustration).

9   Remove the latch mounting bolts and remove the latch.

10 Installation is the reverse of removal.

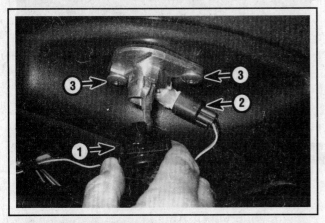

20.3 Trunk lid lock cylinder details:

1   *Trunk lid latch actuator cable*
2   *Lock cylinder electrical connector*
3   *Lock cylinder mounting rivets*

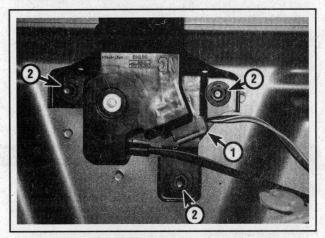

20.8 Trunk lid latch details:

1   *Latch electrical connector*
2   *Latch mounting nuts*

21 Liftgate - removal, installation and adjustment

➡ **Note: The liftgate is heavy and somewhat awkward to remove and install - at least two people should perform this procedure.**

REMOVAL AND INSTALLATION

▶ **Refer to illustrations 21.4 and 21.6**

1 Disconnect the cable from the negative battery terminal (see Chapter 5).

2 Open the liftgate all the way and support it.

3 Using a trim tool, carefully pry out the liftgate trim panels (see Section 13).

4 Press the harness connector for the liftgate in, then down to free the connector (see illustration). Disconnect the harness connector, ground wire and rear window defogger connector, then remove the rubber grommet from the liftgate.

5 Mark around the door hinges with a pen or a scribe to facilitate realignment during reassembly.

6 With an assistant holding the door, pry off the support struts stay bands (see illustration), then pull the support strut(s) from the ball stud at each end of the strut.

7 Remove the hinge-to-liftgate bolts and lift off the door.

➡ **Note: Draw a reference line around the hinges before removing the bolts.**

8 Installation is the reverse of removal.

ADJUSTMENT

9 Having proper liftgate-to-body alignment is a critical part of a well-functioning door assembly. Check the liftgate hinge pins for excessive play. Fully open the liftgate and lift up and down on the door without lifting the body. If a door has 1/16-inch or more excessive play, the hinges should be replaced.

10 Liftgate-to-body alignment adjustments are made by loosening the hinge-to-body bolts or hinge-to-door bolts and moving the door. Proper body alignment is achieved when the top of the door is parallel with the roof section and the sides of the door are flush with the rear quarter panels and the bottom of the door is aligned with the lower door sill. If these goals can't be reached by adjusting the hinge-to-body or hinge-to-door bolts, body alignment shims may have to be purchased and inserted behind the hinges to achieve correct alignment.

11 To adjust the door-closed position, scribe a line or mark around the striker plate to provide a reference point, then check that the door latch is contacting the center of the latch striker. If not, adjust the up and down position first.

12 Adjust the latch striker sideways position, so that the door panel is flush with the rear quarter panel and provides positive engagement with the latch mechanism.

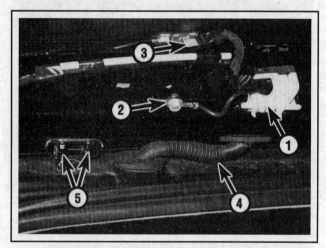

21.4 Liftgate details (left side shown):

1 Harness connector bracket
2 Ground wire retaining bolt
3 Rear window defroster connection
4 Rubber grommet
5 Liftgate mounting bolts

21.6 Remove the strut bands from the strut

22 Liftgate latch and outside handle - removal and installation

LIFTGATE LATCH

▶ **Refer to illustration 22.5**

1 Disconnect the cable from the negative battery terminal (see Chapter 5).

2 Open the liftgate and remove the liftgate trim panel (see Section 13).

3 Working through the large access hole, disengage the outside door handle-to-latch/lock rod. The door latch/lock rod is attached a by plastic clip; the clip can be removed by unsnapping the portion engaging the connecting rod, then pulling the rod out of its locating hole.

4   Disconnect the electrical connectors at the latch.
5   Remove the screws securing the latch to the liftgate (see illustration). Remove the latch assembly through the door opening.
6   Installation is the reverse of removal.

LIFTGATE OUTSIDE HANDLE

7   Open the liftgate and remove the liftgate trim panel (see Section 13).
8   Disconnect the outside door handle-to-latch/lock rod.
9   Remove the rear finish trim nuts and trim.
10 Remove the handle mounting nuts and handle from the liftgate.
11 The remainder of installation is the reverse of removal.

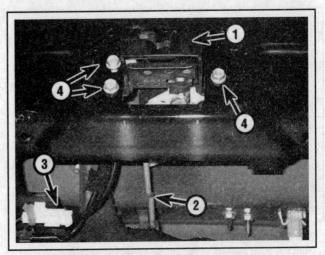

22.5 Liftgate latch details:

1   Liftgate latch
2   Liftgate latch/lock rod
3   Electrical connector
4   Liftgate latch mounting bolts

23 Center console - removal and installation

▶ **Refer to illustrations 23.2, 23.4, 23.5, 23.7, 23.8a, 23.8b and 23.9**

1   Disconnect the cable from the negative battery terminal (see Chapter 5).
2   Using a trim removal tool, carefully pry off the center trim panel from the console (see illustration).
3   Unscrew the shift knob from the shift lever.
4   Using a trim removal tool, carefully pry off the shift indicator panel or boot panel from the console (see illustration) and disconnect any electrical connectors.
5   Adjust the seats to access and remove the two console fasteners from the sides (see illustration), then slide the seats all the way rearward.
6   On 2009 and later models, pry the rear of the console out and remove the two mounting bolts.

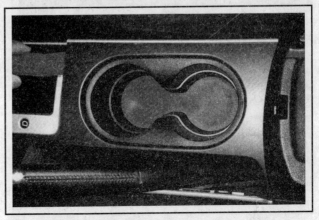

23.2 Carefully pry off the center trim panel from the console

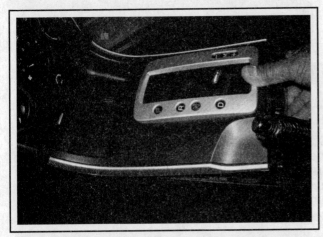

23.4 Carefully pry off the shift indicator panel from the console

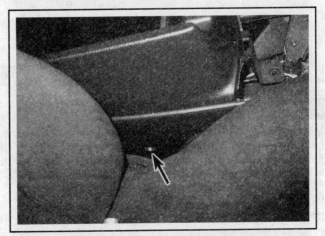

23.5 Console side fastener location (right side shown, left side similar)

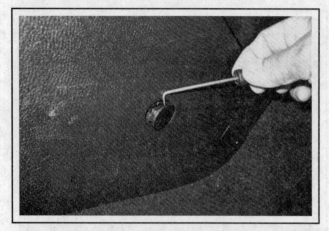

23.7 Remove the fastener trim cap and remove the fastener from the front corners of the console (right side shown, left side similar)

23.8a Front mounting screw locations

7   Remove the fastener trim caps and remove the fasteners from the upper forward corners of the console (see illustration).

8   Remove the screws from the center and front of the console (see illustrations).

9   Open the arm rest at the rear of the console, and remove the liner and mounting fasteners (see illustration).

10 Lift up the console and disconnect all electrical connectors from the console.

11 Remove the center console.

12 Installation is the reverse of removal.

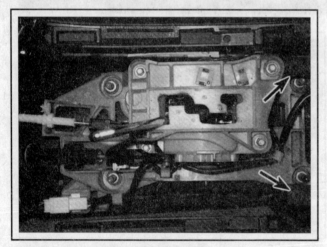

23.8b Center mounting screw locations

23.9 Remove the liner and mounting fasteners

24 Dashboard trim panels - removal and installation

⁕⁕⁕ **WARNING:**

Models covered by this manual are equipped with a Supplemental Restraint System (SRS), more commonly known as airbags. Always disable the airbag system before working in the vicinity of any airbag system component to avoid the possibility of accidental deployment of the airbag, which could cause personal injury (see Chapter 12).

➡ **Note: Refer to Section 6 for fastener and trim removal.**

1   Disconnect the cable from the negative battery terminal (see Chapter 5). Removing various dashboard trim panels provides access to electrical/electronic components such as the instrument cluster, the audio unit, the heater and air conditioning control unit and various instrument panel-mounted switches. To remove the entire instrument panel, all of the trim panels must be removed to access the instrument panel mounting bolts.

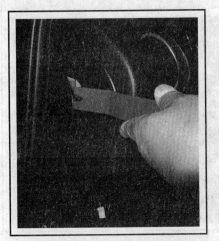

24.2 Pry off the end trim panel

24.5a Remove the instrument cluster trim panel mounting screws

24.5b Rotate the cluster down and out to remove it from the instrument panel

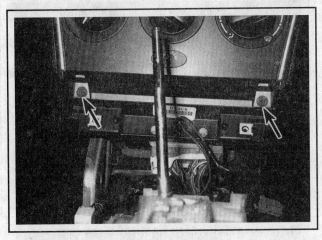

24.12 Remove the center trim panel screws

24.13 Remove the dials and the two mounting screws

LEFT OR RIGHT DASHBOARD END TRIM PANELS

▶ **Refer to illustration 24.2**

2   Carefully pry off the end trim panel (see illustration).
3   Installation is the reverse of removal.

INSTRUMENT CLUSTER TRIM PANEL

▶ **Refer to illustrations 24.5a and 24.5b**

4   Remove the steering column covers (see Section 25). On 2009 and later models, remove the knee bolster trim panel (see Steps 29 through 33).
5   Remove the instrument cluster trim panel mounting screws (see illustrations).
6   Pull the cluster trim panel to the rear to disengage the two retaining clips located at the lower corners of the trim panel.
7   Installation is the reverse of removal. Make sure that the two lower retaining clips snap into place before installing the two upper screws.

INSTRUMENT CLUSTER HOOD PANEL (2009 AND LATER MODELS)

8   To detach the instrument cluster hood panel from its mounting clips, work your way around the outside of the hood panel, carefully prying loose the clips with a suitable trim removal tool. Pull the panel forward to disconnect the rubber strip to the upper steering column cover and remove the hood panel.
9   Installation is the reverse of removal.

CENTER TRIM PANEL

2008 and earlier models

▶ **Refer to illustrations 24.12, 24.13, 24.14 and 24.15**

10 Remove the glove box (see Steps 35 and 36).
11 Remove the center console (see Section 23).
12 Remove the center trim panel mounting screws (see illustration).
13 Remove the A/C and heater unit dials and the mounting screws (see illustration).

24.14 Remove the unit mounting bolts from each side of the instrument panel (right side shown, left side similar)

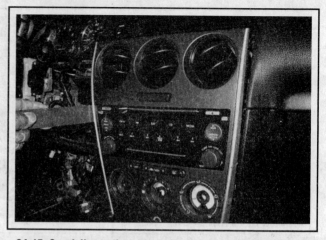

24.15 Carefully pry the center trim panel/assembly out

24.27a Remove the upper storage bin mounting screws . . .

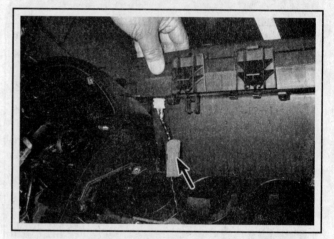

24.27b . . . and disconnect the electrical connector

14 Remove the retaining bolt from each side of the unit (see illustration).

15 Carefully pry around the edges of the center panel and pull the center trim panel out (see illustration). Disconnect the antenna cable from the radio. Disconnect the electrical connectors from the radio and the heater and air conditioning control unit. Remove the center trim panel, radio and heater and air conditioning controls as a single assembly.

16 To detach the air conditioning and control assembly from the center trim panel, see Chapter 3. To detach the audio unit, see Chapter 12.

17 Installation is the reverse of removal.

2009 and later models
Upper trim panel

18 Carefully pry around the edges of the center panel to disengage the clips.

19 Pull the center panel forward to disengage the upper clips. Remove the panel far enough to disconnect the center speaker, hazard switch and information display connectors.

20 Installation is the reverse of removal.

Lower trim panel

21 Remove the upper trim panel (see Steps 18 and 19).

22 Remove the shift knob and console shift indicator panel (see Section 23).

23 Carefully pry the panel forward, using a trim tool to disengage the clips around the perimeter of the panel, and remove the panel.

24 Disconnect any electrical connectors to the panel.

25 Installation is the reverse of removal.

UPPER STORAGE BIN (2008 AND EARLIER MODELS)

◆ **Refer to illustrations 24.27a and 24.27b**

26 Remove the center trim panel (see Steps 10 through 16).

27 Remove the upper storage bin retaining screws, disengage the storage bin mounting clips and remove the upper storage bin (see illustrations).

28 Installation is the reverse of removal.

KNEE BOLSTER TRIM PANEL AND KNEE BOLSTER

◆ **Refer to illustrations 24.32 and 24.33**

29 On 2009 and later models, remove the weather strip sill panel and kick panel (see illustration 26.3a and 26.3b).

24.32 Remove the mounting screws and pry off the knee bolster trim panel

24.33 Knee bolster retaining bolt locations

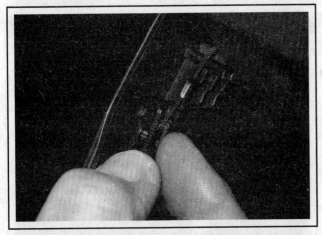

24.35 Disengage the damper clip from this slot on the right end of the glove box (2008 and earlier models)

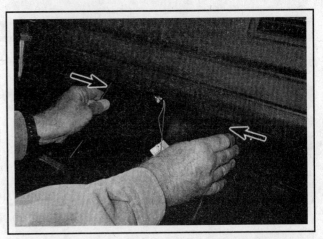

24.36 Push in the hinge pin areas to disengage the pins, then pull out the glove box (2008 and earlier models)

30 On 2009 and later models, remove the instrument cluster hood panel (see Step 8).

31 Remove the hood release lever (see Section 8).

32 Remove the screws from the panel, then carefully pry the panel using a trim tool to disengage the clips around the perimeter of the panel. Remove the knee bolster trim panel (see illustration).

33 Remove the fasteners securing the knee bolster (see illustration) and remove the bolster.

34 Installation is the reverse of removal.

GLOVE BOX

2008 and earlier models

▶ **Refer to illustrations 24.35 and 24.36**

35 Disengage the damper clip from the right end of the glove box (see illustration).

36 Firmly grasp the hinge areas at each end of the glove box, push in to disengage the hinge pins and remove the glove box (see illustration).

37 Installation is the reverse of removal.

2009 and later models

▶ **Refer to illustrations 24.38 and 24.39**

38 Open the glove box and squeeze the strut locking tabs together, then slide the strut off of the glove box tab (see illustration).

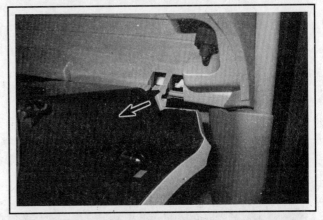

24.38 Squeeze the strut locking tabs together and slide the strut off of the tabs, then squeeze the sides past their stops and lower the glove box (2009 and later models)

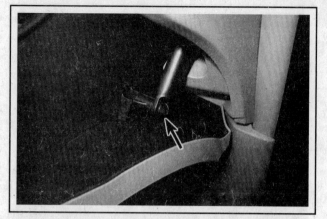

24.39 With the glove box in a 90-degee position, pull the bottom of the glove box outwards to unclip it from the trim panel (2009 and later models)

39 Squeeze the glove box stops in, allow the glove box to come down enough to disengage the glove box from the lower panel and remove the glove box (see illustration).
40 Installation is the reverse of removal.

25 Steering column covers - removal and installation

♦ Refer to illustrations 25.2, 25.3 and 25.4

☀ WARNING:

Models covered by this manual are equipped with a Supplemental Restraint System (SRS), more commonly known as airbags. Always disable the airbag system before working in the vicinity of any airbag system component to avoid the possibility of accidental deployment of the airbag, which could cause personal injury (see Chapter 12).

1 Disconnect the cable from the negative terminal of the battery (see Chapter 5).
2 Remove the mounting fasteners from the lower steering column cover, then press in on the sides of the upper cover and separate the two covers (see illustration).
3 Pull the lower cover down, disconnect the key illumination bulb holder from the cover, then remove cover from the steering column and knee bolster (see illustration).

➡ Note: On 2009 and later models, the key illumination has a separate trim panel that is removed after the lower cover is removed.

25.2 Lower steering column cover mounting fastener locations

4 Lift the upper cover up, then forward to disconnect the plastic pins that hold the rubber strip to the instrument cluster trim panel. Remove the cover (see illustration).
5 Installation is the reverse of removal.

25.3 After separating the column covers, pull the lower cover down then out

25.4 Lift the column cover out to disconnect the rubber strip plastic connectors

26 Instrument panel - removal and installation

▶ Refer to illustrations 26.2, 26.3a, 26.3b, 26.12, 26.13, 26.14, 26.18a, 26.18b, 26.18c and 26.18d

※ WARNING:

Models covered by this manual are equipped with a Supplemental Restraint System (SRS), more commonly known as airbags. Always disable the airbag system before working in the vicinity of any airbag system component to avoid the possibility of accidental deployment of the airbag, which could cause personal injury (see Chapter 12).

➡ Note: This is a difficult procedure for the home mechanic. There are many hidden fasteners, difficult angles to work in and many electrical connectors to label and disconnect/connect. We recommend that this procedure be done only by an experienced do-it-yourselfer.

➡ Note: During removal of the instrument panel, make careful notes of how each piece comes off, where it fits in relation to other pieces and what holds it in place. If you note how each part is installed before removing it, getting the instrument panel back together again will be much easier.

1   Remove the following parts:
   Steering wheel and column (see Chapter 10)
   All the dashboard trim panels and the glove box (see Section 24)
   Air conditioning and heater control assembly (see Chapter 3)
   Instrument cluster and radio (see Chapter 12)
   Front seats (though not absolutely necessary, removing both front seats allows more room to work and eliminates the possibility of damage to the seats during this procedure)
   Center console (see Section 23)

2   Carefully remove the left and right A-pillar (windshield pillar) trim panels (see illustration).

3   Remove the front door opening weather strip, sill panel and kick panels (see illustrations).

4   Disconnect the two electrical connectors in the left kick panel area. Disconnect the bulkhead electrical connector and antenna cable in

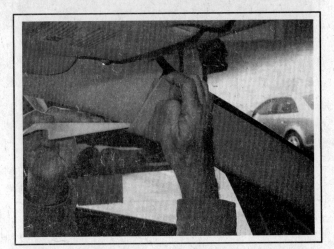

26.2 Carefully pry off the A-pillar trim panels

the right kick panel area, and the satellite antenna, if equipped.

5   In the glove box area, disconnect all air conditioning system electrical connectors.

6   Disconnect all electrical connectors and wiring harness clips located on the floor between the two front seats.

7   Disconnect any other connectors, not already specifically mentioned, that connect wiring between the vehicle and the instrument panel.

8   Mark the relationship of the upper steering column shaft to the lower shaft, remove the steering column pinch-bolt and separate the upper column shaft from the lower shaft.

9   Discard the old pinch bolt and install a new one on reassembly of the steering column.

10 Remove the two hood release handle screws and set the handle aside (see Section 8).

11 Disconnect the in-vehicle temperature sensor, if equipped.

12 Remove the bolts in the instrument cluster opening (see illustration).

26.3a Remove each of the front door opening weather strips . . .

26.3b . . . then the kick panels

26.12 Instrument cluster opening bolts

26.13 Instrument panel center brace bolts (right side shown, left side similar)

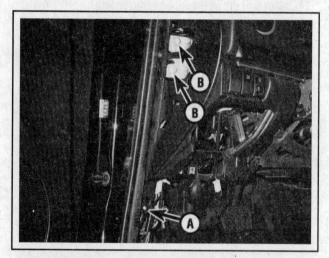

26.14 Left lower instrument panel bolt (A) and left side instrument panel end bolts (B) (left side shown, right side similar)

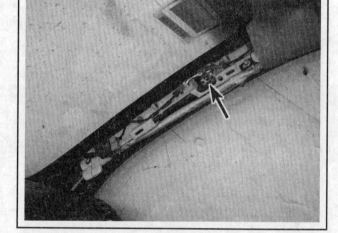

26.18a When the A-pillar trim panels are removed from the A-pillars, the trim panel clips remain stuck in the A-pillars

13 Remove the bolts from the instrument panel center brace (see illustration).

14 Remove the bolts from the left and right lower corners of the instrument panel (see illustration).

15 Remove the instrument panel end bolts (see illustration 26.14).

✷✷ CAUTION:

To avoid damage to the instrument panel when removing these last bolts, have an assistant support the instrument panel. You'll also need an assistant's help when installing the instrument panel and these bolts.

16 With the aid of an assistant, remove the instrument panel from the vehicle.

17 Installation is the reverse of removal.

18 When the A-pillar trim panels were removed from the A-pillars in Step 2, the trim clips remained stuck in the A-pillars (see illustration). Before installing the two A-pillar trim panels, remove the trim panel clips from the A-pillars, tighten the clip retaining screws and install the

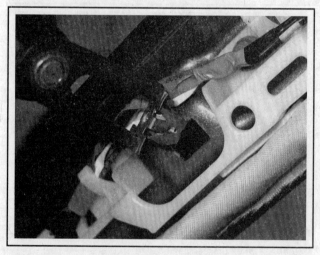

26.18b Remove each clip from the A-pillar . . .

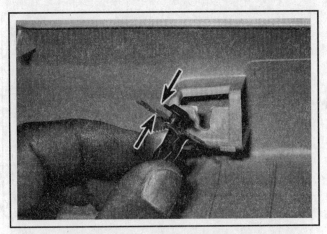

26.18c . . . and adjust the gap between each clip mounting screw and the clip . . .

26.18d . . . so that the clip fits tightly into its mounting bracket on the A-pillar trim panel

clips in their brackets on the undersides of the pillar trim panels (see illustrations).

➡ Note: The trim panels cannot be installed on the A-pillars without putting the clips back where they belong.

27 Seats - removal and installation

FRONT SEATS

◆ Refer to illustrations 27.2a and 27.2b

❋❋ WARNING:

All models covered by this manual are equipped with a Supplemental Restraint System (SRS), more commonly known as airbags. Always disable the airbag system before working in the vicinity of any airbag system component to avoid the possibility of accidental deployment of the airbag, which could cause personal injury (see Chapter 12).

❋❋ WARNING:

Improper handling of the front seats (with side airbag) can cause accidental deployment of the side airbag, which could cause personal injury (see Chapter 12).

❋❋ CAUTION:

The seats are heavy, so have an assistant available to help you lift the seat from the vehicle.

➡ Note: This procedure applies to the driver and passenger seats.

1 Disconnect the cable from the negative battery terminal (see Chapter 5).

2 Remove the covers from the seat mounting bolts and remove the seat mounting bolts (see illustrations).

3 Tilt the seat forward and disconnect all electrical connectors underneath the seat.

4 With the aid of an assistant, carefully lift the seat out of the vehicle.

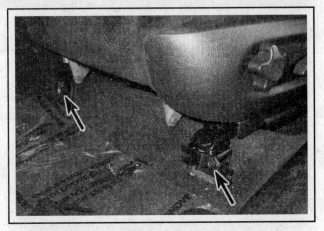

27.2a Front seat mounting bolt covers and mounting bolts (front)

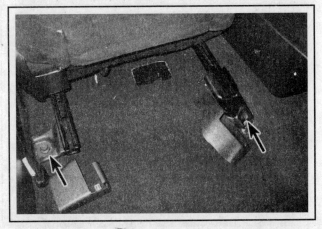

27.2b Front seat mounting bolt covers and mounting bolts (rear)

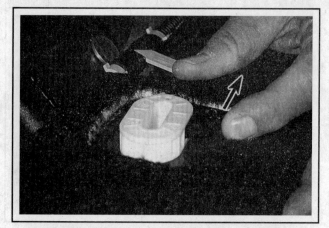

27.6 To disengage the rear seat cushion latches from the wire hoops on the underside of the cushion, pull this lever toward you (seat cushion already disengaged and raised, for clarity)

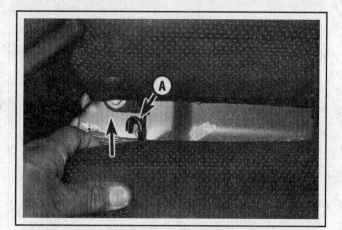

27.7 To disengage each of the two wire hoops (on the underside of the rear part of the cushion) from its corresponding retainer hook (A), push the cushion firmly to the rear (seat cushion already disengaged and pulled forward, for clarity)

✳✳ WARNING:

The seat is heavy, so trying to remove it by yourself could cause injury. Carry the seat with the side airbag module side facing away from you, and set the seat down carefully. Don't drop or place the seat on its side or place anything on top of the side airbag module.

5   Installation is the reverse of removal.

REAR SEAT CUSHION (SEDAN)

▶ **Refer to illustrations 27.6 and 27.7**

6   Open the left rear door, insert your hand between the carpet and the lower edge of the rear seat cushion, then push your hand toward the other side of the vehicle. The release lever for the rear seat cushion latch is located about 18 inches from the left rear door. Pull the release lever toward you (see illustration) and pull up on the front edge of the cushion to disengage the two wire hoops on the underside of the cushion from the latches.

✳✳ CAUTION:

Make sure that these two hoops are fully disengaged from the latches before proceeding, or you could damage the seat cushion.

7   Push the rear seat cushion firmly to the rear to disengage the wire hoops on the underside of the rear part of the cushion from their retainer hooks (see illustration).
8   Lift out the seat cushion, with the aid of an assistant, if necessary.
9   When installing the seat cushion, make SURE that the wire hoops at the lower rear edge of the cushion engage the rear retainer hooks, and that the two latches fully engage the lower front edge of the seat cushion.

REAR SEAT BACKS (SEDAN)

▶ **Refer to illustrations 27.11a and 27.11b**

10   Remove the rear seat cushion (see Steps 6 through 8).
11   To detach the lower part of either rear seat back, remove the two mounting bolts at the bottom (see illustrations).

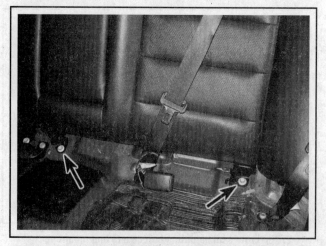

27.11a Left rear seat back lower mounting bolts

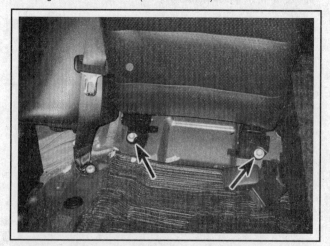

27.11b Right rear seat back lower mounting bolts

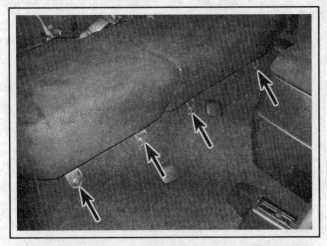

27.14 Rear seat cushion mounting bolt locations (5-door and station wagon models)

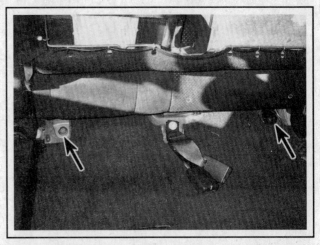

27.15 Rear seat back mounting bolt locations (5-door and station wagon models)

12 To detach the upper part of either rear seat back, open the trunk lid and pull the release handle inside the trunk. The release handle for the left seat back is located on the upper left edge of the trunk opening; the handle for the right seat back is located on the upper right edge of the trunk.

13 Installation is the reverse of removal.

REAR SEATS (5-DOOR AND STATION WAGON)

▶ **Refer to illustrations 27.14 and 27.15**

14 Remove the rear seat cushion mounting bolt covers and bolts (see illustration).

15 Raise the seat cushion up and remove the seat back mounting bolts (see illustration).

16 Remove the seat from the vehicle.

17 Installation is the reverse of removal.

28 Package tray - removal and installation

2008 AND EARLIER MODELS

1 Remove the high-mount brake light housing (see Chapter 12).

2 Release the rear seat backs (see your owner's manual, if necessary) and fold them down.

3 Remove the plastic fasteners (now exposed), lift the front of the package tray up and disengage the clips on the sides of the tray.

4 Disengage the tabs at the rear of the package tray and lift out the tray.

5 Installation is the reverse of removal.

2009 AND LATER MODELS

6 Remove the high-mount brake light housing (see Chapter 12).

7 Release the rear seat backs (see your owner's manual, if necessary), fold them down, and remove the seat backs (see Section 27).

8 Remove the trim cap and screw from the left and right C-pillar trim panels (see illustration).

9 Using a trim removal tool, carefully pry off both C-pillar trim panels.

10 Remove the rear seat cushion (see Section 27).

11 To detach the package tray from its mounting clips, work your way around the outside of the trim panel, carefully prying loose the clips with a suitable door trim removal tool, then pull off the panel.

12 It is not necessary to disconnect any seatbelts to remove the package tray. Instead, pull the package tray forward slightly, then disengage the seatbelts from the tray by threading each belt through the gap in the bottom of each plastic belt guide, then through the gap between the belt guide and the lower edge of the tray.

13 Remove the package tray.

✳ WARNING:

Pay close attention to how the seatbelts are routed. They must be installed exactly the same way. Failure to do so could result in serious injury to someone secured by an incorrectly routed seatbelt in the event of an accident.

14 Installation is the reverse of removal.

Notes

Section

12

CHASSIS ELECTRICAL SYSTEM

1   General information

The electrical system is a 12-volt, negative ground type. Power for the lights and all electrical accessories is supplied by a lead/acid-type battery that is charged by the alternator.

This Chapter covers repair and service procedures for the various electrical components not associated with the engine. Information on the battery, alternator, ignition system and starter motor can be found in Chapter 5.

It should be noted that when portions of the electrical system are serviced, the negative cable should be disconnected from the battery to prevent electrical shorts and/or fires.

2   Electrical troubleshooting - general information

▶ **Refer to illustrations 2.5a, 2.5b, 2.6 and 2.9**

A typical electrical circuit consists of an electrical component, any switches, relays, motors, fuses, fusible links or circuit breakers related to that component and the wiring and connectors that link the component to both the battery and the chassis. To help you pinpoint an electrical circuit problem, wiring diagrams are included at the end of this Chapter.

Before tackling any troublesome electrical circuit, first study the appropriate wiring diagrams to get a complete understanding of what makes up that individual circuit. Trouble spots, for instance, can often be narrowed down by noting if other components related to the circuit are operating properly. If several components or circuits fail at one time, chances are the problem is in a fuse or ground connection, because several circuits are often routed through the same fuse and ground connections.

Electrical problems usually stem from simple causes, such as loose or corroded connections, a blown fuse, a melted fusible link or a failed relay. Visually inspect the condition of all fuses, wires and connections in a problem circuit before troubleshooting the circuit.

If test equipment and instruments are going to be utilized, use the diagrams to plan ahead of time where you will make the necessary connections in order to accurately pinpoint the trouble spot.

The basic tools needed for electrical troubleshooting include a circuit tester or voltmeter (a 12-volt bulb with a set of test leads can also be used), a continuity tester, which includes a bulb, battery and set of test leads, and a jumper wire, preferably with a circuit breaker incorporated, which can be used to bypass electrical components (see illustrations). Before attempting to locate a problem with test instruments, use the wiring diagram(s) to decide where to make the connections.

VOLTAGE CHECKS

Voltage checks should be performed if a circuit is not functioning properly. Connect one lead of a circuit tester to either the negative battery terminal or a known good ground. Connect the other lead to a connector in the circuit being tested, preferably nearest to the battery or fuse (see illustration). If the bulb of the tester lights, voltage is present,

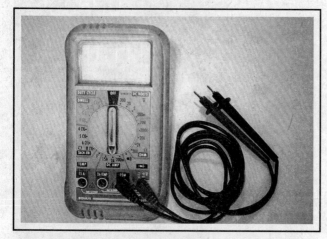

2.5a The most useful tool for electrical troubleshooting is a digital multimeter that can check volts, amps, and test continuity

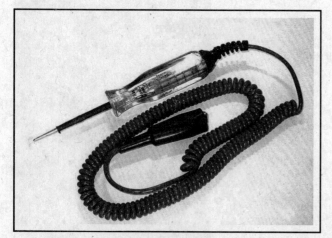

2.5b A test light is a very handy tool for checking voltage

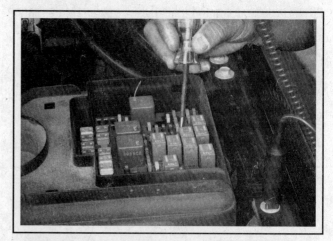

2.6 In use, a basic test light's lead is clipped to a known good ground, then the pointed probe can test connectors, wires or electrical sockets - if the bulb lights, the part being tested has battery voltage

which means that the part of the circuit between the connector and the battery is problem free. Continue checking the rest of the circuit in the same fashion. When you reach a point at which no voltage is present, the problem lies between that point and the last test point with voltage. Most of the time the problem can be traced to a loose connection.

➡ **Note: Keep in mind that some circuits receive voltage only when the ignition key is in the Accessory or Run position.**

FINDING A SHORT

One method of finding shorts in a circuit is to remove the fuse and connect a test light or voltmeter in place of the fuse terminals. There should be no voltage present in the circuit. Move the wiring harness from side-to-side while watching the test light. If the bulb goes on, there is a short to ground somewhere in that area, probably where the insulation has rubbed through. The same test can be performed on each component in the circuit, even a switch.

GROUND CHECK

Perform a ground test to check whether a component is properly grounded. Disconnect the battery and connect one lead of a continuity tester or multimeter (set to the ohms scale), to a known good ground. Connect the other lead to the wire or ground connection being tested. If the resistance is low (less than 5 ohms), the ground is good. If the bulb on a self-powered test light does not go on, the ground is not good.

CONTINUITY CHECK

A continuity check is done to determine if there are any breaks in a circuit - if it is passing electricity properly. With the circuit off (no power in the circuit), a self-powered continuity tester or multimeter can be used to check the circuit. Connect the test leads to both ends of the circuit (or to the power end and a good ground), and if the test light comes on the circuit is passing current properly (see illustration). If the resistance is low (less than 5 ohms), there is continuity; if the reading is 10,000 ohms or higher, there is a break somewhere in the circuit. The same procedure can be used to test a switch, by connecting the

2.9 With a multimeter set to the ohms scale, resistance can be checked across two terminals - when checking for continuity, a low reading indicates continuity, a high reading indicates lack of continuity

continuity tester to the switch terminals. With the switch turned On, the test light should come on (or low resistance should be indicated on a meter).

FINDING AN OPEN CIRCUIT

When diagnosing for possible open circuits, it is often difficult to locate them by sight because the connectors hide oxidation or terminal misalignment. Merely wiggling a connector on a sensor or in the wiring harness may correct the open circuit condition. Remember this when an open circuit is indicated when troubleshooting a circuit. Intermittent problems may also be caused by oxidized or loose connections.

Electrical troubleshooting is simple if you keep in mind that all electrical circuits are basically electricity running from the battery, through the wires, switches, relays, fuses and fusible links to each electrical component (light bulb, motor, etc.) and to ground, from which it is passed back to the battery. Any electrical problem is an interruption in the flow of electricity to and from the battery.

3 Fuses and fusible links - general information

FUSES

▶ **Refer to illustrations 3.1a, 3.1b and 3.3**

The electrical circuits of the vehicle are protected by a combination of fuses, circuit breakers and fusible links. The main fuse/relay panel is in the engine compartment (see illustration), while the interior fuse/relay

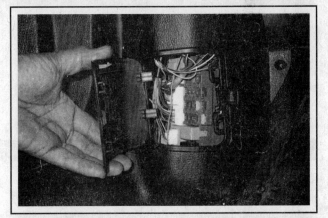

3.1a The interior fuse box is located under the left (driver's) side of the instrument panel, under a cover

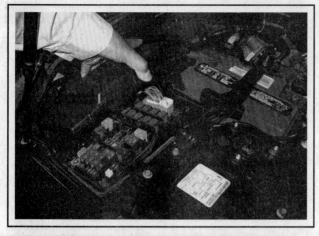

3.1b The engine compartment fuse and fusible link box is located behind the battery

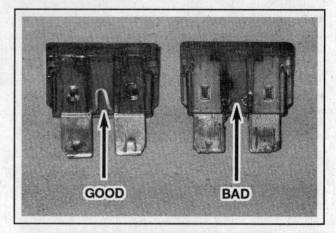

3.3 When a fuse blows, the element between the terminals melts

panel is located inside the passenger compartment (see illustration). Each of the fuses is designed to protect a specific circuit, and the various circuits are identified on the fuse panel itself.

Several sizes of fuses are employed in the fuse blocks. There are small, medium and large sizes of the same design, all with the same blade terminal design. The medium and large fuses can be removed with your fingers, but the small fuses require the use of pliers or the small plastic fuse-puller tool found in most fuse boxes.

If an electrical component fails, always check the fuse first. The best way to check the fuses is with a test light. Check for power at the exposed terminal tips of each fuse. If power is present at one side of the fuse but not the other, the fuse is blown. A blown fuse can also be identified by visually inspecting it (see illustration).

Be sure to replace blown fuses with the correct type. Fuses (of the same physical size) of different ratings may be physically interchangeable, but only fuses of the proper rating should be used. Replacing a fuse with one of a higher or lower value than specified is not recommended. Each electrical circuit needs a specific amount of protection.

The amperage value of each fuse is molded into the top of the fuse body.

If the replacement fuse immediately fails, don't replace it again until the cause of the problem is isolated and corrected. In most cases, this will be a short circuit in the wiring caused by a broken or deteriorated wire.

FUSIBLE LINKS

Some circuits are protected by fusible links. The links are used in circuits which are not ordinarily fused, or which carry high current, such as the circuit between the alternator and the starter motor. Fusible links, which are usually several wire gauges smaller in size than the circuit that they protect, are designed to melt if the circuit is subjected to more current than it was designed to carry. If you have to replace a blown fusible link, make sure that you replace it with one of the same specification. If the replacement fusible link blows in the same circuit, make sure that you troubleshoot the circuit in which the fusible link melted BEFORE installing another fusible link.

4 Circuit breakers - general information

Circuit breakers protect certain circuits, such as the power windows or heated seats. Depending on the vehicle's accessories, there may be one or two circuit breakers, located in the fuse/relay box in the engine compartment.

Because the circuit breakers reset automatically, an electrical overload in a circuit breaker-protected system will cause the circuit to fail momentarily, then come back on. If the circuit does not come back on, check it immediately.

For a basic check, pull the circuit breaker up out of its socket on the fuse panel, but just far enough to probe with a voltmeter. The breaker should still contact the sockets. With the voltmeter negative lead on a good chassis ground, touch each end prong of the circuit breaker with the positive meter probe. There should be battery voltage at each end. If there is battery voltage only at one end, the circuit breaker must be replaced.

Some circuit breakers must be reset manually.

5 Relays - general information

Several electrical accessories in the vehicle, such as the fuel injection system, horns, starter, and fog lamps use relays to transmit the electrical signal to the component. Relays use a low-current circuit (the control circuit) to open and close a high-current circuit (the power cir-

cuit). If the relay is defective, that component will not operate properly. Most relays are mounted in the engine compartment and interior fuse/relay boxes (see illustrations 3.1a and 3.1b).

6   Electrical connectors - general information

Most electrical connections on these vehicles are made with multiwire plastic connectors. The mating halves of many connectors are secured with locking clips molded into the plastic connector shells. The mating halves of some large connectors, such as some of those under the instrument panel, are held together by a bolt through the center of the connector.

To separate a connector with locking clips, use a small screwdriver to pry the clips apart carefully, then separate the connector halves. Pull only on the shell, never pull on the wiring harness as you may damage the individual wires and terminals inside the connectors. Look at the connector closely before trying to separate the halves. Often the locking clips are engaged in a way that is not immediately clear. Additionally, many connectors have more than one set of clips.

Each pair of connector terminals has a male half and a female half.

When you look at the end view of a connector in a diagram, be sure to understand whether the view shows the harness side or the component side of the connector. Connector halves are mirror images of each other, and a terminal shown on the right side end-view of one half will be on the left side end-view of the other half.

It is often necessary to take circuit voltage measurements with a connector connected. Whenever possible, carefully insert a small straight pin (not your meter probe) into the rear of the connector shell to contact the terminal inside, then clip your meter lead to the pin. This kind of connection is called "backprobing." When inserting a test probe into a terminal, be careful not to distort the terminal opening. Doing so can lead to a poor connection and corrosion at that terminal later. Using the small straight pin instead of a meter probe results in less chance of deforming the terminal connector.

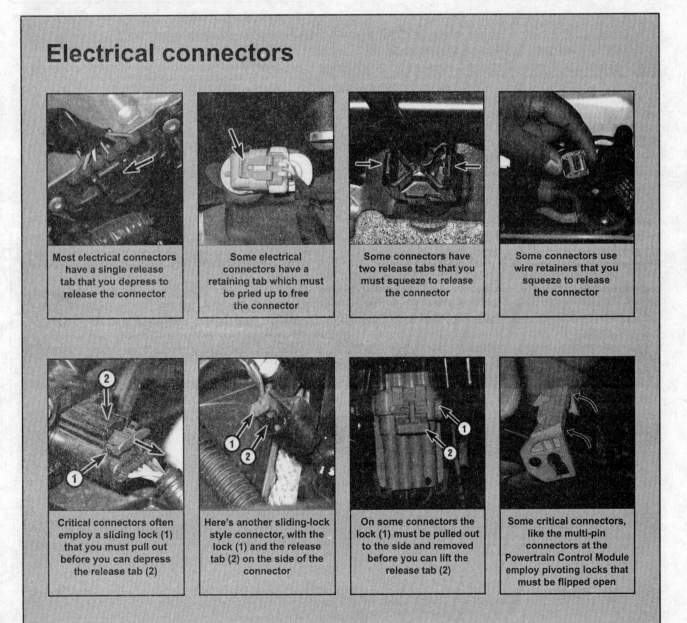

Electrical connectors

Most electrical connectors have a single release tab that you depress to release the connector

Some electrical connectors have a retaining tab which must be pried up to free the connector

Some connectors have two release tabs that you must squeeze to release the connector

Some connectors use wire retainers that you squeeze to release the connector

Critical connectors often employ a sliding lock (1) that you must pull out before you can depress the release tab (2)

Here's another sliding-lock style connector, with the lock (1) and the release tab (2) on the side of the connector

On some connectors the lock (1) must be pulled out to the side and removed before you can lift the release tab (2)

Some critical connectors, like the multi-pin connectors at the Powertrain Control Module employ pivoting locks that must be flipped open

7   Multi-function, headlight and windshield wiper switches - replacement

1   Disconnect the cable from the negative terminal of the battery (see Chapter 5).

HEADLIGHT SWITCH

▶ **Refer to illustrations 7.3 and 7.4**

2   Remove the steering column covers (see Chapter 11).
3   Disconnect the light switch electrical connector (see illustration).
4   Remove the light switch retaining screws and remove the switch (see illustration).
5   Installation is the reverse of removal.

WINDSHIELD WIPER SWITCH

▶ **Refer to illustration 7.7**

6   Remove the steering column covers (see Chapter 11).
7   Disconnect the windshield wiper switch electrical connector (see illustration).
8   Remove the windshield wiper switch retaining screws and remove the switch.
9   Installation is the reverse of removal.

7.3 Headlight switch details

1   *Headlight switch*   3   *Switch retaining screws*
2   *Electrical connector*

MULTI-FUNCTION SWITCH BODY

10   Remove the driver's side lower trim panel, knee bolster (if equipped) and the steering column covers (see Chapter 11).
11   Remove the clockspring and steering angle sensor (see Chapter 10)
12   Disconnect the multi-function switch electrical connector.
13   Disengage the retaining clips and remove the switch.
14   Installation is the reverse of removal.

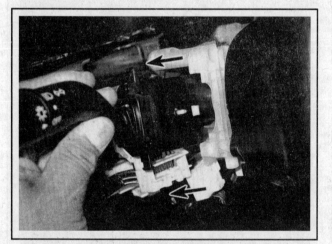

7.4 Pull the switch out from the multifunction switch

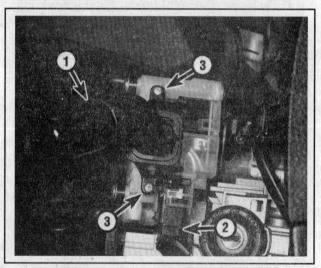

7.7 Windshield wiper/washer switch details

1   *Wiper switch*   3   *Switch retaining screws*
2   *Electrical connector*

8 Ignition switch and key lock cylinder - replacement

✳✳ WARNING:

The models covered by this manual are equipped with Supplemental Restraint Systems (SRS), more commonly known as airbags. Always disable the airbag system before working in the vicinity of any airbag system components to avoid the possibility of accidental deployment of the airbags, which could cause personal injury (see Section 27).

1   Disconnect the cable from the negative terminal of the battery (see Chapter 5).
2   Remove the knee bolster trim panel, the knee bolster and the upper and lower steering column covers (see Chapter 11). Lower the steering column to its lowest position.

IGNITION SWITCH

▸ Refer to illustration 8.3

✳✳ CAUTION:

Do not remove the ignition switch and the key lock cylinder at the same time. According to the manufacturer, doing so could damage the steering column.

3   Disconnect the electrical connector from the ignition switch (see illustration).
4   Remove the mounting screw and depress the release tabs to detach the ignition switch from the steering column.
5   When installing the switch, make sure that it snaps into place. Installation is otherwise the reverse of removal.

KEY LOCK CYLINDER

▸ Refer to illustration 8.7

✳✳ CAUTION:

Do not remove the ignition switch and the key lock cylinder at the same time. According to the manufacturer, doing so could damage the steering column.

6   Turn the ignition key to the ON position (2008 and earlier models) or the ACC position (2009 and later models).
7   Using a suitable tool, depress the key lock cylinder release button (see illustration) and remove the key lock cylinder.
8   To install the key lock cylinder, insert it into the lock cylinder housing and push it in until it clicks into place.
9   Verify that the ignition switch operates correctly in the OFF, ACC, RUN and START positions.
10 Installation is otherwise the reverse of removal.

KEY LOCK CYLINDER ILLUMINATION RING

▸ Refer to illustration 8.11

➡ Note: Removal of the lock cylinder illumination ring is not necessary for lock cylinder replacement.

11 Disconnect the electrical connector from the illumination ring (see illustration).
12 Disengage the lock tabs and remove the illumination ring.
13 Installation is the reverse of removal. Make sure that the ring snaps into place.

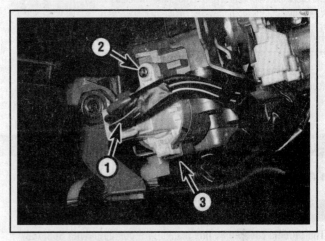

8.3 Ignition switch details

1	Electrical connector	3	Release tab
2	Mounting screw		

8.7 Insert a suitable tool through this hole and push the release button to release the ignition key lock cylinder

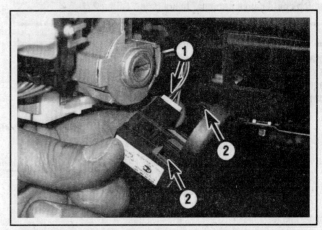

8.11 Key lock cylinder illumination ring electrical connector (1) and lock tabs (2)

9 Instrument panel switches - replacement

※ WARNING:

The models covered by this manual are equipped with Supplemental Restraint Systems (SRS), more commonly known as airbags. Always disable the airbag system before working in the vicinity of any airbag system components to avoid the possibility of accidental deployment of the airbags, which could cause personal injury (see Section 27).

TRACTION CONTROL SWITCH

▸ Refer to illustration 9.3

  1 Disconnect the cable from the negative terminal of the battery (see Chapter 5).
  2 Remove the knee bolster trim panel from the instrument panel (see Chapter 11, Section 24).
  3 Reach through the opening in the end of the instrument panel and push on the back of the switch while simultaneously prying the switch out of the dash with a trim removal tool (see illustration). Disconnect the electrical connectors and remove the switch assembly.
  4 Installation is the reverse of removal.

HAZARD FLASHER SWITCH

  5 Disconnect the cable from the negative terminal of the battery (see Chapter 5).

9.3 Reach behind the instrument panel switch and push the switch out from behind, then disconnect the electrical connector

  6 Remove the center trim panel (see Chapter 11, Section 24).
  7 On 2008 and earlier models, remove the audio unit (see Section 11), the air register mounting screws, and the hazard switch mounting screws.
  8 On 2009 and later models, disconnect the electrical connector to the switch, squeeze the release tabs together and remove the hazard flasher switch from the center trim panel.
  9 Installation is the reverse of removal.

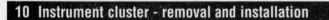

10 Instrument cluster - removal and installation

▸ Refer to illustration 10.4

※ WARNING:

The models covered by this manual are equipped with Supplemental Restraint Systems (SRS), more commonly known as airbags. Always disable the airbag system before working in the vicinity of any airbag system components to avoid the possibility of accidental deployment of the airbags, which could cause personal injury (see Section 27).

➡ Note: If the instrument cluster is replaced, it must be programmed with a specialized scan tool. Take the vehicle to a dealer service department or other qualified repair shop equipped with the necessary tool to have the instrument cluster programmed to the vehicle.

  1 Disconnect the cable from the negative battery terminal (see Chapter 5).
  2 Release the tilt wheel lever and lower the steering wheel to its lowest position. Remove the steering column covers (see Chapter 11).
  3 Remove the instrument cluster trim panel (see Chapter 11).
  4 Remove the instrument cluster mounting screws (see illustration).
  5 Carefully pull out the instrument cluster from the instrument panel and disconnect the electrical connectors.

※ CAUTION:

Once the cluster is removed, set the cluster down with the gauges facing up to prevent grease in the meters from leaking out and staining the face of the gauges.

  6 Installation is the reverse of removal.

10.4 Instrument cluster mounting screw locations

11 Radio and speakers - removal and installation

⁂ WARNING:

The models covered by this manual are equipped with Supplemental Restraint Systems (SRS), more commonly known as airbags. Always disable the airbag system before working in the vicinity of any airbag system components to avoid the possibility of accidental deployment of the airbags, which could cause personal injury (see Section 27).

RADIO

2008 and earlier models

▶ **Refer to illustrations 11.3 and 11.4**

1 Disconnect the cable from the negative battery terminal (see Chapter 5).

2 Remove the lower center console, the glove box and center trim panel (see Chapter 11, Section 24).

3 Pull the center trim panel out enough to disconnect the electrical harness connector and antenna cable (see illustration).

4 Remove the radio mounting screws (see illustration) and separate the radio from the center trim panel.

5 Installation is the reverse of removal.

2009 and later models

6 Disconnect the cable from the negative battery terminal (see Chapter 5).

7 Remove the shift knob and shift panel (see Chapter 7B).

8 Remove the upper instrument panel, decorative trim panel and the upper and lower center trim panels (see Chapter 11, Section 24).

9 Remove the climate control unit (see Chapter 3).

10 Remove the radio unit mounting screws and pull the unit out far enough to disconnect the antenna cable and electrical connectors at the back of the unit.

11 Installation is the reverse of removal.

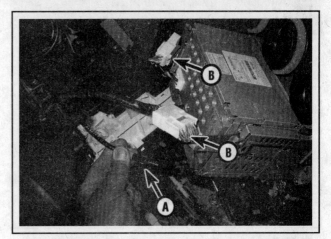

11.3 Disconnect the antenna cable (A) and the electrical connectors (B)

SPEAKERS

Door speakers

▶ **Refer to illustration 11.13**

➡ **Note: This procedure applies to front and rear door speakers.**

12 Remove the door trim panel (see Chapter 11).

13 Unhook the speaker harness from the mount and remove the speaker mounting screws (see illustration).

14 Pull the speaker out of its enclosure and disconnect the speaker electrical connectors.

15 Installation is the reverse of removal.

Door tweeters

▶ **Refer to illustrations 11.17 and 11.19**

16 Remove the door trim panel and the mirror trim panel (see Chapter 11).

11.4 Radio mounting screw locations - there are two on each side and at the top and bottom of the radio unit (2008 and earlier models)

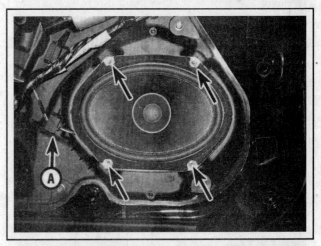

11.13 Unhook the speaker harness (A) and remove the door speaker mounting screws

17 Disconnect the tweeter electrical connector (see illustration).
18 On 2008 and earlier models, remove the tweeter mounting screws.

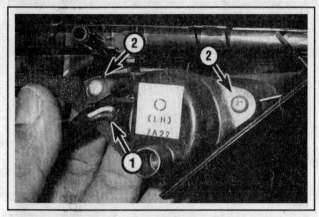

11.17 Door tweeter electrical connector (1) and mounting screws (2) (2008 and earlier models)

11.19 Pull the two plastic locking tabs back and remove the tweeter from the back of the mirror trim panel (2009 and later models)

19 On 2009 and later models, pull the plastic locking tabs back and remove the tweeter from the back of the mirror trim panel (see illustration).
20 Disengage the tweeter harness from the clip on the back of the mirror trim panel and remove the tweeter.
21 Installation is the reverse of removal.

Instrument panel center speaker

22 Remove the center upper instrument panel (see Chapter 11, Section 24).
23 Disconnect the electrical connector, remove the speaker mounting screws and separate the speaker from the panel.
24 Installation is the reverse of removal.

Rear speakers

➡ **Note: Depending on the year and model, there are various configurations of rear speakers and woofers located behind the back seat, underneath the package tray. This procedure applies to any of them.**

25 Remove the high mount brake light.
26 Remove the rear seat cushion (see Chapter 12).
27 Carefully pry off the C-pillar trim panel.
28 Remove the package tray (see Chapter 11).
29 Remove the speaker mounting screws, then lift up the speaker and disconnect the electrical connector.
30 Installation is the reverse of removal.

Audio control switch (steering wheel)

31 Disconnect the cable from the negative battery terminal (see Chapter 5).
32 Remove the driver's side airbag and steering wheel (see Chapter 10).
33 Disconnect the electrical connectors.
34 Remove the mounting screws and remove the audio control switch from the bracket.
35 Installation is the reverse of removal.

12 Antenna, module and cables - removal and installation

ANTENNA

Rear window antenna

1 The rear window mounted antenna is an integral component of the rear window and cannot be serviced separately from the rear window.

Center roof antenna (2008 and earlier models)

2 Carefully pry out the C-pillar trim and center trim from the side of the rear windshield.
3 Remove the rear seats (see Chapter 11).
4 Remove the rear map light (if equipped).
5 Remove the plastic push pin fasteners around the trunk liner and remove the liner.
6 Carefully pull the rear section of the headliner down far enough to access the antenna.
7 Disconnect the electrical connectors to the antenna.
8 Remove the antenna mounting nut and remove the antenna.
9 Installation is the reverse of removal.

Center roof antenna mast (2008 and earlier models)

10 Unscrew the mast from the center roof antenna base.
11 Installation is the reverse of removal.

ANTENNA AMPLIFIER

12 Carefully pry out the C-pillar trim and center trim from the side of the rear window.
13 Remove the rear map light (if equipped).
14 Carefully pull the rear section of the headliner down far enough to access the amplifier.
15 Disconnect the electrical connectors from the antenna amplifier.
16 Remove the amplifier mounting screws and remove the amplifier.
17 Installation is the reverse of removal.

ANTENNA CABLES

18 The antenna cable consists of three cables: front, middle and rear. The front cable is routed through the instrument panel and connects to the middle cable at the base of the A-pillar. The middle cable runs up

through the A-pillar along the edge of the roof and down to the C-pillar where it connects to the rear cable. The rear cable runs from the C-pillar back up to the roof and across to the antenna. If one of these cables must be replaced, the A-pillar, B-pillar, C-pillar, roof trim and headliner must be removed.

➡ **Note: This is a difficult procedure for the home mechanic. We recommend that this procedure be done only by an experienced do-it-yourselfer.**

13 Headlight bulb - replacement

❋❋ WARNING:

Halogen bulbs are gas-filled and under pressure and might shatter if the surface is scratched or the bulb is dropped. Wear eye protection and handle the bulbs carefully, grasping only the base whenever possible. Don't touch the surface of the bulb with your fingers because the oil from your skin could cause it to overheat and fail prematurely. If you do touch the bulb surface, clean it with rubbing alcohol.

HALOGEN-BULBS

1 To access either bulb on the left (driver's side) headlight housing, remove the air filter housing air intake duct (see Chapter 4).

2 To access either bulb on the right (passenger's side) headlight housing, detach and set aside the coolant reservoir tank (see Chapter 3).

Low-beam bulbs

▶ **Refer to illustrations 13.3, 13.5 and 13.6**

3 Remove the round cover from the back of the headlight housing (see illustration).

4 Disconnect the electrical connector from the bulb.

5 Unhook the locking spring from the tab, and remove the bulb from the housing (see illustration).

6 Install the bulb into the corresponding cutouts in the headlight housing (see illustration), and lock it into place with the spring tab. When installing the new bulb, make sure that you don't touch it with your fingers, because the oil from your hands will cause the bulb to overheat and fail prematurely. If you do touch the bulb, be sure to wipe it off with alcohol and a clean soft cloth. Installation is otherwise the reverse of removal.

High-beam bulbs

▶ **Refer to illustrations 13.7 and 13.8**

7 Remove the protective cover (see illustration).

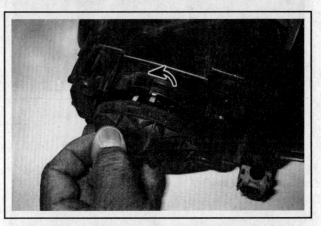

13.3 Rotate the cover counterclockwise and unlock it from the headlight housing

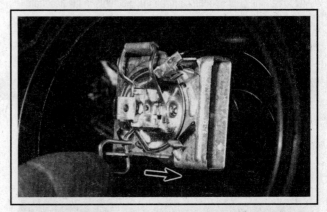

13.5 To remove the low-beam headlight bulb, rotate the bulb counterclockwise and pull it out of the housing, then spread the locking tabs apart and disconnect the electrical connector

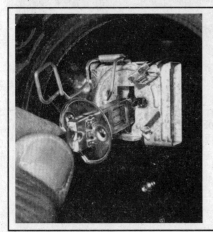

13.6 To install a low-beam bulb, align the lugs on the bulb holder with the cutouts in the headlight housing

13.7 On 2008 and earlier models, depress the tab (arrow) and remove the protective cover from the housing - 2009 and later models are round and pull off

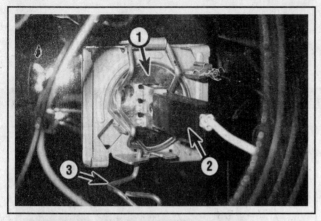

13.8 High beam details (2008 and earlier models)

1   High beam bulb   3   Locking spring
2   Electrical connector

2008 and earlier models

8 Disconnect the electrical connector from the bulb (see illustration).

9 Unhook the locking spring from the tab, and remove the bulb from the housing (see illustration 13.5).

10 Install the bulb into the corresponding cutouts in the headlight housing (see illustration 13.6), and lock it into place with the spring tab. When installing the new bulb, make sure that you don't touch it with your fingers, because the oil from your hands will cause the bulb

to overheat and fail prematurely. If you do touch the bulb, be sure to wipe it off with alcohol and a clean soft cloth. Installation is otherwise the reverse of removal.

2009 and later models

11 Disconnect the electrical connector from the bulb.

12 Rotate the bulb counterclockwise, pull it out and remove the bulb.

13 When installing the new bulb, make sure that you don't touch it with your fingers, because the oil from your hands will cause the bulb to fail. If you do touch the bulb, be sure to wipe it off with alcohol and a clean soft cloth.

14 Insert the bulb into the headlight housing and turn it clockwise to lock it into place.

15 Installation is otherwise the reverse of removal.

XENON (HID) BULBS

✳✳ WARNING:

Some models use High Intensity Discharge (HID) bulbs instead of halogen bulbs. These can be identified by the high voltage warning sticker on the headlight housing. According to the manufacturer, the high voltages produced by this system can be fatal in the event of shock. Also, the voltage can remain in the circuit even after the headlight switch has been turned to the OFF position and the ignition key has been removed. Therefore, for your safety, we do not recommend that you try to replace one of these bulbs yourself. Instead, have this service performed by a qualified repair shop.

14 Headlight housing - removal and installation

▶ Refer to illustrations 14.2a and 14.2b

1 Remove the front bumper cover (see Chapter 11).
2 Remove the pin-type retainer and the headlight housing bolts

(see illustrations).
3 Pull out the headlight housing and disconnect the electrical connectors.
4 Installation is the reverse of removal.

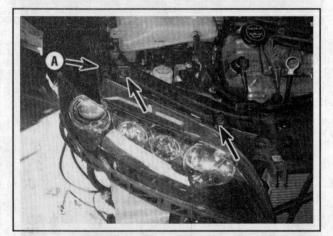

14.2a To remove the headlight housing, remove the pin-type retainer (A) and the upper headlight housing bolts (2007 model shown, other models similar) . . .

14.2b . . . then remove the lower mounting bolts (2007 model shown, other models similar)

15 Headlights - adjustment

▶ Refer to illustrations 15.1 and 15.2

❊❊❊ WARNING:

The headlights must be aimed correctly. If adjusted incorrectly, they could temporarily blind the driver of an oncoming vehicle and cause an accident or seriously reduce your ability to see the road. The headlights should be checked for proper aim every 12 months and any time a new headlight is installed or front-end bodywork is performed. The following procedure is only an interim step to provide temporary adjustment until the headlights can be adjusted by a properly equipped shop.

1 The headlight adjustment screws (see illustration) control up-and-down movement and left-and-right movement.

2 There are several methods of adjusting the headlights. The simplest method requires a blank wall 25 feet in front of the vehicle and a level floor (see illustration).

3 Position masking tape on the wall in reference to the vehicle centerline and the centerlines of both headlights.

4 Measure the height of the headlight reference marks (in the centers of the headlight lenses) from the ground. Position a horizontal tape line on the wall at the same height as the headlight reference marks.

➡ Note: It may be easier to position the tape on the wall with the vehicle parked only a few inches away.

5 Adjustment should be made with the vehicle sitting level, the gas tank half-full and no unusually heavy load in the vehicle.

6 Turn on the low beams. Turn the adjusting screw to position the high intensity zone so it is two inches below the horizontal line.

7 Have the headlights adjusted by a dealer service department at the earliest opportunity.

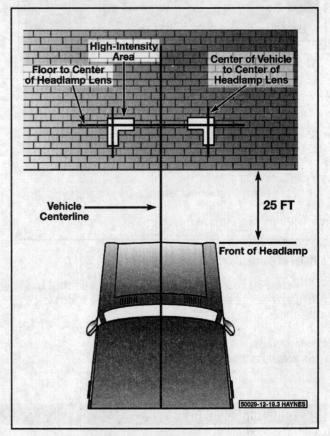

15.2 Headlight adjustment details

15.1 Vertical adjustment screw locations (2007 model shown, other models similar)

16 Taillight housing - removal and installation

TAILLIGHT HOUSING

▶ **Refer to illustrations 16.2 and 16.3**

1 Fold back the trunk floor carpeting mat. Pull out and reposition the flexible trunk side trim panel that covers the taillight housing and the wheelhousing.

❊❊❊ CAUTION:

Do not leave the trunk side panel bent or out of shape too long, or it will be permanently deformed.

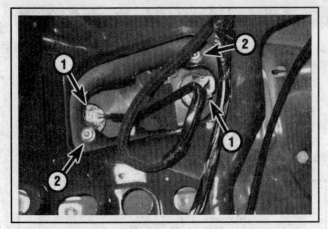

16.2 Taillight housing details

   1   Bulb holder electrical connectors
   2   Housing mounting nuts

  2 Disconnect the electrical connectors from the taillight housing (see illustration).

  3 Remove the taillight housing nuts and remove the taillight housing (see illustration).

  4 Installation is the reverse of removal.

TRUNK LID TAILLIGHT HOUSING

▶ **Refer to illustration 16.6**

  5 Remove the trunk lid trim panel, if equipped (see Chapter 11).

  6 Disconnect the electrical connector from the bulb holders (see illustration).

  7 Remove the light housing mounting nuts and remove the housing from the trunk lid.

  8 Installation is the reverse of removal.

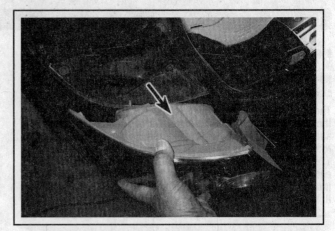

16.3 Slide the taillight housing out from the body

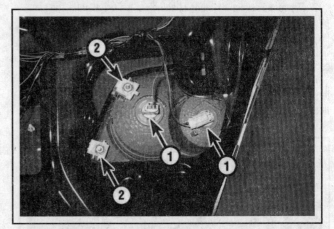

16.6 Trunk lid taillight housing details

   1   Bulb holder electrical connectors
   2   Housing mounting nuts

17 Bulb replacement

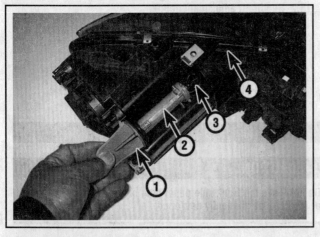

17.3 Front turn signal details

1	*Bulb holder*	*3*	*Bulb*
2	*Electrical connectors*	*4*	*Headlight housing*

EXTERIOR LIGHT BULBS

Front turn signal/parking light bulbs

2008 and earlier models

▶ **Refer to illustrations 17.3 and 17.4**

  1 To access the bulbs on the left (driver's side) headlight housing, remove the battery air intake (see Chapter 5) and the air filter housing air intake duct (see Chapter 4).

  2 To access the bulbs on the right (passenger's side) headlight housing, detach and set aside the coolant reservoir (see Chapter 3).

  3 To remove the front turn signal bulb, turn the bulb holder counterclockwise (see illustration) and remove it from the headlight housing.

Bulb removal

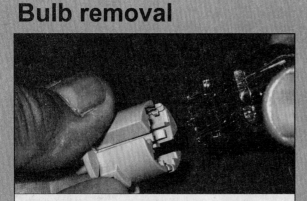

To remove many modern exterior bulbs from their holders, simply pull them out

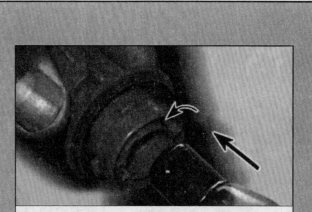

On bulbs with a cylindrical base ("bayonet" bulbs), the socket is spring-loaded; a pair of small posts on the side of the base hold the bulb in place against spring pressure. To remove this type of bulb, push it into the holder, rotate it 1/4-turn counterclockwise, then pull it out

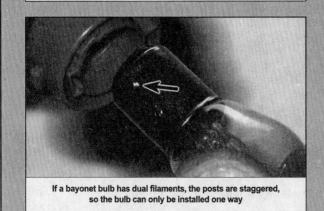

If a bayonet bulb has dual filaments, the posts are staggered, so the bulb can only be installed one way

To remove most overhead interior light bulbs, simply unclip them

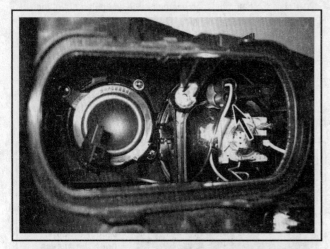

17.4 Rotate the bulb holder counterclockwise and pull it out

4   To remove the parking light bulb, remove the high beam housing cover (see illustration 13.7) and turn the bulb holder counterclockwise

(see illustration) and remove it from the headlight housing. It's not necessary to disconnect the electrical connector to replace the bulb.

5   To remove the bulb, pull it straight out of the holder.

6   Installation is the reverse of removal.

2009 and later models

7   Disconnect the cable from the negative battery terminal (see Chapter 5).

8   Remove the inner fender mounting fasteners (see Chapter 11) and pull the inner fender back.

9   Turn the bulb holder clockwise and remove it from the headlight housing. It's not necessary to disconnect the electrical connector to replace the bulb.

10 To remove the bulb, pull it straight out of the holder.

11 Installation is the reverse of removal.

Front side marker light bulbs

▶ **Refer to illustration 17.13**

12 Remove the inner fender mounting fasteners (see Chapter 11) and pull the inner fender back.

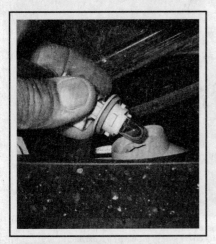

17.13 Reach up through the inner fender, then rotate the bulb holder counterclockwise and pull it out of the sidemarker housing (inner fender splash shield removed for clarity)

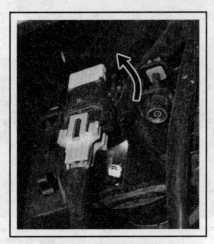

17.25 Disconnect the electrical connector, then rotate the bulb counterclockwise 1/4-turn and pull it out of the fog lamp housing

17.30 Turn the bulb holder counterclockwise and pull it out of the center high-mount brake light housing (2008 and earlier sedan models)

13 Turn the bulb holder counterclockwise and remove it from the side marker housing (see illustration). It's not necessary to disconnect the electrical connector to replace the bulb.

14 To remove the bulb, pull it straight out of the holder.

15 Installation is the reverse of removal.

Front side turn light (2009 and later models)

➡ Note: The front side turn light is not replaceable; the entire side turn light assembly must be replaced in the event of failure.

16 The front side turn lights are located in the outside mirrors.

17 Rotate the mirror in and carefully detach the mounting pin on the back of the mirror glass. Pull the mirror glass holder and remove the mounting clips. Disconnect the electrical connector on models equipped with heated mirrors.

18 Remove the glass holder and outer mirror glass as a single unit.

19 Looking at the mirror, depress the three mounting tabs using a small screwdriver and slide the mirror outer trim off.

20 Disconnect the electrical connector and remove the mounting screw.

21 Remove the side turn light while detaching the tab.

22 Installation is the reverse of the removal procedure.

Fog light bulbs

▶ Refer to illustration 17.25

⁂ WARNING:

Halogen bulbs are gas-filled and under pressure and might shatter if the surface is scratched or the bulb is dropped. Wear eye protection and handle the bulbs carefully, grasping only the base whenever possible. Don't touch the surface of the bulb with your fingers because the oil from your skin could cause it to overheat and fail prematurely. If you do touch the bulb surface, clean it with rubbing alcohol.

23 Raise the front of the vehicle and place it securely on jackstands.

24 Remove the four fasteners and pull back the front part of the inner fender splash shield below the fog light (see Chapter 11, Section 10).

25 Disconnect the fog light bulb electrical connector (see illustration).

26 Turn the fog light bulb counterclockwise and remove it from the fog light housing.

27 To install the new fog light bulb, insert it into the fog light housing and turn it clockwise to lock it into place.

28 Installation is otherwise the reverse of removal.

Center high-mounted brake light bulb

▶ Refer to illustrations 17.30 and 17.33

2008 and earlier sedan models

29 From inside the trunk, disconnect the electrical connector.

30 Rotate the bulb holder counterclockwise and pull it out of the high-mounted brake light housing (see illustration).

31 To replace the bulb, pull it straight out of the bulb holder.

32 Installation is the reverse of removal.

2008 and earlier 5-door models

33 Open the liftgate and remove the access panel (see illustration).

34 Rotate the bulb holder counterclockwise and pull it out of the high-mounted brake light housing.

17.33 On 2008 and earlier 5-door models, open the access panel to remove the bulb

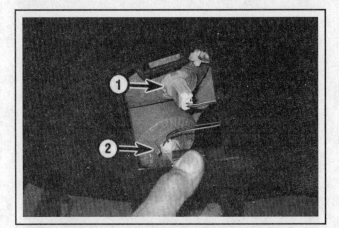

17.47a Remove the access panel for the rear inboard light bulbs . . .

1 *Taillight bulb*	2 *Back-up light bulb*

17.47b . . . and the rear outboard light bulbs (2008 and earlier models)

1 *Brake/taillight bulb*	2 *Taillight bulb*

35 To replace the bulb, pull it straight out of the bulb holder.
36 Installation is the reverse of removal.

2008 and earlier spoiler-mounted, sedan models

37 Remove the two rubber access covers, then remove the high-mounted brake light housing screws. Pull down the housing and disconnect the electrical connector. No further disassembly is possible. The light emitting diodes (LEDs) are an integral part of the housing; they're not separately serviceable.
38 Installation is the reverse of removal.

2008 and earlier wagon models

39 Open the liftgate and remove the upper trim panel.
40 Rotate the bulb holder counterclockwise and pull it out of the high-mounted brake light housing.
41 To replace the bulb, pull it straight out of the bulb holder.
42 Installation is the reverse of removal.

2009 and later models

43 From inside the trunk, disconnect the electrical connector.
44 Push the high-mounted brake light housing to the rear to disengage the front mounting tabs, then tilt it to the rear and pull it forward to disengage the rear mounting tabs. Lift the housing up and out of its mounting hole in the package tray.
45 No further disassembly is possible. The light emitting diodes (LEDs) are an integral part of the housing; they're not separately serviceable.
46 Installation is the reverse of removal.

Taillight bulbs

▶ **Refer to illustrations 17.47a and 17.47b**

47 On 2008 and earlier models, remove the access panel (see illustrations).
48 On 2009 and later models, fold back the trunk floor carpeting mat, then pull out and reposition the flexible trunk side trim panel that covers the taillight housing and the wheelhousing.

⁕ **CAUTION:**

Do not leave the trunk side panel bent or out of shape too long, or it will be permanently deformed.

49 To remove a taillight bulb socket, rotate it counterclockwise and pull it out of the taillight housing. To remove the bulb from the socket, pull it straight out.

➡ **Note: On 2009 and later models, the back-up light bulb must be rotated clockwise to remove it.**

50 Installation is the reverse of removal.

License plate light bulbs
2008 and earlier models

▶ **Refer to illustration 17.53**

51 Remove the rear trunk or liftgate trim panel (see Chapter 11).
52 Remove the rear finish panel mounting nuts and finish panel from the trunk or liftgate.
53 Squeeze the license plate light housing locking tabs together (see illustration) and remove the assembly.

17.53 License plate light housing locking tabs (A)

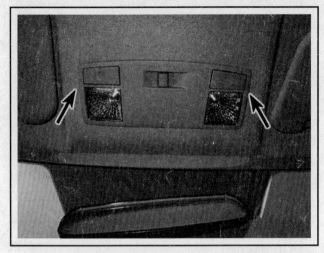

17.64 Carefully pry the housing out from each side with a trim removal tool or screwdriver

17.68 Insert a small screwdriver into the lens recess and carefully pry off the lens

54 Remove the lens from the assembly and pull the bulb from the holder.
55 Installation is the reverse of removal.

2009 and later models

56 Partially remove the trunk lid trim panel (see Chapter 11).
57 Disconnect the electrical connector to the license plate light.
58 Rotate the bulb holder counterclockwise and pull it out of the license plate light housing.
59 To replace the bulb, pull it straight out of the bulb holder.
60 Installation is the reverse of removal.

INTERIOR LIGHT BULBS

Courtesy light bulbs

➡ Note: The courtesy lights, which illuminate the ground below the front doors, are located in the door panels.

61 Using a plastic trim removal tool, carefully pry the courtesy light lens out from the door panel.
62 Pull the bulb straight out of its socket.
63 Installation is the reverse of removal.

Interior map light

▶ Refer to illustration 17.64

64 Carefully pry the interior map light housing down from each side to disengage the mounting clips (see illustration).
65 Disconnect the electrical connector.
66 Rotate the socket counterclockwise and pull it out of the housing. To remove the bulb from the socket, pull it straight out.
67 Installation is the reverse of removal.

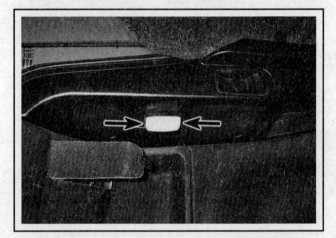

17.71 Squeeze the cargo light lens inwards from the ends

Overhead light

▶ Refer to illustration 17.68

68 Carefully pry off the overhead lens (see illustration).
69 Pull the bulb straight out of its socket.
70 Installation is the reverse of removal.

Cargo light bulbs

▶ Refer to illustration 17.71

71 Squeeze the ends of lens inwards and remove the lens (see illustration).
72 Pull the bulb straight out of its socket.
73 Installation is the reverse of removal.

18 Wiper motor - replacement

FRONT WIPER MOTOR

▶ **Refer to illustrations 18.1, 18.3 and 18.5**

1 Remove the wiper arm nuts and mark the relationship of the wiper arms to their shafts (see illustration). Remove both wiper arms.

2 Remove the cowl panel (see Chapter 11).

3 Disconnect the electrical connector from the wiper motor (see illustration).

4 Remove the two wiper motor and link assembly mounting bolts and remove the wiper motor and link assembly.

5 Carefully separate the linkage from the motor's crank arm (see illustration).

6 Remove the nut that secures the crank arm to the motor shaft (see illustration 18.5).

7 Mark the relationship of the crank arm to the motor shaft and remove the crank arm from the shaft.

8 Remove the two motor mounting bolts (see illustration 18.5) and remove the motor from its mounting bracket.

9 Installation is the reverse of removal.

REAR WIPER MOTOR

▶ **Refer to illustrations 18.11 and 18.13**

10 Disconnect the cable from the negative battery terminal (see Chapter 5).

11 Remove the wiper arm nut and mark the relationship of the wiper arm to the shaft (see illustration). Remove the wiper arm.

12 Remove the liftgate trim panel (see Chapter 11).

18.1 Remove the wiper arm trim cap and the wiper arm nut

18.3 Wiper motor electrical connector (1) and mounting bolts (2)

18.5 Wiper motor assembly details

1   Wiper linkage ball socket connection
2   Wiper motor crank arm mounting nut
3   Wiper motor mounting bolts
4   Wiper motor

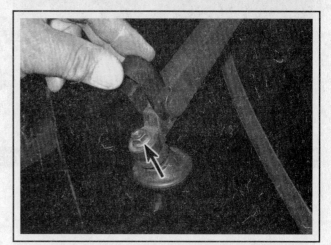

18.11 Remove the wiper arm trim cap and the wiper arm nut

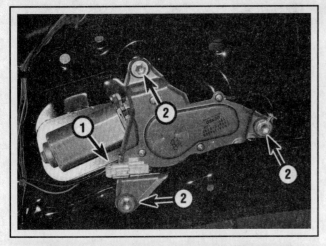

18.13 Rear wiper motor electrical connector (1) and mounting bolts (2)

13 Disconnect the electrical connector from the wiper motor (see illustration).

14 Remove the wiper motor mounting bolts and the wiper motor from the liftgate.

15 Installation is the reverse of removal.

19 Horn - replacement

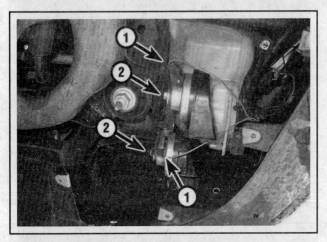

19.4 Horn assembly electrical connectors (1) and mounting bolts (2)

▶ Refer to illustration 19.4

➡ Note: The horn is located at the lower right corner of the vehicle, in the void ahead of the right front wheel well.

1 Raise the vehicle and place it securely on jackstands.

2 On 2008 and earlier models, remove the four right front fender splash shield fasteners and pull down the splash shield to access the horn (see Chapter 11, Section 10).

3 On 2009 and later models, remove the bumper cover to access the horn (see Chapter 11).

4 Disconnect the horn electrical connector (see illustration).

5 Remove the horn mounting bolt, then remove the horn.

6 Installation is the reverse of removal.

20 Daytime Running Lights (DRL) - general information

The Daytime Running Lights (DRL) system used on all models illuminates the low beam headlights at reduced intensity when the engine is running. The only exception is with the engine running and the shift lever in Park. Once the parking brake is released or the shift lever is moved, the lights will remain on as long as the ignition switch is on.

21 Rear window defogger - check and repair

1   The rear window defogger consists of a number of horizontal elements baked onto the glass surface.

2   Small breaks in the element can be repaired without removing the rear window.

CHECK

▶ **Refer to illustrations 21.4, 21.5 and 21.7**

3   Turn the ignition switch and defogger system switches to the ON position. Using a voltmeter, place the positive probe against the defogger grid positive terminal and the negative probe against the ground terminal. If battery voltage is not indicated, check the fuse, defogger switch and related wiring. If voltage is indicated, but all or part of the defogger doesn't heat, proceed with the following tests.

4   When measuring voltage during the next two tests, wrap a piece of aluminum foil around the tip of the voltmeter positive probe and press the foil against the heating element with your finger (see illustration). Place the negative probe on the defogger grid ground terminal.

5   Check the voltage at the center of each heating element (see illustration). If the voltage is 5 or 6-volts, the element is okay (there is no break). If the voltage is zero, the element is broken between the center of the element and the positive end. If the voltage is 10 to 12-volts, the element is broken between the center of the element and ground. Check each heating element.

6   Connect the negative lead to a good body ground. The reading should stay the same. If it doesn't, the ground connection is bad.

7   To find the break, place the voltmeter negative probe against the defogger ground terminal. Place the voltmeter positive probe with the foil strip against the heating element at the positive terminal end and slide it toward the negative terminal end. The point at which the voltmeter deflects from several volts to zero is the point at which the heating element is broken (see illustration).

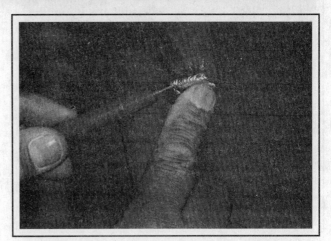

21.4 When measuring the voltage at the rear window defogger grid, wrap a piece of aluminum foil around the positive probe of the voltmeter and press the foil against the wire with your finger

REPAIR

▶ **Refer to illustration 21.13**

8   Repair the break in the element using a repair kit specifically recommended for this purpose, available at most auto parts stores. Included in this kit is plastic conductive epoxy.

9   Prior to repairing a break, turn off the system and allow it to cool off for a few minutes.

10 Lightly buff the element area with fine steel wool, then clean it thoroughly with rubbing alcohol.

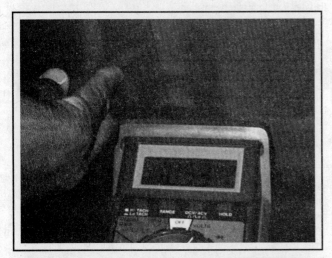

21.5 To determine if a heating element has broken, check the voltage at the center of each element; if the voltage is 5 or 6 volts, the element is unbroken, but if the voltage is 10 or 12 volts, the element is broken between the center and the ground side. If there is no voltage, the element is broken between the center and the positive side

21.7 To find the break, place the voltmeter negative lead against the defogger ground terminal, place the voltmeter positive lead with the foil strip against the heating element at the positive terminal end and slide it toward the negative terminal end. The point at which the voltmeter reading changes abruptly is the point at which the element is broken

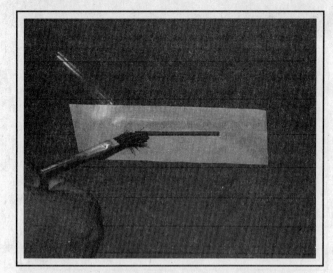

21.13 To use a defogger repair kit, apply masking tape to the inside of the window at the damaged area, then brush on the special conductive coating

11 Use masking tape to mask off the area being repaired.

12 Thoroughly mix the epoxy, following the instructions provided with the repair kit.

13 Apply the epoxy material to the slit in the masking tape, overlapping the undamaged area about 3/4-inch on either end (see illustration).

14 Allow the repair to cure for 24 hours before removing the tape and using the system.

22 Cruise control system - description and check

1 The cruise control system maintains vehicle speed with the Powertrain Control Module (PCM), throttle actuator control motor, brake switch, control switches and associated wiring. There is no mechanical connection, such as a vacuum servo or cable. Some features of the system require special testers and diagnostic procedures that are beyond the scope of the home mechanic. Listed below are some general procedures that may be used to locate common problems.

2 Check the fuses (see Section 3).

3 The Brake Pedal Position (BPP) switch (or brake light switch) deactivates the cruise control system. Have an assistant press the brake pedal while you check the brake light operation.

4 If the brake lights do not operate properly, correct the problem and retest the cruise control.

5 Check the wiring between the PCM and throttle actuator motor for opens or shorts and repair as necessary.

6 The cruise control system uses information from the PCM, including the Vehicle Speed Sensor (VSS), which is located in the transmission or transfer case. Refer to Chapter 6 for more information on the VSS.

7 Test drive the vehicle to determine if the cruise control is now working. If it isn't, take it to a dealer service department or other qualified repair shop for further diagnosis.

23 Power window system - description and check

➡ **Note: These models are equipped with a Body Control Module (BCM). Several systems are linked to this centralized control module, which allows simple and accurate troubleshooting, but only with a professional-grade scan tool. The BCM governs the door locks, the power windows, the ignition lock and security system, the interior lights, the Daytime Running Lights system, the horn, the windshield wipers, the heating/air conditioning system and the power mirrors. In the event of malfunction with this system, have the vehicle diagnosed by a dealership service department or other qualified automotive repair facility.**

1 The power window system operates electric motors, mounted in the doors, which lower and raise the windows. The system consists of the control switches, the motors, regulators, glass mechanisms, the Body Control Module (BCM) and associated wiring.

2 The power windows can be lowered and raised from the master control switch by the driver or by remote switches located at the individual windows. Each window has a separate motor that is reversible. The position of the control switch determines the polarity and therefore the direction of operation.

3 The circuit is protected by a fuse and a circuit breaker. Each motor is also equipped with an internal circuit breaker; this prevents one stuck window from disabling the whole system.

4 The power window system will only operate when the ignition switch is ON, and for a period of time after the ignition key has been turned Off (unless one of the doors is opened). In addition, many models have a window lockout switch at the master control switch which, when activated, disables the switches at the rear windows and, sometimes, the switch at the passenger's window also. Always check these items before troubleshooting a window problem.

5 These procedures are general in nature, so if you can't find the problem using them, take the vehicle to a dealer service department or other properly equipped repair facility.

6 If the power windows won't operate, always check the fuse and circuit breaker first.

7 If only the rear windows are inoperative, or if the windows only

operate from the master control switch, check the rear window lockout switch for continuity in the unlocked position. Replace it if it doesn't have continuity.

8 Check the wiring between the switches and fuse panel for continuity. Repair the wiring, if necessary.

9 If only one window is inoperative from the master control switch, try the other control switch at the window.

➡ **Note: This doesn't apply to the driver's door window.**

10 If the same window works from one switch, but not the other, check the switch for continuity.

11 If the switch tests OK, check for a short or open in the circuit between the affected switch and the window motor.

12 If one window is inoperative from both switches, remove the switch panel from the affected door. Check for voltage at the switch and at the motor (refer to Chapter 11 for door panel removal) while the switch is operated.

13 If voltage is reaching the motor, disconnect the glass from the regulator (see Chapter 11). Move the window up and down by hand while checking for binding and damage. Also check for binding and damage to the regulator. If the regulator is not damaged and the window moves up and down smoothly, replace the motor. If there's binding or damage, lubricate, repair or replace parts, as necessary.

14 If voltage isn't reaching the motor, check the wiring in the circuit for continuity between the switches and the body control module, and between the body control module and the motors. You'll need to consult the wiring diagram at the end of this Chapter. If the circuit is equipped with a relay, check that the relay is grounded properly and receiving voltage.

15 Test the windows after you are done to confirm proper repairs.

24 Power door lock and keyless entry system - description and check

➡ **Note: These models are equipped with a Body Control Module (BCM). Several systems are linked to this centralized control module, which allows simple and accurate troubleshooting, but only with a professional-grade scan tool. The BCM governs the door locks, the power windows, the ignition lock and security system, the interior lights, the Daytime Running Lights system, the horn, the windshield wipers, the heating/air conditioning system and the power mirrors. In the event of malfunction with this system, have the vehicle diagnosed by a dealership service department or other qualified automotive repair facility.**

1 The power door lock system operates the door lock actuators mounted in each door. The system consists of the switches, actuators, Body Control Module (BCM) and associated wiring. Diagnosis can usually be limited to simple checks of the wiring connections and actuators for minor faults that can be easily repaired.

2 Power door lock systems are operated by bi-directional solenoids located in the doors. The lock switches have two operating positions: Lock and Unlock. These switches send a signal to the BCM, which in turn sends a signal to the door lock solenoids.

3 If you are unable to locate the trouble using the following general steps, consult your dealer service department.

4 Always check the circuit protection first. Some vehicles use a combination of circuit breakers and fuses. Refer to the wiring diagrams at the end of this Chapter.

5 Check for voltage at the switches. If no voltage is present, check the wiring between the fuse panel and the switches for shorts and opens.

6 If voltage is present, test the switch for continuity. Replace it if there's not continuity in both switch positions. To remove the switch, use a flat-bladed trim tool to pry out the door/window switch assembly (see Chapter 11).

7 If the switch has continuity, check the wiring between the switch and door lock solenoid.

8 If all but one lock solenoids operate, remove the trim panel from the affected door (see Chapter 11) and check for voltage at the solenoid while the lock switch is operated. One of the wires should have voltage in the Lock position; the other should have voltage in the Unlock position.

9 If the inoperative solenoid is receiving voltage, replace the solenoid.

10 If the inoperative solenoid isn't receiving voltage, check for an open or short in the wire between the lock solenoid and the relay.

11 On the models covered by this manual, power door lock system communication goes through the Body Control Module. If the above tests do not pinpoint a problem, take the vehicle to a dealer or qualified shop with the proper scan tool to retrieve trouble codes from the BCM.

KEYLESS ENTRY SYSTEM

12 The keyless entry system consists of a remote control transmitter that sends a coded infrared signal to a receiver, which then operates the door lock system.

13 Replace the battery when the transmitter doesn't operate the locks at a distance of ten feet. Normal range should be about 30 feet.

BATTERY REPLACEMENT

▶ **Refer to illustrations 24.14 and 24.15**

14 Use a coin to carefully separate the case halves (see illustration).

➡ **Note: On later models, a small screwdriver must be used to separate the transmitter case halves.**

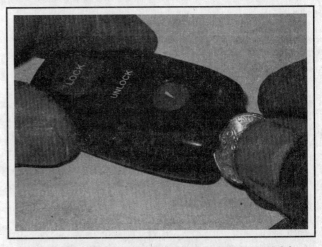

24.14 Using a coin (or a small screwdriver on later models), carefully pry the halves of the transmitter apart

15 Replace the battery (see illustration).

16 Snap the case halves together.

17 If necessary, perform the transmitter programming procedure (see Steps 18 through 23).

TRANSMITTER PROGRAMMING

18 Close all doors and liftgate (if equipped).

19 Open the driver's door.

20 Insert the key into the ignition lock and turn the ignition to the "ON" position, then back to the "LOCK" position three times.

➡ **Note: Do not remove the key from the steering lock during this step.**

21 Open and shut the driver door three times, then leave the door open.

22 Remove the key and press any button on the transmitter.

➡ **Note: The synchronization procedure must be completed within 24 seconds.**

23 The locking system should respond; if not, wait 40 seconds and begin again.

24.15 Carefully pry out the old battery

25 Electric side view mirrors - description

➡ **Note: These models are equipped with a Body Control Module (BCM). Several systems are linked to this centralized control module, which allows simple and accurate troubleshooting, but only with a professional-grade scan tool. The BCM governs the door locks, the power windows, the ignition lock and security system, the interior lights, the Daytime Running Lights system, the horn, the windshield wipers, the heating/air conditioning system and the power mirrors. In the event of malfunction with this system, have the vehicle diagnosed by a dealership service department or other qualified automotive repair facility.**

1 The electric rear view mirrors use two motors to move the glass; one for up and down adjustments and one for left-right adjustments.

2 The control switch has a selector portion which sends voltage to the left or right side mirror. With the ignition in the ACC position and the engine OFF, roll down the windows and operate the mirror control switch through all functions (left-right and up-down) for both the left and right side mirrors.

3 Listen carefully for the sound of the electric motors running in the mirrors.

4 If the motors can be heard but the mirror glass doesn't move, there's probably a problem with the drive mechanism inside the mirror. Power mirrors have no user-serviceable parts inside - a defective mirror must be replaced as a unit (see Chapter 11).

5 If the mirrors don't operate and no sound comes from the mirrors, check the fuses (see Section 3).

6 If the fuses are OK, remove the mirror control switch. Have the switch continuity checked by a dealer service department or other qualified shop.

7 Check the ground connections.

8 If the mirror still doesn't work, remove the mirror and check the wires at the mirror for voltage.

9 If there's not voltage in each switch position, check the circuit between the mirror and control switch for opens and shorts.

10 If there's voltage, remove the mirror and test it off the vehicle with jumper wires. Replace the mirror if it fails this test.

26 Data Link Communication system - description

The vehicles covered by this manual have a complex electrical system, encompassing many power accessories, and a number of separate electronic modules.

The Powertrain Control Module (PCM) is mainly responsible for engine and transaxle control, but also communicates with other modules around the vehicle through a Data Link Communication system, which sends serial port data very quickly between the various modules. Many of the computer functions involved in the operation of body systems are routed through the Body Control Module (BCM), which communicates with the PCM. The Data Link system also includes the Sensing Diagnostic Module (airbag system), the Electronic Brake Control Module and the instrument panel cluster. The BCM further communicates with various body subsystems.

All of the modules in the vehicle have associated trouble codes. When other troubleshooting procedures fail to pinpoint the problem, check the wiring diagrams at the end of this Chapter to see if the BCM or PCM are involved in the circuit. If so, take your vehicle to a dealer service department or other qualified repair shop with the proper diagnostic tools to extract the trouble codes.

27 Airbag system - general information

All models are equipped with a Supplemental Restraint System (SRS), more commonly known as the airbag system. The airbag system is designed to protect the driver and the front seat passenger from serious injury in the event of a head-on or frontal collision. It consists of the impact sensors, a driver's airbag module in the center of the steering wheel, a passenger's airbag module in the glove box area of the instrument panel and a sensing/diagnostic module mounted under the center console. Some models are also equipped with side-curtain airbags and seat belt pre-tensioners.

AIRBAG MODULES

Driver's airbag

The airbag inflator module contains a housing incorporating the cushion (airbag) and inflator unit, mounted in the center of the steering wheel. The inflator assembly is mounted on the back of the housing over a hole through which gas is expelled, inflating the bag almost instantaneously when an electrical signal is sent from the system. A spiral cable (or clockspring) assembly on the steering column under the steering wheel carries this signal to the module. This clockspring can transmit an electrical signal regardless of steering wheel position.

Passenger's airbag

The airbag is mounted inside the right side of the instrument panel, in the area above the glove box. It's similar in design to the driver's airbag, except that it's larger than the steering wheel unit. The trim cover (on the side of the instrument panel that faces toward the passenger) is textured and colored to match the instrument panel and has a molded seam that splits open when the bag inflates.

Side curtain airbags

In addition to the side-impact airbags, extra side-impact protection is also provided by side-curtain airbags on some models. These are long airbags that, in the event of a side impact, come out of the headliner at each side of the car and come down between the side windows and the seats. They are designed to protect the heads of both front seat and rear seat passengers.

SENSING AND DIAGNOSTIC MODULE

The sensing and diagnostic module supplies the current to the airbag system in the event of a collision, even if battery power is cut off. It checks this system every time the vehicle is started, causing the "AIRBAG" light to go on then off, if the system is operating properly. If there is a fault in the system, the light will go on and stay on, flash, or the dash will make a beeping sound. If this happens, the vehicle should be taken to your dealer immediately for service. This module is mounted under the center console. There is also a roll-over sensor located directly behind it on later models.

SEAT BELT PRE-TENSIONERS

Some models are equipped with pyrotechnic (explosive) units in the front seat belt retracting mechanisms. During an impact that would trigger the airbag system, the airbag control unit also triggers the seat belt retractors. When the pyrotechnic charges go off, they accelerate the retractors to instantly take up any slack in the seat belt system to more fully prepare the driver and front seat passenger for impact.

The airbag system should be disabled any time work is done to or around the seats.

✳✳ WARNING:

Never strike the pillars or floorpan with a hammer or use an impact-driver tool in these areas unless the system is disabled.

DISARMING THE SYSTEM AND OTHER PRECAUTIONS

✳✳ WARNING:

Failure to follow these precautions could result in accidental deployment of the airbag and personal injury.

Whenever working in the vicinity of the steering wheel, steering column or any of the other SRS system components, the system must be disarmed.

To disarm the airbag system:

a) *Point the wheels straight ahead and turn the key to the Lock position.*

b) *Disconnect the cable from the negative battery terminal (see Chapter 5).*

c) *Wait at least two minutes for the back-up power supply to be depleted.*

To re-arm the airbag system:

a) *Make sure there is nobody inside the vehicle and that there are no objects near any of the airbag modules, then reconnect the cable to the negative terminal of the battery.*

b) *Turn the ignition switch to the Off position, wait ten seconds, then turn it to the On position. The AIRBAG light on the instrument panel should come on continuously for about six seconds, then turn off.*

➡ **Note: The light might take up to 30 seconds to come on after the key is turned to the On position (during this time the Restraints Control Module is performing a self-check of the system). If the light fails to come on, or if it flashes, or if a chime sounds in patterns of five sets of five beeps, have the vehicle diagnosed by a dealer service department or other qualified repair shop.**

Whenever handling an airbag module:

Always keep the airbag opening (the trim side) pointed away from your body. Never place the airbag module on a bench or other surface with the airbag opening facing the surface. Always place the airbag module in a safe location with the airbag opening facing up.

Never measure the resistance of any SRS component. An ohmmeter has a built-in battery supply that could accidentally deploy the airbag.

Never use electrical welding equipment on a vehicle equipped with an airbag without first disconnecting the electrical connector for each airbag.

Never dispose of a live airbag module. Return it to a dealer service department or other qualified repair shop for safe deployment and disposal.

COMPONENT REMOVAL AND INSTALLATION

Driver's side airbag module and spiral cable

Refer to Chapter 10, *Steering wheel - removal and installation,* for the driver's side airbag module and clockspring removal and installation procedures.

Passenger's airbag module and other airbag modules

Even if you ever have to remove the instrument panel, it's not necessary to remove the passenger airbag module to do so; it can simply remain installed in the instrument panel. We don't recommend removing any of the other airbag modules either. These jobs are best left to a professional.

28 Wiring diagrams - general information

Since it isn't possible to include all wiring diagrams for every year and model covered by this manual, the following diagrams are those that are typical and most commonly needed.

Prior to troubleshooting any circuits, check the fuse and circuit breakers (if equipped) to make sure they're in good condition. Make sure the battery is properly charged and check the cable connections (see Chapter 1).

When checking a circuit, make sure that all connectors are clean, with no broken or loose terminals. When disconnecting a connector, do not pull on the wiring; pull only on the connector.

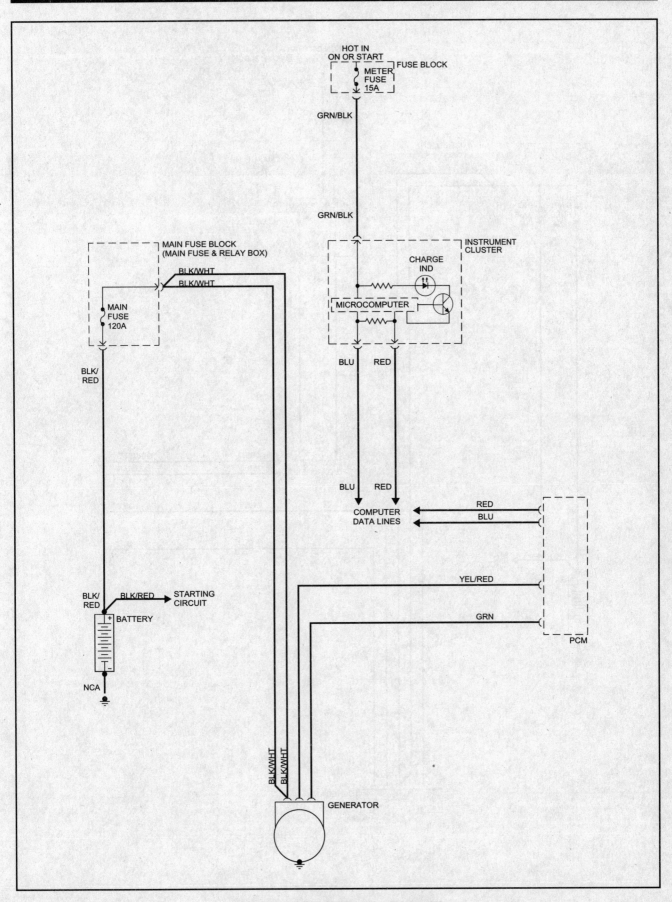

Charging system - 2008 and earlier models

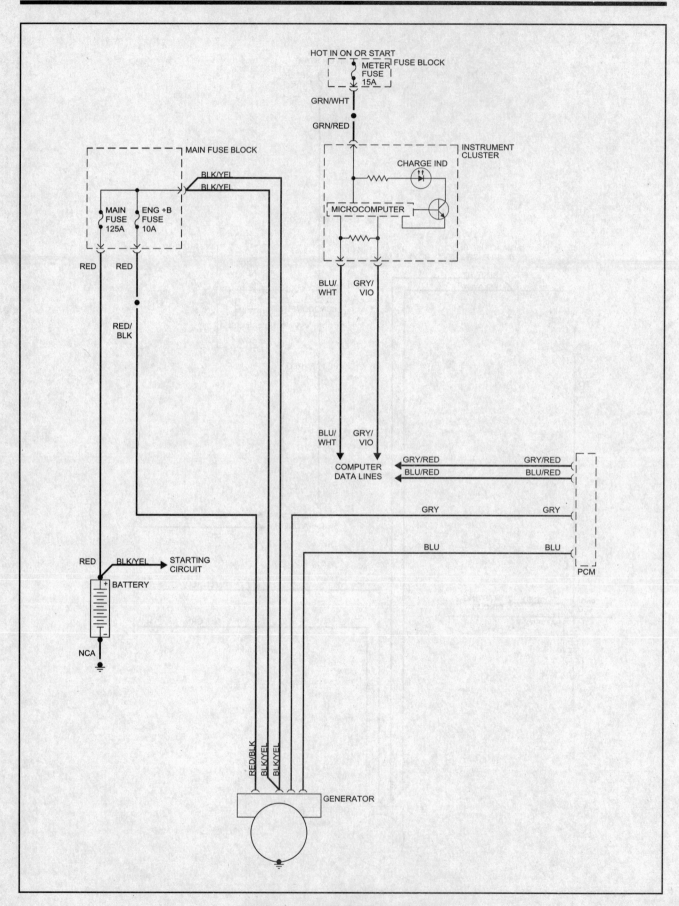

Charging system - 2009 and later models

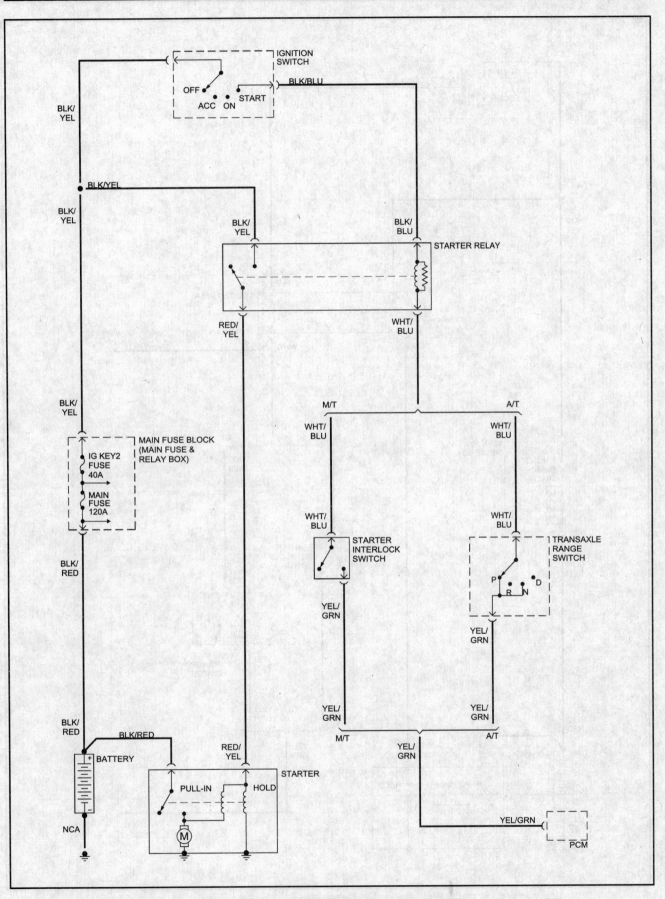

Starting system - 2003 and 2004 four-cylinder models

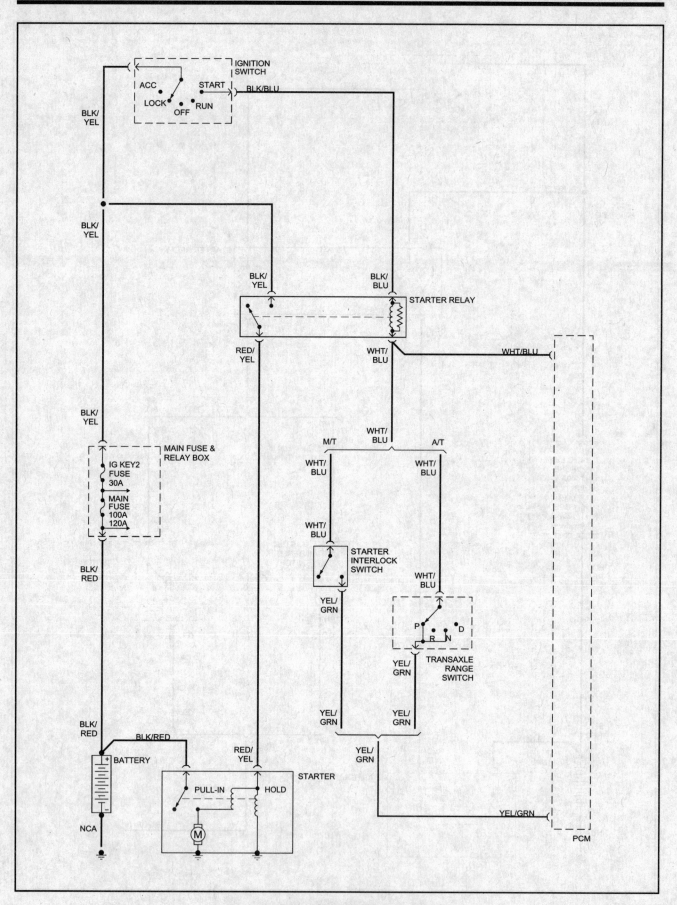

Starting system - 2003 and 2004 V6 models

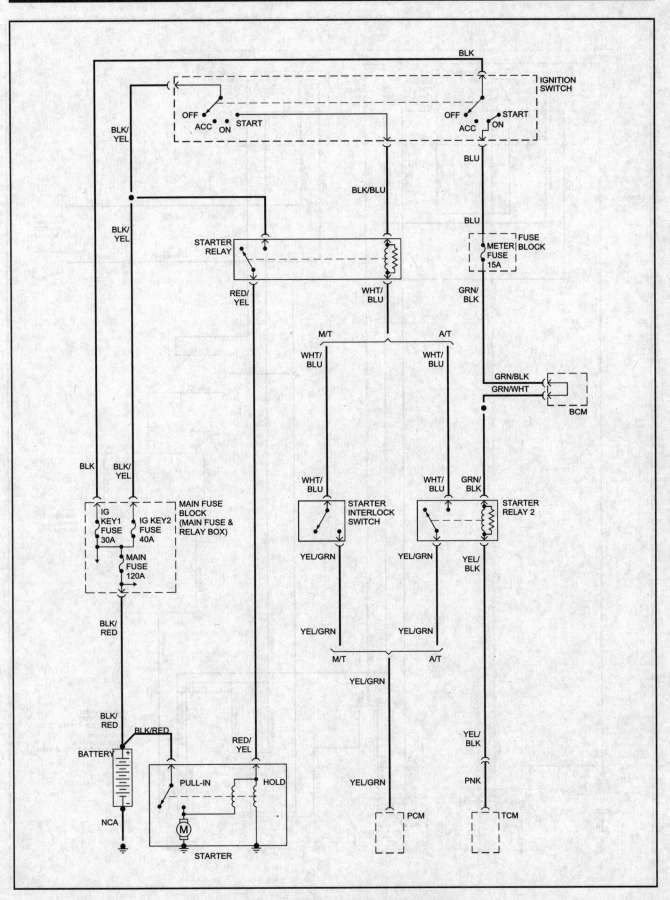

Starting system - 2005 through 2008 models (all)

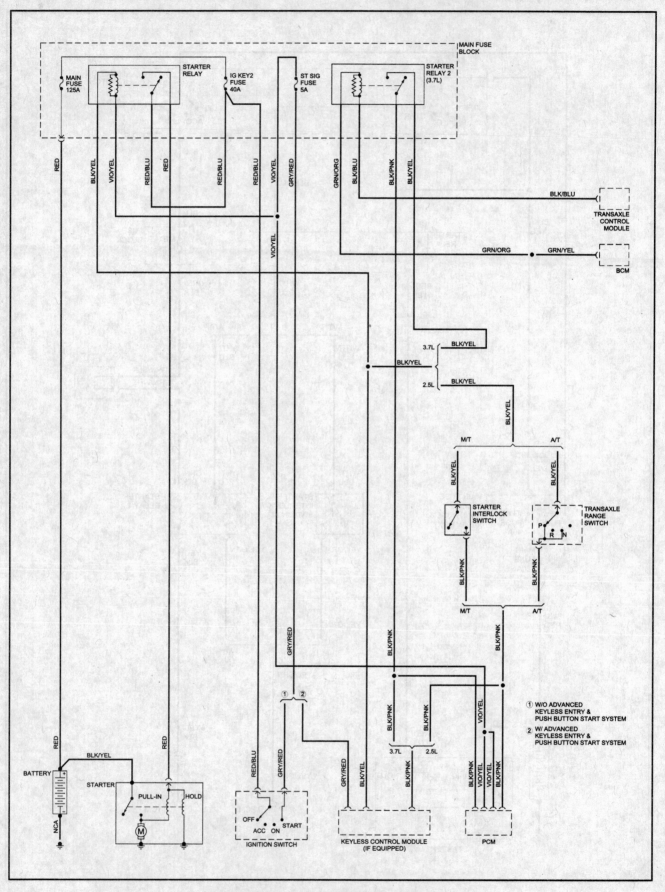

Starting system - 2009 and later models (all)

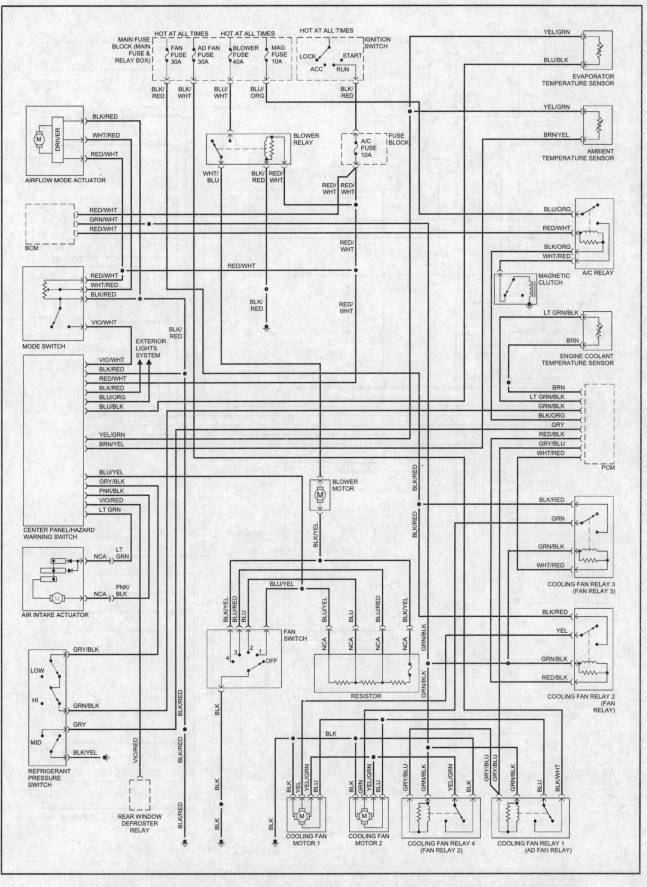

Air conditioning, heating and engine cooling fan system (manual) - 2008 and earlier four-cylinder models

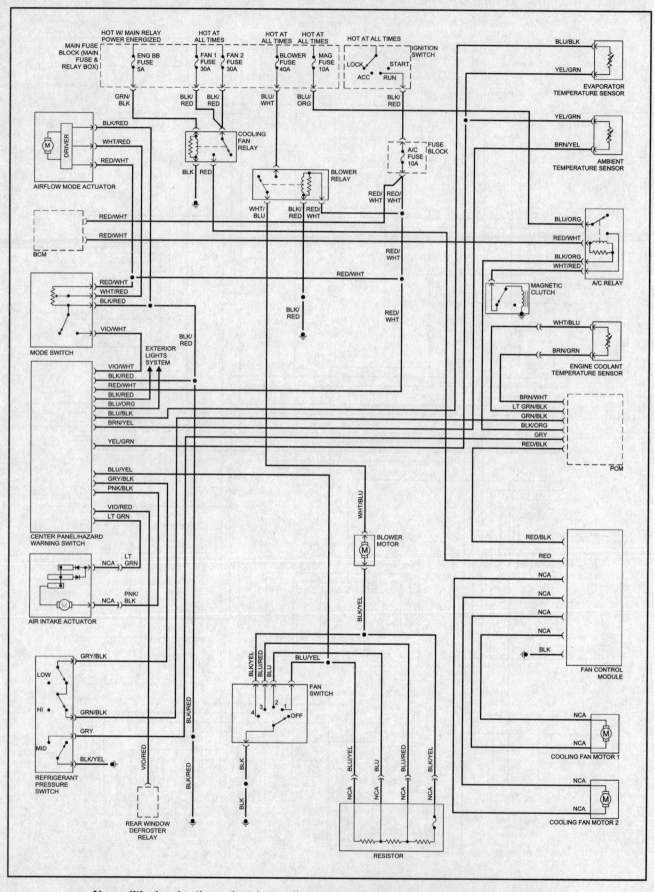

Air conditioning, heating and engine cooling fan system (manual) - 2008 and earlier V6 models

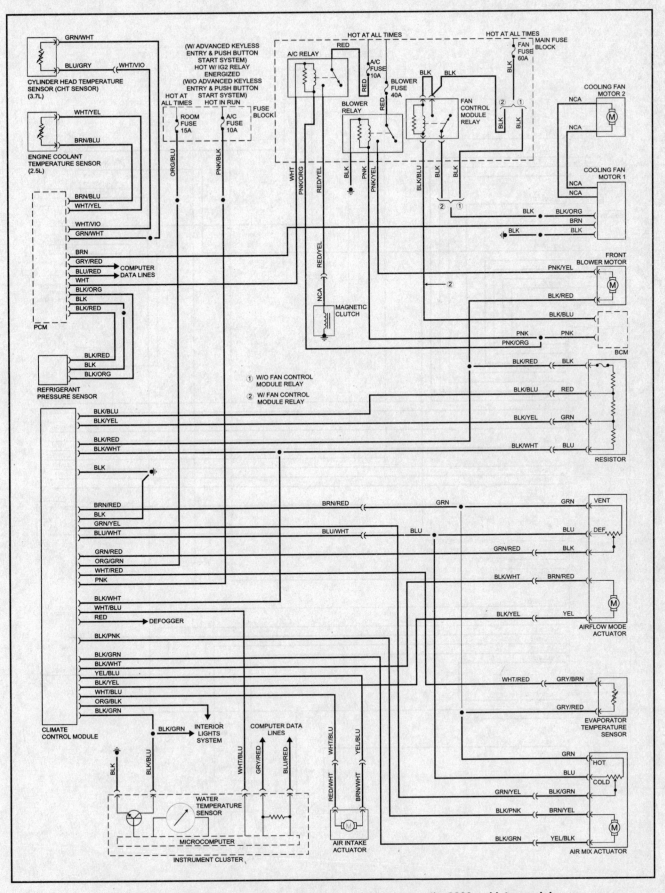

Air conditioning, heating and engine cooling fan system (manual) - 2009 and later models

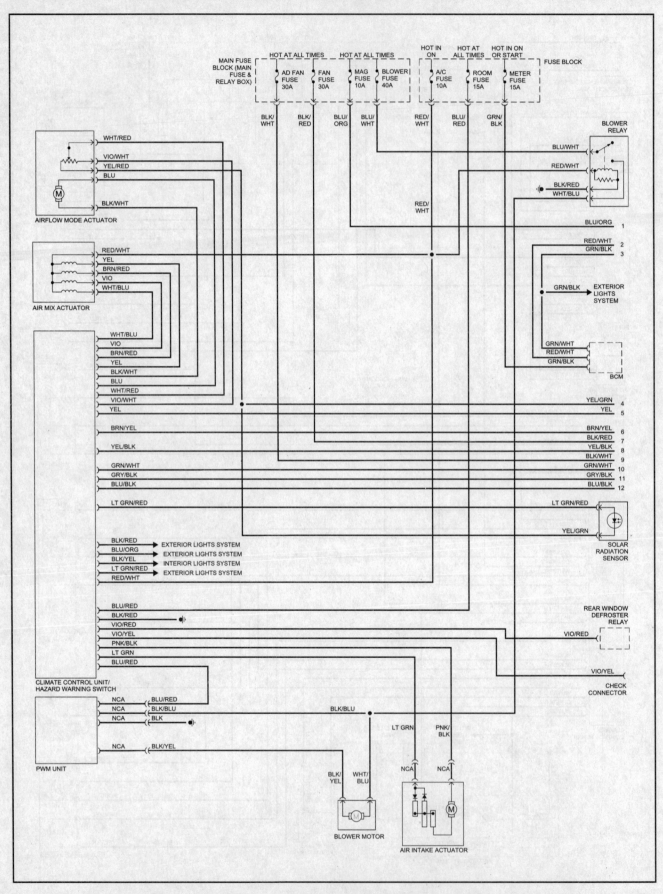

Air conditioning, heating and engine cooling fan system (automatic) - 2007 and 2008 four-cylinder models (1 of 2)

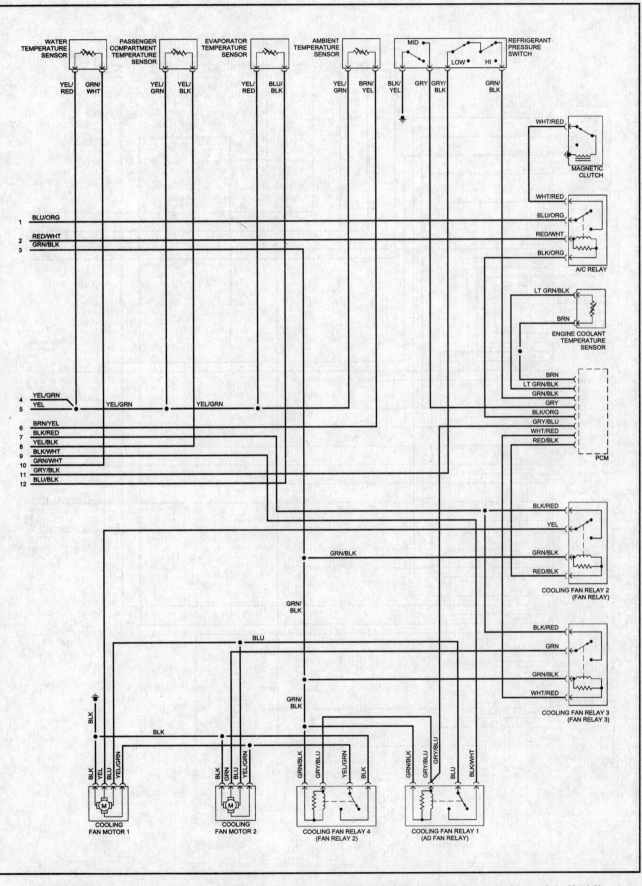

Air conditioning, heating and engine cooling fan system (automatic) - 2007 and 2008 four-cylinder models (2 of 2)

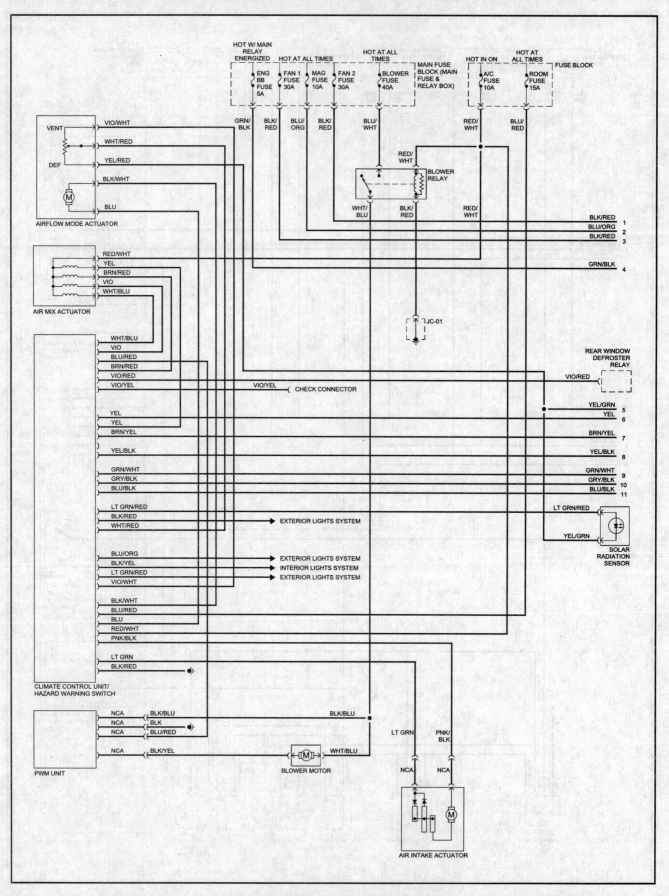

Air conditioning, heating and engine cooling fan system (automatic) - 2008 and earlier V6 models (1 of 2)

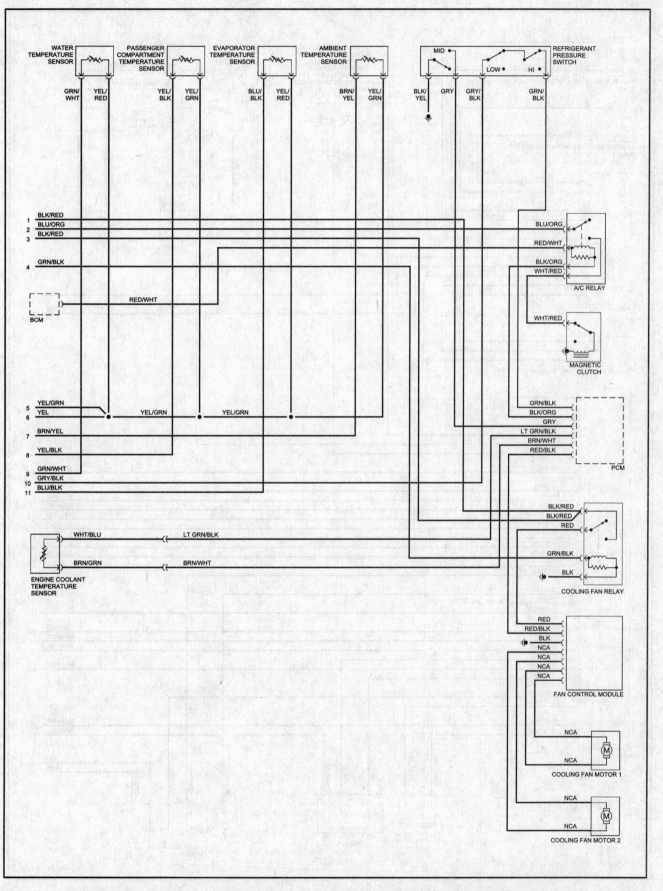

Air conditioning, heating and engine cooling fan system (automatic) - 2008 and earlier V6 models (2 of 2)

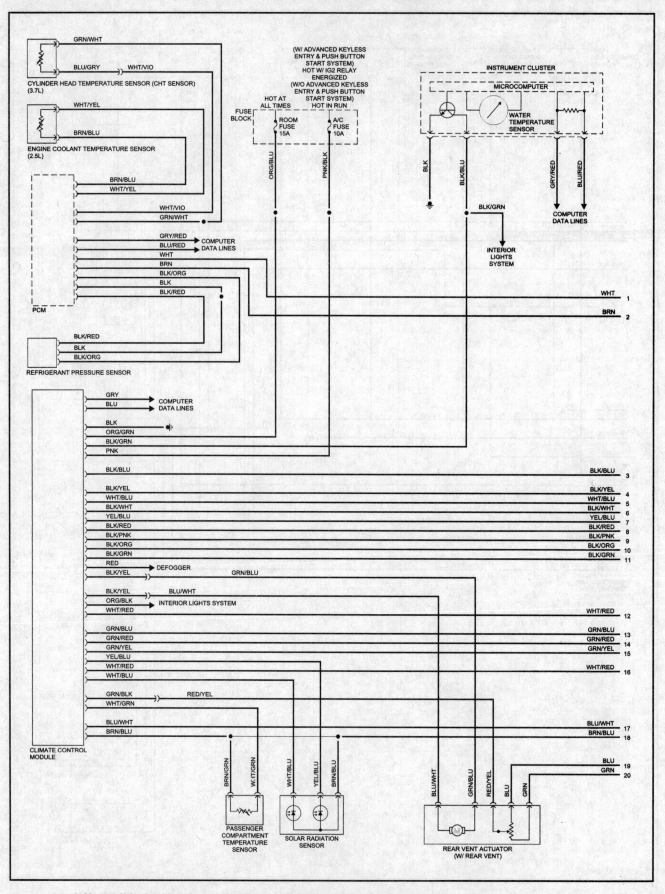

Air conditioning, heating and engine cooling fan system (automatic) - 2009 and later models (1 of 3)

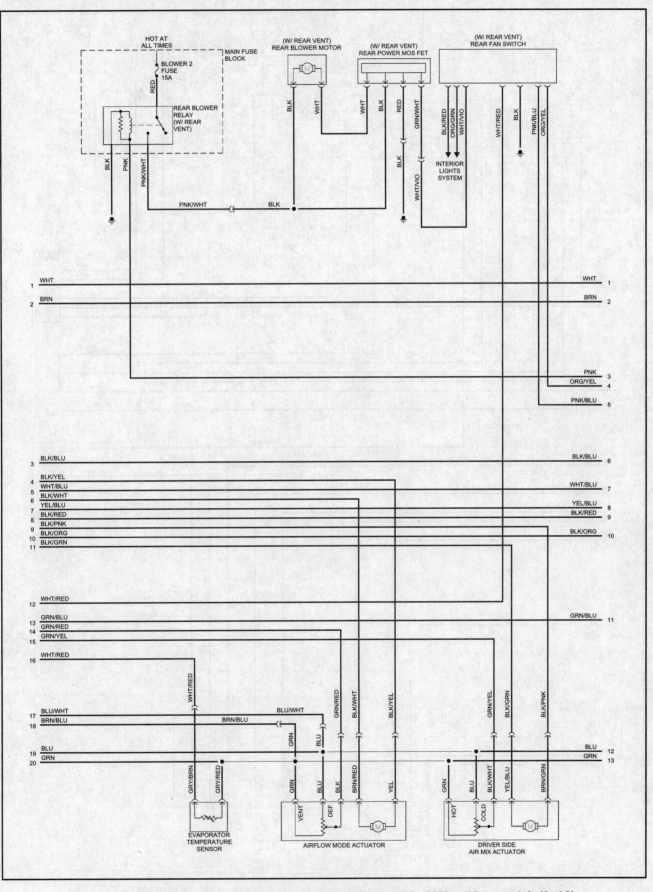

Air conditioning, heating and engine cooling fan system (automatic) - 2009 and later models (2 of 3)

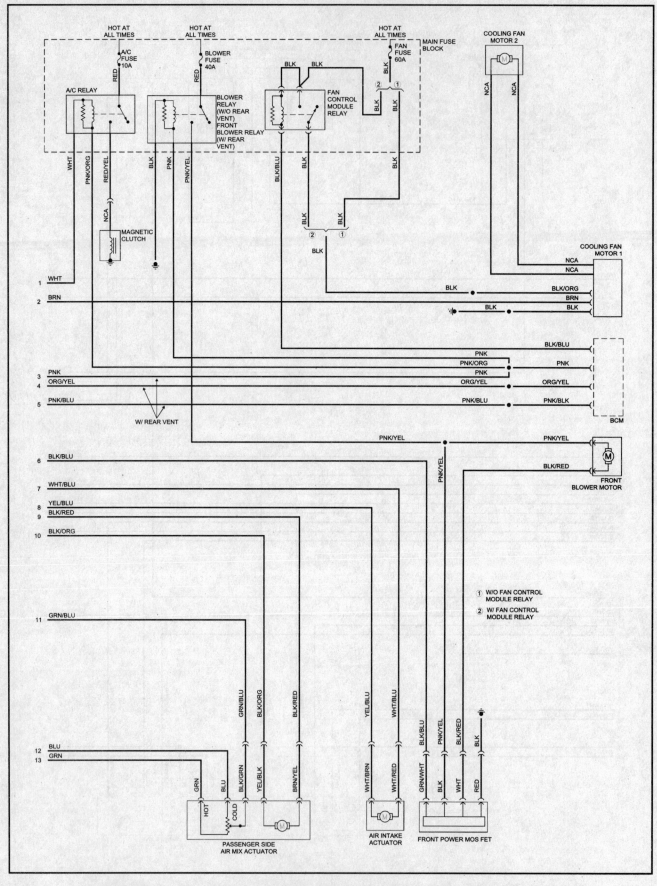

Air conditioning, heating and engine cooling fan system (automatic) - 2009 and later models (3 of 3)

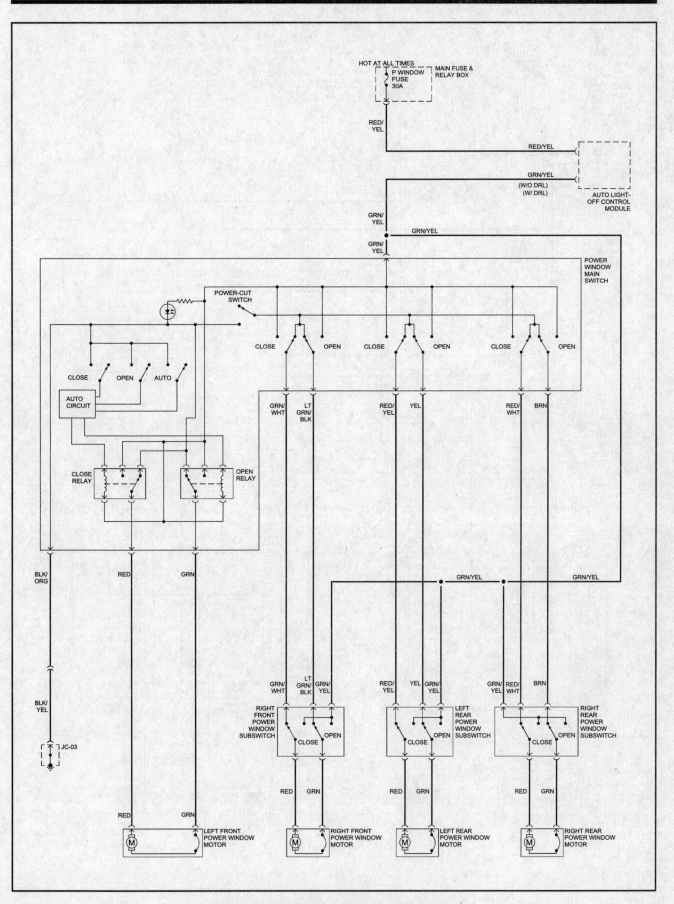

Power window system - 2005 and earlier models

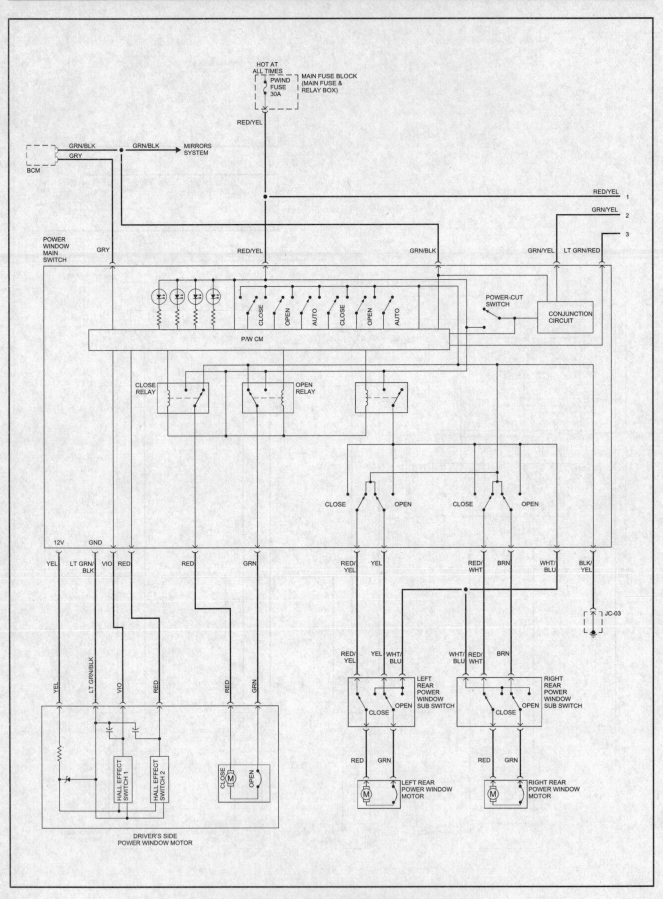

Power window system - 2006 through 2008 models (1 of 2)

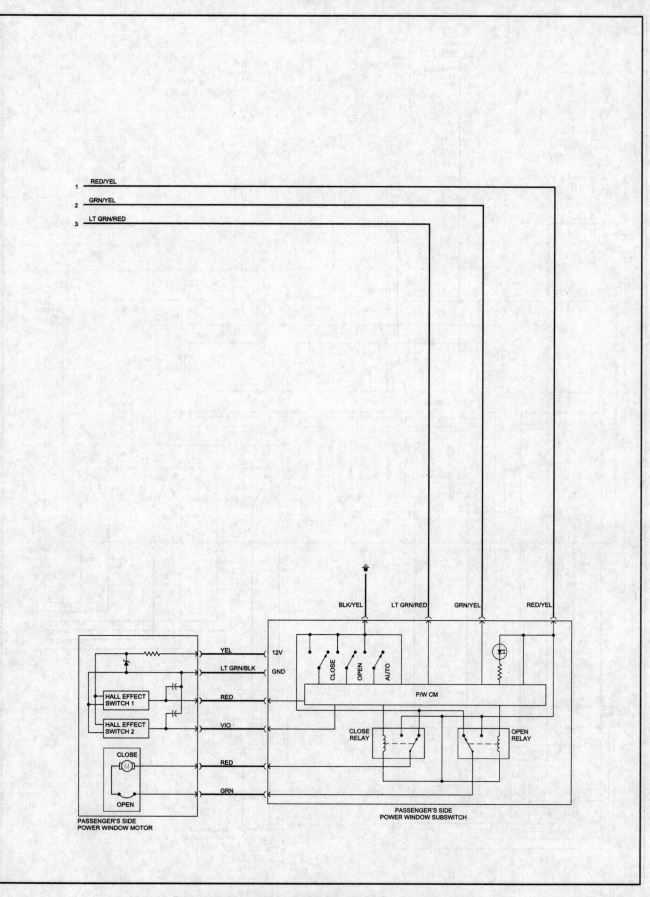

Power window system - 2006 through 2008 models (2 of 2)

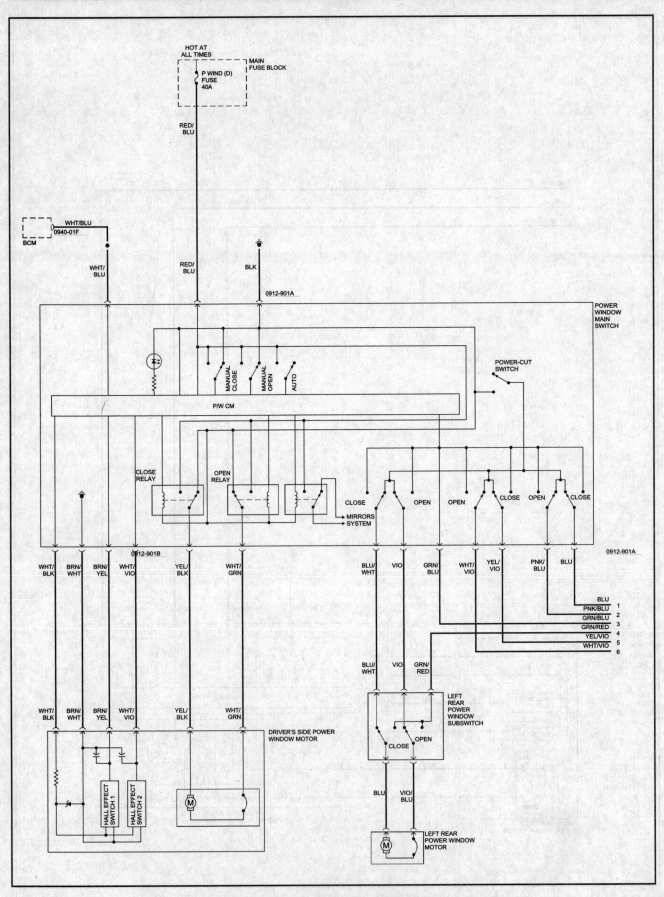

Power window system (with pinch protection) - 2009 and later models (1 of 2)

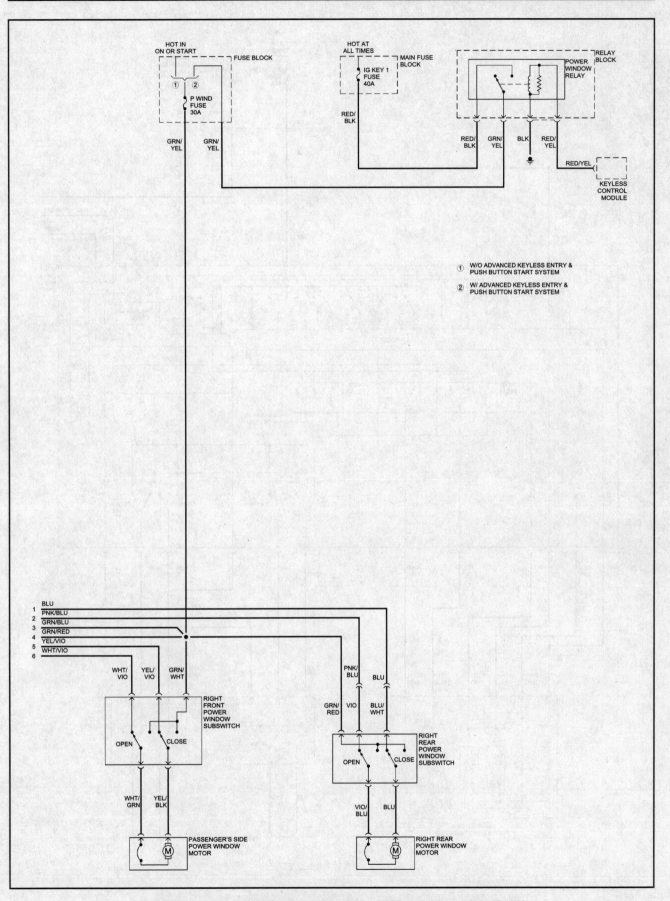

Power window system (with pinch protection) - 2009 and later models (2 of 2)

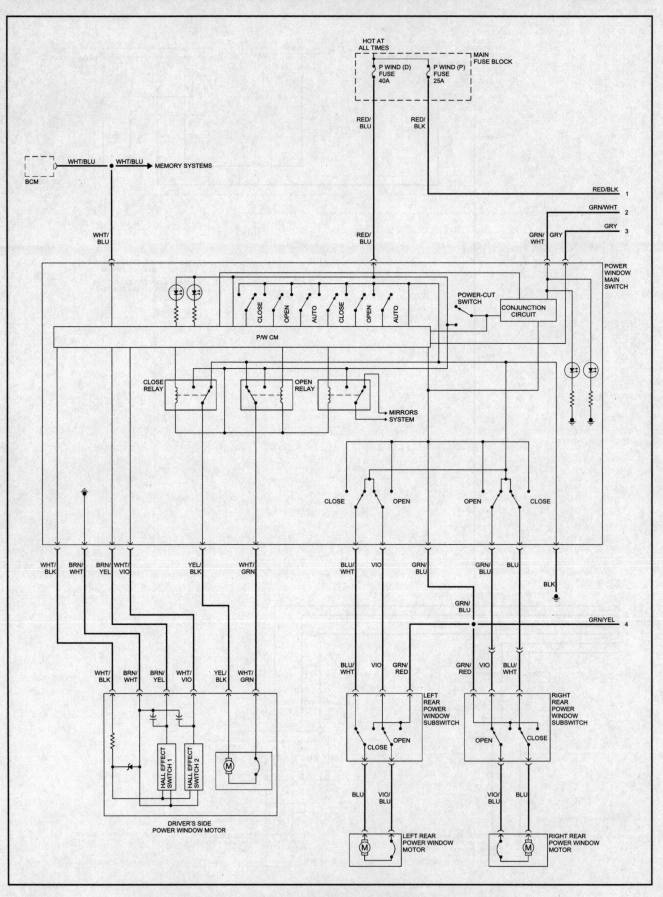

Power window system (without pinch protection) - 2009 and later models (1 of 2)

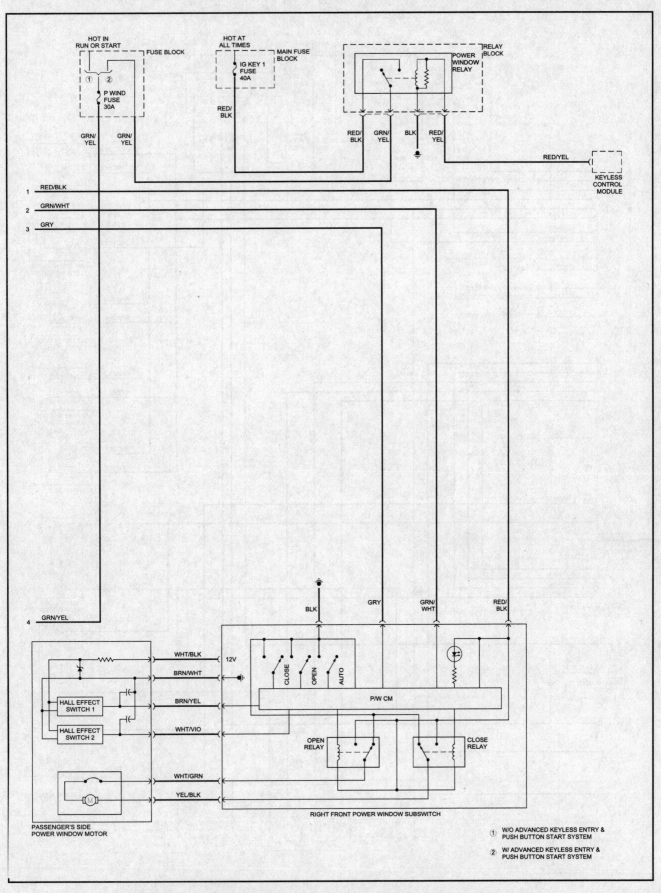

Power window system (without pinch protection) - 2009 and later models (2 of 2)

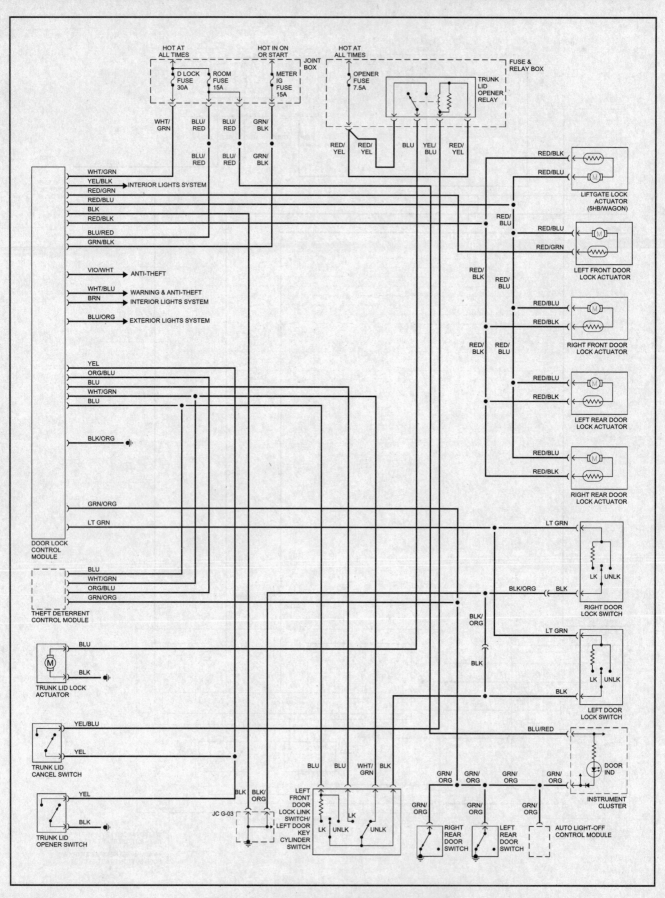

Power door lock system - 2005 and earlier models

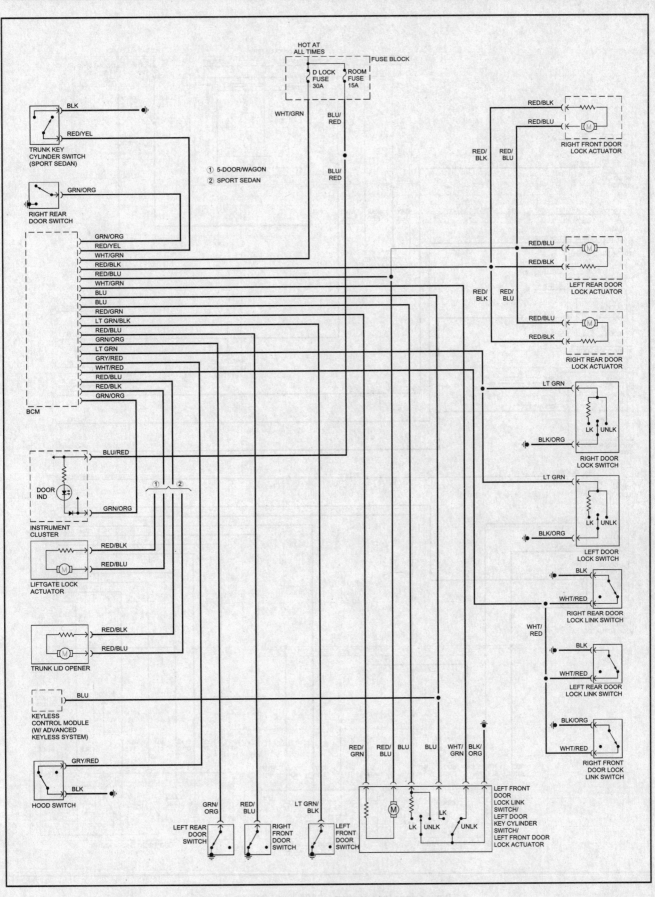

Power door lock system - 2006 through 2008 models

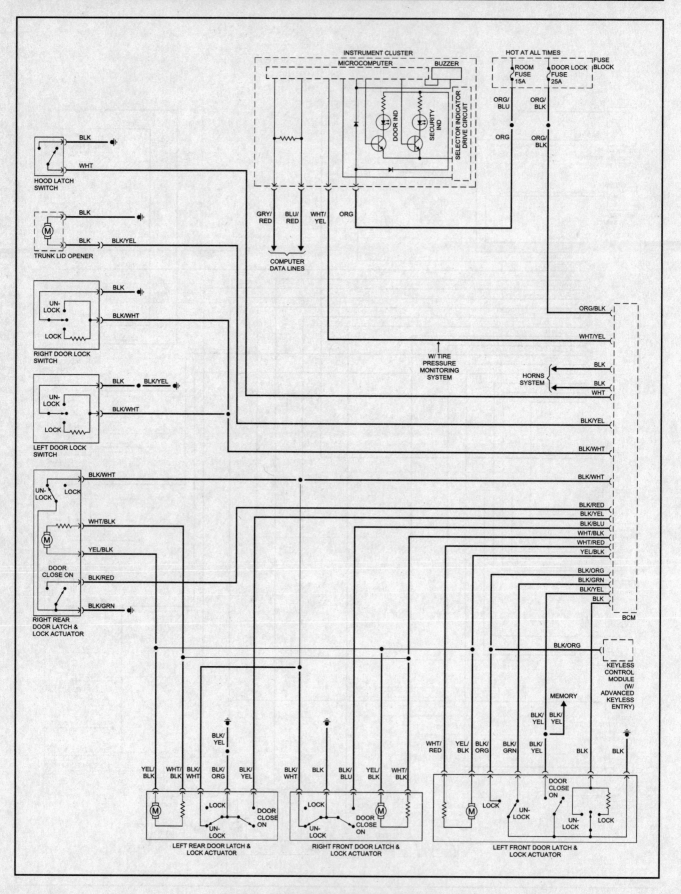

Power door lock system - 2009 and later models

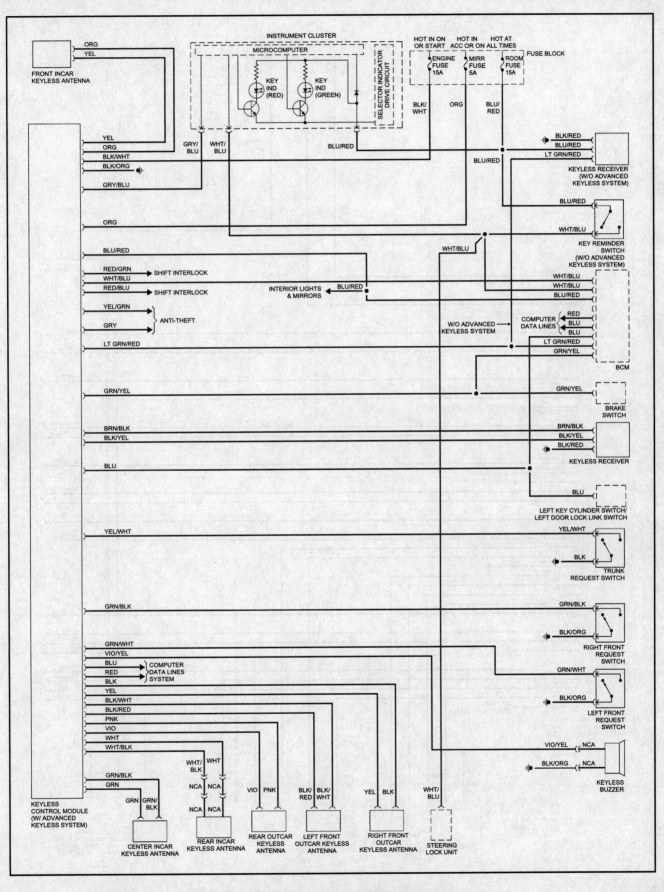

Keyless entry system - 2006 through 2008 models

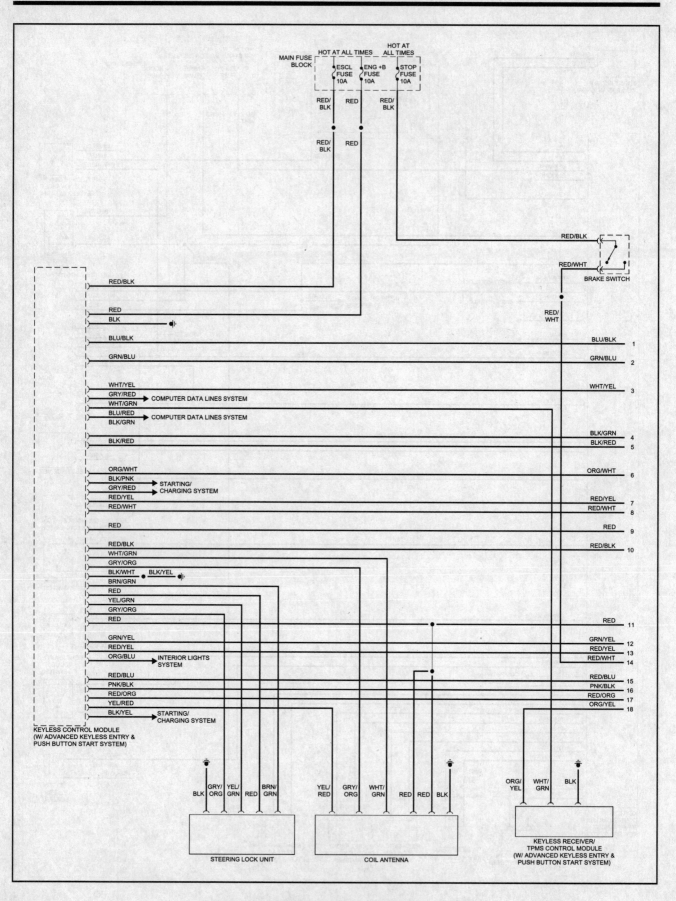

Keyless entry system - 2009 and later models (1 of 3)

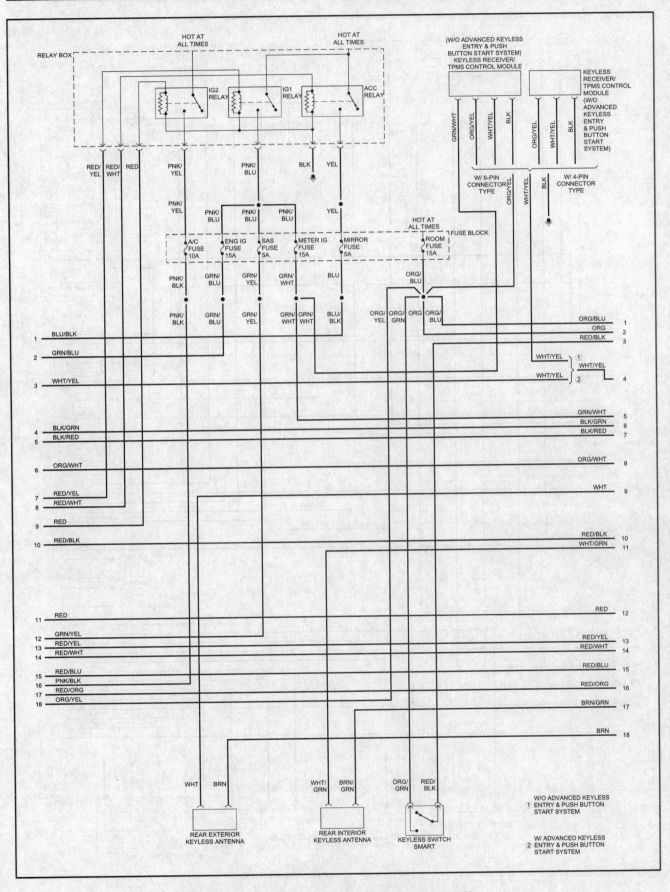

Keyless entry system - 2009 and later models (2 of 3)

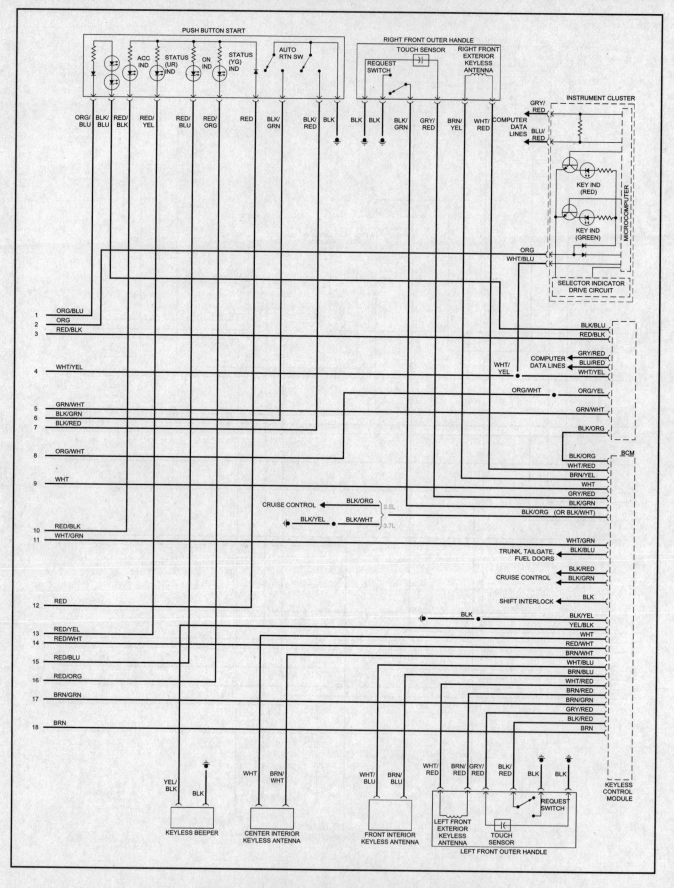

Keyless entry system - 2009 and later models (3 of 3)

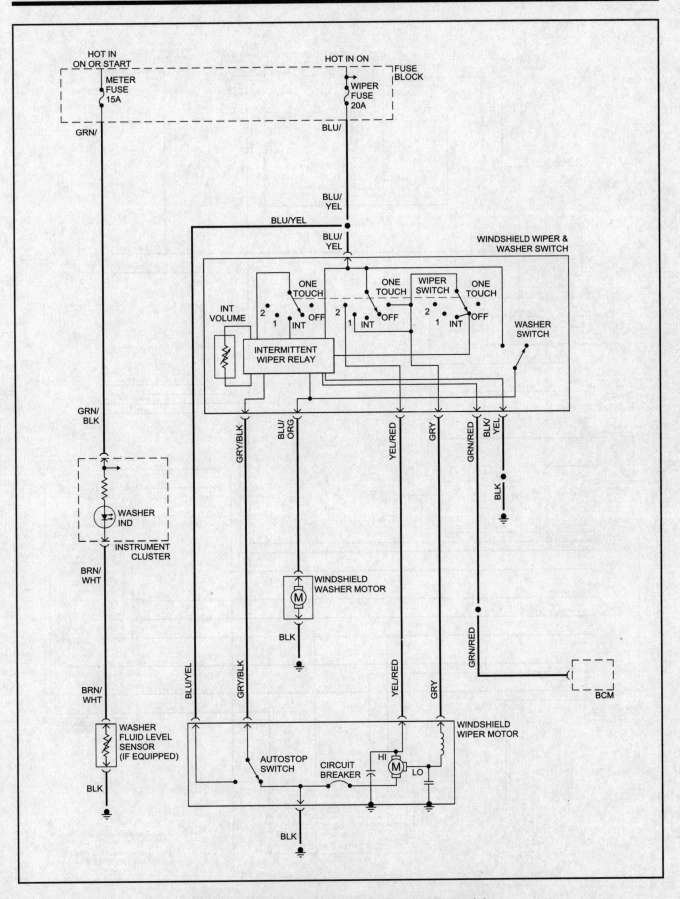

Windshield wiper/washer system - 2008 and earlier models

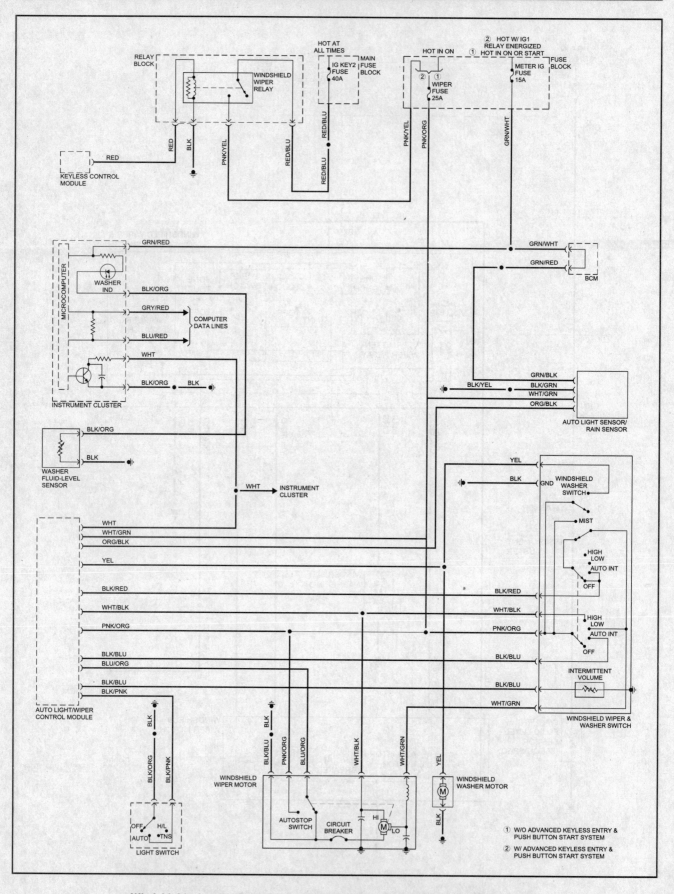

Windshield wiper/washer system (with automatic wipers) - 2009 and later models

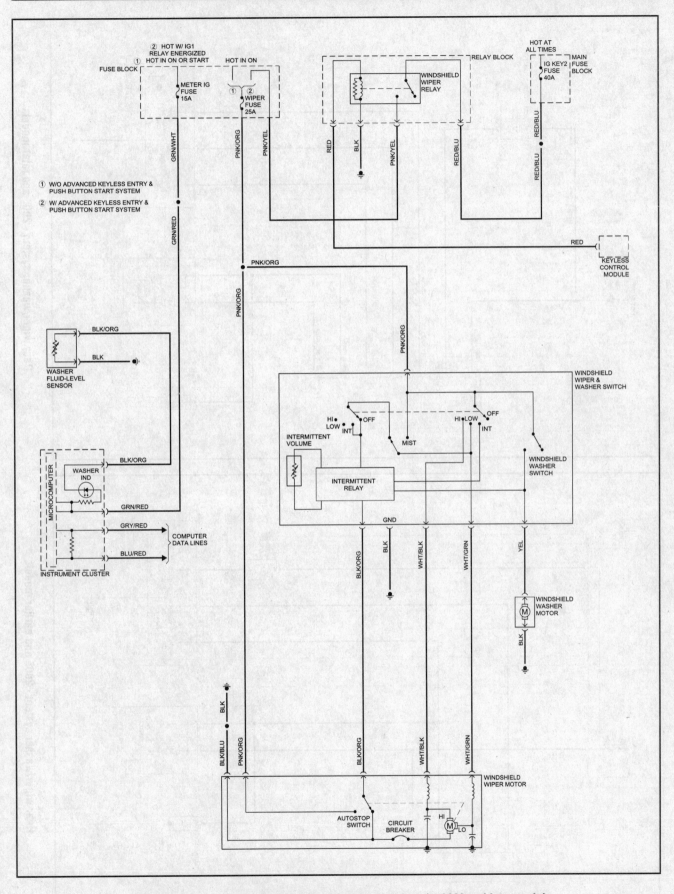

Windshield wiper/washer system (without automatic wipers) - 2009 and later models

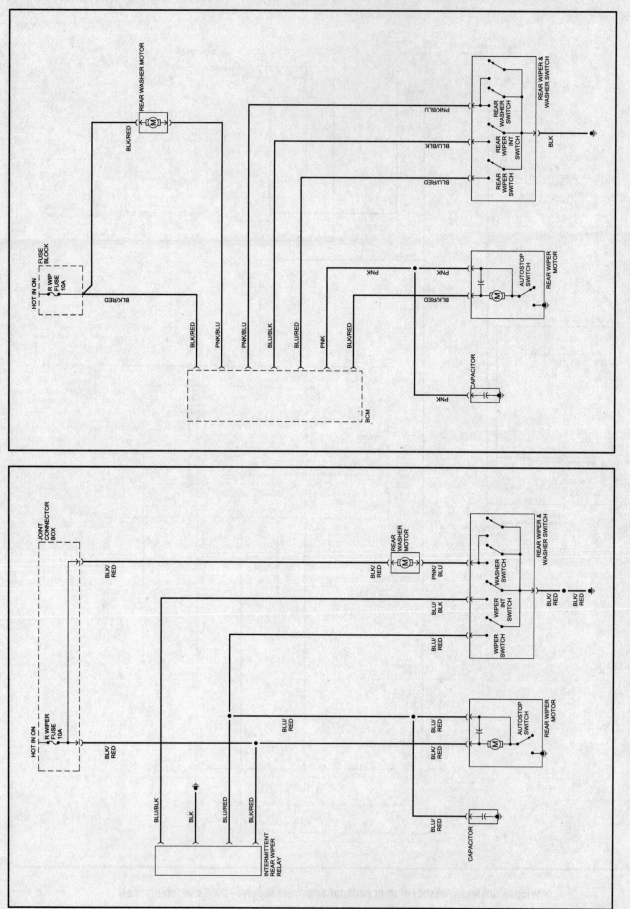

Rear wiper/washer system - 2006 and later models

Rear wiper/washer system - 2005 and earlier models

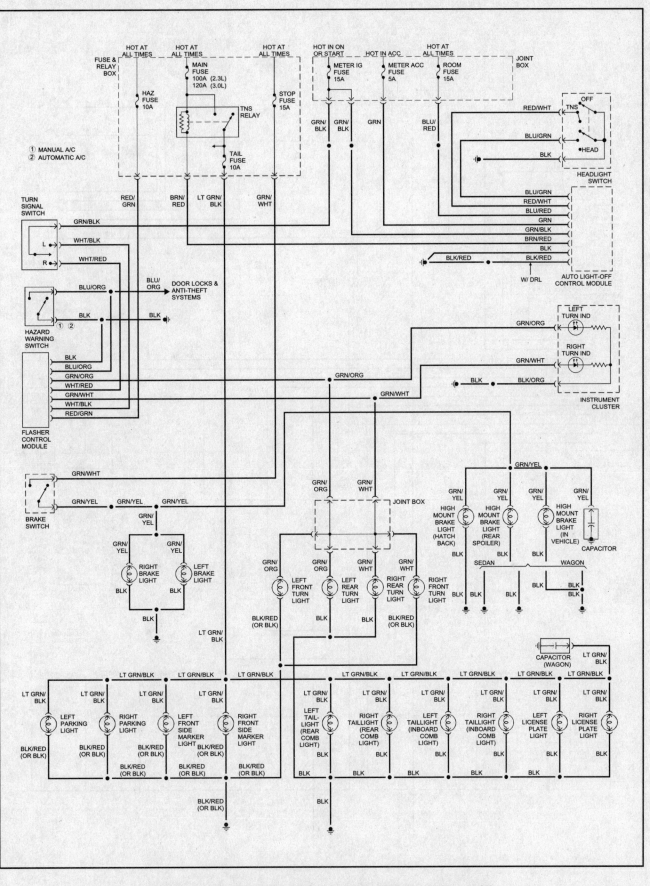

Exterior lighting system (except headlights) - 2005 and earlier models

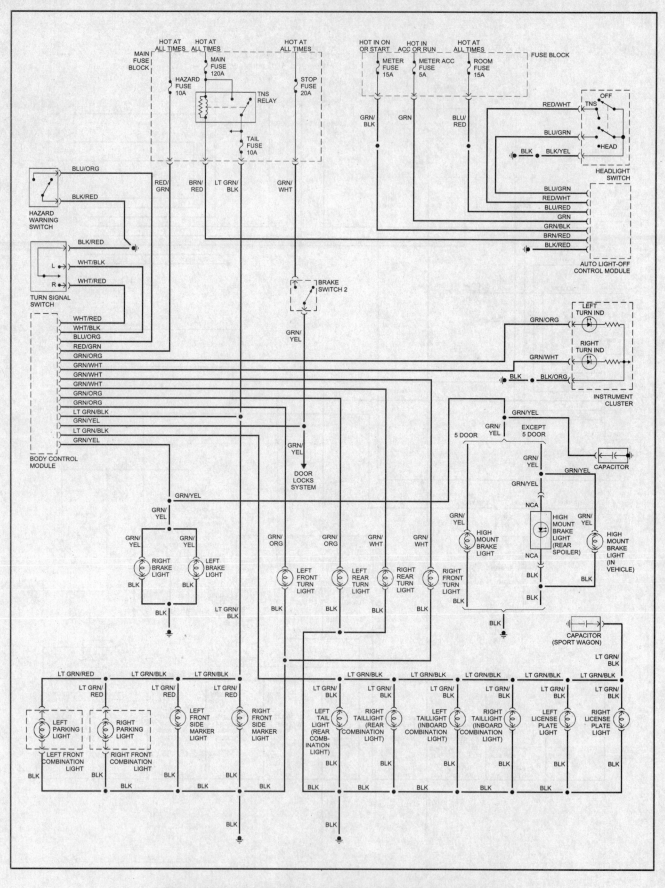

Exterior lighting system (except headlights) - 2006 through 2008 models

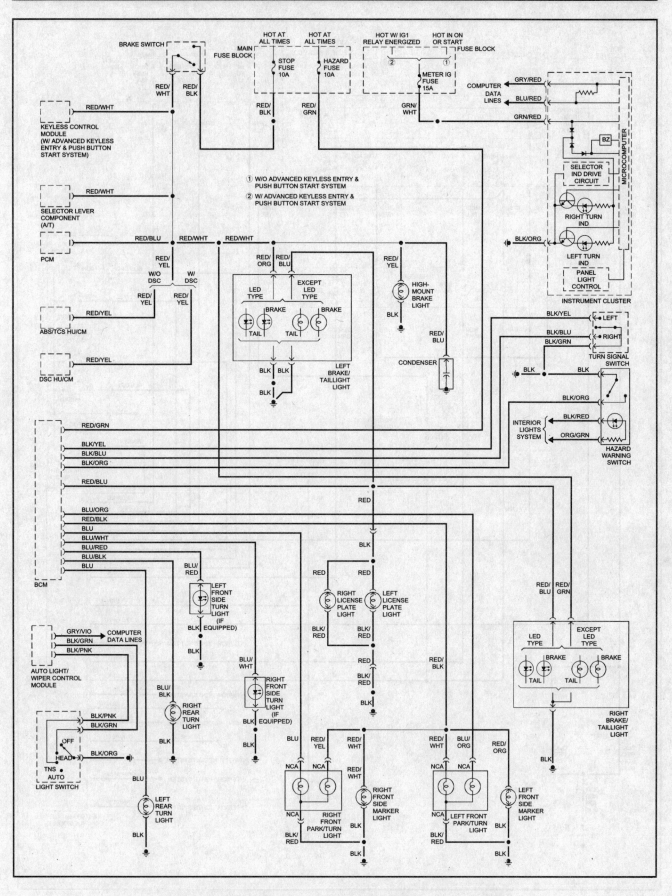

Exterior lighting system (except headlights) - 2009 and later models

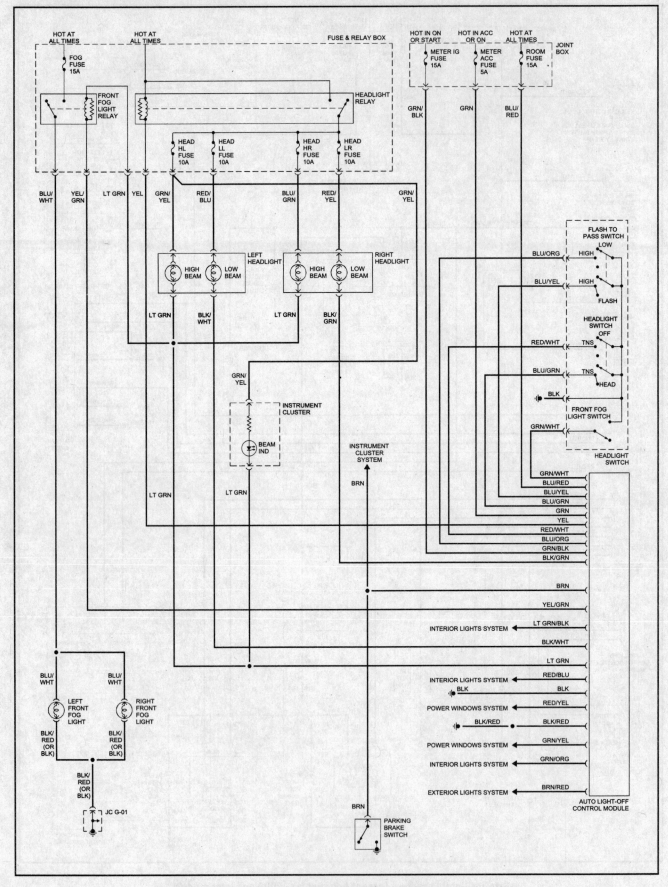

Headlight system (with Daytime Running Lights) - 2005 and earlier models

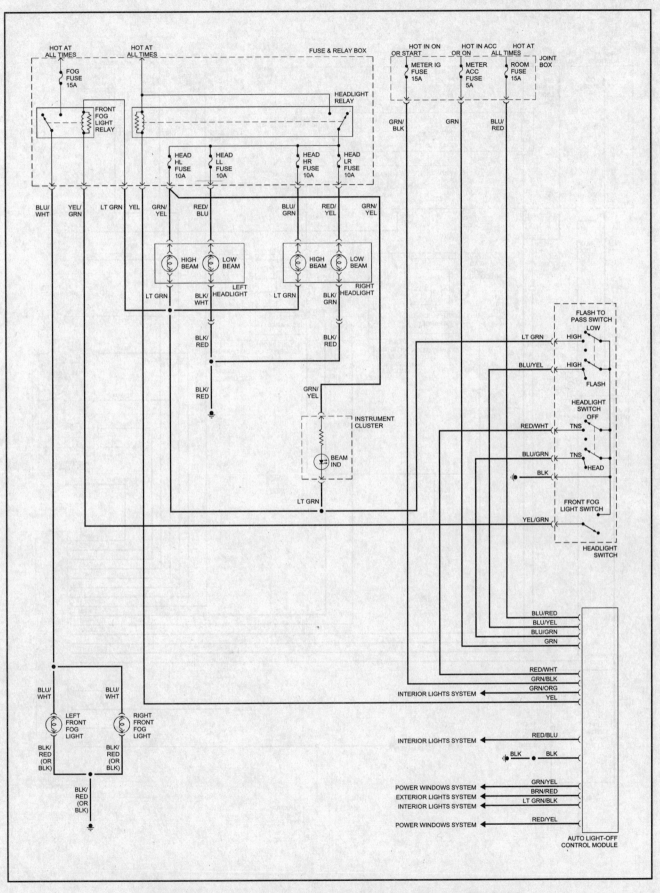

Headlight system (without Daytime Running Lights) - 2005 and earlier models

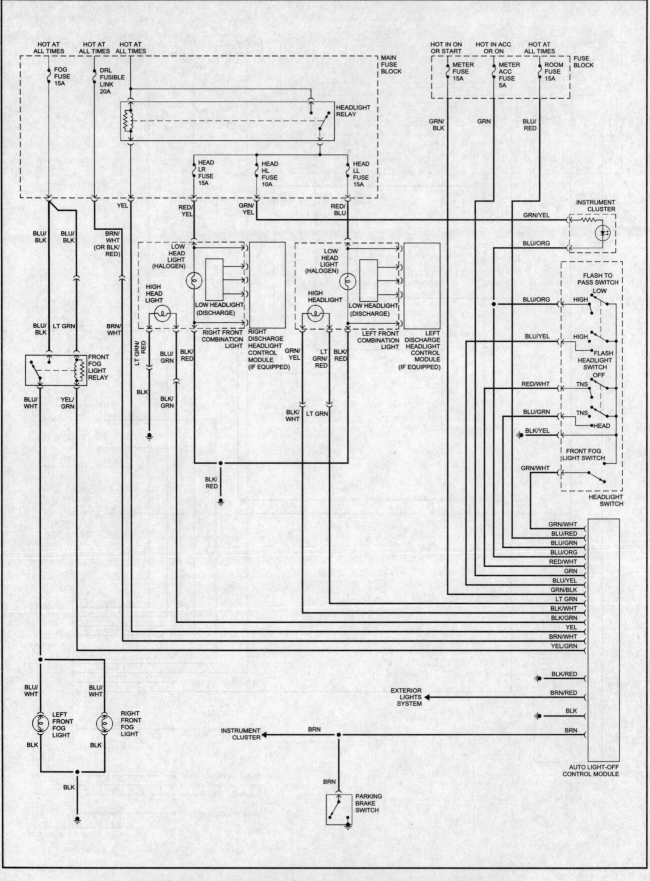

Headlight system (with Daytime Running Lights) - 2006 through 2008 models

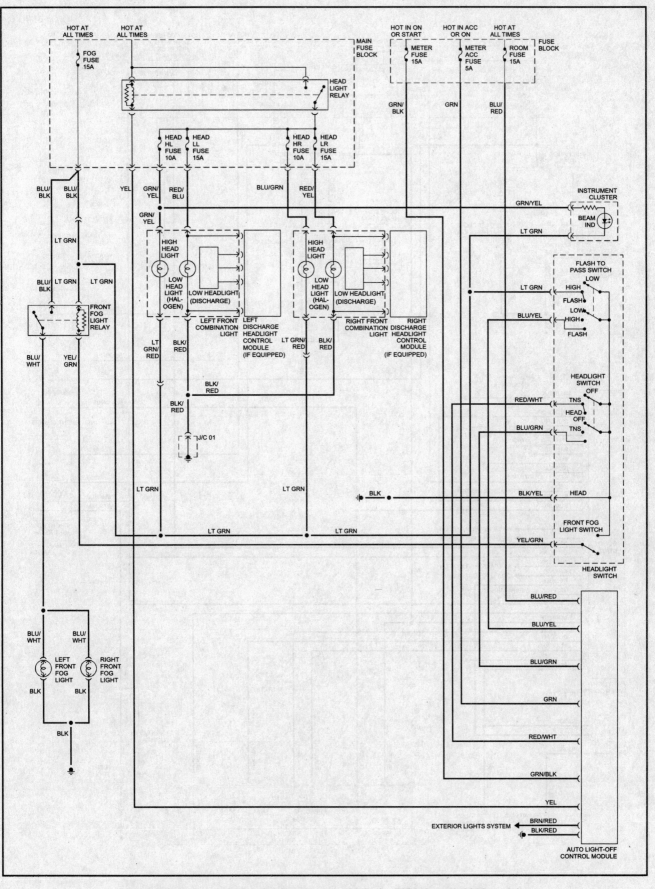

Headlight system (without Daytime Running Lights) - 2006 through 2008 models

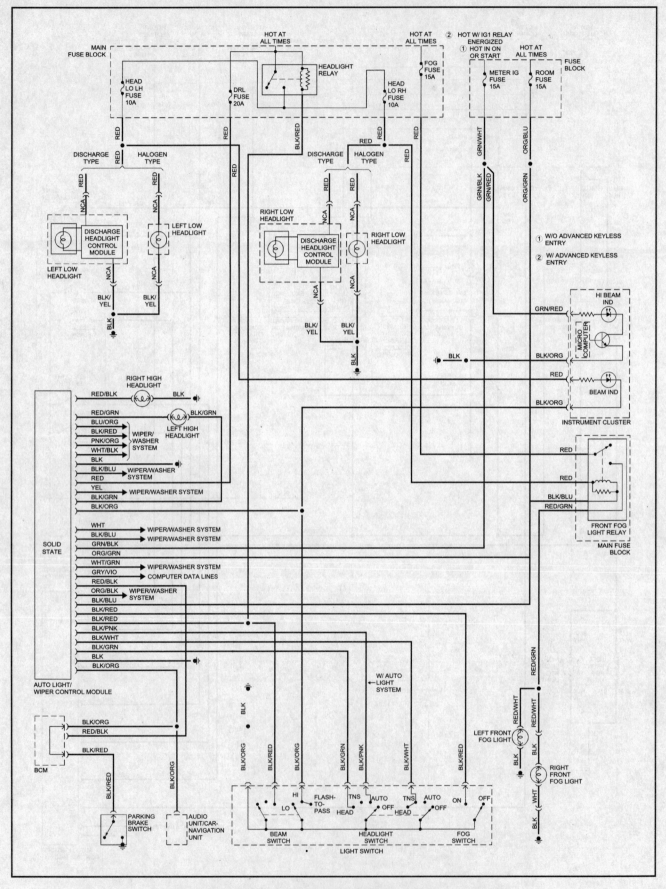

Headlight system (with Daytime Running Lights) - 2009 and later models

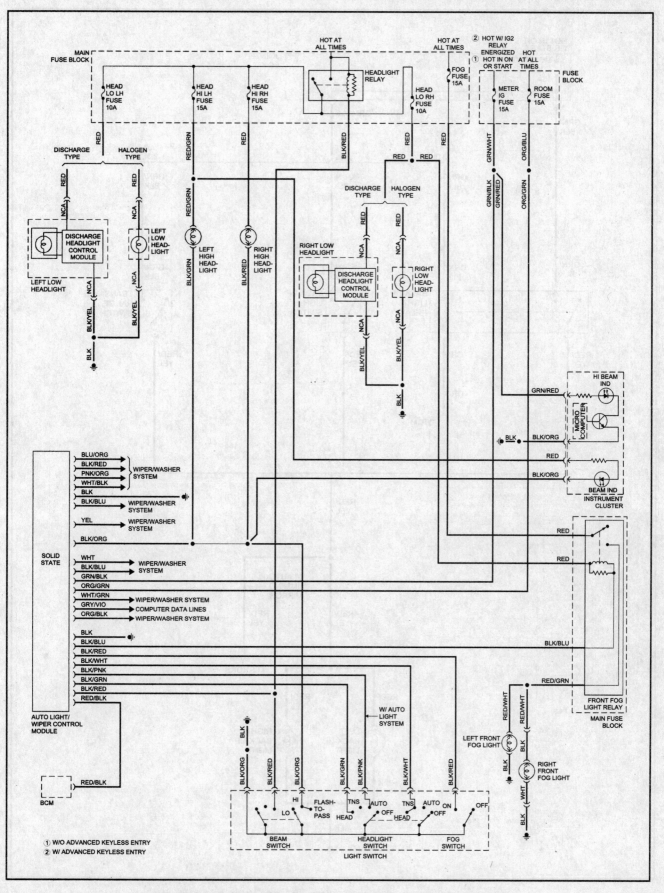

Headlight system (without Daytime Running Lights) - 2009 and later models

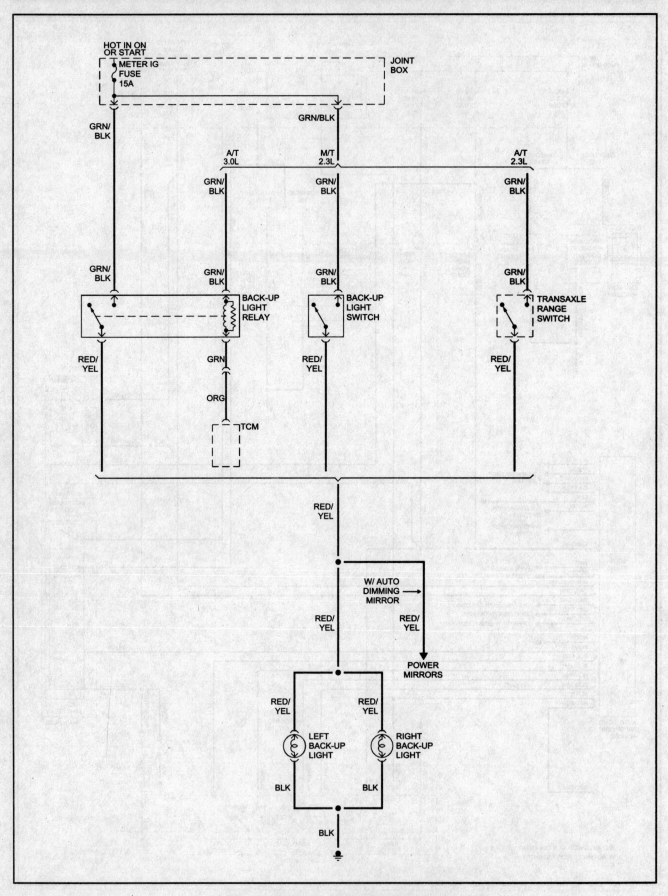

Back-up light system - 2005 and earlier models

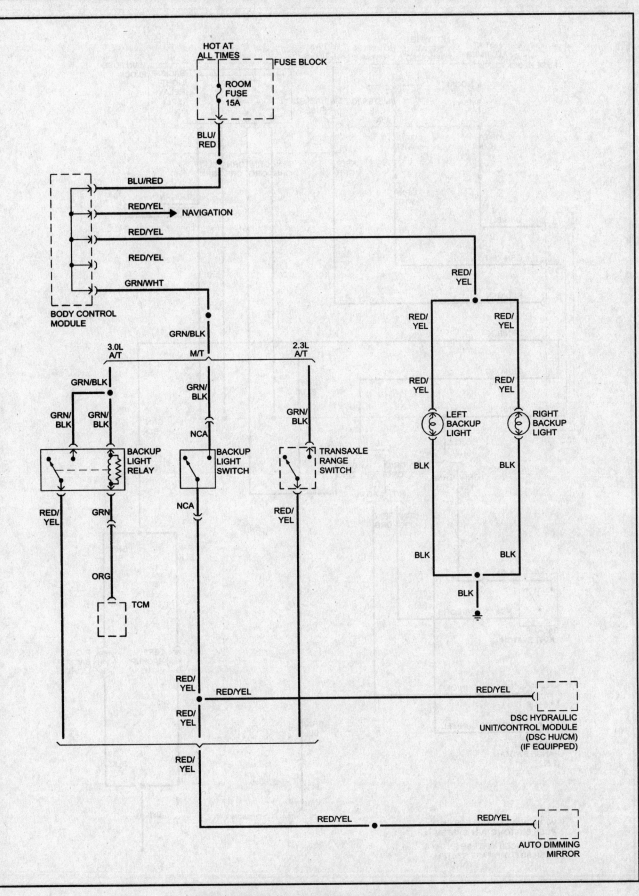

Back-up light system - 2006 through 2008 models

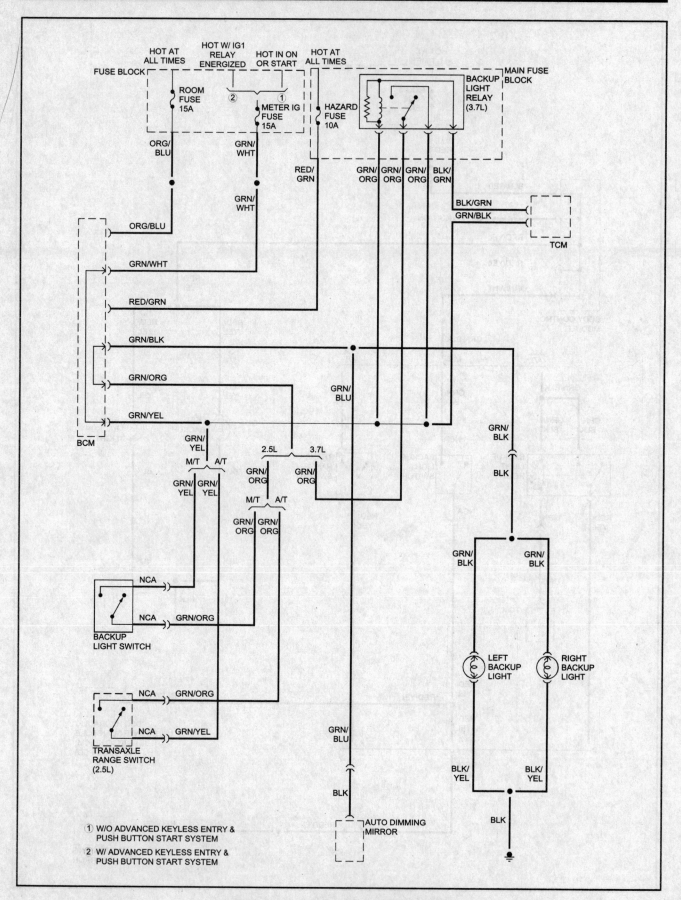

Back-up light system - 2009 and later models

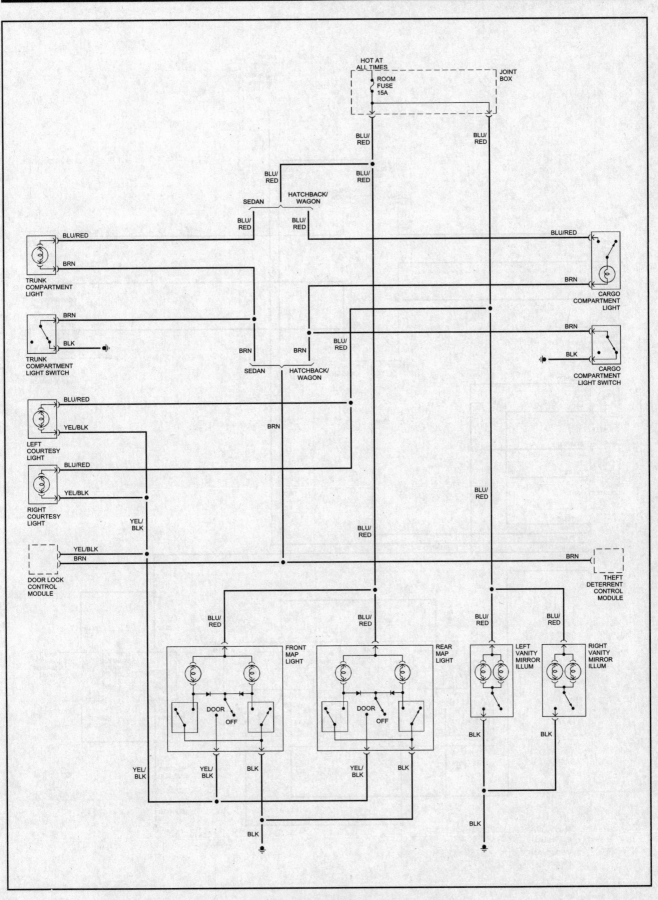

Interior lighting system - 2006 and earlier models

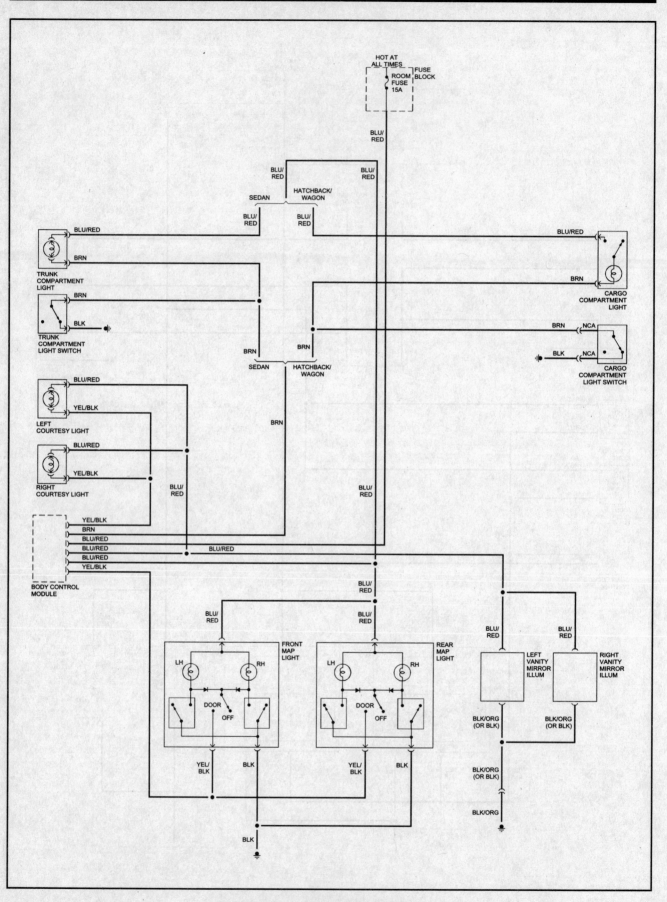

Interior lighting system - 2007 and 2008 models

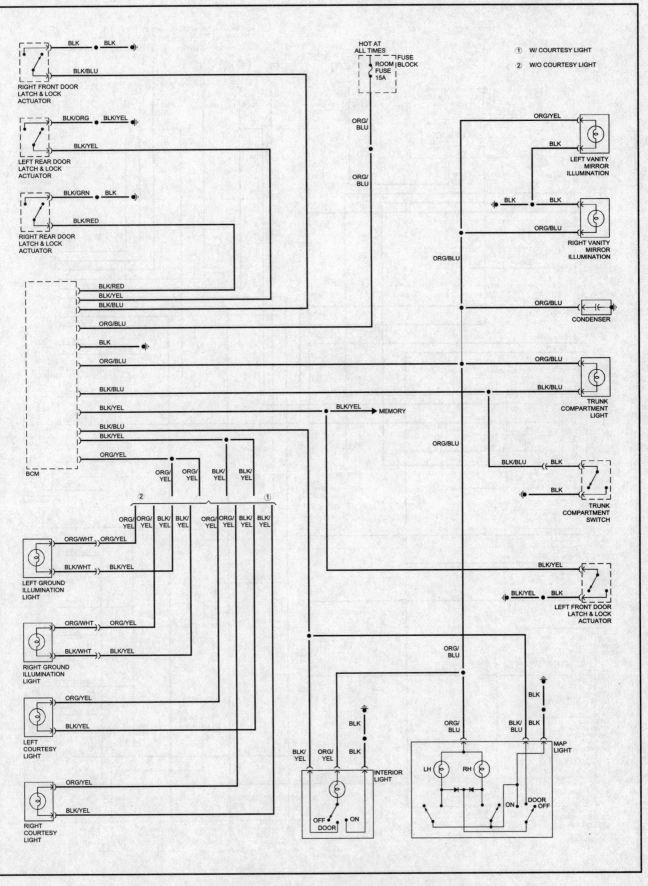

Interior lighting system - 2009 and later models

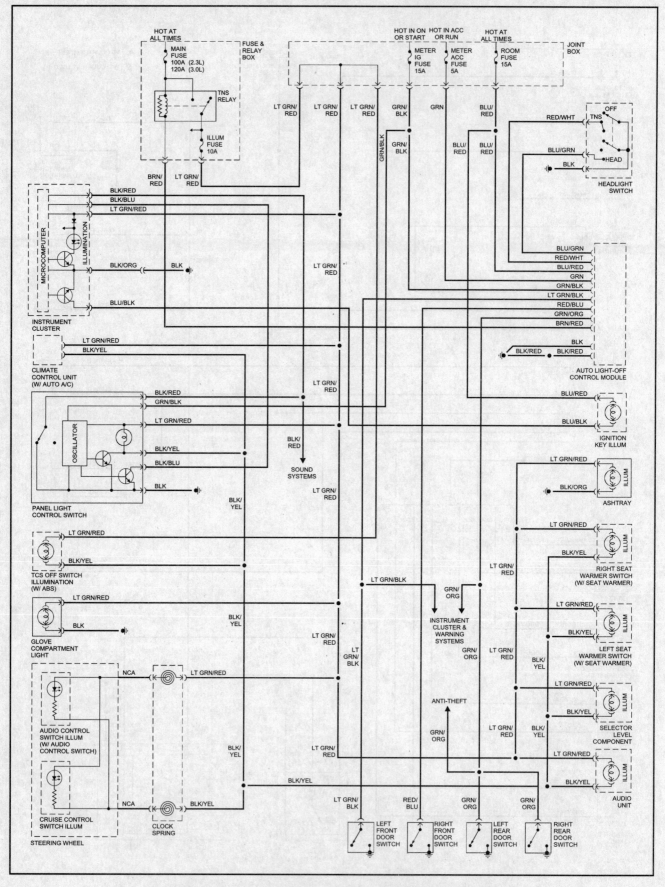

Instrument panel and switch illumination - 2005 and earlier models

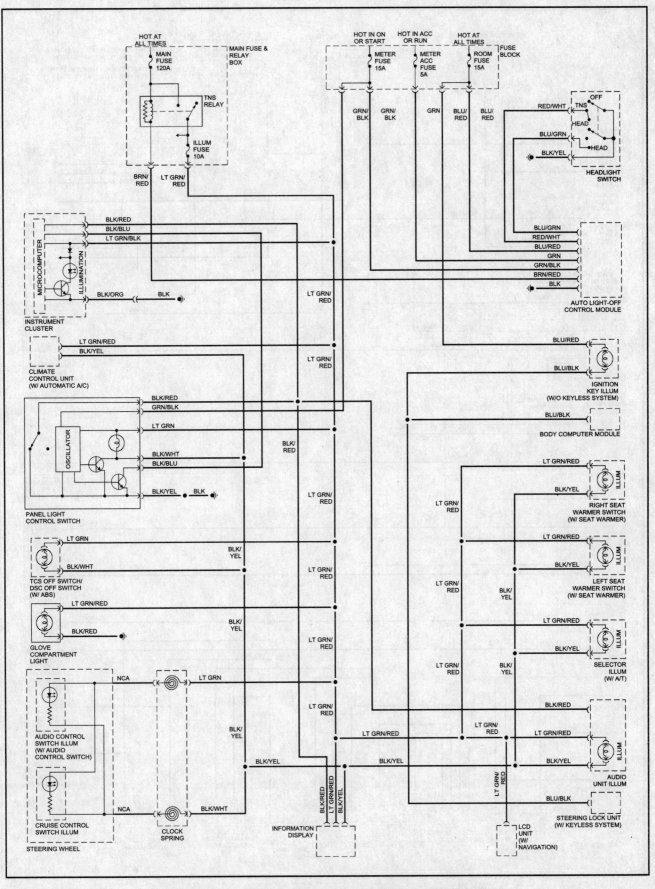

Instrument panel and switch illumination - 2006 through 2008 models

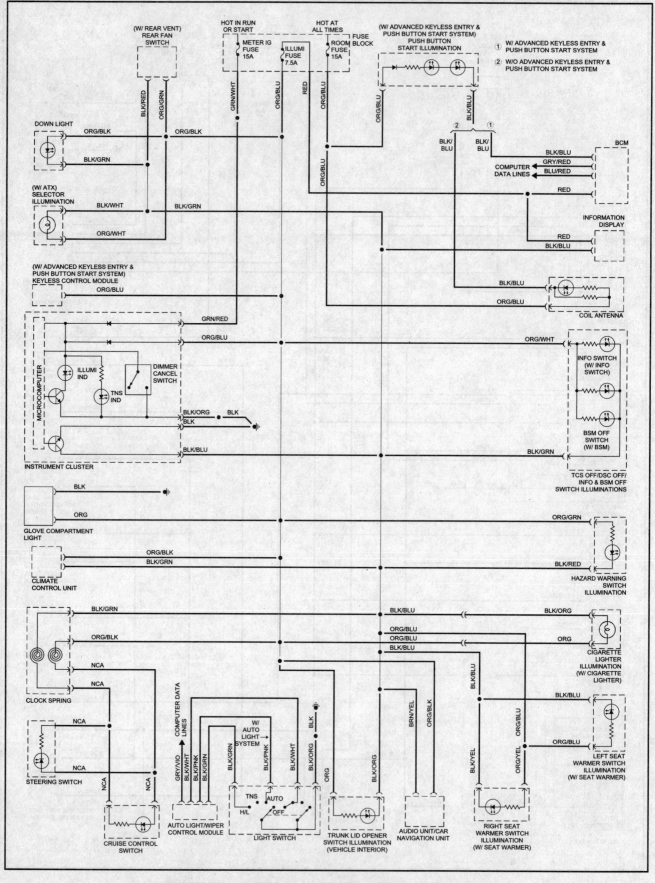

Instrument panel and switch illumination - 2009 and later models

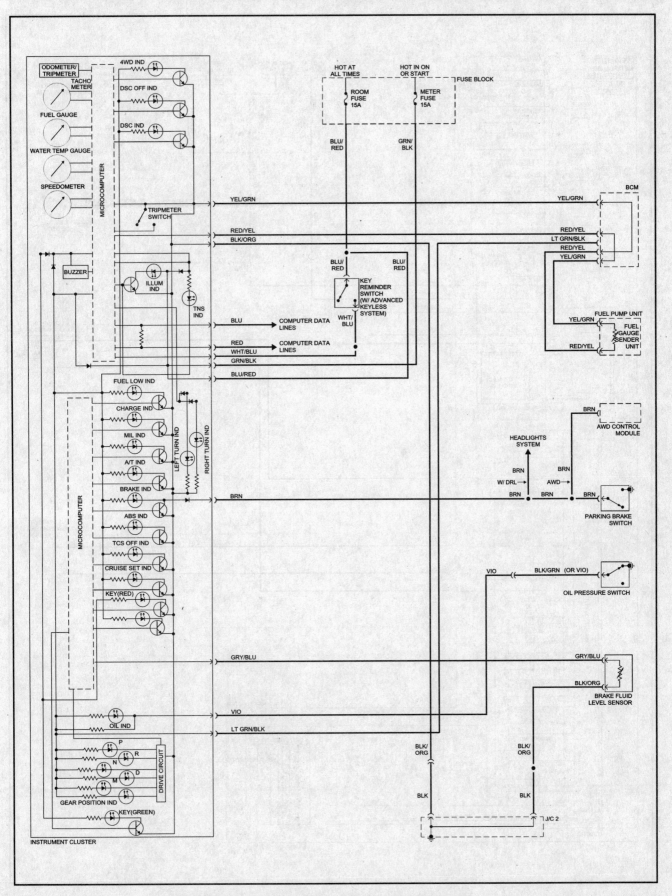

Warning lights and gauges - 2008 and earlier models

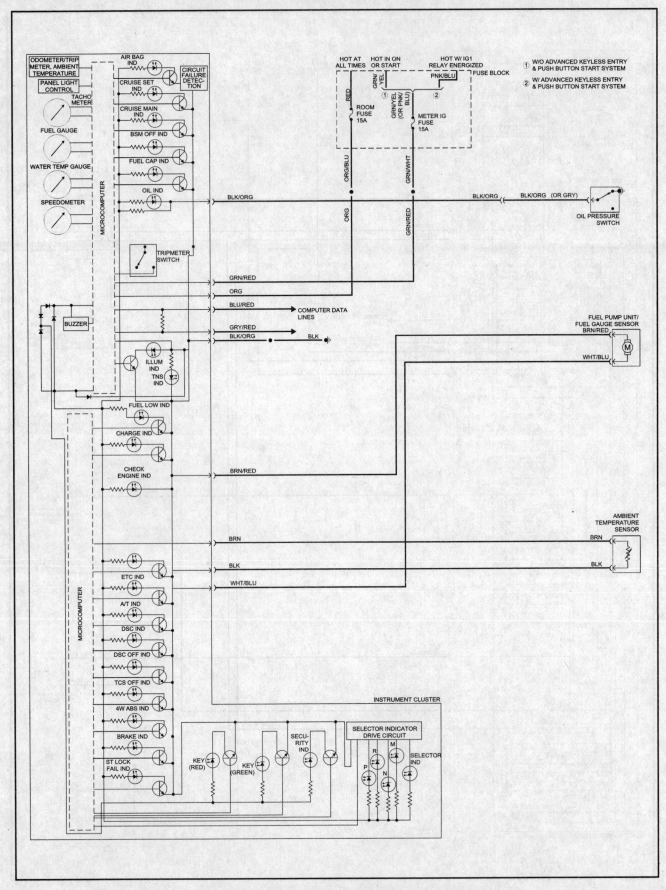

Warning lights and gauges - 2009 and later models

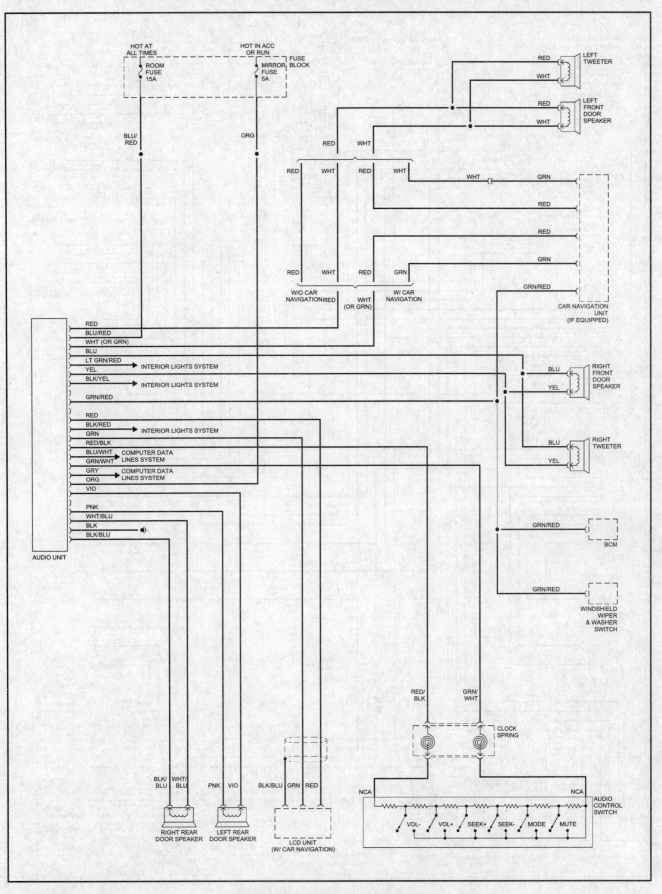

Audio system - 2008 and earlier models

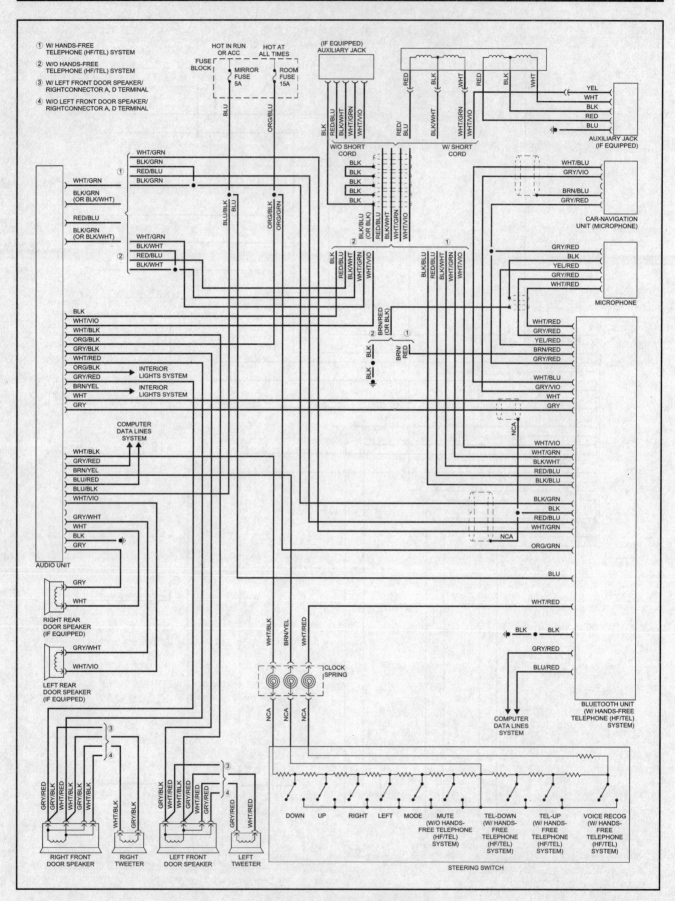

Audio system - 2009 and later models

GLOSSARY

AIR/FUEL RATIO: The ratio of air-to-gasoline by weight in the fuel mixture drawn into the engine.

AIR INJECTION: One method of reducing harmful exhaust emissions by injecting air into each of the exhaust ports of an engine. The fresh air entering the hot exhaust manifold causes any remaining fuel to be burned before it can exit the tailpipe.

ALTERNATOR: A device used for converting mechanical energy into electrical energy.

AMMETER: An instrument, calibrated in amperes, used to measure the flow of an electrical current in a circuit. Ammeters are always connected in series with the circuit being tested.

AMPERE: The rate of flow of electrical current present when one volt of electrical pressure is applied against one ohm of electrical resistance.

ANALOG COMPUTER: Any microprocessor that uses similar (analogous) electrical signals to make its calculations.

ARMATURE: A laminated, soft iron core wrapped by a wire that converts electrical energy to mechanical energy as in a motor or relay. When rotated in a magnetic field, it changes mechanical energy into electrical energy as in a generator.

ATMOSPHERIC PRESSURE: The pressure on the Earth's surface caused by the weight of the air in the atmosphere. At sea level, this pressure is 14.7 psi at 32°F (101 kPa at 0°C).

ATOMIZATION: The breaking down of a liquid into a fine mist that can be suspended in air.

AXIAL PLAY: Movement parallel to a shaft or bearing bore.

BACKFIRE: The sudden combustion of gases in the intake or exhaust system that results in a loud explosion.

BACKLASH: The clearance or play between two parts, such as meshed gears.

BACKPRESSURE: Restrictions in the exhaust system that slow the exit of exhaust gases from the combustion chamber.

BAKELITE: A heat resistant, plastic insulator material commonly used in printed circuit boards and transistorized components.

BALL BEARING: A bearing made up of hardened inner and outer races between which hardened steel balls roll.

BALLAST RESISTOR: A resistor in the primary ignition circuit that lowers voltage after the engine is started to reduce wear on ignition components.

BEARING: A friction reducing, supportive device usually located between a stationary part and a moving part.

BIMETAL TEMPERATURE SENSOR: Any sensor or switch made of two dissimilar types of metal that bend when heated or cooled due to the different expansion rates of the alloys. These types of sensors usually function as an on/off switch.

BLOWBY: Combustion gases, composed of water vapor and unburned fuel, that leak past the piston rings into the crankcase during normal engine operation. These gases are removed by the PCV system to prevent the buildup of harmful acids in the crankcase.

BRAKE PAD: A brake shoe and lining assembly used with disc brakes.

BRAKE SHOE: The backing for the brake lining. The term is, however, usually applied to the assembly of the brake backing and lining.

BUSHING: A liner, usually removable, for a bearing; an anti-friction liner used in place of a bearing.

CALIPER: A hydraulically activated device in a disc brake system, which is mounted straddling the brake rotor (disc). The caliper contains at least one piston and two brake pads. Hydraulic pressure on the piston(s) forces the pads against the rotor.

CAMSHAFT: A shaft in the engine on which are the lobes (cams) which operate the valves. The camshaft is driven by the crankshaft, via a belt, chain or gears, at one half the crankshaft speed.

CAPACITOR: A device which stores an electrical charge.

CARBON MONOXIDE (CO): A colorless, odorless gas given off as a normal byproduct of combustion. It is poisonous and extremely dangerous in confined areas, building up slowly to toxic levels without warning if adequate ventilation is not available.

CARBURETOR: A device, usually mounted on the intake manifold of an engine, which mixes the air and fuel in the proper proportion to allow even combustion.

CATALYTIC CONVERTER: A device installed in the exhaust system, like a muffler, that converts harmful byproducts of combustion into carbon dioxide and water vapor by means of a heat-producing chemical reaction.

CENTRIFUGAL ADVANCE: A mechanical method of advancing the spark timing by using flyweights in the distributor that react to centrifugal force generated by the distributor shaft rotation.

CHECK VALVE: Any one-way valve installed to permit the flow of air, fuel or vacuum in one direction only.

CHOKE: A device, usually a moveable valve, placed in the intake path of a carburetor to restrict the flow of air.

CIRCUIT: Any unbroken path through which an electrical current can flow. Also used to describe fuel flow in some instances.

CIRCUIT BREAKER: A switch which protects an electrical circuit from overload by opening the circuit when the current flow exceeds a predetermined level. Some circuit breakers must be reset manually, while most reset automatically.

COIL (IGNITION): A transformer in the ignition circuit which steps up the voltage provided to the spark plugs.

COMBINATION MANIFOLD: An assembly which includes both the intake and exhaust manifolds in one casting.

COMBINATION VALVE: A device used in some fuel systems that routes fuel vapors to a charcoal storage canister instead of venting them into the atmosphere. The valve relieves fuel tank pressure and allows fresh air into the tank as the fuel level drops to prevent a vapor lock situation.

COMPRESSION RATIO: The comparison of the total volume of the cylinder and combustion chamber with the piston at BDC and the piston at TDC.

CONDENSER: 1. An electrical device which acts to store an electrical charge, preventing voltage surges. 2. A radiator-like device in the air conditioning system in which refrigerant gas condenses into a liquid, giving off heat.

CONDUCTOR: Any material through which an electrical current can be transmitted easily.

CONTINUITY: Continuous or complete circuit. Can be checked with an ohmmeter.

COUNTERSHAFT: An intermediate shaft which is rotated by a mainshaft and transmits, in turn, that rotation to a working part.

CRANKCASE: The lower part of an engine in which the crankshaft and related parts operate.

CRANKSHAFT: The main driving shaft of an engine which receives reciprocating motion from the pistons and converts it to rotary motion.

CYLINDER: In an engine, the round hole in the engine block in which the piston(s) ride.

CYLINDER BLOCK: The main structural member of an engine in which is found the cylinders, crankshaft and other principal parts.

CYLINDER HEAD: The detachable portion of the engine, usually fastened to the top of the cylinder block and containing all or most of the combustion chambers. On overhead valve engines, it contains the valves and their operating parts. On overhead cam engines, it contains the camshaft as well.

DEAD CENTER: The extreme top or bottom of the piston stroke.

DETONATION: An unwanted explosion of the air/fuel mixture in the combustion chamber caused by excess heat and compression, advanced timing, or an overly lean mixture. Also referred to as "ping".

DIAPHRAGM: A thin, flexible wall separating two cavities, such as in a vacuum advance unit.

DIESELING: A condition in which hot spots in the combustion chamber cause the engine to run on after the key is turned off.

DIFFERENTIAL: A geared assembly which allows the transmission of motion between drive axles, giving one axle the ability to turn faster than the other.

DIODE: An electrical device that will allow current to flow in one direction only.

DISC BRAKE: A hydraulic braking assembly consisting of a brake disc, or rotor, mounted on an axle, and a caliper assembly containing, usually two brake pads which are activated by hydraulic pressure. The pads are forced against the sides of the disc, creating friction which slows the vehicle.

DISTRIBUTOR: A mechanically driven device on an engine which is responsible for electrically firing the spark plug at a predetermined point of the piston stroke.

DOWEL PIN: A pin, inserted in mating holes in two different parts allowing those parts to maintain a fixed relationship.

DRUM BRAKE: A braking system which consists of two brake shoes and one or two wheel cylinders, mounted on a fixed backing plate, and a brake drum, mounted on an axle, which revolves around the assembly.

DWELL: The rate, measured in degrees of shaft rotation, at which an electrical circuit cycles on and off.

ELECTRONIC CONTROL UNIT (ECU): Ignition module, module, amplifier or igniter. See Module for definition.

ELECTRONIC IGNITION: A system in which the timing and firing of the spark plugs is controlled by an electronic control unit, usually called a module. These systems have no points or condenser.

END-PLAY: The measured amount of axial movement in a shaft.

ENGINE: A device that converts heat into mechanical energy.

EXHAUST MANIFOLD: A set of cast passages or pipes which conduct exhaust gases from the engine.

FEELER GAUGE: A blade, usually metal, or precisely predetermined thickness, used to measure the clearance between two parts.

FIRING ORDER: The order in which combustion occurs in the cylinders of an engine. Also the order in which spark is distributed to the plugs by the distributor.

FLOODING: The presence of too much fuel in the intake manifold and combustion chamber which prevents the air/fuel mixture from firing, thereby causing a no-start situation.

FLYWHEEL: A disc shaped part bolted to the rear end of the crankshaft. Around the outer perimeter is affixed the ring gear. The starter drive engages the ring gear, turning the flywheel, which rotates the crankshaft, imparting the initial starting motion to the engine.

FOOT POUND (ft. lbs. or sometimes, ft.lb.): The amount of energy or work needed to raise an item weighing one pound, a distance of one foot.

FUSE: A protective device in a circuit which prevents circuit overload by breaking the circuit when a specific amperage is present. The device is constructed around a strip or wire of a lower amperage rating than the circuit it is designed to protect. When an amperage higher than that stamped on the fuse is present in the circuit, the strip or wire melts, opening the circuit.

GEAR RATIO: The ratio between the number of teeth on meshing gears.

GENERATOR: A device which converts mechanical energy into electrical energy.

HEAT RANGE: The measure of a spark plug's ability to dissipate heat from its firing end. The higher the heat range, the hotter the plug fires.

HUB: The center part of a wheel or gear.

HYDROCARBON (HC): Any chemical compound made up of hydrogen and carbon. A major pollutant formed by the engine as a byproduct of combustion.

HYDROMETER: An instrument used to measure the specific gravity of a solution.

INCH POUND (inch lbs.; sometimes in.lb. or in. lbs.): One twelfth of a foot pound.

INDUCTION: A means of transferring electrical energy in the form of a magnetic field. Principle used in the ignition coil to increase voltage.

INJECTOR: A device which receives metered fuel under relatively low pressure and is activated to inject the fuel into the engine under relatively high pressure at a predetermined time.

INPUT SHAFT: The shaft to which torque is applied, usually carrying the driving gear or gears.

INTAKE MANIFOLD: A casting of passages or pipes used to conduct air or a fuel/air mixture to the cylinders.

JOURNAL: The bearing surface within which a shaft operates.

KEY: A small block usually fitted in a notch between a shaft and a hub to prevent slippage of the two parts.

MANIFOLD: A casting of passages or set of pipes which connect the cylinders to an inlet or outlet source.

MANIFOLD VACUUM: Low pressure in an engine intake manifold formed just below the throttle plates. Manifold vacuum is highest at idle and drops under acceleration.

MASTER CYLINDER: The primary fluid pressurizing device in a hydraulic system. In automotive use, it is found in brake and hydraulic clutch systems and is pedal activated, either directly or, in a power brake system, through the power booster.

MODULE: Electronic control unit, amplifier or igniter of solid state or integrated design which controls the current flow in the ignition primary circuit based on input from the pick-up coil. When the module opens the primary circuit, high secondary voltage is induced in the coil.

NEEDLE BEARING: A bearing which consists of a number (usually a large number) of long, thin rollers.

OHM: (Ω) The unit used to measure the resistance of conductor-to-electrical flow. One ohm is the amount of resistance that limits current flow to one ampere in a circuit with one volt of pressure.

OHMMETER: An instrument used for measuring the resistance, in ohms, in an electrical circuit.

OUTPUT SHAFT: The shaft which transmits torque from a device, such as a transmission.

OVERDRIVE: A gear assembly which produces more shaft revolutions than that transmitted to it.

OVERHEAD CAMSHAFT (OHC): An engine configuration in which the camshaft is mounted on top of the cylinder head and operates the valve either directly or by means of rocker arms.

OVERHEAD VALVE (OHV): An engine configuration in which all of the valves are located in the cylinder head and the camshaft is located in the cylinder block. The camshaft operates the valves via lifters and pushrods.

OXIDES OF NITROGEN (NOx): Chemical compounds of nitrogen produced as a byproduct of combustion. They combine with hydrocarbons to produce smog.

OXYGEN SENSOR: Use with the feedback system to sense the presence of oxygen in the exhaust gas and signal the computer which can reference the voltage signal to an air/fuel ratio.

PINION: The smaller of two meshing gears.

PISTON RING: An open-ended ring with fits into a groove on the outer diameter of the piston. Its chief function is to form a seal between the piston and cylinder wall. Most automotive pistons have three rings: two for compression sealing; one for oil sealing.

PRELOAD: A predetermined load placed on a bearing during assembly or by adjustment.

PRIMARY CIRCUIT: the low voltage side of the ignition system which consists of the ignition switch, ballast resistor or resistance wire, bypass, coil, electronic control unit and pick-up coil as well as the connecting wires and harnesses.

PRESS FIT: The mating of two parts under pressure, due to the inner diameter of one being smaller than the outer diameter of the other, or vice versa; an interference fit.

RACE: The surface on the inner or outer ring of a bearing on which the balls, needles or rollers move.

REGULATOR: A device which maintains the amperage and/or voltage levels of a circuit at predetermined values.

RELAY: A switch which automatically opens and/or closes a circuit.

RESISTANCE: The opposition to the flow of current through a circuit or electrical device, and is measured in ohms. Resistance is equal to the voltage divided by the amperage.

RESISTOR: A device, usually made of wire, which offers a preset amount of resistance in an electrical circuit.

RING GEAR: The name given to a ring-shaped gear attached to a differential case, or affixed to a flywheel or as part of a planetary gear set.

ROLLER BEARING: A bearing made up of hardened inner and outer races between which hardened steel rollers move.

ROTOR: 1. The disc-shaped part of a disc brake assembly, upon which the brake pads bear; also called, brake disc. 2. The device mounted atop the distributor shaft, which passes current to the distributor cap tower contacts.

SECONDARY CIRCUIT: The high voltage side of the ignition system, usually above 20,000 volts. The secondary includes the ignition coil, coil wire, distributor cap and rotor, spark plug wires and spark plugs.

SENDING UNIT: A mechanical, electrical, hydraulic or electromagnetic device which transmits information to a gauge.

SENSOR: Any device designed to measure engine operating conditions or ambient pressures and temperatures. Usually electronic in nature and designed to send a voltage signal to an on-board computer, some sensors may operate as a simple on/off switch or they may provide a variable voltage signal (like a potentiometer) as conditions or measured parameters change.

SHIM: Spacers of precise, predetermined thickness used between parts to establish a proper working relationship.

SLAVE CYLINDER: In automotive use, a device in the hydraulic clutch system which is activated by hydraulic force, disengaging the clutch.

SOLENOID: A coil used to produce a magnetic field, the effect of which is to produce work.

SPARK PLUG: A device screwed into the combustion chamber of a spark ignition engine. The basic construction is a conductive core inside of a ceramic insulator, mounted in an outer conductive base. An electrical charge from the spark plug wire travels along the conductive core and jumps a preset air gap to a grounding point or points at the end of the conductive base. The resultant spark ignites the fuel/air mixture in the combustion chamber.

SPLINES: Ridges machined or cast onto the outer diameter of a shaft or inner diameter of a bore to enable parts to mate without rotation.

TACHOMETER: A device used to measure the rotary speed of an engine, shaft, gear, etc., usually in rotations per minute.

THERMOSTAT: A valve, located in the cooling system of an engine, which is closed when cold and opens gradually in response to engine heating, controlling the temperature of the coolant and rate of coolant flow.

TOP DEAD CENTER (TDC): The point at which the piston reaches the top of its travel on the compression stroke.

TORQUE: The twisting force applied to an object.

TORQUE CONVERTER: A turbine used to transmit power from a driving member to a driven member via hydraulic action, providing changes in drive ratio and torque. In automotive use, it links the driveplate at the rear of the engine to the automatic transmission.

TRANSDUCER: A device used to change a force into an electrical signal.

TRANSISTOR: A semi-conductor component which can be actuated by a small voltage to perform an electrical switching function.

TUNE-UP: A regular maintenance function, usually associated with the replacement and adjustment of parts and components in the electrical and fuel systems of a vehicle for the purpose of attaining optimum performance.

TURBOCHARGER: An exhaust driven pump which compresses intake air and forces it into the combustion chambers at higher than atmospheric pressures. The increased air pressure allows more fuel to be burned and results in increased horsepower being produced.

VACUUM ADVANCE: A device which advances the ignition timing in response to increased engine vacuum.

VACUUM GAUGE: An instrument used to measure the presence of vacuum in a chamber.

VALVE: A device which control the pressure, direction of flow or rate of flow of a liquid or gas.

VALVE CLEARANCE: The measured gap between the end of the valve stem and the rocker arm, cam lobe or follower that activates the valve.

VISCOSITY: The rating of a liquid's internal resistance to flow.

VOLTMETER: An instrument used for measuring electrical force in units called volts. Voltmeters are always connected parallel with the circuit being tested.

WHEEL CYLINDER: Found in the automotive drum brake assembly, it is a device, actuated by hydraulic pressure, which, through internal pistons, pushes the brake shoes outward against the drums.

A

MASTER INDEX

F

G